Colección Támesis
SERIE A: MONOGRAFÍAS, 294

A COMPANION TO
SPANISH WOMEN'S STUDIES

Tamesis

Founding Editors
† J. E. Varey
† Alan Deyermond

General Editor
Stephen M. Hart

Series Editor of
Fuentes para la historia del teatro en España
Charles Davis

Advisory Board
Rolena Adorno
John Beverley
Efraín Kristal
Jo Labanyi
Alison Sinclair
Isabel Torres
Julian Weiss

A COMPANION TO SPANISH WOMEN'S STUDIES

Edited by

Xon de Ros
Geraldine Hazbun

TAMESIS

© Contributors 2011

All Rights Reserved. Except as permitted under current legislation no part of this work may be photocopied, stored in a retrieval system, published, performed in public, adapted, broadcast, transmitted, recorded or reproduced in any form or by any means, without the prior permission of the copyright owner

First published 2011 by Tamesis, Woodbridge
Paperback edition 2014

ISBN 978 1 85566 224 7 hardback
ISBN 978 1 85566 286 5 paperback

Tamesis is an imprint of Boydell & Brewer Ltd
PO Box 9, Woodbridge, Suffolk IP12 3DF, UK
and of Boydell & Brewer Inc.
668 Mt Hope Avenue, Rochester, NY 14620–2731, USA
website: www.boydellandbrewer.com

The publisher has no responsibility for the continued existence or accuracy of URLs for external or third-party internet websites referred to in this book, and does not guarantee that any content on such websites is, or will remain, accurate or appropriate.

A CIP catalogue record for this book is available from the British Library

This publication is printed on acid-free paper

CONTENTS

List of illustrations	viii
Acknowledgements	xi
List of contributors	xiii
List of abbreviations	xv
Introduction	1

PART I: MEDIEVAL AND EARLY MODERN

1 Female Foundations in the *Libro de Alexandre* and *Poema de Fernán González*   25
GERALDINE HAZBUN

2 Desire and Transgression in the Female Voice of Early Popular Lyric   41
MARIANA MASERA

3 From Virgin Martyr to Holy Harlot: Female Saints in the Middle Ages and the Problem of Classification   55
ANDREW M. BERESFORD

4 Choosing and Testing Spouses in Medieval Exemplary Literature   69
LOUISE M. HAYWOOD

5 Through Women's Eyes: The Appropriation of Male Discourse by Three Medieval Women Authors   81
NIEVES BARANDA

6 Intellectual, Contemplative, Administrator: Isabel de Villena and the Vindication of Women   97
ROSANNA CANTAVELLA

7 Anatomies of a Saint: The Unstable Body of Teresa de Jesús   109
GEORGINA DOPICO-BLACK

8	Women's Artistic Production and Their Visual Representation in Early Modern Spain CARMEN FRACCHIA	129
9	The Baroque and the Undead: Carnal Knowledge in the Novellas of María de Zayas MARGARET GREER	143
10	Distinct Drama? Female Dramatists in Golden Age Spain ALEXANDER SAMSON	157

PART II: FROM THE EIGHTEENTH TO THE TWENTY-FIRST CENTURY

11	Conversations from a Distance: Spanish and French Eighteenth-Century Women Writers MÓNICA BOLUFER	175
12	What They Saw: Women's Exposure to and in Visual Culture in Nineteenth-Century Spain LOU CHARNON-DEUTSCH	189
13	Luxurious Borders: Containment and Excess in Nineteenth-Century Spain ALISON SINCLAIR	211
14	Women as Cultural Agents in Spanish Modernity SUSAN KIRKPATRICK	227
15	Politics and the Feminist Essay in Spain JOYCE TOLLIVER	243
16	The Theatricalized Self: Women Artists in Masquerade from 1920 to the Present ROBERTA ANN QUANCE	257
17	Gender and Change: Identity and Reform in the Second Republic FRANCES LANNON	273
18	Invisible Catalan(e)s: Catalan Women Writers and the Contested Space of Home HELENA BUFFERY AND LAURA LONSDALE	287
19	The Mother and the Nation: Reading Contemporary Women's Autobiographies XON DE ROS	301
20	Tropes of Freedom: Spectacular Eroticism and the Spanish New Woman On-Screen JESSAMY HARVEY	317

| 21 | Almodóvar's 'Others': Spanish Women Film-Makers, Masquerade, and Maternity
JO EVANS | 329 |

| Works cited | 343 |
| Index | 395 |

LIST OF ILLUSTRATIONS

Women's Artistic Production and Their Visual Representation in Early Modern Spain

Plate 1　Luisa Roldán, *The Virgin and Child with St Diego of Alcalá*, 1690–95. ©Victoria and Albert Museum, London (V&A: 250–1864).

Plate 2　José Ribera, *Assumption of Mary Magdalene*, 1636. Museo de la Real Academia de Bellas Artes de San Fernando, Madrid.

Plate 3　Sofonisba Anguissola, *Self-Portrait at the Easel*, c.1556. Castle Museum, Lancut, Poland.

Figure 1　Bartolomé Esteban Murillo, *Spring as a Flower Girl*, 1660–65. By permission of the Trustees of Dulwich Picture Gallery, London.　136

Figure 2　Diego Velázquez, *Kitchen Maid with The Supper at Emmaus*, c.1620. Courtesy of the National Gallery of Ireland, Dublin.　138

Figure 3　Sofonisba Anguissola, *Isabel of Valois*, 1565. Museo Nacional del Prado, Madrid.　140

What They Saw: Women's Exposure to and in Visual Culture in Nineteenth-Century Spain

Plate 4　Page from a woman's album. Purchased at Paperantic Madrid. VII Salón del Coleccionismo. 11 November 2007.

Plate 5　Dance card. Biblioteca Nacional, Madrid, Ephemera Collection, Catalogue 13-C, no. 3.

Plate 6　Calendar advertisement for Comercio José Ovelar. Biblioteca Nacional, Madrid, Ephemera Collection, Catalogue 36, no. H-12.

Figure 1　Fashions:　194
1A　'Traje de exposición', *Moda Elegante*, 52 (14 April 1893), p. 159.
1B　'Abrigo de terciopelo', *Moda Elegante*, 51 (6 October 1892), p. 435.
1C　'Sombrero de visita', *Moda Elegante*, 49 (14 January 1891), p. 13
1D　'Toque de paja', *Moda Elegante*, 58 (30 March 1899), p. 133.

Figure 2	Woman riding in her tilbury, *Blanco y Negro*, 7 (21 June 1891), cover.	196
Figure 3	Illustration from a chapbook of 1875, *El amigo de las niñas*, by Leopoldo Delgrás (Madrid: Librería de Hernando), p. 5.	199
Figure 4	Postcard. Author's private collection.	201
Figure 5	Advertisements for health and beauty products:	202
5A	*Ilustración Española y Americana*, 33.18 (15 May 1889)	
5B	*Ilustración Española y Americana*, 30 (several weeks running, 1896)	
5C	*Moda Elegante*, 50 (7 April 1893), p. 156.	
Figure 6	Holy picture. Private collection of Antonio Soler Segarra and María Amparo Castillo Martí.	206

The Theatricalized Self: Women Artists in Masquerade from 1920 to the Present

Plate 7	Cover of *La garzona*, by Victor Margueritte, Madrid, 1924(?) Courtesy of the Biblioteca Nacional, Madrid.	
Plate 8	*El niño la está mirando* (1996) by Ouka Leele (© Bárbara Allende). Courtesy of the artist.	
Plate 9	*Semilla* (1993) by Ouka Leele (©Bárbara Allende). Courtesy of the artist.	
Figure 1	'Sala' (or 'Sala Federal'), *Horizonte*, no. 2 (Madrid, 1922), by Norah Borges. © Heirs of Norah Borges.	264
Figure 2	'Norah Borges en el living de su casa', 1930 (from Martínez Quijano 1996: 78). Reprinted by permission of the heirs of Norah Borges.	267
Figure 3	'Guillermo de Torre en el living de su casa', 1930 (?). Frontispiece in Torre [1925] 2000. Reprinted by permission of the heirs of Guillermo de Torre.	268

Plates are between pages 272 and 273

This book is dedicated to the memory of
Professor Alan Deyermond

ACKNOWLEDGEMENTS

The editors are grateful to the John Fell Fund for its assistance with publication costs.

They would also like to acknowledge financial contributions towards the cost of the illustrations from Birkbeck College, Queen's University Belfast, the State University of New York at Stony Brook and Lady Margaret Hall, University of Oxford.

The editors would also like to thank Maria García Liñeira for help with the index, and Elspeth Ferguson, Vanda Andrews and the editorial team at Boydell & Brewer for their excellent work.

LIST OF CONTRIBUTORS

Professor Nieves Baranda is Catedrática de Literatura Española at the Universidad Nacional de Educación a Distancia, Madrid.

Dr Andrew M. Beresford is Senior Lecturer in the School of Modern Languages and Cultures at Durham University.

Dr Mónica Bolufer is Profesora Titular (Associate Professor) in the Departamento de Historia Moderna at the Universitat de València.

Dr Helena Buffery is Senior Lecturer in the Department of Hispanic Studies, University College Cork, Ireland.

Professor Rosanna Cantavella is Catedrática de Filologia Catalana at the Universitat de València.

Professor Lou Charnon-Deutsch is Professor of Hispanic Languages and Literature at the State University of New York at Stony Brook.

Dr Georgina Dopico-Black is Associate Professor of Spanish and Portuguese at New York University.

Dr Jo Evans is Senior Lecturer in Spanish Film and Literature at University College London.

Dr Carmen Fracchia is Lecturer in Early Modern Spanish Visual Studies at Birkbeck College London.

Professor Margaret Greer is Professor in Spanish at the Department of Romance Studies, Duke University.

Dr Jessamy Harvey is Lecturer in Modern Spanish Literature and Cultural Studies at Birkbeck College London.

Dr Louise M. Haywood is Senior Lecturer in Medieval Spanish Studies at the University of Cambridge and Fellow of Trinity Hall.

Dr Geraldine Hazbun is Lecturer in Medieval Spanish Literature at the University of Oxford and Fellow of St Anne's College.

Professor Susan Kirkpatrick is Professor Emerita at the University of California, San Diego.

Dr Frances Lannon, formerly Fellow and Tutor in Modern History, is the Principal of Lady Margaret Hall, University of Oxford.

Dr Laura Lonsdale is Lecturer in Modern Spanish Literature at the University of Oxford and Fellow of The Queen's College.

Dr Mariana Masera is Investigadora (Senior Research Fellow) in the Centro de Poética del Instituto de Investigaciones Filológicas at the Universidad Nacional Autónoma de México (UNAM).

Dr Roberta Ann Quance is Senior Lecturer in Spanish at Queen's University Belfast.

Dr Xon de Ros is Lecturer in Modern Spanish Literature at the University of Oxford and Fellow of Lady Margaret Hall.

Dr Alexander Samson is Lecturer in Golden Age Literature at University College London.

Professor Alison Sinclair is Professor of Modern Spanish Literature and Intellectual History at the University of Cambridge and Fellow of Clare College.

Professor Joyce Tolliver is Associate Professor of Spanish and Gender and Women's Studies at the University of Illinois, Urbana.

ABBREVIATIONS

ADE	Asociación de Directores de Escena de España
AHLM	Asociación Hispánica de Literatura Medieval
AIH	Asociación Internacional de Hispanistas
ALEC	*Anales de la Literatura Española Contemporánea*
Alexandre	*Libro de Alexandre*
ANME	Asociación Nacional de Mujeres de España
AUP	Associated University Presses
BAE	Biblioteca de Autores Españoles
BCom	*Bulletin of the Comediantes*
BFI	British Film Institute
CEDA	Confederación Española de Derechas Autónomas
CL	*Conde Lucanor*
CLAMS	Centre for Late Antique and Medieval Studies
CSIC	Consejo Superior de Investigaciones Científicas
CT	Colección Támesis
CUP	Cambridge University Press
EHT	Exeter Hispanic Texts
GRIF	Groupe de Recherche et d'Information Féministes (Brussels)
HR	*Hispanic Review*
HSMS	Hispanic Seminary of Medieval Studies
IIFV	Institut Interuniversitari de Filologia Valenciana
JHP	*Journal of Hispanic Philology*
LH	Letras Hispánicas
MLN	*Modern Language Notes*
MS(S)	manuscript(s)
NC	*Nuevo corpus de la antigua lírica popular hispánica (siglos XV a XVII)*
NCSRLL	North Carolina Studies in the Romances Languages and Literatures
NRFH	*Nueva Revista de Filología Hispánica*
OUP	Oxford University Press
PFG	*Poema de Fernán González*
PMHRS	Papers of the Medieval Hispanic Research Seminar
PMLA	Publications of the Modern Language Association of America

PPU	Promociones y Publicaciones Universitarias
PSOE	Partido Socialista Obrero Español
QMUL	Queen Mary University of London
QMW	Queen Mary and Westfield College
RAE	Real Academia Española
SUNY	State University of New York
Talavera	*Arçipreste de Talavera / Archpriest of Talavera*
UNAM	Universidad Nacional Autónoma de México
UP	University Press
V&A	Victoria and Albert Museum

INTRODUCTION

In 1978 Beth Miller, editor of the pioneering volume *Women in Hispanic Literature: Icons and Fallen Idols*, complained about the apparent lack of interest in women's studies among hispanists, claiming that 'it was impossible in 1976 to find substantial articles in print applying new feminist perspectives in our field' ([1978] 1983: 25), and hoping that her publication would act as a stimulus for more work in the field. Her call was not unheeded. Three decades later there is an extensive body of scholarship devoted to women's experiences, their historical contexts and their creative works. The substantial bibliography at the end of this Companion is illustrative, if by no means exhaustive. It encompasses work done in a broad variety of disciplines drawing on a range of critical and theoretical models from a feminist perspective, and attests to the fact that women's studies has become a distinct area of studies within hispanism and part of the academic curriculum in many graduate and postgraduate programmes.

Women's studies originated in the humanities as an initiative of the Modern Language Association in 1970 and its development as an academic subject has been informed by the debates in feminist theory. It set out to offer a new form of criticism that draws from other disciplines and whose primary analytical category is gender, understood as a social and cultural construction that reflects and determines differences in power and opportunity, while also considering other determining influences such as class, nationality, religion, sexuality, ethnicity and race that inflect women's experiences and practices.

Critical attention was first directed to images of women in literature and culture, exposing the ideology of patriarchy, with its attendant subordination of women, behind textual versions of the feminine. Alongside the critical revision of the literary canon, research was applied to the rediscovery of a lost tradition, or counter-tradition, of women's writing, seeking for patterns of continuity in themes and preoccupations, and focusing on women's responses to patriarchy – a practice that was termed gynocriticism by Elaine Showalter. Although women's studies first emerged as a discipline in Anglo-American academia, French feminist theory, in the work of Julia Kristeva, Hélène Cixous, and Luce Irigaray, has since the 1980s played a crucial part in offering feminist critics a new conceptualization of the relationship between women, psychoanalysis, and language. Under their influence, the question of the specificity of women's difference, psychological or linguistic (*écriture féminine*), became a touchstone in feminist debate. The rise of post-structuralism and cultural studies in the 1990s brought many changes to the field. A conception of gender identity as fluid and contingent, constructed through discourse, superseded the essentialist view of female difference. At the same time, a new emphasis on reception and an interest in the mass media and everyday life has extended the scope of research into a broader conception of female culture, which includes the role of women as both producers and consumers. From this vantage point some of the most innovative work in recent feminist theory has taken place in film studies and cultural analysis.

We are not going to dwell here on the reasons for the belatedness of this field of inquiry in Spanish studies. A signpost in its development was the 1990 conference on Feminism and Hispanic Literature, held in London and organized by Stephen Hart, who co-edited a collection of selected essays from its proceedings (Condé and Hart 1991). In this volume, representations of women in literature from the early modern period to the present were scrutinized for their ideological construction of gender. In the introduction Hart takes stock of the publications on the subject to date, noting an increase in the number of studies – among them the seminal *Theory and Practice of Feminist Literary Criticism* (Mora and van Hooft 1982), and *Cultural and Historical Grounding for Hispanic and Luso-Brazilian Feminist Literary Criticism* (Vidal 1989), as well as several anthologies and bio-bibliographies of women writers, which together with some special issues by established journals, set the ground for further research. At the same time, social historians in Spain were bringing out valuable surveys on the material conditions of women's lives (Capel 1982, Durán and Capel 1986, Nash 1983, Del Valle 1985, Folguera 1988).

In this and the following decade the process of rediscovery, reassessment, and dissemination of women's writing in Spain gathered momentum with the publication of important anthologies (Janés 1986, Buenaventura 1985, Kirkpatrick 1992, Redondo Goicoechea 1993, Bordonada 1990), bio-bibliographical guides (Galerstein 1986, Levine et al. 1993, McNerney and Enríquez 1994), and the six-volume *Breve historia feminista de la literatura española* (Zavala et al. 1993–2000). Alan Deyermond's article 'Spain's First Women Writers' ([1978] 1983) was a useful point of departure in the medieval field, later to be revised and extended in his 'Las autoras medievales castellanas a la luz de las últimas investigaciones' (1995), which addressed gaps such as the female traditional lyric, Hispano-Arabic, Hebrew, and Catalan poetry. Ana Navarro's *Antología poética de escritoras de los siglos XVI y XVII* (1989) represented the first of Castalia's Biblioteca de la Mujer (Woman's Library) series, and the critical cluster

'Bringing Iberian Women Writers into the Canon' in *La Corónica* proved a later landmark (Bratsch-Prince and Piera 2003).[1] More recently, the four-volume *Historia de las mujeres en España y América Latina* (History of Women in Spain and Latin America), edited by Isabel Morant (2005–06), with some one hundred contributors, is the most extensive (from prehistory to the present day) and up-to-date work in the field.

A crucial move for the establishment of the field in Spanish universities was the creation of academic centres for women's studies: the *Institutos* or *Seminarios de Estudios de la Mujer*. The pioneer seminar was created in 1979 under the aegis of Madrid's Universidad Autónoma (Autonomous University), which from 1981 has also organized the annual forum *Jornadas de Investigación Interdisciplinaria sobre la Mujer* (Interdisciplinary Conference on Women). This academic interest in turn fostered the founding of organizations dedicated to the study of individual authors, such as the Fundación María Zambrano, and the Fundació Mercè Rodoreda. At the same time, a surge of valuable studies on a wide range of authors marked the coming-of-age of the first tradition of scholars on the subject. Other disciplines such as history of art, film studies, sociology, and cultural studies began to extend the scope of the field beyond the literary and the socio-historical, from the visual arts, cinema, popular culture, fashion, publicity, and so on, to the construction of femininity in extra-literary discourses such as the medical (Aresti 2001) and the legal (Larrauri 1994). In the meantime, the general outlook was moving from a focus on women's oppression and subordination, highlighting how their achievements had been excluded and ignored by historiography, to an emphasis on women's agency, their resistance tactics and their strategies to counter discrimination, as well as a re-evaluation of their experiences.

In terms of approach, the prevailing frame of reference has come from Anglo-American feminist models, and while this line has provided a valuable ground for analysis it has also been criticized for overlooking specific cultural differences (see Chown 1983). Some critics have called for a more systematic use of an autochtonous feminist theory in scholarship (Roberta Johnson 2003b, 2005). However, the Spanish theoretical and sociological sources have only recently been widely available. Critics such as Amalia Martín-Gamero (1975), Catherine Jagoe, Alda Blanco, and Cristina Enríquez (1998), and Lisa Vollendorf (2001b) have undertaken the necessary task of gathering documentary information (see also Nash 1994, Aguado and Capel et al. 1994, Enders and Radcliff 1999). Perhaps the area which has undergone a most dramatic expansion is that of information tech-

---

[1] Other surveys and anthologies of medieval or early modern women writers include Marimón Llorca 1990, Pérez Priego 1990, Olivares and Boyce 1993, Surtz 1995, Kaminsky 1996, and Olivares 2009.

nologies. Several internet resources for documentation, bibliography, and general material related to the field of women's studies have been set up in the last decade.[2] Margaret Andrews (2006) draws on Rosi Braidotti's notion of nomadic feminism and feminist cyber theory (1994, 1996) to offer one of the first studies of women's cyberspaces in Spain.

With the benefit of all this scholarly background, the essays collected here engage in literary criticism as well as historical analysis, sociological investigation and interdisciplinary exploration, describing, analysing and documenting a range of women's experiences in Spain from medieval times to the twenty-first century. Given the historical span, as well as the range of approaches and disciplines in women's studies, comprehensive coverage within one volume would be an impossibility. Our decision has been to give the contributors a free hand to write on the topic of their choice within their area of expertise. The result is a collective work in accordance with an established feminist tradition. The essays are variously concerned with texts, discourses, everyday life, and visual culture, and the approaches incorporate current developments in feminist research, theory and practice. Some contributors opted for a survey of an area which has already received critical attention, extending its scope or considering it from a different perspective, whilst others present altogether new material, testing methodological and theoretical boundaries.

The reader will find in this collection of essays a good range of models for scholarship and a sound insight into the main issues and recent critical debates in the field of women's studies, showing its possibilities within the Spanish context and opening up avenues for further research.

The volume is divided into two sections: the first covers topics up to and including the early modern period and the second from the eighteenth century to the present. Each chapter explores a concept, approach, or aspect of feminist theory (such as identity and representation, authorship and authority, masquerade of femininity, cultural agency, strategies of resistance, the mother-daughter bond, discipline and the body, the poetics of domesticity, intersectionality, etc.) while discussing either the work of women or the representation of women. Each essay is followed by suggestions for further reading and there is a bibliography of works cited at the end of the volume.

---

[2] Among them: http://www.mujerpalabra.net/bibliotecademujeres/; http://www.pangea.org/dona/; http://www.entretodas.net/; http://digital.library.upenn.edu/women/; http://www.escritoras.com/escritoras/; http://www.uned.es/bieses/ http://www.audem.com/; http://www.e-mujeres.net/; http://mys.matriz.net/; http:// www.wisps.org.uk/;http://www.aeihm.org/; http://www.ugr.es/~arenal/; http://ailcfh.org/; http://www.fordham.edu/halsall/med/womenbib; http://labyrinth.georgetown.edu/; http://parnaseo.uv.es/Memorabilia/Memorabilia7/bolbibmerida.

Medieval and early modern section

Medieval and early modern Spanish women's studies is a dynamic and developing field of scholarship. The essays contained in this volume present important critical advances, and reflect on progress in the field to date. They also identify gaps and signpost the work that is still needed to achieve a proportion of coverage and a methodological accuracy befitting the diversity and richness of the female cultural heritage with which the medieval and early modern periods in Spain have endowed us.

Women's studies owes much to the historical scholarship that has been conducted in recent years. Worth citing in its own right is the indispensable *La condición de la mujer en la Edad Media* (Fonquerne and Esteban 1986), which covers a wealth of historical and literary topics. This and a further cluster of excellent publications have opened up vistas on women's role in medieval Spanish cities (Dillard 1984), their economic function (Stone and Benito-Vessels 1998), and their experiences of marriage and widowhood (Ratcliffe 1988, Mirrer 1992), and even of pilgrimage (González Vázquez 2000). María del Carmen García Herrero's *Las mujeres en Zaragoza en el siglo XV* (1990) is a pioneering collective biography, a journey through women's experience of birth, nursing, infancy, education, marriage and its ruptures, widowhood, work, and death. Spanish women of the Renaissance and Counter Reformation are also discussed by Barbeito Carneiro 1992, Cruz and Perry 1992, Sánchez and Saint-Saëns 1996, Garrido González 1997, and Dopico-Black 2001.

Studies of women's intellectual history have provided us with further stimulating material. In 1989, a special issue of the *Journal of Hispanic Philology* dedicated to feminist topics included two articles on women's vibrant intellectual experiences in the convent milieu. One redefined female intellectuality in accordance with the specific social, political, economic, and spiritual functions of the convent (Arenal and Schlau 1989b), and the other examined tensions inherent in the writing of nuns' lives through an examination of the confessor-penitent relationship and its attendant dynamics of dominance and submission, self-preservation and self-expression (Donahue 1989).

Valuable explorations into female literacy have been conducted by prominent Spanish scholars, addressing one of the most neglected fields of inquiry in Western cultural history: the possession and use of books (Castillo Gómez 2003, Cátedra and Rojo 2004). Isabel Beceiro Pita (2003) has written on women's relationship with written culture from thirteenth to the sixteenth century; underlining the connections between reading, ideology and social position, she concludes that noblewomen in Castile did not solely have access to religious works, but participated in a culture of reading akin, albeit in limited ways, to that of their male counterparts, which included historical works, poetry and fiction, works by Classical authors, and scientific compendia. Elisa Ruiz García in the same volume re-examines the question of Queen Isabel's books: contrary to popular ideas that the sovereign was devoted to books in a carefree pursuit of pleasure, she reveals that the monarch's books were intended for personal edification as well as for developing the practice of governance and state ideology (2003: 67).

Bibliotecas y lecturas de mujeres (Libraries and Women's Reading) by Pedro Cátedra and Anastasio Rojo (2004) has significantly enriched our knowledge of women's libraries and reading habits in the sixteenth century. The women of Valladolid favoured reading material of a spiritual or liturgical nature, but their collections – in a compelling development of Beceiro Pita's conclusions about Castilian noblewomen – included works of fiction and poetry, which circulated freely in convents, as in private households. Women's reading was mostly books of chivalry, a fact which contributed much to the censure of this genre, regarded as a troubling model for life: 'porque no ay quien tanto siga lo que lee como la muger; que, si es adúltera o enamorada y devota de cavalleros que se precian de tener amigas, no es sino porque la tal muger lee y oye libros de amores y cavallerías' (because nobody follows what they read as much as a woman does; for if she is an adulteress, or a lover, or a friend of gentlemen who pride themselves on their womanizing, it is only because such a woman reads and listens to books of love and chivalry) (Francisco de Osuna, quoted in Cátedra and Rojo 2004: 164). Very occasionally other famous bestsellers like *Celestina* or Montemayor's *Diana* could be found in female possession but works intended to instruct women on how to behave – which were cold and devoid of creative interest – were largely absent from their libraries (2004: 160–1).

Issues of political and military power which affected the women of Spain, particularly royal women, have also been scrutinized by historians, as exemplified by Bernard Reilly's *The Kingdom of León-Castilla under Queen Urraca, 1109–1126* (1982), Magdalena Sánchez's *The Empress, the Queen, and the Nun: Women and Power at the Court of Philip III of Spain* (1998), Barbara Weissberger's *Isabel Rules: Constructing Queenship, Wielding Power* (2004), and Theresa Earenfight's *Queenship and Political Power in Medieval and Early Modern Spain* (2005). This branch of scholarship in particular has raised awareness about the danger of homogeneous readings of women from the perspective of a dominant culture. Recent studies by Luce López-Baralt (1985, 1992), Louise Mirrer (1994, 1996), and María Rosa Menocal (1990) epitomize an interest in the status of subordinate groups in relation to the dominant culture in medieval and early modern Iberia.[3] The branch of analysis which engages with the

---

[3] Other examples of this interest in the relationship between political and religious

specific historical and cultural conditions of the medieval kingdoms and the influence on gender of the counter-hegemonic struggles within them has answered one of Paul Julian Smith's criticisms of Miller [1976] 1983, that it 'fails to address [...] the question of sexual difference itself as a cultural or historical formation' (1989: 15).

The ten essays contained in this section study women writers and the representation of women in the medieval and early modern periods in Spain through a range of critical approaches within feminist theory. They explore the fascinating cultural interface between women as writers or artists and women as they are represented through literature and art. Over the course of the chapters, we are given a range of perspectives on the most compelling women writers of medieval and early modern Spain from Leonor López de Córdoba to María de Zayas, and two women artists at the royal court in the sixteenth and seventeenth centuries. The representation of women is a concern of all these chapters to varying degrees, but particular questions of categorization and configuration of female identities can be traced in a journey through hagiography, poetry (epic, clerical, and lyric), exemplary literature, and the art world of Imperial Spain. As the following synopsis makes clear, the contributors take full advantage of the most appropriate and stimulating directions in feminist criticism to elucidate their material, and to draw out its complexities in full.

In the first chapter, Geraldine Hazbun examines the extent to which female figures lie at the heart of collective identities in the Spanish Middle Ages, as forged in the models of thirteenth-century epic poetry and *mester de clerecía* (clerical art). While these traditionally masculine genres threaten to reinforce perceptions that women are at the margins of authority, power, and identity, she suggests that the hybrid generic status of two major works – the *Poema de Fernán González* (1250s) and the *Libro de Alexandre* (1200) – encourages us to think more carefully about the way in which representations of women in the texts shape the way in which the community imagines itself. Through the optics of New Historicism and contemporary discourse on the cultural construction of community, Hazbun reveals the complexities of the female characters in these works, demonstrating that they surpass rigid traditional stereotypes, and exposing their hitherto undervalued role within the fundamental dynamics of group experience. She argues that women are active participants in the dynamics of heroic success and the correction of its failures, but they are also authoritative signs and symbols of a providential authority. They are instrumental,

---

hegemony and the social, religious, and gender categories on the margins include Pick 2004, Coates 2009, and Grieve 2009.

therefore, in taking these texts to the higher, and more esoteric, plane of meaning that befits their historical time and context of production.

Collective voice has been an extremely important area of research in early modern women's studies. Women's role and representation in early oral and lyric traditions has been examined through studies of the ballads, as well as the popular lyric, compiled and explored extensively by Margit Frenk.[4] Mariana Masera provides a stimulating contribution to this branch of scholarship, demonstrating that one of the distinctive differences between learned and popular lyric poetry of the medieval period is the presence in the latter of female voice with a feminine point of view. Her chapter begins by setting out the significant critical debate surrounding the creative role of women in this poetry, and goes on to provide a detailed survey and analysis of the characteristic features of the female voice and its discourse in the popular lyric. She exposes the reader to the different female voices which populate the early lyric, from the young initiate in love to the woman who waits for her lover, anticipating the delights of the encounter, and explores the distinctive *topoi* and textual markers which reveal the feminine, dividing them into the explicit / textual and the implicit /contextual. Masera draws out the nuances of this rich poetics by identifying different kinds of textual features; she then delves into the implicit, imaginative, context of traditional poetry to explore the frequent use of archaic symbols taken from nature that convey erotic meanings associated with fertility rites and magic. Her chapter reveals that in the popular lyric women express themselves and act with liberty: in contrast with the real world, where social control was strict, trangression is the poetic norm.

Andrew M. Beresford deals with the depiction of the female religious subject in medieval Spanish hagiography, with specific focus on the representation of sexuality and the sublimation of earthly desire into its celestial equivalent. Particular attention is paid to the figure of the *sponsa Christi* (Bride of Christ) and the way in which her sexuality is neither denied nor repressed, but redirected into the love of Christ, sometimes in the most literal and direct of ways. It is argued that, despite taking a surprisingly sympathetic view of female sexuality, the majority of hagiographic legends seek, none the less, to exercise forms of control and regulation, principally in order to bolster the power of the male-dominated Church. Beresford concludes by underlining the extent to which the current fashion for separating types of female saint into supposedly watertight categories is deeply misleading, and how apparently antithetical figures such as virgin martyr

---

[4] See, for example, Frenk 1978 and 2003; on women in the ballad tradition see Anahory-Librowicz 1989, Mirrer 1995, and Castro Lingl 1998; on women as performers see Cohen 2002 and Filios 2005; Haywood 2000 is a collection of studies on the female voice in late-medieval prose and poetry.

and penitent prostitute display remarkably similar characteristics, both of them affixing their sexual desire on Christ.

Medieval exemplary tales of a comic nature are the subject of Louise M. Haywood's chapter. She deals specifically with tales in which spousal suitability is (or explicitly is not) tested in three important collections, each with a significant frame structure: *Sendebar* (1253), *Conde Lucanor* (1330s), and *Arçipreste de Talavera* (1438). A close reading of the tales, backed by historical, medical, and legal discourses of the period and contemporary psychoanalytic and materialist perspectives, exposes the nature of the dangers to men emanating from women in mismanaged marriages. Haywood argues that the tales in question encode a strongly patriarchal social structure. Marriage is the microcosm of a man's conduct in social relations and, as such, a *locus* in which virility is exercised and demonstrated. Under the constraints of such a structure, women are reduced to signifiers of their husband's manliness and capacity to behave appropriately, and, consequently, any means necessary can be employed to reintegrate or domesticate wives. Despite the reductive representation of female characters in the exemplary tales, in which they are desubjectivized and reduced to chattels over which men wield dominion, Haywood observes that historical evidence often suggests otherwise: they enjoyed active and constructive roles.

Nieves Baranda examines the writings of three medieval women: Leonor López de Córdoba, Constanza de Castilla, and Teresa de Cartagena. Despite the uniqueness of each of their individual works, Baranda finds a compelling shared stance among these women which is based on their dialogue with a male-authored tradition. She thus contributes to the array of approaches to women's writing and reading adopted in the first decade of this millenium (see Dinshaw and Wallace 2003). Baranda identifies these writers' awareness of gender not as a limitation but as a fact by focusing on their status as readers. Baranda explores their renegotiation of the texts they inherited and, more specifically, their inscription within these texts of powerful women with whom they identified, who act as a female sign, with characteristics drawn from tradition but values which tellingly diverge from it. While Teresa de Cartagena disregards feminine models in favour of Job, and her reading strategy is equally selective, oriented toward the use of reason and argument to transform her message. Baranda reveals how, as readers of a tradition, these women writers filled the gaps of the texts – as identified by the theory of reception – with their own projections, opening fissures in a masculine literary tradition which they accept, but which they also question.

Rosanna Cantavella provides a comprehensive analysis of another female author, Isabel de Villena, who despite being one of the most important female writers of her time in the Iberian Peninsula has only recently attracted the critical scrutiny she deserves. Cantavella explores Villena's three distinguishing modes, as intellectual, contemplative, and administrator, prefacing her discussion with a compelling survey of landmarks in Villena's biography, including her early years at the Aragonese court, joining a Poor Clare community at the age of fifteen, her election as abbess and administrative duties in the convent, and, of course, the writing of her devotional masterpiece, the *Vita Christi*. The uniquely feminine and pro-feminist narrative style of the *Vita Christi* is examined in detail: the Virgin Mary and Mary Magdalen have key roles in the narrative. But the work is more than a support for the contemplative soul, it also intervenes in the renowned pan-European debate on whether women are essentially good or bad. Villena, we discover, refutes a number of misogynistic clichés from the tradition, particularly from Jaume Roig's *Espill* (Mirror), including female fickleness, lust, inability to love deeply, association with the devil, and idiocy.

In view of the relatively recent flowering of scholarship on Villena, particularly in English, Cantavella concludes by testing the boundaries of the discipline and proposing five lines of future research that will take Villena studies forward and see the author receive the recognition she deserves in the Iberian canon.

The exploration of early modern female authorship and its religious dimensions gains momentum with Georgina Dopico-Black's contribution on Teresa of Avila. Dopico-Black explores the fraught readings that Teresa's body and her autobiography, the *Vida*, have generated, arising from the competing diagnoses that Teresa's raptures provoked and, crucially, the debate over whether they were divine or demonic in origin. This chapter analyses in particular how Teresa reclaims experience as a means of determining the provenance of her charismatic symptoms, allowing her to refute charges of heresy or fraud, and create an experienced-based corpus of theological knowledge, founded, like the new sciences, on the first-hand observation of inner secrets. Integral to this reading of the *Vida* is a challenge continually experienced by Teresa: how to legitimize her right to mystic experiences without overtly defying the hierarchical structure that would be judging her. Dopico-Black identifies two levels of experience in the *Vida*: a direct and unmediated knowledge of the transcendent, that authorizes Teresa to speak among *letrados* (learned men) and the theological science of discernment. Both levels are concerned with truth; in the first instance, experience of union with God provides access to a transcendent Truth; in the second case, experience serves to elucidate the truth-status *of* the revealed truth by discerning its origin as demonic or divine. The *Vida*, it is proposed, functions as a transforming machine, much like early modern theatres of scientific truth production; a site in which doubt is turned into certainty, paradox into divine reason, womanly frailty into strength, prosecutors into defendants.

The visual formulation of women's imagined identity in early modern Spanish culture is the subject of Carmen Fracchia's chapter, which explores the work of two female artists: Sofonisba Anguissola, a sixteenth-century Italian painter who worked at the court of Philip II, and Luisa Roldán, a seventeenth-century sculptor; and three male painters: Diego Velázquez, Bartolomé Esteban Murillo, and José Ribera. Issues of the representation of domestic space, strategies of resistance, and discipline and the body are explored in Fracchia's discussion, while further light is shed on representation of women in the works of these artists through theoretical approaches both pre-modern and contemporary: the concept and the workings of the gaze (Bryson 1983), the construction of gender and the concept of the unified sex (Laqueur 1990), the political and biological formulation of eugenics (Huarte de San Juan 1575), and the workings of the imperial policy of purity of blood *vis à vis* the construction of gender. Fracchia argues that social and ideological constraints took precedence over nature and sexuality in shaping the way female artists worked, and the ways in which they were envisaged by both female and male artists in Imperial Spain.

Margaret Greer extends her previous work on María de Zayas from the perspective of psychoanalytic and feminist theory by focusing on the question of Zayas's treatment of the body. She begins by acknowledging the authorial preface to the *Novelas amorosas* (*Exemplary Tales of Love*), in which Zayas confronts head-on the challenge of writing and publishing in a patriarchal society, justifying her madness in doing so by positing the asexuality of souls and the material equality of male and female organs and flesh. Hence, Zayas avoids using either 'body' (*cuerpo*) or 'flesh' (*carne*), preferring more specific terms like 'material', 'blood', 'senses', 'faculties', and 'organs'. In explicating the kind of carnal knowedge that Zayas offers her readers in the preface and in the novellas, Greer balances early modern, Counter Reformation Catholic conceptions of sexual difference, subjectivity, and the body with the understanding of those categories in the three Lacanian orders of the Real, the Imaginary, and the Symbolic. While paying attention to the particulars of Zayas's language, she also takes advantage of work generated by the recent complete translation into English of Jacques Lacan's Seminar XX, *Encore* (1999).

The theatrical output of Spain's *Siglo de Oro* (Golden Age), the period of artistic accomplishment that extended from the late sixteenth century to around 1680, remains a particularly rich field for the study of women in relation to the dominant cultural and aesthetic order. The two volumes edited by Anita Stoll and Dawn Smith (1991, 2000) epitomize this movement, which takes into account plays written by women (see Soufas 1997a and 1997b) as well as the representation of female figures in male-authored drama. The issue of female actors, as discussed by Alexander Samson, was one of the most controversial and problematic features of the Golden Age theatre for moralists, but it was also and equally one of its most attractive features. Despite a wealth of female roles, there were relatively few playwrights who were also women, and we lack clear evidence of the extent to which any possible female poetics of stagecraft actually reached public audiences through performance in the major commercial theatres. Samson's chapter examines the careers and surviving works of Feliciana Enríquez de Guzmán, Ana Caro Mallén, María de Zayas, Leonor de la Cueva, and Ángela de Azevedo in order to try and answer some of the questions about what a female poetics might be, its public impact, if any, and how and why these women came to write drama in their own words.

Modern section: from the eighteenth to the twenty-first century

The first milestone in the field of modern Peninsular women's studies was Geraldine Scanlon's now classic *La polémica feminista en la España contemporánea, 1868–1974* (Feminist Polemic in Contemporary Spain), in which she traces the truncated history of Spanish feminist movements (1976). The second edition (1986) includes a commentary on the publications that followed in its wake.[5] Under the aegis of the Instituto de la Mujer, founded in 1983, the task of gathering historical, sociological, and bibliographical material occupied scholars in Spain.[6] Meanwhile, the pioneering work of Roberta Johnson (1981), Mirella Servodidio (1987), Janet Pérez (1988), Geraldine Cleary Nichols (1989), Elizabeth Ordóñez (1982, 1991), Joan L. Brown (1991), María del Carmen Riddel (1995), among others, directed critical attention to the writers of the *generación de medio siglo* with excellent results.[7] These studies secured the reputation of many writers – particularly Carmen Martín Gaite and Mercè Rodoreda, but also Carmen Laforet, Ana María Matute, and Esther Tusquets, prompting their inclusion in academic curricula.[8] Owing to the social and political circumstances of

---

[5] See also Martín-Gamero 1975, Levine and Waldman 1980, Davies 1991, Brooksbank Jones 1994, Capel 2004, Ackelsberg 2005.

[6] A state agency concerned with women's welfare and political reform, the *Instituto de la Mujer* was originally dependent on the Ministry for Employment and Social Affairs, but since 2008 it has been under the recently created Ministry for Equality. See the website: http://www.migualdad.es/mujer/. From the late 1980s the Instituto has promoted publications in the field and is the co-producer of two prestigious book series: Feminismos (Cátedra) and Biblioteca de Escritoras (Castalia).

[7] The 'mid-century generation' was a group of dissident writers whose careers started after the mid 1950s.

[8] Recent publications include Schumm 1999; McNerney 1999 and Arkinstall 2004 (on Rodoreda); Ichiishi 1994 (Tusquets); Davies 1998 (Laforet and Matute); María Pilar

the postwar years, works of fiction often became a vehicle for feminist concerns.[9] Those writers who explored and defined the problems facing women in contemporary Spain were, at times prematurely, described as feminists by critics from across the political spectrum, and their works were judged according to ideological rather than formal or stylistic criteria. This may be one reason for the reluctance shown by many Spanish women authors to call themselves feminists, even when their feminism is borne out by their works. The fact that this has been a common attitude in many women both before and after the Civil War of 1936–39 suggests a more complex phenomenon linked to social perception (Roberta Johnson 2005).

Whilst the mid 1990s saw increased research into the eighteenth century (Kitts 1995, Bolufer 1998), a tradition of feminist consciousness was soon traced back to the nineteenth century with María del Carmen Simón Palmer's bio-biographical guide (1991) and the groundbreaking studies of Susan Kirkpatrick (1989), Marina Mayoral (1990a), Catherine Jagoe (1994), and Lou Charnon-Deutsch (1990, 1994, 2000).[10] They explore the consequences of the division between public and private spheres, and the prescriptive ideology of domesticity figured in the 'ángel del hogar' (angel of the hearth) (Aldaraca 1982), which dictated woman's behaviour, restricting her ambitions to the domains of the home and the family, in the literature of Romanticism and Realism. In the same line, the work of Catherine Davies (1998), bridging two centuries and two continents, provides valuable insights into the poetics of modern women writers. In a related study Noël Valis sheds light on the aesthetics originally associated with female domesticity in *The Culture of 'Cursilería': Bad Taste, Kitsch and Class in Modern Spain* (2002). Also in the area of nineteenth-century literary studies, Teresa Vilarós's *Galdós: invención de la mujer y poética de la sexualidad* (Galdós: The Invention of Woman and the Poetics of Sexuality) (1995) is one of the few full-length examples of psychoanalytical feminist reading. The persistence of this ideology of domesticity in modernism is the subject of Roberta Johnson's 2003a study, in which she examines its role in the debates about the nature of the Spanish nation.

Even if narrative fiction has attracted most critical attention, some research has also been directed towards women's poetry (Wilcox 1997, Ugarte 1991, Janet Pérez 1995, Glendinning 1996, Benegas and Munárriz 1997, Bellver 2001), and to their presence in the theatre (García Lorenzo

---

Rodríguez 2000 (from Laforet to Luisa Etxenike); Galdona Pérez 2001 (Laforet, Matute and Elena Quiroga); O'Leary and Ribeiro de Menezes 2007 (Martín Gaite).

[9] Contemporary feminist theory appeared in the magazine *Vindicación Feminista* (Feminist Vindication), directed by the lawyer and writer Lidia Falcón and first published in the summer of 1976.

[10] See also Charnon-Deutsch and Labanyi 1995, Sinclair 1998, Labanyi 2000.

2000).[11] In the field of visual arts, Estrella de Diego's *La mujer y la pintura del siglo XIX español* (Women and Painting in Nineteenth-Century Spain) (1987), opened the discipline of art history to women's studies, which more recently has seen Roberta Quance's *Mujer o árbol* (2000), Pilar Muñoz's survey *Mujeres españolas en las artes plásticas* (Spanish Women in Fine Art) (2003), and Patricia Mayayo's *Historias de mujeres, historias del arte* (Women's Histories, Histories of Art) (2003).[12]

Interdisciplinarity comes naturally to the fore in studies dedicated to modernism and the avant-garde. The first exhibition of avant-garde artists, 'Fuera de Orden: Mujeres de la Vanguardia Española' (Out of Order: Women of the Spanish Avant-Garde), was held in Madrid in 1999. Both Shirley Mangini's *Las modernas de Madrid* (Madrid's Modern Women) (2001) and Susan Kirkpatrick's *Mujer, modernismo y vanguardia en España* (Women, Modernism, and the Avant-Garde in Spain) (2003) include commentaries on the work of women painters.

Publications on post-Franco Spain have seen an upsurge of attention to film and popular culture. Susan Martin-Márquez's study *Feminist Discourse and Spanish Cinema* (1999) is an excellent introduction. The international acclaim garnered by the films of Isabel Coixet (Cristina Andreu 2008), has brought her generation of film-makers into the limelight (Heredero 1998, Camí Vela 2005). The versatility and popularity of the writers of the so-called boom of women's writing after 1975 (Carme Riera, Soledad Puértolas, Adelaida García Morales, Cristina Fernández Cubas, Nuria Amat, Rosa Montero, Lourdes Ortiz), and the iconoclasm of the younger 'Generation X' (Lucía Etxebarría, Belén Gopegui, Almudena Grandes, Ángela Vallvey, Espido Freire), together with the increasing presence of female protagonists and narrators in the Spanish fiction of recent decades, suggest wide possibilities for future research.[13]

Circumstances have changed dramatically for Spanish women in these three centuries, particularly in the last decades of what has been called 'El siglo de las mujeres' (the women's century) (Camps 1998). While current social advances, such as the female majority in Zapatero's 2008 Cabinet, are regarded by some as merely cosmetic, they would have been unthinkable only a few decades ago. But if the realities of women's lives in contempo-

---

[11] For women playwrights see also Nieva de la Paz 1993, Dougherty 1993, Hormigón 1997.

[12] For monographs on individual artists see Fernández Utrera 2001 (on Ángeles Santos and Maruja Mallo), Diego 2007 (on Remedios Varo), Ros 2007 (on María Blanchard), Zanetta 2006 (on Varo, Mallo, and Santos), and Mangini 2010 (on Mallo).

[13] 'Generation X' is the generation of writers born in the 1970s. For the writers of the Transition see, among others, Ciplijauskaité 1988, Manteiga et al. 1988, Knights 1999, Nichols 1992, Davies 1994, Ballesteros 1994. For the younger generation see Tsuchiya 2002, Redondo Goicoechea 2003, Henseler 2003, Henseler and Pope 2007.

rary Spain, in particular the professional elites, are the subject of academic scrutiny (García de León 1982, 1996; Brooksbank Jones 1997), so are those of their counterparts in the Republican period, a generation of women who paved the way for social and political reform and were silenced by Franco's regime.[14] The work of Carmen de Burgos, Rosa Chacel, María Teresa León, Federica Montseny, Carmen Goyri, Margarita Nelken, Clara Campoamor, Victoria Kent, María Zambrano, and many others is being recovered for a tradition whose precursors were Emilia Pardo Bazán and Concepción Arenal.

Also in recent decades, linked to the recovery of historical memory, a new emphasis on oral history has brought to the fore the testimonies of generations of women whose experiences were suppressed under Franco, in the pioneering work of Tomasa Cuevas (1985, 1986) and the studies by Martha Acklesberg (1992), Fernanda Romeu (1994), Shirley Mangini (1995), Mary Nash (1995), and Antonina Rodrigo (1999).

As the contributions in this Companion show, literary criticism is only one of the approaches used by scholars in women's studies. The general emphasis is on the complex system of cultural and ideological discourses and institutions that inform and are informed by representations of women and their roles in society. It would be impossible to represent all the valuable work done to date in the field of women's studies in modern Spain. This brief survey necessarily leaves many gaps and omissions. The essays that follow will provide more specific bibliographical signposts in those areas which have occupied feminist critics' thought in recent years. They offer both reference guidance and examples of fine analysis.

In the first chapter of this section Mónica Bolufer draws on her expert knowledge of women of the Enlightenment to discuss the strategies used by Spanish women writers of the eighteenth century to authorize themselves through translations from foreign texts. Bringing to her analysis a number of case studies – among them that of the proto-feminist Josefa Amar y Borbón, author of the well-known *Discurso en defensa del talento de las mujeres* (Discourse in Defence of the Intelligence of Women) (1786) and *Discurso sobre la educación física y moral de las mujeres* (Discourse on the Physical and Moral Education of Women) (1790), which show her familiarity with the work of her French counterparts – Bolufer examines the translators' interventions and the ways they inscribed their own views in their translations, establishing a relation, both explicit and implicit, with French writers. The context of the essay is especially relevant because

---

[14] For the pre-Civil War tradition see Rodrigo 1988, Zulueta 1992, Vollendorf 2001b, Glenn and Mazquiarán 1998, Davies 1998, Mangini 2001, Herrmann 2010, Folkart 2002, Capdevila-Argüelles 2002. For Francoist gender ideology see Martín Gaite 1987, Graham 1995, Morcillo 2000.

it marks the emergence in this period of a new type of woman writer, belonging to the middle classes, who will supersede the religious and aristocratic models of the past.

The following two contributions deal with the nineteenth-century world of fashion and material culture. Lou Charnon-Deutsch addresses the question whether visual culture, which was expanding dramatically in the second half of the century, defined the scopic field for women to the same degree that it did for men, and considers the inferences that can be drawn from the disparity in what men and women experienced visually in their daily lives in Spain's urban centres. Through a survey of weekly magazines and other visual ephemera such as *cartes de visite*, advertising posters, and photographs, this chapter suggests that while inferences about reception are far from empirically reliable, contaminated as they are by unnuanced theories of the difference between public and private spheres, women surely saw certain objects more often than men, and other objects less often or never. Moreover, they possibly looked at the visual culture available to both sexes differently from men, and were perceived at the time as consumers of visual culture in ways that were gender-specific.

Alison Sinclair looks at beliefs, the material world, social mores, and the policing of those mores in late-nineteenth-century Spain, considering the linked concepts of lust and luxury as forms of excess. She notes that in this period lust is thought of as masculine in its associations, and luxury as feminine. Initially in her examination of material, Sinclair considers how male-authored discourses of medical and religious treatises set out to contain the uncontainable, specifically in the form of passion. Policing does not however operate according to a simple model by which men police the excesses of women. A discussion of female-authored conduct manuals and educational writings explores how they policed the margins in relation to potentially errant sisters, with a particular focus on their tendency towards excess. At the same time, there are examples of how luxury, passion, and fashion are conceptualized (by some women writers) as being at odds with masculinity and thus elements that endanger it. Lastly, drawing particularly on Elisabeth Bronfen, the essay focuses on two novels by women to see how far they operate with or against the policing texts with which they are contemporary.

The essays of Susan Kirkpatrick and Joyce Tolliver explore the ways in which contemporary anglophone feminist analysis both illuminates and circumscribes our understanding of the development of the feminist essay in Spain, focusing in particular on the question of the expressed and implicit political ideologies of the foremost Spanish theoreticians of gender. Pardo Bazán, the noted novelist, intellectual, and feminist, lamented in her 1892 report on the condition of Spanish women that, 'la nueva [España], socialmente hablando, no se ha formado su elemento femenino' (socially speaking, the new [Spain] has not yet formed its feminine element) (Pardo Bazán 1999a: 88). Nevertheless, since the beginning of the century women had been seizing opportunities afforded by the emergence of modern institutions to develop new forms of cultural agency that would rapidly proliferate at the beginning of the twentieth century. In her article Susan Kirkpatrick considers the intersections of feminist thought and ideologies of class and race in women's literary production of the late nineteenth and twentieth centuries in Spain, tracing the ways in which Spanish women found in aesthetic production a means of participating in the emerging modernity. In the early 1800s pioneering women poets adapted aspects of the Romantic movement to legitimate women's public self-expression and create a new feminine identity from which to speak to readers of the developing press industry. Later in the century, women authors of popular fiction played a crucial role in disseminating the bourgeois ideology of female domesticity while paradoxically creating the new social identity of the professional woman writer. Expanding the purview of this new role for women, late-nineteenth-century writers such as Concepción Arenal and Emilia Pardo Bazán began to intervene forcefully in the broad cultural debates through which contemporary Spain began to define itself. With the advent of aesthetic modernism at the beginning of the new century, women found a multiplicity of new avenues and strategies for defining themselves as active subjects in a rapidly modernizing society. As women emerged as key innovators in avant-garde movements encompassing writing, visual arts, and film, they also broke away from the social norms that had limited the public activities of their mothers. While the pull of conservative, religious tradition remained a powerful factor in the lives and attitudes of most Spanish women, their active participation in public life, which had begun with the lyric self-expression of the poets of the 1840s, became a recognized fact with the achievement of women's suffrage during the Second Republic.

Joyce Tolliver's panoramic overview of the Spanish feminist essay complements Kirkpatrick's study of women's agency, within an equally broad historical-cultural context. Focusing on the essay, the chapter considers a range of Spanish theorists from the nineteenth century to the present, arguing that most US feminist scholars, in the past quarter-century or so, have assumed an understanding of feminism that posits the inextricability of gender, race, and class as categories of analysis. As an analytical tool, intersectionality can be fruitful and robust; as the basis for a feminist ethos, it is profoundly idealistic. But when we find it impossible to separate the three aspects of the trinity in our analyses of interventions in the conversations regarding feminism and the woman question of earlier periods, we risk limiting the scope of our analysis to only those figures whose ideologies of class and/or race appeal to a contemporary progressive sensibility. It becomes impossible, by definition, to conceive of any authentic feminism that is not also anti-classist and anti-racist. When we consider the prescient feminist commentary of figures such as Emilia Pardo Bazán, who in an overtly classist gesture signed her later works 'Countess of Pardo Bazán', or, alternatively, the denunciation of the women's suffrage initiative by Victoria Kent, who represented the Radical Socialist Party in the parliament of the Second Republic, we begin to appreciate the historically contingent nature of the academic feminist intersectional postulate. Likewise, a look at contemporary feminist essays by authors such as Carmen Alborch (2001) and Lucía Etxebarría (2000) might lead the non-Spanish reader to ironically deduce that all Spanish women must be of the privileged classes and, of course, white, given the lack of integration of those categories within contemporary feminist commentaries. Tolliver explores these and other cases of ideology trouble that surface when we attempt to read the Spanish gender trouble essay while using the intersectional tools of contemporary feminist analysis.

Roberta Quance discusses the idea of femininity as a masquerade in relation to a range of works from the 1920s to the present, arguing that there are two broadly different approaches to the concept, one which we may call modern and the other postmodern. The modern approach to the question, with roots in Joan Riviere (1929) considers the point of view of the creative woman, who unconsciously adopts a feminine pose to offset what could be perceived as an aggressive foray into traditionally masculine fields. In this way she does not risk arousing male hostility or resentment at her bid for acceptance as an artist on equal terms with men. The other approach to masquerade implicitly challenges the notion of an essential female identity behind any display of feminine gender traits.

While both approaches remain rooted in the psyche of the woman artist or writer, the second development moves quickly to the generalization that all displays of femininity are a masquerade, and that there is no true underlying femininity to be expressed at all. This is the most radical implication of Riviere's critique: that what we perceive as feminine behaviour in signs of women's dress, posture, and interaction with men, is always only a sign of women's role-playing on men's terms. None the less, according to the later development, there can be something liberating in the deliberate, ironic, distancing of the self from its presentation in society. Quance proposes a revival of the concept, first, in its modernist version in order to talk about women artists and writers in Spain who do not always easily fit the mould of heroines and seem in fact to be apostates from modernity, such as Norah Borges.[15] But she also uses the concept to question the radicality

---

[15] Although Norah Borges is Argentine (Buenos Aires, 1901–98) she produced much of her avant-garde work in Spain from 1919 to 1936. She is included here for that reason and also because her case is an exemplary one.

of the stance assumed by women who seem to have had a more knowing, ironic, attitude toward their femininity, such as the *movida* artist Ouka Leele.[16] When parody emerges in a depoliticized space, we can question whether the exponents of a postmodern masquerade are as free to fashion their own identity as they might seem to be.

Frances Lannon analyses the dramatic changes made by the Second Republic to the status of Spanish women and the expansion of opportunities open to them, explaining the complex ways in which gender identity and identities based on class, religion, and politics intersected. Major legislative achievements included the introduction of female suffrage and the granting of equal citizenship to women and men. The chapter emphasizes, however, that some of the efforts to improve, and even transform, the status and life experience of women were embedded in and shaped by other ideological priorities, including rapid secularization. It is argued that the Republic's anticlericalism crucially influenced its approach to both education and marriage, and inevitably alienated large sectors of the population who considered their fundamental values and interests to be under threat. The new status of women was dependent on the Republic's ability to establish its legitimacy and implement its legislation, but neither of these was achieved. The military uprising against the Republic in July 1936 and the eventual victory of the Francoists reversed the gender reforms of the early 1930s. Greater gender equality was a conspicuous casualty of Franco's victory. In a complex way, however, achievable reform had also been undermined by its subordination to the Republic's sectarian ambition.

Recent decades have seen the appearance in the Anglo-American market of numerous studies of Catalan women writers, that have both made a space for new voices in the academic canon and underlined their difference and otherness, normally using the discourses of feminist criticism. Indeed, as has been argued persuasively by, for example, Helena Miguélez-Carballeira (2005), the reception of Catalan women's writing in the anglophone world can be taken as paradigmatic of the development and incorporation of feminist and gender-based criticism in Hispanism generally. This overt appropriation of a series of writers for a particular political agenda has begun to be balanced more recently by attempts to reincorporate these writers into their proper socio-historical context, partly in response to increasing frustration at their resistance to Anglo-feminist projects. Yet these new approaches are marked by a particular critical idiom in which gender and socio-political marginality are intertwined within catch-all ideas of double minority and gender exile, which ultimately take precedence over the real histories (and

---

[16] The *movida* was a countercultural movement that took place in Madrid during the Transition to democracy after Franco's death.

stories) of the writers discussed. In their chapter Helena Buffery and Laura Lonsdale aim to address the place of Catalan women's writing in hispanic studies, assessing the potential as well as the limitations of recent critical paradigms. They seek to navigate and uncover the layering of discourses in the work of canonical writers such as Esther Tusquets and Carme Riera, focusing on some of their more resistant texts in order to map theior relationship to the social and cultural fields in which they are variously located, and identify the particular spaces of representation they create and explore. This chapter draws on Sharon Feldman's concept of a 'Catalunya invisible' (2002) in the cultural production of the 1980s and 1990s, and applies it to Catalan women writers since the Transition, in order to allude to the critical blind spots that have arisen in relation to their work, particularly in the case of authors who have opted to write and/or disseminate their fiction in Castilian. The discussion includes a detailed analysis of Tusquets's *El mismo mar de todos los veranos* (*The Same Sea as Every Summer*) (1978), and Riera's *Cap al cel obert / Por el cielo y más allá* (Towards the Open Sky) (2000 / 2001).

Autobiography occupies an important place in feminist debate. Not only does it have a longstanding association with women's literature but it is also a mode that has been employed in their own work by many feminist theorists and critics. Moreover, through autobiography a generalized concept of female subjectivity has been postulated, based on psychoanalytical models which focus on the relationship between mother and daughter, Xon de Ros examines this relationship in four autobiographical narratives written by women, looking into other aspects of identity articulated through this bond. The case studies examined here extend the discussion of Spanish female autobiography from 1970, with María Teresa León, to contemporary authors Esther Tusquets, Soledad Puértolas, and Laura Freixas.

This chapter considers the ways in which women's autobiography and, within it, the mother-daughter bond, has been theorized by feminist scholars. However, instead of considering it in terms of personal relationships, and since the idea of the nation has often been projected on to a maternal figure, the analysis focuses on the issue of nationality. The essay reveals that the political renegotiations of national allegiances experienced by Spain in recent times can be read in the fraught relations between mothers and daughters in these texts. The mother-daughter relationship is thus seen to link the individual with the collective, and the psychological with the social. The differences in the writers' individual responses suggest the impossibility of generalizing about female experience, and the importance of the circumstances and conditions out of which these texts emerge.

The final chapters are devoted to cinema. The central construction explored by Jessamy Harvey is the so-called Spanish New Woman on-screen, so settled in cinematic scholarship as to become shorthand for a very particular progressive type of post-Franco femininity. From the decade of the 1970s and throughout the democratic period, tropes of freedom attached themselves both to the spectacular erotic female body and the Spanish New Woman. The erotic display of the female body raises the issue of a retrograde objectification of women; so, rather than continue to maintain the trope that the New Woman on-screen is always legible as a positive progressive icon, it would be more useful to discern how she may also convey regressive as well as evolving notions of gender. The first aim of the chapter is to critically inform readers of the evolution of feminist film theory in the anglophone academic sphere and, within hispanism, to provide bibliographical pointers. Secondly, in order to highlight the ways in which the new type of democratic womanhood can convey regressive as well as evolving notions of gender, the chapter goes on to focus on Vicente Aranda's 1994 film adaptation of Antonio Gala's 1993 novel, *La pasión turca* (Turkish Passion). Both novel and film, albeit in different ways, can be interpreted as complex responses to the discourse of New Womanhood and her pursuit of sexual liberation. Although the emergence of the Spanish New Woman on-screen does show, as many critics agree, an individual actively negotiating her own path, this chapter seeks to show how she has had to plot a course within a contradictory culture where politics, sexuality, and the market are closely connected.

Jo Evans's chapter starts from the premise that, for the wider filmgoing public, Spanish film *is* Pedro Almodóvar, and the words 'Spanish film' and 'women' conjure up performers like Carmen Maura, Victoria Abril, and Penélope Cruz more readily than female directors like Chus Gutiérrez, Gracia Querejeta, Patricia Ferreira and Icíar Bollaín. With this in mind, Evans explores women film-makers' relationship to a wider industry in which Almodóvar functions as a metonym for Spanish film. Reversing Laura Mulvey's question about how classical Hollywood film narrative constructs the female spectator (1975), it asks how the film industry constructs the female director and how this is reflected on-screen. Evans then considers their approach to two major motifs of the Almodóvar brand: masquerade and the maternal melodrama. The representation of the diegetic director in Pilar Miró's *Gary Cooper que estás en los cielos* (*Gary Cooper Who Art in Heaven*) (1980) is compared with the response of contemporary directors to the question of women film-makers, focusing on Marta Balletbò-Coll's performance in *Costa Brava* (1995). The discussion of performance is followed by an analysis of the representation of feminine masquerade in Josefina Molina's *Función de noche* (*Evening Performance*) (1980) and Mireia Ros's *La Moños* (1997); from masquerade, the focus moves to the *mater dolorosa* to consider the extent to which the representation of the mother in the films of the boom generation departs from the classical Hollywood melodramas Almodóvar has so successfully updated. Having explored the difference in approach of these women to the representation of masquerade and maternity, the conclusion turns to two recent Spanish women documentary film-makers, Ariadna Pujol and Mercedes Álvarez, to suggest (via Kristeva) that women's performance in an industry dominated by oedipal narratives may always be marked by an unconscious framework that has more in common with the myth of Io than the myth of Oedipus, and that this may make feminine narratives more appropriate to our twenty-first-century interest in global perspectives and mobile identities.

The last two essays in this collection make extensive use of theoretical models elaborated by foreign critics and theorists – as do some of the other contributions. Most of them test, and at times question, their validity in the Spanish context. Attentive to cultural specificity in their discussion of a number of issues that have informed feminist debates, the contributors here engage in a dialogue between Spanish feminist thought – which has been more historical, sociological, and political in nature (Roberta Johnson 2005: 247) – and those foreign theoretical sources.

There are a number of aspects in women's lives and practices which have not found space to be critically examined in this collection. Lesbianism, immigration, ethnic minorities are among them. Likewise, philosophy, journalism, crafts, music and song, dance, sport, science, publicity and the media are other areas of interest in which research has been done elsewhere. Basque and Galician cultures, as well as important historical periods such as Romanticism and Francoism, have been left out for lack of space. Despite these omissions, the editors believe that this Companion, in the breadth of its scope and the diversity of its approaches, contributes significantly to the development of women's studies in hispanism. It will serve both as an introduction to the subject and as a vibrant record of the present state of research, as well as a stimulus to future debate well into the twenty-first century.

Note

Unless otherwise stated, all translations are the authors' own.

PART I: MEDIEVAL AND EARLY MODERN

1

Female Foundations in the *Libro de Alexandre* and *Poema de Fernán González*

GERALDINE HAZBUN

'maguer que pueble en este mundo'*

Recent scholarship on medieval Spanish epic poetry has repositioned female characters within narrative contexts and in the discussions of culture, politics, and society that reach both into and beyond the text.[1] Developing this critical trend, this chapter examines the role of women in two thirteenth-century Spanish narrative poems – the *Poema de Fernán González* (The Poem of Fernán González) (c.1250) and the *Libro de Alexandre* (*The Book of Alexander*) (between 1178 and 1250) – through the optics of new historicism and contemporary discourse on the cultural construction of community.

The *PFG* recounts the emancipation of Castile from the Kingdom of Leon in the tenth century through the efforts of Count Fernán González and his vassals, whereas the *Alexandre* charts the career of Alexander the Great across the Eastern world, turning this classical figure into a medieval

---

A special tribute of gratitude is offered to the late Alan Deyermond in acknowledgement of his role as advisor in respect of the medieval and early modern section of the *Companion*. It represents one of the myriad examples of Alan's extraordinary legacy.

* 'though he may populate this world' (*Libro de Alexandre*, Cañas 2003: 585).

[1] Sponsler 1975 is an early example of this trend. Carolyn Bluestine made a strong but brief case in 1978 for the importance of women to the structure and artistic texture of the *Cantar de mio Cid* (*Song of the Cid*). Studies of epic women in the 1980s include Victorio 1986, Bluestine 1986, Grieve 1987, Ratcliffe 1987, and María Eugenia Lacarra 1988. Alan Deyermond argues persuasively for the importance of sexuality in the earliest Spanish epic cycle, that of the Counts of Castile, identifying what he calls a 'marked feminine element' in Spanish epic poetry (1988: 786). In the following decade, a number of studies were produced by Lacarra (1990, 1992, 1993, 1995, 1999). On the categorization of women's roles in the epic see also Chicote 1996, Castro Lingl 1999, and, most recently, Vaquero 2005, Caldin 2007, and Pattison 2007.

Spanish monarch.² Both works are foundational in their outlook, presenting a single heroic figure who is a successful conqueror of territorial space, and of illustrious descent (*PFG* 178c, *Alexandre* 5–7).³ Inherent in their eminence is an assurance that these men are unique models for a community and shapers of its boundaries, both within the texts themselves and in the historical environments in which they were received. If the thirteenth-century political picture across Europe is reduced to its barest form, the development of nationhood and the monarchical state were changing the nature of group identities. These centralizing, patriarchal forces reinforce the importance of studying female roles in foundational texts of the period, and within the context of dialogue between literature and history. For Lesley Johnson, relatively little critical attention has been given to the relationship between national identity and gender identity in the context of the Middle Ages (1995: 9). Female foundation stories are scarce and, where in existence, shot through with tensions about female access to power (11). Recent commentary on women in the pan-European epic tradition has suggested, however, that given the fundamental place of community in epic literature, the role of women within these texts can 'expand our understanding of both epic and community' (Poor and Schulman 2007: 3).⁴ Both works are set, more particularly, during the phase of Iberian history that hosted the Reconquest, which means that their understanding of colonization, settlement and community is undoubtedly informed by this complex political, religious, and cultural programme. Heath Dillard tells us, and brilliantly demonstrates, that historians tend to overlook the 'vital participation of women in the shaping of Hispanic society during the Reconquest and the medieval expansion of Christian "Spain"' (1984: 1). This is a statement that I wish to build upon, from a literary angle, in this study.

Although epic in spirit and theme, the works in question belong in form to the *mester de clerecía* ('clerical art' or 'clerical function'), a male-authored, clerical literary mode with its roots in Castile.⁵ Gender representation needs to be handled with this in mind. Revisiting discussions of the didactic tendency of the *mester de clerecía*, Julian Weiss highlights the mediatory position of the cleric between Church and state and the range of perspectives this opens up; the 'competing pressures of freedom and constraint'

---

² On the sources of the *Alexandre*, see Michael 1970: 12–27, Willis 1935 and 1965.

³ The stanza and line numbers given for each poem are taken from Juan Victorio's edition of the *PFG* (1988) and Victorio Cañas's edition of the *Alexandre* (2003).

⁴ From the perspective of queer history, Carolyn Dinshaw poses the theoretical question of how medieval communities form themselves in relation to sex (1999: 21–2).

⁵ For definitions of *mester de clerecía*, see Deyermond 1965, López Estrada 1978, Rico 1985, and Weiss 2006: 1–2; more general discussions of this literary movement can be found in Uría Maqua 2000.

placed upon these poems suggest that inroads can be made in examining the position of women (2006: 11). While this confluence of two traditionally masculine genres – epic and clerical poetry – might threaten to reinforce perceptions that women are at the margins of authority, power, and identity, I would suggest that the effect is the opposite and that the hybrid spirit of these works, coupled with their inseparability from the specific historical context of thirteenth-century Iberia, encourages us to think more carefully about the way in which representations of women in the texts shape the way in which, to draw on Benedict Anderson's terminology (2006), the community imagines itself.

The shared cultural and literary backgrounds of these works are borne out at the level of textual discourse through thematic connections, shared literary motifs, and verbal reminiscences.[6] It is in such textual details that I locate the foundational role of women and this necessarily involves close consideration of their relationship with the heroic protagonist. My aim is to demonstrate that women are centrally involved in a powerful dynamic of loyalty and treachery that is at the heart of both texts and of heroic achievement within them. This involves them in both public and private spheres, which contributes to the breadth of vision associated with the hero. What is more, women reinforce the drama of finality and *fama* (fame) which is present in both of these clerically influenced texts and which underpins our perspective on the hero's motives and accomplishments in broader religious and historical terms.

It ought to be stated here that the role women play in dynamics of heroism is one which is complicated by the distinct fallibility of our two heroes.[7] Unlike the Cid, who possesses a finely balanced heroic persona predicated on *fortitudo et sapientia* (strength and wisdom), Fernán González frequently loses his poise, absenting himself from his people, giving in to anger, failing to see through trickery, and even doubting his God (600).[8] Alexander's flaw is a fatal one and one of which the poet is strenuously critical: *cobdiçia* (greed). Not knowing when to stop in his conquests, Alexander attempts to scrutinize the secrets of nature; this incurs the wrath of God and the descent

---

[6] This has led José Hernando Pérez to argue that Diego García was responsible for writing both texts (2001). Other critics have argued, in my view more persuasively, for the influence of the *Alexandre* upon the *PCG*. See, for example, Michael 1970: 286, Uría Maqua 2000: 319–22, Weiss 2006: 169–70.

[7] Note definitions of the traditional hero by Bowra 1952: 4, Vries 1963: 211, and Curtius 1990: 167–70.

[8] Thomas Hart calls the Cid the perfect epic hero since he possesses courage and wisdom in the highest degree (2006: 21). Matthew Bailey has outlined some of the tensions that surround the heroic character of Fernán González (1993: 15).

of the hero to the grave (2672).⁹ The fallibility of the two heroes does not necessarily detract from their positive message for the collective, nor is this my point. What it does do is call into question the exclusivity of their roles at the core of charismatic constructions of group identity. Bernhard Giesen refers to the hero as '*pater patriae*, as the demiurgical creator of the kingdom' (1994: 24), but I would argue that the embedding of women in the constructive process needs to be considered more carefully.

At the heart of both poems is a profound, near-obsessive interest in the practices of loyalty and betrayal which surround heroic achievement. In both cases, loyalty is an essential part of the ethos of leadership (*PFG* 216, *Alexandre* 53), rendering treachery the gravest offence against seigneurial, royal, and divine authority. The Alexander poet austerely moralizes about treachery on numerous occasions, but he reserves sterner words for two incidents. The first is when Alexander discovers the plot to kill Darius (1727abc); the second occurs after the traitors Jobas and Antipater give Alexander the poisoned cup and feather:

> ¡Maldito sea cuerpo que atal cosa faze!
> ¡Maldita sea alma que en tal cuerpo yaze!
> ¡Maldito sea cuerpo que tal cosa le plaze!
> ¡Dios lo eche en laço que nunca se deslaçe! (2618)

> (Damned be the body which does such a deed!
> Damned be the soul which lies in such a body!
> Damned be the body that takes pleasure in such a thing!
> May God bind him so that he never can be free!)

Likewise, the author of the *PFG* is quick to condemn treachery. Describing the corruption of the genealogical line of the Visigothic king Witiza, he links treachery with the complete demise of Spain:

> Fijos de Vautiçanos non devieran nasçer,
> que essos començaron traiçion a fazer:
> volvio lo el diablo, metio y su poder:
> esto fue el escomienço de España perder. (41)

> (The sons of Witiza ought not to have been born,
> since it is they who began to commit treachery:
> the devil presented himself, he put all his power to effect:
> this was the beginning of the loss of Spain.)

Indeed, one of his hero's methods of persuading his vassals to commit to

---

⁹ For a detailed discussion of Alexander's *soberbia* (pride), see Uría Maqua 1996; on his fatal flaw see also Deyermond and Bly 1972: 160–3.

the battlefield is to threaten them with the fate of traitors: lying with Judas in hell (447).

The political advantage of promoting loyalty and denouncing treachery is clear, but in the spirit of medieval misogyny both poems suggest a natural connection between women and devious practice (see Bloch 1991: 20–1, 53, 56–7, 144). In the *Alexandre*, caveats abound: women are weak and forgetful of loyalty (395), they can easily become subjects of male desire (417), they dabble in enchantments (410–11, 416) and they can be deadly, as Cyrus discovers: 'óvola una fembra en cabo a matar' (1000) (a woman finished him off in the end), a deed so troubling it is recalled later in the text (1445). Alexander even recalls, with echoes of the story of La Cava, how:[10]

> Los nuestros bisavuelos por solo un pesar,
> —por una mala fembra que se dexó forçar—,
> por vengar su despecho e por preçio ganar
> sufrieron tal lazerio qual oyestes contar. (768)
>
> (Our great-grandfathers through one sorrowful event,
> – through a bad woman who allowed herself to be raped –,
> to avenge her spite and to recover their worth
> suffered such a plight as you will have heard.)

Added to all of this is the not insignificant fact that the embodiment of treachery in the epic, *Traïçión,* is actually a woman.

In the male-dominated prehistory to Fernán González's life in the *PFG*, the author deliberates on the contrast between purity and corruption. The suggestion of the rape of La Cava, although never explicitly mentioned, haunts these stages of the *PFG* through the uneasy suggestion that in Count Julian's absence something occurs that makes him turn to treachery in his rage (43a). Before this event, Spain is a land of Holy Virgins (11, 155) while after the loss of Spain its women are delivered up to the 'pagan' Almanzor (104). A portrait of pure deviousness is then provided in the form of Queen Teresa of Leon, who devises the strategem that leads to the first capture and imprisonment of the hero. Her scheming is rooted in political motives; added to the fact that she believes the Count has killed her brother, she is described as having a mortal grudge against the Castilians as a 'navarra natural'(Navarrese by birth) (734). In the broader scheme of the poem she

---

[10] La Cava, also known as Florinda, was the daughter of Count Julian; she plays a significant role in traditional accounts of the fall of Spain in 711 since it was her rape by the Roderick, King of the Visigoths, that prompted Julian to take vengeance on Spain by showing the invading Moors how to breach the Peninsula across the Straits of Gibraltar. History and myth have converged in accounts of the invasion to render her part-seductress, part-innocent victim.

is also guilty of the general infidelity of the Iberian monarchs in obstructing Fernán González's objectives, and by extension God's providential purpose: 'los reyes de España, con derecho pavor, / olvidaron a ti, que eres su señor' (the Iberian monarchs, with obvious fear, / forgot about you, who are their lord) (396ab).

All of this begs the question of how women can have a constructive role within these dynamics of loyalty and betrayal, especially when treachery touches two of the most significant women in these poems: the Count's wife, Sancha, and Alexander's mother, Olympias. In the *PFG*, Sancha is a site of contradictions. Before her secret meeting with the Lombard, the poet describes how the pilgrim sees the most incredibly beautiful woman (621ab) and it later becomes clear that she is of 'buen preçio' (a high price) (625a), which in the poem's terminology alludes more to a moral than a material worth.[11] However, the Lombard is stern in his dealings with her; he tells her she is the root cause of the Castilians' extreme affliction (622d), and calls attention to her wretched position: 'muy sin ventura' (very unfortunate) (622a), 'sin piedat e sin buen conosçer' (pitiless and naïve) (623a), 'mucho menoscabada' (greatly lessened [in worth]) (625a). It quickly becomes apparent that the fate of the Count lies in her hands (623bcd). In the Lombard's words, she is guilty of helping the Moors by removing the 'pies e manos' (feet and hands) (624b) of the Christian people, Fernán González. However, this contradiction between innate goodness and active disloyalty is not a lasting one. Her response is to hurry to see the imprisoned Count where she secures his loyal commitment to her by making him promise to marry her and never leave her for another woman (637). Happy with his response, she embarks upon a plan to free Fernán González and deliver him back to his people.

What is striking about this is the active and physical manifestation of her loyalty to the Count and to Castile; during their escape into the thick mountain scrub of the *camino francés* Sancha actually carries him because he is still partly chained up (643d);[12] in fact, she substitutes for the feet of the Christian people. When the Archpriest comes across the pair, she also becomes their hands, striking the first blow against the traitor who threatens their path back to Castile: 'travo l' a la boruca, dio le una grand tirada' (she grabbed his head, she dealt him a great blow) (655c).[13] The poet tells us that

---

[11] See, for example, 156d; see Coates 2008 for further discussion of the subject of worth in the *PFG*.

[12] The *camino francés,* lit. 'French path', is one of the pilgrim routes to Santiago de Compostela.

[13] Commentators are divided over the exact meaning of *boruca*. David Pattison notes that it may mean 'testicles', while another chronicle version refers to her grabbing his *vergüenças* (genitals) (2007: 19–20).

the Count is unable to help her at this point because of his chains; only when he can grasp the Archpriest's knife can he help her to kill him (656).[14] The result of her actions is that Sancha is paid official homage by the Castilians, who kiss her hands and even bestow upon her the epic epithet, commonly reserved for the Cid, of being born in a fortunate hour (683c):

> Fueron besar las manos todos a su señora,
> diziendo, 'Somos ricos castellanos agora.
> Infante doña Sancha, nasçiestes en buen hora,
> por end' vos resçebimos nos todos por señora. (683)
>
> (They all went to kiss the hand of their lady
> saying, 'We are rich Castilians now.
> Princess Sancha, you were born in a fortunate hour,
> and for this we all receive you as our lady.)

The language they use is important because it establishes her position within the economics of loyalty in the poem. Referring to themselves as 'ricos' (rich) (683b), the Castilians acknowledge that without Sancha they would not have been able to *cobrar* (recover), a word with profound connotations, used to describe the Count's territorial, economic, and spiritual recovery of Castile from the time of the invasion of Spain (e.g., 186c, 350c, 357d). In this scene of triumph, it could not be clearer that Sancha's role has been vital in sustaining the heroic vision: 'Sacastes a Castiella de grand cautividat, / fiziestes grand merçed a toda cristiandat' (you took Castile out of great captivity, / you showed great mercy to all Christians) (685ab). Sancha has been instrumental in keeping Fernán González in active service of his people – a commitment of his since the early stages of the poem when he leaves the mountainous terrain of his childhood to embrace public life (181) – but this scene also marks her own entry into a public domain where she can take a full, and at times necessarily independent, part in the Castilians' political project.

In the section of the poem recovered from the *Estoria de España* (History of Spain) the centrality of Sancha to the project of Castilian recovery is sustained.[15] When Fernán González is imprisoned for a second time, she commands absolute loyalty from the Castilians, who are drawn to her charisma (Victorio 1988: 182) but her loyalties are more intimately portrayed

---

[14] Vera Castro Lingl compares this episode with the version in the *Mocedades de Rodrigo*, noting that this later work regenerates the role of the hero and makes him more of an active participant; even when bound in chains Fernán is able to rob the Archpriest of his knife and kill him (1999: 74).

[15] This prosified, chronicle version of the *PCG*'s lost ending is reproduced in Victorio 1988: 179–85.

away from this public sphere. Now married to the Count, she is granted access to his cell for the night on the pretext that she is to undertake a pilgrimage to Santiago de Compostela. Once more, she is responsible for releasing him from his chains, although this time telling the King rather bluntly that 'el cauallo trauado nunqua bien podie fazer fijos' (the stallion that is fettered can never sire a foal) (ibid.). The sexual justification is true; they spend the night together 'amos en uno', which gives us a closer glimpse of their private world; after shared adventure comes mutual conspiracy, 'et fablaron y mucho de sus cosas' (they talked at length of their affairs) (ibid.). However, sex is also part of a ruse; on waking up they swap clothes so that the Count can creep out disguised in Sancha's pilgrim's garb. After this, she shows her loyalty more aptly in the question of lineage, no longer in adventures in the hills. As the hero escapes, now on horseback and alone, Sancha steadfastly safeguards his flight and her own name by invoking kinship ties: 'ca fija so de rey et muger de muy alto uaron, et uos non querades fazer contra mi cosa desaguisada, ca muy grand debdo e con uestros fijos, et en la mi desondra grand parte auredes uos' (because I am the daughter of a king and wife of a very noble man, and you would not wish to do anything offensive to me, for I have a close bond of kinship with your sons, and you would share greatly in my dishonour) (1988: 183). Although the chronicle insists at points on Sancha's fragility, presumably to prevent her from eclipsing Fernán González, it is clear that without her forceful manipulation of sexuality and lineage, the heroic enterprise, and by extension the historical narrative, would stall.[16]

One of the earliest incidents of treachery in the *Alexandre* occurs when Pausanias, overcome with passion for Olympias, Alexander's mother, plots to kill his father Philip (169–86). With Philip left for dead, Alexander, then *Infante* (Prince), is forced to fight Pausanias to protect his mother and the kingdom. When Alexander returns, having killed his foe, he finds his father uttering some hopeful last words which ironically are never fulfilled: 'de mano de traidores, fijo, Él vos defienda' (from the hand of traitors, son, may He defend you) (192d). In fact, Alexander's accession to the kingdom takes place in the context of anxieties about the vulnerability of women in a world of potential traitors, and the concomitant threat they pose to territorial security by dint of their very helplessness. Nevertheless, it would be unreasonable to underestimate Alexander's mother on this basis. From the outset, the poet makes it clear that she is a good and careful woman: 'por nul seso del mundo non la pudo ganar, / ca ella era buena e sabiés bien guardar' (he could not overcome her by any means in the world, / for she was good and knew how to look after herself) (169cd).

---

[16] Castro Lingl calls her a heroine of colossal stature, whose entrance into the life of the hero brings out his heroic distinction (1999: 74).

A serene and cerebral loyalty characterizes Olympias's support of her son's career. She appears little in the work directly but is often on the hero's mind – a private rather than a public role – especially at those times when motivation of others is lacking. Overcoming the desire to stay with one's wife and family is an essential step in the career of a warrior and Alexander frequently reminds his men that he shares this trial with them: 'Yo lexo buena madre e buenas dos hermanas' (I leave behind a good mother and two good sisters) (259a).[17] He allows himself briefly to imagine the pleasure their company would give him:

> Querría mis hermanas e mi madre veer,
> avrién ellas comigo, yo con ellas, plazer;
> mas veo dos contrarios detrás remaneçer
> por do podremos toda la ganançia perder. (1845)
>
> (I would like to see my sisters and my mother,
> I would take pleasure in their company, and they in mine;
> but I see two obstacles remain
> through which we can lose all that we gain.)

This statement is placed in the middle of a key exhortation to combat in which Alexander reconciles absence from one's kin with absolute loyalty to a morally upright cause. In fact, the cause he is fighting is treachery itself: 'nos nada non ganamos / quando los traïdores a vida los dexamos' (we ourselves gain nothing / when we allow traitors to live) (1851).

The distance between Alexander and his family is bridged with letters which highlight their devoted support. When he marries Roxane he writes of the deed, rather endearingly, to 'la su madre cara, / e las sus hermanillas que él niñas dexara' (his dear mother and his little sisters that he left as mere girls) (1965ab). Their response is directly linked to the relationship between women and the oral tradition's public sponsorship and celebration of heroic feats:

> Las dueñas grecïanas, con grandes alegrías,
> renovaron las bodas otros tantos de días,
> metieron en cançíones las sus cavallerías,
> por que serán contadas fasta que venga Elías. (1967)
>
> (The Greek women, with great joy,
> rekindled the wedding celebrations for so many more days,
> they composed songs of this heroic deeds,
> so that they would be told until the end of time.)

---

[17] The *Cantar de mio Cid* also dwells on the warrior leaving his family behind, with even greater poignancy than the *Alexandre*. See Montaner 2007, lines 275–81, 369–75.

The most significant letters in the poem are those which Alexander sends to his mother, added in manuscript O (Osuna, a Leonese version of the fourteenth century) and interpolated between stanzas 2633 and 2634 (stanzas 2468 and 2469 in Cañas 2003).[18] Their existence is testament to the importance that Alexander's mother holds for him, supporting the fact that women are at the foundations of the heroic: the depths of hero's own probing mind. Intended to bring comfort to his grieving mother, the letters also contain advice on setting herself apart from other women and from worldly concerns, and coming closer to continuing Alexander's public reputation by doing so. They urge loyalty to his memory, and to his character through the equation of mother and son: 'devedes punnar en no semeiar a las mugieres en flaqueza de sus coraçones assí como punné yo de no semeiar a los fechos de los omnes viles' (you must strive not to resemble women in the weakness of their hearts just as I strove not to imitate the deeds of base men); 'ya destaiada es la mi nombradía del regnado, e del seso […] avívevos la mi nombradía con vostro bon seso e con vostra sofrençia e con vostro conorte' (The reputation of my kingdom and my wisdom is already famous, keep my reputation alive with your good wisdom and your patience and your strength) (Cañas 2003: 585). The second letter lays further emphasis upon the destination of both their reputations after death:

> Ca la mi nombradia e la mi grant onrra en este sieglo destaiada es, e ficará la nombradía del vostro bon seso e de la vostra sofrençia, la vostra obediença al mandamiento de los sabios, e en esperar lo que Dios mandó del otro que es fincable. (Cañas 2003: 588)
>
> (Because my reputation and my great honour stand out in this world, and you will assure the reputation of your good wisdom and your patience, and your obedience to the edicts of the wise, and in waiting for God's commands from the other world that is lasting.)

The prospect of the 'sieglo […] que es fincable' (the lasting world) is vitally important to both works, and women play a major part in informing the ideal of heroism and the construction of collective identities through their association with a drama of finality. An insistence upon the next life is perhaps unsurprising given the clerical nature of the texts, but it is worth reiterating the particular eschatological anxieties of the clergy of thirteenth-century Iberia, which were tied in to the expectations of the Reconquest (see, for example, Saugnieux 1982). In the *PFG*, time and temporality are a constant preoccupation and while sometimes time is described as moving in circles in accordance with fortune (96ab), or with the desires of God (111d), it is

---

[18] In the edition of Francisco Marcos Marín (1987) the letters are included as an appendix.

certainly finite (210). This certitude is employed to motivational effect by Fernán González. The end is inescapable and must influence the way his men behave:[19]

> Por tanto, ha mester que los dias contemos,
> los dias e las noches en que las espendemos,
> quantos en valde passan nunca los cobraremos. (357abc)
>
> (Therefore, we must take account of the days,
> the days and the nights and how we spend them,
> those that we squander we will never regain.)

Only the noblest and most worthy of man's deeds will be remembered (352c) in a third and more lasting life of *fama*. Sancha upholds Fernán González's chances of achieving *fama* through her critical interventions at moments when he comes close to perishing, a role clearly illustrated when the Lombard visits her to urge her to save the hero from death (623c). Sancha's responsibility for averting his imminent death is repeated by her lady-in-waiting, 'si muere de tal guisa, grand pecado faredes' (if he dies in this way, you will be committing a grave sin) (631d). Moreover, Sancha visits the Count in prison and tells him directly that unless he agrees to marry her he will die there (638a).

These allusions may appear to be intended to inject urgency into the plot, were it not for the fact that the poet frequently associates Fernán González's death with the demise of Castile and the failure of its people to live up to the expectations that their illustrious history and their personal integrity demand. Whenever he is absent, his vassals fret that their shared enterprise is doomed: 'si, ¡mal pecado! muere, Castiella es perdida' (if, God forbid!, he dies, Castile is lost) (339c), and that they are returning to the condition of servitude imposed upon them by the Muslim invasion (607) so explicitly detailed in the opening stages of the poem. His death is thus, in a sense, a collective one. In rescuing him from death, Sancha stands by extension at the confluence of two important ideological strands in the poem: the political and providential destinies of Castile.

That Sancha keeps Fernán González on a providential path is made clear by the poet's choice of language. Before even beginning to rescue him, Sancha states, with biblical echoes (Isaiah 51.11; John 16.20), 'venira sazon que l'vere bienandante' (the time will come when I shall see him happy) (632d), a prediction which is later fulfilled: 'el llanto que fazian en grand gozo tornavan' (the sorrow they expressed turned into great joy) (686d).[20]

---

[19] Deyermond 1990 is fundamental to this discussion.

[20] This echoes the *pesar / plazer* theme in the *Cantar de mio Cid*: e.g., 'Aun todos estos duelos en gozo se tornarán' (line 381).

However, the reactions of the Castilians to her role in extracting the Count from his first imprisonment is more telling still. Not only do they readily admit that she has taken Castile out of servitude, 'grand cautividat' (685a), a biblical allusion echoing the captivity of the Israelites, but they refer to themselves as 'resurrected': 'tenian que eran muertos e que resuçitavan' (they thought they were dead and were being resurrected) (686b). Sancha has removed them, and the hero, from the jaws of death so that Castile's providential destiny can be fulfilled and the Castilians' position within the collective memory assured.

The *Alexandre*'s conception of time is remarkably similar to that of the *PFG*, including several verbal reminiscences.[21] The philosophy that man's life may endure through *fama* if he makes the most of his time on earth is found as early as Aristotle's speech (85d), then throughout the *Alexandre*, culminating in expositions of the worthlessness of earthly glory (2668, 2670–71). This ethos, a motivational one often used by Alexander to inspire his men (e.g., 769–71, 1342–43) and one deeply attached to knightly ideals (Lida 1952: 167), means that death and vistas of the afterlife are ever present in the narrative. Women play a large part in this close relationship between worldly behaviour and piety. A striking incident, used by the poet to glorify his hero, takes place when Endrona, Darius's wife, perishes in prison (1235). Alexander grieves as if this were his own mother (1236b) and proceeds to show her the greatest possible honour, to the extent that he even reaches to wipe her face as she lies dying (1236c). His beneficent treatment is reported to Darius, whose response, an appeal to God, reveals that Alexander's magnanimity virtually crushes his warrior spirit: if he is to lose the kingdom he wishes it to go to Alexander, 'que es rey acabado' (because he is a king through and through) (1258d). This female death has another function: it opens up a commentary on rise and fall, gain and loss, as Darius recognizes the role of providence in man's shifting affairs, 'Señor, en cuya mano somos muertos e bivos [...] los ricos aprimes e alças los mesquinos' (Lord, in whose hand we are dead and alive [...] you oppress the rich and make the poor rise) (1257). This motif, inherent also in the *Poema*, is played out at the level of the narrative when Alexander eventually marries Roxane, daughter of Darius, and new life comes from the death of Endrona. The May

---

[21] Alexander's statement 'Non conto yo mi vida por años nin por días, / mas por buenas faziendas e por cavallerías' (I do not measure my life by years or by days / but by great deeds and acts of bravery) (2288ab) inspires stanza 357 of the *PFG*, quoted above, as well as the phrase, 'Si omne el su tiempo quiere en valde passar, / non quiere d'este mundo otra cosa levar' (If man wishes to spend his time in idleness, he leaves the world with nothing but that) (351ab). The *Alexandre* poet's interest in *fama* is discussed at length by Lida de Malkiel (1952: 167–97; see also 197–207 on the *PFG*).

poem which precedes the wedding, a tribute to this sweet season for lovers, is brimming with symbols of perpetuity and procreation (1950–54).

In quite a different context, a confluence of life and death is also found in the episode where Alexander meets Thalestris, Queen of the Amazons.[22] The poet tells us that these warrior women exist in a society apart, 'tierra quel dizién femenina' (a land they call female) (1863b), from which men are excluded except for three occasions a year when the women go to established locations at the borders of their territory to sleep with them (1865). The aim of this is procreation. If a female child is born it remains with its mother, while male offspring are sent to the father (1866ab).[23] We discover that Alexander's fame has even reached the confines of this all-female space; the beautiful Thalestris visits Alexander on account of his great repute: 'traes grant ventura, / grant seso e grant fuerça, esfuerço e mesura' (you bring great fortune, great wisdom and great strength, fortitude and restraint) (1885ab). What she wants, in contradiction to tradition, and what he agrees to, is to conceive a male child with him, because it will have an illustrious lineage, unrivalled in the whole world (1886c).[24]

Supportive of Alexander's *fama* and the perpetuity of his name, this episode may also have links with the poem's eschatological drama. In traditional legends of Alexander, the Amazons are associated specifically with the defence of Christendom against the tribes of Gog and Magog, and more generally with guarding the gates beyond which lie demonic hoards or marauding invaders like the Alans, Huns, and Saracens (DiMarco 1991: 69–73). Vicent DiMarco cites 'geographical confusions' and 'narrative coincidences' as main reasons for this and it does appear that in our poem relatively few stanzas (some 213) separate the meeting of Alexander and Thalestris from the scene where Alexander finds an unfamiliar multitude beyond a pass in the Caspian mountains (2101–16). He is told by an anonymous sage that they are Jews, and that as betrayers of the Lord they were either killed or sent into captivity. After this notice, Alexander orders that they should be incarcerated there for all time and prays to God, who in response closes off the rocky pass. The threat they pose to humankind is sufficiently stressed as to conflate the poem with the Revelation of St John (2115). The *Alexandre* narrative does not seem, however, to have progressed

---

[22] This episode captured the imagination of the poet. On his amplification of the Latin text, see Catena 1986.

[23] This information concurs with views of the image of Amazons in the classical world.

[24] Estelle Irizarry confirms that the poet's elaboration of Thalestris's visit is 'evidently directed toward enhancing the king's stature' (1983: 56); she also reads links between the Amazon women and Sancha in the *Poema* as a way of elevating the Infanta's strength and courage 'to legendary status' (58). Sharon Macdonald notes that the classical Amazons traditionally rejected marriage and sons (1987: 6), a view confirmed by Else Kirk, doubly emphasizing the attraction of Alexander's fame (1987: 31).

to the stage of active involvement between the Amazons and the Jews, beyond the abiding impression that the poet wishes his reader to consider geographical boundaries in more conceptual and symbolic terms.[25] The fact that Thalestris is not portrayed as resistant to the values of the society in which Alexander lives, but actively seeks to share in them through a son with Alexander, also rules out DiMarco's argument that the subversion implied by women's rule could be associated as one of the signs of the end of the world (1991: 75). In this case, the Amazons serve principally to reinforce the hero's fame, and to justify its extension to the next generation.

While the ending of the *PFG* remains lost, the *Alexandre* concludes with the death of the hero, a point in the poem where gender dynamics are of heightened interest. Alexander's offence is against the symbolic mother, Nature, 'que cría todas las crïaturas' (who nurtures all creatures) (2325a), as he attempts to pry into her secrets: 'quísolas Alexandre por fuerça conocer' (Alexander wanted to know them through force) (2327). Deyermond makes the excellent point that this line contains 'in the combination of "por fuerça" with the sexually suggestive "conocer" a hint of rape' (1996: 152). The descriptions of Nature as 'sobjugada' (overcome) and 'aontada' (dishonoured) (2326) appear to support this view. This attempted penetration of the feminine order displeases God, the Patriarch, 'al Crïador que crió la Natura' (the Creator who created Nature) (2329a) and challenges the suggestion that heroic masculinity is at the heart of this community, as popular reaction to his death would seem to suggest:

> los unos dizián: '¡Padre!', los otros: '¡Ay, señor!';
> otros dizián: '¡Rey!', otros: '¡Emperador!';
> todos, grandes e chicos, fazien muy grant dolor. (2658bcd)
>
> (some cried 'Father!', others: 'Oh, my lord!',
> others cried 'King!', others: 'Emperor!'
> All men, great and small, expressed deep sorrow.)

However, Weiss astutely notes that Alexander is killed by a father figure, Antipater, in an ironic inversion whereby 'Providential order is protected by an act of betrayal' (2006: 120). His masculinity, having become excessively proud and uninhibited, is killed off by a symbolic anti-father, who ultimately safeguards the patriarchal order. Because of conflicting evidence in the poem's closing stanzas, it has been debated whether Alexander is

---

[25] Deyermond makes the supporting point that the *Alexandre* poet is adept at linking microcosm and macrocosm, adding that the he 'is fascinated [...] by geography, by the broad sweep of history, by intellectual curiosity, by the harmonious blending of different areas of knowledge in a unified theory' (1996: 153).

damned or not.[26] Returning to the interpolated letters from Alexander to his mother may shed further light on this eventuality. Plainly, the letters between mother and son mean that the connection with the feminine / maternal that was so fractured by Alexander's breach of Nature is re-established in the minds of the audience, with absolving effect. More importantly, the letters take the reader's imagination beyond Alexander's death. As his posthumous interlocutor, Olympias keeps Alexander's voice alive, giving him a platform where a purer voice can speak out, one that is structurally removed from the narrative of pride and downfall, and one that stands therefore as a more fitting testament to the heroic and its meaning for future generations. Left to resume the dialogic construction of an heroic vision, now that the narrator's voice has tailed away, Olympias confirms that the ethos of the poem is one of continuation and providential expectation.

In conclusion: women are active participants in the dynamics of heroic success and the correction of its failures, but they are also authoritative signs and symbols of a providential authority. They are instrumental, therefore, in taking these texts to a higher plane of meaning, one that would no doubt have been appreciated, if not actively sought, by its medieval readers. Within this clerical context, and in their proximity to the hero, women help to extend the collective imagination of the audience; they are a profound part of literature *in* society at a critical juncture in Spain's medieval history. Men are the colonizers and conquerors in this world, but they must leave it: 'el omne, maguer que pueble en este mundo, a ir es dél, e del regnado, maguer que dure, a dexar es' (man, though he may populate this world, is due to leave it and although the kingdom may last, he has to leave it behind) (Cañas 2003: 585). It is woman, both in text and context, who lays solid foundations for the next.

Further reading

Anderson, Benedict, 2006. *Imagined Communities: Reflections on the Origin and Spread of Nationalism*, rev. edn (London: Verso)

Johnson, Lesley, 1995. 'Imagining Communities: Medieval and Modern', in *Concepts of National Identity in the Middle Ages*, ed. Simon Forde, Lesley Johnson, and Alan V. Murray, Leeds Texts and Monographs, 14 (Leeds: UP), pp. 1–21

Lacarra, María Eugenia, et al. (eds), 1990. *Estudios históricos y literarios sobre la mujer medieval*, Biblioteca de Estudios sobre la Mujer, 4 (Málaga: Diputación Provincial)

---

[26] Critics who conclude that Alexander repents include Lida (1952:194–6) and Willis (1956–57: 212–24). Ian Michael has argued that the hero is damned (1960, 1965, and 1970: 263–6).

Poor, Sara S., and Jana Schulman (eds), 2007. *Women and Medieval Epic: Gender, Genre, and the Limits of Epic Masculinity* (New York: Palgrave Macmillan)

Veeser, H. Aram (ed.), 1989. *The New Historicism* (London: Routledge)

2

Desire and Transgression in the Female Voice of Early Popular Lyric

MARIANA MASERA

for Alan Deyermond †

¡Ayres, ola!, ¡que me abraso en amores toda!:* woman's song – male invention or female reality?

The *cancionero popular medieval* (corpus of medieval folksong) is made up of songs that were sung to while away the monotony of daily tasks, to celebrate high days and holidays, and to accompany courtship and carnival.[1] These songs were in the main composed and transmitted orally, and they survive in variant versions, some very ancient, some more recent, which are adopted and adapted by the poetic schools of different times and regions. The early folksongs that have come down to us were committed to writing in the fifteenth, sixteenth, and seventeenth centuries because of an interest, first on the part of composers, then of poets and dramatists, in renewing the language of learned poetry.[2] During this time, the songs for which we have a written record – only a fraction of the numbers that must have existed – 'have passed through various filters: the filter of writing, the filter of the aristocratic, urban culture which embraced them, and the filter of the poets and playwrights who pressed them into service' (Frenk [1994] 2006:19). Even so, despite the long period of assimilation, the corpus of traditional lyric

---

* Breezes, hello! I'm burning up with love! (*NC* 269). All lyric quotations are taken from Frenk's *Nuevo corpus* (2003), hereinafter *NC*. This collection is in my view the most complete, as much for the number of texts it contains – more than 3,769 – as for its critical apparatus.

[1] According to Frenk, the term 'popular' is preferable because it takes us back to the culture from which the lyric originates, and which sustains it, that of the Middle Ages and of the sixteenth and seventeenth centuries (2003: 9, n.1).

[2] For details of this process of appreciation of the popular lyric, see Frenk 1971: 1–48.

'reveals an idiosyncratic imaginary world, quite different from the worlds it inhabits in time and space, and it unveils certains forms of sensibility, of experiencing the world, which cannot be other than those of the popular culture to which they belonged' (ibid.).

One of the most compelling and distinctive features of the popular lyric of medieval Spain is the pervasiveness of the female voice. Not only does this voice come from the mouth of a woman but it also reveals an outlook which is different from that of the male voice predominant in court poetry of the period. I understand 'female voice' in the sense defined by James Monroe: 'When one speaks of a feminine lyric one is referring to a literary voice, to a persona, not to actual feminine authorship, much less to feminine performance' (1981–82: 134). Nevertheless, I agree with Margit Frenk when she says that in the corpus of traditional lyric there exists a woman's song which, besides being placed in the mouth of a woman, has added to it, and sometimes running counter to it, viewpoints we recognize as specifically feminine ([1993b] 2006: 354).[3]

As many scholars have shown, women's songs are not exclusive to the Iberian Peninsula. Elvira Gangutia suggests that the origin of the love songs sung by women goes back to an archaic East-West community. They originated in specific cults which never had access to the world of Ancient Greece, but whose songs were reawakened by Hellenism and the empire, although fragmented into a thousand different nuances (Gangutia 1972: 377). The importance of women's songs in a wider European literary tradition has also been highlighted by Doris Earnshaw: '*Chansons de femme*, or women's songs, occupy a place of special importance in the study of medieval Romance lyric. Dating from the tenth century, they are the earliest lyrics in the vernacular languages of Western Europe' (1988: 1).

For some years now the debate over the origins of the woman's-voice lyric before the troubadours has generated divergent opinions. On the one hand, we can point to the repeated references in ecclesiastical documents to women's songs, held up for censure as 'cantica diabolica, amatoria et turpia, obscina et luxuriosa cantica' (dissolute, amorous, and depraved songs, filthy and lewd songs) (Lorenzo Gradín 1990: 8; cf. Frenk 1985: 44–8). We must also take into account the fundamental presence of the female figure as a character in the poetic genres on the margins of the distinctly male-voice

---

[3] On woman's-voice poetry in general see Plummer 1981, Lemaire 1987, Earnshaw 1988, Lorenzo Gradín 1990; on woman's-voice lyric in medieval Iberia see Ashley 1981, Lemaire 1983, Lorenzo Gradín 1990, Masera 2001. John G. Cummins in his anthology relates the currency of the female voice to the fact that 'the female members of a Spanish community sing more than men' (1977: 22). On woman's voice and the women poets of late-medieval Spain see Deyermond 1983, Whetnall 1984, López Estrada 1986, and Pérez Priego 1990.

troubadour lyric: the *pastorela* (shepherdess song), the *alba* or dawn song, the *chanson de toile* (weaving song), and the song of the *malmaridada* (unhappily married woman) (Frenk 1985: 79).

In the Iberian Peninsula, the Mozarabic *kharja* (tenth to eleventh centuries), the Galician-Portuguese *cantiga de amigo* (song of the lover) (twelfth to fourteenth centuries) and the Spanish *estribillo* (refrain) (collected from the fifteenth century onwards), constitute the three great poetic traditions which have in common the presence of a woman's voice, notably the monologue of a young girl in love who speaks of her feelings; a voice which in the two later traditions is linked to the world of nature. This voice, which was absent from the learned lyric of the time, and which is quite different in tone and expression from that of the male-voice songs, becomes a distinctive feature which can be understood as deriving from, or influenced by, the traditional lyric of popular origin.

Although the antiquity of the woman's-voice love song is an acknowledged fact there still exists a polemic among critics with regard to the creative role of women. Among those who accept the possibility of female authorship there is Theodore Frings (1949), who considers that the creative woman is 'at the beginning of all love poetry', an opinion held by other scholars who maintain that these songs are 'remnants of precourtly, oral and traditional culture, songs of women's groups in village and manorial society' (Earnshaw 1988: 1–2).[4] For others such as Leo Spitzer, however, 'this woman has in primitive world literature a role imposed upon her by man, answering him with the very words of longing he has suggested to her' (1952: 22). This view is shared by Giuseppe Tavani (1969), among others, who believes that women's songs – referring in particular to the *cantigas de amigo* – are 'the work of the male troubadour, who sang them for the entertainment of an aristocratic audience' (Earnshaw 1988: 2).[5]

On this question, with regard to the popular lyric of medieval Spain, specifically the refrains that were written down between the fifteenth and the seventeenth centuries, I concur with Frenk who, in the face of those who maintain that it is all a question of rhetoric and that rhetoric is neutral, emphatically champions the living tradition of this lyric, and 'its relationship with the social lives and the inner worlds of women' ([1994] 2006: 360). It should not be forgotten that these female voices belong to an oral tradition,

---

[4] For Lemaire, writing changed the old oral songs: 'my thesis is that men have used that new technology to exclude women from various fields in culture, e.g., as authors of love poetry' (1986: 740).

[5] Critics who do not accept the notion of female authorship of these lyrics include Beltrán (1976: 48, 54) and Gaylord (1982).

to a common imaginary, and the songs are there to help girls express their desires rather than to represent the reality of a world without restrictions.[6]

A la guerra van mis ojos:[*] **the markers of voice and associated *topoi*[7]**

The medieval Spanish popular lyric hosts not one female voice but a plurality of voices belonging to several different women, from the young initiate in love to the married woman waiting for her lover and looking ahead to the delights of the encounter. The female voice can be identified in these songs from various markers, both textual (explicit) and contextual (implicit), which can further be subdivided into two categories: the symbolic and the non-symbolic. The textual or explicit features are of three kinds: markers that denote the speaker, markers that point to the addressee or interlocutor, and markers which indicate the person who is being spoken of, or the *delocutor*.[8] Let us look at some examples:

> ¡Hala, hala, hala, hala,   (Hey, hey, hey, hey,
> que no estoy para vos guardada!   I'm not destined for you!)
> (*NC* 710)

In this song the speaker is identified as female by the grammatical gender of the last word, 'guardada' ('destined'). In the next two examples the speaker declares herself to be the object of amorous advances by a male admirer.

> Déxate, Juan, de burlar,   (Stop flirting, Juan,
> que no quiero aquillotrar.   I don't want to make love to you.)
> (*NC* 694)
>
> Ayer vino un caballero,   (Yesterday a gentleman came,
> mi madre, a me namorar;   my mother, to make love to me;
> no lo puedo yo olvidar.   I can't forget him.)
> (*NC* 282)

In most female-voice love songs the woman emerges as the subject of her own discourse (the marker of the speaker); this is not the case with male-

---

[6] See Frenk's articles 'Lírica tradicional y cultura popular en la Edad Media hispánica' ([1994] 2006), and 'Poesía de la aristocracia y poesía del pueblo en la Edad Media' ([1992] 2006).

[*] My love is going to the war (*NC* 177A).

[7] I take the term *topos* (pl. *topoi*) to mean the stable configuration of various motifs that reappears with frequency in literature (Ducrot and Todorov 1989: 257). The motif that keeps recurring, a phenomenon known as the leitmotif, will be treated as a *topos*.

[8] For alternative methodologies regarding the identification of gender markers in medieval woman's-voice lyric see Earnshaw 1988 and Klinck 2003.

voice songs, in which the man's discourse centres on the woman and the most frequent marker is that of the addressee.[9] This is evident in one of the *topoi* exclusive to the female voice of the popular lyric, which is common to the various medieval poetic traditions, namely the *topos* of self-praise (see Frenk 1971: 68).

> Pues que me tienes, Miguel, por esposa,
> ¡mírame, Miguel, cómo soi hermosa! (*NC* 122)
>
> (Since I am your wife, Miguel,
> look at me, Miguel, how beautiful I am!)

Another *topos* peculiar to the female voice is 'waiting', which belongs to the universal theme of absence, provoked by the delay of the lover. This causes the suspicion and frustration of the girl in love since jealousy does not take long to appear, as seen in the words of the woman fretting about her lover's neglect:

> A la queda han tocado,   (They have sounded the curfew
> y mi bien no viene: and my lover does not appear:
> otros nuevos amores   a new love
> me lo detienen.   is keeping him from me.)
> (*NC* 568C; see also *NC* 572)

No textual marker is needed to indicate that the following song is a woman's, since the *topos* of waiting is combined with the symbol of the door:

> Llaman a la puerta,   (Someone is knocking at my door
> y espero yo a mi amor: and I am waiting for my lover:
> ¡que todas las aldabadas   all the knocks
> me dan en el coraçón!   strike at my heart!)
> (*NC* 292)

No quiero ser casada / sino libre enamorada:* marriage or freedom

A recurrent theme of the medieval popular lyric is marriage, about which the girls have differing views. Some want to get married, some don't, and yet others threaten their parents if they don't carry out their wishes. There are also songs involving girls who refuse to follow the destiny that has been lined up for them, such as becoming a nun, although at times the convent

---

[9] The many male-voice songs which are marked for speaker include *NC* 260, 641, 689.
* I don't want to be a married woman / but a free-spirited lover (*NC* 216)

seems to be the preferred option. The importance of this theme is attested by the number of texts displaying the range of female attitudes to matrimony, whether 'Madre, casarme quiero' (*NC* 197) (Mother, I want to get married), or 'No quiero marido, no' (I don't want a husband, no), or about the unhappy nun, the *malmonjada*, or the reluctant novice:

Dizen que me case yo: ¡no quiero marido, no! (*NC* 218)[10]	(They say I should marry: I don't want a husband, no!)
Prometió mi madre de me dar marido, hasta que el perexil estuviesse florido. (*NC* 202)	(My mother promised to give me a husband, as soon as the parsley was in flower.)
Mongica en religión, me quiero entrar, por no mal maridar. (*NC* 215 A)	(I want to enter the convent as a nun, so as not to marry badly.)
No quiero ser monja, no, que niña namoradica so. (*NC* 210)	(I don't want to be a nun, no, for I am a girl in love.)

The rebellion of the daughter is another *topos* that belongs to this convention. Sometimes the girl in love can be heard complaining of the guardianship imposed by her mother; in other songs she boasts of flouting this vigilance:[11]

Aguardan a mí: ¡nunca tales guardas vi! (*NC* 153)	(They watch over me: such guards I never did see!)
Madre, la mi madre, guardas me ponéys: que si yo no me guardo, mal me guardaréys. (*NC* 152)	(Mother of mine, you put me under surveillance but if I don't guard myself, you will guard me badly.)

---

[10] There is just one text featuring a man who does not want to get married: '–Cásate, manzebo. / –No quiero casarme: / más quiero ser libre / que no cautivarme' (*NC* 217) ('Marry, lad. / I don't wish to marry: / I'd rather be free / and not be trapped').

[11] For the motif of the rebellious daughter see Lorenzo Gradín 1990: 185.

¡Hola, hola / que no tengo de dormir sola!:* desire and transgression

The *topos* of the kiss forms part of the theme of erotic games. It is striking how often the sexual initiative comes from the woman, who takes delight in mischief and naughtiness:

Pues por besarte, Minguillo,	(Because I kissed you, Minguillo,
me riñe mi madre a mí,	my mother scolds me,
buélveme presto, carillo,	so give me back soon, dearest,
aquel beso que te dí.	the kiss that I gave you.)
(*NC* 1684 B)	

Some songs reveal a desiring woman who wants to be with her lover; in others, desire is transformed into a performative principle, into an invitation for him to take her with him, suggesting, symbolically, the erotic encounter:

Por el río me llevad, amigo,	(Take me down to the river, lover,
y llevádeme por el río.	and take me down to the river.)
(*NC* 462)	

The comings and goings of the woman in this love poetry are closely tied up with her sexual desire, which, when fulfilled, leads the speaker to make transparent excuses for her actions, such as, for example, inventing an errand from her mother.[12] The young girl complains mischievously about the risk entailed in going alone to certain places with strong erotic associations, such as the olive grove:

A que horas me mandais	(At this hour you send me
aos olivaes!	to the olive groves!)
(*NC* 316)	

In many songs the woman is seen in motion, which may be due to a number of factors, such as her occupation, which always carries suggestive connotations: 'Ývame yo, mi madre, / a vender pan a la villa' (*NC* 120 B), (I went, mother, / to sell bread in the town), or 'guardando el ganado / la color perdí' (*NC* 139) (while tending the flock / I lost my colour); or her attendance at church: 'Ansí vaya, madre, / virgo a la vigilia' (*NC* 185 C) (So may I go, mother, / a maiden to the vigil); or on a pilgrimage: 'Viniendo de la romería' (*NC* 273 A) (Coming back from pilgrimage), and 'Yo me iva, mi madre, /

---

* Hey, hey, / I don't want to sleep without a lover! (*NC* 169A)

[12] On the motif of the transparent excuse see Gornall 1988.

a la romería' (*NC* 313) (I went, mother, / on a pilgrimage).[13] All these texts refer to women who are notorious for their amorous proclivities: the baker's girl, the dark-skinned girl, and even the girls who go on a pilgrimage, which in the love lyric serves as a rendezvous for lovers. Thus almost any kind of activity involving a woman may signify an erotic encounter.

>No sé qué me bulle
>en el calcañar,
>que no puedo andar.
>
>Yéndome y viniendo,
>a las mis vacas,
>no sé qué me bulle,
>entre las faldas
>que no puedo andar.
>(*NC* 1645 B)
>
>(I don't know what is stirring
>in my heel,
>that I cannot walk.
>
>Coming and going,
>to my cows
>I don't know what is stirring
>between my skirts
>that I cannot walk.)

One of the most erotic lyric moments is the early morning, whether it figures in *albas*, dawn songs, when lovers part at daybreak or, more often, in *alboradas*, when lovers meet at dawn. These have existed since ancient times in many traditions, and the Spanish popular lyric is no exception:

>Ya cantan los gallos,
>buen amor, y vete,
>cata que amanece.
>(*NC* 454 B)
>
>(Cocks are crowing,
>good love, be gone:
>look, the day is breaking.)
>
>Al alba venid, buen amigo,
>al alva venid.
>(*NC* 452)
>
>(Come at dawn, my love,
>come at dawn.)

Another *topos* of great persistence in the various poetic traditions, and which is omnipresent as a marker of woman's voice in the medieval popular lyric, is the loneliness of the girl in love. This can be expressed as a complaint at being alone without her lover, or as a form of lure after his mistreatment of her, or in an invitation to an erotic encounter, where it is usually reinforced by a symbol:

>Sola me dexastes
>en aquel yermo,
>¡villano, malo, gallego!
>(*NC* 673)
>
>(You left me alone
>in that barren land
>peasant, evildoer, coward!)

---

[13] There is the occasional male-voice song which relates the activity of the woman to her work, such as *NC* 551. On eroticism and women's work see Masera 1999.

¡Ay toda la noche, toda!	(Oh, all night, all night!
¡Ay, toda la noche sola!	Oh, all night alone!)
(*NC* 581)	
A los baños dell amor	(To the baths of love
sola m'iré	I shall go alone
y en ellos me bañaré.	and bathe myself in them.)
(*NC* 320)	(Whilelm 1990: 253)

From all these examples, we can appreciate how spoken *topoi* of the female voice functioned: the listener recognized them and was then able to identify the text as a woman's song.[14]

Mal ferida iva la garça / enamorada:* symbolism and women's songs

However, as various studies have shown, the most striking poetic feature of the female-voice lyric is the constant presence of symbols from the world of nature.[15] This has led some critics to categorize the female voice as archaic and primitive (Earnshaw 1988: 135), although studies reveal a very rich and complex poetics. Traditional symbols come mainly from the natural world of plants, flowers, water. They are ancient symbols associated with human sexuality, linked to myths of the renewal of nature, whose ultimate objective is the preservation of life (Morales Blouin 1981: 33). Traditional symbols are also constant and collective (Reckert 1970: 32), which means that a small number of them are frequently repeated in a large body of texts. Their constant recurrence in the corpus is no accident; on the contrary, 'the body of symbols appearing in folk songs is a language, a code system, and it has to be understood by its users' (Frenk 1993a: 21). In other words, the existence of a symbolic language presupposes the mindset and the capability to perceive and decode it. For this reason, the study of myths and symbols opens the door to a world of meanings that were previously hidden. So in order to arrive at a better understanding of the symbols of traditional lyric a knowledge of their context is essential.

Traditional symbols tend to cluster together, illuminating one another. Hatto has declared that on some occasions, 'so concrete is traditional poetic language and so often do parallel situations occur over wide intervals of

---

[14] Other attitudes of the female voice which do not serve as exclusive markers, since they also appear in other voices, are: lament, protest, warning, plea, curse, declaration, affirmation, reproach, desire, preoccupation, justification, request, rejection, order, and advice.

* The heron was sorely wounded / and in love (*NC* 512 A)

[15] A study of symbols in the various Peninsular traditions can be found in Hatto 1965, Reckert 1970 and 1993, Deyermond 1979–80, Olinger 1985, and Frenk 1993a.

time and space that (although parallels never meet) the key to one poem may sometimes unlock another, however remote their external circumstances' (1965: 65). The relationship between the symbols that appear in different cultures has led researchers to think that their occurrence in different places and at different periods demonstrates their archetypal nature.[16] There are other hypotheses according to which the antiquity of some symbols can only be explained by their common origin in a remote past (Deyermond 1979–80, Frenk 1993a). And indeed, the rich poetic harmonies that emerge in female-voice song can only be unravelled through a constant dialogue with the tradition to which they belong. Woman and her erotic desires are associated with the moon, the wind, water, and trees:

> Salga la luna, el caballero,
> salga la luna, y vámonos luego. (*NC* 459)

(As soon as the moon comes out, my lover,
as soon as the moon comes out, let us go.)

Un mal ventecillo,	(A wicked little breeze
loquillo con mis faldas	playing the fool with my skirts:
¡tira allá, mal vento!	leave me alone, wicked wind!
¡qué me las alças!	What are you lifting them for?)
(*NC* 973)	(Reckert 1993: 59)
Orillicas del río,	(On the banks of the river,
mis amores ¡é!	my love, hey!,
y debajo de los álamos	and beneath the poplars
me atendé.	you wait for me.)
(*NC* 461)	

Aunque soi morena, no soi de olbidar:[*] the symbolism of the dark-skinned girl

The dark-skinned woman is one of the standard protagonists of traditional European lyric which has persisted down to the present day.[17] On a literal

---

[16] According to Cummins, the survival of symbols and motifs in contemporary Spanish folksong suggests 'that field-work can still add to our knowledge of the tradition, revealing startling links between the lyrics current today and those preserved in published or written form from earlier periods' (1977: 2).

[*] Although I am dark / I should not be forgotten (*NC* 140) (Wardropper 1986: 489)

[17] The motif of the dark girl is treated by Lucretius in *De rerum natura* (IV.1160–70). Robert D. Brown points out that for other classical authors, a 'dark complexion in women was considered inferior to pale [...] and darker complexions are often excused or euphemized in erotic literature' (1987: 283).

level, dark skin is associated with the paradigm of rustic beauty in comparison with aristocratic beauty, which is fair-haired and white-skinned. However, it has been shown that the colour also functions as a symbol.[18] Danckert has demonstrated that the colour of dark skin, as a female attribute (*Schwarzbraun*), indicates sexual availability and thus the *morena* (*Braunmeydelein*) (brown girl) represents the woman who has already had amorous experiences (1976: I, 404). This is the meaning it has in the Spanish traditional lyric (Frenk [1993b] 2006: 367), where the dark-skinned woman accounts for her colour by means of symbolic expressions with erotic connotations which reveal a girl who has already experienced love:

Con el ayre de la sierra, tornéme morena. (*NC* 135)	(With the breeze from the mountains I turned dark.)
Madre, la mi madre, si morena soy, andando en el campo me á tostado el sol. (*NC* 138)	(Mother, my mother, if I am dark, walking in the fields the sun has burned me.)

These texts are open to two simultaneous interpretations: from a literal reading we glean that her dark colouring is a consequence of the toil of the rustic woman; a symbolic reading gives us the sun and wind as symbols of the male principle, of sexual passion (Olinger 1985: 79). The same applies to the following example, where is it clear that it is not any old river to which the girl is heading, but the river of love:[19]

Por el río del amor, madre, que yo blanca me era, blanca, y quemóme el ayre. (*NC* 136)	(Along the river of love, mother I was white, white, and the wind burned me.)

Generally, symbols are grouped in clusters and this imbues them with a heightened lyricism which reaches almost hermetic extremes, as in this song in which the girl's desire leads her to cross liminal spaces between her body

---

[18] For the dark-skinned girl as a model of rustic womanhood see Wardropper 1960: 415, Cummins 1977: 99–102, and Gornall 1986. On the dark-skinned girl as a symbol see Morales Blouin 1981, Olinger 1985: 119–69; Frenk 1993a: 9, and Vasvári 1999.

[19] See Reckert on the river as a symbol of fertility in Iberian lyric (1970: 35); Deyermond 1979–80 on the river as a symbol of male passion; on water symbolism in the traditional lyric see Morales Blouin 1981 and Battesti-Pelegrin 1985.

and the world, represented by the elemental symbols of the door and the fountain.[20]

> A mi puerta nasce una fonte: (At my door a spring gushes out:
> ¿por dó saliré que no me moje?   how shall I get round it dry?)
> (*NC* 321)   (Reckert 1993: 62)

Her fear is similar to that of another girl who must cross the river without getting her shoes wet:

> ¡Río de Sevilla,   (River of Seville,
> quién te passasse   if only I could cross you
> sin que la mi servilla   without my shoe
> se me mojasse!   getting wet!)
> (*NC* 2352 A)

Why are the protagonists so afraid of getting wet? In the first place, as we have seen, the river is one of the most erotic places for lovers' meetings. Secondly the motif of crossing the river is a symbol 'linked to the renewal of sexual vigour, the affirmation of coitus, and the promise of fertility' (De Lope 1985: 255). That is to say, the water can be interpreted as the male sexual principle. We can attribute the girl's fear to the fact that 'crossing the water' can be understood as a rite of passage, whereby the wetting of the shoe also represents the girl's sexual transformation.

We are presented with a female voice which feeds on an archaic but far from primitive symbolic system that is often combined with *topoi* from other traditions; this produces songs of great poetic density that reveal a world of different sensations and resonances.

Airezillo en los mis kabellos, / i aire en ellos:* female voice and male voice

Women's songs in the traditional medieval corpus are as frequent as those of men: the female voice existed alongside the male voice, on equal terms (Masera 2001).[21] This is one of the important respects in which the traditional lyric of the medieval and early modern periods differs wholly from its learned counterpart, which was predominantly male-voiced. Earnshaw's

---

[20] For the sexual symbolism of doors see especially Vasvari 1999; for fountains see Deyermond 1979–80.

  * A gentle breeze in my hair, / breeze in my hair (*NC* 974)

[21] On the male-voice lyric, see also Cabo Aseguinolaza 1989 and Masera 2000.

analysis of woman's voice as a discourse intercalated in male-voice genres – a kind of borrowed speech – suggests that:

> [as the] inhabitant of marginal areas of the society, the female speaker brings unity to the social picture in her function of complementary voice. She serves as a channel for pathos, dissent, irony, and humor [...] Representative of both the juvenile and archaic values, her voice is the foil against which the centrist male voice is created and recognized.
>
> (1988: 121)

Moreover, according to Earnshaw, the female voice in medieval Romance lyric, particularly in the hispanic repertoire, tends to stand out from the male, since the woman's discourse is often 'archaic, erotic, primitive, incantatory' (1988:135).

The analysis of these texts demonstrates that in the medieval corpus of popular lyric women's songs are frequently female-voice songs. This female voice is identifiable by means of markers, some of them explicit, or textual, while others are implicit, or contextual, both of which evince a longstanding and intense relationship between song and tradition. We can also see that this woman's-voice discourse, infused with ancient nature symbols, derives from an wholly rural environment. Even though the presence of symbols and of specific *topoi* indicates that the female-voice lyric forms part of a distinctive poetic register, a style characteristic of oral tradition, this does not exclude the possibility of its being a genre of women's own making.

Further reading

Cummins, John G. (ed.), 1977. *The Spanish Traditional Lyric* (Oxford: Pergamon)
Frenk, Margit, 1993a. *Symbolism in Old Spanish Folk Songs*, The Kate Elder Lecture, 4 (London: Dept of Hispanic Studies, QMW)
Masera, Mariana, 2001. *'Que non dormiré sola, non': la voz femenina en la antigua lírica hispánica* (Barcelona: Azul)
Reckert, Stephen, 1993. *Beyond Chrysanthemums: Perspectives on Poetry East and West* (Oxford: Clarendon Press)

3

From Virgin Martyr to Holy Harlot: Female Saints in the Middle Ages and the Problem of Classification

ANDREW M. BERESFORD

The influence of the cult of the saints in the Middle Ages was almost beyond reckoning. As intermediaries between this world and the next, saints performed a vital function, serving both as conduits to the divine and authorities in their own right. No aspect of everyday life was either too worldly or too insignificant for them to exercise their powers. For toothache, rather than quack potions and cures, believers could solicit the intervention of St Apollonia. For a healthy supply of breast milk, on the other hand, nursing mothers could offer prayers to St Agatha. Wayfarers could look to St Christopher, believing it impossible for them to die on a day when they had seen his image, while as battle was struck, soldiers would offer a hearty appeal to St James, their protector and national patron. Images of the saints enlivened even the darkest corners of churches and religious institutions, and in an age of universal faith, they would have been seen not just by the clergy, but peasant and noble alike. Painting, sculpture, stained glass, richly decorated altar tables, and most importantly of all, the ornately bejewelled funerary caskets or reliquaries of the saints themselves, offered not merely a feast of colour, but a sense of common purpose and a source of reassurance. Saints even structured time itself, with the feasts of Christmas and Easter supplemented in the liturgical-sanctoral calendar not merely by feasts of the Virgin Mary such as the Assumption (15 August), but a succession of daily celebrations. Some, such as those of Dominic (8 August) and Francis (12 August), commemorated the founders of religious orders, while others championed secular trades and professions. A third group functioned as patrons of cities, familiar examples being Leocadia of Toledo (9 December) and Isidore of Seville (18 March), while a fourth fused spiritual and secular, with that of John the Baptist (24 June) coinciding with the summer solstice, and that of the Holy Innocents (28 December) providing a pretext for wholesome pranks and games.

The profusion of saintly reverence was expressed most tangibly in the Middle Ages in the form of devotional literature, but while some works were never committed to writing, and some have been lost, others now languish in dusty libraries, available only in manuscript form. As a result, it is difficult to gain an impression of the extent of pious devotion or of the position of female saints within it. The earliest vernacular hagiographic texts were cast as narrative poetry, and two of the seven major works to have survived deal with female subjects: an early thirteenth-century account of the prostitute saint, Mary of Egypt (Alvar 1970–72), and a slightly later treatment of the life and visions of Oria, a Benedictine anchoress (Dutton 1981). These are accompanied by a fourteenth-century lyric dealing with Mary Magdalen (Gómez Redondo 1996), and a series of others that appear in the various songbooks or *cancioneros* compiled from the 1360s onwards; these include treatments of Catherine of Alexandria, Leocadia of Toledo, and Clare of Assisi (Dutton 1990–91). The production of this poetry is sporadic, and its subject matter unrepresentative of trends in popular devotion. This is partly the result of social problems such as famine, plague, and dynastic and political instability, but also a lack of literacy, particularly in the nobility. The most significant contributory factor, however, can be explained by analogy, for while Castile invested much of its effort in the Reconquest, as a result producing only a relatively impoverished poetic tradition, in Catalonia, where the conflict ended earlier, there was an upsurge in hagiographic production. Evidence can be seen in the *Cançoner sagrat de vides de sants* (Sacred Songbook of Saints' Lives), a collection of fifty-nine poems (twelve of them dealing with female subjects) composed at the turn of the fifteenth century (Foulché-Delbosc and Massó y Torrents 1912). An analogous distinction appears in relation to drama, with treatments of saints such as Agatha not matched by equivalents in Castilian until the Golden Age (Romeu 1957).

The majority of medieval Castilian hagiographic works were cast as prose. Some were embedded into sermons and disseminated as part of the liturgy, but critics have been reluctant to work with this material, and a book-length survey is long overdue. The most spectacular oversight, however, is in relation to Jacobus de Voragine's *Legenda aurea* (*Golden Legend*) (c.1260), a compendium of 182 readings arranged according to the chronological position of feast days in the liturgical-sanctoral calendar. Voragine's collection represents the high point of medieval hagiographic production, with a text that was widely copied and adapted before being reworked into the majority of European vernaculars. Theories explaining its spectacular rise to prominence are legion, but what is most noticeable in relation to other forms of hagiography is that his narratives are economically expressed, exquisitely structured, and almost completely uncluttered by theological moralizing. The emphasis, in fact, often falls on the incredible, with sensationalized accounts of torture and resistance accompanied by vivid and evocative descriptions of divine intervention and retribution. In the legends of female saints this sometimes leads to sexualization, with the emphasis falling on the erotic and sacrificial nature of the relationship between the individual and Christ. These qualities make Voragine not merely one of the greatest of all medieval storytellers, but a significant influence on popular piety, with his works, by the close of the fifteenth century, coming second only to the Bible in the number of manuscript and printed editions (Seybolt 1946a and 1946b, Reames 1985, Bussell Thompson 1990).

Voragine's compendium came early to the Peninsula and was translated into Catalan as the thirteenth-century *Vides de sants roselloneses* (Roussillon Lives of Saints) (Maneikis Kniazzeh and Neugaard 1977). A major study of this text has not yet been conducted, but much of it appears to have been reworked without significant modification. Exceptions can be seen in the omission of several martyr narratives, many of them dealing with female subjects, and the interpolation of sections dealing with local saints such as Feliu de Guixols and Narcís de Girona. The fact that an equivalent version did not appear in Castilian until almost half a century later is unsurprising. What is not so is that it can be found in two entirely independent recensions known as Compilations A and B, or the *Gran flos sanctorum* (Flowers of the Saints) and the *Estoria de los santos* (Tales of the Saints) (Thompson and Walsh 1986–87). The first was almost certainly produced in a monastic environment and is characterized by the incorporation of formulas, suggesting that it was designed with the requirements of oral delivery in mind – perhaps for the benefit of monks as they ate in the refectory or within the context of sermons that could have been delivered to male and female alike. Its lucid and engaging quality has not been explored in satisfactory detail, and only a minuscule sampling of its 200 or so sections has been either edited or subjected to analysis. Preliminary research, however, has shown that it is arguably the finest narrative collection to have been composed in Spain during the Middle Ages, and that its content was by no means slavishly assembled. In fact, a significant number of Voragine's accounts are replaced by older (usually longer) versions, many of them finely crafted and rich in detail. Two notable examples are a version of the legend of Mary of Egypt reworked from the Latin of Paul the Deacon (Thompson and Walsh 1977) and a retelling of Pseudo-Ambrose's passion of St Agnes (Beresford 2007a).

The texts of Compilation A can be found in a family of five medieval manuscripts (Escorial h–II–18 and h–III–22, and MSS 780, 12688, and 12689 of the Biblioteca Nacional, Madrid) that differ relatively little from one another. Accounts of some saints can be found in one manuscript, and some in two or three, but no saint can be found in all four. The simplicity of this arrangement differs from that of Compilation B, which offers a series of abbreviated versions that continued to evolve as they were copied. The result is that the six extant medieval manuscripts (Biblioteca Menéndez Pelayo 8 and 9, Escorial K–II–12, h–I–14, and M–II–6, and Fundación Lázaro Galdiano 419) differ not only from those of Compilation A, but from one another. In certain cases (Petronilla being a good example) the result is the production of six versions, each with a subtly differing tone and emphasis. Unfortunately, only a small proportion has been made available for scrutiny, the major exception being an edition of Biblioteca Menéndez Pelayo 8 (Baños Vallejo and Uría Maqua 2000). The purpose of Compilation B has not yet been established, but in contrast to the sermon-like tone of Compilation A, it displays a markedly less polished approach to the demands of syntax and rhetoric. This suggests that copies could have been used as digests for sermon material, possibly by novices learning their craft. The physical production of the manuscripts (with paper rather than parchment, and without the benefit of costly illumination) supports this hypothesis; so too does the fact that some have been badly damaged, suggesting that they were valued merely as a means to an end. The evidence, however, is inconclusive, and some arguments point to other possibilities. One of the most compelling is the absence of marginal annotation, which shows that if the texts were used by novices, they were unusually well behaved. A more persuasive argument can be seen in relation to content, which in contrast to that of Compilation A, tips the balance between theology and entertainment more noticeably towards the latter. It may be, in view of this, that the manuscripts were commissioned for the purpose of private reading by members of the lower nobility, possibly as educational tools intended, at least in part, to establish or reinforce paradigms of gendered behaviour. A further complication, however, is that some of them could have been rewritten with the requirements of specific individuals or denominations in mind, possibly in order to inculcate differing conceptions of sanctity, or more broadly, of the relationship between the Church and the individual. This can be seen in the process of selection, with some manuscripts favouring certain types of saint at the expense of others.

The provenance of three further collections is uncertain. MS 9247 of the Biblioteca Nacional offers a variant version of the legend of St Pelagia (Rodado Ruiz 1990, Beresford 2007b), while MS 10252 embraces a series of twenty-four readings arranged according to subject matter. Its table of contents indicates that it should have included the legends of fourteen female saints, but the text breaks off prematurely. A third manuscript, Escorial h–I–13 (Moore 2008), lies on the border ground between hagiography and romance, and with the exception of two works, where the emphasis is on male suffering, the seven remaining narratives concentrate on female subjects whose faith and virtue remain unshaken despite constant affliction and temptation; a high point is a version of the legend of Mary of Egypt (Walker 1977). Fleeting allusions to female saints can be found in *exemplum* collections such as Clemente Sánchez de Vercial's *Libro de los exenplos por a.b.c* (Book of *Exempla* by ABC) (Keller 1961) and the *Espéculo de los legos* (Mirror for the Laity) (Mohedano Hernández 1951). The same is true of Fray Martín de Córdoba's manual for young ladies, the *Jardín de nobles donzellas* (Garden of Noble Maidens) (Goldberg 1974). The most significant late medieval source for hagiography, however, is Álvaro de Luna's *Libro de las virtuosas e claras mugeres* (Book of Virtuous and Famous Women), which devotes its final section to a study of female sanctity (Vélez-Sainz 2009: 457–552). The provenance of the author's material is uncertain, but while some phrases echo the wording of Voragine's *Legenda aurea*, and others, the Compilation A reworking, his approach is different, with a series of idealized and rhetorically elaborate portraits of female sanctity.

The corollary to the profusion of medieval hagiographic writing is that the legends of most saints can be found in more than one version, and some, in several. The texts, moreover, were designed for different purposes and directed at differing audiences. We need also to bear in mind the chronology of production and the impact of developments not only in religious practice, but the expression of popular piety, which, like the Church itself, evolved in various ways from the early thirteenth century through to the Renaissance. The result is that as with other forms of narrative, the identities of the saints (and the themes associated with them) become malleable, and are shaped not merely by constants, but the imposition of specific agendas. In view of this, it becomes as important to consider the underlying ethos of a legend as it does the variation between versions. Equally essential is the application of a coherent and transparent methodology, particularly with regard to the analysis of broad conceptual or intellectual developments, lest critics accidentally assimilate plot lines or aspects of theme, image, or characterization, in the process creating hybrid versions, dissimilar from those that circulated in the Middle Ages. A case in point is the legend of Mary of Egypt, which is one of only a handful to have received adequate editorial attention. In all of the extant versions Mary is presented as a penitent prostitute who wanders naked in the desert in order to atone for her sins. Yet while the early poetic version is aimed at a popular audience, placing the emphasis on eleventh-hour repentance, the Compilation A text offers a longer, scholarly account, with a more expansive exploration of humility, notably in monasticism. The four Compilation B texts offer pithier treatments and are shaped by agendas that have not been fully explained, while the *Estoria de Santa María Egipçiaca* (Story of St Mary of Egypt) (Escorial h–I–13), despite being derived from the same source as the early poem, is divergent in content and emphasis. Finally, the last of the medieval versions, that of Álvaro de Luna, is notable for its narratorial interjections and heightened emotional tone. It view of this, it becomes dangerous to assume either that there is a single Mary of Egypt or a definitive account of her legend. In fact, she, as with all saints, lives in a variety of subtly differing incarnations.

Regardless of such methodological obstacles, critics, in order to quantify the vast body of medieval hagiographic production, have tended to pigeonhole saints into a series of relatively watertight categories. These correspond to historical phases and developments in Christianity, and so the earliest belong to New Testament. The most notable examples in the two early Castilian compilations (the subject of this study) are Martha, sister of Lazarus and Mary, and Petronilla, traditionally identified as the daughter of St Peter.[1] Neither of the two has been edited or subjected to analysis, but while the former focuses on the period after the dispersion of the disciples and incorporates a number of fanciful miracles (including one in which a dragon shoots explosive dung at its pursuers, consuming all those who are touched with flame), the latter offers a curiously bipartite account, with the initial portion offering an illustration of the relationship between the saint and her father, and latter stages, a description of conflict and martyrdom. The early sections of the legend of Mary Magdalen also fall partly into this category, but as a result of the influence of popular tradition (notably as she atones for a life of wanton lechery), she is more effectively classified as a holy harlot.

The most numerous category, accounting for approximately half of all female saints, is that of the virgin martyr, a figure who belongs to the age of the Roman persecutions, and who dies by imitating Christ in the most literal of ways – a process known as *imitatio Christi*. The legends of the virgin martyrs are varied and engaging, but they have seldom proven popular with critics, who have all too frequently viewed them as variations on a series of common themes and stock situations. This erroneous impression is partly the result of a lack of generic understanding (formulaic construction is fundamental to most medieval narrative genres), and partly the result of a paucity of detailed textual studies, with only a handful of the twenty or so legends (the majority existing in more than one version) receiving adequate critical attention. They have also suffered as a result of developments in aesthetic taste, with their vivid scenes of torture and heroic resistance producing reactions of nausea and disgust rather than empathy, admiration, and communal solidarity.

Notable in this respect is the legend of Agatha, in which her breasts (the very symbol of her femininity) are implacably severed, and that of Christina, who throws chunks of amputated flesh at her father, encouraging him to

---

[1] See Altman 1975 and Elliott 1987. Buxton 2008, in contrast, classifies texts according to narrative structure.

devour that which he once engendered. The importance of gore, however, has been overemphasized, and it is unfortunate that other texts, many of them exploring differing aspects of the female religious experience, have been ignored. These include the legends of Juliana, who thrashes the devil with chains before hurling him into a privy, Catherine of Alexandria, who serves as a rare model of female erudition and intellectual sophistication, and the Virgin of Antioch, whose martyrdom is explored in a uniquely emotive and rhetorically abstract manner. A related problem is that the legends have sometimes been discussed out of context or in an anachronistic light, with some critics, eager to accuse medieval monks of prurient sexual fantasizing – notably in relation to the sexualization, fetishization, and morbid physical destruction of the female body – forgetting that male martyrs are treated in remarkably similar ways. This, of course, calls for caution, and for an approach to gendered interpretation based on a holistic appreciation of the aetiology of persecution and its impact on Christian writing. More fundamentally, it behoves readers to think again about female saints, appreciating that a nuanced understanding of gender paradigms cannot successfully be developed in isolation from a consideration of equivalent patterns in the depiction of male sanctity.

Not all martyrs, however, are virgins, and while some, such as Anastasia, can be classified as widows, some are mothers. This important distinction, which is fundamental to an understanding of gender paradigms and their impact on theoretical debates on corporeality (Bell 1985, Bynum 1987, Robertson 1991, Wolf 1997), has not yet become the subject of academic inquiry. The result is that basic questions, such as the relationship between virginity and motherhood (and their reception in Christianity and Rome), have not yet been even partially answered. This may to some extent be attributed to a lack of interest in women's issues in the Middle Ages, but it could also be on grounds of taste, with the maternal martyr offering one of the most unpalatable accounts of sacrifice. A good example is the legend of Felicity, who is scourged when eight months pregnant; this leads her baby to be born prematurely, but in place of compassion, she is stripped, dragged through the streets, and thrown to wild beasts. Equally severe is the legend of Julitta, in which her three-year-old son, Quiricus, has his brains dashed out on a flight of steps before she is decapitated. A third significant narrative is that of the Seven Brothers, in which their mother, a different Felicity, is forced to endure their martyrdom, in each instance praising their resilience and offering words of encouragement before she too is put to death.

With the accession of Constantine and the incorporation of Christianity into the official structures of the Roman Empire, martyrdom began to lose its relevance. The cult of the martyrs, which depended on the diametric opposition between Christianity and Rome, had presented the battle between the two as a microcosm of the wider conflict between good and evil. Yet with the promulgation of the Edict of Milan in 313, the new religion embarked on a different phase of development, with the emphasis now falling on an internalization of spiritual conflict. This process, which can be viewed as a self-inflicted martyrdom, or more strictly, asceticism, shifted the emphasis of sanctity from an antithetical relationship between the individual and society, to a gradational structure in which the achievement of exemplary status became conditioned not merely by the manner of one's death, but an ability to lead a life of virtue (Altman 1975). This ensured that although saints would continue, via the notion of *imitatio Christi*, to function as refractions of the divine, their worth would be gauged not simply by parallels with the Crucifixion, but other correspondences. These included humility, patience, poverty, the avoidance of temptation, and ultimately, the ability to change society. It is in the last of these that the position of female saints becomes problematic, for although there are differences between the sexes in the depiction of martyrdom (notably the representation of the physical body and the tortures to which it is subjected), the exclusion of women from the structures of ecclesiastical power ensured that they would never again be able to enjoy such prominence. Men could become theologians, bishops, or popes, but in contrast to the egalitarian spirit of the words of St Paul, in the post-Constantinian world there was no equivalent female path to sanctity.[2] The effect on cognate literature was the imposition of a degree of chronological fossilization, with female saints embodying the virtues of a form of sanctity that had, by the time its composition, lost most of its relevance.

The bifurcation between the genders can be seen in relation to Paula, who, as a fifth-century Roman matron, is Voragine's only example of a non-legendary female ascetic before Elizabeth of Hungary, who died over 800 years later. In addition to the fact that Paula and Elizabeth are widows, they also belong to the highest echelons of society – a correlation that cannot be dismissed as coincidental. Unfortunately, as neither of the two has received critical attention, their significance has not been understood.

The spectacular absence of non-legendary female saints is partly attenuated by the interpolation of Castilian treatments of Bridget of Kildare and Clare of Assisi. It says much, however, not only about Voragine's process of selection, but his theological understanding of women, that the only other female ascetics included from the post-Constantinian period are legendary figures such as transvestites and holy harlots, individuals who lie at the fringes of orthodox belief. The first of these has yet to be studied in Castilian, but as John Anson (1974) has shown, the thematic nucleus consists of a false

---

[2] 'There is neither Jew nor Greek, slave nor free, male nor female, for you are all one in Christ Jesus' (Galatians 3.28). See also Schulenburg 1978.

allegation, with the transvestite accused either of seduction or of having fathered a child – crimes of which she would have been incapable. The tales thus stand in a unique position in the hagiographic canon, as explorations not merely of alterity, gender inversion, and the shadow-self, but social attitudes towards male and female spirituality. The second grouping, that of the holy harlot, displays similar characteristics, as in each instance a fallen woman undergoes a process of metamorphosis by eschewing a life of iniquity in order to embark on the path of redemption. This leads to the establishment of a binary structure and an evocative contrast between extremes of experience, with virtue pitted against sin, faith against despair, and salvation against damnation (Ward 1987, Beresford 2007b).

A brief survey of the two Castilian compilations reveals the extent to which categorization performs a valuable function in drawing out broad distinctions between different types of saint. The process, however, is not without pitfalls, and the most obvious danger is that the simplistic nature of the parameters that have traditionally been applied can lead ineluctably to distortion. The distinction between martyr and ascetic, for instance, focuses critical attention purely on the manner of the saint's death, while a binary division between virgin and non-virgin effectively places the transvestite alongside the virgin martyr, and (rather more uncomfortably) the mother and the widow alongside the penitent prostitute. Although there are, of course, exceptions, the result is that a traditional element of medieval misogyny (the polarization between innocent Mary and experienced Eve) becomes enshrined in the language and methodology of critical discourse. A more complex problem is that as hagiographic cults are products of evolving social and religious circumstances, they can be classified in varying ways. An example can be seen in Joyce E. Salisbury's work on a tenth-century Latin manuscript, Escorial a–II–9, which despite being produced in Spain offers an impression of female sanctity dominated by Eastern ascetic traditions. The result is that Pelagia is most effectively classified not as a harlot, but a transvestite (1991: 97–110). A more extreme metamorphosis is that of Apollonia, who is presented in Voragine's Latin as a voluntary martyr of advancing years, but in the *Cançoner sagrat* as a teenage princess put to the sword by her father (Beresford 2001). This, of course, reiterates the extent to which readers of hagiography must exercise caution either when generalizing or comparing texts from different sources. A further aspect of distortion comes as a by-product of longevity, with the cults of the saints undergoing several stages of development before being reworked into Castilian. This ensures that aspects of characterization and representation expressed initially in acts of popular devotion, and then in early lyric and narrative works, become fossilized in an act of partial ventriloquism alongside modifications introduced as part of a dual process of medievalization – the first phase taking place with Voragine in the 1260s, and the second, in the transition to Castilian. Needless to say, the impression that this creates is at times unstable and inauthentic.

A more fundamental drawback to traditional modes of classification is that they encourage readers to focus not on elements of the text that are most intellectually or conceptually significant, but those that are superficially obvious – reducing the process of reading in this way merely to a consideration of common generic points of contact. This, of course, is to the detriment of a more nuanced understanding in which readers could focus their attention not simply on comparable narrative events and structures, but factors that catalyse their development. It also limits the scope of critical activity by encouraging readers to explore individual strands of sanctity rather than common denominators present in texts that appear initially to exhibit dissimilar characteristics. A case in point is the representation of Christ as celestial bridegroom and the cognate manipulation of attitudes towards the control and regulation of female sexuality. This process takes place internally in a number of virgin martyr narratives, where it results in the aggressive display and defence of virginity (Winstead 1997), but also in relation to the inculcation of related aspects of dogma in the female members of the audience to whom the compilations could potentially have been externally disseminated.

A familiar example is that of Agnes, who formalizes her status as *sponsa Christi* (bride of Christ) by literalizing the language and rhetoric of sexual relationships.[3] In the Compilation A version we are told initially that Agnes 'amó solamente al fazedor de la vida' (loved only the creator of life) (*Istoria*, line 16), but before long we realize that her love is neither ethereal nor incorporeal. In fact, it is a deeply erotic and sexualized form of adoration (if not infatuation) that presents Christ as a virile and attractive husband, attentive to her physical and spiritual needs. In Compilation B, in a borrowing from the rhetoric of courtly love (as expressed in fifteenth-century love poetry), he even becomes a refined and courtly 'entendedor' (sympathetic slave to love) (*Vida*, line 8), able to fathom the ennobling power of the virgin's desire and to treat her as she deserves.

The consequences of Christological literalization are most abruptly felt when the thirteen-year-old Agnes rejects a rival suitor (the prefect's son) as she returns from school. In so doing she juxtaposes various levels of consciousness, contrasting notions of celestial and terrestrial, perfect and

---

[3] The final section of this article borrows ideas from *La istoria de la vida de Santa Ynés* (The History of the Life of St Agnes), and *La vida e passion de Santa Ygnés* (The Life and Passion of St Agnes) (Beresford 2007a: 71–84; 85–92), and *La ystoria de la santa muger Tarsis* (The Story of the Holy Woman Thaïs) and *La vida de Santa Tays* (The Life of St Thaïs) (Beresford 2007b: 133–34; 135–6), but establishes original links between them. Texts are identified throughout by short title and line number.

imperfect, and chaste and sexual. Christ, her 'otro amador' (other lover) (*Istoria*, line 34), has bestowed various symbolic gifts upon her: a ring and a dress betokening marriage, a necklace, pearls, and jewels of great worth; he is handsome, powerful, and of the highest lineage. The most literal revelations, however, come later, initially as she speaks brazenly of their nuptial bed ('el su tálamo me está ya aparejado') (his nuptial bed has been readied for me) (line 48), and then as she advances to a more audacious admission – the fact that they have already engaged in a form of sexless coitus: 'los sus abraçamientos castos son a mí muy amables, e el su cuerpo es ayuntado al mío' (I adore his chaste embraces, and his body is joined with mine) (lines 51–52). With these words Agnes offers a frank exploration of the paradox of mystical union, envisioning Christ not in abstract terms, but as a figure of flesh and blood as real as the boy she is rejecting.

Her feistiness appears initially to betoken a degree of empowerment and a rejection of secular temptation, but beneath this it is noticeable that by adopting the traditionally submissive rhetoric of wifely deference she has succeeded only in exchanging one form of phallocentric submission for another. The message to women is not, therefore, that they should deny their sexuality, but that they should sublimate sexual instinct into spiritual reverence by affixing their desire on Christ. In this way the Church can control and regulate their sexual impulses, and in so doing gain power not merely over their hearts and minds, but those of men. It is perhaps for this reason that Agnes's martyrdom returns with breathtaking candour to the notion of divine marriage by presenting the knife that penetrates her throat as a deflowering penis, setting the seal not simply on her worldly demise, but the solemnization of her celestial marriage to Christ. The blood that drips from the wound in her neck, of course, evokes an image of a ruptured hymen, but the impression of sexualized physical penetration is purposefully ironic, drawing attention not merely to her corporeal integrity, but the sexual favour and reward that the boy could never experience and that Christ would never claim. As *sponsa Christi*, Agnes is thus preserved intact in perpetuity, and as the redness of her blood drips onto the whiteness of her wedding dress, we are reminded most of all of Communion, the New Covenant, and the ritualistic mingling of human and divine.

Traditional methods of classification encourage readers to search for comparable patterns in the legends of other virgin martyrs, and they are by no means difficult to find. A striking example is that of Agatha, who claims, when her breasts are severed, that she has ancillary breasts within her soul: 'Yo he otras tetas entregas en la mi alma que consagré al Señor desde la mi niñez, e con ellas dó yo a los mis sesos fartura de leche' (I have other breasts intact within my soul consecrated to the Lord since infancy, and I use them to feed my brain an abundance of milk) (Beresford 2010: 187, lines 93–94). The parallel, however, although informative, is also constraining, as it does not encourage readers to consider the way in which equivalent ideas are exploited by other branches of hagiography. A thought-provoking analogue can be found in the legend of the prostitute saint, Thaïs, who repents when confronted by Paphnutius, an abbot in disguise. The circumstances of Paphnutius's visit recall the familiar courtly notion of *amor de lonh* (love from afar), where the lover becomes enamoured of his lady on the basis of reputation rather than sight. Yet Paphnutius's love is as sexless as that of Christ, and by setting out from the desert in order to lead her into a trap (in the process forcing her to understand the nature of sin), it is as manipulative as it is unsentimental. Posing as a client, Paphnutius enters her boudoir, a luxurious dwelling with several rooms in which she has plied her trade with impunity – in the process amassing a fortune. The Compilation B text (*La vida de Santa Tays*), conscious of this anomaly, places pimps at her threshold, but in both of the extant versions Paphnutius enters without impediment and greets her with a coin. Thaïs accepts payment and entreats him to climb onto a bed bedecked with precious coverlets, but he now puts his plan into effect, urging her to find a more private place. Thaïs agrees, but the pattern is repeated several times. Before long, she becomes frustrated and alerts her client to an incontrovertible fact: there is no such thing as a private place as God is always watching.

At this point the analogue becomes clearer. Thaïs has been involved in a triangular relationship, binding prostitute, client, and pimp in a nexus of evil. Paphnutius sets out to shatter that relationship, and in so doing, seeks not merely to reclaim her soul, but those of her clients, who, in a dazzling inversion of the law of supply and demand, are perceived to be guilty merely of having succumbed to her libidinous charms. The result is the establishment of an impressive number of parallels. The abbot arrives materially poor but spiritually rich; Thaïs, who is spiritually poor but materially rich, receives him in her boudoir. The 'muger pública' (public woman) (*Ystoria*, line 1, *Vida*, line 1), engaged in hedonistic sin, is confronted by public man on a personal mission, determined to lead her, via a process of cathartic repentance, to a state of revirginalized grace. The rooms through which they travel function as a representation of the depth of Paphnutius's penetration into her soul. The private, female space, where men have never been, is penetrated physically (but not sexually) by a public man, accustomed only to the silence and reverence of desert solitude. The conversation between them is equally binary, pitting heaven against hell, present against future, and salvation against torment. The harlot, who had initially urged Paphnutius to raise himself onto her bed, sinks to his feet with tears in her eyes; and just as Paphnutius had entered with a coin, hoping to reclaim a single errant soul, Thaïs resolves to depart with her fortune, impressing the finality of her conversion on the inhabitants of an entire city.

The final portion of the narrative establishes a different triangular relationship – one that functions as a mirror image of the first. To atone for her sins, Thaïs enters an anchorhold, spending three years wallowing in her own excrement. Paphnutius, her confessor, seals the door with lead and leaves her, reminding her before he departs that she is unfit even to pronounce the name of God. The shaping of the scene, with the transition from boudoir to anchorhold (from a zone of public iniquity to one of private virtue), reminds the reader of the *hortus conclusus* (enclosed garden) tradition, and the consecration of virginity within stoutly protective walls. In this way it focuses attention on the control and regulation of female sexuality, and the role of Paphnutius in severing the connection between Thaïs and her clients. This, of course, can be read as a sublimated sexual conquest that allows him, as a representative of the Church, to gain power not just over Thaïs, but the expression of sexuality in the society in which she lives. His actions, however, are more akin to those of a pimp, as the emphasis falls not on conquest or prohibition, but the transference of sexual availability to a different client – the spiritual bridegroom. It is for this reason that news of her forgiveness is transmitted in allegorical form, with a vision of a bed guarded by celestial virgins functioning both as an echo of the bed in which she once earned a living and a representation of the nuptial bed that she and Christ will share. In this respect, the revirginalized Thaïs differs little from Agnes, as in each instance the message transmitted to female believers is not that they should deny their sexuality, but that they should affix their desires on Christ – in the process sublimating their base (and potentially destructive) sexual instincts into a more rewarding and socially beneficial form of devotion.

The extent to which variants of this pattern are embedded into other forms of hagiography will not, of course, be known until a greater proportion of the corpus is edited and made available for scrutiny. An important task in the interim, however, will be the development of more nuanced approach to matters of classification, with a move away from narrowly defined labels (such as martyr, ascetic, virgin, and non-virgin) allowing readers to develop a more sophisticated understanding not simply of the factors that catalyze hagiographic representation, but the cognate processes of manipulation and indoctrination that affected female believers in the Middle Ages.

Further reading

Baños Vallejo, Fernando, and Isabel Uría Maqua (eds), 2000. *La leyenda de los santos: 'Flos sanctorum' del ms. 8 de la Biblioteca de Menéndez Pelayo*, Estudios de Literatura y Pensamiento Hispánicos, 18 (Santander: Año Jubilar Lebaniego / Sociedad Menéndez Pelayo)

Baños Vallejo, Fernando, 2003. *Las vidas de los santos en la literatura medieval española*, Colección Arcadia de las Letras, 17 (Madrid: Laberinto)

Beresford, Andrew M., 2007a. *The Legend of Saint Agnes in Medieval Castilian Literature*, PMHRS, 59 (London: Dept of Hispanic Studies, QMUL)

——, 2007b. *The Legends of the Holy Harlots: Thaïs and Pelagia in Medieval Spanish Literature*, CT, A238 (Woodbridge: Tamesis)

——, 2010. *The Severed Breast: The Legends of Saints Agatha and Lucy in Medieval Castilian Literature* (Newark, DE: Juan de la Cuesta)

4

Choosing and Testing Spouses in Medieval Exemplary Literature

LOUISE M. HAYWOOD

'e avíala él provado en algunas cosas'*

Medieval Iberian women's studies is a diverse and fast-developing area of study, focusing on the lives of historical women, secular and religious, on women's writing and artistic production, on the exploration of the anonymous canon, and on the representation of women in work produced by men, including the use of queer and feminist theory, and resisting reading strategies.[1] Heath Dillard, for example, has produced a magisterial study of the roles of non-noble women in Castilian town society, and her evidence reveals that their capacity to act as agents is much greater than students of literature would ever assume (1984). None the less, there remains much work to be done: for example, to take two of the most canonical literary productions, there is no systematic, theoretically informed study of the representation of women in Juan Ruiz's *Libro de Buen Amor* (*Book of Good Love*) (c.1330), although initial attempts at the categorization of female characters have been undertaken with considerable success. Nor is there a study of the representation of women in either of the encyclopaedic histories of Alfonso X in their entirety, although, again, studies of thematically or generically linked material have been successful. Exemplary literature, especially comic tales dealing with the couple, has particularly engaged the attention of scholars using feminist approaches, and I shall discuss these here.

---

* 'and he had tested her in different things' (*Sendebar*) (María Jesús Lacarra 1996: 65)
[1] I should like to thank Andreea Weisl-Shaw (Corpus Christi College, Cambridge) for reading a draft, and members of the research seminars at Cambridge, Manchester, QMUL (particularly Barry Taylor, British Library), and the joint Durham/Newcastle seminar to whom earlier versions of parts of this paper were presented for their comments and suggestions. I remain responsible, of course, for any deficiencies that remain.

In comic tales of marriage, the husband, rather than the wife, tends to be the butt of the humour, and no more misogyny is in evidence than that usually found in medieval representations of women (Goldberg 1983) and ratified by contemporary theology, medicine and natural philosophy. In other words, women are conceived of in relation to the more perfect male specimen as physically and intellectually imperfect beings, whose physiological and psychological flaws make them prone to carnal and spiritual temptation, and who deploy their intellect for deception, self-protection, and deviousness. Owing to limitations of space, I shall focus on some tales in which spousal suitability is (or explicitly is not) tested, and confine my discussions to three collections: *Sendebar* (1253), a translation from a lost Arabic version of a tale collection ultimately of Sanskrit origin, commissioned by Don Fadrique of Castile, son of King Ferdinand the Holy and brother of Alfonso X, the Learned; *Conde Lucanor* (1330s; hereafter *CL*) by Don Juan Manuel, a grandson of Alfonso; and *Arçipreste de Talavera* (1438; hereafter *Talavera*) by Alfonso Martínez de Toledo, a trained lawyer, sometime Archpriest of Talavera and chaplain of John II of Castile.[2] Each frame tale provides a pretext for the collection. In *Sendebar* an incestuous and traitorous stepmother trades tales with the ruler's seven advisors, the prince, and his tutor. In the first part of *CL*, the only one comprising tales, the eponymous Count seeks instruction from his wise advisor, Patronio, on ethical, political, and governmental issues. *Talavera* is presented as a compendium of instructive materials on the evils of sexual desire and women, whose narrator purports to have witnessed some of the material recounted. *Talavera* comprises five sections, and my analysis is concerned with Section 2, Chapter 7, which deals with disobedient women.

The frame tale of *Sendebar* links the extensive polygamy of King Alcos with intradiegetic male characters who are subject to lust, such as the King whose only flaw is his excessive love of woman, or the man whose desire is pricked by merely hearing of a woman (*Sendebar*, tales 1 and 13). The link between these tales and the frame is underscored by the positioning as first tale of that a lust-prone King. Alcos's polygamy, however, is excused by the fact that he is King of Judea, and not subject to medieval Christian practices, 'avía noventa mugeres. Estando con todas, según era ley, no podía aver de ninguna de dellas fijo' (he had ninety wives. According to custom, he lay with them all but could not have a child [son] with any of them) (Lacarra 1996: 65). In keeping with medieval medical thinking, the implied frequent and excessive sexual intercourse required of Alcos, 'según era ley', depletes his strength and virility and, as *Sendebar* appears to suggest, may contribute

---

[2] All citations from the three texts are taken, respectively, from Lacarra 1996 for *Sendebar*, Juan Manuel 1994 for *CL*, and Martínez de Toledo 1981 for *Talavera*.

to his sterility. His favourite wife, 'cuerda e entendida' (clever and astute) (ibid.), whom he has tested (see the epigraph to this chapter), suggests that they pray to God for a son. This son later demonstrates his own nobility of character by resisting the sexual advances of one of his stepmothers. The son's chastity (and wisdom) contrasts strongly with his father's sexual proclivity (and indecision in the face of persuasion).

Although there is no mention of the stepmother's qualities or of her having proved herself, she occupies an esteemed position in Alcos's affections: 'la qual más amava e onrávala más que a todas las otras mugeres qu'él avía' (whom he loved more and he honoured her more than all the other wives that he had) (Lacarra 1996: 74); perhaps more so than the prince's mother. The qualities of the wives are contrasted: both are favoured by Alcos's great love, but only the prince's mother, not his stepmother, has demonstrated virtue. The debate in the frame tests the stepmother's claim that the prince has attempted to rape her. The King's advisors fail to discredit her by adducing examples that generalize out from individual female characters to women in general, and it is the prince's testimony and learning that ultimately convince the monarch.[3] The failure of the stepmother's rhetoric and persuasive acts, such as setting up her own funeral pyre, leads to her execution by scalding in a hot cauldron. Her guilt, of course, is never in question for the audience, since the opening frame reveals her treachery, conspiracy to dethrone the King, and attempt to seduce the Prince, an individual within the prohibited degrees of consanguinity from a medieval Christian perspective.

I do not wish to exaggerate the role of spousal testing in *Sendebar*'s frame tale, since it rests on brief details that differentiate the prince's mother and stepmother (and also the prince and his father). None the less, it is the untested wife, whose virtue or lack thereof goes unmentioned, that threatens the King and the stability of Judea. I suggest, therefore, that *Sendebar* dramatizes the threat posed to a man, his status, and his estate by inappropriate spousal selection, which is witnessed also in contemporary legal codes. For example, *Siete partidas* (Legal Code) II.vi.1 treats the qualities of royal brides, and concludes by emphasizing lineage and custom as hereditary goods untarnished by time:[4]

> Cate que sea de buen linaie e de buenas costumbres, ca los bienes que se siguen destas fincan sienpre en el linaie que della desçende, mas la fermosura e la rriqueza pasar de ligero: onde el Rey que asy non lo catase, errarie en sy mismo e en su linaie.   (Alfonso X 1991: 73)

---

[3] See Weisl-Shaw 2010 on the structures of persuasion.

[4] *Siete partidas* II.vi.1 and II.vii.12 recommend the same qualities for a princess's spouse.

([The king] should see that his wife be of good family and of good habits, for the benefits which result from these two qualities, will all abide in the line which descends from her; but beauty and riches pass away more easily. For which reason the king who does not bear this in mind will sin against himself and his offspring)   (Alfonso X 2001: 298)

Thirteen *CL* tales deal with marriage and evince an interest in marital conduct, the selection of good wives, or the consequences of failure to test, select, or manage wives appropriately. However, the concern with spousal testing also extends to male partners. In *CL25*, Saladin advises his prisoner the Count of Provence to select a son-in-law who is *omne* (literally, 'a man'), a term reinforced through rhetorical emphasis to mean 'a man of outstanding quality' (England 1999: 358). All of the male parties involved, Saladin, the Count, and his son-in-law, benefit from the advice's effectiveness.[5] The marriage mediates a triangular relationship between the three men to the 'pro et onra' (advantage and honour) of them all. That is, it establishes a homosocial relationship between them (Sedgwick 1985).

CL tales dealing with the selection of a bride are equally concerned with character traits, and present spousal selection as the basis for marital harmony. For example, *CL27* is a doublet in which successful testing (*CL27B*) and the failure to test (*CL27A*) are contrasted. Each tale's components refract elements of the other to contrast the conduct of the protagonists and their wives. In *CL27A*, the Emperor Fradrique chooses a bride of high lineage but fails to investigate her character (Juan Manuel 1994: 116), thus ignoring contemporary advice concerning spousal selection, discussed above. Consequently, despite some good qualities, the Empress's contrary nature is soon revealed so that the Emperor 'vio que, sin el pesar et la vida enojosa que avía de sofryr, quell era tan grand daño para su fazienda et para las gentes' (Juan Manuel 1994: 117) ('realised that, aside from the life of pain and torment which he would suffer, his failure to find a solution was very damaging for his household and his vassals', England 1987: 175, adapted)

In *CL27B*, the renowned warrior Alvar Háñez subjects three sisters to a character test by claiming that age and battle wounds make him susceptible to violent, drunken rages, and that his behaviour in bed is unclean. He chooses Doña Vascunaña on account of her appropriately submissive responses (Bobes Naves 1991: 99–100). After the marriage, he responds to criticism about the autonomy he allows her by submitting her, before a sceptical witness, to another set of tests. Vascunaña demonstrates absolute

---

[5]   I consider that Saladin's reputation is enhanced on account of his good advice, magnanimity, and munificence; Palafox takes the view that Saladin, by losing the Count, whom he holds hostage, suffers 'las consecuencias de sus malas acciones en aras de su propio buen consejo' (1998: 70; see also 78).

submission to his will (England 1977: 81, Bobes Naves 1991: 98–100) by valuing his word above the evidence of her senses.[6] She knows and absolutely trusts her husband to the extent that she will act always to his benefit and honour (Juan Manuel 1994: 125). The *exemplum* concludes with Patronio's summary of the appropriate conduct of husbands in marriage:

> deve mucho guardar que por lo que a él mucho non cunple nin le faze gran mengua, que non le faga pesar nin enojo, e señaladamente en ninguna cosa en que pueda aver pecado, ca desto vienen muchos danios: lo uno, el pecado e la maldad que el omne faze, e lo ál, que por fazerle enmienda o fazerle plazer por que pierda aquel enojo avrá a fazer cosas que se tornarán en danio de la fazienda e de la fama. Otrosí, el que por su fuerte ventura tal muger oviera como la del emperador, pues al comienço non pudo o non supo poner ý consejo, non ay sinon pasar por su ventura como Dios gelo quisiere endereçar. (Juan Manuel 1994:126–7)

> (in matters which are not of great importance to him, he should take great care not to upset or offend her, for this is the source of great damage. On the one hand, there is the sin and the wrong-doing; and on the other, the fact that, in order to make amends or please her so that she will cease to be angry he will have to do things which will be damaging to his well-being and reputation. Furthermore, any man who has the misfortune to have a wife like the Emperor's, and who in the initial stages has failed or been unwilling to do anything about it, has no choice but to accept the fate allotted to him by God.) (England 1987: 189)

The wife's behaviour flows from her husband's management of their relationship. The Emperor exemplifies failure to prevent difficulties at the outset and anyone in his position should resign himself to his situation.

CL27A belongs to the tale type of the 'Disobedient Wife' punished (Stith Thompson T.254), also in evidence in *Talavera* II.vii. In *CL* and two of the *Talavera* tales, about a Scottish wife poisoned (II.vii A) and a wife murdered by a crossbow trap (II.vii B), the husband liberates himself from his contrary wife by forbidding her, in front of witnesses, something which she later uses to fatal effect.[7] In *CL27A* the Emperor forbids his wife an unguent for

---

[6] I am very grateful to Consuelo de Andrés Martínez for providing me with a copy of her unpublished paper 'La violencia doméstica en el *Libro del conde Lucanor*', presented to the annual conference of the Association of Hispanists of Great Britain and Ireland, at the University of Kent, in April 2000. I draw on her analysis here.

[7] In a previous draft I referred to the *Talavera* tales only by number but the anonymous readers pointed out that this might be confusing for readers unfamiliar with the tale collections. Naming the tales, however, raises an interesting problem from a feminist perspective. The 'Disobedient Wife' tale type, for example, offers an unsatisfactorily androcentric label when 'Wife Brutally Dominated' may appear to be a more accurate label at least for the tales under discussion here. However, the latter imposes an anachronistic view of the rights of

poisoning arrows and recommends instead a salve to promote the healing of sores and wounds. In *Talavera* the husbands forbid a flask of wine (II.vii A) and a stout chest concealing a cocked crossbow (II.vii B). However, a concern with sin is evident only in *CL*27A and the *Talavera* tale of the Scottish wife poisoned (II.vii A).

In *CL*27A, before resorting to the forbidden ointment ruse, the Emperor requests a separation from the Pope on account of the damage that the Empress causes. The Pope commends the issue 'al entendimiento et a la sotileza del emperador, ca él non podía dar penitencia ante que el pecado fuesse fecho' (Juan Manuel 1994: 117) ('to the Emperor's wits and understanding, as he could not impose penance before the sin was committed', England 1987: 177). The papal counsel may be read as condoning in advance the Empress's murder but the Emperor uses every stratagem possible to alter her conduct before resorting to the ruse, and the moralization condemns any conduct that threatens status, including spiritual. Fradrique's appeal to the pope for a separation brings into play a Christian ethical framework, 'la ley de los christianos' (Juan Manuel 1994: 117), which prohibits separation on the grounds of character, and introduces the question of the Emperor's culpability. The Emperor's attempt to outwit his wife by telling the truth might be seen as sinless, but his intention renders him sinful. That the Pope might be willing to offer absolution may suggest approbation of the act, but this is belied by the fact that in the *exemplum* the tale of Emperor Fradrique is coupled with that of Alvar Háñez, who tests the character of three prospective wives by warning them of his bad habits and chooses his wife according to her response.

In the first Disobedient Wife tale in *Talavera* (II.vii A), Scottish Wife Poisoned, there is no appeal to a third party, and the wise man – its protagonist – is censured: 'usó de arte segund el mundo, aunque segund Dios escogió lo peor' (Martínez de Toledo 1981: 151) ('he acted in accordance with the uses of the world, although according to God he chose the worse', Simpson 1959: 134). In the three other *Talavera* tales of this type, the husband makes his wife appear responsible for her own death by prohibiting use of the fatal item before witnesses, and in *CL*27A, the Emperor prohibits the Empress's use of the poisoned ointment before the entire court, which tries to dissuade the Empress from using it. In Scottish Wife Poisoned (*Talavera* II.vii A), the narrator explicitly states that the husband wishes his wife to appear responsible and uses direct speech to report the plotting of the ruse and the husband's hypocritical lamentation over the death.

The condemnation of the sinful husband is clear in *CL* 27A and *Talavera* II.vii A, and the contrast between worldly and Christian values is explicit

---

women within marriage. I have tried to opt for neutral descriptive titles that focus on the wife as theme.

in both. This is not the case in II.vii B or the other three Disobedient Wife tales in Talavera. The narrator describes them as a potentially inexhaustible *enumeratio*, 'destos enxienplos mill millares se podrían escrevir, pero de cada día contescen tantas destas porfías quell escrevir es por demás' (Martínez de Toledo 1981: 155) ('I could tell you a thousand cases like these, but so many of them happen every day that it would be a waste of time', Simpson 1959: 137).

In *Talavera* II.vii B, the husband seeks revenge for an undescribed slight by concealing a cocked and loaded crossbow in a locked chest; his wife cannot subdue her curiosity about the chest's contents, and is killed opening it. In II.vii C and II.vii D, the wives' stubbornness is their principal fault, and exhibited in speech. In II.vii C the husband tricks his wife, whose argumentative nature makes his life difficult, into a trivial argument that exposes her contrary nature. When he pushes her into a river, he convinces potential rescuers to go upstream after her since she is so contrary that the current will be unable to sweep her downstream. Public knowledge of her stubbornness hinders her rescue, and she drowns. In a similar verbal duel in II.vii D, the wife's stubborn opposition, again in an inconsequential disagreement, causes an excess of melancholy in her husband, who beats their donkey so seriously that they alter the objective of the pilgrimage that they have undertaken to pray for its recovery.

Despite the fact that both *CL* and *Talavera* express objections to the husband's treatment of his spouse, the misogynistic focus on unruly women is more marked in *Talavera* than in *CL*, where the need to select, discipline, and control is central, and where the dangers to the husband are further explored. In *CL*35, for example, the bride's father warns the bridegroom of the malignant and potentially fatal consequences of the marriage (Juan Manuel 1994: 149), suggesting a strong taboo against marrying a women of 'maneras [...] malas et revesadas' (1994: 148) ('evil and contrary ways', England 1987: 217). The young man dominates the girl through a display of male aggression, behaviour deemed appropriate in male characters (Mirrer 1994). Once they are alone, before she acts or speaks, he kills a series of domestic animals in increasing order of value (England 1977: 80) for failing to respond to commands. Finally, he assimilates all living creatures to a single order (Andrés 1998: 252–3), over which he asserts dominion, stating that any unruliness will be punished by death.

His threat is reinforced by the cumulative nature of the killings, and the carefully staged escalation in violence: 'muy sañudo et todo ensangrentado [...] muy mayor saña que contra el perro [...] con la mayor saña que podía mostrar' (Juan Manuel 1994:149–50) ('Very angry and all bloodied, even greater anger than against the dog, with the greatest show of anger he could muster', England 1987: 221). His final gesture enacts the threat of decapitation and dismemberment associated in modern psychoanalysis with the socialization of women (Andrés 1998: 254–5) as analogous to castration anxiety (Cixous 1989: 42–3):

> Et assentósse et cató a cada parte, teniendo la espada sangrienta en el regaço. Et desque cató a cada parte et a otra et non vio cosa viva, volvió los ojos contra su muger muy bravamente et díxol con grand saña, teniendo la espada en la mano: —Levantadvos et datme agua a las manos.
> (Juan Manuel 1994: 151)
>
> (He sat down and looked all around with his blood-stained sword in his lap; and having looked all around and seeing no living creature, he turned with great ferocity towards his wife, and sword in hand said to her very angrily, 'Get up and bring me water for my hands!') (England 1987: 221)[8]

His success in terrorizing his wife into submission is demonstrated when she pleads the following morning with their extended family to keep silent. As summarized in the closing couplet, 'si al comienço non muestras qui eres, / nunca podrás después, cuando quisieres' ('If from the outset you do not show who you are, / you will not be able to later when you want to', England 1987: 223), his action is timely, and it brings him esteem in the extended family, and guarantees his legal place as the principal beneficiary of his father-in-law's wealth.

Prior to the couplet, the *exemplum* ends with a short coda in which his father-in-law belatedly and unsuccessfully attempts to dominate his own wife by killing a cockerel. Its slaughter symbolizes his (self-)emasculation by failing to govern his own wife and daughter, and to act promptly: as his wife rebukes him, 'A la fe, don fulán, tarde vos acordastes, ca ya non vos valdría nada si matássedes çient cavallos; que ante lo oviérades a començar, ca ya bien nos conosçemos' (Juan Manuel 1994: 152) ('Dear me, husband, you have come to your senses too late. It would do you no good to kill even a hundred horses: you should have started earlier, because we know each other too well now', England 1987: 223). Just as the bridegroom is the son of a good man whose habits he shares, so the bride, prior to her marriage, shares her mother's unruliness. Her father's rueful warning about married life can be understood in hindsight as an ironic commentary on his own married life. As in *CL25*, on the selection of a bridegroom who is 'omne', all three of the men involved in the exchange benefit as a direct result of the marriage, thereby raising homosocial bonds between them; and, further, the father-in-law in *CL35* is instructed by it, albeit too late for his own marriage.

The threat posed by an unruly woman in *CL35* is realized in *CL27A* on Emperor Fradrique and his wife: the unruliness of the Empress is portrayed unambiguously as detrimental to the wellbeing of the Empire, as noted above.

---

[8] See Andrés 1998: 253 on the blood of animals as symbolic of loss of virginity.

In order to contain the danger associated with her, the Emperor submits her to a three-step process. Before much of the court, he warns her against using a poisonous herb, anoints his own blemishes with an unguent and then offers this to the Empress, 'si le fuesse mester, que de aquel pusiesse en cualquier llaga que oviesse' (Juan Manuel 1994: 118) ('to put the ointment on any sores she had if the need arose', England 1987: 177).

It has been observed that the representation of an Empress as diseased strikes an incongruous and comic note, yet little has been made of the fact that the Emperor is also depicted as being physically imperfect. These details are lacking from the other versions of this tale type with which I am familiar. I suggest, therefore, that his actions can be interpreted allegorically. According to this analysis, the Emperor's injuries represent wounds in the body politic that he can heal by integrating the Empress or by eliminating her from it. Consequently, Fradrique offers her a choice whereby her own bad conduct leads irrevocably to her downfall. Her failure to use the ointment that he recommends confirms her contrariness; it figures her refusal to conform to social norms as an obedient wife and to heal that which is corrupt within the body politic, herself. I suggest that her failure to act as a wife should is thematized as disease and malaise affecting her, her husband, and his estate. The Empress ignores Fradrique's words and the message that his actions convey, and she focuses instead on her own appetite, attending to the fissures in her own body, her *llagas* (sores), external signs of her own malaise and stubbornness.

The Emperor failed twice in his selection of a spouse. First, he failed to attain prior knowledge of her character; the importance of which is reinforced in the coda about the father-in-law in *CL27* and portrayed as an important factor in spousal selection in *Siete partidas* II.vi.i (cited above). Secondly, he failed to correct her at the outset, as summed up in the concluding couplet of *CL27*. His double failure affects his own wellbeing and that of the Empire. The tale illustrates the point that a man's conduct as bridegroom and husband has social as well as personal and spiritual implications, such as the fact that he commits a sin in order to rid himself of the Empress, and its effect on his reputation and possibility of salvation; whereas failure to correct her would give rise to further social and personal ill.

My argument about the tale of Emperor Fradrique depends, in the first place, on the recognition that the Empress's behaviour affects the Empire and the physical wellbeing of the Emperor. In *CL27* Don Juan Manuel clearly states the former, and in his *Libro infenido* (Unfinished Book) he warns against the very real dangers unruly wives pose to body and estate, even cross-referring to his *Conde Lucanor*:[9]

---

[9] In *CL*44, men's bodies and their imperfections are symbolic of their own or another's state of sin (Haywood 2005).

los más de los omnes yerran en la manera que deven traer con sus mugeres. Ca unos fazen tanto que ellas quieren, *que les es muy dannoso para las faziendas et para los cuerpos et para las famas. Et muchos fazen tan poco por ellas, et aun les dan tantos enojos, que les es muy dannoso para las almas, et aun para los cuerpos et para las faziendas et para las famas.* Et muchos cayen en ellos yerros porque dizen que sus mugeres son tan buenas et aman tanto a sus maridos, que por fuerça an ellos a fazer lo que ellas quieren. Et otros dizen que sus mugeres son tan fuertes et tan bravas et tan porfiosas, que por fuerça an a pasar et fazer lo que ellas quieren, por non aver mala vida con ellas. Et destas maneras ay tantos omnes que yerran en esto, que sería grant marabilla que todas las maneras en que yerran, que se podiesen poner en scripto. [...] Et pues en otro libro lo he puesto, non quiero poner en éste en quál manera se deven guardar los tales commo vos de tales yerros commo estos.

(Juan Manuel 1952: 130–1; my italics)

(most men err in the way that they deal with their wives. *Thus some men do whatever their wives wish, which is very damaging to their estates, bodies, and reputations. And many other men do so little for them, and even annoy them so much, that it is very damaging for their souls, and even for their bodies, and estates, and reputations.* And many fall into these errors because they say their wives are so good and love their husbands so well, that they must do what their wives wish. And others say that their wives are so strong and so fierce and so wilful, that they must do what their wives wish, so as not to have a bad life with them. And in these ways there are so many men who err in this, that it would be a great marvel were all the ways in which they err possible to put into writing. [...] And as I've put it in another book [*CL*], I don't want to put in this one in what way those such as you can guard against such errors as these.)

My second premise is that he makes allegorical use of the commonplace of the ruler as microcosm of the empire. Juan Manuel himself uses the techniques of allegory in four, or possibly five, *CL exempla*, and the association between the ruler's body and the body politic has been well documented in the early modern period, having been used as a political metaphor from as early as the twelfth century (Kantorowicz 1957, Hale 1971).[10] José Manuel Nieto Soria (1988: 90–8) has shown that organicist images, particularly of the king as head of a realm composed of vassal members, were prevalent in thirteenth- and fourteenth-century Castilian discussions of the relationship of king to kingdom, such as in the juridical *Espéculo* (Mirror) and in the *Libro de los cien capítulos* (Book of One Hundred Chapters).

---

[10] The four certain allegorical *exempla* are *CL*26, *CL*43 , *CL*48, and *CL*49: see Scholberg 1997: 153–4. Alexander Krappe (1933: 294–7) and Daniel Devoto (1972: 209–15) argue that *CL*33, about a falcon, an eagle and a heron, is a political allegory in which the eagle represents the king, and the falcon, a vassal.

As a metaphor it was certainly familiar to compilers of the *Siete partidas* (see II.I.5 and II.XII.26) (Alfonso X 1991: 45; 129–30), where it appeared relating the king to the head and soul of the body, and to the head and heart. I have been unable to locate precisely the image of the ruler as microcosm in Juan Manuel's writings, but he expresses the core idea of the human body as microcosm of the wider world in his *Libro del cavallero et del escudero* (Book of the Knight and the Squire) (1326): 'Mas, asý commo el omne, que es mundo menor, es conpuesto et se mantiene por el alma et por el cuerpo, bien así el mundo mayor se mantiene por las obras spirituales et tenporales' (Juan Manuel 1989: 43) (Further, just as man, who is the lesser world, is composed of and maintained by his soul and by his body, so too the greater world is maintained by spiritual and temporal works). The evidence presented does not, I think, prove my argument conclusively, but it does suggest strongly that it is a plausible interpretation. If my interpretation is correct, the unruly Empress's behaviour contravenes taboos concerning appropriate wifely behaviour, and she is fittingly punished when she cannot be reincorporated into the body politic. For the Emperor, her elimination cleanses and purifies the ill in the body politic and, by extension, his own sores. However, her unruly behaviour was only able to develop and cause problems because he failed to establish her character prior to marriage and to assert his authority at the beginning of the relationship, and he cannot escape the tarnish of his actions on his reputation and eternal soul.

In the *CL exempla* discussed here Juan Manuel explores issues that arise from the need to assimilate women as property under patriarchy. The principal form this anxiety takes is as a taboo against women's unruly behaviour, and it is sufficiently powerful to pollute the persons and estates of their husbands. The unruliness of untested and untried women is also thematized in the frame narrative of *Sendebar*, where the threat to social and moral order posed by the stepmother could not be clearer. As an advice book, *CL* teaches appropriate forms of action for men and, as the concluding verses to *CL27* exemplify, generalizes out from marriage to the wider world. The frame tale of *Sendebar*, with its contrasts between the moral status of mother and stepmother and son and father, performs a similar function.

Anxieties arising from marriage as a microcosm of male conduct are particularly explored where spousal selection is at issue. This anxiety is sometimes linked to status issues when the father marries his daughter down the social hierarchy. In *CL25* Patronio's advice and the *exemplum* deal with the importance of selecting a son-in-law of the appropriate character, not lineage: he must be 'omne'. In *CL35* the young woman's father regards her as unmarriageable, but is fortunate in that the young bridegroom proves equal to his own ambition. Both of these sons-in-law act in ways that redound to the benefit of the reputation and estates of their extended families, and their actions guarantee the future of their lineages. Juan Manuel's treatment of these issues focuses on the husband's quality of character rather than birth. Two of the *CL* tales discussed (*CL*27A of Emperor Fradrique, and *CL*35, in which a son-in-law subdues his bride by killing their animals), convey anxiety associated with marriages in which women take a dominant role and the effect that this has on their husbands' estates. A man's inability to assert his authority over his wife may be indicative of his inability to act as a man of his station should and to take the appropriate stance at the beginning of any social interaction. This last point is made most clearly in the contrast between the father and son-in-law in *CL*35. As I have argued, the ability to assimilate a wife into an appropriate place in the domestic hierarchy signifies a husband's authority and, as an adjunct to this, his ability to defend and improve his own honour and advantage: a man's authority extends from the domestic context into his dealings with the world at large. Juan Manuel makes these views explicit in his *Libro de los estados* (Book of the Estates) (completed 1330–32) and the later *Libro enfinido* (1334–37). Marriage is the microcosm of a man's conduct in social relations, and if his wife is unruly then misrule will govern his estate.

Exemplary tales in which women are depicted as mirrors of their husbands, and particularly of their husband's ability or failure to dominate in a given social context, encode a strongly patriarchal social structure. In such a structure, marriage is a *locus* in which virility is exercised and demonstrated. Under the constraints of such a structure, women are reduced to signifiers of their husband's virility and his capacity to behave appropriately, and, consequently, any means necessary can be employed to reintegrate or domesticate wives. Despite the reductive representation of female characters in medieval exemplary tales of this type, in which women are desubjectivized and reduced to chattels over which men wield absolute dominion, studies such as those by Heath Dillard (1984) and Peter Linehan (1997) show that many historical medieval women enjoyed freedom of speech and action.

Further reading

Archer, Robert, 2005. *The Problem of Woman in Late-Medieval Hispanic Literature*, CT, A124 (Woodbridge: Tamesis)

Cadden, Joan, 1993. *Meanings of Sex Difference in the Middle Ages: Medicine, Science, and Culture* (Cambridge: CUP)

Mérida Jiménez, Rafael M., 2008. *Damas, santas y pecadoras: hijas medievales de Eva*, Icaria, Mujeres y Cultura, 98 (Barcelona: Centre Dona i Literatura)

Lacarra, María Eugenia, 1988–89. 'Notes on the Feminist Analysis of Medieval Spanish Literature', *La Corónica*, 17: 14–22

Lacarra, María Jesús, 1979. *Cuentística medieval en España: los orígenes* (Zaragoza: Universidad)

5

Through Women's Eyes: The Appropriation of Male Discourse by Three Medieval Women Authors*

NIEVES BARANDA

Medieval women writers in Castile are few in number, clustered mainly in the fifteenth century, and bear no resemblance to the predominant European model of the female visionary, or *santa viva* (living saint).[1] It is entirely possible that the women writers we are aware of today are not the only ones to have existed, given the problems of survival that have afflicted Spain's cultural heritage of this period, but currently the authors of prose works may be listed as follows: Leonor López de Córdoba, Constanza de Castilla, and Teresa de Cartagena. If we include women writing in Catalan, we can add Isabel de Villena (1430–90), the author of a compelling *Vita Christi*.[2] With regard to poetry, the number of known women poets is scarcely greater, comprising Mayor Arias, María Sarmiento, Queen Juana, and Vayona, with one poem apiece, and Florencia Pinar, the author of five short poems.[3]

The biographical profiles of all these women, together with their works, appear to mark them out as fundamentally different. This difference relegates them the margins of the standard literary histories, though today they

---

* Translated from the Spanish by Geraldine Hazbun.
[1] See Dronke 1994, Ferrante 1997, Rivera Garretas 1997, and Cirlot and Garí 1999.
[2] See Rosanna Cantavella's chapter in this volume. Studies of Villena which share a similar approach to mine are Hauf 1990: 323–97 and Twomey 2003b. Another Catalan nun, Sor Ramoneta Oller, seems to have composed various religious treatises at the end of the fourteenth century: see Pernarnau Espelt 1982.
[3] On these poets, see the edition by Pérez Priego (1990) and studies by Whetnall (1992) and Gómez-Bravo (2003). For all of these female writers, an extensive volume of studies can be consulted in *BIESES, Bibliografía de escritoras españolas*: http://www.uned.es/bieses. For an overview of the period and considerations which complement my discussion here, see Baranda 2005: 123ff.

enjoy a certain visibility thanks to their unique status as women. But this very uniqueness, which has rescued them for traditional historiography from the 1970s onwards, has isolated them from one another: analysed within the context of a literature that is both male-authored and androcentric, they lose part of their meaning. To recover this meaning, we must align ourselves with gender studies, history constructed from the perspective of gender, that is, taking into account the specific femaleness of the object of study. By applying this analytical approach, we can uncover the full significance of these female writers. Gender studies is a discipline that does not restrict us to a single formula, given the range of available methodologies which are constantly broadening our horizons and opening up new and complementary aspects of the works.

One of the now classic approaches adopted by feminist criticism concerns the practice of reading, and highlights women's need to adapt their ways of reading to the practices of the dominant masculine group, which demand identification with their own values, in which women occupy a silent and subordinate position. The empirical foundations of this approach are too well known to require further elaboration (see Flynn and Schweickart 1986); the problem is that the irrecoverable loss of the experience of women readers of the past, especially the medieval past, deprives us of first-hand knowledge of how women negotiated androcentric texts from a female point of view, and whether and if so to what extent a resistant reading was possible, that is, a reading which did not identify with the assumptions of misogyny. The appropriate sources are scarce for medieval Spain because of the poor survival rate of collections of letters, women's diaries, or personal documents. For this reason I believe we are justified in turning our attention to female writers; they are by definition readers, and their dialogue with tradition can show us how they renegotiated the texts they inherited and how they inscribed in them women with whom they could identify.

One way or another, this procedure is engaged in by all three of the writers I am going to discuss, since they include in their works a female sign with traditional characteristics, but they also display values which diverge from tradition.

Leonor López de Córdoba (1362–1430)

The *Memorias* (Memoirs) of Leonor López de Córdoba is a short first-person narrative telling part of the life story of a highborn noblewoman from birth up to the year 1396 or 1400, depending on which date we assign to the outbreak of plague which affects the city of Córdoba at the end of her story. What Leonor relates is a long succession of misfortunes which befell her and her family when Henry II came to power after the assassination of

King Peter I in 1369 and the cruel persecution of all his supporters.[4] First she gives an account of her lineage, traced through the genealogy of her parents, since the nobility of her family ties is a measure of the gravity of the injuries sustained, the appeals made, and the injustices suffered. Her father, portrayed as a loyal servant of the dead king and his daughters, is betrayed by the followers of Henry, who execute him and incarcerate his family. In a Seville prison, where they are confined for nine years until the death of Henry (†1379), Leonor loses all of her family and servants, so that when freedom comes only she and her husband are left, stripped of their worldly goods. This is when they initiate proceedings to recover their honour, status, and possessions appropriate to their noble rank, a task shouldered by Leonor when the feeble efforts of her husband, without military or financial backing, come to nothing. Leonor is taken in by her aunt in Córdoba and from this position, humiliating for one who has enjoyed great riches and a house of her own, she gradually succeeds in recovering some of her property by recourse to prayers, supplication to the Virgin, and sacrifice.

Leonor concludes her account with burial of her son, a victim of the plague. Although the whole family group has fled Córdoba, plague enters the house in Aguilar with a sick Jewish boy whom she had adopted as a child and so feels obliged to care for. Her adopted son survives, but her biological son dies. While she is mourning this loss, her aunt, at the insistence of her daughters, who bear ill feelings towards Leonor, asks her to leave: 'Y así, víneme a mis casas de Córdoba' (Vozzo 1992: 66) ('and so I returned to my house in Córdoba', Constable and Lacey 1997: 301). The text says nothing about her later life, how she finally attains her longed-for honour in the form of power and wealth. Not long after the events narrated she is appointed lady-in-waiting to the Queen (Katherine of Lancaster) and becomes her favourite, until she falls from grace in 1412 and is exiled from the royal court.

The first difficulty of interpretation presented by this unique text arises in deciding when exactly and why it was composed, questions that have given rise to conflicting critical responses. If we date it to 1412, as argued by Ayerbe-Chaux 1977–78 and Vozzo 1992, the *Memorias* can be read as a skilful defence against the calumnies that had led to Leonor's estrangement from the Queen and her banishment from court, because in it she portrays herself as the constant victim of slander and harassment. This possibility, however, does not explain the absence of reference to any of the actual accusations levelled against Leonor at that time. If, on the other hand, we date the *Memorias* to around 1396, its purpose may have been to support

---

[4] The most accessible modern edition of the text is Ayerbe-Chaux 1977–78; English translations can be found in Kaminsky 1996: 19–32, and Constable and Lacey 1997.

for Leonor's bid for royal favour; since we have documentary evidence that at that time she received a royal concession for Cordoban soap, this earlier dating seems very plausible. What is more, this hypothesis makes sense of other features of the text: its configuration as a legal document committed to writing in the presence of a notary; the insistence upon veracity; the skewing of historical events relating to the siege of Carmona in order to portray Leonor's father as protector and saviour of the royal princesses (one of whom was Queen Katherine's mother); the emphasis on Leonor's lineage and her exemplary behaviour in the face of misfortune; and the fact that the end of her account coincides with the time of writing. Viewed in this way, the *Memorias* of Leonor López de Córdoba can be understood as a type of letter of introduction to the Queen, a 'testimony of services rendered' composed to solicit royal favour or a concession of some kind.[5]

López de Córdoba had to find a socially acceptable and rhetorically plausible way of writing about herself, a woman, avoiding the sin of pride which was inherent in this act, but mustering sufficient authority to be credible. Also, the deeds recounted had to be significant in themselves and sufficiently meritorious to warrant recognition, but they could not be the kind of deeds related in chronicles or male-authored memoirs, since the services proffered by Leonor were not in the sphere of arms. In the absence of an obvious written tradition, Leonor acts with great perspicacity, choosing a medium in which the written word carries the weight of legal truth: the deposition sworn before a notary. This solves the problem of making *natural* sense of a first-person account, when the sole protagonist is also the person dictating, because in the textual space she has appropriated, Leonor can introduce herself as a witness: 'Juro por esta significancia de †, en que yo adoro, cómo todo esto que aquí es escrito es verdad, que lo vi y pasó por mí' (Vozzo 1992: 44) ('I swear by the meaning of the cross that I adore, that all that is written here is true, that I saw it, and it happened to me', Constable and Lacey 1997: 294).

However, this framework is not enough on its own and Leonor immediately opens up a new sphere of meaning by inserting her tale into another tradition, that of the miraculous, namely, the collections of miracle stories which were compiled as a showcase for the Virgin's benevolence and to inspire the devotion of the faithful. Leonor's didactic intent raises her story to a level beyond autobiography (a concept with no meaning at that time) towards the *exemplum*, whose protagonist, male or female, is best placed to bear witness. Leonor continues:

---

[5] The case for this dating was put forward by Marcelino Amasuno in 1996, and is now the most widely accepted. For a summary of the critical issues relating to the *Memorias*, see Gómez Redondo 2002: 2334–50.

y escríbolo a honra y alabanza de mi señor Jesucristo y de la Virgen Santa María su madre, que lo parió, por que todas las criaturas que estuvieren en tribulación sean ciertos que yo espero en su misericordia, que si se encomiendan de corazón a la Virgen Santa María, que ella las consolará y acorrerá, como consoló a mí. (Vozzo 1992: 46)

(I write it for the honor and glory of my Lord Jesus Christ, and of the Virgin, St Mary his mother, who gave birth to him, so that all creatures that were in tribulation may be secure – as I put my faith in her mercy – that if they commend their hearts to the Virgin St Mary, she will console and succor them, as she consoled me.) (Constable and Lacey 1997: 294)

The account of her life which follows is modelled on hagiographical convention (Valero-Costa 2002), as Leonor explains the slow process of recovering her honour after leaving prison in terms of suffering, sacrifice and/or prayers to the Virgin, and miracles. A careful analysis of the account reveals no direct temporal or causal connection between the different incidents, but Leonor isolates them and links them up in a sequence to suggest they were ordained by divine design. When she is living with her aunt, she wishes to be spared the humiliation of going out into the street in order to have a proper meal each day, a sign of servitude. Leonor's many prayers are answered when her aunt agrees to open an inner door, but a maid interferes and, we are told, goes on to suffer a cruel death. Implicitly the maid dies because she opposed the divine plan. López de Córdoba doesn't state this in so many words, nor does she say when the death of the woman takes place; she simply sets out events in a sequence which steers the logic of the account in the direction she wants.

Another of the moments symbolizing this divine aid is the vision in which Leonor is given to understand that the Virgin will help her to obtain the longed-for home of her own. In the narrative she acquires the house after having raised the Jewish orphan; it is a gift from her aunt in recognition of Leonor's having spent seventeen years living with her. Leonor concludes:

Y tengo que por aquella caridad que hice en criar aquel huérfano en la fe de Jesucristo, Dios me ayudó a darme aquel comienzo de casa. Y de antes de estos [sc. días], yo había ido treinta días a maitines ante Santa María el Amortecida, que es en la Orden de San Pablo de Córdoba, con aguas y con vientos, descalza, y rezábale sesenta y tres [sic] veces esta oración que se sigue, con sesenta y seis avemarías, en reverencia de los sesenta y seis años que ella vivió con amargura en este mundo, por que ella me diese casa. Y ella me dio casa, y casas (por su misericordia) mejores que yo las merecía. (Vozzo 1992: 60)

(I believe God helped me by giving me that beginning of a house because of the charity I performed in raising the orphan in the faith of Jesus Christ.

> For thirty days before this, I had gone to Matins to the image of St Mary the Fainting, which is in the Order of San Pablo of Córdoba, barefoot and in all weathers, and I prayed to her the prayer that follows sixty-three times, with sixty-six Ave Marias, in reverence for the sixty-six years that she lived with bitterness in this world, so that she would give me a home, and she gave me a home, and houses better than I deserved, out of her mercy. (Constable and Lacey 1997: 299, slightly modified)

Through this selection and sequencing of events, the life of Leonor acquires an exemplary character, much like that of the unjustly accused and persecuted queen in the miracle story, since her tale begins in a state of prosperity, followed by a sudden and undeserved reversal of fortune, and then begins her slow ascent, thanks to her acceptance of the divine plan and the manifest help of the Virgin (see María Jesús Lacarra 2007).[6]

Her *Memorias* portray Leonor López de Córdoba as an apparently conventional reader, since she constructs female models which conform to tradition, as the passive subjects of a fate forged by a history of violence constructed by men. Faced with her destiny as a woman, the only route open to her is the physical inactivity proper to her gender and adapted to an interior space (the home), and intense activity of a spiritual kind, which is where she finds her reward, in this world or the next. However, the conventionality is only apparent. A closer reading reveals that Leonor does not simply follow these models, she transforms herself into one of them, rising through her narrative construct to attain the standing of an example to other women.

Constanza de Castilla (c. 1395–1478)

The historical crisis that peaked with the assassination of Peter I in 1369 affected Leonor López de Córdoba, but it also had a direct impact on the life of Sor Constanza de Castilla. This Dominican nun was a granddaughter of the assassinated king, offspring of the marriage between Prince John and Elvira de Eril, the daughter of his gaoler in Soria. The two children of this union were the protegés of Queen Katherine, who safeguarded them from the threat they posed to the new dynasty by directing them into the religious life. For neither sibling was this a lesser fate: while her brother Pedro rose to became Bishop of Palencia, Constanza, having taken the veil at an early age, after thirty-eight years was elected Prioress of Santo Domingo el Real, one of the most important convents in Madrid. Through her connections to

---

[6] On the hagiographical motif of the persecuted queen, see Domínguez Prieto 1998.

spheres of influence and successive queens-consort, Constanza de Castilla expanded the convent and brought it greater prestige.

Surviving documentation reveals that Constanza de Castilla worked tirelessly in the defence of her own interests and those of the convent, and her writings have the same concerns at their heart. MS 7495 of the Biblioteca Nacional, Madrid, is a miscellaneous volume containing a collection of devotions of varied purpose, application, and theme, some in Castilian and some in Latin.[7] The author describes them as follows:

> lo que yo he conpuesto, escripto en este libro, así la de oraçión de tu vida e passión, commo de las oras de los clavos, commo en la ordenaçión de las oras de la tu encarnaçión, commo en los quinze gozos e siete angustias e letanía de Nuestra Señora (Wilkins 1998: 90)[8]
>
> (what I have composed or written in this book, whether the Meditation on your Life and Passion, or the Hours of the Nails, or the Order of the Hours of your Incarnation, or the Fifteen Joys and Seven Sorrows and Litany of Our Lady)

Since most of these are well-known prayers which would have formed part of the communal devotions in a Dominican convent of the period, we might be tempted to discount the work as the result of mere copying or compilation to create a prayerbook for personal use. However, although this is effectively what we are presented with, a book of private devotions, it is also much more than that, because these prayers have been passed through the filter of an author who in the act of rewriting has imposed her own reading on an tradition which might otherwise seem monolithic and immutable.

The book opens from a position of anonymity, which can be explained by Constanza's need to distance herself from the sin of pride that the act of naming would imply: 'Esta oraçión que se sigue conpuso una soror de la orden de Sancto Domingo de los Predicadores, la qual es grant pecadora' (The following prayer was composed by a nun of the Order of St Dominic of the Preachers, who is a great sinner) (Wilkins 1998: 3). However, this initial reticence is short-lived, soon giving way to repeated mentions of her name –'Yo Costança' (1998: 24, 37, 85, 90, 108) ('I, Constanza') – and an explicit reference to her lineage, which enabled Huélamo (1993) to positively identify the author as Constanza de Castilla:

---

[7] Ana María Huélamo (1993) gives a detailed description of the manuscript; from internal and external evidence she argues for a date of composition of c.1465, the year in which Constanza stepped down from her duties as prioress.

[8] Other studies of this author and her work include Surtz 1995: 41–67 and Wilkins 2003; for a more traditional reading, see Gómez Redondo 2002: 3071–74.

Señor, [...] te suplico que ayas merçed de todas las ánimas que están en purgatorio, principalmente las de mi padre e madre, e del señor rey don Pedro, e de la señora reyna doña Catalina, e de mi señora doña María e de todos los que yo cargo tengo. (Wilkins 1998: 31)

(Lord, [...] I implore your mercy on all the souls in purgatory, especially those of my father and mother, and his majesty King Peter and her majesty Queen Katherine, and my lady Queen Maria, and on all those who are in my care.)[9]

Throughout the whole of the first part, comprising the *Oración* (Meditation) on the Life and Passion of Christ, Constanza recurs like a leitmotif as the penitent sinner, admitting her faults, praying for herself, pleading for God's grace. This corresponds in part to a standard procedure in medieval devotionary literature, whereby an author not only reviews his past sins but embodies them personally as a mark of humility and with didactic intent. So Constanza's presence in the text, the direct tone of her entreaties to God, and the repetitive structure in which scenes from the Life of Christ, particularly his Passion, are linked to specific virtues which the author requests for herself transport us to an intimate place: Constanza's awareness of the perfection which she fails to attain, and for which she strives in the contemplation of Christ. This insertion of the author into the text is not restricted to her name or her personal entreaties; it permeates the work, making the whole book a woman's prayer, for the feminine grammatical markers prevail over the masculine, even in the most impersonal passages.

Sor Constanza's reading of canonical texts is not applied just to herself. Undoubtedly the most original part of the work is her re-creation of Christ's Passion. This occurs in two of the pieces: the long introductory Meditation on the Life of Christ, and the Hours of the Nails. The Meditation is divided into forty-four short chapters, each scene associated with one or more virtues; it also contains intercalated prayers and hymns. She pays closest attention to the scenes of the Passion, in which the visual elements, the most dramatic physical aspects which arouse pity and horror at the suffering of sacred persons, are re-created in minute detail. Constanza, a well-read and educated woman, has learnt from devotional treatises on the Passion, from *Vitae Christi*, the procedure for re-creating those scenes graphically, breaking them down into their component elements, and enhancing them with humane touches. Like the *Vitae Christi* authors she occasionally introduces the syntagm 'Et posumus credere', or 'Sentimos [...] e piadosamente

---

[9] Constanza's grandfather, Peter I, as noted above, was assassinated in 1369; Katherine of Lancaster, the widow of Henry III, had died in 1418; Queen Maria, the first wife of John II of Castile, died in 1445.

creemos' (we feel [...] and piously believe) (Wilkins 1998: 21, 74), the kind of expression used to justify the personal gloss and the devout flight of fancy.[10]

After Christ, the Virgin is the most important figure in these scenes and in the Hours of the Nails. The narration stresses the intimate suffering humanity of Mary, inviting identification by the reader or listener as she stirs his senses and feelings. The Virgin is both spectator and participant in the scene, because she suffers in sympathy with her son. Nevertheless, Constanza questions the total passivity which characterizes the Virgin in Catholic tradition. In the Hours of the Nails, Constanza wonders how it is that Mary went out to watch the sacrifice of her son and asks: '¿Por quél temor que a las mugeres retrae a ti non detovo aquel día de ver tan grandes crueldades, señaladamente en el fijo tuyo? [...] creemos aquel día las costunbres e condiciones ser mudadas por amor natural del tu fijo' (Why did that fear that makes women withdraw not stop you that day from seeing such great cruelty, dealt especially to your own son? [...] we believe that on that day customs and rules were altered through natural love for your son) (Wilkins 1998: 73–4).[11] Implicitly, the prayerbook stresses certain traditions that question the Virgin's unbroken silence by including a copy of the Virgin's (apocryphal) letter to St Ignatius of Antioch. The theme of other letters in this tradition is essentially Marian, since they sing the Virgin's praises and refer to her role as transmitter of the teachings of Christ.

There is no evidence to suggest that Sor Constanza saw or felt that her authority to write was in question, or that her gender caused tensions around her. In her repeated recourse to the humility *topos* she characterizes herself merely as a sinner, but not as specifically different from men. Indeed, throughout her life she always acted with great freedom and initiative, supported by her royal lineage, her position in the convent, and her close connections with the court. Thus she uses the Virgin Mary to represent an exceptional woman who is able to act against convention without forfeiting her exemplary status: she writes like a teacher, she defies womanly custom when attending the crucifixion. Underlining these aspects of Mary's behaviour is a form of reading the Virgin as a type of powerful woman, a mirror reflecting the sort of prerogative rarely exercised by nuns, but essen-

---

[10] Meditations on the humanity of Christ date back to the thirteenth century, but the genre undergoes a great surge in popularity at the end of the fourteenth, in the form of the *Vita Christi* tradition; the genre is also represented in the Offices of the Cross and the Passion in many Books of Hours. It would be interesting to compare Constanza's practice in this respect with that of Isabel de Villena: see Hauf 1990 and Courcelles 2001.

[11] See also Surtz's commentary on this question (1995: 52–6, 61ff.).

tial for Constanza in her task of managing and expanding the heritage of the convent.[12]

Teresa de Cartagena (1424/30–c. 1480)

Like Leonor and Constanza de Castilla, Teresa de Cartagena cannot be said to regard her female condition as inferior or marginal when she embarks on her first work, the *Arboleda de los enfermos* (*Grove of the Infirm*).[13] In this longish treatise she refers to herself as a woman on only three occasions. First in the prologue, where she alludes to 'la baxeza e grosería de mi mugeril yngenio a sobir más alto non me consienta' (Cartagena 1967: 38) ('And since the lowliness and grossness of my womanly mind do not allow me to rise higher', Seidenspinner-Núñez 1998: 24). This is no more than a formula of the humility *topos*, a standard component of the *captatio benevolentiae* used by writers of the period. The second instance is of the same sort and serves as closure to an excursus (Cartagena 1967: 69); the third occurs just before the final section of the book, on the theme of patience: 'Mas porque mi grosero juyzio mugeril haze mis dichos de pequeña o ninguna autoridad' (Cartagena 1967: 96) ('Yet because my coarse womanly judgement gives my words little or no authority', Seidenspinner-Núñez 1998: 74.) This is certainly an odd assertion coming from someone who has spelt out her arguments at some length without showing any concern so far for a womanly lack of authority. The presence of the author in the text is a common connecting device in medieval works, used for introducing new topics or sections, as Teresa uses it to begin the section on patience. Consolation in infirmity – the suffering caused by her total deafness over a period of years – is the central theme of the *Arboleda de los enfermos*.

Teresa de Cartagena belonged to an eminent family of *converso* origin, the Santa María / Cartagena clan, relatives of the Chief Rabbi of Castile, Salomón Ha Levi, who converted to Christianity in 1390, taking the name of Pablo de Santa María and going on to become Bishop of Cartagena.[14] Intellectual prowess was one of the distinguishing marks of this family, which is reflected in the excellent education that Teresa must have received,

---

[12] See Ángela Muñoz Fernández's summary and analysis of Constanza's life in the light of documentary evidence (1995: 123–59).

[13] The only modern edition of the *Arboleda de los enfermos* and the *Admiraçión operum Dey* is by Lewis Hutton (Cartagena 1967), but Juan Carlos Conde is preparing a new edition for Editorial Cátedra. The English citings here are from the translations of both works by Dayle Seidenspinner-Núñez included in her critical study of 1998.

[14] For the latest biography see Seidenspinner-Núñez and Kim 2004.

including access to the libraries of various of its members, some of whom achieved renown as historians and essayists as well as holders of high office in administration and the Church. Although it used to be assumed that she was put in a convent because of her infirmity, recent research has established that Teresa's deafness did not manifest itself until she was in her thirties, years after she took vows. She first professed as a Poor Clare, but by the time she was twenty-four she had transferred to a Cistercian convent, most probably the important convent of Las Huelgas, in Burgos.

It is thought that the *Arboleda* was written between 1473 and 1479, the fruit of a lengthy process of soul-searching and mature deliberation: Teresa tells us that she had been suffering from deafness for about twenty years when she started it. The work caused widespread controversy, which we know about from the *apologia* she composed herself, and which constitutes her second work, *Admiraçión operum Dey* (*Wonder at the Works of God*). In this much shorter treatise, Teresa takes as her point of departure the criticism meted out to her as a woman, and defends her right to write, basing her defence on the argument that it is God who distributes learning and chooses in whom he wishes to deposit it. She employs a strategy traditional among female religious writers of displacing the authority of their work on to God, disavowing their own learning and wisdom with the object of reducing to nothing their responsibility as authors.[15]

However, the fact that she locates herself within the tradition of the *querelle des femmes*, and that her *Admiraçión* is an *apologia*, forces Cartagena to question herself, to justify her position as a woman in a gendered world, and to defend her transgressive intellectual activity in a way that had not come to the fore in the *Arboleda*. And this gender awareness, imposed upon her as a reaction to criticism, conditions her reading of the female sign by placing it at the centre of debate, and in a position of defensiveness. In terms of the approach I have adopted it is impossible to compare *Admiraçión* with the work of either Leonor or Sor Constanza, so I shall restrict my discussion to the *Arboleda*.

The *Arboleda* is a work of consolation, a genre which aims to find positive meaning in life's great problems, in order to overcome them: a topic of considerable importance in the European Middle Ages. Boethius's *Consolation of Philosophy* is one of the most famous and influential examples, but the genre took many forms (prose, verse, treatise, epistle, etc.), and it was quite common at the time when Cartagena was writing. As a treatise, *Arboleda* has a complex structure, its elaboration grounded in a thorough knowl-

---

[15] For this and other techniques used by Teresa, see Surtz 1995: 28ff. and Moore 2003. On *Admiraçión operum Dey* see especially Gómez Redondo 2002: 3053–70, Rivera Garretas 1992, Seidenspinner-Núñez 1993 and 1997, Quispe Agnoli 1995, and Cortés Timoner 2004.

edge of the learned techniques of weaving a text out of ideas which link up, separate, and come together again; techniques derived in part, although not exclusively, from sermon composition. In common with the sermon it has didactic intent, a unifying *thema*, allegories deriving from the material world, and a comprehensive argument, sweeping the reader along to its conclusions with any doubts put firmly aside. The usual authorities included works of pagan antiquity as well as the Bible and the Church Fathers, but Teresa's models and sources for the *Arboleda* are strictly religious. As well as biblical and patristic sources, which are cited in Spanish, Lewis Hutton found traces of direct influence from more recent texts, such as the *Libro de consolación* of Pedro Luna (Pope Benedict XIII) and two works by Ramón Llull (see Cartagena 1967: 17–26); María del Mar Cortés Timoner has since found echoes of Alfonso de Cartagena (Teresa's uncle), and the *Libro de las tribulaciones* of López de Minaya (2004: 45, 149–59).

Out of such apparently intractable materials, Cartagena constructs an extremely personal work, in which the reader is made continually aware of the sensitivity with which she experiences deafness. Obviously, the consolatory genre, by its very nature, tends to include mentions of personal misfortune (bereavement, imprisonment, impoverishment, etc.), since without them it would make little sense. None the less, in this work of self-consolation the personal becomes the point of departure, a source of authority, and a weapon in the armoury of persuasion. There can be no doubt that this personal presence, the most idiosyncratic aspect of the *Arboleda*, which some critics regard as autobiographical (see Rodríguez Rivas 1992), is what lends it its greatest interest; not just because of its exemplarity, but because it is possible to extrapolate a positive message from the lengthy process of reflection leading up to the acceptance of deafness, a message that can be extended to all the sick.

Teresa begins her work in the first-person singular, *yo* ('I'), as she discusses her illness, her refusal to accept it, and her eventual understanding of the spiritual benefit that it confers; this discussion culminates in a confession of her sins. From this point on, the *yo* gives way to *nosotros los enfermos* (we, the sick), a company of fellow sufferers united as 'aquellos que en el convento de dolençias tenemos hecha profesyón' (Cartagena 1967: 58) ('we who have professed in the convent of afflictions', Seidenspinner-Núñez 1998: 42), and the treatise becomes more coherent and more complex in its argument. This fellowship she mentions is not just a didactic ploy, but a strong background feeling which keeps surfacing and which divides up world's population, not into men and women, but into the healthy and the sick, who receive an unequal share of the good things of this world: 'Trabajamos por traer a nuestras manos los gozos humanos y ellos no quieren venir. Todo el bien deste mundo es manjar de los sanos' (Cartagena 1967: 62) ('We strive to bring within our reach human joys and they refuse to come. All the blessings of this world are food reserved for the healthy', Seidenspinner-Núñez 1998: 46). These and other more personal comments reveal a strong tension between Teresa's observation of the reality she suffers and the need to find a explanation for and an ultimate blessing in the disability, which is the object of her treatise. That is why she rejects the arguments marshalled by other sources and develops a theory of her own which she lards with expressions indicating personal opinion ('It seems to me') rather than certainty.

By means of this argumental progression she arrives at her final section, on the virtue of patience. Here she rejects the wise men of her time: not only do they fail to console, but their advice turns out to be harmful for the sick. To sidestep their teaching she reverts to the sages of classical antiquity who, 'no en París ni en Salamanca aprendieron las leyes, mas en la escuela de obras perfectas asý florescieron, que fueron y son muy famosos maestros' (Cartagena 1967: 96) ('learned their laws not in Paris nor Salamanca but in the school of perfect works, where they were and continue to be great teachers', Seidenspinner-Núñez 1998: 75). Thus with one elegant sweep of the pen she brushes aside all the learned authorities of her time. For this subject, the knowledge that comes from study alone is not enough – it demands experience, *'facere et docere'* (Cartagena 1967: 96), of which she is a consummate master.

Like other learned authors of her time Cartagena controls the art of argument by the deployment of *auctoritates*, and, through a hierarchical organization which privileges experience as a source of the knowledge that matters, she rejects traditional notions in order to set up her own. For example, if canonical doctrine requires a sick person to bear his affliction cheerfully and in silence, Teresa rejects it by reformulating the connotations of *paciencia*:

> la paçiençia no está en no se quexar ni aflegir onbre en sus dolores poco ni mucho, ca esto a la discreçión de cada uno se queda e mucho más a la calidad e cantidad del dolor que syente, mas consiste y está enteramente en que non ofendamos a Dios nin digamos palabras de sobervia.
> (Cartagena 1967: 99)

> (patience is not in whether or not one complains about one's pains, for this pertains to the discretion of the individual and even more to the quality and quantity of the pain that he experiences; rather, patience consists wholly in not offending God or uttering words of pride.)
> (Seidenspinner-Núñez 1998: 77)

In *Admiraçión*, because of the polemic surrounding her capacity to write, Teresa is obliged to interpret the world as a woman and to transform herself into an object of discourse. But female identity is not relevant to the *Arboleda*. The key to reading the *Arboleda* is infirmity. Infirmity has raised Teresa's awareness of belonging to a group of the dispossessed and, accordingly, has led her to reject as partly devoid of meaning the worldview of the dominant group of the privileged well. Her resistant reading is not of a woman but of a sick person, and from it she exposes the untruth of those who from a position of health try to impose models of behaviour, particularly models of salvation, on the sick. That is why she has recourse to Job, because re-reading Job allows her to validate new norms constructed upon her experience of infirmity and pain.

When I began this analysis I thought I was going to show how the fact of being women conditioned these writers' approach to writing, since they must have felt under scrutiny and conscious of transgressing an essential rule for their gender: *mulier in ecclesia taceat*. However, gender awareness is apparent in their texts not as a limitation, but as a fact. When they read their sources, they take from them the aspects they can identify with, while seeming to discard or downplay those aspects which do not conform to their position in the world or their outlook. In each case, these women belong to the upper echelons of society, whose status is determined more by the power that they can wield by virtue of their lineage, education, or rank than by their gender, with the result that they identify with female models of power: the unjustly accused queen, the charismatic figure of the Virgin Mary. These, among the most orthodox models approved by society, are accepted by these writers, but not unreservedly: they sift through their significant attributes to select the ones most relevant to themselves, arranging them in such a way as to favour their own position.

Only Teresa de Cartagena disregards female models and reaches for Job. Her reading strategy strips this exemplary figure of certain meanings and invests him with others, not the ones traditionally assigned to him, but ones which suit her position as a sick woman. Hers is a special case, though, in that the substitution is explicit, because Teresa, an intellectual who has passed through the classrooms of Salamanca, can use argument and persuasion to transform her message. As readers of a tradition, these writers fill the gaps in the text – identified by reception theory – with their own projections, two of them relating to the powerful woman (powerful first and woman second), and one to the dispossessed invalid. In this way their *lecturas-escritas* (written readings) open fissures in a male-authored tradition which they accept, but which they also question.

Further reading

Baranda, Nieves, 2005. *Cortejo a lo prohibido. Lectoras y escritoras en la España moderna* (Madrid: Arco)

Muñoz Fernández, Ángela, 1995. *Acciones e intenciones de mujeres: vida religiosa de las madrileñas (ss. XV–XVI)* (Madrid: Horas y Horas)

Segura Graíño, Cristina (ed.), 1992. *La voz del silencio, I. Fuentes directas para la historia de las mujeres (siglos VIII-XVIII)* (Madrid: Asociación Cultural Al-Mudayna)

Surtz, Ronald, 1995. *Writing Women in Late Medieval and Early Modern Spain: The Mothers of Saint Teresa of Avila* (Philadelphia: University of Pennsylvania Press)

Whetnall, Jane, 1992. 'Isabel González of the *Cancionero de Baena* and Other Lost Voices', *La Corónica*, 21.1: 59–82

6

Intellectual, Contemplative, Administrator: Isabel de Villena and the Vindication of Women

ROSANNA CANTAVELLA

Isabel de Villena is a relative newcomer in the field of women's studies. Some present-day handbooks on medieval hispanic literature still overlook her work, even though she may be considered the most important woman writer of her day in the Iberian Peninsula and an admirable advocate for her sex. An introduction to her life and work is therefore necessary.[1]

She was born Elionor de Villena in 1430, of noble birth but illegitimate. Her mother's identity is unknown; Enrique de Villena, nobleman and man of letters, has traditionally been regarded as her father. She was certainly of royal descent, as revealed by her coat of arms and acknowledged by several contemporary writers:

> D'aquella tan alta, tan fort y gran çoca
> del arbre real dels reys d'Aragó,
> sou vós una branca ab virtut no poca. (Bernat Fenollar)
>
> (Of that tall and strong and illustrious trunk
> of the royal tree of the House of Aragon
> you are a branch of no small virtue.)
>
> A vós, la pastora tan digna d'aquelles
> que tant conversau humilment ab elles,
> vestint rica porpra de tan real sanch. (Pere Martines)
>
> (To you, their honoured shepherdess,
> who used so humbly to converse with them [your nuns],
> though you wear the rich purple of the blood royal.)[2]

---

[1] This chapter forms part of the research project FFI2008–00826, funded by the Ministerio de Ciencia e Innovación, with an additional grant from the Generalitat Valenciana, ACOMP/2009/162.

[2] García Sempere 2002: 225, lines 6–8; 229, lines 59–61. See also the dedication to

From early childhood she is associated with the Valencian court of her devout cousin Queen Maria, the consort of Alfonso the Magnanimous, King of Aragon.

With the help of several papal bulls Queen Maria had arranged the expulsion, for indecent behaviour, of a community of Augustinian monks from the Holy Trinity monastery – ideally situated just outside the walls of prosperous fifteenth-century Valencia – and moved a community of Poor Clares (nuns of the Franciscan Order), from Gandia, to take up residence in this convenient location.[3] The convent was dear to the Queen's heart, and she regarded it with special favour: the daughters of the best Valencian families professed there. People from all walks of life contributed funds to its maintenance, for there were further papal bulls promising them ample heavenly indulgences if they did so.[4] The Queen's cousin Elionor de Villena, then aged fifteen, was the first novice to take the veil at Holy Trinity, choosing the name Isabel.[5] This first profession might have been regarded by Queen Maria's contemporaries as a political gesture, aimed at showing the citizens of Valencia that the convent was under firm royal control. The Holy Trinity was adjacent to the palace, and the Queen had her own rooms inside the convent. When she died she was buried there, and Valencia's most important families followed her example.[6]

In 1462 Isabel de Villena was elected abbess of the convent. There is a legend that the Archangel Michael campaigned in person on her behalf.

Villena in Bishop Miquel Pérez's translation of Thomas à Kempis's *Imitatio Christi*: 'essent gran senyora, e de real linatge, haveu menyspreat de aquest trist món les honors e riquees' (although you are a great lady of royal descent, you have spurned the honours and riches of this miserable world) (Pérez 1491: fol. 2v). Bishop Jaume Pérez addresses her as 'most noble daughter of an illustrious royal line' in the dedication to his commentary on the *Magnificat* (1485: fol. 104r). The most complete record of her supposed genealogy is Sales y Alcalá 1761, ch. 6, reproduced in Villena 1916: III, 379–81; see 384 for her family tree). Her coat of arms appears on the title page of the 1497 incunable (Villena 1916: I, 3); a later version, from the convent's *Llibre major de títols*, is reproduced in Villena 1992: I, 100.

[3] See Martínez y Martínez 1945:167–85; also Benito Goerlich 1998: 45–57, which is the best modern account of Villena's life in the Trinity.

[4] On the Trinity's funding and papal bulls see Benito Goerlich 1998: 50–51. The convent's *Llibre de casa de la Reina* records the names of every almsgiver (see Villena 1992: I, 132–3).

[5] She took the veil on 28 February 1445 and made her final vows on 25 March 1446 (Benito Goerlich 1998: 49).

[6] On the Queen's rooms in the Trinity, see Sales y Alcalá 1761: 29 and Benito Goerlich 1998: 49–50; on her tomb, ibid., pp. 53–7. On the origins of the nobility's custom of being buried in privileged positions inside religious foundations established by them or their forebears, see Westerhof 2008. Also buried in the Trinity was the *infanta* Maria, illegitimate daughter of King Ferdinand II of Aragon: she took the veil aged five, in 1483: see Benito Goerlich 1998: 65–6, who gives the names of other famous families which can be found among the nuns of the Trinity.

And Villena probably needed this backup, since she had to overcome the handicap of illegitimacy, which should have excluded her from this position had the rules of the Order been strictly applied. Queen Maria could not help her with this: she had died in 1458. However, another papal bull, issued three years after Villena's election, lifted the obstacle of illegitimacy. It was precisely the need for a papal bull, nevertheless, that indicates that her election had met with significant opposition.[7]

But Isabel de Villena proved herself to be a worthy abbess, not least because of her excellent abilities as an administrator. She carried out, with an economic policy to match, the building improvements to the convent that her two predecessors had pursued under the patronage of Queen Maria. It was Villena in fact who transformed the Holy Trinity into the bright gem of late Gothic architecture that it is today. When she died in 1490 (in one of the recurrent outbreaks of the plague epidemic), the major building works were already completed, though her successor, Aldonça de Montsoriu, continued with the programme. Villena's administrative contribution to the Trinity convent was, therefore, outstanding.[8]

She is, however, more remembered for her intellectual achievement as the author of a *Vita Christi*, which she left unfinished at her death, with only the last few chapters still to be written. Aldonça de Montsoriu had it printed in 1497 at the request of Queen Isabel of Castile – a niece of Villena –, who took a particular interest in the work. From the perspective of women's studies, Villena's *Vita Christi* is quite remarkable, the result of an all-female intellectual enterprise in the fifteenth century.

Villena's book follows the general pattern of this devotional genre: its aim is to move the readers' or listeners' sensibility by inducing in them an identification with Jesus's life, works, and sufferings. The *Vita Christi* tradition was part of an emotional, contemplative spirituality which especially appealed to the Franciscan vision of Christianity. Many books of this kind were composed and circulated in Western Europe between the thirteenth and sixteenth centuries, mainly in Latin, but also in the vernacular.[9] And Villena's was not the first *Vita Christi* to be written in Catalan: she knew, and

---

[7] In a bull dated 7 March 1465, Pope Paul II 'granted a dispensation from the *defectu natalium*, in order to remove the legal impediment which rendered Sor Isabel de Villena's election as abbess null and void' (Benito Goerlich 1998: 61). On the story of her election see also Sales y Alcalá 1761: 51.

[8] 'One of her most admirable feats is to have completed in such a short time [...] the work started by Queen Maria. Moreoever, this work was developed to a higher standard of sumptuousness and grandeur than originally planned' (Benito Goerlich 1998: 63). For a detailed account of the building works, see also Mata López 1967: 43–50. Isabel de Villena was a meticulous accountant and kept a record of every donation towards the building costs in the Trinity's *Llibre de censals* (transcribed in full in Villena 1992: I, 116–27).

[9] The anonymous *Meditationes vitae Christi*, Ubertino da Casale's *Arbor vitae cruci-*

used as one of her sources, the earlier *Vita Christi* by Francesc Eiximenis (†1409), also a Franciscan (see Hauf 1987:105–64 and 2006).

But although it adheres faithfully to the tradition, Villena's *Vita Christi* displays some unique characteristics. Villena has a natural storyteller's instinct, she maintains a steady aristocratic outlook, and her narrative is interspersed with Latin quotations accompanied by often erudite expositions, which reveal a considerable knowledge of theology. But the *Vita Christi's* main feature is undoubtedly its feminine and pro-feminist narrative style.[10] Unlike earlier *Vitae Christi*, the narrative of Jesus's doings in this world does not cover only the life of Jesus: the book opens with Mary's conception in the womb of St Anne and closes with Mary's Assumption and Coronation. Even the episodes of Jesus's public life tend to be told from the perspective of their impact on his mother. This is not so much a *Vita Christi* as a *Vita Mariae*.

The character of Mary Magdalen has also a leading role. In Villena's *Vita Christi* she is introduced unambiguously as a young lady in love with Jesus. The chapter when she first meets him constitutes one of the most extraordinary love scenes in the whole of medieval Catalan literature:

> E, venint sa majestat per preïcar e pujant en lo predicatori, mirà de fit la dita Magdalena ab aquells ulls de clemència, tirant-li una sageta d'amor dins lo seu cor; la qual, sentint-se així nafrada i tirada, estava tota alterada, mudant los seus pensaments. E lo Senyor, qui eternalment l'havia elegida e sabia quant havia d'ésser gran i excel·lent aquesta dona, dreçà tot lo sermó a ella, parlant de les grans misericòrdies divinals e com ell era vengut del cel per reconciliar los pecadors e fermar pau entre lo seu pare eternal e ells, dient: *Misericordiam volo et non sacrificium: non enim veni vocare iustos sed peccatores ad penitentiam.*(Matt. 9.13) [...] E Magdalena, oint aquestes coses e sentint-se dins si tirada per gràcia singular de la clemència divina, veent-se ja lligada e fermada ab aquella cadena d'amor, la qual com més anava més creixia dins ella, baixà los ulls en terra, posant-se lo ventall davant la cara, e començà a rompre en grans llàgrimes, dient dins son cor: *Paratur cor meum Deus.* (Ps. 107.1) [...] E, creixent la flama d'amor dins d'ella, acabat lo sermó tornà-se'n a casa sua a peu, no volent ja cavalcar, avorrint de cor ço que tant solia amar. (Villena 1987: 46–7)[11]

---

fixae, and Ludolph of Saxony's *Vita Christi* are some of the most influential examples of the genre, which was widely cultivated. For the English tradition, see Sargent 2005.

[10] Joan Fuster was the first to point this out in a series of articles published in the 1950s and later collected in vol. 1 of his *Obres completes*: see Fuster 1968a and 1968b. These chapters are essential reading for any student of Villena.

[11] This anthology provides a selection of the numerous passages illustrating Villena's espousal of the cause of women.

(And when his majesty came to preach, and climbed up into the pulpit, he gazed down at Mary Magdalen with those eyes of clemency, shooting an arrow of love into her heart; and she, feeling at the same time stricken with pain and irresistibly attracted, was visibly shaken, and confused in her mind. And the Lord, who had chosen her from the beginning of time and knew what a great and excellent lady she was to be, addressed his whole sermon to her, as he spoke of the boundless mercies of God, and how he had come down from heaven to reconcile sinners and to bring peace between them and his eternal father, and saying: *What I want is mercy, not sacrifice. And indeed I did not come to call the virtuous, but sinners to repentance.* [...] And Mary Magdalen, listening to these things and feeling drawn towards the special grace of God's mercy, seeing herself already bound and tied by a chain of love which was growing and growing inside her, with eyes downcast, she covered her face with her fan, and burst out weeping, saying in her heart: *My heart is ready, God.* [...] And with the flame of love burning within her, when the sermon was over she walked back home, for she no longer wished to ride, heartily detesting that which she used so much to love.)

Mary Magdalen was of prime importance to Christian spirituality, as she symbolized both the contemplative soul and the hope of salvation for repentant sinners. But Villena cleverly takes this convention one step further, and presents her as a woman falling in love with Jesus, the man as well as the godhead; a love which he returned, for Villena's Jesus honours the Magdalen with a special regard. This was the ideal narrative perspective for the character with whom a community such as the nuns of the Trinity, the *Vita Christi's* first audience, could most identify.

Furthermore, Villena restricts her account of Jesus's public life to just those episodes in which female characters figure as the beneficiaries of his words or miracles. The deliberateness of this selection is explicitly declared by the Vita Christi narrator:

> E d'aquests miracles los principals féu sa clemència en dones e a petició d'aquelles, car per amor e reverència de la senyora mare sua les amava e favorejava en totes coses, en tant que havien a conéixer les gents que lo càrrec e vergonya que les dites dones portaven per la desobediència de la primera, era ja tot passat e a elles en molta glòria tornat.
> (Villena 1987: 41–2)[12]

(And his clemency performed the most important of these miracles on women, or at their request, because out of love and reverence for his mother he loved them and favoured them in everything, so that people

---

[12] See Cantavella 1990 for a comparison between Villena's interpretation of this Gospel passage and the interpretations of other authors.

might know that the burden and shame borne by women because of the first woman's disobedience had now passed, and was transformed for them into great glory.)

This passage alone would be highly indicative of Villena's particular way of championing the dignity of her sex. But she goes even further: specific responses to a great number of literary antifeminist topics have been identified and catalogued in the *Vita Christi*. Villena and the French writer Christine de Pizan are the only women known to have participated in the notorious European-wide debate about whether women are essentially good or bad.[13] Villena uses her *Vita Christi* – besides its obvious main purpose as an aid to the contemplative soul's identification with Jesus, his mother, and Mary Magdalen – to refute the charges of those medieval texts which presented the female sex in a negative light. The principal, longest work of this kind in the whole of Europe was written by a contemporary of Villena's and a fellow Valencian: Jaume Roig. One of Roig's daughters had professed in the Trinity, and Roig himself was the convent accounts manager for a long time, so there is no question of Villena not knowing the *Espill* (Mirror) (see Benito Goerlich 1998: 53, 66). Villena methodically demolishes the misogynistic literary tradition, specifically that of the *Espill*, theme by theme: charges against women such as inconstancy, lust, inability to love deeply, associating with the devil, and stupidity. She demonstrates the patent falseness of this last charge by her own intellectual prowess as well as by her construction of highly intelligent female characters.[14]

It has also been mooted by, for example, Ramon Miquel y Planas (in Villena 1916: I, xx–xxi), that Villena's emotive style and attention to domestic detail are indications of a feminine mode of writing. And, although all examples of the *Vita Christi* genre – because their aim is to move the Christian soul – offer high doses of emotivity, the different, distinctive feminine style of Villena's *Vita Christi* is in my view indisputable. However, I have never been able to see this as the inevitable consequence of its author being a woman, so much as the result of a conscious narrative choice about how best to reach her primary audience, the nuns. The abundance of erudite quotations and glosses show that the abbess possessed more than enough learning

---

[13] See Cantavella 1986 and the prologue to *Protagonistes femenines* (Villena 1987).

[14] On the *Espill* see Jaume Roig 2006, and Cantavella 1992 and Solomon 1997 for its place in the *querelle des femmes* tradition in Western Europe. The first scholar to suggest that Villena used the *Vita Christi* to contest the misogyny of the *Espill* was again Fuster (1968b). Hauf shows a certain degree of scepticism on the subject (see Villena 1995: 56), but I was able to prove Fuster's thesis topic by topic (Cantavella 2000). One of the many exemplars of female intelligence in the *Vita Christi* is Jesus's mother, who after the Ascension becomes the highest theological authority on earth, as well as the editor of the Gospels (Chapter 278). See also Papa 1994a.

to have written, had she so wished, a purely intellectual, non-gender- or emotion-marked discourse. Villena's feminine style is deliberate, as I have argued elsewhere (Cantavella 1986: 42).

An extraordinary narrative focus on domesticity is one feature of this style, along with her characteristic use of diminutives. Martí de Riquer considers this to be 'estil de monja, en el bon sentit de l'expressió' (a nun's style, in the best sense) (1964: III, 480). Riquer's is not the only patronizing comment on the *Vita Christi*. Like many other women writers Villena has in the past been on the receiving end of a number of dismissive or disparaging remarks about, for example, her competence as a theologian.[15] Unsubstantiated assessments such as these illustrate the difficulty of gaining recognition for women's intellectual achievements from even the most distinguished and perceptive of scholars. Aldonça de Montsoriu is not spared either, and her authorship of the prologue – the prologue of a book she herself had had printed – has also been questioned.[16]

In Trinity convent lore Isabel de Villena is traditionally credited with the authorship of two other books: a collection of sermons, and a lavishly illuminated manuscript with the same contemplative purpose as the *Vita Christi*, called *Speculum animae*. These works, which were long believed lost (Sales y Alcalá 1761: 90–1), have recently been rediscovered.[17] The book of sermons has been identified as MS 4327 of the Biblioteca Nacional, Madrid, (formerly attributed to Francesc Eiximenis): the texts match up with some chapters from the Passion sequence in Villena's *Vita Christi*, but are contained within the framework of literary sermon.[18] The *Speculum animae* has also been identified as the text of MS Espagnol 544 of the Bibliothèque Nationale, Paris; but its editors have concluded that, although a product of the same contemplative environment, it was probably written and illuminated after Villena's death (Benito Goerlich and Hauf 1992).

---

[15] 'el *forte* de la monja rau més en la forma que no en el contingut [...] convertir sor Isabel en una teòloga professional com Eiximenis o Ubertí [...] seria desmesurat' (this nun's *forte* lies in the form more than the content [...] to regard Sor Isabel as a professional theologian of the calibre of Eiximenis or Ubertino [...] would be going too far) (Hauf 1991: 111, n.29).

[16] 'Crec probable que Miquel Peres siga també l'autor del pròleg, firmat per sor Isabel [*sic*] de Montsoriu, que encapçala l'edició del VC' (I think it likely that Miquel Peres was also the author of the prologue to the *Vita Christi* which is signed by sor Isabel [*sic*] de Montsoriu) (Hauf 1991: 109).

[17] A third text ascribed by Almiñana to Villena, a sonnet thanking Bishop Pérez for dedicating his translation of the *Imitatio Christi* to her (see Villena 1992: I, 149), is clearly apocryphal, a fake by mossin Jaume Barrera, a friend of Villena's editor Ramon Miquel i Planas, who made them up in 1912, as Jaume Riera i Sans showed in 1993. It was anachronically written in imitation of the poetry of John of the Cross (1542–91).

[18] See Villena 1995: 26–33. Curt Wittlin was the first to draw attention to the correspondence between MS 4327 and Villena's *Vita Christi* (see Hauf 1991: 104–5).

Isabel de Villena's fellow Valencians were by no means unaware of her many virtues as a contemplative, an administrator, and an intellectual. She acquired several important book collections for the convent, thereby enriching it to an extraordinary degree:

> Podemos considerar el convento como una universidad para mujeres, a la que los privilegiados envían a sus hijas a educar. Y para ello no faltarán medios, ya que contarán con bien nutridas bibliotecas, tanto particulares como conventuales, que se incrementarán con importantes donaciones. Coincidiendo con el mandato de sor Isabel de Villena legaron su biblioteca, al convento, varios canónigos de la Catedral de Valencia, destacando la de mosén Eixarch, la de la reina Maria y la de la noble Ursula de Montpalau. (Galiana Chacón 1991: 100–1) [19]

> (We may regard the convent as a university for women, to which the privileged classes send their daughters to be educated. And it will not lack for means, as they will be able to count on some substantial book collections, both personal and monastic, which will grow as a result of some important donations. During Isabel de Villena's time as abbess, several canons of the Cathedral of Valencia bequeathed their libraries to the convent, most notably Mossén Eixarch, [as did] Queen Maria and Ursula de Montpalau.)

Isabel de Villena was the dedicatee of at least three books by her contemporaries, all of whom look up to her as a figure of intellectual as well as spiritual authority.[20] It is assumed that Villena's convent would have been a centre for the religious literary life of her time: 'El patio del convento de la Trinidad [...] se articulará como un espacio privilegiado, como lugar de coloquio e incluso como lugar de redacción de documentos' (The enclosed garden of the Holy Trinity [...] was to become a privileged space, a place for learned debate, even a place for drafting documents) (Galiana Chacón 1991: 99; see also Hauf 1989: 541–52). Little wonder that Agustín de Sales called her the oracle of Valencia (1761: 51).

It is clear that we still don't know very much about the life or work of this first-rate author. Recent decades, however, have seen a rapid growth in interest in her *Vita Christi*. For example, Villena has finally made an appear-

---

[19] Jaume d'Eixarc, who for many years helped Villena with the convent accounts and was later buried there, appointed her as his executor – a task which she apparently took on, in spite of a legal ban on women executors (see Cortés and Pons 1993).

[20] Miquel Pérez praises her as an exemplary contemplative (1491: fol. 2); Jaume Pérez presents her as the spiritual inspiration for his commentary on the *Magnificat* (1485: fol. 104); Bernat Fenollar and Pere Martines ask her to edit their *Istòria de la Passió* (also known as *Lo Passi en cobles*) in any way she likes: her improvements will be jewels in their text, since 'you are a learned doctor in intellectual matters'; they also praise her exemplary spiritual life (García Sempere 2002: 225–9, lines 14–66).

ance in modern English-language surveys on hispanic women writers. She can be found in *Women Writers of Spain* (Galerstein 1986), the *Dictionary of the Literature of the Iberian Peninsula* (Bleiberg et al. 1993), *Double Minorities of Spain* (McNerney and Enríquez 1994), and *Women in Medieval Iberia* (Mérida Jiménez 2002); and in 2001 Kathleen McNerney published an English translation of Chapter 93 of the *Vita Christi*. Advocates of Villena's work have brought it to the attention of academics in France and the German-speaking world (Aichinger 2003; Courcelles 2000 and 2001), and the *Protagonistes femenines* anthology (Villena 1987) has recently been translated into French (Villena 2008). This late flowering of Villena scholarship is all the more creditable given the absence of a modern critical edition of the *Vita Christi*: readers still have to make do with Miquel y Planas's edition of 1916.[21]

The number of academics working on Isabel de Villena keeps growing. Their publications have dealt with a diversity of themes, the main one being the question of the feminine and pro-feminist character of the *Vita Christi*, which is only natural, given its pre-eminence in the text.[22] But other, less studied, areas also demand consideration. I should like to emphasize the need to develop, as a matter of priority, five lines of inquiry in Villena studies.

The first is, I believe, the most pressing: archive research into Villena's life. It is rather disgraceful that we still have to fall back on tradition for so many key facts in the life of such a prominent public figure as Isabel de Villena. Enrique de Villena's paternity seems to be confirmed by heraldry and indirect family records, but who was her mother? Although this issue remains unresolved, we are none the less beginning to build on our knowledge of her life, thanks to scholars such as art historian Daniel Benito Goerlich, and palaeographers Josepa Cortés and Vicent Pons.[23]

The second line of inquiry is the study of Villena's work in its religious context, textual as well as visual. This line, begun by Albert Hauf, has contributed important information about Villena's indebtedness to devo-

---

[21] But note the anthologies Villena 1986, 1987, and 1995. There is a complete edition by Josep Alminana and Juan Costa (Villena 1992), but it is the work of amateurs with a secessionist agenda.

[22] I explored this theme in my doctoral thesis of 1987 (II, 353–61) and in my introduction to Villena 1987. Several scholars have since outlined their views: see Marçal 1990, Alemany 1993, Orts Molines 1993, Papa 1994b, and Piera 2003 and 2006.

[23] According to Benito Goerlich, Pons and Mari Luz Mandigorra are in the process of transcribing those parts of the *Llibre de títols* in the Trinity convent archive that cover Villena's era (1998: 67). Few scholars have gained admittance to this most inaccessible and accident-prone of archives, so we should not pin too much hope on their success. The whereabouts of what is left of the Holy Trinity documents outside the convent can be checked in Mateu y Llopis 1956.

tional texts by earlier and contemporary authors (see Hauf 1990 and 1998). Marinela García Sempere has also pursued this path fruitfully, identifying a *planctus Mariae* as a source for a passage in the *Vita Christi* (2000). Judith Berg's breakthrough iconographical study of 1979 was followed by Hauf 1999 on the religious application of *ut pictura poesis* in Villena's graphic descriptions.[24]

The third line of inquiry has to be the in-depth study of textual aspects of the *Vita Christi*: a narrower but more intensive kind of research. It cannot yet be concerned with interpretation, however. As a medieval writer Villena was raised in the tradition of deference to the authority of the classics and to literary precedent. We cannot embark on interpretations of her work until we understand how much of the *Vita Christi* is her own material, how much is the voluntary or involuntary reproduction of other, earlier, texts and opinions, and what criteria dictate her choice of quotations. Only then will we be able successfully to separate out her intentions and her originality from the complex web of intertextualities that informs every medieval work of learning. In this area, articles by Roxana Recio (1993) and David Barnett (2006) lead the way.[25]

The fourth line of inquiry needs to tackle Villena's handling of the social and cultural references of her age. Villena is an aristocratic writer, who depicts saintly characters conducting themselves as though in a royal court, as Fuster has observed (1968a:163–9). The abbess also reveals a detailed knowledge of aristocratic clothing and jewellery, which she applies symbolically in her representation of the Virgin Mary as a royal queen. As a member of the Franciscan Order, Villena is also an Immaculist: her belief in the dogma of the Immaculate Conception is firmly projected in *Vita Christi*. In this socio-cultural field of research, Lesley K. Twomey's work excels (see 2003a, 2003b, 2005, and 2007).[26]

The fifth line of inquiry involves the application of new technologies to Isabel de Villena's work. Rafael Alemany's research team has produced the most important results so far: complete concordances of the *Vita Christi*, and a digital version of the 1497 incunable (Alemany et al. 1996; Alemany

---

[24] See also Alejos Morán 1984. One of Benito Goerlich's suggestions for future research is Villena's probable influence on the Valencian painting of her day (1998: 76).

[25] Barnett compares the Visitation episode in Villena's *Vita Christi* with those of Eiximenis and Ludolph of Saxony, two of Villena's sources: neat, clear, and informative, it is a model of what can be achieved. A specialist in translation studies, Recio analyses the Latin interpolations in Chapters 117–22 and the particular way Villena translates them; she concludes that Villena's practice is indeed personal in the medieval context.

[26] These articles are due to appear in a collected volume entitled *The Fabric of Marian Devotion in Isabel de Villena's 'Vita Christi'* (Twomey, forthcoming).

1997). Having recently joined the team, I am currently compiling a complete bibliography of primary and secondary sources on Villena.[27]

Let us hope that in ten years' time much more will be known about Isabel de Villena, her life, and her work. Her memory deserves to be preserved, not only because she was a woman writing in a world of men, but also because of the high quality of her literary output. So, to conclude, one cannot but endorse Montserrat Piera's call for Villena's work to be included in the Spanish literary canon (2003: 117–18).

Further reading

Villena, Isabel de, 1916. *Llibre anomenat 'Vita Christi'*, ed. Ramon Miquel y Planas, 3 vols (Barcelona: Biblioteca Catalana)

Villena, Isabel de, 1995. *Vita Christi: selecció*, ed. Albert Hauf, Millors Obres de la Literatura Catalana, 115 (Barcelona: Edicions 62 / 'la Caixa')

Barnett, David, 2006. 'The Voice of the Virgin: Accessible Authority in the Visitation Episode of Isabel de Villena's *Vita Christi*', *La Corónica*, 35: 23–46

Cantavella, Rosanna, 2000. 'Isabel de Villena', in *Breve historia feminista de la literatura española (en lengua catalana, gallega y vasca)*, Zavala et al. 1993–2000: VI, 40–50

Recio, Roxana, 1993. 'Las interpolaciones latinas en la *Vita Christi* de sor Isabel de Villena:¿traducciones, glosas o amplificaciones?', *Anuario Medieval*, 5: 126–40

---

[27] The aim of the bilicame project is to prepare a complete bibliography of medieval Catalan authors (primary sources and critical literature), which will be made available on the web, completion date to be announced in the Biblioteca Virtual Joan Lluís Vives (www.lluisvives.com). The full text of the 1497 incunable of the *Vita Christi* can now be consulted in this virtual library. The University of Valencia has also digitized its copies of the 1513 and 1527 editions, which are freely consultable through its catalogue (http://trobes.uv.es).

7

Anatomies of a Saint: The Unstable Body of Teresa de Jesús

GEORGINA DOPICO-BLACK

Teresa reading Teresa

From as early as 1554, when Teresa de Jesús experienced her first raptures, both her body and her soul became the object of competing diagnoses that endeavored to determine whether her ecstasies were divine, demonic or, most egregious of all, human in origin. Not least among them were the diagnoses of the future saint herself whose *Vida* (*Life*) can be read as a response to growing suspicion throughout the sixteenth century of charismatic female spirituality and of mystical practices that sought unmediated communication with God. Ecstatic bodies, in particular those of mystic women, thought to be especially vulnerable to diabolic seductions, posed a vexing interpretive challenge: identical symptoms could have radically opposing etiologies, since God and the devil had access to the same alphabet of rapturous signs. How, then, to know with any degree of certainty that a rapture was a sign of sanctity and not grounds for exorcism?

For Teresa, symptomatized and pathologized by both Church and Inquisition as a potential heterodox, this process took on special urgency. In this essay, I explore Teresa's efforts to interpret the symptoms of her body and the movements of her soul and, specifically, the strategies she mobilized in order to claim diagnostic authority over the radically unstable text of her interior, substituting a demonic etiology with a divine one. I explore how Teresa reclaims experience – *espiriencia* – as that which allows her to distinguish the provenance of her charismatic symptoms, providing a cogent rebuttal to those who would accuse her of heresy or fraud and, moreover, an experienced-based *corpus* of theological knowledge, founded, like the new sciences, on first-hand observation of interior secrets.

One might argue that there is nothing remarkable in Teresa's turn to experience as a means to authorize her discourse. Indeed, the Thomistic premise of *cognitio dei experimentalis* had been used by Gerson, Bonaventure, and

Bernard of Clairvaux to define mysticism. Francisco de Osuna, quite likely Teresa's principal source on affective spirituality, had affirmed the importance of experience (and of experienced guides) on the path to direct knowledge of God. But there are two important distinctions to be drawn. First, in the Spain of the mid sixteenth century, any claim of an immediate (that is, unmediated) knowledge of God through experience was deemed dangerously close to Lutheran heresy or demonic possession, particularly if such claims were put forth by a woman.[1] The challenge for Teresa, then, was to legitimize her right to mystic experiences without overtly challenging the hierarchical structure that would be judging her. Several critics have done remarkable work in this direction. Alison Weber has argued that the requirement to justify her spiritual favors while demonstrating obedience puts Teresa in a 'double bind'; she suggests that the rhetoric of humility which pervades the *Vida* provides a way out of the double bind, by inscribing inferiority in order to then wield it as an arm of resistance (1996: 45–8). James Fernández offers a different but equally suggestive reading; he argues that autobiographical discourse – especially Teresa's – is structured on a back-and-forth movement between two forms of address: apostrophe (the invocation of a higher authority – God, in Teresa's case) and apology (submission to a concrete human authority – for Teresa, her *letrado* or learned confessors) (1992: 29). Drawing on Weber's and Fernández's insights, we might say that Teresa relies on experience in order to negotiate a position of knowledge that is precariously balanced between subjectivity and subjection.[2]

The second distinction between Teresa's use of experience and that found in earlier mystic treatises such as Osuna's has to do with what was most crucially at stake for Teresa: it was not only knowledge about God through experience, but also a second-order knowledge *about* that knowledge and more specifically, about its provenance. Experience can be said to work on at least two levels in Teresa's discourse: it legitimates her access to the supernatural, and also guarantees the accuracy of her interpretation, underwriting a theory as well as a praxis of *discretio spiritum*. In both cases truth is the central concern. In the first instance, experience is the very union with God that provides access to a transcendent Truth; Teresa's challenge is to defend her claims to that Truth against those who either lack experience or who allege she has no right to it. In the second case, experience serves to elucidate the truth status *of* the revealed truth by discerning its origin as demonic

---

[1] On the ways in which experience operated within both Reformation and Counter Reformation theology, see Jay 2006. On the concept and history of *cognitio dei experimentalis,* see also Geybels 2008.

[2] Other recent studies of the *Vida* include Hollis 1990, Slade 1995, Ahlgren 1996: 67–84, Pérez-Romero 1996, and Carrera 2005.

or divine. Teresa relies on experience as a means of producing hermeneutic certainty, gaining diagnostic authority over her own symptoms.

*Espiriencia, mujercillas, mística teología**

The first nine-and-a-half chapters of Teresa's *Vida* mostly follow the conventions of nuns' autobiographies: they are a confession of her past life (beginning with a spiritual calling in childhood, heeded, then postponed, then taken up again), and an account of her fledgling efforts at interior prayer.[3] It is in Chapter X that the *Vida* takes a decidedly different turn. From that point forward, she narrates the account of what happens to her in ecstasy and, beginning in Chapter XI, daringly offers an excursus on mystical theology which, she claims, is based not on book learning, but fully grounded in experience. Teresa does not ignore her transgressiveness; in the penultimate paragraph of the *Vida* she will confess that she has been very bold in writing about 'cosas tan subidas' (1990: 481) ('these sublime subjects', 1957: 314).[4] It is precisely in the passage from Chapter X to Chapter XI, as Teresa is about to begin recounting and interpreting the spiritual gifts that have given rise to so much apprehension, that she requests that García de Toledo, intended reader of this particular version, either tear up or burn her manuscript if it does not conform to the truths of the Holy Catholic Faith (1990: 189), corroborating the extent to which such conformity weighed on her. She also makes a plea for anonymity, claiming that no good will come of the circulation of her name. It is one of several moments in the *Vida* that splits the text in pieces, creating an almost Augustinian before and after that will be repeated, not coincidentally, in the chapter that closes the theological excursus:

> Yo digo lo que ha pasado por mí como me lo mandan; y si no fuere bien, romperálo a quién lo envío, que sabrá mijor entender lo que va mal que yo, a quien suplico por amor del Señor, lo que he dicho hasta aquí de mi ruin vida y pecados, lo publiquen (desde ahora doy licencia, y a todos mis confesores que ansí lo es a quien esto va) y, si quisieren, luego en mi vida; porque no engañe más al mundo que piensen hay en mí algún bien y cierto, cierto, con verdad digo, a lo que ahora entiendo de mí, que me dará gran consuelo. Para lo que de aquí adelante dijere, no se la doy

---

* Experience, poor little women, mystical theology

[3] For background on early modern hispanic nuns as autobiographers, see Arenal and Schlau 1989a, Donahue 1989, and Surtz 1995.

[4] All citations of the *Vida* refer to Dámaso Chicharro's edition (Teresa de Jesús 1990); English versions are taken from J. M. Cohen's translation (Teresa de Jesús 1957).

[licencia para publicar]; ni quiero, si a alguien lo mostraren, digan quién es por quien pasó, ni quién lo escribió, que por esto no me nombro, ni a nadie, sino escribirlo he todo lo mejor que pueda por no ser conocida, y ansí lo pido por amor de Dios. (Teresa 1990: 188)

(I merely relate what happened to me, as I have been commanded. If the recipient of this does not approve of it, he will tear it up, and he will know better than I what is wrong with it. But I implore him, for the Lord's sake, to let what I have so far said about my wretched life and my sins be published. I give permission for this, here and now, to him and to all my confessors, of whom he is one. They may publish this now in my lifetime, if they like, so that I may no longer deceive the world, which thinks there is some good in me. I am speaking in all sincerity when I say that, in so far as I understand myself at present, this will give me great comfort. This permission does not apply to what I am going to say from now on. If the rest is shown to anyone I do not wish him to be told whose experience it describes, or who wrote it. That is why I mention neither myself nor anyone else by name and have done my best to write in such a way as not to be recognized. I beg your Reverence, for the love of God, to preserve my secrecy.) (Teresa 1957: 74)

Teresa's rending of the text in two might be seen as a pre-emptive move to ward off the threat of violence over the body of her manuscript that her confessors hold. That she herself deposits that power in their hands (by insisting they destroy it if it is non-conforming) is a red herring; they in fact have had the power all along. But what is extraordinary is the way Teresa's invitation to her confessors to destroy the secret text if it is unorthodox covertly transfers that culpable non-conformity from her person on to her text. In fact, Teresa creates two texts from one: the first, a public autobiographical confession that by outing her as a sinner will bring her consolation; the second (contained within the first, another secret interior), a clandestine text that recounts and interprets her mystic experiences. She tellingly frames this secret text in a double passivity: a grammatical one that uses the passive voice to displace agency ('what happened to me') and a rhetorical one that reinscribes her obedience ('as I have been commanded') as she enters shaky ground.

It is no coincidence that at this juncture, as Teresa is erasing herself from her own story, she should reaffirm the extent to which the account that follows cannot exist without her. Three times in the chapter's final paragraph she makes reference to experience, framing it as the *sine qua non* that, more than simply supplementing book learning, seems at times to supplant it:

Por claro que yo quiera decir estas cosas de oración, será bien escuro para quien no tuviere espiriencia. Algunos impedimentos diré, que a mi entender lo son para ir adelante en este camino, y otras cosas en que hay peligro, de lo que el Señor me ha enseñado por esperiencia, y después tratádolo yo con grandes letrados y personas espirituales de muchos años, y ven que en solos veinte y siete años que tengo oración, me ha dado Su Majestad la espiriencia, con andar en tantos tropiezos y tan mal este camino, que a otros en cuarenta y siente y en treinta y siete que con penitencia y siempre virtud han caminado por él. (1990: 189)

(However clearly I may wish to explain this matter of prayer, it will be very obscure to anyone who has not the experience. I shall describe certain impediments, which I believe prevent men from advancing on this path, also certain other sources of danger about which the Lord has taught me by experience. More recently, I have also discussed the subject with men of great learning and persons who have led spiritual lives for many years; and they have seen that in the twenty-seven years during which I have practised prayer, ill though I have trodden the road and often though I have stumbled, His Majesty has granted me experiences for which others need thirty-seven, or even forty-seven, although they may have progressed in penitence and constant virtue.) (1957: 75)

Teresa makes clear that no matter how eloquently she recounts this matter of prayer, her meaning will remain elusive to those who lack the experience that at once forces and authorizes her to speak. It is one of many instances throughout the *Vida* in which Teresa draws a distinction between the initiated and uninitiated in affective spiritual practices; this distinction will find an echo in her categorization of confessors as *espirituales* (spiritual) and *letrados* (educated) (among these she will draw a further distinction between fully fledged *letrados* and *medios letrados* (half-educated) confessors). In suggesting that the uninitiated – those who lack first-hand experience of the rapture she describes – will be unable to understand her, she subtly wrests from them the authority to judge her.

What comes next seems, at first blush, to respond to an apostolic or pedagogic impulse; Teresa offers to map the pitfalls on the path of interior prayer for the benefit of those who wish to advance on the path. But that impulse, which is potentially dangerous for a woman in her circumstance, is doubly (if only implicitly) sanctioned: first, by the assertion that it is God who has taught her, and secondly, by the vetting of the 'grandes letrados y personas espirituales' (men of great learning and persons who have led spiritual lives) with whom she has consulted. Teresa achieves a delicate balance here, moving between a dyadic and a triangular geometry. This is a recurrent movement in the *Vida*. On one hand, she affirms the intimacy of her one-on-one relation with God, who imparts His teachings to her without the need of a mediator, by experience, and, on the other, she wards off potential criticism by submitting those teachings to third-party adjudicators whose complicity she actively seeks. Rather than relinquishing authority in the hands of those mediators, however, Teresa enlists them as witnesses in her defense who *see* that her experience is God-given. It is important to note that Teresa does not try to gloss over the disparity they also see (her receiving divine gifts despite being unworthy), but incorporates the fullness of their gaze into her narrative, thereby increasing its truth value. What immediately follows is the turn to God that so often resolves *aporias* in Teresa's discourse: 'Blessed be He for all things, and may He, for His name's sake, make use of me. My Lord knows that all I desire is that He may be praised and magnified' (1957: 75). Here that turn works to dispel doubts about the paradox she has just raised and which informed the murmurings of those who argued that she was either a demoniac or a fake: why God would have chosen Teresa's body, 'un muladar tan sucio y de mal olor' ('a foul and stinking dunghill'), as the site on which to plant his spiritual gifts, 'huerto de tan suaves flores' (1990: 189) ('a garden of such sweet flowers', 1957: 75). Far from ignoring or writing off the contradiction, Teresa takes full ownership of it, emptying it of any suspect content: the paradox itself becomes proof of divinity, the stuff of miracles.

It is a paradox Teresa returns to time and again throughout the *Vida*; this is not surprising, since it was at the heart of the argument of those who claimed she was either possessed or a charlatan. At times she humbly confesses her insufficiency before God, at other times she lays claims on that insufficiency as a means to neutralize its charge. One of the most dramatic instances of this occurs in a passage that Weber has insightfully read in the context of the changing tides of the word *mujercilla* (poor little woman) in the wake of the trials of the *alumbrados* (Illuminists), and as a defense veiled as a concession (1996: 31–7).[5] Admonishing those who question the provenance of her raptures (skeptical that God would confer divine favors on Teresa in a mere matter of days, and yet withhold them from men who have worked long years to obtain them), she writes:

> Para mujercitas como yo, flacas y con poca fortaleza, me parece a mí conviene (como ahora lo hace Dios) llevarme con regalos, porque pueda sufrir algunos trabajos que ha querido Su Majestad tenga. Mas para siervos de Dios, hombres de tomo, de letras y entendimiento, que veo hacer caso de que Dios no los da devoción, que me hace disgusto oírlo, no digo yo que no la tomen, si Dios la da [...] mas que cuando no la tuvieren, que no

---

[5] The *alumbrados* or Illuminists were groups of men and women, both lay and religious, many from *converso* families, who met in private homes, outside of the Church hierarchy, in order to discuss and interpret the Scriptures. Weber writes: 'Although the groups did not share a unified doctrine, they held the common belief that the individual was capable of understanding the Scripture when inspired or "illumined" by the Holy Spirit' (1996: 22). Many of these groups, who believed salvation came by grace alone, were led by women.

se fatiguen; y que entiendan que no es menester, pues Su Majestad no la da, y anden señores de sí mesmos. (1990: 197–8)

(As for a poor woman like myself, a weak and irresolute creature, it seems right that the Lord should lead me on with favours, as He now does, in order that I may bear certain afflictions with which He has been pleased to burden me. But when I hear servants of God, men of weight, learning, and understanding, worrying so much because He is not giving them devotion, it makes me sick to listen to them. I do not say that they should not accept it if God grants it to them [...] but they should not be distressed when they do not receive it. They should realize that since the Lord does not give it to them they do not need it. They should exercise control over themselves and go right ahead.) (1957: 81)

The question of mystical experience here becomes gendered: it is not that Teresa receives spiritual gifts *in spite of* being a woman but rather *because* she is a woman. The incongruity inherent in her receiving favors provides the best proof of their orthodoxy. It is a brilliant strategy that patronizes her accusers, who are advised to exercise control over themselves, and categorically disarms them, turning the tables on their skepticism through a process analogous to what Josefina Ludmer has defined as 'tricks of the weak' (1984: 53).[6] Paraphrasing Ludmer, we might say that from her assigned place of *mujercita flaca* (a weak little woman) Teresa changes the meaning both of that place (a foul dunghill) and of what is (or can be) installed there (a garden of such sweet flowers). One might be tempted to see Teresa's move here within a longer tradition that associates affective female spirituality with experience, but leaves theological exegesis to men of letters and understanding (see Perry 1990: 91–2). There is no question that Teresa writes, wittingly or not, in the protective shade of charismatic foremothers – as well as in the ominous shadow of the *alumbradas* (Illuminists) – who similarly accessed the transcendent through experience. But if this would seem to inscribe Teresa's use of experience on one side of a set of seemingly intractable alignments (man/woman, mind/body, rational/affective, theoretical/experiential), it is worth remembering that this passage occurs in the midst of a chapter on *mística teología* (to use Teresa's words) that is authored by a woman and in which the experiential *determines* the theoretical. Despite the qualifier that she may have read or heard it somewhere (1990: 193), the fourfold metaphor of the waters that begins in Chapter XI is an attempt to transform the experience of interior prayer into the discourse of a mystic science. Far from reinscribing the rift between mystic experience and mystic theology along gendered lines, Teresa dissolves it.

---

[6] See also James Fernández's remarks on the applicability of Ludmer's term to Teresa's practice (1990).

Discretio spiritum

I turn now to the second level at which experience operates in the *Vida*. If the first level of experience is based on a direct and unmediated knowledge of the transcendent that authorizes Teresa to speak among *letrados*, the second level is explicitly associated with the theological science (or grace) of discernment and with a kind of knowledge *about* knowledge that legitimates Teresa's ability to interpret her raptures and confirm their divine provenance, thus guaranteeing their truth. At the heart of both the principle and practice of discernment is a confrontation between doubt and certainty.[7] As Michel Foucault writes: 'For Christians, the possibility that Satan can get inside your soul and give you thoughts you cannot recognize as Satanic but that you might interpret as coming from God leads to an uncertainty about what is going on inside your soul. You are unable to know what the real root of your desire is, at least without hermeneutic work' (2003: 203).

The hermeneutic work of discernment – understood by the Church as the product of both a God-given grace and a learned method – stages the encounter between faith and science, heavily mediated by doubt: it provides a way to know, a system for moving from interpretive instability to interpretive stability. Moshé Sluhovsky writes, 'Theologically, discernment of spirits (*discretio spiritum*) is a divine grace (*gratia gratis data*); philosophically, it is an interpretive challenge'(2007: 170). For Teresa, the way to confront that challenge, the movement from hermeneutic instability to stability, customarily takes one of three forms (although I discuss these separately, they often overlap): *a posteriori* external confirmation (objectivity), isolation of doubt –and of those who would doubt her– as demonic (the devil's due), and a turn to the effect as the legible, perceptual trace of invisible or indeterminable phenomena (traces).

Objectivity

The first of Teresa's strategies for dispelling doubts about the orthodoxy of her mystic raptures is, in many ways, the most straightforward. It consists of a second experience of God that confirms (or, on occasion, strategically denies) divine authorship of a first experience. In the *Cuentas de conciencia* (Examinations of Conscience) as in the *Vida*, God often reappears to dispel Teresa's doubts concerning the provenance of a rapture or, as frequently, of a message she has received during rapture. Although this strategy is efficient in foreclosing the possibility of misdiagnosis (that is, of misconstruing the

---

[7] The history of discernment within the Catholic Church finds its roots in 1 John 4.1: 'Believe not every spirit, but try the spirit if they be of God'. Sluhovsky 2007 traces the history of this elaborate system from the time of John to the sixteenth century.

demonic as divine or the divine as demonic), insofar as God Himself returns to set the record straight, it could be said to create an infinite hermeneutic circle: how can Teresa know, after all, that the second vision or mystic experience is not itself a demonic illusion that falsely confirms untruth as truth?

Part of the answer to this question can be found in the continuous nature of Teresa's exchanges with God, who returns, time and again, to offer a second (or third or fourth) opinion when the first opinion (typically offered by a *letrado* or *medio letrado* who lacks mystical experience and prompts Teresa's self-doubt) is erroneous. James Fernández has noted that this constant communication with God is one of Teresa's most frequent and astute tactics, whereby she ends up skirting the question of her orthodoxy or heterodoxy, burying it in the text itself (1990: 299). Along these lines, we might see these *a posteriori* confirmations by God in relation to the tenuous balance the text negotiates between a specular geometry (based on an unmediated relation with God) and a triangular one (in which the confessor occupies the third position). Here, God occupies not only the second position, the *Tú* (Thou) that grounds the *Vida* (and dissolves with the writing *yo* in mystic union), but also a fourth position that displaces the third (making the confessor's skepticism all but irrelevant) and gives Him – and Teresa through Him – the last word, dispelling any doubt about her orthodoxy.

Another part of the answer has to do with the way in which this second level of experience (the belated confirmation) is granted a different epistemic status in the text from the initial affective experience it guarantees. Although both are sited in the identical interior space (Teresa's soul), the second experience rarely consists of an ecstatic dissolution with the divine; rather, it most often takes the form of a message that is almost prosaic in nature and that is externalized through the medium of voice. If rapturous union is radically subjective, at once interpellating and annihilating the subject, the voice of God that confirms rapture is presented as entirely objective, almost as an eyewitness testimony. The interpretation the voice offers can go either way, at times confirming a divine etiology, at times warning of the opposite. But the provenance of the voice itself and the certainty it provides are never in question.

> Cuando es demonio, no sólo no deja buenos efectos, más déjalos malos. Esto me ha acaecido no más de dos o tres veces, y he sido luego avisada del Señor cómo era demonio. [...] El gusto y deleite que él da, a mi parecer, es diferente en gran manera. Podría él engañar a quien no hubiere tenido otros de Dios. (1990: 313)
>
> (Locutions that come from the devil not only lead to no good, but leave bad effects behind them. These I have experienced, though only on two or three occasions, and each time I have had an immediate warning from the Lord that they came from the devil [...] The pleasures and joys which the

devil bestows are, I believe, more various; and with his pleasures he might well deceive anyone who has not experienced, or is not experiencing, pleasures from God.) (1957: 177–8)

If God here informs Teresa that an earlier experience was demonically authored, it is worth noting that He is not telling her something she did not already know. The passage points to the multilayered nature of Teresa's diagnostic method, which generally makes use of more than one criterion to reach interpretive certainty. Here, for example, Teresa relies on a difference in the quality of pleasures – and on the effects those pleasures produce – in order to render a diagnosis which is later substantiated by God. The status of certainty that the text bestows on God's voice copiously overflows on to Teresa's act of discernment, reinforcing its affiliation with truth. But that certainty was in a sense already predetermined by experience, which makes her immune to the devil's capacity to deceive the inexperienced. If the devil can possess Teresa, he cannot, however, fool her into thinking he is God.

The devil's due: Teresa's dance with doubt

Given the suspicion of demonic intervention that Teresa's visions and ecstasies aroused, the overwhelming presence of the devil in her autobiography seems almost scandalous. Far from banishing him from her text in an effort to keep suspicions at bay, Teresa gives him pride of place in the *Vida*; according to Weber, he is named more than 200 times throughout her works (1992: 171). As we have just seen, Teresa even confesses to having been rapturously possessed by the devil, albeit only on two or three occasions and never confusing his ephemeral pleasures with God's lasting ones. The inclusion of the diabolical is entirely logical. The devil occupied an important position in the spiritual landscape of early modern Europe, which was populated by creatures both demonic and divine (see Dulumeau 1978 and Camporesi 1991). A text that purports to be a confession of ecstatic spiritual experiences would have been suspiciously lopsided without him. Nevertheless, Teresa pulls off a brilliant slippage in her text between the devil and doubt; she aligns those who question the divine provenance of her raptures with the devil himself, making doubt, not seduction, the devil's finest tool. This slippage, that isolates doubt and reduces it to a known quantity, constitutes a second strategy for dispelling uncertainty, both about the sources of her ecstasies and about her ability to properly identify and name them. Teresa turns the tables on those who seek the devil in her raptures, boldly suggesting that the devil is to be found not in the object of their scrutiny, but in the gaze that looks for him.

Teresa's tactic is a daring one, but it is not entirely original. Osuna had laid the groundwork for it in his *Tercer abecedario espiritual* (1527) (Third Spiritual Alphabet), where he responds to those who denounce quietist practices on the grounds that its followers love God not for Himself, but for the sensual pleasure He provides (1972: 212). In a move Teresa will emulate, Osuna transforms the accusations of his critics into the devil's work. Throughout the *Tercer abecedario,* the devil operates much as he will in the *Vida*, as a counterfeiter who falsifies and devalues good intentions. But where Teresa will go farther than Osuna, and take greater risks, is in conflating doubt itself (both the doubts of her detractors – those who harbor suspicions about the divine etiology of her ecstasies – and the self-doubts they arouse in her) with the devil.[8]

As a rhetorical strategy, it is nothing short of brilliant. Doubt, not rapture, is revealed as the symptom whose etiology is demonic. Any reading (not excepting her own) that misrecognizes the divine, construing it as diabolical, is reduced to a mere deceit of the devil. Confessors who suspect she is merely possessed are thus aligned with the demonic: the devil is duping them, not her. This is not to say that Teresa denies that the devil operates directly upon her; on the contrary, at different moments throughout the *Vida*, and notably in Chapters XXX–XXXII, she describes the battles and temptations she endures at the devil's hands. But even outright temptations by the devil are very often reduced to a question of doubt. Referring to the disobedience to her superiors that her founding in secret represents, Teresa writes:

> Acabado todo, sería como desde a tres u cuatro horas, me revolvió el demonio una batalla espiritual como ahora diré. Púsome delante si había sido mal hecho lo que había hecho, si iba contra obediencia en haberlo procurado sin que me lo mandase el provincial. (1990: 424)

> (When it was all finished – it must have been some three or four hours later – the devil plunged me into a spiritual battle once more, as I shall now relate. He suggested to me that what I had done might have been wrong and that I might have been violating my obedience by bringing it all about without a mandate from the Provincial.) (1957: 267)

The expected resolution doesn't come until several paragraphs later, when God provides 'a ray of light which showed me that this was the devil's work. Then I recognized the truth and knew that it was all an attempt to scare me with lies' (1957: 268). What God grants Teresa here is nothing other than the grace of discernment, allowing her to see her doubt for what it was: a demonic snare intended to keep her from doing God's work of reform. The temptation and its disclosure (that exposes doubt as demonic) authorize her disobedience. God Himself quiets her uncertainty.

One of the places where the conflation of devil and doubt appears most clearly in the *Vida* is in its treatment of humility. Weber has written exten-

---

[8] On Teresa and doubt, see Subirats 1983, Fernández 1990, and Van Ginhoven 2010.

sively on how a rhetoric of humility structures Teresa's spiritual autobiography, noting a split of humility into 'a true and a counterfeit virtue' (1996: 74). We might find in Teresa's conceptions of true and false humility responses to the two principal charges leveled against her: that she was a fake, authoring her own raptures, or that her raptures were demonic in origin. True humility consists of simply accepting God's favors without questioning His reasons for making her their object, or presuming she has done anything to deserve them:

> Y como este edificio todo va fundado en humildad, mientras más llegados a Dios, más adelante ha de ir esta virtud, y si no, va todo perdido. Y parece algún género de sobervia querer nosotros subir a más, pues Dios hace demasiado, sigún somos, en allegarnos cerca de sí. (1990: 202)

> (Moreover as the whole edifice is founded on humility, the nearer we draw to God the more this virtue must be developed, and if it is not, all is lost. It seems a sort of pride in us too that makes us wish to rise higher when God is already doing more for us than we deserve by drawing us, in our condition, nearer to him.) (1957: 85)

> Aquí es muy mayor la humildad y más profunda, que al alma queda, que en lo pasado; porque ve más claro que poco ni mucho hizo, sino consentir que la hiciese el Señor mercedes y abrazarlas la voluntad. (1990: 241–2)

> (The soul's humility is now greater and more profound than it was before. It clearly sees that it has done absolutely nothing except consent to the Lord's granting it graces, and embraces them with its will.) (1957: 118)

Musings on true humility almost invariably lead to the same point: how little Teresa has to do with the favors she receives: 'no havía fuerzas en mi alma para salvarse, si Su Majestad con tantas mercedes no se las pusiere' (1990: 249) ('my soul would have no power to achieve salvation if His Majesty did not bestow it on me with His great mercies', 1957: 124). In distancing Teresa from any culpable agency in producing or controlling her ecstatic experiences, this positively-charged humility goes a long way towards responding to what was perhaps the most dangerous of the diagnoses her symptomatic body and soul elicited: that her raptures were neither divinely nor diabolically authored, but products of her own hand.

Counterfeit humility, in contrast, is that which leads Teresa to abandon God's path, not thinking herself worthy of His favors. There is example after example in the *Vida* of the dangers of false humility, which is repeatedly exposed as an invention of the devil (1990: 168):

> Éste fue el más terrible engaño que el demonio me podía hacer debajo de parecer humildad, que comencé a temer de tener oración. (1990: 157)

(Now the devil began to practise a most terrible deception on me, under the guise of humility. Seeing myself to be so utterly lost, I began to be afraid to pray.) (1957: 50)

Y no le tiente el demonio [al que tiene oración mental] por la manera que a mí a dejarla por humildad. (1990: 171)

(Let him [who has begun mental prayer] not be persuaded by the devil, as I was, to give it up out of humility.) (1957: 62)

no cure de unas humildades que hay [...] que les parece humildad no entender que el Señor les va dando dones [...] Creamos que quien nos da los bienes, nos dará gracia par que, en comenzando el demonio a tentarle en este caso, lo entienda, y fortaleza para resistirle. (1990: 185–6)

(Let him take no notice of certain kinds of humility [...] Some think it humble not to recognize that the Lord is bestowing gifts on them [...] Let us believe that He who gives us the blessings will also give us grace to detect the devil when he begins to tempt us in this way, and makes us strong enough to resist him.) (1957: 72)

In each case, false humility is associated with demonically inspired doubt. This can manifest itself as either the doubt imposed externally by examiners who accuse her of vainglory, or its internalization as self-doubt. In exposing these accusations (and the 'humility' they prescribe) as the devil's ruses, Teresa disarms those critics who question her claims of divine rapture by suggesting she has been seduced by the devil but is too vain to realize that God would not bother with her. She will go so far as to say that she fears those who see the devil everywhere (especially the confessors who counsel 'humility') more than she fears the devil himself (1990: 319). The devil, while ultimately rendered powerless, cannot be dispensed with. Doubt needs a place at the table; truth cannot be produced in its absence. Indeed, doubt must be conjured in order to be defeated. In the *Vida*, the devil fulfills this function. Through him doubt is localized and disciplined: 'una higa para todos los demonios, que ellos me temerán a mí' (1990: 319) ('I snap my fingers at all the devils; they shall be afraid of me', 1957: 183).

Traces
More than the other two, the third strategy for discerning spirits and dispelling doubts is a science of reading traces. It seeks to translate supernatural phenomena that are most often externally imperceptible and of indeterminate provenance into visible, or tactile, or otherwise perceptual proof, to make evidence out of things unseen. It is, moreover, the method Teresa recurs to most frequently throughout the *Vida* and the one she recommends *as* a method: the experienced soul, she suggests, will be able to correctly

judge the source of a rapture based upon careful examination of the effects it produces, of the traces it leaves behind. A number of chapters of the autobiography, and the later *Camino de Perfección* (*The Way of Perfection*), can be read both as a theory of discernment that takes up weighty theological questions and as a manual on discernment that provides a virtual how-to for interpreting ecstatic effects. The symptoms of demonic and divine rapture may be identical to the untrained eye or inexperienced soul, but what remains, the traces each one leaves, are not.

> Si es del demonio, alma ejercitada paréceme lo entenderá; porque deja inquietud y poca humildad y poco aparejo para los efectos que hace el de Dios. No deja luz en el entendimiento ni firmeza en la verdad. (1990: 229)
>
> (If it comes from the devil, I think an experienced soul will realize it. For it leaves disquiet behind it, and very little humility, and does not do much to prepare the soul for the effects which are produced when it comes from God. It brings neither light to the understanding nor strength to the will.) (1957: 108)

Even if the rapture *is* demonic in origin, something that can be easily ascertained by the experienced soul based on the markedly different after-effects of one and the other, the malady matters less than the diagnosis: possession by the devil is reduced to a manageable threat if he is correctly identified as such.

The importance that experience acquires in this third method gives rise to a significant tension in the *Vida*. The subjective agency that Teresa had so urgently denied in relation to rapture (as it could be taken as proof of either demonic vainglory or forgery) surreptitiously resurfaces here. If the first kind of discernment relies on apprehending (grasping the meaning of) God, who reappears to objectively confirm that a vision or rapture was divine, and if the second relies on apprehending (capturing by exposing) the devil, who provokes the doubts that define rapture as demonic, this third class of discernment relies primarily on the experienced, discerning human subject, Teresa herself, who is best armed to determine the truth about her own raptures, based on the effects they leave.

The problem was already implicit in Osuna's *Tercer abecedario* particularly those passages that recognize the degree to which the subject participates in discerning the movements of his or her own soul (and Osuna believed women to be fully capable of discerning, under the guidance of an experienced confessor) (1972: 118). But the landscape had changed considerably in the almost three decades separating the 1527 publication of the first volume of the *Abecedario* and Teresa's first drafts of her spiritual autobiography in the mid 1550s. The challenge for Teresa, once again, was to find a middle ground that allowed her to lay claim to interpretive authority over her own body and soul, and at the same time to distance herself from the appearance of excessive agency; in other words, to walk the fine line between subjectivity and subjection. One way out of the dilemma is to emphasize the sense of absolute certainty that accompanies divine rapture and makes examination of the sort advocated by Osuna almost gratuitous: 'When God's spirit is at work there is no need to cast around for ways of inducing humility and shame' (1957: 110). If God is the author of the ecstatic experience, the effects of true humility and almost overwhelming shame are so clear that there is no need for any kind of research, or *a posteriori* hermeneutic work.

But Teresa's more customary approach is to turn to God in the face of a potential impasse. In the following passage, she does just that, elegantly negotiating a compromise:

> Bien creo no estará en este engaño quien tuviere talento de conocer espíritus y le hubiere el Señor dado humildad verdadera; que éste juzga por los efectos y determinaciones y amor, y dale el Señor luz para que lo conozca. Y en esto mira el adelantamiento y aprovechamiento de las almas, que no en los años; que en medio puede uno haber alcanzado más que otro en veinte. Porque, como digo, dalo el Señor a quien quiere y aun a quien mejor se dispone. (1990: 462–3)

> (I am quite sure that no one who has a gift for spiritual discernment, and to whom the Lord has given true humility, will remain under this delusion for long. He will judge things by their fruits, and by the good resolutions and love to which they give rise; and the Lord will give him the light by which to recognize these. God considers a soul's advancement and progress, but takes no account of time. One soul may have achieved more in six months than another in twenty years, since, as I have said, the Lord gives at His own pleasure, and to him who is readiest to receive.) (1957: 298)

Sluhovsky reads this passage as affirming a kind of equal opportunity principle. 'Teresa's definition of the successful discerning personality,' he writes, 'is not bound by gender, position in the church or degree of learning' (2007: 214). This democracy – or better, meritocracy – of discernment is an important part of the self-defense Teresa articulates in these lines, but it is not the whole story. In fact, that defense is considerably more complex than it appears. Discernment in this formulation depends on both human and divine agency: the hermeneutic activity whereby the mystic subject distinguishes demonic from divine ecstasies according to the effect each leaves (a talent that Teresa directly links to experience at numerous times throughout the *Vida*) and the God-given humility and light that confirm the judgment. In one respect, this is nothing but a re-elaboration of discernment as both a science and a grace. But even the language of 'God-given' Teresa invokes does not so much elide as camouflage the subject's agency. God bestows his divine gifts (including that of discernment) according to His own desire and, what is more, according to how well the subject has prepared herself to receive it.

We might see in Teresa's compromise between talent and light something resembling Cisneros's marriage of acquired and infused knowledge, *scientia experimentalis* and *sacra doctrina*.[9] But this is doubly problematic for Teresa. As a woman, she cannot claim to possess acquired knowledge, book-learning, as the basis for discernment. However, if she relies solely on infused knowledge to determine the provenance of spirits, she runs the risk of re-entering the hermeneutic circle described above. If what is at stake is precisely the divine nature of her visions and experiences, how can one of those selfsame visions provide the needed proof of its orthodoxy? As a kind of materialization of immaterial phenomena, and as the memory of that materialization, effects and experience furnish Teresa with a subtle way out of the predicament. To begin with, the experience of past raptures – the Rosetta Stone by which effects can be deciphered – provides the means through which infused learning takes on the status of (and arguably supplants) acquired learning. This type of substitution takes place throughout the *Vida*, both in dramatic climaxes, as when Teresa's confessors take away her books and God announces that He will be her new book, but also, more prosaically, through the operations whereby experience – even (especially) experience that cannot be adequately articulated by the intellect or translated into language – is somehow fixed in memory. Secondly, as the perceptible traces of ineffable experiences, effects quite literally substantiate, give substance to, an invisible presence, whether divine or demonic. Like the voice of God who confirms a prior rapture, effects confer the luster of objectivity on acts of interpretation. In so doing, they provide a way out of the hermeneutic circle and affirm Teresa's right to self-diagnose her ecstatic symptoms.

Contingency and certainty

Throughout the *Vida,* effects serve as a means to reach interpretive certainty, to prove either the divine nature of Teresa's ecstasies or her immunity to demonic deceit. But there is an instance that seems to put everything into question, raising the possibility that diagnosis can be erroneous, that effects can be misconstrued. After declaring that an experienced soul will immediately recognize demonic seduction based on the effects it leaves, Teresa writes:

[9] See Howe 2002: 289. On Cisneros, see also Gómez de Castro 1984 and Rummel 1999.

Puede hacer aquí poco daño o ninguno [el demonio], si el alma endereza su deleite y suavidad, que allí siente, a Dios, y poner en Él sus pensamientos y deseos, como queda avisado. No puede ganar nada el demonio, antes permitirá Dios que con el mismo deleite que causa en el alma, pierda mucho; porque éste ayudará a que el alma, como piensa que es Dios, venga muchas veces a la oración con codicia de él. (1990: 229–30)

(Here the devil can do little or no harm, if the soul directs to God the delight and calm that it then feels, and fixes its thoughts and desires on Him, as it has already been advised to. Indeed, the devil can gain nothing. On the contrary, by God's grace, the joy that he arouses in the soul will cost him dear. For this joy will help the soul, who will think it to be of God, and so will often come to its prayer with a desire for Him.)
(1957: 108)

The shift from the idea that the experienced soul will be able to recognize the etiology of its own ecstatic movements to the possibility that it can be mistaken is not insignificant. It may be that Teresa is simply keeping with accepted early modern theological wisdom, which accords God greater power than the devil; in the end God wins, as the soul is drawn to prayer. But in suggesting that it is the pleasures the devil affords the body and soul of the possessed that end up doing God's work, Teresa seems to diverge radically from accepted dogma. It is a rare moment in the *Vida* when the misdiagnosis of spirits is presented as possible, as well as quite beside the point. Ultimately, the subject can redirect if not the causality then at least the net effect of demonic possession, emptying it of its fatal, heterodox charge. If the soul turns the fullness of the ecstatic experience – pleasure and tenderness, thoughts and desires – towards God, neither the provenance of the symptoms nor their misrecognition will matter. It seems a risky position for Teresa to advance, despite the final outcome of divine victory: 'no tornará muchas veces el demonio, viendo su pérdida' (1990: 229) ('he will realize that he has lost the game and very often will not try again', 1957: 109). In a text that is trying to rule out the possibility of mistaking the devil for God, why raise it?

One answer might be that the self-defense Teresa's *Vida* provides is successful precisely because it accounts for all possible contingencies. Both etiologies prove her innocence in the end, and, what is more extraordinary, all interpretive eventualities are considered, from the most orthodox to the most heterodox:

- If it is God who authors Teresa's ecstasies, there is no room for doubt: 'de ninguna manera podía dudar que estaba [Dios] dentro de mí u yo toda engolfada en Él' (1990: 184) ('as made it impossible for me to doubt that He was within me, or that I was totally engulfed in Him', 1957: 71). The paradox inherent in a frail, unlearned woman's receiving spiritual gifts

against all conventional wisdom is the best proof that her raptures are divine.
• If Teresa doubts or is doubted, God returns to dispel uncertainty. Doubt itself, and the false humility prescribed by those who traffic in doubt, are revealed to be effects of the devil. Those doubts are more to be feared than the devil himself.
• If perchance it is *not* God, and the devil seduces Teresa, she will know. The devil may possess her but cannot deceive her.
• If in the moment of rapture, she does *not* discern the devil's hand, because he can produce symptoms and pleasures identical to those of God, the traces rapture leaves behind will clarify matters. She will be able to accurately interpret ecstasy's effects.
• And then, what might be seen as the most radical turn of all, if the diagnosis errs and the traces deceive: even in this case, the effects – the desire for further prayer – subvert and render harmless (and even profitable) the devil's original seduction, as well as the misdiagnosis itself.

The threat of interpretive instability this last possibility holds out is not so much dispensed with as incorporated and de-clawed. In the end, the *Vida* leaves no tenable position of uncertainty concerning Teresa's orthodoxy, even if the ecstatic body remains radically unstable.

Teresa's beatification in 1614 and her complete incorporation into the Church as a canonized saint in 1622 might be seen as the culmination of a long process of diagnostic scrutiny that could have gone either way. It may be that the Church decided she was more useful, or less menacing, as saint than as heretic. Indeed, Teresa's growing, almost cult-like, popularity throughout the teens and well into the twenties may have made any other decision inexpedient. As a mystic, a women, and a reformer, Teresa stood triply on the fringes of Church orthodoxy. Her absorption into official *doxa* as a saint was, among other things, an economic and efficient way of rendering her corpse (or her memory, or her autobiographical text) stable at last, of transforming the pathology of the mystic's non-normative body and soul into the very example of sanctity. This reading, perhaps too cynical about the Vatican's motives, is not meant to exclude other possibilities. Throughout her life, Teresa was precariously balanced between the condemnable exemplarity of demonic impostor and the commendable exemplarity of living saint. But if the former position was clearly the more risky of the two, the latter was not entirely unproblematic. Rather it remits to a paradox located at the very core of Christian theology concerning sacramentality and the principle of *imitatio Christi*: how is Christ's example at once both singular – a supreme sacrifice which initiates a new Law and with it a new temporality – and repeatable, a sacrifice reenacted via the Eucharistic sacrament performed at every mass? What is more, if not repeating Christ's example can lead to a kind of heresy, repeating too closely can lead to a kind of idolatry. In the case of Teresa, the canonization that rehabilitates her within Church orthodoxy and transforms her, finally, into an example of saintliness holds – or hides – a similar paradox, one inscribed in the *Vida*, particularly when it is read, as it was by her nuns, as an instructive text.

The Vatican's institutional discernment apparatus, which diagnoses her as a saint, can redeem Teresa for *doxa*, but it cannot altogether erase the traces – the effects – of her former illegibility recorded in the autobiography. Teresa's canonization suggests that in the end the *mujercita flaca* who claimed to experience God directly was successful in making her case, in proving as truth the divine etiology of her ecstasies and her right to bear witness to the experiences of her own body and soul. The *Vida* itself has much to do with this: it effectively functions as a transforming machine, a site in which doubt is turned into certainty, paradox into divine reason, womanly frailty into strength, prosecutors into defendants. These transformations, I have argued, are not so different from those staged on early modern theaters of scientific or quasi-scientific truth production, and in dissection theaters, that similarly achieve certainty by exposing an interior and untangling the layers hidden therein.

Further reading

Certeau, Michel de, 1992. *The Mystic Fable, I: The Sixteenth and Seventeenth Centuries*, trans. Michael B. Smith (Chicago, IL: Chicago UP)

Fernández, James, 1992. *Apology to Apostrophe: Autobiography and the Rhetoric of Self-Representation in Spain* (Durham, NC: Duke UP)

Haliczer, Stephen, 2002. *Between Exaltation and Infamy: Female Mystics in the Golden Age of Spain* (Oxford: OUP)

Sluhovsky, Moshé. 2007. *Believe Not Every Spirit: Possession, Mysticism and Discernment in Early Modern Catholicism* (Chicago, IL: Chicago UP)

Weber, Alison, 1996. *Teresa of Avila and the Rhetoric of Femininity* (Princeton, NJ: Princeton UP)

8

Women's Artistic Production and Their Visual Representation in Early Modern Spain

CARMEN FRACCHIA

This chapter explores the depiction of women's imagined identity in early modern Spanish culture by one female painter, one female sculptor, and three male painters: Sofonisba Anguissola (c.1532, Cremona – 1625, Palermo), Luisa Ignacia Roldán or La Roldana (1652, Seville – 1706, Madrid), José Ribera (1591, Játiva, Valencia – 1652, Naples), Diego Velázquez (1599, Seville – 1660, Madrid), and Bartolomé Esteban Murillo (1617, Seville –1682, Seville). Samples of their work will be selected from a range of artistic genres such as devotional painting and sculpture, portraiture, self-portraiture, allegorical painting, and *bodegones* (genre painting), which were produced in three key urban centres: at the Hapsburg Court in Madrid; in Seville, the second most important European trade centre with the Atlantic World; and in Naples, the capital of the Spanish viceroyalty in Italy.

In this analysis of their visual forms the workings of the gaze will play a key role. The visual form as an activity of the sign unfolds, according to Norman Bryson, within the social formation, or else within the field of power. Bryson explains that painting, and by extension sculpture, 'as art of the sign, which is to say an art of discourse, is coextensive with the flow of signs through both itself and the rest of the social formation' (1988: xxii). Viewers, by the act of viewing and through their cultural codes of recognition, are interpreters of signs and, therefore, the process of viewing is an activity which constantly transforms the material of the visual into meaning. Thus, the gaze is an interpretative tool of social power relations. In order, therefore, to grasp the cultural significance of the subjectivity of women at this period, we need first to explore the social reality of women artists working in early modern Spain, which is inextricably bound up with concepts of gender and sexuality. Therefore, emphasis will be given in this chapter to some of the conditions attendant on image production in early modern Spain and Italy: the status of the art, the lineage and social position of artists, the situation of women artists and their strategies of resistance, and the prescriptive views of art theorists on the depiction of the female figure. The relationship between early modern visual production and patriarchal values and the ways in which women's imagined identities were shaped by the visual form will also be considered.

While the artistic production of Ribera, Velázquez, and Murillo is internationally acclaimed, Anguissola has been acknowledged only since the 1960s and little is known about the work of Roldán, despite the fact that, like Velázquez, she worked at the Spanish court. This is indicative of the position that women artists, and women in general, occupied in the social order and in the collective imaginary of the sixteenth and seventeenth centuries in Imperial Spain. Whereas a series of important scholarly works have been published on women and gender in the fields of literary and cultural studies, very few publications shed light on women artists in the field of early modern Spanish visual studies. The sketchy records of women artists in the artistic sources and their intermittent visibility in the European artistic historiography, are not, as feminist art historians Rozsika Parker and Griselda Pollock maintained in 1981, the consequences of a natural phenomenon; they are, at least in part, the result of the long patriarchal tradition of the art treatise and humanist thinking. Thus, as Pollock later asserts, the histories of women artists are connected to 'the ideological and social formations which shaped their interventions in artistic practice' (1988: 41).

Women artists have always existed: the evidence is found in documentary, artistic, and literary sources, where their names and their work have been recorded (Greer 1979). Spanish art theorists provided, in line with classical tradition, a list of women painters, sculptors, illuminators, gilders, and printmakers, albeit with little or no information about their work. Conversely, there also exist signed works by women artists whose names are not recorded in art historiographical sources or in convent archives, as is the case with Josefa Sánchez who signed a crucifix in the Convent of San Antonio, Real de Segovia (Muñoz López 2003: 81). The legacy of this neglect is that the greater part of women artists' *oeuvre* remains difficult to identify. By contrast, the work of the few women artists who were acknowledged during their lifetimes and praised as exceptional by art theorists is more accessible to the modern audiences. This is the case with Anguissola and Roldán and, to a lesser extent, with the painter Josefa Ayala de Óbidos (c.1630, Seville – 1684, Óbidos) (see Brooke 1997). There is a connection between the celebration of the rarity of the female artist (Woods-Marsden 1998: 191–9) and the neglect of most women's work by Spanish art theorists. The root of the problem lies in the mechanics of artistic production and the ideology which shaped women's position in the artistic milieu.

Women rarely emerged as independent artists or as running their own workshops, since they were not permitted by law to sign work contracts. The only option for a woman was to be accepted as apprentice by a male relative, whether father, husband, or uncle, in his family workshop. The position of women in the family workshop follows the pattern of social reality for urban women, as the case of Luisa Roldán reveals. She trained with her father, Pedro de Roldán (1624–99), one of the most productive and famous sculptors in Seville, and with her siblings, including two sisters, Francisca and María Josefa, who were also sculptors. In 1671, she gained independence from her father when she married the lesser-known sculptor Luis Antonio de los Arcos (†1702/3), who polychromed her work and signed her contracts (Hall-van den Elsen 1997). Few of her large-scale wooden sculptures and reliefs for altarpieces in Seville and Cadiz were signed by Roldán, so most of her earlier production is unidentifiable. However, three sculptures in Cadiz Cathedral were recently identified as hers following the discovery during restoration of autograph documents inside the heads of these hollow figures. In the document inside the *Ecce Homo*, signed on 29 June 1684, the artist refers to herself as an *insigne escultora* (famous sculptor) and claims the authorship of this statue with the help of her husband, who may have painted it. Inside the statues of *San Servando* and *San Germán*, the patron saints of Cadiz, a document names Luisa Roldán as the author of the work, which was scupted after designs by her father and painted and gilded by her husband (García Olloqui 2000: 75, 83–5). The sculptures of the saints, it transpires, had been commissioned from Luisa Roldán by Cadiz Town Hall on 10 March 1687. The use of hidden documents was a strategic device adopted by assistants in artistic workshops across Western Europe and in the New World, to assert their authorship when they were responsible for a work signed by their master.[1] However, when Roldán was appointed *Escultora de Cámara* (Court Sculptor) by Charles II in 1692 and *Escultora del Rey* (Sculptor to the King) by Philip V in 1701, she signed her work with the elegant new title (Trusted 1996: 70).

Like Roldán, most women artists during this period trained with a male relative, as did Josefa Ayala, and the Flemish painter Catherina van Hemessen (c.1527/8, Antwerp – sometime after 1587), who worked at the Spanish Court from 1556 to 1558 (Grössinger 1997: 64–5). This was not, however, the case with Sofonisba Anguissola, who also worked at the Hapsburg court in Madrid from 1560 to 1573. Her father, Almicare Anguissola, was not an artist, but a nobleman, who, unusually, promoted his daughter's artistic education and her work (Greer 1979: 180–2). Anguissola learned Latin, how to play music, and to paint, in line with the liberal ideas on the educa-

---

[1] An autograph document by the artist Juan de Mesa (1583–1627) was found inside the sculpture *St Francis Xavier* (Martín González 1993: 33, n.30); outside Spain there are the two cases of documents inside a sculpted figure: a medieval *Crucifix* in Siena, Italy, and an *Ecce Homo* in Potosí, Bolivia (Trusted 2007: 155–6, n.132).

tion of the noblewoman set out by Baldassare Castiglione in his *Book of the Courtier* of 1528 (Sutherland and Nochlin 1976: 23–4; Woods-Marsden 1998: 189–90). Anguissola's class, education, and international reputation as a painter were assets to her employment at the Spanish Court, where she was invited in 1559 to become lady-in-waiting and painter to Queen Isabel de Valois, the third wife of Philip III.[2] The artist was never paid for her art work: as befitting a noblewoman, she was given expensive gifts, clothing, and jewellery in lieu of money.[3]

Painting was, in line with Italian Renaissance values, considered a liberal, noble, and intellectual pursuit and the Renaissance artist was invested with a noble status by the Tuscan humanist and architect Leon Battista Alberti (1404–72), who misunderstood the social position of the artist in antiquity. At a time when the paradigm of the modern artist was being set up in Italy (Parker and Pollock 1981: 86), in Spain the visual artist was still regarded as an artisan until 1677, when painting was legally recognized as an intellectual calling and divorced from manual skills by the Spanish state (Brown and Engass 1992: 167). Anguissola's social class was certainly an advantage in the period predating this change; artists, classified as artisans unless they belonged to the court, were subject to the payment of *alcabala* (a sales tax), as were tailors, shoemakers, and silversmiths. Spanish art theorists attempted to dissociate the artist from the artisan class and the tax burden in order to defend the intellectual nature of their work. El Greco (1541, Crete – 1614, Toledo) and the art theorist Vicente Carducho (1576, Florence – 1638, Madrid), along with other painters, fought a legal and political battle to raise the social status of the 'medieval artisan-artist' to the realm of the nobility (Brown and Engass 1992: 167–8). Their aspirations came up against a new source of conflict in the middle of the sixteenth century, when the state approved the imperial policy of purity of blood that prohibited people of Muslim or Jewish ancestry from occupying positions of power (Elliott 2002: 219–24). If an artist wanted to claim noble status, a thorough investigation of his lineage was required, as the well-known case of Velázquez reveals (Brown 1978: 251–2). Most male artists had an artisan background; artists from the nobility, like Anguissola, were extremely rare (Parker and Pollock 1981:17). Association with the new aspirations of the visual artist made it possible for women artists from the nobility to be acknowledged as professionals by contemporary art theorists. However, the identification of the

---

[2] For the recognition Anguissola received from the artistic elite in Rome and Florence, and from Michelangelo, see her biographer, Vasari (1878–85: v, 81; vi, 498–502; vii, 133); and Jacobs 1997: 189–90.

[3] The artist did, however, received a salary as a lady-in-waiting, and gifts of money from Philip II for her dowry in 1569. See Perlingieri 1992: 60, 72–3, 83, 88; and Kusche 1997: 72.

'female sex with the notion of the artist' was compromised in the rhetoric of the Renaissance by the notion of God the Father as The Divine Artist and the artist's aspirations of aiming at divinity (Parker and Pollock 1981: 86–7).

The aims of painters and their practices were inscribed in the Catholic discourse of salvation by Francisco Pacheco (1564–1644), who was the censor of sacred art for the Inquisition and Velázquez's father-in-law. In his *Arte de la pintura* (*Art of Painting*) (1649), Pacheco declares that among the aims of the painter, 'el principal será, por medio de el estudio y fatiga desta profesión, estando en gracia, alcanzar la bienaventuranza' (Pacheco 1990: 249) ('The principal purpose will be this: to attain a condition of blessedness through the study and toil of his profession as undertaken in a state of grace', Pacheco 2007: 31).

When in 1724 painter Antonio Palomino (1655–1726) wrote a biography of the *eminente escultora* (eminent sculptor) Luisa Roldán, he legitimized the concept of the female sculptor as an extraordinary phenomenon, emphasizing her Christian sensibilities and her working methods:

> Y aseguran, que cuando hacía imágenes de Cristo, o de su Madre Santísima, además de prepararse con cristianas diligencias, se revestía tanto de aquel afecto compasivo, que no las podía ejecutar sin lágrimas.
> (Palomino 1986: 349)
>
> (It is said that when she did an image of Christ or of His Blessed Mother, besides preparing herself by fulfilling her Christian duties, she became so immersed in feelings of compassion that she could not execute it without tears.) (Palomino 1987: 342)

Roldán's work consists mainly of representations of the most popular Counter Reformation subjects: the Life and Death of the Virgin, Christ, and the Saints. She carved and sculpted scenes such as *The Holy Family*, *The Nativity*, and *The Education of the Virgin* (Trusted 1996: 70–74). Much of Palomino's biography is taken up with the impossibility of finding words to express the powerful emotional and religious effects of Roldán's realism, which was the desired outcome for the arts in Counter Reformation Spain. In Roldán's innovative court *oeuvre* of small-scale, portable, painted terracotta sculptures, such as *The Virgin and Child with St Diego of Alcalá* (1690–95, Victoria and Albert Museum, London) (Plate 1), the mystic event is conveyed with a clear immediacy and intimacy by the realism of the scene and the lively interaction between the two androgynous angels, the cherubs, the Franciscan saint and the Christ Child, established by the complex intertwining of gaze and speech. The figure at the centre of the composition is the Virgin, who is looking down at the Holy Child sitting on her lap. She is portrayed as a quiet, content, and modest mother, representing the qualities of modesty and virtue, identified by Palomino as the reason for Roldán's artistic achievements, in addition to her superior skills: 'era su modestia suma, su habilidad superior, y su virtud extremada' (Palomino 1986: 349) ('her modesty was great, her skill superior, and her virtue extraordinary', Palomino 1987: 342).

Roldán's feminine attributes were the ones expected from, and prescribed to, an upright Christian woman in Spanish society of the time, as the vast output of plays, poems, and conduct manuals by male Christian authors testifies (Dopico-Black 2001). In the visual field, Pacheco codified the iconographical conventions of image-making according to art regulations set up by the Council of Trent in 1563 (Mâle 1932). The Tridentine image was inherently didactic, and used as a tool for the regulation of private and public behaviour. Prescriptions about artistic production placed emphasis upon accuracy in the representation of religious subjects; the aim was to provide an intelligible and realistic image for the viewer by adhering to the cathartic effect of medieval apocryphal tradition and by adding appropriate symbols to the figures depicted so that they could be readily identified by the audience.

Among Pacheco's iconographical formulations we find rules on how to depict women in the most challenging religious and mythological narratives. Pacheco's formula for the most popular depiction of the Virgin, the Immaculate Conception, epitomizes the imagined identity of women in early modern Spain:

> Hase de pintar, pues, en este aseadísimo misterio esta Señora en la flor de su edad, de doce a trece años, hermosísima niña, lindos y graves ojos, nariz y boca perfectísima y rosadas mexillas, los bellísimos cabellos tendidos, de color de oro; en fin, cuanto fuere posible al humanísimo pincel. (Pacheco 1990: 576)
>
> (In this most lovely mystery the Lady should be painted in the flower of her youth, twelve or thirteen years of age, as a most beautiful young girl, with fine and serious eyes, a most perfect nose and mouth and roseate cheeks, wearing loose her most beautiful golden hair, in short, with as much perfection as the human brush is capable of achieving.) (Pacheco 2007: 36.)

The dogma of the Immaculate Conception was based on the belief that the Virgin alone of all humanity was conceived without the stain of Original Sin, since she did not belong to the realm of the divine (Warner 1976: 236–54). The natural realism of the portrayal of a very young contemporary girl in paintings of the *Immaculate Conception* by Spanish artists (Suzanne Stratton 1994) and in Roldán's polychromed terracotta has an immediate resonance with the viewer, with whom the Virgin cannot engage. These depictions, in which the Virgin's gaze is directed away from the viewer either by her downcast eyes or by her upward gaze towards God the Father, allow the viewer a voyeuristic licence to scrutinize the Virgin's body (Berger 1972). She is the protagonist of these images, but her subjectivity has been denied and her body becomes a 'site on which to inscribe interpretative anxieties' (Dopico-Black 2001: 68) in early modern Spain, where chastity, according to Juan Luis Vives, was considered the most important virtue, and superior to soberness and to other feminine virtues such as 'obedience, humility, silence' (Aughterson 1995: 67, 70–1).

The depiction of women's bodies in religious narratives was also regulated to avoid the production of lascivious images because of 'their possible inspiration to immoral behaviour' (Brown 1978: 72). The use of the female life model, 'who poses no danger', but is an 'honest' woman, was limited by Pacheco, who permitted the artist to copy her face and hands: 'del natural sacaría rostros y manos [...] de mujeres honestas, que a mi ver no tiene peligro'(Pacheco 1990: 377). If a religious scene required the depiction of a naked woman, he recommended the eclectic use of visual sources, from the best paintings, drawings, sculptures, and prints of the past, but not from a life model. This precept was a reinforcement of the 1640 ruling against lascivious images in the Index of the Inquisition:

> To partly avoid the grave scandal and damage [...] caused by worldly and lascivious painting, we order: That no person dares to bring into this country paintings, prints, statues or other lascivious sculptures, nor to use them in public places or squares, streets or shared rooms in houses. It is also forbidden to painters to paint them [...] under pain of full excommunication. (Portús 2002: 37)

However, while the ruling classes continued to expand their collections of lascivious or mythological scenes, the rest of the population had access to the visual formulation of the male gaze in the erotic religious images of female saints. The most popular was *The Penitent Magdalene* in prayer by a grotto with her gaze up to heaven, usually portrayed as a healthy young woman with one or both shoulders or breasts glimpsed through a veil of hair, cloak, or ragged garments (Haskins 1993). In the *Assumption of Mary Magdalene* of 1636 (Museo de la Real Academia de Bellas Artes de San Fernando, Madrid) by José Ribera (Plate 2), the composition make reference to the iconographies of the *Immaculate Conception* and the *Assumption of the Virgin,* but the penitent's robes and attributes confirm that this is the depiction of a fallen woman who is nevertheless deserving of redemption. She is enveloped in a red cloak with her hands crossed over her breasts and is being carried up to heaven, with the Spanish Bay of Naples in the background, by cherubs bearing a jar of ointment, a skull, and scourges. Her upward gaze allows viewers the freedom to enjoy the youth and beauty

Figure 1. Bartolomé Esteban Murillo, *Spring as a Flower Girl* (1660–65)

of an erotic female figure inscribed in a religious context which requires an emotional stimulus to piety.

The inherently contradictory iconography of Mary Magdalene is also found in covertly erotic depictions of women in allegorical genres. In Murillo's *Spring as a Flower Girl* of 1660–65 (Dulwich Picture Gallery, London) (Fig. 1), the modestly dressed girl becomes the erotic object of the male gaze (Berger 1972: 45–64). Her direct engagement with the viewer, her smile, her partially uncovered hair, and her lightly tanned skin tone, used by the artist to differentiate between the sunburnt poor and the pale aristocracy, indicate that the portrait of an ordinary girl, not destined for immortality, could only be justified by allegorization (Brooke and Cherry 2001: 112). As a girl with a rose in her turban, offering roses to her viewers from an open woven shawl of Mexican design, and located in the outskirts of a city, in a landscape, and not inscribed in the private domain, she becomes the personification of Spring. The divide between 'men's public function and place and women's private function and place' (Aughterson 1995: 165) was becoming increasingly polarized as one of the consequences of the progressive attitude towards the limited education of the elite woman in early modern Europe.

In Counter Reformation societies, however, convents remained centres for the vocational education of women for life, and learned nuns, as public figures, were also the subjects of portraiture. In Spain, Velázquez immortalized the strong personality of a 66-year-old Toledan Poor Clare renowned for her organizational skills and founder of the first enclosed convent in the Far East, in Manila in the Spanish Philippines. In his portrait *The Venerable Mother Jerónima de la Fuente* of 1620 (Museo del Prado, Madrid), the male artist fashions the nun's subjectivity by allowing her a direct engagement with the viewer through her powerful gaze. This is an exceptional representation of a strong and independent nun and missionary legitimized by her religious attributes, a crucifix in her right hand and a sacred book in the other. Her full-length figure stands at the centre of the canvas against a flat background to prevent any distraction from her gripping gaze (*Velázquez* 2006: 142). Despite the fact that in the real world, women did not 'lack the ability to manage large affairs, to think about important religious truths, or to become missionaries' (Ortega Costa 1989), women's place in the domestic sphere was also sanctioned by representations of popular episodes from the daily life of the Christ Child. In his *Holy Family with Little Bird* of c.1650 (Museo del Prado, Madrid), Murillo depicts an intimate and domestic sacred scene in the interior of St Joseph's workshop. As the provider for his family, St Joseph occupies the centre of the composition and watches over the Christ Child, who is holding a little bird and playing with a dog. In this way the painter emphasizes the connection between obedience to authority and the patriarchal family, in line with St Ignatius Loyola, who believed that devotion to the image of the Holy Family could help believers to make the

Figure 2. Diego Velázquez, *Kitchen Maid with The Supper at Emmaus* (c. 1620)

association with this mechanism of control (Villaseñor Black 2006). Murillo's Virgin, on the other hand, is relegated to semi-darkness in the left-hand corner, behind a work basket full of cloth, seated at her spinning, and quietly observing her divine son. None of the characters depicted engages with the viewer, who becomes a secret and privileged witness to an accessible sacred scene, in which the social divide between the sexes (Laqueur 1990: 134) has been established and sanctioned by the sacrament of matrimony promoted by the Council of Trent. In *bodegones*, or scenes set in a kitchen or tavern, Velázquez locates lower-class women in a domestic space. In his *Kitchen Maid and the Supper at Emmaus* of c.1620 (National Gallery of Ireland, Dublin) (Fig. 2), he paints the only extant portrayal of a mixed-raced woman in her workplace, the kitchen, as the site where most female slaves worked in Spanish urban centres. The submissive and modest-looking slave with her downcast eyes, echoing the subjects in religious images, is contextualized in the discourse of salvation, but also in the 'type of domestic production without which the Spanish Golden Age elite could not have survived' (Fracchia 2004: 29). Velázquez's painting draws the viewer's attention to the process of Christianization of slaves, which did nothing to inhibit the practice of slavery in early modern Spain, or the sexual exploitation of female slaves, or the donation of slaves to religious institutions or to newly married couples (Fracchia 2007).

Women's bodies were regulated by the production of the visual form. Their depiction was a manipulative vehicle for setting the standard required for the social control of sexual practices, in order to keep intact the lineage, honour, and sexual purity of Old Christians by preventing contact with New Christians suspected of having Muslim or Jewish blood. Images of women were also shaped by notions of anatomy and the workings of the body. The concept of 'one-sex body' which considered the male as one canonical body, and the female anatomy as imperfect and inferior, was the predominant ideology in European society from antiquity to the eighteenth century (Laqueur 1990: 63–113). In order to construct an ideal rational and handsome political ruler for the Spanish state, Doctor Juan Huarte de San Juan (1529–88) in his *Examen de ingenios* (*Examination of Men's Wits*) of 1575 advocated the perfect combination of the inner humoral balance of male and female bodies. Huarte spelt out the stages necessary for attaining the exact 'moderate' degree of coldness and humidity in the female body and dryness and heat in the male body to produce a ruler such as Philip II, to whom the book was dedicated (see Arquiola 1988: 301–2). The Spanish physician further maintains that the humoral balance can be deduced from the physical appearance of men and women. A woman's humoral balance is evident in the correct pitch of her voice, her weight, her pink-and-white skin tones, fair hair, and 'extreme' beauty, an index of her fertility.[4]

Huarte's description is no different from Pacheco's prescription of the appearance of the Immaculate Conception, or from Anguissola's full-length portrait *Isabel de Valois* of 1565 (Museo del Prado, Madrid) (Fig. 3). In this portrait the Queen is looking at the viewer, to whom she is presented in luxurious attire and covered with jewellery against a dark background, with her face bathed in full light, which makes her pale pink skin tone even more prominent. She engages with the viewer, but the rigidity of her pose and the lack of expression in her face, formal requirements for a royal portrait rooted in the Germanic restrained pose (Portús 2004: 93), articulate a distance between the viewer, the subject, and her imaginary space.[5] The miniature portrait of her husband, Philip II, which Isabel holds in her right hand and shows to the viewer, distracts our attention from her direct gaze. She has been defined by the image of her husband, as depictions of saints or the Virgin are defined by their engagement with God the Father. In the same way, the contemporary court painter Alonso Sánchez Coello (c.1531–88), defines Isabel Clara Eugenia, Governor of the Spanish Netherlands, by the miniature portrait of Philip II, her father, which she shows to her viewers in *Isabel Clara Eugenia and Magdalena Ruiz* of c.1587 (Museo del Prado, Madrid).

Anguissola adhered strictly to the pattern of Spanish rules for royal portraiture, and since she never signed her official portraits in Spain, this has created a problem with the authorship of her Spanish paintings, which were traditionally ascribed to Anthonis Mor (c.1520–77) or Sánchez Coello

---

[4] According to Elvira Arquiola, Huarte's thesis is the first attempt in Spain to set out the biological formulation of eugenics (1984: 95–105, 110–11).

[5] On Germanic traditions in Spanish royal portraiture see also Brown 2004.

Figure 3. Sofonisba Anguissola, *Isabel of Valois* (1565)

(Kusche 1989). However, in her *Self-Portrait at the Spinet* of 1561 (Spencer Collection, Althorp, Northampton), Anguissola portrays herself as a noblewoman, with her chaperon in the background, and an inscription stating that this work was made by the 'virgin' Anguissola for her father during her stay at the Hapsburg Court (Mainz 1997: 40). The artist had earlier defined her gender and her profession in the association between herself and her father in the oval miniature *Self-Portrait* of c.1556 (Museum of Fine Arts, Boston), in which she is holding up in both hands a big shield with the mysterious inscription of her father's name (Woods-Marsden 1998: 203). Her *Bernardino Campi Painting Sofonisba Anguissola* of c.1559 (Pinacoteca Nazionale, Siena), produced either in Italy or in Spain, which shows her art master painting her portrait, and both male painter and female subject looking out from the canvas directly at the viewer (Woods-Marsden 1998: 208–10), also justifies her gender position in the artistic milieu.

Given the social and ideological constraints on self-expression by women, and in an age in which artists seldom used themselves as the subjects of their paintings (Parker and Pollock 1981: 18), it is all the more remarkable that Anguissola developed the genre of self-portraiture. In at least twelve self-portraits Anguissola depicts herself, most frequently, as a member of the cultured elite, as a musician, a learned humanist, or a noblewoman, to signify her social class and education in order to be accepted as a painter. Thus in her self-portraits she chooses to define herself by a variety of social attributes: a musical instrument, a book, expensive jewellery and dress, or sober clothing without jewellery, or by the background presence of a servant; less frequently by the attributes of her profession. It is claimed (Tinagli 1997: 119; Woods-Marsden 1998: 204) that Anguissola never saw the *Self-Portrait at the Easel* of 1548 by her predecessor at the Spanish Court, Catherina van Hemessen (Kunstmuseum, Öffentliche Kunstsammlung, Basel), which is considered to be the first European self-portrait by a woman painter. I suggest that Anguissola might nevertheless have been aware of this composition when she fashioned herself as a painter in her *Self-Portrait at the Easel* of c.1556 (Castle Museum, Lancut, Poland) (Plate 3). As in van Hemessen's self-portrait, Anguissola also interrupts her work to concentrate her attention on her spectators and she directs the viewer's gaze with the brush in her right hand, which points towards her ambiguous-looking depiction of woman and child, usually interpreted as the Madonna and Child, but more plausibly as Venus and Cupid. Her sober dress and hairstyle indicate her status as a noblewoman at work, while her class justifies her gender and profession, unlike Velázquez's self-portrait in *Las Meninas* (*The Maids of Honour*) of 1656 (Museo del Prado, Madrid). Velásquez needs to legitimize his recent elevation to the nobility by depicting himself as a painter next to the heiress to the throne at the centre of the canvas, and to the royal couple faintly reflected in the mirror in the background.

The genre of self-portraiture that was developed by Anguissola more than by any other artist in early modern Europe before Rembrandt van Rijn (1606–69) escaped the constraints of patronage and, to certain extent, artistic tradition. It gave a degree of freedom to female and male artists to explore the self in innovative ways, as did the modernity of the *bodegón,* which allowed Velázquez to represent new subjects such as the female slave, albeit with her subjectivity denied. By contrast, the image-making process in the more established genres of court portraiture and religious and allegorical paintings was highly regulated in early modern Spain, as were the various ways of looking at depictions of women. However, ideological and artistic prescriptions did not, as we have seen, eliminate the ambiguities and contradictions inherent in depictions of women in three of the key centres of visual production in Hapsburg Spain. Patriarchal values were also responsible for creating a different pattern of artistic production for women artists; for relegating them to a greater invisibility in the artistic historiography than their male counterparts; and for regarding as exceptional the successful and complex cases of Anguissola and Roldán.

I would argue that the underlying current at the root of images of women was the fear of women's subjectivity and their sexual agency as destabilizing factors in a patriarchal society. Rather than their nature or sexuality, the social and ideological constraints upon female artists shaped their way of working and the visual representation of the imagined identity of women by female and male artists in Imperial Spain.

Further reading

Calvo Serraller, Francisco (ed.), 1991. *Teoría de la pintura del Siglo de Oro* (Madrid: Cátedra)

Harrison, Charles, Paul Wood, and Jason Gaiger (eds), 2007. *Art in Theory 1648–1815: An Anthology of Changing Ideas* (Oxford: Blackwell)

Morán Turina, Miguel, and Javier Portús, 1997. *El arte de mirar: la pintura y su público en la España de Velázquez* (Madrid: Istmo)

La mujer en el arte español, 1997. VIII Jornadas de Arte, Departamento de Historia del Arte 'Diego Velázquez', Centro de Estudios Históricos, CSIC (Madrid: Alpuerto / CSIC)

9

The Baroque and the Undead: Carnal Knowledge in the Novellas of María de Zayas

MARGARET GREER

The seventeenth-century writer María de Zayas y Sotomayor opens her *Novelas amorosas y ejemplares* (*Exemplary Tales of Love*) with an authorial preface in which she confronts head-on the challenge of writing and publishing in patriarchal society.[1] She justifies her 'madness' in doing so by positing the asexuality of souls and the material equality of male and female organs and flesh. Women's intellectual limitations, she says, are due only to men's tyranny in locking them up and denying them education. Her stated objective in writing is that of re-educating both men and women, so that men will no longer exercise verbal and physical cruelty toward women, and women will learn to mistrust desire – their own as well as that of men. In story after story, she displays the effects of those desires on the flesh of women, maimed or killed, blackened by their own sin or redeemed in saintly death. Various characters, male as well as female, return in the flesh from beyond the grave to warn the living or to accuse their guilty torturers in stories that often anticipate Gothic novels or early horror movies.

While providing a general introduction to Zayas's Baroque novellas of desire, love, and death, this essay will extend my previous work on Zayas from the perspective of psychoanalytic and feminist theory by focusing on the question of Zayas's treatment of what we commonly call the body. English has two words to distinguish 'meat' from 'flesh', but Spanish, like its Latin parent, *caro, carnis*, has only one: 'carne'. The Latin root gives us the loaded adjective 'carnal', with similar connotation in both languages. Zayas, however, uses neither 'flesh' nor 'cuerpo' (body) in her preface to

---

[1] My thanks to Laura R. Bass and the Henry W. Sullivan for reading an earlier version of this article and for their helpful comments on it, and to Henry Sullivan for the Lacanian body–organism distinction, explained in 'Don Quixote & the "Third Term"' (1999).

the reader in arguing for equality of the sexes, preferring the general word 'matter' and more specific terms:

> si esta *materia* de que nos componemos los hombres y las mujeres, ya sea una trabazón de fuego y barro, o ya una masa de espíritus y terrones, no tiene más nobleza en ellos que en nosotras si es una misma *la sangre; los sentidos, las potencias* y *los órganos* por donde se obran sus efectos, son unos mismos; la misma alma que ellos, porque las almas ni son hombres ni mujeres: ¿qué razón hay para que ellos sean sabios y presuman que nosotras no podemos serlo? (Zayas 2000: 159, my italics)

> (if this *material* of which we men and women are made, whether a combination of fire and mud, or a mass of spirits and clods, is no more noble in them than in us, if our *blood* is the same, our *senses, faculties* and *organs* through which their effects are wrought, are all the same, the soul the same as theirs – since souls are neither male nor female – what reason is there that they would be wise and presume we cannot be so?)
> (Zayas 2009: 47, my italics)

In explicating the kind of carnal knowledge that Zayas offers her readers in the preface and the tales she spins, I will balance early modern, Counter Reformation Catholic conceptions of sexual difference, subjectivity, the body, and death with the understanding of those categories in the three Lacanian orders of the Real, the Imaginary, and the Symbolic. While paying attention to the particulars of Zayas's language, I will also be taking advantage of work generated by the recent complete English translation of Lacan's Seminar XX, *Encore* (1999).

We know frustratingly little about Maria de Zayas's life with certainty, other than that she lived in the first half of the seventeenth century, that she belonged to the aristocracy, and was from Madrid, but published her work in Zaragoza, and was in Barcelona in 1643 during the Catalan rebellion against the monarchy of 1640–52. That she was born in Madrid in 1590, the daughter of Fernando de Zayas y Sotomayor and María de Barasa, seems reasonably certain, according to the baptismal certificate published by Manuel Serrano y Sanz. Fernando de Zayas was an infantry captain who served as administrator for the seventh Count of Lemos, Pedro Fernández de Castro, and was awarded the habit of the elite military-religious Order of Santiago in 1628.[2] She was a resident of Madrid in 1617, when her signature appears as one of the associates of the Confraternity of the Defenders of the Immaculate Conception (Barbeito Carneiro 1992: 166–7). She was apparently composing poetry, drama, and her first novellas in the 1620s and partic-

---

[2] Serrano y Sanz 1975: 271, 583–5; Barbeito Carneiro 1992: 165–7. He gave the mother's name as Catalina, not María, as the certificate shows.

ipating in some fashion in the literary academies of Madrid. In his popular miscellany *Para todos* (For Everyone), published in 1632, Juan Pérez de Montalbán wrote: 'Doña María de Zayas, dézima Musa de nuestro siglo, ha escrito a los certámenes con grande acierto, tiene acabada una comedia de excelentes coplas y un libro para dar a la estampa en prosa y verso de ocho Novelas exemplares' (Doña María de Zayas, tenth muse of our century, has entered poetry competitions with great success, has completed a play in excellent verse, and has ready for publication a book of eight novellas in prose and verse) (cited in Moll 1982: 178). The play in question may have been her one extant drama, *La traición en la amistad* (*Friendship Betrayed*), which survived in manuscript and was first published by Manuel Serrano y Sanz in his volume on Spanish women writers.[3] Jaime Moll suggests that the publication of Zayas's novellas in Madrid was then blocked, as was the publication of other works of entertainment in Castile from 1625–1634 as part of the reform effort of the Count-Duke of Olivares in the early years of the regime of Philip IV, and was therefore shifted to Zaragoza, in Aragón (Moll 1982).

Zayas published two volumes of ten novellas each, in the tradition launched by Boccaccio's *Decameron*, a tradition that took root rather belatedly in Spain, but acquired great popularity in the wake of the publication of Cervantes's *Novelas ejemplares* (*Exemplary Novels*) in 1613. Zayas's first volume, entitled *Novelas amorosas y exemplares*, was published in 1637 in Zaragoza and the second, generally known as the *Desengaños amorosos* (*Tales of Disillusion with Love*), appeared ten years later, again in Zaragoza. In fact, the two tomes constitute a single collection, for the framing narrative begun in the first part is only concluded at the end of the second volume.

The only other definite scrap of information we have about her is a burlesque portrait in the *Vejamen* (Vexation) penned by Francesc Fontanella, a poetic 'roast' of all the poets who participated in a competition in Barcelona in 1643. In a fictional dream, he satirizes the poetic failings of all the competitors and of Zayas 'in the flesh' as well, painting her as a bewhiskered woman who tries to usurp masculine discourse for which she does not have the physical 'equipment', that is, a 'sword' under her 'sayas', playing on the name Zayas (a close homonym of the word for 'skirt'):

Doña María de Sayas
viu ab cara varonil,
que a bé que 'sayas' tenia,
bigotes filava altius.

---

[3] Serrano y Sanz 1975: I, 590–620. The play is also available in more recent editions, including a bilingual one (Zayas 1999). For a discussion of the play, see Alexander Samson's essay in this volume.

> Semblava a algun cavaller,
> mes jas' vindrà a descubrir
> que una espasa mal se amaga
> baix las 'sayas' femenils.
> En la dècima tercera
> fou glosadora infeliz,
> que mala tercera té
> quant lo pris vol adquirir.
> O! Senyora Doña Saÿa [*sic*],
> per premiar sos bons desitgs
> del sèrcol de un guardainfant
> tindrà corona gentil! (Kenneth Brown 1987: lines 725–40)

(I saw Lady Mary of the Skirts with a manly face, who although she wore 'skirts', was twirling a haughty mustache. She looked like a gentleman, but it will be revealed that a sword can hardly be hidden beneath feminine 'skirts'. In the third stanza, she was unfortunate at glossing and she has a poor procuress when she wants to win the prize. Oh, Lady Dame Skirt, to reward your good desires, you will have a charming crown [made] of the hoop of your farthingale.)[4]

We have no further information about Zayas after the publication of the *Desengaños*. Serrano y Sanz published two death certificates in Madrid for women named María de Zayas, one in 1661 and another in 1669, but also commented that it was a common name (1975: II, 583–7).

Zayas's novellas were very popular in Spain and in translation in other European lands in her own day, but her tales of love and of masculine cruelty to women would be banished from the national canon of high culture formulated in the nineteenth century and re-publication of her works ceased until the mid twentieth century. They were victims of the liberal reforming desire of a male intellectual elite to control the production and reading of novels, achieving a mass popular audience. Like the novels of nineteenth-century Spanish women writers, they were classed as low, idealist, and feminocentric works of entertainment devoured by uncritical readers (Jagoe 1993: 226–7, 234–40). That negative judgment was reinforced by later foreign critics schooled in Victorian standards of literary decency, who condemned her stories as unseemly, obscene, even sadistic. The dissident Spanish novelist Juan Goytisolo, however, saw Zayas's works in a very different light. He asserted that her combination of the erotic with burlesque touches, magic, and violence is what makes her fictions live for readers today:

---

[4] I thank Belén Atienza for her help in translating the Catalan. For a more detailed analysis of the portrait and other conjectures on her life, see Greer 2000: 17–35.

En un país cuya literatura ha servido desde siglos de vehículo transmisor
– a menudo admirable – a la institucionalización de sus complejos y frustraciones sexuales, las *novela*s de María de Zayas se destacan de modo
señero y nos conmueven aún con la frescura de su insólito y audaz desafío.
(1977:109)

(In a country whose literature has for centuries served as a transmitter –
often an admirable one – for the institutionalization of its sexual complexes
and frustrations, the novels of María de Zayas alone stand out and still
move us with the freshness of her singular and daring challenge.)

Today, four decades after Goytisolo lauded Zayas's 'daring challenge', dozens of scholars have analyzed its nature and extent from multiple and still multiplying angles. Zayas criticism is still a small fraction of the attention dedicated to Cervantes, but her novellas are proving to offer similarly polyvalent texts, to be reinterpreted by succeeding waves of scholars in light of their personal and generational concerns. Julia Kristeva wrote that certain texts can occupy the position of the analyst, inviting readers to engage with them like analysands, making the point of transference 'the structure and function of language [...] [to] open the way for all linguistic, symbolic and social structures to be put in process / on trial' (1984: 209–10). Kristeva had in mind avant-garde poetic texts, not the more apparently conventional narratives Zayas wrote, which are at once formulaic, melodramatic page-turners of love, desire, and the violence they can create; and tales that invite her readers to explore the bases and consequences of human identity and sexual relations, and the role that language plays in shaping them, then as now. Although in what follows I often write 'Zayas says' and equivalents both from custom and for economy of language, I do not necessarily mean by that to attribute the statements I make and the conclusions to which they lead to the conscious prescience of the seventeenth-century woman writer, but to the language of her texts.

Zayas rejected, either explicitly or implicitly, the traditional hierarchical binary definitions of human sexual identity. The quote from her preface about the identical 'material' of which men and women are made rejects the Aristotelian difference of woman as matter and man as defining form. Later in the same preface she upsets the differentiation of the sexes in the humoral theory of medicine formulated by Galen and rendered again in the influential treatise of Juan Huarte de San Juan's *Examen de ingenios para las ciencias* (*Examination of Men's Wits*) of 1575 (1989: 110–13). In Huarte's humoral theory, women possessed the same sexual organs as men, but turned inside their bodies rather than outside like men's, because of a deficiency of body heat. Their cold and damp composition also made them intellectually inferior to men (1989: 327, 608, 610–14). Zayas does not dispute that women's humoral balance is more cold and damp, but reverses its value, saying that if women were given books and teachers, 'fuéramos tan aptas para los puestos y para las cátedras como los hombres, y quizá más agudas, por ser de natural más frio, por consistir en humedad el entendimiento' (Zayas 2000: 160) ('we would prove as apt for posts and professorships as men, and perhaps of sharper wit, since our disposition is colder, given that the understanding is humid', Zayas 2009: 48). The second, more dominant, version of the creation story in Genesis 2.3 made woman a secondary creation from Adam's rib and, as the guilty heir of Eve's transgression, duly subordinated to man by the Pauline injunction to silence. But Zayas's assertion of the equality and asexuality of souls is in accord with the first creation story, in Genesis 1.27, 'So God created man in his own image [...] male and female he created them'.

The frame-tale narrator of the *Fourth Tale of Disillusion* in Zayas's darker and more violent second volume of novellas intensifies the challenge to men's assumed superiority. Therein, she paints male vituperation and restriction of women as a socially organized defense mechanism against threatening female ability, backing it up with a list of contemporary women known for their learning and their capacity to govern wisely. She caps this with a striking comparison that equates disempowerment of women with castration of men: 'los hombres de temor y envidia las privan de las letras y las armas, como hacen los moros a los cristianos que han de servir donde hay mujeres, que los hacen eunucos por estar seguros de ellos' (Men deprive them of learning and arms out of fear and envy, as the Moors make eunuchs of Christians who are to serve where there are women, so they can be sure of them) (Zayas 1983: 231). The privileged object in the second half of her equation is access to women as sexual objects; in the first half, it is access to Symbolic order power. This equation is, in my opinion, an uncanny anticipation of the operation of what Lacanian psychoanalytic theory calls secondary castration, the marking of sexual difference on the basis of 'having' versus 'being' the phallus, and of the unequal effects that operate in the hierarchy of gender roles in patriarchal culture.

Freud described the sexual difference on the basis of anatomy, having or not having a penis, and made the fear of losing it, or the castration complex, the central fact in shaping masculine sexual identity. Lacan, rereading Freud, denaturalized the marker of sexual division, which he termed the phallus, and he categorized the masculine / feminine difference as that of 'having' versus 'being' the phallus. The phallus in this differentiation is *not* the penis of the human organism, or even the man associated with it, but rather the signifier that Lacan chooses to designate the necessary attachment of speaking subjects to the Symbolic order and the genders they will assume therein. The literal fear of losing the penis is not the central fact in shaping masculine sexuality, nor is the desire for that organ that which conforms the feminine gender. The crucial 'castration' in forming the speaking human subject is the first (Symbolic) separation from the mythical *jouissance* or enjoyment of the infant's seamless union with the (m)Other, a separation effected by the third term, the phallic function of the signifier, of language that the mirror-stage infant takes up to negotiate that loss. Language works through a system of differentiation between a chain of signifiers, creating meaning by such differentiation (as Saussure illustrated). But it is always incomplete, an imperfect medium for achieving full knowledge, comprehending truth and being, or for communicating need, desire, and the demands for recognition that we address to the Other. For subjects thus constituted in the Symbolic, what is crucial is the question of 'seeming', acting the part according to sexual ideals of gender roles instilled early on in the lives of boys and girls. Playing these roles involves virile display by masculine subjects, as well as the feminine masquerade, both designed to lure the desire of the Other, as it operates both in the Imaginary and Symbolic orders. As Colette Soler points out, 'The phallus is [...] always veiled, which means concretely that the conditions of desire are unconscious for each of us' (2002: 103).

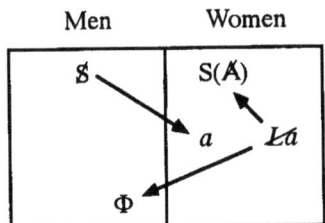

Zayas's novellas demonstrate throughout that however effectively those gender roles are learned and acted out, the full complementarity of the sexes they posit is a fantasy. Lacan observed that 'there's no such thing as a sexual relationship' (1999: 58–9), in the sense that two human beings in love never fit together perfectly like the halves of the divided jewels of myth and fable. Although the fantasy of harmony between the sexes goes back at least as far as Plato's *Symposium* (Fink 2002: 29), there is no direct, unmediated relationship between masculine and feminine subjects. Lacan's diagram of sexuation above shows why.[5] The upper row gives the symbols with which Lacan represents gender identification, not necessarily equivalent to sex; regardless of the genital configuration of the organism, males and females can place themselves on either side of the graph with regard to gender identification. The lower set of symbols indicates the direction of desire. For those subjects on the masculine side of the graph there is only one arrow, pointing toward

---

5   The graph as shown appears in Fink 1995: 114.

an *objet a* of desire on the feminine side. A masculine subject, forced by the *Nom/Non du père* to identify with difference, away from the maternal, seeks to recoup that loss by pursuing a substitute object on the feminine side. On the feminine side of the graph, however, there are two arrows. One points toward the symbol for the phallus on the masculine side, one that in fantasy would anchor her to the Symbolic order power of wealth and words, imagined as the domain of men in patriarchal cultures. The other arrow that remains on the feminine side signifies recognition of lack in the phallic signifier and a drive toward a fantasy of *jouissance* beyond the phallus, beyond language. It may be read as asexual, as aimed at religious ecstasy, or both. Recognizing its existence helps explain why in Zayas's plot structures we find her heroines alternating between attraction to men and retreat to a safe haven (typically a convent) on the feminine side (see Greer 2000: 87–157). Simplifying considerably the explanation of the nature of desire that results from the incorporation of the gaze of the Other, we can say that whether one is man or woman, homosexual or heterosexual, it is always a desire for recognition, the desire to be desired by the other (small o) who is one's *objet petit a,* the object that offers the fantasy of full complementarity.

The heroine of Zayas's very first novella identifies the loss of her mother as the condition for her tale of desire and registers its initiation as a physical wound. Jacinta tells her rescuer, Fabio:

> Faltó mi madre al mejor tiempo, que no fue pequeña falta, pues su compañía, gobierno y vigilancia fuera más importante a mi honestidad, que los descuidos de mi padre [...] Quería el mío a mi hermano tiernísimamente, y esto era sólo su desvelo, sin que se le diese yo en cosa ninguna.
> (Zayas 2000:179–80)

> (My mother died at the most important time, which was no little lack, since her company, governance and vigilance would have been more important for my chastity than was my father's lack of attention [...] My father loved my brother most tenderly and this was his only preoccupation, for I have never given him any whatsoever.) (Zayas 2009: 67)

In this emotional vacuum, she dreams of a handsome young man, who stabs her in the heart with a dagger when she uncovers his face, so that she awakens screaming in pain but totally enamored. When the man she dreamed appears in the flesh as Felix, their clandestine love leads to three deaths: first, that of a female cousin and rival for his love, who commits suicide and whose body turns black and swollen, marking the sin of jealous despair; then Jacinta's brother, whom Felix kills in self-defense; and finally Felix, whose death she foresees in a dream in which she opens a casket thinking he has sent her jewels, but sees instead his severed head.

Thus even in her first volume, Zayas weaves death into her love stories, enlisting Eros and Thanatos as drives at work in differing degrees in most of her narratives. Love fades, or is serialized, and repeatedly brings death in its wake. In this volume, in which female and male narrators alternate in dramatizing the lure toward the opposite sex and the fears they imagine it poses, victims claimed by death are more often male than female. Sometimes it is the 'other woman', the heroine's female antagonist, who either commits suicide or, in the second novella, is executed by the cross-dressed aggrieved heroine herself. In the sixth, *Disillusionment in Love and Virtue Rewarded*, Fernando seduces Juana with promised marriage, then marries but abuses Clara, having fallen under Lucrecia's spells; Juana, warned by a former lover reappearing from purgatory, enters a convent and later helps Clara undo Lucrecia's power and force her suicide, whereupon the weakened Fernando dies.

We can presume that Zayas was aware of the challenge and contradiction of using the genre of the love story, whose standard objectives are desire for a sexual object or the social goal of marriage, to warn both men and women away from the dangers of desire. One of the three fantasy tales that do end in happy marriage with which she concludes the first volume, promising its continuation in a sequel, is the aptly named eighth novella, *Triumph over the Impossible*. It is a male-narrated fantasy of love that conquers the ultimate human enemy, death. Rodrigo's prayers to Christ in Leonor's tomb are answered and she revives, to marry him rather than the rival to whom her parents had wed her.

In Zayas's second volume, *Tales of Disillusion*, Thanatos reigns throughout, and the body count mounts with every tale. All the explicit narrators are women, who are instructed only to tell 'true cases'. Of the sixteen 'good' women whose stories are recounted, only three survive at the end of their stories, to become nuns after a series of trials: in the *First Tale of Disillusion*, after being raped, sold into slavery, and kidnapped; in the fifth, after being cemented in a chimney for years, and in the ninth, after multiple assassination attempts from which the Virgin Mary rescues her. Of the others, one is poisoned by her husband (*Second Tale*), one bled to death by a husband (*Third Tale*) and another by a father-in-law (*Seventh Tale*); one, falsely accused and imprisoned by her husband, starves to death (*Fourth Tale*), one beheaded (*Eighth Tale*), one strangled with her own hair (*Seventh Tale*) and the others stabbed to death or otherwise slain by their husbands and male relatives. We can only speculate on why Zayas escalated the violence against women to hyperbolic levels in this second volume. Critics who construct a pseudo-autographical loop between the novellas and the unknowns of Zayas's life tend to attribute it to a presumed disappointment in love and/or her advancing age. Others link it to the prevailing Counter Reformation and Baroque philosophy of *desengaño* or disillusionment with all worldly satisfactions and pleasures of the flesh, repeatedly depicted in *memento mori* paintings by Juan Valdés Leal and other artists. Surely, the increasingly pessimistic mood and sense of national decline in seventeenth-century Spain played its part in the tone of the second volume. Whatever motivated it, the body count is much more than a numbers game in Zayas's text. Spanish 'contar' means both to count and to recount or relate a story, and it is in this sense that bodies recount as well as adding up. Not only those of women, but men's bodies as well, the latter particularly in the form of the undead. Zayas's women are haunted in life by the constant threat of a violent death and tell their tales with their dying and dead bodies in this volume; men, on the other hand, can be compelled to speak truth from the other side of the grave. But just what is this body, and how is it a channel to the truth of the subject?

Lacanian theory subverts insistent Western binaries between mind and body, body and soul, woman and man, matter and form (Barnard 2002: 15).[6] Looking again at Zayas's argument for equality of the sexes I quoted at the outset, we can see that she does not disavow the body–soul binary, but underlines its application to men as well as women. Zayas's shifting approaches to the supposedly material side of that binary are a clue to its complex composition. This material of which men and women are made is equal, she says, whether it be a compound of 'fire and mud', or 'spirits and clods', the same blood, senses, faculties, and organs through which they take effect. Where, in this continuum, does one cross from the simply material to the realm of the mental and spiritual? Lacanian theory helps explain why Zayas – and centuries of more sophisticated scientific and theological writers – found it so hard to establish that frontier.

In the Borromean knot of the Real, the Imaginary, and the Symbolic that interact in human subjectivity, the Real is the traumatic cause that escapes Imaginary order representation and Symbolic order articulation, one that reveals its existence in distorted formulations around sites of anxiety. In Paul Verhaeghe's words, 'The real of the organism functions as the cause, in the sense that it contains a primordial loss that precedes the loss in the chain of signifiers. Which loss? The loss of eternal life, which paradoxically is lost at the moment of birth [...] as a sexed being' (2002: 132). It pushes the subject to seek in vain to close the gap it leaves, and often surfaces in slips of the tongue (ibid.). Zayas left us one example in a slip of the pen between the first and second edition of her preface to the *Novelas amorosas*. After arguing that women with voracious reading habits like her own can compensate for the education denied them by men, she continues: 'Pues si esto es verdad, ¿qué razón hay para que no tengamos promptitud para *los*

---

[6] For an exploration of how some of Zayas's contemporaries, both male and female, challenged those binaries, see Bultman 2007.

hombres? Y más si todas tienen mi inclinación' ('Well if this is true, what reason is there that we should not have readiness *for men*, especially if all women have my inclination' (Zayas 1637: fol. q7r, my italics). In the second edition, that was corrected by the author herself, 'for men' is changed to 'for books', the more logical continuation of her argument. That slip shows that despite her spirited arguments for women's equality, the traumatic effect of the Real in her unconscious left by sexual difference in the patriarchal social order remains active. The masculine judge and jury that control access to the literary elite in her unconscious will still linger, twenty stories later, as a trace in her authorial farewell to readers.

What we imprecisely call the body is not an autonomous material organism; rather, the Other of language constructs the body, marking it up from the day of birth (or before, with uterine sonograms) with the declaration, 'It's a boy' or 'it's a girl'. Other chains of signifiers follow – pretty girl, strong boy, smart, difficult, black, blond, good/bad baby – so that by the time children enter the mirror stage, become aware of their separateness from the (m)Other or primary nurturer and begin to emerge as speaking subjects, their bodies have been shaped by the Other. As Verhaeghe says, 'The body we "have" exists only through the mind; it is the Other that constructs the body' (2002: 110). The child's own body image is formed not by intimate experience of the material organism, but by analogy with her perception of other human bodies and the reflection she sees in the mirror, shaped by language. Because this image forms a core of identity thus shaped in alienation by interaction of the Imaginary and Symbolic orders, however, visual and verbal images of bodies can have powerful effects, erotic, repellant, painful, or all of those effects at once, as Jacinta's dream wound in the first novella attests. Implicitly recognizing this, Laura, the protagonist of the *Fifth Tale of Love, Fuerza del amor* (*The Power of Love*) dramatizes her suffering in the flesh by comparing it to that of Prometheus in the ballad of lament she sings when her husband, Diego, is in the arms of his lover:

> Y tú, afligido Feníceo [i.e., Prometeo]
> aunque tus carnes veas
> con tal rigor comidas
> por el águila fiera;
> Y si atado al Cáucaso
> padeces, no le sientas,
> que mayor es mi daño.

> (Don't lament, afflicted Prometheus, although you see your flesh so cruelly eaten by the fierce eagle. If you suffer tied to the Caucasus, my wound is greater) (Zayas 2000: 359).

As in Laura's invocation of Prometheus and other mythical sufferers, Zayas's verbal images of tormented bodies can avail themselves of the intersubjective nature of body images to imprint the tales they tell on the empathetic reader.

Tale-telling bodies in the second volume are mostly, but not exclusively, those of women. In the *Third Tale of Disillusion,* Zayas's rewriting of Cervantes's *El curioso impertinente* (The Tale of Foolish Curiosity), God briefly resuscitates a hanged man to save the life of Roseleta's would-be seducer Juan, who has prayed to the Virgin Mary for forgiveness on his way (as he thinks) to sin; the Virgin's intervention does not save Roseleta, whose husband Pedro bleeds her to death, then marries her antagonist Angeliana, who has had affairs with both Juan and Pedro. In the *Eighth Tale of Disillusion*, when Mencía's greedy father and brother Alonso kill her to prevent her marriage to Enrique, grandson of a commoner, her undead voice and still-bleeding corpse save him from slaughter and her corpse keeps bleeding while he becomes a monk and builds a chapel in which to bury her. When the father later disinherits Alonso for also marrying against his will, Alonso beheads his wife, throws her body in a well and buries the head. When Alonso is captured and about to be executed, he has the head brought to him to beg her forgiveness before his death. In both instances, Zayas makes the miraculously preserved beauty of female flesh (a common motif of exhumed saints' remains) speak for women's innocence and condemn patriarchal greed. In both cases, however, the dictates of the greedy patriarch operate at a distance from the scene of the murder, and the ironic coda is that the disowned grandson inherits his wealth.

What the *Third Tale of Disillusion* uncannily anticipates, therefore, is Verhaeghe's Lacanian explanation (2002: 132–5) of how the sexual relationship masks a primordial discordance at the heart of human existence, the death-in-life that is inevitable in sexed reproduction. The attraction of eternal life, Zoë in classical Greek, can only be achieved by sexually undifferentiated one-celled organisms, yet the individual life, Bios, tries to return to it. For the speaking human subject, the Real loss of being operated by castration and the assumption of sexual difference, interpreted phallically through the Other of language, drives the desire to satisfy that loss in the joining of a man and woman, which masks that primal discordance. Verhaeghe concludes:

> It is during this process that the body is constructed, the body that we have (not the body that we are), clothed in an ever-secondary gender identity. The originally circular but not reciprocal relationship between life and death, between jouissance and subject, is reproduced and worked over between man and woman. (2002: 135)

Looking at the peculiar forms of undeath in two other Zayas tales will help us reveal her implicit knowledge of this masking process in operation.

Counter Reformation theology, of course, stressed constant remembering of the inevitability of death and encouraged mortification of the flesh to purify oneself by sacrificing earthly pleasures in order to secure eternal life (see Greer 2000: 254–85). The entire second volume is supposedly related during Carnestolendas (Carnival), which literally means 'taking off the flesh'. In the *Fifth Tale of Disillusion,* Zayas gives us a gruesomely graphic description of the flesh of the heroine, Inés, in a death-like rot, her blond hair turned white and matted with crawling vermin and her flesh eaten to the bone. Inés's husband, brother, and sister-in-law have kept her barely alive, walled up in a tiny space for years because, by using a magic spell, another man has repeatedly brought her in an unconscious trance into his bed. Although her beauty is restored when she is rescued and enters a convent, she remains blind, a detail most readers find unjust. As I have written elsewhere, I see this blindness as a misplaced, synecdochic punishment inflicted on the eyes of the woman whose beauty arouses desire in the eyes of others and her relatives' thirst to punish her in the flesh (2000: 274–9). That punishment also serves, I believe, to deflect the eye from the paralyzing spectacle of her death-in-life.

Lacan in *Seminar XI* separates the eye that sees from the gaze, a primary drive that is always in the field of the Other: 'the eye viewing the object is on the side of the subject, while the gaze is on the side of the object. When I look at an object, the object is always already gazing at me' (Zizek 1991: 109). Slavoj Zizek, following Lacan's analysis in 'Kant with Sade', says that in the perverse voyeurism of pornography, however, the spectator effectively occupies the position of the object, and is 'reduced to a paralyzed object-gaze' (1991: 110). Reiterated emphasis on Inés's continuing blindness in her twenty years of saintly life in a convent serves, I suggest, to undo the reader's fall into voyeuristic participation in her worm-eaten flesh. It protects *our* eyes from *her* gaze, as it lingers in the imagination.

The *Tenth Tale of Disillusion*, with which Zayas closes her *Tales of Disillusion with Love*, is the problematic story of a 'bad' woman, Florentina, who seduces her sister's husband and provokes a bloodbath that only she survives. It too contains an undead figure, the still-moaning dead body dug up in the basement of a household of loose women in the first episode. I believe that the episodic structure of Zayas's stories enables her to negotiate, by leaving unspoken the key term in the unconscious logic that links the episodes, an irresolvable tension between class loyalty to the ideology of patriarchal aristocracy and gender solidarity with the women she purports to defend. In this story, I see the key term as 'the enemy within' – the Portuguese in the Spanish monarchy, servants in the aristocratic household, and sexual desire as the resilient enemy within the body of woman (see Greer 2001). At a yet more fundamental level, the enemy within is death itself, that keeps wordlessly moaning its masked mystery in the corpse dug up in the house of pleasure. Neither the love notes nor the papal bull in its pockets have afforded it eternal life. Don Gaspar takes it as a divine warning away from that house of pleasure, but turns to pursuing Florentina, inaccessible until he finds her near death in the street, moaning even more frighteningly than the corpse in the cellar.

Zayas ends her collection by having Florentina, the surviving protagonists of other tales, and the frame-tale heroine retreat to the convent. She sends all these Imaginary bodies back to the feminine side of the sexual graph, the safe haven from death at the hands of cruel males, and the approved path to everlasting life through devotion to a Catholic masculine divinity and His perfect Mother. Yet in the last paragraph in her own authorial voice, blurring narrative levels by addressing Fabio, Jacinta's understanding rescuer in the first novella, Zayas assures him this is a happy ending and tells him he may seek out the frame-tale Lisis there 'with chaste intention' should his desire to see her continue. The danger of sexual desire may be contained, but desire for Symbolic order recognition from a masculine judge and jury is one last vestige of the Undead.

Further reading

Brownlee, Marina, 2000. *The Cultural Labyrinth of María de Zayas* (Philadelphia: University of Pennsylvania Press)

Grieve, Patricia E., 1991. 'Embroidering with Saintly Threads: María de Zayas Challenges Cervantes and the Church', *Renaissance Quarterly*, 44.1: 86–106

Kaminsky, Amy, 2001. 'María de Zayas and the Invention of a Women's Writing Community', *Revista de Estudios Hispánicos*, 35: 487–509

Montesa Peydro, Salvador, 1981. *Texto y contexto en la narrativa de María de Zayas* (Madrid: Dirección General de la Juventud y Promoción Sociocultural)

Vollendorf, Lisa, 200la. *Reclaiming the Body: María de Zayas's Early Modern Feminism*, NCSRLL, 270 (Chapel Hill: University of North Carolina Press)

10

Distinct Drama?
Female Dramatists in Golden Age Spain

ALEXANDER SAMSON

> The players themselves consist of men and women: the men are indifferent actors, but the women are very good, and become themselves far better than any ever I saw act those parts, and far handsomer than any women I saw. To say the truth, they are the only cause their plays are so much frequented.

So wrote Sir Richard Wynn of Gwydir, Charles I's groom of the bedchamber, about the Spanish *comedias* (plays) that the prince and his entourage attended regularly in Madrid, in his published account of their stay there in 1623.[1] His observation that women played women, as opposed to the boys who took female parts in Jacobean London, and his remark on their sexual attractiveness underlying the *comedia*'s popularity, reflect moral anxieties obsessively explored in the outpouring of anti-theatrical polemic in both England and Spain from the period. Warnings about the dangerous incitement to lust of women parading themselves in public, whether on stage as in Madrid or mingling freely in the crowd in London where they were not segregated as they were in the *corrales* (theatres), in the *cazuela* (lit. 'stewpot') with its jealously guarded entrance, were commonplace.[2] Women were banned for a brief time from the Spanish stage between 1596 to 1598. However, commentators such as Juan de Mariana accepted that boys in drag were a greater evil, potentially tempting spectators into 'mayor torpeza y maldad' (greater evil and obscenity).[3] The *primera dama* (leading lady) in acting

---

[1] See Wynn [1623] 1996: 100–1, quoted in Shergold 1967: 266.
[2] The standard source on these polemical debates in Spain is Cotarelo y Mori 1904. For an excellent discussion of the analogous controversies in early modern England, see Laura Levine 1994.
[3] In his *Tratado contra los juegos* (Treatise against Games/Gambling) of 1609, cited by Ivan Cañadas in his insightful consideration of female roles (2005: 45).

companies was habitually paid more than her male counterpart, who was often the manager as well, perhaps a measure of the commercial significance of actresses for the *comedia* and underlining the truth of Wynn's observation (Cañadas 2005: 47; see also McKendrick 2006). Their violation of female decorum by making public spectacles of themselves led female actors to be compared to and seen as little more than prostitutes, *rameras*. The debate about women's place in the theatre underlined how, despite the divergent staging practices in England and Spain, the figure of the unruly woman haunted both stages. A lot of research has focused on how gender was staged and represented in these contexts, where boys dressed as women, or married women played sexually available maidens, and women cross-dressed as men.[4] Although women played women in Spain, female parts were mostly written by men, in acting companies run mostly although not exclusively by men. Despite injunctions insisting that all female members of acting companies be married, and regular reports returned to the authorities on all members of companies by their managers, widowed and unattached women do appear on rolls clearly identified as *viuda* or *soltera*, widow or single (Oehrlein 1993: 219).

While considerable attention has been devoted to female voices and the roles played by women on the early modern stage, less has been written on the surviving corpus of plays by women, although there are signs of growing interest in this drama, not least in the theatrical profession.[5] Many of the plays have only become available in accessible editions comparatively recently, a great debt being owed to the work of Teresa Scott Soufas. A major subdivision of the dramatic output of women, only a tiny proportion of which is extant, is convent drama. The best-known example of this genre, which is even less regularly performed and written about than the commercial theatre discussed here (for the obvious reason that it is mostly in Latin), are the witty dialogues written by Sor Marcela de San Félix, Lope de Vega's daughter; these are extant despite her burning almost all of her poetic output on the instructions of her confessor (for her dramatic output, see San Felix 1988). A similar fate befell the most famous woman dramatist of this period, Sor Juana Inés de la Cruz, who is not included in the current

---

[4] Lope de Vega referred to this practice: 'Las damas no desdigan de su nombre, / y si mudaren de traje, sea de modo / que pueda perdonarse, porque suele / el disfraz varonil agradar mucho' (Ladies should not forsake the name and, if they do change their appearance, let it be in a way that can be forgiven, because masculine disguise is usually highly pleasing) in his *Arte nuevo de hacer comedias en este tiempo* (*New Art of Writing Plays in this Time*) ([1609] 2006: 146). For a useful summary of the controversies in Spain, see O'Connor 2000: 29–118.

[5] On *dramaturgas* see Cecilla 1998 and the section on women playwrights in Thacker 2007 (88–91).

survey since she was writing in colonial Mexico.⁶ There were many other nuns who produced drama in the Iberian Peninsula, such as María de San Alberto, Cecilia del Nacimiento, and Sor María do Ceo.⁷

Feliciana Enríquez de Guzmán, born before 1580 in Seville, wrote two classicizing dramas that sought to respect 'los preceptos antiguos' (the ancient precepts) and 'Leyes de tiempo y lugar' (unities of space and time) (Soufas 1997b: lines 3 and 5).⁸ The *Tragicomedia de los jardines y campos sabeos* (Tragicomedy of the Sabean Gardens and Lands) and its *Segunda parte* (Part Two) were first published in 1624 in Coimbra and Lisbon respectively, with a second edition of both appearing together in Lisbon in 1627, although the date of the dedication indicates that both were composed before 1619. She was married for the first time at the age of thirty-six to a widower, Cristóbal Ponce Solís y Farfán, who died a few years later, leaving the *patronazgo* of a chaplaincy to her.⁹ Within four months of his death she was married again, to Francisco de León Garavito, to whom she dedicated the second play. Very little is known about her life. As a result, a reference in Lope de Vega's *Laurel de Apolo* (Apollo's Laurel Wreath), to a Feliciana who disguises herself as a man in order to study at the University of Salamanca and falls in love with a fellow student, has been taken entirely fancifully as referring to Enríquez de Guzmán. Nevertheless, the dates of her plays and her forthright rejection of Lope's *comedia nueva* (commercial plays), and poets who 'han pagado tanto tiempo torpe y venalmente al ignorante y bárbaro vulgo por tener treguas y paz con él' (have paid court for too long dishonourably and out of greed to the ignorant, barbarous multitude, in order to enjoy a truce and be at peace with them) (Soufas 1997b: 229), places them firmly in the context of the literary storm between the *lopistas* and neo-Aristotelians.¹⁰

Her first play deals with the betrothal of Clarisel, a Spartan prince, and Beloribo, king of Macedon, to the princesses Belidiana and Clarinda. *Segunda parte* takes the story forward to their eventual marriages to two different

---

⁶ On religious women's writing, see Surtz 1995. Plays by Sor Marcela and Sor Francisca de Santa Teresa have been partially published in Doménech Rico 1996.

⁷ See Arenal and Schlau 1989a, San Alberto 1998, Nacimiento 1970, and the forthcoming edition of María do Ceo by Valerie Hegstrom. I would like to thank Valerie for her indispensable help with bibliography on these lesser-known figures.

⁸ For background on Enríquez de Guzmán, see Louis Celestino Pérez 1988: 1–30 and Soufas 1997b: 225–8. See also the recent study by María Reina Ruíz (2005). All quotations from the plays are taken from Soufas 1997b: 225–71.

⁹ The term *patronazgo* refers to inherited income from entailed lands.

¹⁰ For background on this, see Porqueras Mayo 1972. Enríquez de Guzmán's critique of Lopean drama continues in the 'Carta ejecutoria' (Letter Patent) in which she orders that 'todas las comedias guardasen de aquí adelante la traza y arte, leyes y preceptos de la dicha tragicomedia [*Segunda parte*]' (from now on all plays must observe the form and method, law and precedents found in this tragicomedy) (Soufas 1997b: 268).

princesses, Maya of Spain and Hesperia of Italy. A profusion of mythical, mythological, and historical figures intermingle on stage in what is a highly static and undramatic demonstration of poetic virtuosity. Even the supposedly comic *entreactos* (interludes) rely heavily on verse narration of plot and complex, allusive, and erudite witticism rather than action, dialogue, and dramatic irony. Despite internal references that might suggest performance, such as stage directions and a prologue opening 'En este sitio, señores' (In this place, gentlemen), the unwieldy number of characters, uncertain plot, and long set pieces (the second act of *Segunda parte* is entirely occupied by Adonis, Venus, Vulcan, and some cupids) suggest that, if anything, these texts were written to be read as poetry rather than performed dramatically for an exclusive palace or courtly audience.

Born around 1600, possibly in Granada, Ana Caro Mallén de Soto spent much of her life in Seville. She won prizes for her poetry, some of it still extant, which ranged from a *romance noticiero* (newsbearing ballad) to *relaciones de fiestas* (festival texts), *loas* (playlets), and a get-well sonnet for Doña Inés Jacinta Manrique de Lara. Dubbed the tenth muse of Seville by her contemporary Luis Vélez de Guevara in his picaresque novel *El diablo cojuelo* (*The Lame Devil*), she was a friend of María de Zayas, a fact alluded to by Alonso de Castillo Solórzano in his novel *La guarduña de Sevilla y anzuelo de las bolsas* (The Seville Thief and Pickpocket) of 1642 and attested to by the eulogistic *décimas* (verses) she contributed to the preface of Zayas's *Novelas amorosas y ejemplares* (1637) (*Exemplary Tales of Love*), as well as by allusions in the stories themselves: 'los teatros la han hecho estimada' (the theatres have made her famous) (Zayas 1948: 230).[11] There is no direct evidence that the plays by any other of these women were actually performed. However, Lope de Vega and Juan Pérez de Montalbán were both familiar with dramatic texts by Caro and Zayas, and Rodrigo Caro in his *Varones ilustres de Sevilla* (Illustrious Men of Seville) described her as 'insigne poetisa que ha hecho muchas comedias, representadas en Sevilla y Madrid' (distinguished poet who has written many plays, which have been performed in Seville and Madrid) (quoted in Soufas 1997a: 2). Although her *autos sacramentales* (religious plays based on the sacraments) are no longer extant, Ana Caro received payments of 300 *reales* on two occasions for pieces written for Seville's Corpus Christi celebrations, *La puerta de la Macarena* (The Macarena Gate) in 1641 and another of 1645 whose title has not survived.[12] She wrote another *auto sacramental* in 1642 entitled *La cuesta de Castilleja* (The Hill of Castilleja) (Soufas 1997a: ix and xii).

---

[11] Biographical information on Ana Caro, and on most of the other women cited here, can be found in Levine et al. 1993 (see especially Kaminsky 1993), and Zayas 2000: 154ff. Also worth consulting is de Armas 1986: 66–7.

[12] The *real* was a silver coin: 12 *reales* = 1 gold ducat.

The earliest edition of Caro's *El conde Partinuplés* (Count Parthenopeus), written in the late 1630s or early 1640s, is in a printed anthology of 1653, the *Laurel de comedias: quarta parte de diferentes autores* (Laurel Wreath of Plays: Part Four by Different Authors).[13] This play was depicted by her contemporary Juan de Matos Fragoso in *La corsaria catalana* (The Catalan Corsair) in the hands of a theatre manager (Soufas 1997b: 133). Ana Caro stands out as perhaps the only female dramatist to write for the commercial stage who did have a professional outlet for her work.[14]

The plot of *El conde Partinuplés* derives from a French chivalric novel about Partonopleus de Blois which was translated into Spanish in 1497.[15] It dramatizes the dilemma faced by Rosaura, Empress of Constantinople, when her subjects demand she marry to avoid 'ver tu corona / dividida en varios bandos / y arriesgada tu persona' (seeing your rule divided by factional struggle and your person at risk) (Soufas 1997b: 137–62, lines 78–80), given the prophecy of her father on his deathbed that:

> un hombre ¡fiero daño!
> le trataría a mi verdad engaño,
> rompiéndome la fe por él jurada,
> y que si en este tiempo reparada
> no fuese por mi industria esta corona,
> riesgo corrían ella y mi persona. (lines 177–82)

> ([A] man, oh fearsome ill!, would repay my truthfulness with deceit, breaking his sworn promise, and if this damage were not repaired by my efforts in time the crown and even my life will hang in the balance.)

The competing duties of married female monarchs had been explored in theoretical works throughout the previous century, following the reigns of a series of women from Queen Isabel (1474–1504) to her granddaughter Mary Tudor (1553–58) and her half-sister Elizabeth I (1558–1603), as well as a series of female regencies from Margaret of Hungary and Mary of Guise to Catherine de Medici. In a treatise published as Elizabeth's reign began, John Aylmer speculated whether if a queen's husband 'breake any lawe, if it were capitall, she myghte strike with the sword, and yet be a wife good inought for the dutye that she oweth to him', asserting that, on the other hand, 'if for

---

[13] A seventeenth-century copy in the Biblioteca Nacional, MS 17189, is believed by Alberto Blecua to postdate the printed text, which is generally taken to be the *princeps* (see Soufas 1997b: 134–5). See also Lola Luna's edition (Caro 1993a).

[14] She is characterized as an 'escritor de oficio' (professional author) by Luna (1995: 11–26).

[15] For recent criticism on the play see Soufas 1997a: 46–58, Carrión 1999, de Armas 1999, and Whitenack 1999.

her wedlocke dutie to him, she will neglect the commonwealth: Then is she a loving wife to him and an euel head to the countrye'.[16] Rosaura, although loath to submit to any man:

> ¿qué gusto puedo tener
> cuando ¡ay Dios! me considero
> esclava, siendo señora,
> y vasalla, siendo dueño? (lines 285–8)
>
> (what pleasure, oh God!, can there be in envisaging myself a slave, when I am a mistress, a vassal being used to command?)

determines to try to ensure her safety by spying on potential suitors, availing herself of her cousin Aldora's magical powers.

This element of the play requires heavy use of stage machinery, painted backdrops, and the discovery space, as characters are mysteriously transported from one place to another, attacked by a lion, invisibly served a banquet, flown through the air, or appear on stage on horseback. Rosaura's preference for Partinuplés, the heir to the French throne, needs to overcome two major obstacles. The first of these is what inspires her initial choice: his engagement to Lisbella, who besieges Constantinople in order to reclaim the Count, but renounces her love for him and accepts her rival's victory. The second obstacle, a reworking of the Cupid and Psyche myth, departs from Partinuplés's peeping at Rosaura while she is asleep, disregarding her insistence on keeping her identity a secret, and ironically reversing the gaze that has allowed Rosaura to spy on him while he hunts in the royal party at the beginning. She condemns him to death, but is obliged to accept him as her husband when, having been rescued by Aldora, he emerges as the victor of a tournament organized to decide who will win her hand. In a final twist the Count renounces the Kingdom of France for love of Rosaura, and bestows it on Lisbella.

Caro's other extant play is a *comedia de capa y espada* (cape and sword play), *Valor, agravio y mujer* (Courage, Offence, and Woman) (late 1630s), which survives in one contemporary manuscript copy.[17] Its complexities and ambivalence are signalled from the opening scene, when the villain of the piece, the seducer and abandoner of Leonor, Don Juan de Córdoba, rescues the Countess Estela and her cousin Lisarda from armed bandits who, not content with stealing their jewels, are about to rape them. His chivalrous

---

[16] *An Harborowe for Faithful and Trewe Subjectes Agaynst the late blowne Blaste, concerninge the Gouernment of Wemen* (Strasburg: 26th April, 1559), sig. Giii.

[17] Biblioteca Nacional, MS 6620. See the edition by Luna (Caro 1993b). Recent criticism on this play includes Soufas 1991, Williamsen 1992, Maroto Camino 1996, Gorfkle 1996, Soufas 1997a: 116–25, and Mujica 1999.

bluster, '¿a qué aspiran? / ¿A experimentar rigores / de mi brazo y de mi espada?' (what are you hoping to get? A feel of the force of my arm and sword?) (Soufas 1997b: 163–94, lines 159–61) is greeted with the bandit leader's underwhelmed '¡Dispara, Rufino!' (Shoot him, Rufino!) (line 168). The morality of masters and servants reflects and parallels each other in the subplot, in which Juan's servant Tomillo attempts to rape Flora, but is thwarted by her spiking his chocolate drink and despoiling him of his purse. Both Juan and Tomillo are *burladores burlados* (tricksters tricked)

Much has been written about the ways in which the transvestitism of Leonor, her transformation into Leonardo, connotes an essentialist shift in her identity:

> En este traje podré
> cobrar mi perdido honor [...]
> Engañaste si imaginas,
> Ribete, que soy mujer;
> mi agravio mudó mi ser. (lines 464–5, 508–10)
>
> (dressed like this I will be able to recover my lost honour [...]
> You deceive yourself if you think, Ribete, that I am just a woman; my injury changed my very being.)

She has been transformed into a 'nueva amazona' (latterday amazon) (line 501) or, as Ribete suggests, 'el nuevo traje te ha dado / alientos' (the new outfit has given you balls) (lines 506–7). However, the internal logic of the play underlines the ambiguity of her transformation and its relationship with dress: 'Yo soy quien soy!' (I am who I am) (line 507). Some of the best comedy in the play depends not on her occupation of an androgynous space as a *mujer varonil* (virago), but on an ambivalent, shifting, gender identification, as for example when she provokes Juan into a swordfight, but switches sides when Ludovico joins the combat against him. The homoerotic interest of Estela in

> este Adonis galán,
> este fénix español,
> este Ganimedes nuevo,
> este dios de amor, mancebo,
> este Narciso, este sol (Soufas 1997b: lines 915–19)
>
> (this elegant Adonis, this Spanish phoenix, this latterday Ganymede, this love god, cherub, this Narcissus, this sun)

despite her rescuer Juan's earnest courtship, is another example of the way that Caro 'not only meant Leonor's male attire to be read as a revelation rather than a cover-up, but also that its ending satisfied her beyond the exigencies of convention' (Rhodes 2005: 310). An ironic intertextual reference by Ana Caro to herself as playwright appears in a dialogue between Leonor's co-conspirator Ribete, who comments 'quieren poetizar / las mujeres, y se atreven / a hacer comedias ya' (women want to write poetry and nowadays even dare to come out with plays) (lines 1168–70), and the *gracioso* (clown / comic servant) Tomillo, who retorts: '¡Válgame Dios! Pues, ¿no fuera / mejor coser e hilar? / ¡Mujeres poetas!' (God forbid! Is it surely not better for them to sew and spin? Women poets!) (lines 1171–3).[18] The fact that it is Ribete, 'elegido por mi amigo' (chosen to be my friend) (line 537), who makes this comment underlines the metafictional irony, since he is instrumental in his cross-dressed mistress's plot to avenge herself.

Discussions about the proto-feminism or otherwise of these plays and playwrights, with the implicit problems this presents of definition and anachronism, do not detract from the fact that they contain original and unusual explorations of female agency, constantly pushing against the limits of *comedia* conventions, by redeploying devices like cross-dressing and deforming honour revenge plots, and in their very self-consciousness as literary products by women. The argument advanced that *Valor, agravio y mujer*'s closure is a conservative reassertion of patriarchal values with Leonor's marriage to her craven seducer Don Juan and his weak 'Te adoraré' (I will adore you) (line 2724) (see Stroud 1986: 610), has been countered by critics such as Rhodes, who argues that reading it through 'the lens of justiciary poetics, *Valor* becomes a comedy in which Caro advances a moral principle: the verbal articulation of a promise has enduring value because noble integrity guarantees the contractual validity of performative speech' (2005: 312). The double standard of the honour code is similarly and pointedly exposed by Leonor's brother Fernando who, despite Juan's boasts about his amorous exploits, is happy to befriend him – until he discovers that the woman who has been dishonoured is his own sister: 'mal pagaste de mi pecho / las finezas' (you have betrayed the loving ministrations of my heart) (lines 2643–4). Initially Fernando refers to Juan's 'heroico valor' (heroic worth) (line 444), but in the final act he joins Estela and others condemning Juan as 'mal caballero, ingrato' (dishonourable and ungrateful) (line 2602).

The title's incongruous conjunction of contradictory categories, 'valor' (value, worth, valour, courage, or lustre), 'agravio' (offence, injury), and 'mujer' (woman), is explored in the text through a series of subtle shifts in the meaning of the first term. Leonor describes her revenge being achieved through her 'valor' ('courage' or 'worth', line 555). It is ironically applied a few lines later to Juan's enjoyment of the Infanta's favour for his 'bizarro valor' ('dashing gallantry', line 581). Ludovico honours him for his 'gran

---

[18] Discussed by Cañadas (2005: 49), who describes the play as first-rate.

valor' ('great worth', line 762). Leonor as Leonardo underlines 'el valor de mi sangre' ('the illustriousness of my family', line 660) and praises her brother's famed 'valor' ('generosity', line 746). Her plea that the world 'ha de ver en mi valor' ('must see some worth or value in me', line 866) is partially fulfilled in Juan's recognition of Leonardo's 'valor tan grande' ('great worthiness', line 1449), and finally brought about with Leonor's explanatory codicil, 'tanto puede en un pecho / valor, agravio y mujer' ('that is what courage, offence and woman are capable of achieving in one breast', lines 2721–2).

The play is constantly concerned with destabilizing an audience's ability to read value(s), in the sense of something's relative worth as opposed to its inherent value. Legal records show that women did have legal recourse if they were seduced with promises of marriage or 'estupro bajo palabra de matrimonio'. However, sexual behaviour in Spain conformed precisely neither to Catholic doctrine that of course condemned such deceit, nor to the honour code that responded by annihilating the offending stain (see Dyer 2003: 441). Whether or not the justice narrative in the play draws a morally flawed Don Juan back to the strictures of honourable behaviour, it presents a markedly different vision of women making unexpected sexual choices, washing their lost honour in blood, or offering men a way out of dishonour through marriage.

María de Zayas's work *La traición en la amistad* (*Friendship's Betrayal*) has generated the greatest enthusiasm perhaps of any of the works considered here, especially in the theatre.[19] A recent translation and bilingual edition (Zayas 1999) have been followed by two productions in America: at the Spanish Drama Festival 'El Chamizal Siglo de Oro', directed by David Pasto in 2003; and by the Washington Women in Theatre, directed by Karen Berman in 2006.[20] Another production by the Compañía Nacional de Teatro Clásico (National Theatre) toured Spain in 2004 and there have been two further editions (Zayas 2003, 2006). One of its central themes is female friendship and solidarity and its betrayal.[21] Just over half the dialogue in the play is delivered by female characters, and its settings are dominated by the interior, domestic, spaces they inhabit. The opening scene shows Marcia confessing her sudden love for Liseo to her friend Fenisa, who on seeing his portrait, falls for him as well and then in the soliloquy that follows asks:

---

[19] For a biographical sketch of Zayas, see Margaret Greer's essay in this volume.
[20] For more information on the theatre productions, see López-Mayhew 2004, Mujica 2008, and Voros 2008.
[21] On the theme of female friendship in Zayas, see Gorfkle 1998, Wyszynski 1998, Maroto Camino 1999, and Vollendorf 2005.

> ¿Soy amiga? Sí. Pues, ¿cómo
> pretendo contra mi amiga
> tan alevosa traición? (Soufas 1997b: 277–308, lines 163–65)
>
> (Am I her friend? Yes. Then, how could I so maliciously betray her?)

In contrast, as soon as Marcia learns from Laura that Liseo has revealed unwittingly in his sleep that 'Marcia y Fenisa me adoran' (Marcia and Fenisa adore me) (line 789), she takes her side and sets about avenging the wrong done to her new friend Laura and herself by her confidante Fenisa.

Fenisa has trysts with Liseo, Juan, and Lauro, and confides in her servant Lucía that: 'Diez amantes me adoran, y yo a todos / los adoro, los quiero, los estimo / y todos juntos en mi alma caben' (Ten lovers adore me and I adore, love, and cherish them all, my soul has enough room for all of them) (lines 1518–20).[22] This remark immediately precedes her attempted seduction of Marcia's long-suffering admirer Gerardo, the only person to actually spurn her advances. In fact some critics have argued that Fenisa is a kind of female Don Juan and that the play represents Zayas's reworking of Tirso's version of the legend (Larson 1994: 129–38). She is also a female counterpoint to Liseo, who courts her, and Marcia, and the abandoned Laura. Lucía asks Fenisa, '¿Pues cómo puede ser que a todos / quieras?' (How is possible for you to love all of them?) (lines 2388–9), to which she answers:

> a todos cuantos quiero yo me inclino [...]
> a los feos, hermosos, mozos, viejos,
> ricos, pobres, sólo por ser hombres.
>
> (I favour all those who I love [...] ugly, beautiful, young, old, rich, poor, just because they are men.) (lines 2392, 2394–5).

In one of her soliloquies, she challenges the audience's moral condemnation of her: 'amando mucho, mucho siento; / no es razón que tu audiencia me condene' (loving many, I feel deeply, it is not fair that your audience condemns me) (lines 2367–8), and she cries when she learns that Juan has gone back to Belisa and Liseo has left her for Marcia. Her altercation with Belisa over Juan, in the Pasto staging a scene transformed from 'a cat fight, into a sword fight', is another indication of the depth and complexities written into this part (Larson 2008: 88). The *gracioso* León comments on the fight: 'si no viniera, / ellas, con hermoso brío, / se asían de las melenas' (if she [Marcia] hadn't come, they'd have been pulling each other's hair with enticing vigour) (lines 2790–2).

---

[22] As Sharon Voros puts it: 'Fenisa's brazen overtures to men have attracted the lion's share of scholarly commentary' (2008: 230).

By the end of the play Marcia and Belisa have tricked Liseo into signing himself over in marriage to Laura. León's misogynistic interventions, often undercutting his master Liseo's inflated glosses on his lust, provide some of the funniest moments in the play. His subsequent sufferings at the hands of a livid Fenisa, and his upstaging by Belisa, might suggest that Zayas is providing a kind of poetic justice for the women in the audience. Lucía addresses the female part of the audience directly to question Fenisa's capacity to love so many: 'digan, señoras, ¿no miente / en decir que quiere a todos?' (What do you think, ladies? Is she not lying when she says she loves them all?) (lines 2481–2). Liseo insists as he brings the play to a close that: 'no ha un año que en la corte / sucedió como se cuenta' (not a year ago exactly the same thing as you have heard happened at court) (lines 2909–10). While León, in one of the play's most subversive moments, offers Fenisa up to any interested male spectators:

> Señores míos, Fenisa,
> cual ven, sin amantes queda;
> si alguno la quiere, avise
> para que su casa sepa. (lines 2911–14)
>
> (Gentlemen, Fenisa, who you see here, is left without a lover, if anyone wants her, let us know so we can give you her address.)

This metatheatrical collapsing of the distance between the moral, gendered worlds of the stage and audience holds the mirror up to their own responses, being simultaneously comic, degrading, liberating, and provocative.

Fenisa's eventual exclusion by the other women could be read as the punishment for her 'traición en la amistad', but as each of them pairs up with a man guilty of exactly the same fickle, capricious, refusal to choose one partner, a more radical reading might suggest that it is Fenisa's friendship and female solidarity that has been betrayed. As in Ana Caro's *Valor, agravio y mujer*, female friendship is intertwined with eroticism and power. Marcia's interest in 'hermosura' (beauty) is apparent when she tells Laura 'los ojos / me tienen enamorada' (your eyes have made me fall in love with you) (lines 909–10), exclaiming when Laura fully unveils, 'Hermosa sois' (You're beautiful) (line 915). And Belisa continues even more suggestively:

> No hay más bien
> que ver cuando viendo estoy
> tal belleza: el cielo os dé
> la ventura cual la cara;
> si hombre fuera, yo empleara
> en vuestra afición mi fe. (lines 915–20)

(There is no greater joy than to look at your beauty, let heaven give you as much luck as with your face. If I were a man I would worship only you.)

Zayas won renown in the literary academies of the day for her poetry, was known as the Spanish Boccaccio for her *novelas*, and like her friend Ana Caro she was dubbed the tenth muse. The critical attention her work has received is a fair reflection of its importance.[23]

Leonor de la Cueva y Silva's *La firmeza en la ausencia* (Constancy in Absence) is a representative, well-wrought kingship play about a *galán* (courtier), Juan, who finds himself in competition with his king, Filiberto, for the love of Armesinda. The king's disorderly passions lead him to claim tyrannically to his sister that his person 'no está sujeto a ley' (is not subject to law) (Soufas 1997b: 198–224, line 511), except 'La del gusto' (that of his own pleasure) (line 513). The play dramatizes Franco-Spanish rivalry, with Juan, it has been suggested, being loosely modelled on the Gran Capitán, Gonzalo Fernández de Córdoba, and dispatched to repel a French invasion of Naples (an allusion to the battle of Garigliano in 1503), in the hope of his death. Armesinda's awareness of the evanescent nature of reputation is underlined by her claim that the letter from her lover, 'en seis años de amor / es el primero' (in six years of love it is the first) (lines 381–2), something they have agreed so as not 'perder honra y fama' (not to lose integrity and reputation) (line 391). At the king's instigation, Juan's friend Carlos tells Armesinda, first, that he has married another woman, then, that he is dead. Neither stratagem avails in overcoming her constancy, as she weighs up, in a series of moving soliloquies, the options left to her of entering a convent or committing suicide, and anatomizes the pathological nature of male jealousy and desire. The play underlines her stoic resistance to Filiberto's cajoling, threats, and deceptions, demonstrating that fickleness, far from being a typically female failing,

> Mal ha dicho quien ha dicho
> que la mudanza se engendra
> solamente en las mujeres,
> por su femenil flaqueza (lines 1170–3)

(He was wrong who said that changeability is bred only in women, as a result of their female weaknesses)

is in fact symptomatic of men: 'tan varia naturaleza / como en el hombre se ve' (just such a variable nature as is to be seen in men) (lines 1164–5). One

---

[23] There is now an extensive secondary bibliography on the play: see Zayas 1999, 2003, 2006.

of the most interesting readings of the play suggests that Armesinda's resistance relies on 'her assumption of the courtly role of faithful but unrequited lover caught in the suspended state of desire', a strategy that renders her resistant to the material realm and absent from physical desire by occupying a male subject position (Soufas 2000: 147; see also Soufas 1997a: 59–69 and Voros 1997).

Leonor de la Cueva probably deserves to be better known, not just for this play, her one surviving excursion into drama, but also for her poetry, preserved in a manuscript miscellany, probably her own, copied alongside work by Cervantes, Lope, Góngora, and Juan de Salinas. She was born in 1611 in Medina del Campo into the minor nobility and, it used to be thought, remained unmarried until her death in 1705 at the age of ninety-four (Levine et al.1993: 125–30; Soufas 1997b: 195–7). As a result of the recent discovery by Sharon Voros of her last will and testament and other documents, we now know, as well as the date of her birth, that she was married to Baltasar Blázquez de Frías; we can also identify the contents of her personal library.[24] Two of her brothers were soldiers, while another became a canon in the city. Her uncle was the poet Francisco de la Cueva y Silva. The manuscript of her play, MS 17234 of the Biblioteca Nacional, originally belonged to the Dukes of Osuna.

The most prolific among these playwrights was Ángela de Azevedo. Born in Lisbon, she moved to Madrid with her parents, who were in royal service, and became a lady-in-waiting to Isabel de Borbón, Philip IV's queen from 1621 until 1644. She was married, but took the veil after her husband's death and entered a Benedictine convent with her only daughter (see Soufas 1997b: 1–3). Her three plays all survive in printed copies. *Dicha y desdicha del juego y devoción de la Virgen* (Fortune and Misfortune at Cards and Devotion to the Virgin) is the story of two pious but poor young nobles, Felisardo and María, and how devotion to a shrine to the Virgin enables them to overcome material and spiritual obstacles to their happiness and prosperity. The play comments on the changing relationship between social status and wealth, the immorality of the marriage market, and how economic problems in Spain were promoting gambling and the bargaining of young women for financial advantage.[25] *La margarita del Tajo* (The Pearl of the Tagus) is a *comedia de santos* (saints' play) based on hagiographical tradition and ballads about the fourth-century Portuguese martyr Santa Iria (St Irene). It depicts Irene's struggle to cling on to her virtue in the face of pursuit by

---

[24] See Voros 2009 for an analysis of the library and new documentary information. I would like to express my gratitude to Sharon for sharing this material with me.

[25] On this play see Soufas 1997a: 73–90 and de Armas 2003. More generally on Azevedo, see Ferrer Valls 2006 and Gascón 2006: 127–44.

the married nobleman Britaldo and the lascivious monk Remigio (see Soufas 1997a: 90–104). *El muerto disimulado* (Playing Dead) is a deliciously witty *comedia de enredo* (love comedy) involving a pair of cross-dressed siblings. The sister Lisarda disguises herself as a man in order to seek out and kill her brother's murderer. Meanwhile, her brother, Clarindo, who has been miraculously restored to life, disguises himself as a woman in order to test Jacinta's fidelity and to spy on his friend and suspected assassin, Álvaro. The author comments on the incredibility and complexity of her plot through Lisarda, '¿En qué comedia se han visto / más extrañas novedades / ni enredos más excesivos?' (In what play have you ever seen more strange novelties and excessive twists and turns in the plot?) (lines 2863–5), and later through the gracioso Papagayo: '¿qué diablo de poeta / maquinó tantos delirios?' (what devil-poet came up with these delirious ragings?) (lines 3128–9).[26]

The dramatists discussed here are only a selection of the women who wrote plays in early modern Spain. A number of other dramatists' works still languish in relative obscurity: Bernarda Ferreira de la Cerda, *Cazador del cielo* (Heavenly Huntsman); Sor Maria do Ceo, *Preguntarlo a las estrellas* (Ask the Stars), *En la más oscura noche* (In the Darkest Night) and *En la cura va la flecha* (Healing Arrow), and several *autos sacramentales*, including *Mayor fineza de amor* (The Greatest Love Compliment), *Amor y fe* (Love and Faith); María Egual, *Los prodigios de Tesalia* (The Thessalian Prodigies) and *Triunfos de amor en el aire* (Triumphs of Love in the Air); and Juana Teodora de Sousa, *El gran prodigio de España, y lealtad de un amigo* (Spain's Greatest Prodigy and the Loyalty of a Friend).[27] In this group of survivals, a number of works possess real distinction, from Ana Caro's plays about women subverting partriarchal norms and transcending their status as objects of sexual exchange to María de Zayas's explorations of the corollary of homosocial friendships among women. Their ironic inversions and reversals of *comedia nueva* and *drama de honor* (honour play) conventions not only function as commentaries on their own place on the stage as female dramatists, but also point up the limits of male-centred dramas both

---

[26] For some recent material on this play, see Stoll 1999, Maroto Camino 2001, Múzquiz-Guerreiro 2005, Gascón 2006: 83–97, and Hegstrom 2007.

[27] Soufas (1997a: 169), and see Simón Palmer 1992, a catalogue of women's writing in the Biblioteca Nacional. There are other dramatists about whom even less is known, such as Mariana de Carvajal, Isabel Señorina de Silva, Beatriz de Sousa, and Paula Vicente. For a complete list see Hegstrom and Williamsen 1999: 319–24, Appendix I. There is also a useful survey by Doménech Rico 1997 and another short introduction by Hegstrom and Stoll 2002: 112–15. For a complete account of women's writing in early modern Spain, see Mujica 2004; on women as readers/writers, see Luna 1996.

on and off the stage. While mothers are generally absent from male-authored *comedias*, in these plays there is a corresponding lack of fathers.

It is difficult to generalize about what makes the material produced by these *dramaturgas* distinct from that of their male contemporaries.[28] However, they focus more profoundly on female friendship, offering more nuanced explorations of women's roles, granting them agency in driving the plot rather than acting as mere vehicles for male conflict, and demonstrating a sustained interest in self-fashioning, the transformative possibilities of speech, and identity (see Larson 2000). There is a social asymmetry involved in comparing this corpus with the rest of Golden Age drama, since all of the women considered here are of noble background. This is why they were educated enough to be able to compete with writers like Lope and Alarcón and others, whose origins were considerably more modest and whose impetus to write for the theatre was financial as well as artistic. It is nevertheless surprising that they chose to write drama rather than confining themselves to the more acceptably aristocratic medium of manuscript poetry.

Despite anxieties about female decorum and an ongoing feminist / antifeminist strand in humanist writing, women dramatists wrote self-confident, original, and subversive plays in early modern Spain. It is hard not to want to imagine how seventeenth-century audiences might have responded to León's invitation at the end of *La traición en la amistad* for any man present to shout out if he wanted Fenisa's address, a brilliantly comic and ironic moment, crossing the boundary between actors and audience, and playing on the centrality of women to the *comedia* observed by Sir Richard Wynn. Much work remains to be done in making silenced female dramatists from the early modern period speak again.

Further reading

Doménech Rico, Fernando, 1997. 'Autoras en el teatro español: siglos XVI-XVIII', in *Autoras en la historia del teatro español (1500–1994)*, ed. Juan Antonio Hormigón, 2 vols (Madrid: ADE), I, pp. 391–604

Hegstrom Oakey, Valerie, and Amy Williamsen (eds), 1999. *Engendering the Early Modern Stage: Women Playwrights in the Spanish Empire* (New Orleans, LA: UP of the South)

Serrano y Sanz, Manuel, [1901] 1975. *Apuntes para una biblioteca de escritoras españolas desde el año 1401 hasta 1833*, 2 vols, BAE, 268–71, 2nd edn (Madrid: Atlas)

---

[28] See Voros 2000 for an attempt to discover whether their use of terms such as *ingenio* (wit) is different.

Soufas, Teresa Scott, 1997a. *Dramas of Distinction: A Study of Plays by Golden Age Women* (Lexington: UP of Kentucky)
——, 1997b. *Women's Acts: Plays by Women Dramatists of Spain's Golden Age* (Lexington: UP of Kentucky)

# PART II: FROM THE EIGHTEENTH TO THE TWENTY-FIRST CENTURY

11

Conversations from a Distance: Spanish and French Eighteenth-Century Women Writers

MÓNICA BOLUFER

The year 1797 saw the publication in Spanish of *Conversaciones de Emilia*, a translation of Louise d'Épinay's *Conversations d'Émilie* which had appeared in Leipzig in 1774 and in Paris in 1775 (see Épinay 1797 and 1996). The Spanish translator, Ana Muñoz, is an unknown woman for whom we have no biographical data and no references concerning other literary works. Her presence in the text is discreet: although her name appears on the cover together with that of the author, she did not write a foreword of her own, as was customary at the time, nor did she make additions to the work in the form of interpolated passages or explanatory notes. Despite this, her decision to provide the publisher with a translated work rather than an original text and to choose a pedagogical treatise by a famous French woman writer is significant with regard to the strategies developed by Spanish women writers in the eighteenth century. Their choices may be seen as a kind of conversation between translator and author, in this case only implicit but adopting more explicit forms in other cases of foreign women writers translated by women of letters in Spain.

In the course of the eighteenth century an increasing number of women decided to express their thoughts in writing, at a time when printed matter was circulating more widely and having an ever greater influence on public opinion (see Serrano y Sanz [1901] 1975, Bolufer 1998, ch. 7, Palacios 2002, López-Cordón 2005, García Garrosa 2007). In view of the modest parameters of the Spanish publishing market and the shortcomings in women's education, it is not surprising that the number of those who did so was much smaller than in England or France, as also was the total number of writers and works published. However, of the approximately 2,900 authors of both sexes about 200 were women.[1] This was a significantly greater number than in

---

[1] Francisco Aguilar Piñal offers a complete catalogue of manuscript and printed works written in Spain in the eighteenth century (1981–2000).

previous centuries, though the fact that many of those women were the authors of only one or very few works shows their difficulties in establishing a literary career.

What was a 'woman writer' in that period? She could not, of course, be identified as a professional, nor could the male writer, at a time when it was almost impossible to make a living from writing in Spain (Álvarez Barrientos 2006). In any case, the condition of woman writer did imply, as for her male counterpart, a certain desire that her works should reach a wider audience, either in semi-public form, such as the circulation of manuscripts in select circles or performance in private theatres, or through the printed word. Who were they? First of all there were women belonging to religious orders, who had made up the majority of women writers in the sixteenth and seventeenth centuries and still represented over a third of the total in the eighteenth. They were followed by noblewomen, often members of the court aristocracy, who used to combine their own writing with patronage of artists and writers or running salons (*tertulias*). But there was also an increasing number of women from the middle class, belonging to the commercial bourgeoisie or the world of families in the liberal and bureaucratic professions.

With few exceptions, Spanish women writers in the eighteenth century cultivated all the genres, themes, and literary forms characteristic of the age, ranging from essays on pedagogical or moral themes to plays, poetry (in all forms), and, more rarely, novels. A new feature in that century is the fact that many of those women translated foreign works, an increasingly frequent activity and one that found growing favour among the public. The second half of the eighteenth century and the first decades of the nineteenth were a boom time for translations, encouraged by the multiplication of cultural relations with other countries, growing interest in what was happening abroad, greater access to the learning of foreign languages, the increase in the instruments available (such as grammars and dictionaries) and the general development of publishing and reading (Donaire and Lafarga 1991, Lafarga 1999). Over 2,100 publications of translated works appeared between 1750 and 1808, mostly taken from French (55%), followed at a considerable distance by Italian (18.9%) and Latin (16.4%), with a much smaller presence of other languages, such as English (3.74%), Portuguese (2.49%), or Greek (1.54%). French also played an important part as an intermediary language for texts written in other languages, which were generally translated from versions in French.

In the eighteenth century, translation had a special significance as a cultural and publishing practice. It was used by the Spanish enlightened elites to express and strengthen their links with the European culture of the Enlightenment, mainly (but not solely) French, as part of an international community which shared similar moral and social values and aesthetic and literary tastes. For the publishers, translating was a way of responding to the demand of an expanding market, particularly in the case of much sought-after new genres, such as the periodical press or the sentimental novel. For the translators it was a source of income, it enabled them to present themselves as being abreast of new intellectual trends and it gave them a way of expressing their ideas by their choice of text and the alterations they made to it.

Among those who devoted themselves to this activity there was a considerable number of women, a new phenomenon satirically portrayed by José Vargas Ponce in his *Proclama de un solterón: a las que aspiran a su mano* (A Bachelor's Declaration to Ladies Who Seek His Hand) (1827): 'Otrosí, traductoras abrenuncio / Harto habla una mujer sin diccionario' (Furthermore, I renounce women translators, / A woman talks quite enough without a dictionary).[2] With their versions women translators helped to connect Spanish culture to the trends of thought and aesthetic sensibilities of European literature. Jansenist religiosity (Letourneux, translated by the Countess of Montijo), pedagogical and moral concerns (Rollin, by Catalina Caso; Vicessimus Knox, by Josefa Amar), philosophical reflection (Zanotti and Condillac, by Josefa de Alvarado, Marchioness of Espeja), neoclassical drama (Racine and Voltaire, in translations by Margarita Hickey), the philosophical novel (Mme de Graffigny, by María Romero; Samuel Johnson, by Inés Joyes), the didactic or sentimental novel (Saint-Lambert, by María Antonia del Río; Elizabeth Sommerville, by Juana Bergnés; Michel-Ange Marin, by Cayetana Aguirre), agronomy (Griselini, in a translation by Josefa Amar), literary history (from the Italian of Lampillas, also by Josefa Amar), and travel writings (Sir George Staunton on China, by María Josefa Luzuriaga); and in the early nineteenth century Francisca Larrea translated Maistre, Byron, and Schlegel.

Most of these women translated French texts, as was customary at the time, or else French translations of works originally written in other languages, such as Italian or, less often, English. For some, such as Josefa Amar and Margarita Hickey, translation was a prelude and accompaniment to their own writing; for others, such as Catalina Caso and the Countess of Lalaing, it was their only literary activity of which we have any evidence. Translating enabled them to apply their knowledge of foreign languages, which became a customary component in the education of young women of good family in the eighteenth century. Above all, however, it allowed them to make themselves heard in public from a somewhat sheltered position, in keeping with the attitude of modesty expected of their gender. Translation was like a veil which, depending on the circumstances, let them show themselves openly or

---

[2] On women translators, see López-Cordón 1996 and Bolufer 1998: 331–9. So far I have found 27.

else conceal themselves bashfully behind the author's name. It offered the possibility of making oneself known via an intermediary, but also of raising oneself almost to the level of an author by one's treatment of the original text.

In fact, authorship and translation are not radically different forms of intellectual activity. In the light of modern literary theory, translation contains creative dimensions of adaptation and appropriation (Krontiris 1992). The margin was even broader in the eighteenth century, for in the absence of a modern concept of intellectual property translations could be distinctly different from the original text; remaining true to the spirit and style in terms of form, because of the prevailing ideal of free rather than servile translation, but not betraying the Spanish language with barbarisms and forced constructions. Yet also at a deeper level, because the very selection of the work to be translated (involving considerations of opportuneness and marketability, but also of literary taste and affinity for the content), forewords of justification, erudite or explanatory notes about terms and usage foreign to Spanish readers or, more radically, alteration (and often censorship) of the text to adapt it 'to the customs of the country' could end up by transforming the work itself into something different from the original and the task of translation into a largely creative process (Urzainqui 1991).

Depending on the translators' intentions, training, or opportunities, their interventions ranged from a few brief lines of introduction to a much more intense transformation of the work and even some additions of their own. For example, when the Countess of Montijo published her translation of *Instruction pour le sacrament du mariage*, she did not add a preface of her own but a foreword by her spiritual director, who emphasized the translator's affinity for the text selected (Letourneux 1774, foreword by Bishop José Climent). On the other hand, some took advantage of the foreword to set out their ideas about the process of translation, such as Margarita Hickey (1789), or incorporated erudite notes, such as Josefa Amar (Lampillas 1789), or even went so far as to add a text of their own, independent of the original work, such as the 'Apología de las mujeres' (An Apology for Women) included with her translation of *Rasselas* by Inés Joyes (1798; see Bolufer 2008 and 2010).

It is noteworthy that among women translators there was a special predilection for translating works by other women, particularly French women writing on pedagogical or moral themes, such as Mme de Lambert, Mme d'Épinay, Mme Le Prince de Beaumont, Mme de Graffigny, or Mme de Genlis. For Spanish women writers trying to make their way in the literary world, choosing a work by another woman represented a double strategy of affirmation. With regard to the public, it enabled them to justify their incursion into the printed word, on the supposition that they were primarily addressing readers of their own sex (even if that was not always the case).

For themselves, following in the footsteps of another woman who was more or less established could strengthen their own feeling of entitlement to take up the pen, and provide them with a kind of complicity, in the recognition in someone else's written reflections based on experiences which to some extent they had in common.

Even more predictable is the fact that the writers they translated were nearly always French. French was by far the best-known language among enlightened Spanish elites, and, regardless of whether they already had works translated into Spanish, French women of letters had a certain renown with the Spanish public. In his *Defensa de las mujeres* (Defence of Women) of 1726, a celebrated assertion of the intellectual equality of the sexes, the enlightened Benito Jerónimo Feijóo showed his admiration of the extensive presence of women in French intellectual life: 'Las Francesas sabias son muchísimas: porque tienen más oportunidad en Francia, y creo que también más libertad, para estudiar las mujeres' (There are very many learned French women: because French women have more opportunity and, I think, more freedom to study in France) (Feijoo [1726] 2004: Discourse XVI, p. 62). Praise of writers such as the Hellenist Mme Dacier, the novelists Mme de Lafayette and Mlle de Scudéry, and the moralists Mme de Lambert and Mme de Sévigné appears in periodicals and catalogues of famous women published in Spain (*Memorial literario* [The Literary Magazine], June 1785; Thomas 1773; Bolufer 2000). And a traveller such as the Duke of Almodóvar, in his *Década epistolar sobre el estado de las letras en Francia* (Ten Letters on the State of Literature in France) (1781), devotes the whole of his last letter to women writers, from scientists such as Mme du Châtelet to contemporary novelists: Mmes de Genlis, Élie de Beaumont, Puisieux, Riccoboni, Le Prince de Beaumont, and Beauharnais (Almodóvar 1781: Letter X). All these references familiarized Spanish readers with women writers in the neighbouring country and may have predisposed them to take an interest in translations of their work.

For her part, the famous Spanish author and translator Josefa Amar (1749–1833?) shows an extensive knowledge of pedagogical literature and special appreciation of the work of women writers: 'En Francia es largo el catálogo de literatas insignes' (The list of famous women of letters in France is long) (Amar [1790] 1994: 70), she says in her most important work, *Discurso sobre la educación física y moral de las mujeres* (Discourse on the Physical and Moral Education of Women) (1790), and both in that work and in her *Discurso en defensa del talento de las mujeres* (Discourse in Defence of the Intelligence of Women) (1786) she mentions Mmes de Sévigné, Lafayette, Dacier, Le Prince de Beaumont, and Genlis. She especially admires Marie-Thérèse de Marguenat de Courcelles, Marchioness of Lambert (1647–1733), whom she quotes, for example, to evoke the pleasure of reading and study as ways of achieving a certain independence of mind and finding happiness for oneself without making it depend on others: '¡Qué fortuna es saber vivir consigo mismo, apartarse de sí con violencia, y volver con gusto a encontrarse! Entonces no se apetece el bullicio de las otras gentes' (How fortunate is the ability to live with oneself, withdraw violently from oneself, and take pleasure in finding oneself again! Then the bustle of others becomes unappealing). These words are taken from the *Avis d'une mère à sa fille* (A Mother's Advice to her Daughter), a debt which Josefa Amar does not hesitate to acknowledge: 'Así habla la célebre marquesa de Lambert, que conocía bien a fondo el corazón humano' (These are the words of the celebrated Marchioness of Lambert, who had a profound knowledge of the human heart) (Amar [1790] 1994: 195). Indeed, despite the profound differences between a Parisian aristocrat and *salonnière* and a middle-class Spanish woman with a less brilliant life, Mme de Lambert and Josefa Amar share many concerns. These include their intense moralism, their clear awareness of the inequalities that pervaded women's lives, their deep conviction of women's (and their own) intellectual ability and their fondness for private pleasures (study, reading, reflection) as guarantees of moral and emotional independence. Thus, in the pages of the *Discurso sobre la educación* of 1790, a kind of dialogue of complicity is created between the French writer who had died over half a century before and the Spanish author, who took the prestige of the other woman as a basis for developing her own ideas and presenting herself publicly as a respectable and respected writer.

Although Mme de Lambert was read by Josefa Amar in the original French, her *Obras* (Works), a selection of her moral and philosophical essays, had already appeared in Spanish in 1781, translated by Cayetana de la Cerda y Vera, Countess of Lalaing (?–1798). This choice seems far from accidental (Lambert 1781). She was a lady whose prestige among the aristocracy of the court is known to us, but we have no information about her education and intellectual activity. Nevertheless, her only known works, this translation and an unpublished one which we shall discuss later, enable us to form an approximate idea of her as a cultured woman with an excellent knowledge of French, possessing exquisite literary and philosophical tastes and a clear idea of her right of access to the public world of letters. The *Obras* are preceded by a foreword in which the Countess expresses her affinity for Mme de Lambert, a representative of the fusion of stoicism and epicureanism in the aristocratic moral tradition of the *Grand Siècle* (Marchal 1991).

By their nature, Mme de Lambert's works must have found their audience among a minority in the aristocracy or people of refined tastes, to which both her translator and her admirer Josefa Amar belonged in their different ways. A wider public was reached by three other standard authors in the moral and educational sphere: Jeanne-Marie Le Prince de Beaumont (1711–80), Louise Tardieu d'Esclavelles, Countess of Épinay (1726–83), and Stéphanie Ducrest, Countess of Genlis (1746–1830). These three women had a common concern for education, inseparable, as was usual in that century, from an intense moral interest and a special but not exclusive attention directed towards readers of their own gender. All three enjoyed great celebrity, both in their own country and elsewhere, as is shown by the spread of their works, re-published and translated into various languages during the course of the eighteenth and nineteenth centuries (Bolufer 2002).

As we have seen, Mme d'Épinay's most famous work, *Conversations d'Émilie*, intended to serve for the instruction of her niece, was translated into Spanish. It is a work in which she took the liberty of replying to Rousseau, showing her disagreement with the educational model that he expounded in *Émile* (1762). In contrast to Rousseau's Sophie, an image of femininity limited in terms of intellectual and moral capabilities, Mme d'Épinay's Émilie is a girl who asks questions, argues, reasons, and learns to think for herself; one assumes her to be endowed with a full intellectual potential and no forbidden areas are designated in her education, nor are explicit limits indicated.

The *Conversations* were highly praised and repeatedly reprinted in their own country and translated into various languages. They were published in Spanish in 1797, translated from the fifth French edition. We know nothing about the motives of the translator, Ana Muñoz, for choosing this work, or her possible affinity for it. We know only that the Spanish press hailed it as a work 'para utilidad principalmente de las madres de familia' (of use mainly for mothers with children), commented that it had been widely read in Europe and undermined its profoundly secular content by presenting it as a book about 'cristiana y política' (a polite Christian) education in the *Gaceta de Madrid* (Madrid Gazette), no. 91, 14 October 1797, p. 960). Its first two *Conversations* were also published in 1797 in a Madrid periodical, without identifying the author (*Miscelánea instructiva y curiosa* [Instructive and Curious Miscellany], vol. 3, nos 8 and 9, pp. 250–4, 356–94).

From the vast output of Mme Le Prince de Beaumont (70 volumes), ten books were published in Spanish between 1770 and the early years of the nineteenth century.[3] They included her famous *Magasins* (*des enfants, des adolescentes*) – dialogues between a woman teacher and her pupils in which discussions and tales alternate with lessons about morality and instruction in various disciplines – and also her moral tales and several novels: *La Nouvelle Clarice* (written in response to Samuel Richardson's *Clarissa Harlowe*), *Mémoires de Mme la baronne de Batteville* and *Lettres de Mme du Montier*.[4] Only the last of these books was translated by a woman, Antonia del Río y Arnedo (1775–1815), also the author of a version of *Sarah Th.*, by the French writer Jean-François de Saint-Lambert (Río y Arnedo 1795). In the

---

[3] On her work, see Stewart 1993, Havelange and Le Men 1988; on its dissemination in Spain, Bolufer 2002.

[4] For the Spanish translations of these works see Le Prince de Beaumont 1778, 1787, 1797, 1795, and 1796–98, respectively. See also Le Prince 1779–80, 1782, 1807.

preface to her translation of the *Lettres* (*Cartas*), Río y Arnedo renounces the possibility of including a foreword of her own, shielding herself behind the author's prestige:

> sería en mí una temeridad imperdonable querer añadir un ápice a las sabias y oportunas reflexiones de aquella mujer insigne. Hable, pues, por sí y por mí la misma Madama de Beaumont, supuesto que nada se puede decir más fino ni más convincente que el discurso preliminar que ella pone a su obra.
> (Le Prince de Beaumont 1796–98, translator's preface)

> (it would be an act of unpardonable temerity on my part to seek to add anything to this illustrious woman's wise and timely reflections. Let Mme de Beaumont speak both for herself and for me, therefore, since nothing could be said more finely nor more convincingly than the preliminary discourse that she includes in her book)

The translator was a cultivated woman from a distinguished family, and she achieved considerable success with these two books when she was only 21, as shown by their republication in 1805, and in 1798, 1800, and 1801, respectively. As her literary options were restricted by the rules of decorum that weighed on women writers, she chose, like many others, to make herself known by translations, but she introduced alterations to the original texts, adapting them to the restrictions of Spanish censorship. Moreover, despite her protestations of humility, she used the preface as a forum in which to express herself. There she presented herself as a woman of unimpeachable moral principles who desired to contribute to the reform of customs, and a writer conscious of the weakness of her talent: an image adapted to the modesty expected of women of letters, but revealing a literary ambition which she maintained throughout her life. After marrying in 1798, she accompanied her husband, a lawyer, on his posting to Charcas (New Spain), where she continued reading, accumulating a substantial library, and sending the occasional short translation to the newspapers (Rípodas 1993). Thus her literary activity testifies to her passion for reading and writing, but also to the limits within which eighteenth-century women had to develop their intellectual vocation.

The novel translated by María Antonia del Río relates the misadventures of Mlle de Montier, a virtuous but impoverished young woman whose husband, a rakish nobleman, is unfaithful to her. Yet she forgives him and never wavers in her virtue, not even after her husband's death, when she renounces the possibility of marrying the man she loved and consecrates her life to God. The story is a good example of the complexity of the work of Mme Le Prince de Beaumont, who presents female sexual virtue as a categorical demand of the order governing the family and society, but at the same time she shows her acute awareness of the moral inequality in marriage and the unhappiness that it brought to women, obliged to display a heroism not required of men (Stewart 1993: 24–49). Perhaps the translator identified with the very unidealized view of marriage and the bitterness conveyed by this apparently conventional novel, like other works by Mme Le Prince de Beaumont, all of which were well received in Spain, as acknowledged by the periodical press (*Gaceta de Madrid*, no. 106, 15 December 1795, p. 1281). *Cartas de Mme de Montier* and *La nueva Clarisa* (translated in 1797) had numerous subscribers, nearly a third of them women (27.8% and 28% respectively), which indicates their popularity with an extensive readership made up of both sexes.

Very different was the fate that befell another of her books, *Les Américaines*, a dialogue which seeks to prove the truth of the Catholic religion by applying the Cartesian method of methodical doubt, clearly showing Mme Le Prince de Beaumont's rationalist mind and her endeavour to defend the faith from the advances of secularity and scepticism in the eighteenth century. Having translated Mme de Lambert in 1781, in 1790 Cayetana de la Cerda, Countess of Lalaing, asked the Council of Castile for permission to print her translation, *Las americanas* (permission had been refused to an earlier translator, José Morcillo, in 1782), thus setting in motion a process which was to last 14 years.[5] Her request was rejected on 17 March 1791, on the basis that, by setting out the arguments of atheists and Protestants against Catholicism too explicitly, the book might lead readers to waver in their faith, and that writing on religious controversies was reserved for the clergy.

The fact that it was a book written by a woman, translated by another woman, and presented in the form of a dialogue between female characters was not unrelated to this adverse judgement, in which reference was made to St Paul's famous epistle to Timothy which orders women to be silent and submit to men in religious matters (I Tim. 2.11–15). Moreover, the censors considered the book even more dangerous because they thought it was implicitly addressed to an uneducated (female) readership, for whom discussion about truths of faith would do more harm than good: 'Las que sean capaces de percibir las razones que prueban la verdad de la revelación serán tan raras, como las aves del todo blancas' (Those women who are able to perceive the reasons that prove the truth of revelation will be as rare as birds that are completely white).

This decision did not satisfy the translator, who, by virtue of her upbringing, rank, and character, was not cowed by a refusal. Her response (16 October 1791) expressed her disagreement with the report in a firm, defiant tone, defended the merit of Mme Le Prince de Beaumont and the

---

[5] Archivo Histórico Nacional, *Consejos*, legajo 5556, expediente 35.

appreciation of her by influential people in Spain, and requested that the case be passed on to no less a person than the Inquisitor General. She defended the text's orthodoxy with legal and theological arguments and, offended by the censor's doubts, most particularly praised the talent and erudition of her sex and made it clear that the book was addressed to a select readership which included cultured women like herself, capable of understanding and appreciating it, and not at all to a popular, ignorant audience: 'no ha de andar en manos de las calceteras y lavanderas' (there is no reason for it to fall into the hands of hosiers and washerwomen). Her declaration shows her as a cultured woman with a knowledge of Latin, possessed of a religious attitude close to Enlightened Christianity and with a clear feeling of belonging to a minority distinguished no less by intelligence than by rank.

Predictably, the censor stood firm and sternly rejected the Countess's arguments, including her defence of the intellectual ability of her sex, as exaggerated and of little relevance to the case. Despite further protests from the translator, the case was finally dismissed on 22 March 1804. This did not prevent other works by Mme Le Prince de Beaumont from continuing to be translated and read in Spain, as we have seen. The key to her success here, as in other countries, lay to a large extent in her ability to expound moral principles in an entertaining way, drawing on her broad educational experience, and to adapt her writings to the various aspirations and to the intellectual level of her readership. Such was her celebrity that after her death a Spanish cleric published a discourse in her praise in which he defended the orthodoxy of her writings and her life and pointed out that Mme Le Prince de Beaumont had travelled to Spain and stayed with the Duke and Duchess of Híjar, who vainly attempted to engage her as a tutor for their daughters (Obregón 1784). It is clear, therefore, that in Spain she had a large and faithful readership and powerful patrons who were not happy about the ban on translating *Les Américaines* (in 1782 and 1791) and took action to clear her name of any suspicion.

Similar success in Spain was achieved by Mme de Genlis, known outside France primarily for her moral and educational writings, although she cultivated many genres, including also poetry, fiction, literary criticism and political pamphlets.[6] From her abundant *oeuvre* (over 140 books) about twenty titles were translated into Spanish, including the pedagogical novel *Adèle et Théodore* (*Adela y Teodoro*, 1785), *Les Veillées du château* (*Las veladas de la quinta*, 1788) and *Les Annales de la vertu* (*Los anales de la virtud*, 1792), followed by seventeen more in the nineteenth century (Bolufer 2002). Like Mme d'Épinay, Mme de Genlis shared the new pedagogical ideals of her century, but, also like her, disagreed with the essayists of the time, espe-

---

[6] On Mme de Genlis, see Laborde 1966, Clancy 1982, Plagnol-Diéval 2000, Orr 2005.

cially Rousseau, concerning their model of education for women. Though her programme for women's education was limited in content and oriented towards training them for a different, subordinate role with regard to the male, the ambitious, wide-ranging reading plan that she designed for Adèle, her ideal pupil, reveals her confidence in women's intellectual ability and her determination to open the doors of knowledge, without violating social conventions.

Mme de Genlis's writings were very successful in Spain with readers of both sexes and of various positions in society. Women readers gave her their support, as is revealed by the fact that *Las veladas de la quinta* was dedicated by the translator to the members of the Ladies' Committee of the Madrid Economic Society, who responded by raising a collective subscription. The Spanish press commended her books, read in their French versions by adherents of the Enlightenment such as Gaspar Melchor de Jovellanos, María Rosario Romero (Mme de Graffigny's translator), and Josefa Amar, who praised her in her *Discurso sobre la educación* (Amar [1790] 1994: 266). Moreover, María Jacoba Castilla Xarava, the translator of Mme de Genlis's *Adélaïde*, dedicated her version to women and stressed its moral utility 'en un tiempo en que la virtud y el decoro están ausentes de nuestras concurrencias' (at a time when virtue and decorum are absent from our midst) (Genlis 1801, translator's preface).

As subscription lists and readers' praises reveal, these authors and their works were not identified as being addressed exclusively to a female audience, though they were seen as being especially suitable for women. A Spanish periodical attributed the responsibility for the increase in reading among women to foreign books, including those of Mme Le Prince de Beaumont (*Correo de los Ciegos* [Courier of the Blind], no. 224, 14 January 1789, p. 1412). Their great popularity also appeared, in fictional form, in another periodical, which recommended the works of Mme Le Prince de Beaumont and Mme de Genlis to women because they were useful, 'comunes y baratas en las Librerías de esta Corte' (common and cheap in the Bookshops of this City) (*Diario de Madrid* [Madrid Daily], 28 October 1797, p. 1269). An alleged reader responded that those books were already being read by women of all social levels:

> Ha extrañado mi Amiga que la tenga Vmd. por tan ignorante que no sepa todo lo que contiene su apreciable carta, y *especialmente los tratados de la Condesa de Genlis, y la Beaumont, cuando la cocinera de su casa los tiene leídos en sus ratos desocupados. [...] una Señora ilustrada [...] no mendiga traducciones y sabe el mérito de esas obras por sus originales.*
> (*Diario de Madrid,* 10 November 1797, p. 1339; my italics)
>
> (My Friend was surprised that you should hold her to be so ignorant as not to know all that your estimable letter contains, and *especially the essays of the Countess of Genlis and Mme Beaumont, when the cook in her house*

has read them in her moments of leisure. [...] an Enlightened Lady [...] does not beg for translations and knows the merit of those works from their originals.)

The obvious exaggeration and humorous tone of the letter leads us to interpret it not as a real contribution from a reader but as one of the fictitious contributions customary in the press of the period. However, the comment suggests that these books circulated among a varied readership or, as the censor of *Las americanas* warned, among all those people (of both sexes) who had 'gusto por los libros y dinero para comprarlos' (a taste for books and money to buy them): cultured men and women who read them in the original language, but also more modest or less educated readers who knew them from translations. The fame they attained in Spain must have helped to normalize the image of the woman writer and associate it with certain literary genres – essay, dialogue, short story and novel – and themes – moral and educational – which were considered suitable for female readers; it is not surprising, therefore, that women featured prominently among those who translated them.

One last example of the implicit dialogue established between French women authors and their Spanish women translators is provided by María Rosario Romero in the preface to her translation of Françoise de Graffigny's *Lettres péruviennes* (1747) in 1792. The novel describes the journey to Europe of Zilia, an Incan princess captured by the Spaniards and, later, by the French, a literary device which allowed the author to offer a critical view of her own society, particularly of morality, social relations, and the status of women, and at the same time to reflect on the position of the woman writer and her opportunities for expression and self-representation (Theresa Ann Smith 2003 and 2006: 178–96).

All these aspects must have carried weight in the choice made by the translator, whose affinity for the chosen text is evident. However, María Rosario Romero went beyond mere translation. In her own footnotes, she extended the author's criticisms of France to Spanish society, and she patriotically corrected Mme de Graffigny by softening or omitting many of the reproaches she made about the Spanish colonization of the American continent; moreover, she altered the sense of the original story by adding a final letter about Zilia's conversion to Christianity, showing her own preference for Enlightened forms of religiousness and her indifference to merely external devotion. She also included in her preface a short autobiographical narrative of her progress as a reader, from her early love for 'las novelas de María de Zayas, y otros escritos de ese jaez' (María de Zayas's novellas, and other writings of that ilk), to her later development under male guidance (that of her brother) of a taste for morally instructive and literary reading. The distinction between 'improper' fiction (represented by the narratives of María de Zayas) and 'proper' novels (those of Mme de

Genlis) was evidently used here to authorize the translator as a respectable woman writer according to the new eighteenth-century standards of female propriety.

Making translations, very often of the work of women writers whose fame in their own country was already established, was thus one of the favourite options for Spanish women writers in the eighteenth century, though certainly not the only one. Converting the writing of other women, often their contemporaries, into their own language enabled them, to some extent, to engage in 'conversations' of agreement or disagreement, implicit or expressed in their rewriting of the original works. Gender complicity was not the only kind of rapport established by women translators, who produced versions of works by male authors, also selected, in many cases, on the basis of some affinity: of literary tastes, religious orientation, intellectual preferences, or ideological attachment.[7] Yet, undoubtedly, women writers and translators were united by their common experiences as women who, despite their different status and points of view, shared, in many cases, certain ideas (such as a sceptical view of marriage and a conviction of women's intellectual ability and entitlement), as women of letters who aspired to make a place for themselves in the literary world. By using, in many cases, French female authors of proven prestige as a basis for their activity, Spanish women writers were able to establish themselves in a position which in the eighteenth century, even more in Spain than in France, was still ambiguous and insecure, thus strengthening their aspiration to a new public legitimacy for women's intellectual and literary activity.

Further reading

Bolufer, Mónica, 2009. 'Between Tradition and Modernity: Women of Letters in Eighteenth-Century Spain', in *Eve's Enlightenmen: Women's Experience in Spain and Spanish America, 1726–1839*, ed. Catherine Jaffe and Elizabeth F. Lewis (Baton Rouge: Louisiana State UP), pp. 17–32

García Garrosa, María Jesús, 2007. 'La creación literaria femenina en la España del siglo XVIII: un estado de la cuestión', in *Cambio social y ficción literaria en la España de Moratín*, ed. Teresa Nava Rodríguez (Madrid: Universidad Complutense), pp. 203–18

López-Cordón, María Victoria, 2005. 'La fortuna de escribir: escritoras de los siglos XVII y XVIII', in *Historia de las mujeres en España y América Latina*, ed. Isabel Morant, 4 vols (Madrid: Cátedra), II, pp. 193–234

---

7 For example, those between Le Tourneux and the Countess of Montijo, and Samuel Johnson and Inés Joyes (see Bolufer 2008, ch. 4).

Smith, Theresa Ann, 2003. 'Writing out of the Margins: Women, Translation, and the Spanish Enlightenment', *Journal of Women's History*, 15.1: 116–43
—, 2006. *The Emerging Female Citizen: Gender and Enlightenment in Spain* (Berkeley and Los Angeles: University of California Press), ch. 4, 'Negotiating a Female Public: Writers and Reformers', pp. 111–47, and ch. 6, 'Between Reason and Passion: Citizenship in Translation', pp. 178–96

* This essay is part of the research project HAR2008–04113 (MICINN) and the COST Action ISO901.

12

What They Saw: Women's Exposure to and in Visual Culture in Nineteenth-Century Spain

LOU CHARNON-DEUTSCH

People living in the West are bludgeoned daily with thousands of man-produced images, most of which get discarded into the wastebaskets of minds and spaces, crowded out by other, more lasting and consequential images. Of necessity we have become skilled at mentally screening out the trivial visual documents of everyday. Lacking this immunity, we would be psychologically overwhelmed, just as we might if suddenly our lives were entirely image-deprived in this image-affluent era. We sometimes forget that circumstances in the nineteenth century were much different. Original art had begun to lose its aura with the capacity for mass reproduction on the horizon, but the daily consumption of machine-produced images was not the barrage it is today, and even serially produced images were still able to enchant in an era when the technology for their production had not yet been perfected to allow truly massive runs whose ubiquity would dull interest. Still, print imagery was quickly becoming a familiar part of everyday life, and women, who mostly did not produce printed images, were nevertheless implicated in this revolution as the most frequent human figures depicted in non-photographic images and as consumers of certain classes of images. This survey looks especially at the ephemera of everyday life that no longer is so accessible to cultural historians.[1] While it may be an exaggeration to say that the 'second half of the nineteenth century lived in a sort of frenzy of the visible' (Jean-Louis Comolli, cited in Schwartz 1995: 8), it is nevertheless the case that new technologies were facilitating what Antonio Ramírez

---

[1] I am deeply indebted to Vanessa Herrero for the painstaking gathering of information at the Biblioteca Nacional, Madrid, and for her insights about the images surveyed for this article. Rosario Ramos Pérez and her staff at the Ephemera Collection of the Biblioteca Nacional also gave generously of their time and deserve my thanks. Cristina Soler was also generous with her sources and help in the collection of material for this article.

describes as the 'aceleración iconográfica' (acceleration in image production) (1999: 105) that prompted new forms of political and social forms of communication (Riego 2001: 47). Visual stimulation through newer, more affordable kinds of ephemera like those surveyed for this study was part of everyday life for most urban dwellers.

It is by now a cliché that the private and public spheres as described by social historians held out vastly differing educational and social possibilities for men and women in the nineteenth century. An analogous issue is whether visual culture, which was expanding dramatically, defined the scopic field for women differently than it did for men. If there is a qualitative as well as quantitative disparity in what men and women experienced visually in their daily lives in Spain's urban centers, what inferences can be drawn from this disparity? Through a survey of weekly magazines, books, art, and other visual ephemera such as visiting cards, wall calendars, albums, almanacs, fans, posters, prospectuses, and marquees, holy pictures, congratulatory notes, and photographs, in this essay I shall attempt to show that while inferences about reception remain largely speculative, it is at least possible to review categories of images whose ideal consumers were presumed to be women and suggest a relationship between ideal femininity and the quest for beauty in visual representation. Women surely did see certain objects more or less often than men, possibly looked at visual culture available to both sexes differently than men, and were widely perceived as consumers of visual culture in gender-specific ways.

For both men and women, the technical and aesthetic quality and the quantity of visual material possessed by an individual depended on class and geography. In rural areas access to pictorial material was comparatively restricted; in urban areas the images studied here were more readily available. It is also the case that the cultural experience of the unemployed and the working poor differed significantly from that of the bourgeoisie. While they may have occasionally purchased one of the colorful lithographs illustrating popular French texts that Amédée Achard found for sale 'on every corner' as early as the 1840s (2005: 59), fine engravings and original works of art would be beyond the means of everyone except the wealthiest. The seamstress sewing a ballgown for an elegant figure on a dance invitation reproduced in Ramos Pérez (2003: 53) might have caught a glimpse of invitations to events such as the one in which she is depicted, but her white-clad mistress would have filed away the invitation in her album for her private, repeated viewing. Certain classes of women: the working poor, seamstresses, domestics, the truly indigent, were unlikely to frequent the few museums open to the public, or purchase certain types of printed material such as coloured visiting cards, prints, photograph albums, or illustrated gazettes.

However, if their work took them away from home or workshop these women would have been exposed to an abundance of pictorial diversions, including store windows, advertisement posters and flyers, or even popular spectacles like the occasional cosmoramas, dioramas, and magic-lantern shows that were popular from the early decades of the century (Parsons 2003: 27). And, like the family who manages a coachhouse in Jacinto Picón's novel *Dulce y sabrosa* (Sweet and Delectable) (1891), they might have clipped images from advertising posters or magazines to relieve the bareness of their walls. Even those subsisting on meager incomes would have kept an album or cigar box in which they put away prized keepsakes which included printed objects of all types. As Galdós noted in his essay 'El coleccionista' (The Collector), 'Hoy, hasta los pobres se ven tocados de la manía de reunir y clasificar cachivaches de cualquier orden' (Today, even the poor are caught up in the obsession with collecting and classifying trinkets of every type) (Pérez Galdos 1923: 197), an example of 'pasiones inocentes en el seno de las familias más modestas' (innocent passions in even the most modest of families) (204). Galdós's character Isabelita in *La de Bringas* (*That Bringas Woman*) (1884) collects 'all the detritus of nineteenth-century popular culture' (Gold 1988: 325), including bottle labels, cigar bands, postage stamps, and holy pictures of the Sacred Heart and Catholic visionaries. The album of Enriqueta Sanfiz (dated 1885), housed in the Biblioteca Nacional, Madrid, gives an idea of the types of print visuals that women thought worth collecting and that could be found in the homes of many women. It included pages torn from the almanacs of 1881–83, calendar illustrations, commercial cards, congratulatory and greetings cards (*felicitaciones*), trolley and omnibus tickets, postcards, dress model figurines, and other ephemera. Cecilia Gasset de la Ricada's album (dated 1874), is divided into six parts: 'Ornithological Alphabet,' 'Military Gallery,' 'The British in America,' 'Children,' 'The Hunt,' and 'Don Quijote de la Mancha'. Several pages are a collage of figures snipped from advertising sheets (*marquillas*) and assembled into scenarios to tell an amusing story. Pages cut from women's albums such as the one I found recently at a paper fair in Madrid [Plate 4] are prized collector's items still today, adorned with *troquelados*, or colorful stamped figures printed in sheets and purchased in stationary stores as gifts or rewards for young women. These cutouts of animals, flowers, angels, women, and decorative borders were the building blocks of the album's sometimes cluttered compositions.

Women of means who were out in society were expected to attend many social functions involving a variety of printed visual material. Balls and charity events were favorite pastimes of the monied classes and a great deal of etiquette was involved in these events. In addition to colorful advertisements, invitations, and programs, women attendees would receive dance cards, such as the one in Plate 5, with romantic images pressed into their cover. Photograph albums, another standard item in many homes, included both formal family portraits and images of Spanish royalty and other celebrities that studios mass produced at modest prices. Collecting photographs of royalty and the notables of the day helped define the liberal state whose citizens were expected to be knowledgeable about their leaders and cultural icons (Riego 2001: 344, 384–85).[2] Evidence exists that even working-class dwellings would have at least one framed photograph on the wall, like the one Bernardo Riego reproduced (2001: 383) of a rustic couple that marks them as belonging to what was dubbed the 'popular' classes, or the photographs of the dying or deceased children that were thought to aid in the recognition and memory of the departed.

Museums and high art in general were accessible only to the wealthy and limited members of the urban working class who could find time on weekends to frequent the museum when there was no entrance fee. Although the Prado Museum in Madrid was open to the public from 1868, the appreciation of high art was still considered the domain of those with the means to collect original art. Galdós recognized this disparity through his character Isidora Rufete in *La desheredada* (*The Disinherited*) (1881), who is surprised to learn that the Prado permitted entry to the *pueblo*, or ordinary folk, because she saw no one meeting that description on her visit (Pérez Galdos [1881] 2005: 83–6). Stepping into the hallowed halls of the museum was then, as now, like crossing the line from the profane to the sacred, reserved for those who 'find themselves legitimated in their privilege, that is, in their ownership of the means of appropriation of cultural goods' (Bourdieu et al. 1990: 113). Over the century, many private and secluded collections were increasingly made public and incorporated into national museums (Vázquez 2001: 161), but critics repeatedly denigrated the middle classes for their tepid interest and appreciation of high art (70). Exposure to high art among the middle classes was mostly in the form of black-and-white magazine reproductions derived from engravings *after* original works of art. Depictions of visits to museums and expositions give ample evidence of the elite status of museum frequenters. M. Picolo and Luis Jiménez's sketches for the *Ilustración Española y Americana* (Spanish and American Illustrated) of women attending the Paris Exhibition of 1889 suggest that the elegantly clad women are themselves the greatest work of art, something that would please the editors of *La Moda Elegante* (Elegant Mode), who every year offered

---

[2] Photography quickly promised a new way of knowing not just the exotic corners of the world, but the everyday city scenes and inhabitants, and ever larger numbers of people desired to expand their vision of their immediate surroundings by filtering it through the photograph that could be purchased and collected in albums, one of the most popular and enduring hobbies of the leisure classes. For more on this, see Charnon-Deutsch 2008.

numerous samples of 'exhibition gowns' like the regal woman facing front in Fig. 1A, clad in silk, feathers, velvet, and precious stones.³

Illustrated magazines were one of the most important contributors to women's visual culture, especially during the latter part of the century, when they became more affordable for the middle classes. Earlier in the century women's magazines were big on moral instruction but largely devoid of imagery, occasionally offering crudely sketched black-and-white images of saints, mannequins, and other items. In terms of graphic imagery, Isabel Segura and Marta Selva divide women's magazines into fashion magazines and Marian magazines, the latter concerned with women's moral education and largely devoid of images (1984: 93). As the printing industry evolved, women's magazines became more varied and their illustrations more sophisticated, but they were rarely a match for periodicals geared to a general reader. Among the more notable examples published in the second half of the century are: *Correo de Moda* (Fashion Courier) (Madrid, 1851–86), *La Mujer* (Woman) (Madrid, 1851–52), *La Violeta* (The Violet) (Madrid, 1862–65), *La Educanda* (The Educator) (Madrid, 1861–65), *La Margarita* (The Daisy) (Madrid, 1871–72), *Album del Bello Sexo* (Album of the Fair Sex) (Barcelona, 1882–?), *La Guirnalda* (The Garland) (Madrid, 1867–83), *La Mariposa* (The Butterfly) (Barcelona?, 1886-88), *El Iris del Bello Sexo* (The Rainbow of the Fair Sex) (Santiago, 1841), *Instrucción para la Mujer* (Instruction for Women) (Madrid, 1882), and the various *Semanarios* (weeklies) that had a strong influence on women's culture: *Semanario de las Familias* (Family Weekly) (Madrid, 1882-83), *Semanario de la Mujer* (Woman's Weekly), *Semanario de la Familia Pintoresca* (Picturesque Family Weekly) (Barcelona, 1875–81), *Semanario Popular* (Popular Weekly) (Madrid, 1862–65).

A few magazines, *Ilustración de la Mujer* (Woman's Illustrated) (Madrid, 1873–76), *Ilustración de la Mujer* (Barcelona, 1883–85) and *La Moda* (Fashion) (Cadiz, 1842–1927), continued by *La Moda Elegante* (Madrid, 1876–82?), are among the exceptions to the image-starved women's magazine trade. In addition to lavish illustrations, *La Moda* counted on the collaboration of noted writers such as Pilar Sinués, Margarita Pérez de Celis, and Ángela Mazzini. *La Moda Elegante* similarly offered dozens of well-executed line engravings of dress and hat models (see Figs 1C and 1D), together with feature articles by Pilar Sinués, Isabel Cheix, Faustina Sáez de Melgar, and other notable arbiters of women's morals and fashions.[4] Elegant dresses designed specifically for events like art exhibitions or visits to art

---

[3] See Charnon-Deutsch 2000 for a survey of the over-representation of women, or what Mary Ann Doane calls their 'being-for-the-gaze-of-others' (1989: 109).

[4] *La Moda Elegante* offered its readers four different editions. Subscription to the most expensive, the de luxe edition, cost 36 pesetas a year, the cheapest, 16 a year. Even at the cheapest price, most working-class families would not have been able to afford this magazine.

Figure 1. Fashion illustrations from *Moda Elegante*:
1A 'Traje de exposición' (exhibition gown) (April 1893)
1B 'Abrigo de terciopelo' (velvet coat) (October 1892)
1C 'Sombrero de visita' (visiting hat) (January 1891)
1D 'Toque de paja' (straw hat) (March 1899)

studios such as the one in Fig. 1B, are an indication both of the presumed class status of the magazine's subscribers, and the fact that fashion-minded ladies were expected to be seen at (as well as to see) these events.[5] The short lived and irreverent *Mundo Femenino* (Woman's World) (1886–87) offered frequent cartoons which featured women in uncommon scenarios, riding horses, bicycles, and even, in one magazine cartoon, men; but, in general, magazines directed exclusively at women were not where women were most exposed to the visual print culture that went beyond fashion illustration. Rather, women of means would savor the more widely distributed weeklies such as the *Seminario de las Familias*, that evolved into the *Ilustración Española y Americana*, or one of the other similar large-format illustrated magazines that catered to the upper-middle classes: *Ilustración, Ilustración Ibérica, Ilustración Artística, Ilustración de Madrid* (Illustrated, Iberian Illustrated, Art Illustrated, Madrid Illustrated), among others. Women with access to these premier weeklies would savor dozens of new engravings of paintings and original sketches every week and could have the issues of the magazines bound for their personal libraries.

Reading periodicals, however, was considered a modern, and therefore frivolous, activity, something the arbiters of feminine conduct advised Spanish women to avoid even as magazines were increasing their appeal to women. According to the editor of *Ilustración Artística*, Lorenzo Casanova's painting, *La vida moderna* (Modern Life), of a woman reading a magazine that was shown at the Parès Salon in Barcelona in 1884 exemplified the 'sensuality' that characterizes modern times 'dedicated to material pleasure.' Towards the end of the nineteenth century and into the twentieth, large-format illustrated magazines ceded readership to the more compact medium-format magazines such as *Blanco y Negro* (Black and White), that debuted in 1891.[6] A combination of factors ensured that *Blanco y Negro* was an instant success. Urban readers were increasingly receptive to news doled out in small batches, often with a heavy dose of humor and numerous accompanying images that functioned as a kind of shorthand messaging system. With its weekly fare of sketches, photographs, cartoons and short articles, *Blanco y Negro* invited the reading public to envision Madrid as an exciting and heterogeneous city where women as well as men, the elite as well as the middle classes, could see themselves displayed. In keeping with the tradition of the large format magazines, sketches of fantasy women vastly outnumbered images of real women. But increasingly *Blanco y Negro*'s artists depicted working-class

---

[5] The *traje de exposición* (exhibition gown) appeared in the 14 April 1893 issue, vol. 52, no. 14, p. 159. The materials for the dress included silk, satin, velvet, stork feathers, and brocaded silk.

[6] *Blanco y Negro* ran until 1936, when it became a Sunday supplement to the *ABC* daily newspaper.

Figure 2. Woman riding in her tilbury, cover illustration of *Blanco y Negro* (June 1891)

women and women in poses that marked them as modern and independent, such as the one riding in her tilbury in Fig. 2. This engraving by watercolor painter Ángel de Huertas was featured on the cover of every issue during the first year of production. It established a modern woman as the magazine's chief visual anchor: cracking her whip, she appears to be riding off into the future in a tilbury drawn by a white butterfly and a black dragonfly, the magazine's logo.

Aside from magazines, the consumption, design, and execution of decorative or ornamental arts comprised women's major exposure to visual art. As part of their early training, young women whose parents could afford tutors or who were fortunate to attend one of the few primary schools for women, received at least a superficial instruction in the fine arts and would have readily available images to copy in their sketches or watercolors. Since it was generally assumed that women had a superior sensitivity, they would have or need to have, a greater familiarity with beautiful objects (Diego 1987: 166). But the notion that morality and beauty were inseparable when it came to women, meant that formalized instruction precluded the use of models in their training which was, in the main, expected to be superficial. Most women artists gravitated towards still life, scenery, and decorative arts. Sketching and painting in watercolor were signs of a certain level of class distinction, but also activities that conduct manuals recommended 'provided they don't occupy time that in theory should be dedicated to other more strictly feminine obligations' (172). The widespread assumption was that domestic duties took precedence over leisure activities like painting, sketching, and reading magazines. But nearly all women learned some form of decorative craft, especially when the object was utilitarian: objects of all sorts would have been embellished with artistic flourishes through embroidery, needlepoint, tapestry, crochet, lace, or appliqué.

With the perfection of lithography and woodblock engraving, and towards the end of the century of advanced photo-engraving technologies, illustrated books became readily available to most classes, many of them geared to a female reader. Ubiquitous penny novels, such as The Children's Museum series published by Sucesores de Hernando in Madrid, featured colored scenes on the front and small black-and-white drawings scattered throughout their fourteen pages. Costing less than a peseta and small enough to fit in the palm of the hand, these booklets were the precursors of the twentieth-century comic book, but those destined for a female or children's market were usually moralistic tales that reinforced religious and home instruction. By mid century popular novels purchased by subscription and paid for in installments (*novelas por entrega*) commonly included between four and ten illustrations, many of them woodblock prints tipped in the book on removable pages, and very refined. We tend to forget these commonplace visuals because modern editions of the novels often lack the original illustrations, and novels today do not typically include illustrations. When removed from books and tacked on the wall, headboard, or mirror, these engravings provided accessible art to families who could not afford the luxury of framed engravings or original art (Ferreras 1972: 30). Many of these engravings sought to capture the dramatic moments of the novel, especially confrontations between rival suitors and star crossed lovers, while others bore a clearly indoctrinating message such as the image of a good mother and a bad mother from *Las buenas y las malas madres* by popular novelist Manuel Fernández y González (reproduced in Charnon-Deutsch 2000: 82).[7]

Because home schooling was the norm for girls before universal primary education legislation was introduced (legislation, we should recall, that the government never fully implemented in the case of girls), many mothers were familiar with the primers available for home instruction as well as textbooks their sons used in school.[8] Images in children's storybooks and textbooks reinforced Catholic virtues as well as prevailing gender arrangements which, as Thomas Laqueur has argued (1990), had begun to exaggerate the complementary but different nature of men and women that helped implant the ideal of the *ángel del hogar* (angel of the hearth). In Spain as elsewhere in Europe it was thought that 'men and women are physiologically and culturally different; for this reason they should have specific social functions and should receive a different form of education, since their aptitudes and behavior have to be distinct' (Folguera Crespo 1997a: 430). The popular primer *Tesoro de las escuelas* (The Schools' Treasury) boasted 1,000 images, many showing the schoolboy Juanito, whose life is told in Part Three, 'The Duties of Children.' Although a young girl is pictured on the cover, girls would find themselves largely absent from this and most other primers of knowledge. A few chapbooks included lessons for both boys and girls. *Los peligros de la infancia* (The Perils of Infancy), by Pierre Blanchart, follows over a dozen naughty or careless children as they learn the dire consequences of their disobedience, inattention, and cruelty.[9] Scattered among the dangers for girls are stories about the consequences of feminine vanity or failure to care for siblings, in other words, subtle indoc-

---

[7] Fernández y González had male fans as well. His biographer, F. Hernández-Girbal, maintained that Fernández y González's *Luisa* (which reportedly sold 200,000 copies in just a few months), was being read by construction workers, schoolchildren, seamstresses, office workers, and soldiers (1931: 120).

[8] According to Folguera Crespo, the 1825 Education Act had very little impact on girls, 'the network of public schools was very small and in any case the resources invested in feminine education were meager' (1997a: 430). See especially Jagoe 1998 for information regarding women's education in Spain.

[9] Other texts published by the Pascual Bookshop in Valencia include titles such as: 'The Artisan's Friend', 'Poetic Gems', 'The Dawn of Infancy', 'A Child's Mentor', and 'Well-spoken'.

Figure 3. Illustration from *El amigo de las niñas* (The Young Girls' Friend), by Leopoldo Delgrás (1875).

trination about their future roles as homemakers. There were, in addition, several chapbooks exclusively destined for the instruction of young girls, among them *El pensil de las niñas* (The Young Girls' Bower) of 1846, by José Codiba y Barhomeu, *La ciencia de la mujer al alcance de las niñas* (A Knowledge of Women for Young Girls) of 1855, by Señora de Arteaga y Pereira, and the generously illustrated *El amigo de las niñas* (The Young Girls' Friend), by Leopoldo Delgrás (1875). Typical of these chapbooks, *El amigo* is about a young girl who receives daily lessons from her father, shown in Fig. 3, about how to be generous, sweet, submissive, industrious, self-sacrificing, and unassuming. There is no need for an 'agglomeration of lessons' on 'sublime' or 'scientific' knowledge, when there are so many other indispensable lessons for a young girl to learn (Delgrás 1875: 68–69).

Many types of ephemera would fall into the hands of those who could not afford even the inexpensive weekly illustrated magazines such as *Blanco y Negro* or the prints and photographs for special occasions. In *Ephemera* Ramos Pérez surveys the host of new publications that from the 1850s were becoming available both for advertising and for personal use, thanks to advances in printing technology, including: 'lithography, chromolithography, photography [...] phototype, tricolor chromography, photogravure, phototypographic reproduction [...] steel engraving (to produce holy pictures), and watercolor sketches, ink drawings, and gouache [in preliminary sketches for labels]' (Ramos Pérez 2003: 12).[10]

Because women (and their servants, if they had them) were the primary caretakers of the house, many ephemeral items would have come to them first. Groceries, dry goods, letters, calling cards, and all types of household goods were delivered by *repartidores*, regular delivery men who sent greetings cards to their clients at Christmas time, sometimes in the form of a poem on the reverse of the card, requesting in return their *aguinaldo*, or yearly tip. These chromolithographs were sometimes highly sophisticated, with artistic flourishes appealing to women's aesthetic sensibilities. Like many other established businesses, José Ovelar's store in Villa del Prado, a town outside Madrid, offered its clients wall calendars with extraordinary, refined lithographs of women, like the one in Plate 6, embellished with silk sashes, lace shawls, fur trimmings, flowered borders, and feathered millinery. Along with foodstuffs and fabrics, José Ovelar's calendar was selling elegance, youth, and beauty.

Other ephemera of everyday life that catered to women were in the form of stationery, postcards, greetings cards, and fans that sported sirens, nymphs, garlands, and flowers. The postcard in Fig. 4, sent by a man to a certain Adelina in 1902, reports that he loves her 'above anything in the world'.[11] Image and its caption supplement the verbal message with its idealization of the figure of the woman who awaits her absent love: 'While he from his shore departs, she prays to the Virgin to protect him.' Items of everyday use could also serve as advertisements. For example, the manufacturer of Andreu pharmaceuticals offered its female clients a *paipay* (round-shaped fan on a stick) with a scene from the opera *Lohengrin* above the words 'Gift from Andreu to its Clients' printed in large letters on the bottom, a novel way to advertise its products that heralded the twentieth-century practice of attaching advertising to practical items.[12] Products aimed specifically at a male clientele, like cigars, matchboxes, cigarettes, cravats, and hats, although highly decorative, were decidedly less embellished with romantic insignia. However, some that were decorated with romantic scenes and flowers would seem quaint today: trolley and train schedules, business cards, and marquees. So it should be pointed out that the flowery trend in decorative arts was not aimed exclusively at women, even if women were more apt to be the ideal receptors of most advertising imagery.

---

[10] See Ramos Pérez (2003: 14–15) for a list of the classifications of ephemera housed in the Biblioteca Nacional. This is the most important collection of ephemera in Spain, but other collections exist, notably in Barcelona.

[11] My thanks to Alejandro Sanz-Bermell Martínez for deciphering the partially obliterated message on this postcard.

[12] My thanks to Flora Klein Andreu for supplying an image of the Andreu *paipay*.

VISUAL CULTURE IN NINETEENTH CENTURY SPAIN 201

Mientras el de su playa, veloz se aleja,
ella pide à la virgen que le proteja

Figure 4. Postcard from the author's private collection

Figure 5. Advertisements for health and beauty products:

5A *Ilustración Española y Americana* (May 1889)
5B *Ilustración Española y Americana* (1896)
5C *Moda Elegante* (April 1893)

From the 1860s, companies began to adopt modern advertising techniques by establishing brand recognition through a repeated figural icon. By 1900 most brands of soap, perfume, and other articles of feminine consumption had established a recognizable identity through the use of product prospectuses, business cards (postcard-sized images advertising businesses with an image on one side and sales information on the reverse), advertising posters, boxes, and wrapping paper featuring a female figure that served as the product's mascot. Some of the first Spanish businesses to establish a brand using a woman icon were the registered trademarks of Wertheim & Wheeler and Wilson sewing machines. At a time when women made their own clothes (or had them made by seamstresses) in the home, a sewing machine was an important acquisition. Wertheim & Wheeler and Wilson advertised their machines with high-quality trade cards like the one reproduced in Eguizábal and Santiago Páez (2002: 256).

By the end of the century a beautiful woman like the one on Olivar's calendar became the favored look to sell not just practical items like sewing machines, but beauty products appealing overwhelmingly to women. Raúl Eguizábal and Elena Santiago Páez argue that in a society in which women had little opportunity to earn money, their other assets (in addition to a dowry) included beauty, and advertisements appealing to women to enhance their beauty like the posters they produced in their 2002 book or the magazine advertisements in Fig. 5 for women's hair tonic were understandably in abundance. But today, beauty-for-sale is an even more inescapable aspect of everyday life, and yet women in Western societies have ample opportunities to work. It seems more accurate to argue that as they moved to capitalistic modes of production manufacturers sought to expand markets for their goods and find new ways to outsell competitors and stimulate consumption. They quickly discovered that certain goods could be cheaply produced and sold at higher prices if they appealed to those who were in charge of the family's shopping.

By 1900 the visual field readily available to readers through print media had expanded tremendously, an indication of the growing addiction to visualism that characterized other industrialized nations already in possession of a mass media long before that date. As competition between rival brands emerged in manufacturing sectors, the importance of brand recognition grew and, with it, the need to modernize advertisements by introducing a higher standard of artistic production. The advertising poster served to 'provoke demand, increase sales of surplus goods, and artificially maintain the production-consumption ratio'(Ramírez 1999: 191). Around the turn of the century and for several decades afterwards, this type of advertisement achieved a very high level of artistic refinement. Far surpassing magazine advertisement in terms of potential viewers, the poster offered an urban sensory experience that could be enjoyed in public spaces. Well suited to iconic reproduction on specialized paper, it attracted many artists, especially during competitions for the best posters.[13] Thousands of these turn-of-the-century posters excel for their adroit combination of advertisement and modernist graphics, selling Jaime Boix chocolates, La Palma cookies, Codorníu champagne, del Mono anisette, and other luxury products. The street poster did the work for commerce, industry, and entertainment events that billboards, television, and the internet do for us today.[14] Unlike the magazine, the poster was free in the sense that it could be viewed by rich and poor, women and men alike, in public spaces: street corners, kiosks, theaters, dance halls, commercial façades, and shop windows. In an integral way posters participated in the urban social ritual of the *paseo* (evening stroll), on view for everyone at every turn, arguably the 'most characteristic means of communication in the nineteenth century' (Eguizábal and Santiago Páez 2002: 35).

Rather than concerts, operas, and other exclusive entertainments of the bourgeoisie, event posters, another ubiquitous urban fixture, advertised middle-class entertainments and spectacles like the cabaret, the circus, carnivals, and bullfights. Even these entertainments were prohibitively expensive for a large percentage of the urban population, but the posters advertising them acted as magnets that fostered desires. Because of the public nature of the poster's content and venue it cannot be considered to have women as its ideal receptor, but, as Eguizábal points out, colorful images accompanying the announcements were sometimes laid out in such a way that they could be useful as wall art, and 'publicity images thus became part of the more intimate surrounding; before the onset of intrusive media like the radio, the public had already spontaneously made publicity part of their immediate surroundings, in the sacrosanct spaces of the home' (2002: 54), where most women spent their time. For example, the chocolate producer Jaime Boix offered a collection of posters with images of subjects in the typical dress of the 49 provinces of Spain, which became a favorite collector's item. The top part of the poster could be cut off and saved as a splendid color image of provincial dress.

Because 'representation can no longer be conceived without its spectator, who is structurally and socially positioned by the image itself' (Dubreuil-Blondin 1993: 152), it is important to speculate about ideal image reception. What can be surmised about the types of images to which women were exposed in the nineteenth century? For one thing, the images to which women were most frequently exposed were increasingly brightly colored and

---

[13] For example, in Madrid the Círculo de Bellas Artes (Fine Arts Circle) offered prizes for posters advertising various public entertainments.

[14] Eguizábal and Santiago Páez divide up the Biblioteca Nacional collection into eleven categories: circus, theater, bullfights, festivals and exhibitions, travel and transport, products, horse races, publications, dances, political, and miscellaneous (2002: 94).

highly ornamental, adorned with objects coded as 'beautiful' in the conventional sense: flowers, birds, bowers, ribbons, lace, and courting scenes. If the supply of these images elicited demand, it also seems that the demand elicited supply. Judging by the success of idealized portraits, women clearly enjoyed seeing myriad images of their wishful selves, when they were dressed elegantly, young, beautiful, innocent (or, conversely, exotic and sexually alluring), and surrounded by beauty. Their response to this sudden onslaught of woman-images, however, was bound to be both exciting and alienating. The proliferation of the female image, more than a display of true femininity, was a kind of campaign to privilege some images over others. As such it was an exemplary practice feeding into and from various discourses of power. The fact that this may not have been a consciously directed practice and that women themselves provided some of the impetus for it does not mean that image production played no role in engineering gender relations. My conclusion is that the production of 'beautiful' images played a key role in shaping notions of proper and desirable feminine behavior and could thus be considered a regulatory practice.

Still, it is difficult to arrive at a nuanced theory of response beyond saying what kinds of images were fashioned to please women for obvious reasons. Postulating ideal beholders, for which there is ample evidence, is not quite the same thing as assessing reception or determining the cultural impact of images. Behind every popular image there is a story with many layers of meanings that subtend production and consumption. For example, given the great popularity of intricate holy pictures like the one in Fig. 6, whose caption exhorts St Joseph to let the owner of the postcard hold Jesus in her heart forever, it is possible to speculate that they function as amulets in women's lives.[15] But the move from pleasurable contemplation to emotion and religious fervor may also be deduced from the care that the Catholic Church invested in their production and dissemination. Recognizing their reception in the deepest sense entails understanding what possible benefit would accrue to the vested interests of powerful institutions such as the Catholic Church by inculcating religious fervor in women through sentimental religious iconography.

The relationship between beholder and image was clearly very intimate, judging by the popularity of pasting images into private albums, for which there is ample anecdotal and material evidence, or collecting and binding magazines at the end of each year. It is obvious that many women treasured idealized, colorful, romantic keepsake images. Bearing in mind that the images were created and produced by men, however, we must add to

---

[15] I wish to thank Antonio Soler Segarra and María Amparo Castillo Martí for allowing me to photograph their collection of holy pictures and the rare children's chapbook *Los peligros de la infancia*.

Figure 6. Holy picture (from the collection of Antonio Soler Segarra and María Amparo Castillo Martí)

the equation the very probable hope that women, who were beginning to express an interest in greater educational and career opportunities, would identify with the images of delicate femininity in particular ways. Similarly, given that advertisement was more and more using a woman-image to sell products, images were beginning to embody the desire of manufacturers to invest new values in the products being advertised that had less and less to do with their use value. At the same time, understanding that so many of the images that circulated were simultaneously advertising products as well as indirectly endorsing class pretensions means that image reception cannot be studied in isolation from questions of cultural capital, class aspiration, taste, and stereotypes of female acquisitiveness.

A careful study of nineteenth-century graphic images should convince us of David Freedberg's argument that 'the power of images is much greater than is generally admitted' (1989: 419). Images need to be taken seriously not just as cultural forms, but as cultural forces. From literature come stunning examples of how important the visual image was for nearly all the characters in Galdós's *Novelas contemporáneas*: for Isidora Rufete who misrecognizes herself in the portrait of the daughter of the Marquesa de Aransis in *La desheredada*, for Amparo in *Tormento* (Torment) (1884) who is tormented by the photograph of her father, which seems to accuse her of her great sin every time she glances at it, and for Frasquito Ponte in *Misericordia* (Compassion) (1897), who sacrifices his last pennies to buy Obdulia a print of Napoleon's wife.

To gauge the power of images like the ones studied here in the lives of real women is more difficult. Nevertheless, from the ubiquity of certain types of images we know that they were circulating everywhere as part of urban life, and from their popularity the following conclusions may be drawn. Small decorated objects and ephemera seem especially important for their keepsake value at a time when the vast majority of women could not boast a 'room of their own' (Folguera Crespo 1997b: 458) but were nevertheless encouraged to admire beauty in its most conventional forms. Women's exposure to visual graphics was equal to or exceeded that of men, but their aesthetic experiences differed to the degree they could afford some types of visual culture and not others. Many graphic objects that women saw daily were explicitly linked to commercial interests that used the power of beauty, color, and refinement to persuade women to purchase objects that held out the illusory promise of being something beyond what they really were. Illustrations that accompanied women's reading material tended to be infused with moralistic or religious overtones, exhorting women to be nurturing, forbearing, dutiful, and hardworking. The cloying sentimentality of many images often appealed to women's desire for refined courtship rituals or invited them to see the beauty of tremendous sacrifices made in the name of love or duty. Women's role as educators of young children exposed them to visual experiences that encouraged a childlike regard for the simplistic and unchallenging representations of family life. Even in the most trivial or simplistic cultural forms social and moral authority exerted itself. As such, the images of popular culture directed toward women were not only constitutive of culture, they mediated pre-existing ideological and social formations, serving the interests of those in positions of privilege and power, both secular and religious. While exhortations from the pulpit and conduct manuals warned women to be concerned with the wealth of their soul rather than their personal adornments and beauty, the well financed secular publishing industry sent the opposite message about the importance of physical beauty and elegance.[16] Thus the visual culture daily available to women shows evidence of an epic ideological battle for women's hearts and minds as well as their pocketbooks: the creed of physical self-improvement and the creed of religious improvement. The commodity nature of image production then reinforced a rather schizophrenic notion of ideal femininity embracing at once two competing visions of ideal femininity.

In my work on representations of women in late nineteenth-century magazines I speculated about what it was that men lacked that they fetishized the female body to such a degree during the time leading up to the turn of the century. Similarly, I can't help asking what it was that prompted women to favor and collect certain kinds of images displaying what we could call 'trite' beauty. Certainly women were being interpellated by advertisements to picture themselves in fantasy realms inhabited by beautiful women, and thus fantasy had been commodified and 'integrated into a totalising capitalist system which is driven by consumption.' (Jon Stratton 1996: 15). But it also seems to be the case that the new emphasis on consumption implied that women were incomplete, that they needed beauty products and objects of beauty to enhance their worth which could be bought. Invested with desire, 'the image can never correspond to the "reality" of the commodity – or the person' (1996: 72), and I conclude that this disjunction between reality and representation is at the heart of what women saw.

Further reading

Museo Virtual de Arte Publicitario, 2002. Centro Virtual Cervantes, http://cvc.cervantes.es/actcult/muvap/:

Riego, Bernardo, 2003. *Impresiones: La fotografía en la cultura del siglo XIX (Antología de textos)* (Girona: Centre de Recerca i Difusió de la Imatge / Ajuntament de Giron)

---

[16] See excerpts from *Llamamiento a la juventud de señoras cristianas dedicado a la Asociación de Madres Católicas* (An Appeal to Young Christian Ladies Addressed to the Association of Catholic Mothers) in Aguado and Capel et al. 1994: 331–2).

Ruiz Gómez, Leticia, 1998. *La colección de estampas devocionales de las Descalzas Reales de Madrid* (Madrid: Fundación Universitaria Española)

Satué, Enric, 1985. *El libro de los anuncios, II: La época de los artesanos (1830–1930)* (Barcelona: Alta Fulla)

Vélez, Pilar. 1998. *El cromo a Catalunya, 1890–1936* (Molins de Rei: Ajuntament)

13

Luxurious Borders: Containment and Excess in Nineteenth-Century Spain

ALISON SINCLAIR

> The sacrifice of the daughter represents
> the renunciation of the mother
> (Elisabeth Bronfen, *Over Her Dead Body*)[*]

Lust and luxury can both be conceptualized as forms of excess, with fashion promoted as one of the prime manifestations of excess among women. Whereas in Bataille's view on excess (1967) there is something positive to be perceived about the phenomenon, a different view emerges from women's conduct manuals in the nineteenth century, in which discourses of anxiety and containment may be observed in relation to the feminine. In this chapter I argue that in the late nineteenth century there is a shift of attention to areas of excess that moves from lust to luxury, and that this is fundamentally an avoidance tactic, by which masculine excess is sent to the background while feminine excess is used for the marking of social borders. Although lust may be sporadically reclaimed for the feminine, the policing of it remains as strong as does the policing of luxury, habitually expressed through the concept of fashion, and woman's taste for it. The reasoning for these vicissitudes of containment derives largely from the theories of Lou Charnon-Deutsch (1990) and Elisabeth Bronfen (1992), by which masculine anxiety is translated into the need for the containment of the feminine.

Surplus and excess

The concept of surplus is to do with things that we do not need: surplus is excess to requirements. But the way in which excess figures in late

---

[*] Bronfen 1992: 33

nineteenth-century texts in Spain indicates that excess is something that is threatening, that goes over the borders, and that threatens to disrupt the organizational lines of a wobbly and evolving social structure. Jo Labanyi's excellent study of *Gender and Modernization in the Spanish Realist Novel* (2000) indicates in numerous ways how excess (unproductive surplus) could be thought about or accommodated in society, and discusses how we can see a correlation between emergent economic theory and the literary productions of the nineteenth century. A complementary view can be obtained by considering, as Charnon-Deutsch and Bronfen suggest, a psychoanalytic approach to society by which anxiety triggers its own excesses, namely those of containment.

Georges Bataille's robust view of excess is one that offers a bridge between these two approaches and allows us to account for the excess or surplus that taxed nineteenth-century writers. He argues that our economy is one that is ultimately not purely economical: we produce more than we need, and we tend to lose and destroy things, so that excess 'must be spent, willingly or not, gloriously or catastrophically' ([1967] 1988: 21). For Bataille surplus can be positive in that it moves energy into different areas. Once its limits for containment are reached in one sphere, the energy or excess has to flow over in order to be contained in a further sphere. The context of the late nineteenth century in Spain is less positive about this move of excess, but it does demonstrate the same mobile dynamic. Specifically, Bataille's concept of moving excess helps to explain how the excess of *lujo* (lust) gets moved sideways into the moral economy, and is made to change places with the more easily identifiable and understandable *lujuria* (luxury).

In her foundational study of the *ángel del hogar* (angel of the hearth) Bridget Aldaraca presents a detailed discussion of the concepts of luxury and lust, *lujo* and *lujuria* (1991: 88–117). She offers as an initial epigraph the definitions of these terms:

> *el lujo*: excess in ostentation and comfort (*Diccionario de autoridades*)
> *la luxuria*: the unruly: appetite or excessive use of sensuality or carnality
> (*Diccionario de autoridades*)
> *luxus* (Latin): excess, licentiousness
> (*Diccionario crítico etimológico de la lengua castellana*)

Further to this, definitions for these terms taken from María Moliner's *Diccionario del uso del español* (*Dictionary of Spanish Usage*) (1966) read:

> *lujo*: ostentación de riqueza; cosa cuya realización supone cierta libertad, sobra de dinero, de tiempo; abundancia o gran número de ciertas cosas, que pueden no ser necesarias, pero tampoco estorban (*luxury*: ostentation of wealth; something that implies a certain level of freedom, excess of money or time, in order to be attained; abundance or great number

of certain things that do not have to be necessary, but which are not a problem)

lujuria: lascivia. Deseo sexual exagerado o vicioso; abundancia o exceso de algunas cosas (*lust*: lasciviousness. Extreme or vicious level of sexual desire; abundance or excess of certain things)

What is significant about Moliner's definition is that it adds on to *lujo* the concept of freedom. *Lujo* constitutes, therefore, the route to a form of social distinction, in that there is a choice to engage in ostentation. Engaging in *lujo* at least (if not *lujuria*) sets us not just apart from the crowd, but above it. In terms of *luxuria* or lust, Moliner again moves on from the idea of the unruly as posited by the *Diccionario de autoridades* cited by Aldaraca, and links it to *lascivia*. By so doing, she moves *luxuria* to being not just a question of excessive desire or carnality, but to the idea of talking about it. The person who is *lascivo* according to the Moliner definition is one dominated by sexual desire, 'y que lo demuestra en sus palabras, gestos, etc.' (and shows it in their words, gestures, etc.). It thus relates to a talking-up of sexual activity, promoting interest in it, marketing desire, and, as such, demonstrates an affinity of activity with *lujo*.

Aldaraca points out that the link between the two forms of excess is that 'Women dress to attract men, but it is also their attraction to finery which causes them to sell themselves or to pilfer their husband's estate in order to satisfy their insatiable vanity' (1991: 92–3). One vice leads to another, and if woman is victim of fashion, man is victim of passion for the woman embellished by fashion. We can see this illustrated in the pastoral advice offered by the Jesuit Pedro Calatayud, though the excess consists in having too much bare flesh on view, leading to spiritual homicide:

> Pero sabed que estas desnudeces son capaces de excitar muy malos deseos en el corazón de los hombres, y que estos malos deseos dan muerte a su alma, si les dan consentimiento; con que así, cuando en ese traje inmodesto y provocativo os exponéis a la vista de los hombres, sois rea de un homicidio espiritual. (Calatayud, cited in Claret 1859: 220)

> (But you should know that these forms of displaying naked flesh are able to awake most evil desires in the hearts of men, and that these evil desires bring death to his soul, if he allows it; therefore, when by wearing clothes that are immodest and provocative you expose yourselves to the gaze of men, you are guilty of spiritual homicide)

Aldaraca also astutely notes that the problem with feminine luxury is that it is an unknown and immeasurable quantity, and that it evades retribution. A husband cannot shoot a wife, Aldaraca crisply notes, 'when she is caught *in flagrante* in the ribbon store' (1991: 107).

There is a clear correlation between two sorts of spending that we can observe in the advice offered in conduct manuals and the advice to priests and in works of literature. The woman who cedes to vanity and spends in the literal sense of spending money on fashion engages in a field of excess that is difficult for the man to calculate, and she offers two offences. She is engaged in 'unproductive excess'. In relation to this we could note that Antonio María Segoviano in one of his Sunday lectures in 1869 defended consumption that was not excessive (and hence in a sense could be considered productive) but criticized women for necessarily being non-productive consumers (Aldaraca 1991: 100–1). Such activity is also one which legislation curtailed. Article 62 of the 1889 Código Civil (Civil Code) declared that women were allowed to spend household finances on what was necessary for the domestic economy, but not on fripperies (more examples of the sinfulness of the ribbon store) (relevant articles of this code are quoted in Jagoe et al. 1998: 265). But in spending, in the literal, material sense, woman also offered the second offence of being an individual. As Bryan Turner points out, with a reformulation of Descartes, 'I consume therefore I am', in spending woman establishes her identity (Turner 1996: 7).

Thus two of Galdós's female protagonists, Rosalía de Bringas in *La de Bringas* (*That Bringas Woman*) and Isidora Rufete in *La desheredada* (*The Disinherited*) illustrate forms of Turner's assertion that are emotionally inflected. Noël Valis, in her splendid study of *cursilería*, considers Rosalía with her passion for fashion and indicates how her activities fit into a model of a social negotiation, one that derives from experienced difference and the desire that such difference should not be there (Valis 2002: 156–71). Meanwhile, Isidora, with her desire to prove that she has been assigned to a lower social stratum than is right, engages in spending in order to provide herself with the appurtenances of a higher level. One type of excess (the madness of her alcoholic father) has dominated the opening pages. Isidora's desire to be assigned to (and contained in) a higher social stratum, a desire expressed partially in her spending excess, is thus also the impulse *not* to be tied to her father with his negative genetic inheritance.

Isidora's example points to an interesting aspect of excess, by which one form of excess (spending) is part of a desperate strategy to have other social borders. Material artefacts are a tangible sign of what we would wish to be thought of as being, and offer a (fragile) superstructure of consolation for life's hardness, its emptiness, and its unsatisfactory social arrangements. Georg Simmel's writing on the philosophy of fashion (1923) articulates for us the social negotiations implied in fashion: we want to be players in the field, but to be distinguished among them. As Pierre Bourdieu will comment later, the consumer is part of the communication ring. When women in the nineteenth century consume, they are moving on to a social stratum distinct from that of being objects of passion (1984: 2).

Discourses of policing and control

Michel Foucault (1961) has reminded us of the ways in which sexual practices have, or have not, been in public discourse at different periods. In nineteenth-century Spain, as in many other European countries, the visibility of sexuality is through medical discourse about sexual activity, shared in part with religious discourse (Sinclair 2005). The type of medicine that came to hold sway in Spain in the mid-nineteenth century was that of 'hygienic medicine', its practitioners classed as *médicos higienistas* (see Sinclair 1998, ch. 5, and 2005). An example here illustrates how they were in agreement with leaders of the Church in perceiving that passions were detrimental to wellbeing: the two bodies of 'controllers' (doctors and confessors) united in their attempts to dissuade the public from excess.

My example is from Pedro Felipe Monlau, who in his 1857 treatise on personal healthcare outlined the detrimental effects of passionate excess:

> Los efectos de las pasiones son terribles. Como que en su esencia no son más que transgresiones higiénicas, pueden producir todas las enfermedades conocidas. La mitad de las tisis pulmonares, así adquiridas como hereditarias, reconocen por causa el *amor* o la *lujuria*. La gota y las flegmasías agudas del tubo intestinal, en los más de los casos, no son sino tristes frutos de la intemperancia, y sobre todo de la *gula*. Las enfermedades crónicas del estómago, de los intestinos, del hígado, del páncreas y del bazo, son generalmente debidas a la *ambición*, a los *zelos*, a la *envidia*, o a largos y profundos pesares. (Monlau 1857: 379–80)

> (The effects of the passions are terrible. Since by their nature they are simply transgressions against what is required for health, they can produce all known illnesses. Half the cases of tuberculosis, whether caused by contagion or through heredity, are due to *love* or to *lust*. Gout and acute inflammations of the intestine, in the majority of cases, are simply the result of intemperance, above all of *gluttony*. Chronic disorders of the stomach, of the intestines, of the liver, the pancreas and the spleen, are the result of *ambition*, of *jealousy*, of *envy*, or of extended and profound grief.)

Here the discourse of the deadly sins is brought into service to strengthen medical control of excess. Be excessive, and it will end in tears. The discourse of sin is pushed to the margins of the body, where it is made explicit. Consonant with modern theory on psychosomatic disorders, excess in the department of the emotions and the desires is coupled to signs of physical excess.

Female-authored texts of containment

It was not only male writers in nineteenth-century Spain who uttered dire warnings about excess. Conduct manuals authored by women are equally unequivocal in their attitude. But at the same time we can see in them a capacity for moderation. The 1861 conduct manual of Emilia Serrano de Tornel, an early feminist, articulates in a no-nonsense way how one can follow fashion and yet be restrained. She attacks fripperies (the idea of being caught *in flagrante* in a ribbon shop again comes to mind):

> Un aderezo, un prendido, un traje de baile, son muchas veces, lectoras queridas, la base de grandes catástrofes; la exageración del lujo, el exceso de los gastos en blondas, sedas y terciopelos, ¿no colocan a cada cual en otra esfera, en otro mundo que, no siendo el de su posición social, da por resultado seguro las deudas, los alcances, las reyertas y disenciones con el esposo, que ve aterrado tal desorden? (Serrano de Tornel 1861: 62)

> (A trimming, a fastening, a ball gown, dear readers, are frequently at the base of great catastrophes; exaggeration in luxury, excess in spending on lace, silks, and velvets, and do you not see how they place individuals in another sphere, in another world, which, not being that of their own social position, gives rise to debt, monetary losses, disputes and quarrels with one's husband, who is struck with terror at the sight of such disorder?)

The road to perdition, it would seem, is indeed strewn with lace trimmings. But a potential solution is perceived by Serrano de Tornel, who advises that what is essential is keeping an eye on the figures (rather than fashion for the figure). She posits that:

> El gran tacto de la mujer debe ser, saber equilibrar los gastos, y que cubiertos los necesarios de la casa, pueda acudir a vestirse con el decoro que reclama su posición, la de su esposo y la de su nombre; pero sólo como la corresponda, y no aspirando la obrera a igualarse con la clase media, ni ésta a parodiar a la aristocracia. (Serrano de Tornel 1861: 64)

> (Woman's great skill has to be to balance out costs, and, once the necessary expenses of the household have been met, she can then set about dressing with the dignity required by her position, that of her husband, and that of her family name; but only according to what is appropriate, so that the working-class woman should not aspire to be part of the middle classes, nor should a woman of that class parody the aristocracy.)

From this we can see that the point is not a simple economic one, of women who squander the family finances (although that is obviously an issue), but is to do with staying in one's class (an issue of proper containment).

By the 1880s, however, there seems to have been more of an accommodation to the idea of spending. Joaquina García Balmaseda, for example, believes that *lujo* is not a problem if controlled by arithmetic:

> No es, pues, el lujo censurable cuando el lujo no hace olvidar la *aritmética*. La mujer que sabe contar y arreglar sus gastos con relación a sus ingresos, puede gastar y debe gastar lo que permite su fortuna, que para alguien se han de fabricar los chales de la India y las joyas de gran valor. (García Balmaseda 1882: 28)

> (Luxury is not therefore to be censured when it does not cause *arithmetic* to be forgotten. The woman who knows how to count and set her expenses in order in relation to her income, may spend, and indeed should spend, what her fortune allows her, since shawls from India and precious jewellery have to be made for someone.)

Again and again, women's writings continue to declare that the prime danger is excess, and that vanity (linked inevitably to woman's excessive spending) is woman's chief sin. María Clemencia Castaños lists the sins to which women are prone: they are subject to 'la vanidad, el orgullo, la envidia, la pereza' (vanity, pride, envy, sloth) (in that order) (1884: 13). And vanity of woman is what produces the sin of *luxuria* in man (Galiana y Albaladejo 1861: 4).

Advice against *lujo* also took the form of the recommendation of simplicity in dress, often in a manner that suggested simplicity of mind in the reader, for example, on the purpose of clothes. Luciana Monreal de Lozano indicated – albeit implicitly – that the invention of underwear diminished the need for frequent washing. As she informed her readers, the ancients had managed without underwear by washing once or twice a day (1884: 23). Curiously, this runs contrary to what Galdós was to suggest in *Fortunata y Jacinta* (1884–86), which is that the improvements in plumbing at the period encouraged more washing, and a greater market for fine underwear, an economic shift of which his character Isabel Arnáiz takes advantage (Pérez Galdos 1997: I, 150–6).

We can regard washing as one of the ways of keeping the body (with its tendency to smell and dirt) under control; it is our way of dealing with the body's natural excess that is perpetually self-renewing. This advice on washing can be bracketed with one of the concerns of fashion, the importance of the corset. Thus if women are given to excess in the form of fashion, and the spending required to attain it, paradoxically, the actual nature of fashion in this period is to do with containing rather than spending. Thus when advice is offered in a *Compendio de higiene para niñas* (Compendium of Hygiene for Girls) it singles out four items of clothing that most require attention: 'el corsé, sombrero, calzado y corbata' (corsets, hats, shoes, and neckties) (Barberá y París 1897: 50). The last three in the list presumably require attention since they are obvious markers of fashion and status. But prime place is given to the corset. And as the author warns (and as Bryan Turner observes), this containing garment ensured not just the effect of fragility in women, but the actual fragility of women, because it could suppress menstruation (Barberá y París 1897: 51; Turner 1996: 192–3). The woman conforming to the stereotypical image of the feminine simultaneously moved out of the functioning body of the feminine. Corseted (contained) women might actually move further out of a world of heterosexual exchange, in which they were object. Through being consumers they could express an independent identity; so, too, unexpectedly, they could move out of the form of the feminine precisely through the fashions of the feminine. Corsets were thus double containers of excess.

Fashion was therefore an embodiment of excess that might paradoxically provide its own containing solution (both for the physical excess of woman, her exuberant flesh, and for her bodily and potentially messy femininity). In relation to man, however, it was more problematic. There was the perception, mentioned earlier, that it might incite man to his own excess, passion. But it was also thought of something that might 'contaminate' him and be injurious for his masculinity. Labanyi has commented on the feminizing effect of fashion on man (2000: 155–56, 232–34), and it was a recurrent concern in women writers of the late nineteenth century. This was so much the case for the feminist Concepción Jimeno de Flaquer that what she says on the topic in the *La mujer española* (The Spanish Woman) (1877) she repeats almost *verbatim* in *Evangelios de la mujer* (Gospels for Women) (1900: 110–11):

> Es vergonzoso, criminal y humillante ver a un hombre en un almacén de modas, ocupándose en hacer apologías de las últimas, plegando y desplegando telas delicadísimas, que ofrecen en sus manos el terrible contraste que presenta a nuestra vista el raso y la estameña.
> ¿No es doloroso que el hombre, dotado de robusta naturaleza, de gran musculatura y de fuerza atlética, se apodere de pequeños trabajos, únicos que puede desempeñar la mujer por su delicada contextura y su pobre organización física?
> Es deplorable que un hombre gaste el vigor de su juventud en trenzar cabello, en peinar bucles y rizar sortijillas y tirabuzones.
> Los peluqueros no debían existir. (Jimeno de Flaquer 1877: 119–20)

> (It is shameful, criminal, and humiliating to see a man in a dress shop, occupied in conversing about fashion, folding and unfolding delicate fabrics, which in his hands present the terrible contrast between silk and sackcloth. Is it not to be lamented that men, endowed with robust constitution, strong muscles, and athletic strength, should devote himself to small tasks that only woman, with her delicate being and poor physical state, should carry out. It is deplorable that a man should waste the strength of

his youth in plaiting hair, combing curls, and making tight or loose ringlets. Male hairdressers should not exist.)

In the way that we think of the effects of passive smoking, it appears then that passive fashion could endanger the proper sexuality of men.

A further issue of wellbeing in relation to fashion, this time the wellbeing of the nation, is the concern of a text of 1882, 'El lujo en los pueblos rurales' (On Luxury in Country Towns), written by Rosario Acuña Villanueva for the *Gaceta Agrícola* (Farmers' Gazette). Here the man who follows fashion becomes a caricature of what he should be, as he runs after the chimeras of an artificial world. In the following vignette, the agricultural labourer takes on the attributes of *lo cursi*, a term variously translated as 'affected', 'pretentious', 'sentimental', 'chichi', and characteristically reserved for feminine behaviour:

> el labrador de nuestros pueblos, cuidándose con minucioso esmero sus blancas manos, adornado de los mil dijes con que la moda convierte al hombre en caricatura, buscando en las impresiones del juego, de la embriaguez o de la liviandad, un olvido voluntario a sus angustias financieras, disimulando el estado ruinoso de su moralidad bajo una máscara de ilustración, procurando ocultar el egoismo de su corazón, helado en el vacío de un hogar sin amor y sin belleza, por medio de un apasionamiento ridículo a las bellas artes. (Acuña Villanueva 1882: 27–8)

> (the labourer of our villages, taking care of his white hands with delicate care, adorned with the countless trinkets with which fashion turns man into a caricature, seeking in the experience of gambling, drinking, or loose living to forget his financial difficulties, hiding the disastrous state of his morality beneath a mask of learning, trying to hide the selfishness of his heart, frozen in the emptiness of a home without either love or beauty, through a ridiculous passion for the arts.)

The link between fashion, vanity, and passion is now suggested as being somewhat other than that initial simple model by which woman, prey to her vanity, becomes engaged in fashion and incites the passion of man. Here the *labrador*'s conversion into a being of fashion and artifice ultimately affects the nation. The *lujo* to which he is prey is a 'mal invasor, repugnante siempre en los grandes centros de las naciones, y mucho más en los hogares del agricultor' (an invading evil, always repugnant when found in capital cities, and much more so when found in the home of the farm labourer). It is not the *lujo* of the rich man, whose income obliges him to enjoy as many pleasures as are offered him by civilization, but a *lujo* that affects the life of the countryside, with dire effects on the nation. It is a 'lujo ruín, estrecho, lleno de privaciones y de congojas' (a wretched, narrow form of luxury, full of deprivation and anxiety), one that leaves the ignorant (and deceived) labourer with neither bread nor virtue (Acuña Villanueva 1882: 5–6).

Discourses of desire and imagination

In this final section I shall turn to literature, to two little-known novels of the period written by Spanish women, which differ in their ways of dealing with vanity and passion, those two forms of excess of female and male. The two texts are *El lujo* by Ángela Grassi y Trechi (1865) and *María Magdalena* by Matilde Cherner (1878). The first considers *lujo*, and the second *luxuria*. The first is arguably predictable in the light of the discourses from the conduct manuals that we have seen, and takes a conservative and critical approach to its topic. The second is circumspect about *lujo*, but allows space for passion, and in this case the theory of Bronfen allows for a complexity of reading.

In *El lujo*, the desire for finery is presented as something passed down within the family, forming part of the earliest environment. Nurture is virtually equated with nature. Claudina and Marcos, the brother and sister affected by this contagion, are orphaned early in the text, with no further inheritance than that of their parents' social ambitions (a trope that will reappear in altered form in *La desheredada*, by Galdós). With the passage of two years, and a move to an urban environment, Claudina's appearance indicates that a severe physical degeneration has taken place, one that is linked to her being affected by the desire for *lujo*. Indulging in *lujo* in this novel is thus presented less as a misdemeanour than as a matter of victimization. The warning offered by the narrative about social, moral, and physical danger is sharpened by the fact that sophistication and a life of luxury appear to lead to death. An early observation in the novel points to Claudina's envy of her companion Teresa for her fashionable clothes and possessions. This envy provides Claudina's 'entry' into a world of desire and luxury. By Chapter 7, Teresa, now aged thirty, looks ten years older. This premature ageing is perceived as what results from her having been a victim of her desires. But her downfall is also attributed to a lack of basic arithmetic. The sage advice of writers such as Serrano de Tornel on how to keep an eye on expenses is something that has clearly passed Teresa by.

My other example demonstrates how women novelists at this time did not restrict their output to cautionary tales about the fate that awaited those who gave in to vanity. An interesting border case is that of Matilde Cherner, who wrote under the male pseudonym of Rafael Luna. Her self-positioning as author is in itself significant and an indicator of how she tries to straddle the two spheres of man and woman. The plot of her novel promotes the idea of passion, apparently subscribing to the idea of a heterosexual relationship based on desire. Her story of a fallen woman is unconventional in that it mixes two strands, presenting as its protagonist a woman who is superior, and intellectual, and who eventually experiences, or rather succumbs to, passion. Thus all options, *lujo* and *luxuria*, domains of masculine and feminine, appear to be combined.

At the outset the novel presents a classic exemplary tale warning of the sexual evils that lie in wait for women, despite their virtuous behaviour and control of excess. Our heroine María Magdalena (in her early teens, and her name presaging her fate), is presented as one who in no way is guilty of her fall. When she and her mother fall on hard times, they live with greater and greater economy, sinking into poverty and starvation and eventually her mother dies. Distraught, María Magdalena wanders around the streets, looking for the river so she can drown herself. She collapses and faints, only to find herself in the house of Celestina, the local brothel-keeper (whose name points to the archetypal example of a woman of this profession in Spain). Initially caring for her, Celestina then forces María Magdalena into a life of prostitution.

Cherner indicates a fundamental difference between victim and abuser. The Celestina figure shows all the ravages and physical deformities that twenty years later would be the sort associated by the Italian criminologist Cesare Lombroso with a life of excess and crime (see Lombroso 1896). She has a flattened nose, eyes that are lash-less, round and agitated, reddened by alcoholic abuse, heavy brows, heavy and bony hands, and the whole is coupled with an attitude of fear, calculation. By contrast, her victim, when seen on her deathbed, lacks such features. Only twenty, mortally ill, her features tell of former social distinction:

> su bello y expresivo semblante no había perdido nada de su encanto y distinción. Aunque la palidez que cubría su rostro podía creerse hija del mal y la postración, el óvalo perfecto de su cara, sus finas facciones, sus cejas y pestañas sumamente negras y el delicado tinte moreno que animaba un tanto su sedosa tez, la denunciaban como de pálido e interesante color. (Cherner 1878: 18)
>
> (her beautiful and expressive face seemed to have lost none of its charm and distinction. Even though the pallor flooding her face could be judged to be born of evil and prostration, the perfect oval of her face, her fine features, intensely black eyebrows and eyelashes, and the delicate olive hue that enlivened her silky complexion declared her colouring to be pale and interesting.)

Her fine hands protect her from the roughness of the sheet, with delicacy, providing a boundary against excess of roughness:

por bajo de la barba, sin duda para impedir que la grosera tela de la sábana rozara su rostro, asomaban las puntas de unos dedos finos y torneados, adornados de uñas largas y ovaladas, teñidas, a causa del mal, de un ligero color azulado. (Cherner 1878: 19)

(below her chin, doubtless to prevent the rough material of the sheet from touching her face, there appeared the tips of fine and shapely fingers, adorned with long oval nails, tinged, because of her illness, with a faintly blue colour.)

The observer of these differences is Benavides, a doctor who acts as a masculine textual mediator for the girl's story (before she dies she leaves him with a written account of her life), policing the margins between innocence and a life of immorality, between fashion, passion, and intellectual superiority. If the fallen heroine is distinguished by her superiority, the labelling of that superiority comes from that habitual authority of the period, the doctor, man of science and observer of physical and moral decadence.

The name of the young victim, or rather her assumed name from the brothel, is Aspasia. This link to the consort of the Greek statesman Pericles denotes Cherner's intention to demonstrate how a woman can survive on the margins of acceptance and distinction. The historical Aspasia, educated and intelligent, was known for her literary gatherings and, through her intelligence, was powerful and respected. The Aspasia of the novel similarly is able to create a life of distinction for herself within the brothel. This distinction is based not upon her physical beauty, but on her literary and social activity, particularly through her creation of a literary circle. She follows in the best traditions of the courtesan.

But the narrative of Aspasia contains a rogue element, and in this we can see how even this unconventional woman novelist brings her heroine to heel, punishing her through the weakness to which her passion exposes her. There is a dual presentation of Aspasia, as victim and as woman who rises above her fate as victim, remaining untouched by the environment of the brothel. Aged fourteen or fifteen when she is taken into the brothel, her memoirs record how 'Causábanme instintivo disgusto las caricias que los hombres prodigan, con demasiada insistencia a veces, a las niñas de corta edad' (Instinctively I was upset by the caresses that men, all too often, lavish on girls of tender years) (Cherner 1878: 31). She recounts how for a year after her enforced entry into a life of prostitution she reacted mechanically to the demands made on her, her salvation being her ability to separate body and mind: 'Toda aquella corrupción, todas aquellas monstruosidades de que era víctima mi pobre cuerpo, jamás llegaron a contaminar mi alma, siempre pura en medio de aquellas abominaciones, ni mi corazón y mis sentidos, que no tomaban en ellas la más mínima parte' (All that corruption, all those monstrous things my body was subjected to, never came to touch my soul, which remained pure in the midst of such abomination, nor were my heart and senses affected, never taking the smallest part in it all) (Cherner 1878: 69).

This separation between mind and body stands in contradistinction to what Bronfen perceives as the significance for woman and her body, where a lack of boundaries and meanings is the precise cause of masculine anxiety, and consequently of masculine desire for containment and control. Bronfen argues convincingly for a double meaning of woman and her body in the world of man. Woman is irrevocably associated on the one hand with nature, and, in her persona as Other, with the connotations of 'womb-tomb-home'. Through the persona of Eve, she is associated with temptation, passion. Eve and the Virgin Mary lead equally to difficulty, both 'are equated with aspects of death and as such also mark the limit and vanishing point of the culture they give birth to' (Bronfen 1992: 66). Aspasia, in her fall (into the brothel), repeated by her 'fall' into romantic love with La Sierra, is an Eve figure, contrasting with that of Aspasia, the woman who, between these two episodes, acts as inspiration and centre of an intellectual circle (a new type of Virgin figure).

This splitting of the central female figure of the novel, mirrored by what Aspasia sees as the split she has achieved between mind and body, also echoes Bronfen's comments on Freud's discussion of the *fort-da* game of the child. This game is to do with separation (from the maternal, and hence dangerous, body, mastery and control). Woman is made into an object, no longer able to threaten. Separating from her is a move that offers individual definition (and safety) to the child. Her body is a 'trope for the "soma" which must be restrained or renounced by the child as it moves from the position of primary narcissism to that of the speaking subject bound by symbols and laws of the community' (Bronfen 1992: 32).

Aspasia is above fashion, vanity, and *lujo*. As such, she evades the traditional pitfall for the feminine. But – hovering in a social context where she is virtually masculine (she decides her fate, exacts respect, has distinction) – she finally falls victim to a masculine fate, that of passion. Charnon-Deutsch has reminded us that male characters in male-authored novels of the nineteenth century habitually do well in terms of relationships and general survival and enjoyment, thus encouraging the male reader as he learns 'that even the most mediocre of men can inspire passion in nearly every woman he meets' (Charnon-Deutsch 1990: 37). Not so Aspasia, who is subjected to the fate of the woman as victim a second time over. Having fallen because she could not help it, because she was abused, she now 'falls' passionately for a student. And, consonant with a variety of unsatisfactory male characters in male-authored novels (see the discussion of Luis's initial problems with his masculinity in Valera's *Pepita Jiménez*, and other issues of masculinity in Charnon-Deutsch 1990: 21–40), we find that in his diminished masculinity La Sierra is an unworthy recipient of that passion. His physical attributes point to a masculinity that hovers on the borders of insecure sexual definition:

> Su figura tan esbelta, que casi parecía endeble, era nerviosa y recia en vez de afeminada, trasluciéndose su poderosa musculatura en la flexibilidad y desarrollo de sus delgados miembros.
> Contando apenas veinte años, eran aún imberbes sus facciones, por más que hubieran ya del todo perdido la frescura de su primera edad, apareciendo apáticas y decaídas cuando no las animaba algún afecto.
> (Cherner 1878: 95)

> (his slender figure, so slender it appeared almost weak, was nervous and strong instead of effeminate, his powerful musculature shining through in the flexibility and development of his slim limbs. Barely twenty years old, his face was as yet beardless, even though his features had already lost their initial freshness, now seeming apathetic and fallen unless they were affected by some emotion.)

Aspasia's passion for a man who is worthy in her eyes rather than in those of the rest of the world is described as an illness to which she succumbs. Yet its advantage, from the point of view of how Aspasia is viewed by the narrator, and consequently presented to a reader we might presume to be female, appears to allow her to penetrate the world of the masculine. She sees clearly into the world of the passions, which – giving her some sense of personhood – restores her to where she was before her initial 'fall':

> La fiebre que consumía mi cuerpo y embotaba mis fuerzas, daba lucidez y energía a mi espíritu, permitiéndole sondear los misterios de nuestras humanas pasiones, y dejándole entrever en aquel amor, fuente para mí de toda pura dicha, la rehabilitación de mi pasada existencia.
> (Cherner 1878: 100)

> (The fever that consumed my body and blocked my strength gave clarity and energy to my mind, allowing it to penetrate the mysteries of our human passions, and allowing it to glimpse through that love, source for me of all bliss, the recuperation of my past existence.)

The mediation of the story of Aspasia through a male narrator and the doctor, Benavides, means that her story appears as a between-men transaction. Having moved into the world of the masculine, she is kept in place by a framework of masculine recognition and definition. But in the middle of it, we have not only her separation of mind and body, reflecting that of the child/man who has to separate from the mother/death, but also the fact that she writes her memoirs. Her fate is made known to the narrator through this written account that is handed to the doctor, so that she has defined her own self, at least within the text. Cherner, her female creator, having explored the limits of distinction for her heroine, finally conforms to social policing, and does not allow her to thrive. There are strong shades of Bronfen 1992 here, both in the internal plot and in the narrative structure in which it is contained.

Conclusion

The boundaries on *lujo* and *luxuria* seem to be relatively simple when we are in the area of discourses of authority, that is, conduct manuals, whether written by men or women, although the women are frequently practical in their sense of limitation. But when it comes to fiction, and particularly to the type of minor works of fiction I have referred to, there are some deviations. None the less, while excursions into risky border areas, as exemplified by Cherner, allow some crossing into unknown territories of conduct, they retain frameworks that re-impose policing. Furthermore, the restraints or constraints of the models are impressive. Thus even when female-authored fictions promote the idea of passion (with the example of Matilde Cherner writing as Rafael Luna) what is subscribed to is still a heterosexual relationship based on desire, objects, etc., despite the promotion of the heroine-as-intellectual (Aspasia). Women may seek to elude this template of stereotypical femininity through consumerism that is restrained and policed. The issue is whether the policing is not of sexuality but of the consumerism that would allow them to escape the template of patriarchy and heterosexuality, and whether it is of a form of sexuality that would allow them agency and independence.

> The construction of Woman-as-Other serves rhetorically to dynamise a social order, while her death marks the end of this period of change. Over her dead body, cultural norms are reconfirmed or secured, whether because the sacrifice of the virtuous, innocent woman serves a social critique and transformation or because a sacrifice of the dangerous woman re-establishes an order that was momentarily suspended due to her presence. (Bronfen 1992: 181)

Further reading

Aldaraca, Bridget, 1991. *El ángel del hogar: Galdós and the Ideology of Domesticity in Spain* (Chapel Hill: University of North Carolina Press)

Bronfen, Elisabeth, 1992. *Over Her Dead Body: Death, Femininity and the Aesthetic* (Manchester: Manchester UP)

Jagoe, Catherine, Alda Blanco, and Cristina Enríquez de Salamanca, 1998. *La mujer en los discursos de género: textos y contextos en el siglo XIX* (Barcelona: Icaria)

Labanyi, Jo, 2000. *Gender and Modernization in the Spanish Realist Novel* (Oxford: OUP)

Valis, Noël, 2002. *The Culture of 'Cursilería': Bad Taste, Kitsch, and Class in Modern Spain* (Durham, NC: Duke UP)

14

Women as Cultural Agents in Spanish Modernity

SUSAN KIRKPATRICK

What form will modernity take in Spain? This question, expressed as anxiety about Spain's failure to be modern enough, on the one hand, or about its abandonment of national tradition on the other, dominated public discussion at the end of the nineteenth century. That Spain *was* modernizing was an underlying economic reality (Ringrose 1996: 56–80), but institutions, ideologies, and social groups were engaged in an increasingly contentious struggle to shape the social and cultural contours of the new Spain. Most thought, however, that if women had a role in this process, it was as guardians of tradition and social stasis. Even Emilia Pardo Bazán, the only significant feminist intellectual of the time, stated flatly that, 'siempre que la mujer española revela interés político, se adhiere a la España antigua; la nueva, socialmente hablando, no se ha formado su elemento femenino' (whenever Spanish women reveal a political position, they adhere to the old Spain; socially speaking, the feminine component of the new Spain has not been formed) ([1892] 1981: 31–2). From the perspective of the twenty-first century, however, study of print culture tells a somewhat different story about Spanish women's participation in the modernizing process.

Although Spanish women were categorically denied any political rights, and their exercise of economic power was severely restricted by legal and social codes, already at the dawn of the nineteenth century some women privileged by birth and by location in more cosmopolitan centers found a way to be part of public discourse through aesthetic activity –painting, writing, translating. As the century progressed and the devastation caused by the Peninsular War (1808–14) and the loss of colonial empire gave way to uneven but accelerating economic modernization, women took up the pen in increasing numbers to find release, solidarity, and subjective identity in poetic expression and the creation of fiction. In tandem with the development of the press industry in Spain, a growing female reading public found in these women authors a recognizable articulation of their personal aspirations and frustrations. In this process was shaped a bourgeois feminine identity that – though predominantly conservative, as Pardo Bazán noted – incorporated contemporary ideological currents and was highly similar to predominant models of feminine identity in France and England, countries considered exemplars of modernity by Spaniards. In particular, one social role or identity consolidated by the nineteenth-century women writers – that of the woman writer – formed a basis from which young women coming of age at the beginning of the twentieth century could assert their own agency as cultural or aesthetic producers. Still denied political rights and only with great difficulty gaining access to economic independence, young Spanish women seized on new modes of cultural production as pathways to fuller participation in their society, and in so doing ultimately became visible agents of Spain's twentieth-century modernity.

Toward the end of the eighteenth century Spain's elite urban milieux saw the formation of institutions associated with the emergence of a modern public sphere. In the academies, cultural societies, and periodical publications through which elite Spaniards began to form opinions and interests distinct from the Church–State power monopoly that had governed for two centuries, a few women found the opportunity to make their voices heard. While fewer than 10% of Spanish women as a whole were literate, the educated women in families receptive to enlightenment values participated in salons and even in the Royal Academy of Art. A few lettered women found in the theater and in the burgeoning press an outlet for their writing (Bolufer 1998: 309–17). The prodigious Josefa Amar y Borbón (1749–1833), widely viewed as the feminine face of the Spanish Enlightenment, published books and treatises; others adopted a mediating role as translators, influencing discourse in the realm of letters through selection and interpretation (Bolufer 2003, Theresa Ann Smith 2006).

The case of the poet Gertrudis Maria Hore (1742–1801) offers a striking example of how a late-eighteenth-century woman negotiated the co-existing and often conflicting strata of old and new, residual and emerging institutions and practices in order to participate in cultural production. A member of the mercantile elite, she was an active participant in the salon culture of mid-eighteenth-century Cádiz and Madrid, writing verses in the fashionable rococo style and circulating them in manuscript among her friends and admirers. Much of this poetry, like that of Hore's male peers, featured erotic and sensual content lightly veiled by idealizing pastoral conventions (Constance Sullivan 1992). Suddenly, at the age of 35, Hore entered a convent. Whether she was coerced by considerations of family honor or moved by sincere religious vocation is unknown, but her reclusion did not prevent her from continuing to write. Indeed, like many intellectual women of the ancien regime, she found in the convent a propitious space for creative activity; unlike her predecessors, however, she discovered a modern way to make her work public – the periodical press. In 1787, nine years after entering the convent, she sent a selection of her poems to a leading vehicle of Enlightenment ideas, the newspaper *El Correo de Madrid* (Madrid Courier), initiating a decade during which her poems appeared not only in that paper but also in *Diario de Madrid* (Madrid Daily) and the *Diario de Barcelona* (Barcelona Daily). In reaching beyond the convent walls to an incipient periodical-reading public, Hore helped to lay a foundation for women's participation in modern print culture.

Hore's exact contemporary Josefa Amar y Borbón directly addressed the question of women's role as cultural agents in her *Discurso en defensa del talento de las mujeres* (Discourse in Defense of the Intelligence of Women and of Their Fitness for Government and Other Offices in which Men are Employed), written in 1886 as an active intervention into a raging debate about whether to admit women to the Madrid Royal Economic Society of Friends of the Nation. Despite her forceful arguments that women were equal to men in intellectual capacity, the royal decision, reflecting predominant opinion, created a separate *Junta de Damas* (Women's Auxiliary) rather than give women full membership in the Society.[1] In effect, the role offered to the women who wished to contribute to the progress of their country was that of mothers of the nation and it was reflected in the *Junta*'s agenda, which focused on foundling hospitals and training for destitute women (Smith 2006). Emanating from Jean-Jacques Rousseau, this view that women's place in society was determined by their reproductive function dovetailed with the gender ideology of Spain's Catholic tradition and would channel women's activity as producers of culture throughout the following century.

Cataclysmic events – the Napoleonic invasion and takeover of the Spanish state, eight years of guerrilla warfare, the rebellion of overseas colonies, and the reactionary policies of the restored Bourbon monarchy – disrupted the continuity of cultural as well as economic and social life in the first quarter of the nineteenth century. The impact on civil society, educational institutions, and the press, new arenas in which privileged women had begun to participate, was severe. Nevertheless, the politically unstable period of liberal reform initiated in 1832 was underpinned by gradual economic recovery and expansion, and new bourgeois forms of sociability emerged. As social clubs dedicated to literature and the arts sprang up in Spain's larger cities and a newly flourishing press industry sought wider markets, women belonging to the middle classes – landed gentry, lesser nobility, urban merchants, and professionals – began to take part in public culture. The first sign in the print archive of this development was the unprecedented publication of three volumes of poetry by woman authors between 1841 and 1843, which began

---

[1] It should be noted that Amar had already been admitted to full membership in the Aragonese Economic Society.

a trend: 67 books of poetry by women were published in the four following decades, and that rate doubled in the final twenty years of the century. The proliferation of woman-authored poems published in the periodical press, however, was even more significant in terms of circulation (Simón Palmer 1991). Even though after 1850 women writers shifted more of their output toward fiction, almost without exception those who gained national recognition launched their writing careers with a book of poetry.

The special place of poetry in Spanish women's emergence as producers of print culture merits some elaboration. The growth of the press industry was an important factor, but the consolidation of liberal ideals of self-realization in conjunction with the triumph of a conservative brand of Romanticism in Spain was also crucial. Women who had no formal education but possessed a feeling heart and enthusiastic imagination were authorized to think of themselves as poets by a Romantic aesthetic that viewed art as primarily the expression of emotion and imagination rather than the product of intimate knowledge of the classical tradition. Furthermore, in a society that prized as Spain did the religious piety of its women, historical romanticism à la Chateaubriand offered a personalized discourse of feeling closely associated with religious devotion that Spanish women could adapt for self-expression. From this mix, women writers of this period were able to forge the idea of a natural association between women and poetic expression.

Carolina Coronado (1823–1911), a pioneering figure among the new cohort of women poets, defended their existence against detractors by insisting 'La *poetisa* existe de hecho y necesita cantar, como volar las aves y correr los ríos, si ha de vivir con su índole natural, y no comprimida y violenta.' (the poetess exists in fact and must sing, as birds must fly and rivers must flow, if she is to live in accord with her nature and not violently constrained) (1846). Drawing on the liberal precept of an inherent right to self-expression and an assumed natural feminine lyricism, Coronado counters the hostility stemming from the continuing ideological weight of Spain's long tradition of secluding women at home, away from public attention. She and her contemporaries thus claimed a new kind of authority for their literary production – the authority to write from their hearts and nature, that is, to write *as* women, rather than in spite of being women.

Although Spain's women poets strategically presented their writing as the unconstrained expression of a natural, feminine inner self, considerable cultural work was required to produce and disseminate an image of feminine subjectivity that accommodated social norms, yet allowed women to recognize their inner experience. The poets who originally published in the 1840s – Coronado, Gertrudis Gómez de Avellaneda (1814–73), and Josefa Massanés (1811–87) – situated themselves as lyrical subjects in relation to verbal forms and social discourses that ranged from neo-classical didacticism, through Romantic sentimentality, to Byronic rebellion, but avoided expressions of ambitious or erotic desire that might be deemed inappropriate for virtuous women (Kirkpatrick 1989). The reception of this poetry by other women set off a chain reaction, as more women inspired by these models wrote and published – and in addition wrote to each other, forming epistolary networks of support and solidarity.

This interactive process of women reading and writing was sometimes described in their poetry, in no case more dramatically than by Vicenta García Miranda (1816- ?), a small-town widow who began writing in the 1840s. In a long poem recounting her coming-to-writing, she represents reading the verses of Carolina Coronado not only as a transformative experience, but as a kind of physical shock:

> Un eco solamente de otra lira,
> lira de otra mujer, que honra su sexo, [...]
> penetró en mi alma tan sonoro,
> y se extendió vibrando por los senos
> [...] de mi fiel corazón
> que al choque eléctrico
> pensé que en mil pedazos se rompiera,
> no cabiendo el júbilo en el pecho.
> (Kirkpatrick 1992: 48; first published 1855)

> (The mere echo of another lyre, the lyre of another woman, an honor to her sex [...] penetrated my soul with such resonance and spread vibrating through my faithful heart [...] till I thought the electric impact might break it in a thousand pieces, unable to contain such jubilation in my breast.)

Agitated and jubilant, García Miranda suffers a kind of vertigo upon encountering in Coronado's poetry the verbal image of a feminine poetic subject. Then, assuming that identity as her own, she is able to speak in the same poetic language: 'al ceder este estado tan violento, moduló mi garganta unos sonidos' (as this violent state subsided, my throat began to modulate some sounds). According to the story that García Miranda elaborated in letters as well as in this poem, she was only able to act as a poetic subject after reading a text that clearly identified the enunciating subject as feminine, even though she had earlier experienced inchoate longings and perceptions that later she came to understand as signs of her poetic vocation. Once launched, she wrote and published voluminously, addressing her poems to other women and participating enthusiastically in a developing discourse about women's experience.

Women's intervention as poets in mid-nineteenth-century print culture thus played a role in creating a kind of evolving verbal mirror in which literate nineteenth-century Spanish women came to see themselves as subjectively inhabiting a given social identity. Thus formed, the feminine poetic tradition functioned as part of a complex discourse that regulated women's self-representation throughout the rest of the century. After 1850, the evolving differentiation of the print market and the emergence of new techniques of distribution such as serial publication gave popular fiction and conduct manuals a predominant share of print products aimed at a feminine market. At the same time, the emerging contours of modern, capitalist Spain were modifying traditional gender ideology to project an ideal of bourgeois womanhood, the *ángel del hogar* (angel of the hearth) – pure, selfless, maternal, and exclusively domestic. Women such as Angela Grassi (1823–83), Faustina Sáez de Melgar (1834–95), and Pilar Sinués de Marco (1835–93), who had started their writing careers as poets, became dominant practitioners of the fiction through which the image of the domestic angel was elaborated, and in so doing shaped it in decisive ways. Whereas contemporary male ideologues of gender difference inveighed, as had their early modern forebears, against the morally poisonous effects of reading and writing for women, these writers consistently represented literacy as an integral part of the domestic woman's activities.

Alda Blanco, who has cogently analyzed how female authors of domestic novels converted a transgression (women writing) into a virtue by linking literacy and education to women's maternal role as moral instructors, singles out a telling passage from the icon of Spanish domestic fiction, Sinués's *El ángel del hogar* (1859), in which an exemplary mother gives her diary to her daughters to serve as a kind of conduct book. Blanco adds that:

> the author, Sinués, inscribes herself in this book as the mother of her readers and likewise recommends that they write, adopting a non-fictional narrative form – the diary, the prescriptive essay – for their texts [...] Although writing in this articulation is for the private sphere and private consumption, such diaries should circulate among daughters in an exchange that converts them into a public discourse for domestic space. (1998: 33)

Thus mid-nineteenth-century Spanish women naturalized women's writing, as Blanco puts it (1998: 26), in both lyric poetry and domestic fiction, justifying their new role in the production of print culture even as they helped constitute new feminine identities.

A closer look at the configuration of these women's self-representation as subjects reveals that textual strategies, genres, and social constraints formed a complex system of elements in tension. With its marked didacticism, woman-authored fiction propagated a highly regulated image of the forms of subjectivity necessary to the performance of women's domestic and maternal mission – tender-heartedness, patience, self-denial, purity, piety, and prudence. As narrative, this fiction inevitably traces a process by which female subjects are molded into angels of the hearth. In many cases, as in

Sinués's *El ángel del hogar*, that transformation takes place through moral education and example. In others, the female protagonist is taught her nature and place in society through life's harsh lessons, as is the case of the rebellious and self-seeking (and talented) central character of *La gaviota* (The Seagull) (1849) by the highly successful Cecilia Boehl von Faber (Fernán Caballero). Sometimes the difficulty of becoming a proper woman is represented: Sinués's novella *La sortija* (The Ring) (1887) relates the internalized rage and depression suffered by its protagonist before, with the help of a circle of supportive women friends, she can put aside her resentment and develop the submissive, altruistic qualities that will make her worthy of marriage (see Urruela 2001).

In counterpoint to the disciplinary aspects of women's fiction, the lyrical self-expressive tradition developed by Spanish women poets of this period allowed more personal articulations of desire, perception, and imagination. By offering a mirror in which middle-class women could identify as positive a broader spectrum of their inner life than permitted by didactic novels, lyric poetry made the identity of the domestic angel more attractive and assumable for women. From the beginning, a theme of nineteenth-century women's poetry was the feminine subject's struggle for freedom to express itself in the face of oppressive social conditioning. In an 1845 poem exhorting other women to write, Carolina Coronado used the image of suffocation to suggest the forced suppression of thought and feeling in women:

>   En el pasado siglo, intimidadas,
>   las hembras desdichadas
>   ahogaron entre lágrimas su acento [...]
>   No injustamente
>   su inspiración naciente
>   sofoquéis en la joven fantasía. [...]
>   [Q]ue penas y placeres
>   en silencioso tedio consumían
>   ahogando en su existencia
>   su viva inteligencia
>   su ardiente genio. (Coronado 1993: 345).

'In the last century, intimidated, unfortunate women *stifled* their voices in tears ...'. Coronado urged her sister poets not to follow their example: 'Do not unjustly suffocate the dawning inspiration of young fantasy'. The same verb (*ahogar*) is repeated a few stanzas later when she imagines the suffering of women of the past, 'who swallowed pains and pleasures in tedious silence, *stifling* lively intelligence and ardent genius in their existence'. Coronado and her women contemporaries perceived the act of writing poetry as the undoing of suffocation, as *desahogo* (relief). By creating an outlet, a breathing space for individuated feeling and thought, writing poetry

– and reading poetry by other women – brought relief from the heavily normative constraints imposed on middle-class women.

Although normative social pressures clearly shaped the women poets' characteristic enunciation of pious sentiment, filial tenderness, virtuous reflections, and chaste yearnings, more individuated and thus less angelic impulses are revealed in subtexts and sudden outbursts. With some frequency, the poet's desire thrusts against restrictions imposed by society, producing expressions of protest, complaint, and frustration – the very feelings that Sinués's protagonist must banish in order to become a properly adjusted female subject. A case in point is a poem by Victorina Sáenz de Tejada, a destitute and orphaned gentlewoman (precisely the situation of many heroines of didactic fiction), that expresses in only slightly veiled terms resentment of a male poet's freedom of life and artistic scope:

> 'Tú, en alas del raudo genio
> el éter puro cruzando,
> puedes cual águila alzarte
> a donde impera el rey astro;
> yo soy pobre pajarillo
> en mi jaula aprisionado;
> para volar tengo aliento,
> pero me falta el espacio [...]
> Por eso cantar tú debes
> y al siglo arrancar un lauro,
> que es tu porvenir la gloria
> y para mí sueño vano.
> Canta esperanzas y amores,
> gloria, nobleza, entusiasmo,
> y déjame a mí en silencio,
> tedio cruel devorando.
> (Kirkpatrick 1992: 268; first published 1865)

> (You, crossing the pure ether on the wings of speeding genius, can soar like an eagle to the realm of the sun; I am a poor little bird imprisoned in my cage; I have the spirit to fly but lack the space. [...] Therefore you should sing and win laurels from the world, for you the future is glory, for me a vain dream. Sing, then, of hopes and loves, glory, nobility, enthusiasm, and leave me in my silence, consumed by cruel tedium.)

In counterbalance to domestic fiction's insistence that by disciplining feelings women could come to regard the home as a space of happy fulfillment rather than a cage, this poem offers its readers an opportunity to share in venting frustration. There was less scope to express erotic – as distinct from ambitious – desire, however, since sexual purity was fundamental to any Spanish woman's claim to moral authority. Still, women poets found space for the expression of desire in the homoerotic. The practice and rhetoric of passionate friendship among women was widespread and had a notable place in women's fiction, but the erotic charge of its expressions was particularly intense in the poems women wrote to each other. For example, a poem by Dolores Cabrera y Heredia (1826–78) ends with these lines:

> si pudiese contemplar
> tus ojos negros y bellos,
> y tu frente y tus cabellos
> arrebatada besar,
> y el viento hiciese mover
> tus rizos sobre la mía [sic][...]
> el placer me mataría,
> ¡si es que nos mata el placer!
> (Kirkpatrick 1992:100; first published 1850)

(If I could gaze upon your beautiful black eyes, and enraptured kiss your hair and forehead; and if the wind moved your curls across my brow [...] I would die of pleasure, if it is true that pleasure kills!)

Such sensual intensity was absent from the domestic novel and from poetry about amorous relations with men, but it found an outlet in the sizeable corpus of women's friendship poems (Mayoral 1990b).

Women's fiction and women's lyric poetry, then, were interwoven in a complex system producing and reproducing in public culture self-representations that acted in a number of ways. In elaborating a version of feminine subjectivity based on assumptions of women's natural difference and their affinity for the domestic sphere, both genres helped install a gender ideology that preserved and justified the subordination of women while at the same time adapting older norms to a gradually modernizing bourgeois society.[2] Domestic fiction explicitly advocated women's participation in writing and reading practices as part of their strictly maternal and moral mission – in contradistinction to the traditional prohibition of women's reading. In its more contestatory aspects, lyric poetry was practiced and understood as the expression of suffering caused by women's disadvantageous position in society, yet in general this poetry functioned as a safety valve, allowing women to vent their anger and frustration with little damage to the subordinating system.Yet, in the final analysis, both genres worked subtle transformations in cultural understandings and representations of women, above all, by inserting women into the cultural conversation as writing subjects.

---

[2] However, as Joyce Tolliver points out in her essay in this volume, writers such as Sinués and Sáez de Melgar were more critical of prevailing norms in their sketches of Spanish life and customs.

It should be noted that, far from being marginalized, the woman writers who configured this discourse enjoyed considerable prestige during the reign of Isabel II (1843–68). Íñigo Sánchez Llama has analyzed in detail how the arbiters of high culture, such as the Royal Academy of Language and the literary critics of the time, promoted an aesthetic canon based on Catholic precepts, moral didacticism, and the historical nationalism of the more reactionary wing of Romanticism, all values that reflected the highly conservative liberalism prevailing among Spain's politically predominant groups at the time. A high proportion of women's literary production conformed closely to these values and, consequently, became part of what Sánchez Llama has termed the Isabelline canon (2000: 79–80, 91–104). The paradigmatic case is that of Cecilia Boehl von Faber (1796–1877), whose first published novel, *La gaviota* (1849), integrated depictions of Spanish customs with a fervent defense of Catholicism, traditional Spain, and the ideology of feminine domesticity, and was rapturously received by the critical establishment, which proclaimed its author 'Spain's Walter Scott' (Sánchez Llama 2000: 96). Although the home-centered fiction published by Grassi, Sinués, and Sáez de Melgar earned more measured praise, its convergence with the predominant aesthetic canon endowed it with considerable cultural authority.

As the more modern sectors of the economy grew and the establishment of a liberal state became more urgent, however, aesthetic canons changed too. The Revolution of 1868 dethroned Isabel II and, after a turbulent eight years, ended in 1875 with a political compromise that provided stability into the twentieth century – a constitutional monarchy that functioned through a pact among oligarchic groups. Didacticism and neo-Catholicism lost their prestige as other aesthetic canons accompanied the rise of a brilliant new Spanish realist novel. Now seeking to promote an imagined nation based on more secular and forward-looking values, critics and writers revealed how deeply the bourgeois division of the social field into separate, gendered spheres had become rooted in Spanish culture: they projected the realist aesthetic as objective, modern, authentically Spanish, and masculine, devaluing the earlier novelistic canon as imitative, sentimental, and essentially feminine – especially in terms of its authors and readers (Blanco 1995). By this time women writers had firmly established careers (they had in fact created the new social identity of the woman writer) and continued to influence readers in Spain and in Spanish-speaking America through their writing and through the journals they directed. Yet they were regarded as speaking to a feminine rather than a national audience.

The partition of late-nineteenth-century Spanish print culture into a masculine sphere of high seriousness, aesthetic vigor, and universal scope, on the one hand, and a feminine sphere defined as domestic, imitative, and limited, on the other, did not remain unchallenged. Two women intellectuals in particular opened a breach in the wall delimiting feminine activity. Concepción Arenal (1820–93), who was required to cross-dress in order to attend law courses in Madrid, also found it necessary to conceal her identity when writing articles and editorials for the mid-century liberal press, either under the name of her ailing husband or, after his death, anonymously. Devoting herself to work among prisoners and the poor, she became in effect a pioneering sociologist when she began to publish under her own name her conclusions about the consequences of poverty and ways to address them (Irizarry 1993). She played an active role in prison reform in Spain, and her work on prisons was known throughout Europe. In the public conversation about women's nature and place in society, her respected voice struck an independent note. Arenal directly addressed the ideology of feminine domesticity in *La mujer del porvenir* (The Woman of the Future) (1861) and *La mujer de su casa* (The Woman of the Home) (1883) with a critique of the idea that women were suited by nature to function only in the home, arguing instead for women's right to equal education and economic independence. Arenal's arguments that society would benefit if women were involved in addressing social problems provided intellectual reinforcement for women's increasing engagement in charitable and abolitionist organizations.

In the following generation, Emilia Pardo Bazán (1851–1921) became the most influential advocate of the idea that women were equal to rather than essentially different from men.[3] Asserting that, 'en el reino de las letras no hay, como en las iglesias protestantes, *lado de las mujeres y lado de los hombres*' (unlike a Protestant church, the domain of letters does not have a woman's side and a men's side) (1890: x), she boldly crossed the lines that fenced off women's writing and climbed to the top of Spain's nineteenth-century pantheon as a realist novelist, erudite essayist, and cosmopolitan literary critic. By the last decade of the century, she was not only a celebrated writer, but also actively intervened in important modernizing cultural institutions: she founded the leading intellectual journal of her time, *La España Moderna* (Modern Spain), single-handedly published a feminist periodical, and set up a press dedicated to translating significant European feminist works into Spanish. For a vanguard figure, Pardo Bazán was in many ways too far out in front of the mass of Spanish women, as she herself conceded when she concluded that publishing a cookbook was the only way she could sell her book series to women.

The continuing sway of the domestic ideal of feminine identity in Spain notwithstanding, at the end of the nineteenth century women's participation in public culture was by far broader and more diverse than at the begin-

---

[3] For a detailed discussion of Pardo Bazán's feminist positions, see Tolliver's essay in this volume.

ning of the century. A somewhat higher percentage of women, roughly 28%, could read and write (Martínez Cuadrado 1973:124), reflecting an anemic but increasing commitment to women's education. Sinués, Arenal, and Pardo Bazán were only the most visible of the many women writers advocating – with varying emphasis – improvements in educational and vocational opportunities for women. The growing acceptance of this agenda was registered in the 1892 Spanish-Portuguese-American Pedagogical Congress. In comparison with the pedagogical congress that had taken place a decade earlier, in 1892 an unprecedented number of women participated actively, either on the organizing committee or on the panels presiding at sectional meetings, and these women reflected the widening spectrum of professional positions occupied by Spanish women: teachers, normal school instructors, directors of private girls' schools, writers, physicians, and university students.

Heated debates pitted those who argued for women's equality with men in most areas of social life against those who resisted any departure from women's traditional subordination; in the end the resolutions adopted by majority vote moved toward a middle ground, supporting the goal of giving women an educational basis for economic independence in case they were widowed or remained single (Capel Martínez 1986: 128–9, 143–4). The consensus was reflected in the establishment of normal schools to train women teachers, as well as schools in commerce, telegraphy, languages, and typesetting for women of the urban lower middle classes who might need to support themselves by working outside the home (Scanlon 1986: 35). The everyday reality that peasant and working-class women worked in fields or factories had never been acknowledged by the ideologues of feminine domesticity. As a consequence, middle-class women who came of age around 1900 were able to define for themselves in the Spain of the new century more diverse roles than their mothers had known.

Legal codes and economic barriers restricting women's activity had not changed significantly by 1900, but the women writers of the nineteenth century had firmly established a pathway to participation in print culture. Although the language of lyrical sisterhood and didactic sentimentality was now outmoded ('evita como al fuego a las palabras bonitas que suenan y corren con dulce murmullo de arroyo' (avoid like fire pretty words that tinkle along with the sweet murmur of a brook), Pardo Bazán advised a young woman poet, 1890: x), women were finding a wide variety of new outlets for their productions. If Blanca de los Ríos (1862–1956), who began her career with a promising collection of poetry in 1881, became the doyenne of scholarly studies of Golden Age drama in the early twentieth century, her contemporary Sofía Casanova (1862–1958), also the author of well-received collections of verse, went in quite a different direction to become a successful journalist, supplying Madrid newspapers with stories from the front during the First World War and the Russian Revolution.

Thus, at one end of the spectrum of public intellectual life, women were pushing at the doors of the university system, which began officially admitting women with no restrictions in 1910. The government made Pardo Bazán Spain's first female university professor in 1916, although students protested this unprecedented move by refusing to attend her lectures. By 1920 there were more than 400 women at university, a small percentage of the total student body, but a significant beachhead (Scanlon 1986: 56). As the case of Casanova suggests, the other end of the spectrum – the rising mass media – also offered expanding opportunities for women to participate in shaping Spanish modernity. Advancing print technologies such as the incorporation of photography and the increasing literacy of the Spanish public worked together to create new products and new markets in which women had an ever greater role.

No figure better exemplifies the many facets of women's cultural activity at the beginning of the twentieth century than that of Carmen de Burgos (1867–1932). Separated from an abusive husband and with a young child to support, she took advantage of emerging educational opportunities for women by attending normal school, and then obtaining an appointment as a normal school teacher in Madrid. Once settled in the capital, she moved into the field of journalism, a highly masculine space in which conditions were ripe for a feminine voice. Burgos supplied this with weekly columns for women readers under the pen name *Colombine*. She boldly used her success in this genre to stir up public debate on topics that cut across older ideals of domestic virtue. In 1903 she conducted an opinion poll on divorce among her readers, and in 1906 solicited readers' opinions on woman suffrage. Such audacity, far from harming her career, attracted public attention and sold newspapers. She became a much sought-after writer and public speaker. Although like most of her predecessors she based her ideas about women's place in society on their reproductive role, unlike them, she considered women's maternal mission the basis for their duty to participate in public life in support of progressive causes that would reduce exploitation and improve the well-being of families (Burgos 1912).

Another area in which Burgos expanded on and modernized nineteenth-century print products for women was the practical manual. Reflecting a widening female readership, the increasing prosperity of the middle classes, and the development of consumer society, the conduct manual morphed into books on home decoration, etiquette, and beauty. Burgos published a stream of titles in this mass-market-oriented venue, offering advice on household management, sewing, decorating, charm, and beauty. Although much of this was hack work, Burgos advanced in these books the message that women in their domestic activities were also aesthetic subjects, engaged in the creation of beauty, taste, and culture (Kirkpatrick 2003: 165–210). And it was through literary creation that Burgos intervened in yet a third new arena of print culture that took off like wildfire in the first decade of the twentieth century – the highly profitable paperback short novel series pitched both in price and style toward a mass audience.

In the course of her lifetime, Burgos published over 100 novellas in these series, using the genre's formal characteristics – linear narrative, vivid language, intense emotional effects, unexpected twists – to convey her perceptions of changing relations among the classes and the genders in the modern, urban Spain that was coming into being. Anja Louis has recently analyzed how Burgos' melodramatic stories fed into the public debate about marriage, divorce and women's equality (2005). Burgos was, in fact, one of a cohort of women writers (including Concha Espina and María Martínez Sierra, in addition to Casanova and de los Ríos) who in cultivating the short novel made a significant mark on Spanish culture. As Amparo Hurtado has observed, the novellas published by these women 'contribuy[eron] [...] de modo especial a "normalizar" la voz femenina en el panorama general de la literatura y la sociedad española de hace un siglo' (contributed in an especially significant way to the 'normalization' of the feminine voice in the general panorama of Spanish literature and society a century ago) (1998: 151).

Indeed, wide-ranging as Burgos's interventions may be, they are representative rather than exceptional in relation to women's expanding role in early twentieth-century public culture. Among her exact contemporaries some, such as Concha Espina, achieved critical prestige as novelists, others wrote for the theater, many contributed to the periodical press, some undertook research projects, others gave public lectures. As the rapidly growing anarchist and socialist movements developed their own print media, women writers like Teresa Mañé (Soledad Gustavo) (1866–1939) gave voice to working-class women's perspective. As Shirley Mangini (2001) has amply demonstrated, by the 1920s the feminine component of modern Spain had stepped into the public sphere to play a visible role in shaping Spain's modernity. Thus Spanish women born at the turn of the century had within their horizons more varied options for social identity, options that included identification as a woman with modernity itself. One member of this generation, the writer Rosa Chacel (1898–1994), who became an active member of Spain's brilliant literary and artistic vanguard of the 1920s and 30s, dramatized the change in her experimental short story 'Chinina Migone' (1928). In the story, a couple rooted in nineteenth-century values is devastated when their only child, socialized in the new culture of the cinema, bobs her hair and leaves home to pursue a career in the movies. Chacel thus inextricably links that most modern of arts, cinema, with women of the younger generation as active agents of the transformation of both life and art in twentieth-century Spain. While the pull of conservative, religious tradition remained a powerful factor in the lives and attitudes of most Spanish women, their active participation in public life, which had begun with the lyrical self-expression of the poets of the 1840s, was politically institutionalized with inclusion of women's suffrage in the Constitution of 1931.

Further reading

Blanco, Alda, 2001. *Escritoras virtuosas: narradoras de la domesticidad en la España isabelina* (Granada: Universidad)

Kirkpatrick, Susan, 1989. *Las Románticas: Women Writers and Subjectivity in Spain, 1835–1850* (Berkeley: University of California Press)

Mangini, Shirley, 2001. *Las modernas de Madrid: las grandes intelectuales españolas de la vanguardia* (Barcelona: Península)

Morant, Isabel (ed.), 2005–06. *Historia de las mujeres en España y América Latina*, III, *Del siglo XIX a los umbrales del XX* (Madrid: Cátedra)

15

Politics and the Feminist Essay in Spain

JOYCE TOLLIVER

In the first decade of the twenty-first century, Spanish women seem to have made great political strides. For the first time in history, there are more women than men in the presidential Cabinet, and Spain is among the top ten countries in the world in terms of representation of women in its legislature. In 2007, the Ley Orgánica Para La Igualdad Efectiva de Mujeres y Hombres (Equal Gender Rights Law) was passed, criminalizing discrimination based on sex, strengthening rights of maternity and paternity leave, and mandating equitable representation of women among upper management of companies employing more than 250 workers. It is tempting to attribute the improvement in women's legal status not only to the hard work of feminists during the past quarter-century or so, but also to the socialist victory in the 2004 election, and indeed it would be wrong to deny credit to the current Spanish socialist party for the advances they have made in gender equity. Nevertheless, a consideration of the history of Spanish feminism, in its broadest sense of advocacy of gender equity, will remind us that the correlation between leftist ideology and feminism is anything but perfect. In contrast to the history of feminism in the United States (but not so very unlike the history of feminism in Great Britain), supporters of gender equity and contributors to Spanish feminist thought have not always, or even typically, allied themselves with socially progressive ideologies. The reverse is also true: by no means can we trace a correlation in Spanish history between progressive social theories, such as anarchism or socialism, and a support of feminist causes.

It is a commonplace that feminism came late to Spain, compared to the United States, England, and to other European countries. And it is indeed true that the so-called first wave of feminism, widely associated with the campaign for women's suffrage, was virtually non-existent in Spain, in comparison with the United States and other European nations: women were not given full voting rights in Spain until 1931.¹ But the feminists of the time of the Pankhurst sisters, Susan B. Anthony, and Elizabeth Cady Stanton had the work of their own feminist foremothers to inspire them, writers such as Mary Wollstonecraft. When we consider this earlier, Enlightenment, phase of feminist thought, Spain's chronology is not so far behind the rest of Europe. In fact, at the time of the publication of Wollstonecraft's *A Vindication of the Rights of Woman* in 1792, Josefa Amar y Borbón (1749–1833) had already published *Discurso en defensa del talento de las mujeres y de su aptitud para el gobierno y otros cargos en que se emplean los hombres* (1786) (Discourse in Defense of the Intelligence of Women and of Their Fitness for Government and Other Offices in which Men Are Employed) and *Discurso sobre la educación física y moral de las mujeres* (1790) (Discourse on the Physical and Moral Education of Women). But even Amar y Borbón did not invent her feminist theories from whole cloth, having benefited from the work of a monk from her great-grandfather's generation, Benito Jerónimo Feijóo (1676–1764), whose massive *Teatro crítico universal* (Universal Critical Theatre) (1726–40) includes, in the first volume, the well-known essay *Defensa de las mujeres* (Defense of Women).²

Given the Church's opposition to feminism in nineteenth- and twentieth-century Spain, it may surprise contemporary readers to reflect upon the fact that one of the most important works of Spanish feminist thought was penned by an eighteenth-century Benedictine monk. Feijóo's proto-feminist stance illustrates just one of the several ways in which present-day scholars must adjust our perspective as we think about feminist writing in Spain. Not only must we consider the particular development of feminist thought firmly within the context of the particularities of Spanish culture, we must also be careful not to impose a twenty-first century model of feminism upon our readings of works from earlier periods. As Sarah Childs points out, today, 'much, if not all, contemporary feminist theorizing recognizes intersectionality – that gender is cross-cut by other identities' (2008: 20). That is, contemporary definitions of feminism are shaped by the precept that it is artificial to disentangle the various socially constructed categories of identity: we cannot analyze the dynamics of gender or sexuality in isolation from social class, race, or other categories. Likewise, our analysis of social class

---

¹ In 1924, under the dictatorship of Miguel Primo de Rivera, single women over 23 could vote in local elections only. By contrast, extended male suffrage was granted in 1907.

² Of course, Wollstonecraft herself was not the first British woman to write a tract explicitly arguing for gender equity; a century earlier, Mary Astell had published *A Serious Proposal to the Ladies* (1694), which, as Karen Offen explains, 'advocated founding a women's university and community for women who did not wish to marry but preferred to pursue lifelong learning in the company of other similarly disposed women' (2000: 38); likewise, in France, the late seventeenth century saw the production of such proto-feminist works as Poullain de la Barre's *De l'Égalité des deux sexes* (1673) (On the Equality of the Two Sexes).

or of race must acknowledge the inextricability of the categories of gender and sexuality.

Indeed, one could argue that contemporary academic feminists have made perhaps their most significant contribution to western feminist theory through the recognition that these three forms of oppression are inextricably intertwined, and essential to the formation of patriarchy. But when we find it impossible to separate these aspects of the patriarchy in our analyses of interventions in the conversations regarding feminism and the woman question of earlier periods, we run the risk of limiting the scope of our analysis to only those figures whose ideologies of class and/or race appeal to a contemporary sensibility: it becomes impossible, by definition, to conceive of any authentic feminism that is not also anti-classist and anti-racist. When it comes to scholarship on feminism, it is dangerous to assume that an authentic feminist, by definition, should always work to dismantle *all* oppressive institutions; that there must be a symmetry between what one thinks, writes, and says about gender issues, and what one thinks, writes, and says about other aspects of the patriarchy.

In our feminist analyses, intersectionality is theoretically robust. However, to impose our intersectional model on earlier writings is fundamentally anti-historicist. As Karen Offen's study of European feminism makes clear, the term 'feminism' (and its equivalents in other languages) only entered the lexicon fairly recently, probably not before the 1870s. When it did enter the language – and it seems to have appeared first in French – it was 'commonly used as a synonym for women's emancipation' (Offen 2000:19). Taking into account a broad range of evidence drawn from archival sources that document women's emancipation movements in a variety of Western cultures, Offen suggests the following baseline definition of feminism: 'the name given to a comprehensive critical response to the deliberate and systematic subordination of women as a group by men as a group within a given cultural setting' (2000: 20). This definition, obviously, is an historical, and not a philosophical or theoretical one; it does not attempt to link the critical response to women's subordination to a critical response to other types of subordination (such as those based on race or class). In fact, speaking strictly as a feminist historian, and contrasting her own historian's perspective with a feminist philosophical perspective, Offen rejects the notion that 'feminism is – or should be – "a movement that challenges all injustices".' Instead, it is, she says, 'a theory and a practice that challenges *one* injustice' (2000: 15–16).

A reading of some of the primary texts of what we now call Spanish feminism will quickly reveal the excision of the challenge to gender injustice from challenges to other sorts of injustice. In particular, many authors who made prescient and incisive challenges to the pervasive gender ideology of their day were anything but egalitarian when it came to class. Rosalía de Castro, for instance, wrote a biting satire of the denigration meted out to women writers, 'Las literatas' (The Bluestockings) (1866). And yet one of her primary supporting arguments was an ironic portrayal of a Cuban barber with pretensions to authorship:

> ¡Cómo se conoce que vienes de aquella tierra! –exclamé yo para mí– [...] aquella feliz provincia en donde todos, todos (yo creo que hasta las arañas) descienden en línea recta de cierta antigua, ingeniosa y artística raza que ha dado al mundo lecciones de arte y sabiduría.

> ('How clear it is you come from that land! I exclaimed to myself [...] that happy province where everyone, everyone (even the spiders, I dare say) descends in a direct line from a certain ancient, ingenious, artistic race that has given the world lessons in art and wisdom', trans. Mary Ellen Fieweger, in Castro (1996: 472)).

The speaking voice thus points out the absurd hypocrisy of the prejudice against women writers, but at the expense of a sarcastic barb at both the servant classes and the Spanish colonial subjects.

Likewise, Emilia Pardo Bazán (1851–1921) is often criticized for her class prejudice, even though, as Susan Kirkpatrick notes in her essay in this volume, she was the most powerful champion of gender equity of her generation. The criticism is not ungrounded. She expended considerable effort to reinstate the non-hereditary title of Count that had been bestowed upon her father by the Pope and to convert it to a hereditary one, thus becoming the Countess of Pardo Bazán (and arranging for her son to become a Count upon her death). She concludes the prologue to her *Cocina española antigua* (Old-Fashioned Spanish Cuisine) (1913) with a little tip, which she calls 'lo más femenino de este libro' (the most feminine thing about this book): ladies who want to do their own cooking should make sure to leave the preparation of onions and garlic to their cooks: 'Es su oficio, y nada tiene de deshonroso el manejar esos bulbos de penetrante aroma; pero sería muy cruel que las señoras conservasen, entre una sortija de rubíes y la manga calada de una blusa, un traidor y avillanado rastro cebollero' (That is their job, and there is nothing wrong with handling those pungent bulbs; but it would be cruel indeed if ladies retained, alongside their ruby rings and lacy cuffs, a treacherous, common scent of onion) (Pardo Bazán 1913: 18). On a less frivolous note, Pardo Bazán was explicit about her disdain for Spanish middle-class women as a group, whom she criticized not only for their vacuity and indolence – faults that she considered to be the result of their deficient education and the social prohibition against ladies working outside the home – but also for their vulgar attempts to imitate the aristocracy in their dress and customs (Pardo Bazán [1892] 1999a).[3]

---

[3] Pardo Bazán portrayed working-class women more generously in this essay, pointing

Carmen de Burgos (1867–1932), known later in her life as The Red Lady, for her support of the Republican cause, defended equal civil rights for women, supported the legalization of divorce, and protested the gender discrimination of laws included in the newly-drafted Civil Code of 1889.[4] So outraged was Burgos by Article 438 that she used it as the title of one of her novellas and reproduced the text of it as an epigraph to her novel *El Artículo 438*, of 1921. This article specified that a husband who killed his wife upon discovering her in an adulterous relationship would be punished only by banishment; any physical attacks not resulting in death would not be punished. Her essay collections *La mujer moderna y sus derechos* (The Modern Woman and Her Rights) (1927) and *El divorcio en España* (Divorce in Spain) (1904a) are surprisingly modern feminist critiques. And yet Burgos also stated that feminism was necessarily an elitist movement, one that was irreconcilable with anarchism: 'Las mujeres del pueblo, entiéndase esto bien, no son nunca feministas, sino esencialmente anarquistas' (The common woman, it must be emphasized, is never a feminist, but essentially an anarchist) (1904b: 7). Federica Montseny (1905–94), the Spanish anarchist leader, was also known for her firm rejection of feminist postulations and initatives, asserting the primacy of humanism over feminism.

The historical separation of feminism from other types of challenges to injustice is perhaps seen most vividly in the relationship of Spanish feminism to the socialist and anarchist movements in the first decades of the twentieth century. The Asociación Nacional de Mujeres Españolas (National Association of Spanish Women) – which Geraldine Scanlon describes both as the early twentieth century's most important Spanish feminist organization *and* as politically conservative and socially elitist (1986: 203) – strongly supported the inclusion of Article 36, guaranteeing women's right to vote, in the new Republican Constitution. Victoria Kent (1898–1987), on the other hand, who represented the Radical Socialist Party in the Cortes Constituyentes (The Constituent Assembly), argued that to give the vote to Spanish women would be fatal to the Republic, since women were not yet politically sophisticated enough to support the socialist cause. Margarita Nelken (1896–1968) was also one of the three women representatives in the Spanish legislature in 1931, during the Second Republic, when the ques-

---

out ironically that there was no gender inequality when it came to work for the rural women, whose hard physical labor was essential. She took up the problem of middle-class women's lack of preparation for the workforce in several of her fictional works, including *Memorias de un solterón* (Memoirs of a Bachelor) (1896) and the short stories 'Náufragas' (Shipwrecked) and 'Casi artista' (Almost an Artist) (1909); her story 'La manga' (The Sleeve) (1910) portrays the economic havoc wreaked on middle-class families by the perceived need to dress their daughters to attract well-off husbands.

[4] In her essay in this volume, Kirkpatrick discusses Burgos as a multifaceted cultural agent.

tion of women's suffrage was debated. As Judith Keene points out, Nelken 'eschewed feminism as an ideology suited only to bourgeois women' (1999: 335); she shared the logic of most socialists of the time, which postulated that once class conflict was eliminated, gender discrimination would also disappear.

Clara Campoamor (1888–1972), representing the Radical party, was the only one of the three female legislators who supported women's voting rights. Citing thinkers such as the eighteenth-century philosopher Fichte, she argued that

> sólo aquel que no considere a la mujer un ser humano es capaz de afimar que todos los derechos del hombre y del ciudadano no deben ser los mismos para la mujer que para el hombre [...] Una Constitución que concede el voto al mendigo, al doméstico y al analfabeto – que en España existe – no puede negárselo a la mujer. (1931)

> (only he who does not consider women to be human would affirm that all human and civil rights should not be the same for women as for men [...] A Constitution that gives the vote to beggars, to servants, and to illiterates – of which there are some in Spain – cannot deny it to women.)

Campoamor's speech, which she made in explicit response to Kent's argument against passing Article 36, was definitive in the women's suffrage debate: although by a narrow margin, the legislators voted to approve the Article. (It is perhaps not surprising that women voters were blamed for the right-wing victory in 1933, in spite of the fact that, as Gerald Alexander demonstrates (1999: 357–9), there was no evidence for any causal connection – and in fact, in 1936, when women were still voting, it was the Popular Front that won.)

A consideration of the debates over women's suffrage in the Second Republic makes it clear that feminism and leftist politics were by no means perfectly allied (see Frances Lannon's essay in this volume). Even more surprising to contemporary readers might be the notion that women who were politically aligned with conservative politics in the Franco years may have considered themselves to be advancing women's rights – or, indeed, that anyone would openly advocate women's rights during the forty-year-long dictatorship. This was a period when the hard-won right to universal woman suffrage was lost, divorce was again illegal, and the discourse of the government and of the Church represented a return to the nineteenth-century ideal of the angel of the hearth.[5] Indeed, María Teresa Gallego

---

[5] During the Franco dictatorship, in national elections each household had a vote, and the head of the household was legally defined as the husband or father.

Méndez's carefully documented study of the Sección Feminina de la Falange (Women's Section of the Falangists) during the early years of the Franco dictatorship concludes that, at least up to 1945, 'la Sección Femenina era una entidad, bastante activa, *antidemocrática* y *antifeminista*' (the Women's Section, quite an active organization, was *anti-democratic* and *antifeminist*) (1983: 198). On the other hand, Victoria Lorée Enders reports on a series of interviews that she held with former members of the Sección Femenina, who were surprised and hurt by the hostility shown them and their cause by women of the post-Franco generation – a hostility that they perceived to be rooted in a lack of understanding of the history and mission of the Sección Femenina. These women speak of the efforts of the Sección Femenina to introduce physical education for girls into public education, in spite of the disapproval of members of the clergy, and their efforts in the fields of education and professional training for women, among other achievements for which, in their view, they have never received the credit due them. Enders suggests that the way in which feminist history has often treated the Sección Femenina represents a blind spot, resting on critics' claim to 'an epistemic privilege – that they have a grasp on motivational causality' (Enders 1999: 379). Enders opens her essay on the Sección Femenina with a reference to the musings of Ida Blom, who speculates about 'whether Euro-American theories explaining gender inequalities may apply to all cultures, whether theories generated within other cultures may be applied to Euro-American history, or whether specific culturally determined theories are needed' (Blom 1991: 140, cited in Enders 1999: 375). The inside look at the Sección Femenina obtained by Enders does, she says, '[verify] the need for 'specific culturally determined theories in the pursuit of women's and gender histories' (1999: 378).

One way to deepen our understanding of the writings of proponents of women's rights and equity in cultures not our own, and during historical periods not our own, is to attend to the distinction that Offen makes between what she calls relational feminism and individualist feminism. As she explains, relational feminists

> proposed a gender-based but egalitarian vision of social organization. They featured the primacy of a companionate, non-hierarchical male-female couple as the basic unit of society, whereas individualist arguments posited the individual, irrespective of sex or gender, as the basic unit. Relational feminism emphasized women's rights *as women* (defined principally by their childbearing and/or nurturing capacities) in relation to men. It insisted on *women's* distinctive contributions in these roles to the broader society and made claims on the commonwealth on the basis of these contributions. (Offen 1988: 136)

Offen generally associates individualist feminism with the Anglo-American tradition since the publication of John Stuart Mill's *On the Subjection of Women* (1869), and relational feminism with Latin cultures, broadly speaking. She points out that these two modes of feminist thought are not to be interpreted as an absolute dichotomy. A single historical period may feature the co-existence of these two modes, although at times there have been more active debates among feminists representing one mode or the other. Our understanding of *fin de siglo* (*fin de siècle*) Spanish feminist thought is illuminated when we consider Offen's assertion that 'between 1890 and 1920 [...] the aims and goals of relational and individualist approaches appeared increasingly irreconcilable, as different groups of women began to articulate differing claims. The feminist family tree stands revealed as a two-forked tree, with many smaller branches' (1988: 143).

Mary Nash's discussion of the positions held by Federica Montseny, in contrast to that of the anarchist group Mujeres Libres (Free Women), illustrates the nature of these bifurcating, yet connected smaller branches. She says that for Montseny,

> the solution to the problem [of the sexes] lay in establishing libertarian communism and, more specifically, in developing a new human personality for males and females [...] .The prototype of the new woman advocated by the anarchist leader was one full of confidence and awareness that the destiny of humankind depended on her. However, this model of superwoman proposed by Montseny, the product of individual consciousness and self-transcendence, would have been extremely difficult for the average Spanish woman – whom Montseny herself had qualified as ignorant and backward – to emulate. In contrast to Montseny's individualistic approach to the problems of female and human emancipation, Mujeres Libres proposed a double strategy based not only on individualism but also on a collective response that would offer women the fundamental support and training to enable them to achieve freedom as women.
> (Nash 1995: 86)

The two parts of Offen's feminist history tree were palpably present before Montseny's time, to be sure. We might place Pardo Bazán's feminist writings generally in the category of individualist feminism, given her repeated postulation of the essential androgyny of the intellect and indeed of the human spirit.[6] It is not coincidental, indeed, that her Biblioteca de la Mujer (Women's Library) included a translation of *On the Subjection of Women*. In fact, Pardo Bazán succinctly summarized the basic tenet of individualist feminism in her 1892 essay 'La educación del hombre y la de la mujer:

---

[6] On Pardo Bazán's poetics of androgyny, see Tolliver 1998: 11–42.

sus relaciones y diferencias' (Men's and Women's Education: Their Relationships and Differences), when she criticized the pervasive concept that women's value, and indeed her very identity, were inconceivable outside of her relationship with men. This mode of thinking, she says, determines the nature and quality of women's education in Spain, which is based on the notion that: 'el eje de la vida femenina [...] no es la dignidad y felicidad propia, sino la ajena del esposo e hijos, y si no hay hijos ni esposo, la del padre o del hermano y cuando éstos faltaren, la de la entidad abstracta género masculino' (the center of a woman's life is not her own dignity and happiness, but rather that of others, of her husband and children, and if there are no children or husband, then that of her father or her brother, and when there is no father or brother, the entire male gender as an abstract entity) ([1892]1999b: 152).

On the other hand, considering the individualist / relational contrast as a continuum, rather than a dichotomy, we tend to find a more clearly relational slant in the ideas on the woman question advanced by such *fin de siglo* writers as Pardo Bazán's contemporary Concepción Gimeno de Flaquer (1850–1919); earlier writers such as Gertrudis Gómez de Avellaneda (1814–73), Concepción Arenal (1820–93), and Faustina Sáez de Melgar (1834–95); or even the later figures María (Lejárraga) Martínez Sierra (1874–1974) and Margarita Nelken (1896–1968). Arenal's books *La mujer del porvenir* (The Woman of the Future) (written in 1861, published in 1868) and *La mujer de su casa* (The Woman of the Home) (1883) at times seem to represent an individualist strain of feminism, as when she analyzes and dismisses the pseudo-scientific studies that alleged that women's intellectual inferiority was determined by the smaller size of her brain. She points out that if one considers the size of the brain relative to the size of the rest of the body women's brains are about the same; real differences, she says, are the result of education ([1861] 1993: 63). Her defense of women's intellectual aptitude is based on an argument of essential equality between the sexes, but her discussion of the professional aptitudes of women is couched in a discourse that asserts the moral superiority of women, rather than their equality to men. Because of this moral superiority, she defends women's right to the priesthood, but she also maintains that this same superiority, manifested as emotional sensitivity, makes women unfit for work in politics or on the judge's bench (ibid., 119).

The case of Faustina Sáez de Melgar represents a degree closer to the relational end of the continuum. Catherine Davies places Sáez de Melgar, along with Pilar Sinués de Marco and Concepción Gimeno de Flaquer, firmly in the category of nineteenth-century women writers who opted to 'kow-tow to prevailing ideas in order to secure openings and a respectable career' (1998: 25). Many of Sáez de Melgar's works uphold the domestic feminine ideal of the angel of the hearth, as envisioned in the work of that title – *El ángel del hogar* (1859) – and other works by Sinués.[7] But her 1886 collection of vignettes in essay form, *Las mujeres españolas, americanas y lusitanas pintadas por sí mismas* (Spanish, Spanish-American, and Lusitanian Women as They Portray Themselves) often challenges the dominant idea of natural feminine subservience, as well as Pardo Bazán's relative notion of women's subjectivity. This massive collection includes short essays on women of different provinces and colonies of Spain, as well as on female 'types' such as the gypsy woman (written by Blanca de los Ríos) and the flower girl (written by Josefa Massanés). As Alicia Cerezo points out (2008: 27), the work is remarkable in that many of the essays pointedly criticize prevailing gender norms, and at times are in direct opposition to the very traditional portrayal of women in the graphic illustrations accompanying the textual portraits.

One of the most interesting of these essays is 'Las heroínas catalanas' (Heroines of Catalonia) written by Concepción Gimeno de Flaquer, about the women of Gerona and surrounding villages who defended the city in the eight-week siege by Napoleon's troops in 1808. Gimeno begins her essay in terms that seem to firmly uphold Davies's view of the author as an accommodationist: 'La mujer ama el hogar, la tranquilidad, la vida dulce, apacible y sedentaria; el hombre, más impetuoso y más inquieto siempre, ama la vida activa, los viajes, la equitación, la caza' (Women love the home, peace and quiet, a sweet, pleasant, sedentary life; men, always more impetuous and restless, love the active life, travel, horse-back riding, and hunting) (Gimeno 1886: 233). Nevertheless, she quickly moves on to a more much contestatory stance, denouncing the absence of women from history in general and, in particular, the oblivion into which the woman warriors of Gerona have fallen. She laments the general lack of respect for women: 'como hoy el más imberbe mozalvete [*sic*] se convierte en impugnador de la mujer, nos parece muy justo que los hombres serios refieran nuestros nobles hechos para que alguna vez se hable bien de nosotras, ya que tantas veces se habla mal' (since nowadays even the most fresh-faced youngster can throw out a challenge to a woman, it only seems fair to us that serious men relate our noble deeds, so that someone speaks well about us women for once, since so often we are spoken ill of) (ibid., 234). In a gesture that presages contemporary feminist archival research, she makes use of personal letters that she has come upon in order to rescue the historical record of the women

---

[7] Kirkpatrick (see her essay in this volume) rightly points out that the fictional works of Grassi, Sinués, and Sáez de Melgar all contributed significantly to the creation of the *ángel del hogar* ideal. Nevertheless, see Urruela 2001 for a provocative and intelligent analysis of Sinués's representation of the domestic ideal as a challenge to the happiness and autonomy of many women. On the complications of Sáez de Melgar's domestic fiction, see Alicia Andreu 1995.

– of all social classes – who fought against the French troops in the 1808 siege, listing several women's names and briefly relating the adventures of others. This sort of bait-and-switch technique is one Gimeno uses often in her works on the woman question, such as *La mujer española: estudios acerca de su educación y sus facultades intelectuales* (The Spanish Woman: Studies on Her Education and Intellectual Abilities) (1877).

María Lejárraga, who was mainly active as a feminist in the early decades of the twentieth century, published most of her writings under the name of her husband, Gregorio Martínez Sierra. A trained schoolteacher, she was devoted, throughout her life, to the cause of women's education, and, in 1931, founded the Asociación Femenina de Educación Cívica (Women's Association for Civic Education). In collaboration with Gregorio, she wrote *Feminismo, feminidad, españolismo* (Feminism, Femininity, and Spanishness) (Martínez Sierra 1917), a collection of essays dealing with a wide range of issues related to questions of gender. In defending women's suffrage, in promoting social activism on behalf of poor women and children, in advancing the cause of women's education, and in defining and defending feminism itself, her stance is generally relational. She contests the notion that feminists are ugly man-haters (a notion that has resurfaced, or persisted, in our own time), she defends women's essential pacifism as a manifestation of their maternity, and she advocates women's suffrage on the grounds that the participation of women in the political process can only improve the nation. Many chapters of *Feminismo, feminidad, españolismo* report on advances for women in other European countries and in the United States, and in fact the volume is an interesting resource for the sort of comparative international feminism advocated, generations later, by contemporary historians such as Blom and Offen. An unexpected intersection of leftist politics and relational feminism is perceivable in her report on the *Liga de Amas de Casa* (Housewives' League), a US organization whose stated primary aim is the protection of the home; the primary mean to this traditional-sounding end, however, is to 'organizar, es decir, reunir a todas las amas de casa, haciéndoles comprender la importancia de la solidaridad para realizar los fines educativos, defensivos y constructivos que se propone' (organize, that is, unite all housewives, leading them to understand the importance of solidarity in carrying out the educational, defensive, and constructive goals to which the group aspires) (Martínez Sierra 1917: 194).

It is easy for contemporary feminist scholars to overlook, or even to dismiss, the relational mode of feminism found in works of earlier periods. Anglo-American scholars may be more likely to have formulated definitions of feminism based on an individualist model, as Offen suggests; post-Franco Spanish feminist theoreticians have tended to theorize feminism according to this model as well. In the years following the death of Franco, when it was clear to many feminists that it was vitally important to make up for the gains lost to women in the previous half-century or so, feminist theories based on difference, such as those of Luce Irigary and Hélène Cixous, seemed to represent an intellectual luxury that feminism could ill afford. In fact, the so-called Continental theories of feminism were seen, in some ways, to do more harm than good to Spanish feminism. According to Mercedes de Grado, 'estas propuestas, lejos de reconciliar las disputas entre socialistas y radicales, no hicieron sino ahondar las diferencias y provocar un cisma' (these postulations, far from reconciling socialist and radical [feminists], only deepened their differences, and provoked a schism) (Grado 2004: 30).

Currently, while relational feminism is certainly represented in Spain, especially by feminism of difference thinkers such as Rosa Rodríguez Magda, it is individualist feminism that predominates, particularly in the form of feminism of equality, a feminism based on Enlightenment principles. This branch of the Spanish feminist tree 'considera que los principios democráticos definidos por los teóricos ilustrados nunca se han llegado a implantar completamente, por haber excluido a las mujeres como colectivo o grupo social. Así, el feminismo de la igualdad considera que tales proclamas son aún una reivindicación pendiente' (believes that the democratic principles laid out by Enlightenment theoreticians never really took root, because they excluded women as a collective or social group. So, for equality feminism, these principles have yet to be put into action) (Grado 2004: 35).

The feminist activist Lidia Falcón (1935-) has been a central figure in the development of equality feminism in the post-Franco years. She founded the journals *Vindicación Feminista* (Feminist Vindication), a name she also used later for an intellectual center and a feminist press), and *Poder y Libertad* (Power and Freedom). Like most of the Spanish feminist writers discussed so far, she is a creative writer – specifically, a playwright – as well as a key figure in Spanish feminist thought. Her analyses are based on Marxist principles, which led her to found the Partido Feminista (Feminist Party), based on the conviction that women as a group would not successfully change their status as second-class citizens until they organized politically *as a group*; until that happened, she thought,

> sería imposible que alcanzasen las cotas de influencia social y política necesarias para adquirir el protagonismo que por su número e importancia económica se merecen. Para ello es preciso que las mujeres en vez de seguir en el estadio de alienación de pertenecer a una clase en sí adquieran, en términos marxianos, la conciencia de clase para sí. (Falcón 1992: 21)

> (it would be impossible to attain the degree of political and social influence necessary to achieve the leading role appropriate to their numbers and their economic importance. In order to do this, instead of continuing in the alienated stage of forming a separate class by themselves, women must, in Marxist terms, develop their own class-consciousness.)

Celia Amorós (1944-) is a professor of philosophy at the Universidad Complutense in Madrid. Her feminist theories, steeped in her own study of the Enlightenment period, represent today's perhaps most influential contribution to contemporary Spanish feminist philosophy, in their analysis of the ways in which Enlightenment thought was gendered. She suggests a reformulation of those principles, but with women, rather than men, as the generic human. Clearly aligned with Offen's individualist feminism, she considers postmodern feminist philosophy, and particularly the feminism of difference, to rest upon shaky ground, both philosophically and in practical terms. She rejects Rodríguez Magda's proposal for a feminist critique based on a parodic enacting of normative gender roles :

> El problema que esta propuesta nos plantea, entre otros, es que sospechamos que la mayoría de las mujeres, hiperrepresentadas en las bolsas de pobreza, por ejemplo, no están de humor como para ponerse como prenda divertida y seductora las máscaras de siempre; no todas quieren ni pueden permitirse el lujo de la ironía de asumir a guisa de disfraz el uniforme genérico de las idénticas de currantes de base, que les toca llevar puesto todos los días. (Amorós 2000: 458)

> (The problem that this proposal raises, among others, is that we suspect that most women, over-represented below the poverty line, for example, are in no mood to put on, as a fun, seductive, wardrobe item, the same old masks; not all women want, or can afford, the irony of disguising themselves in the generic uniform of the minimum-wage working drudge, which they are forced to wear every day.)

As we study the complexities of feminist and political ideology in modern Spanish culture, we must do so with an awareness of our own cultural and historical situation. As Blom and other feminist historians have reminded us, it is not the case that feminism appears in the same guise in every culture; clearly, the contours of feminist thought have shifted also from historical period to historical period. Above all, we must be conscious of the fact that our own feminist theories have been produced within, and reflect the perspectives of, a particular culture and a particular historical period. We must be careful, in studying gender analyses of cultures or historical periods that are not our own, to avoid committing what Michèle Barrett and Anne Phillips call the 'generational fallacy': the 'simplistic teleology of assuming that later theory is therefore better theory, and the best theory of all is the position from which we happen at the moment to be speaking' (1992: 7). That is, as we teach and research the history of Spanish feminisms and gender ideologies, we would do well to remain conscious of 'the position from which we happen at the moment to be speaking,' and to realize that that position is likely to be different from the positions taken by the writers whose works we study. Ultimately, our study of the history of Spanish feminist writing must pay as much attention to the *history* of feminism as we typically pay to the *philosophy* of feminism. When we do this, I suspect we will find that to expect all feminist texts, by definition, to rigorously challenge *all* aspects of the patriarchy is, as Offen (2000: 16) says, simply asking too much.[8]

Further reading

Fagoaga, Concha (ed.), 1999. *1898–1998, un siglo avanzando hacia la igualdad de las mujeres* (Madrid: Dirección General de la Mujer)

Folguera Crespo, Pilar (ed.), 1988. *El feminismo en España: dos siglos de historia* (Madrid: Pablo Iglesias)

Glenn, Kathleen M., and Mercedes Mazquiarán de Rodríguez, 1998. *Spanish Women Writers and the Essay: Gender, Politics and the Self* (Columbia: University of Missouri Press)

Merced, Leslie Anne, 2004. 'Writing in the Raw: Rhetorical Moves of Female Essayists during the Spanish *Fin de Siglo*', unpublished doctoral thesis, University of Illinois, Urbana-Champaign

Nash, Mary (ed.), 1983. *Mujer, familia y trabajo en España (1875–1936)* (Barcelona: Anthropos)

---

[8] I am grateful to Megan Kelly, the consummate research assistant, for her able assistance with this project.

16

The Theatricalized Self: Women Artists in Masquerade from 1920 to the Present

ROBERTA ANN QUANCE

The idea of femininity as a masquerade was first proposed by Joan Riviere in 1929 and later popularized through film criticism of the 1980s (Doane 1991) and the critique of gender set forth by Judith Butler (1990). I will argue that there are two broadly different approaches to the concept, one which we may call modern and the other, postmodern. To illustrate the differences between the two I will be looking at the work of visual artists and writers from the twentieth and the twenty-first centuries, including one artist, Norah Borges, who, while not Spanish-born, helped to legitimate the Spanish avant-garde, and another, Remedios Varo, who did her best work in Mexico.

The modern approach to the question is rooted in the point of view of the creative woman, who unconsciously adopts a feminine pose to offset what could be perceived as an aggressive foray into traditionally masculine fields. In this way she does not risk arousing male hostility or resentment for her bid for acceptance as an artist on equal terms with men. This may have been the case with Borges, who was extremely deferential to her husband. The other approach to masquerade has been applied to sexually bolder women, like Frida Kahlo (1907–54), who are – arguably – always in costume, implicitly challenging the notion of an essential female identity. But, generally speaking, women of this period were aware, at the very least, that they had to balance their creative boldness with an image of traditional feminine demeanour in order to gain acceptance in male-dominated circles.[1] In Rosa Chacel's diaries *Alcancía (Ida)* and *Alcancía (Vuelta)* (Money Box

---

[1] See, for example, Chacel's diva pose for the 1925 portrait by husband Timoteo Rubio, reproduced in colour in Chacel 1980, plate III. In the cover photograph of Josefina de la Torre in Mederos 2001, we see the artist wearing a (modern) tennis sweater and skirt but projecting a shy schoolgirl demeanour.

– Departure, Money Box – Return) (1982), the concern with appearance is a leitmotif.

While both versions remain rooted in the psyche of the woman artist or writer, the second development moves quickly to the generalization that all displays of femininity are a masquerade and that there is no true femininity underneath at all. This is the most radical implication of Riviere's critique: that what we perceive as feminine behaviour in signs of women's dress, posture, and interaction with men is always only a sign of woman's role-playing on men's terms. None the less, some have invoked masquerade in favourable terms, to suggest that there can be something liberating in the deliberate, ironic, distancing of the self from its presentation in society – as if a woman could never be anything but in drag and to know this is to position oneself above it all. I would like to revive the concept in its modernist version to talk about women artists and writers in Spain who do not always easily fit the mould of heroines and seem in fact to be apostates from modernity, such as Norah Borges, or women who turned their backs on their avant-garde creation. It is not clear that they did so freely.

Spain presents a special problem in that the Franco regime (1939–75) brutally excluded and anathematized key aspects of modernity (all liberal values derived from the Enlightenment, including laicism and gender equality), making it all but impossible for artists and creators to build on the art and literature from before the Civil War. But this violent truncation of liberal development points up the radical edge of Riviere's critique of femininity as a reactionary phenomenon. It should make us sceptical of any display of conventional femininity we find in the art and literature developed under Franco and even during Spain's transition to democracy, which sought to bury the Francoist past without fully bringing to light its legacy or reopening old wounds. The postmodern use of the concept of masquerade is a potentially ambiguous one, with roots in a world view that sought to re-establish women as the keepers of the faith and home and which flourishes in depoliticized space. By returning the concept of female masquerade to its modern root – where the issue is, for the woman, gaining acceptability in the eyes of men – and by historicizing its use, we can question whether exponents of a postmodern parody of femininity are as free to fashion their own identity as they might seem to be.

The postwar period in twentieth-century Spain is riddled with the epitaphs of the dead and of those who left the country in protest or fear of Francoist repression and who for a good many years after the victory were as good as dead to the people who remained. Students of poetry will think of Juan Ramón Jiménez, Jorge Guillén, or Pedro Salinas; readers of the novel will remember Rosa Chacel or Francisco Ayala (to speak only of the generation that came into its own before the war). But there were other casualties, and some of the women artists who debuted in Spain in the 1920s and 1930s must be counted among them. To approach their work sympathetically is to consider the image of women contained therein and often too their self-representation as signs of a masquerade that protected them from hostility in their environment. I will start by briefly contrasting their activities before the war with their near-effacement afterwards, for the extent to which the concept of femininity as a masquerade is relevant to their life and work has to do with the defeat of feminist ideals which took place under the Franco regime.

Consider the case of a relatively unknown artist who has recently attracted attention, Delhy (Adela) Tejero, who was born in Toro (Zamora) in 1904 and died in 1968. Her date of birth makes her a contemporary of several leading women writers of the 1920s and 1930s: Rosa Chacel (1898–1994), Concha Méndez Cuesta (1898–1986), María Teresa León (1903–88). María Zambrano (1904–91), Ernestina de Champourcín (1905–99), and Josefina de la Torre (1907–2002). Delhy had been fortunate enough to have her family's permission to study at the Academia de Bellas Artes de San Fernando (San Fernando Academy of Fine Art) in Madrid, where she met the budding painters Maruja Mallo (1902–95) and Remedios Varo (1908–63). Less rebellious than they, Delhy made friends more readily at the Residencia de Señoritas (Young Ladies' Hall of Residence) with aspiring poet Marina Romero.[2]

Although Delhy did not remain in Spain during the Civil War – but travelled to Paris and Rome –, she returned home shortly after the Francoist victory and experienced at first hand the brutal realities of postwar Spain. The diaries she kept over the years show that she deeply regretted her missed chances in life. Delhy had turned down offers of help with her career from her classmate Mallo and the well-known Uruguayan painter Joaquín Torres-García. She recognized later that her Catholic upbringing had got in the way: she had been scandalized by Mallo's blasphemy and Torres-García's interest may have struck her, or those close to her, as improper – she does not say. In one telling passage she reproaches her home town and her religious upbringing for its hold on her:

> Toro, ese Toro que tanto me ha perjudicado, ¿pero por qué no me lancé a la vida con todas sus consecuencias? Porque la fuerza, la materia, y la sensibilidad, yo hubiera empleado todo esto en un arte nuevo, en el de ayer. Voy a recordar las cuatro o cinco veces que llamó esto a mi puerta y creo que si yo hubiera echado el resto ..., pero al ser de Toro y de mi familia —sobre todo la religión ha debido tener mucha culpa.
> (Tejero 2004: 265)

---

[2] The Residencia de Señoritas was an establishment founded in Madrid in 1915 for young women on university courses.

(That town, Toro, that has done me so much harm – why didn't I throw myself into life and take all the consequences? Because the force, the material, the sensibility – I would have used it all in making a new art, the art of yesterday. I want to recall the four or five times I heard life knocking at my door and I do believe that if I had thrown all the rest aside ..., but being from Toro and from my family – above all, religion must have been to blame.)

None the less, for all the mysticism evident in her diaries, Delhy had been a transgressor, taking lovers and remaining single all her life.

Even the more successful women of the period were held back by the values of a conservative milieu. In 1930 Ramón Gómez de la Serna wrote a passionate public plea (cited in Quance 2000) on behalf of the brilliant young painter Ángeles Santos (b.1911), author of one of the most admired paintings of the day, *Un mundo* (A World) of 1929 (see Casamartina i Parassols 2003: 163), whose parents had committed her briefly to a sanatorium after what they took to be a nervous breakdown. On her release, Santos eventually settled into marriage and learned to paint in a serene, impressionist style, like her husband Julián Grau. This could not be more removed from her brooding avant-garde canvases.[3]

Roles for women had been changing swiftly since World War I, and in Spain, as Geraldine Scanlon and others have shown, campaigns for women's suffrage grew perceptibly in the 1920s. There can be no question that changes in the image of women had bombarded popular consciousness, as even a casual look through the illustrated women's magazines of the time – *Blanco y Negro* (Black and White), *La Esfera* (The Sphere) – will reveal: see *Veinte ilustradores españoles* (Twenty Spanish Illustrators) (2004). Women, it was said, had been liberated from the corset by trend-setting designers such as Paul Poiret and Madame Vionnet; in popular magazines they were often shown in glamorous garb or in poses that emphasized their lithe, athletic bodies. Even the heroines of the Russian Revolution were presented seductively, as in the serialized novel by 'El Caballero Audaz' (The Audacious Gentleman), *La Venus bolchevique* (The Bolshevik Venus), which ran in *Crónica* (Chronicle) in 1932, with illustrations by Delhy Tejero; or the film *Ninotchka* (1939) by Ernst Lubitsch.

---

[3] This episode in the artist's life is unclear. Ángeles Santos spent a month in a *sanatorio* (mental hospital) in Madrid in the spring of 1930 after her parents apparently grew alarmed at her agitated state of mind. Gómez de la Serna (1930) links this to parental repression of young and rebellious women artists. According to a chronology of her activity (Casamartina i Parassols 2003: 231–2), Santos did not resume painting until 1935, when she met her future husband.

But in view of the swift and brutal repression that followed the war, which included a concerted campaign to drive women back into the home and into a position of subservience (Morcillo 2000: 47), one is entitled to ask whether the prewar display of charm and glamour was not simply a version of masquerade: not the truth about modern women but a carnival-like guise that masked certain fears women had – and which they were encouraged to have – which could be preyed upon by conservatism (Lawlor and Plymen 2000: 83).

To begin to grasp the roots of the modern interpretation of masquerade one must first take into account the influential view propagated by the philosopher José Ortega y Gasset regarding the gender of the times. At several different points over the course of the 1920s Ortega expressed the view that the modern times one was living were masculine ones: 'El cariz que en todos los órdenes va tomando la existencia europea anuncia un tiempo de varonía y juventud. La mujer y el viejo tienen que ceder durante un período el gobierno de la vida a los muchachos' (The turn that life all throughout Europe is taking in every order of things augurs a time of manliness and youth. Women and old men will have to cede their place for a time to boys) ([1925] 1998: 52). Ortega cast himself as an observer of the *Zeitgeist*, not as one who enjoined this sort of view on anybody. This was, it seemed to him, the way things were.

In fact, as we know and as Rita Felski has argued (1995), he was giving voice to a widespread genderization of modernity, which pitted women, women's world, and the values traditionally attached to womanhood against prominent values of modernity: rationalism, secularism, science, technology, urbanity. In the colloquial, essayistic style he cultivated in the press, he brought this idea home to the younger generation by relating his views to the contemporary scene and by commenting on sociological phenomena himself or encouraging others to do so: flirtation, fashion, love, politics, sport, bullfighting – almost nothing was deemed too ephemeral for his comment. Nor was Ortega's tendency to perceive these subjects through the prism of gender any more remarkable. (Because he could and did treat these subjects as seriously as he did more traditionally philosophical topics, it could be argued that his views became all the more influential.)

The young women of the time whom we associate with the Generation of 1927 grew up with desires and expectations that had been shaped by the feminism of the 1920s, and by some of the older generation of women who had led the fight for women's education and suffrage, even though few, if any, of the younger figures considered herself a card-carrying feminist (Mangini 2001). Almost all of them became members of the Lyceum (1926–36), or at the very least participated in the club's cultural activities. This is not to say that the club directly ignited their ambitions, but it seemed to ratify them. In 1929 art critic Enrique Lafuente observed that a generation of artists had arrived on the scene in a display of artistic feminism (Quance 2000: 51). This, it seems to me, is an accurate way of understanding the *inquietudes* (aspirations) of the young women at the time. Their feminism was an instinctive one that could not be separated from their intellectual ambitions. It expressed itself primarily through the urge to write or paint and in general to emulate the young men with whom they came into contact. Theirs was the first generation that had actually broken free of intellectual and social segregation. And by coming into contact with young men, by beginning to seek out young men's company as a companion – and not necessarily as a possible *novia* (sweetheart) – they came naturally, it would seem in the eyes of some, to want to be young men.

In France the novel of the moment was *La Garçonne* (The Bachelor Girl) (1922) by Victor Margueritte, which was soon translated into Spanish as *La garzona*. The image on the front cover (Plate 7) set the tone for a style that became popular in the 1920s and was widely imitated: that of the lithe and elegant young woman who cropped her hair short and began to claim more sexual freedom. Only a few years earlier, on the other hand, the fashion had been more along the lines of Cléo de Mérode, the celebrated French actress who wore her locks long and beribboned. The young Norah Borges was photographed with this look in 1915 (see Martínez Quijano 1996: 74).

Riviere's 1929 article is predicated on the assumption, widespread thoughout the period, that there was such a thing as intersexuality or varying degrees of sex and gender status, ranging from the purely virile to the purely feminine (Marañón 1960: 141–53). It should be noted that this concept of degrees of femininity or masculinity suggests that there was no clear recognition at the time of a distinction between sex and gender, even if the concept of intersexuality or bisexuality contained the seeds of the distinction. Thus Riviere could argue that when an intellectual woman displayed excessive signs of femininity – submissiveness to men, coquettish behaviour, marked concern with her appearance – this could sometimes be a kind of mask she donned in order to compensate for other kinds of behaviour she had internalized as masculine.

The women Riviere studies as a psychoanalyst were ambitious women who had moved into fields previously dominated by men, such as the liberal professions: they were, according to Riviere, unconsciously compensating through their exaggerated pose of femininity for signs of aggressivity they feared might antagonize the men in their circle. According to her, these women had actually assumed some aspects of masculinity which they then undertook, unconsciously, to camouflage. Their display of femininity could not be taken for granted or at face value; it was instead a sign of psychic conflict. Elvira Burgos (2008: 174) observes that Riviere did not believe such inward masculinity implied desire for the same sex. In making a great show of their willingness to defer to men, the women seemed to wish to hold men's interest as objects of heterosexual desire.[4]

To an extent, the psychoanalytic concept can help us understand sympathetically and from the point of view of the creator some of the inner contradictions to which the first generation of artists and writers were prey. Consider the example of the avant-garde artist Norah Borges (Buenos Aires, 1901–98), sister of the celebrated Jorge Luis Borges. Although she is not the first female member of the Hispanic avant-garde (Marie Blanchard precedes her), she is the first to make a name for herself in Spain. Her contribution to *ultraísmo* was so important that some have claimed it legitimized the movement.[5] Borges's reputation gradually faded, however, after she returned to Argentina after the Civil War. Vindicated today as a key figure in both Spain and Argentina, she has been remembered as a retiring woman, who cultivated a self-effacing and deferential demeanour with respect to her husband, fellow *ultraísta* Guillermo de Torre.[6] Torre was a young Spanish poet and critic who courted her assiduously as soon as they met in March 1920, and competed for her hand with other admirers.

The Argentine art critic and collector May Lorenzo argues that her work exemplifies *la vanguardia enmascarada* (the masked avant-garde) (2007, 2009). This, the subtitle of Lorenzo's 2009 study, implies that the work itself presents ambiguous signs of the artist's adherence to avant-garde aesthetics. And that, perhaps, despite her mastery of expressionism and cubism, the artist was not entirely committed to the new art. Was that art implicitly masculine? And, if so, in what sense? Did Borges become more feminine as European art everywhere gradually experienced a return to order after World War I? These questions remain to be studied as specifically semiotic problems; however, the eventual softening of the angular lines of Norah's expressionism, her retreat from the techniques of analytical cubism visible in some of her woodcuts, also follows the story of her growing commitment to Torre, their courtship and eventual marriage (Lorenzo 2007: 24), and her return to an artistically more conservative milieu.

---

[4] But see Butler (1990: 43–57) for discussion of the ambiguity of what lies behind the masquerade. Butler starts from the Lacanian perspective according to which the female 'is' the phallus for the male observer.

[5] *Ultraísmo* refers to an avant-garde movement in Spain which flourished between 1918 and 1922. It amalgamated futurism, dada, cubism, expressionism, and *creacionismo* (creationism). In Argentina it was to thrive for slightly longer and under somewhat more classical premises.

[6] Ana Martínez Quijano cites Bioy Casares on Borges: 'Tan fina, tan delicada, de ninguna manera quería ensombrecer la imagen de su marido, por eso a veces permanecía callada' (So nice, so delicate, in no way did she wish to overshadow her husband's image, and so she sometimes refrained from speaking) (1996: 21).

Figure 1. *Sala* or *Sala Federal* (Hall or Federal Hall), linocut by Norah Borges (1922)

To apply the concept of masquerade more generally to women's work of this generation, it may be more helpful to insist on a stricter application of Riviere's ideas. An illustration Borges provided for the second issue of the late-*ultraísta* journal *Horizonte* (Horizon) in 1922 offers a way into the subject. The linocut Borges contributed to the journal (Fig. 1) was not an illustration in the usual sense of the word, but an independent work of art that the little magazines used to illustrate new trends.[7] Although it is not

---

[7] I am correcting my 2001 reading of the artwork, which contrasted Borges's linocut with a poem by Buñuel on what appeared to be the facing page. The copy of *Horizonte* I had consulted in the Biblioteca Nacional, Madrid, proved to be defective: the print appeared opposite different texts in that issue, including a poem dedicated to Norah Borges by Adriano

clear from the print itself that this is a self-portrait, one of the young women depicted is shown in a pose that is remarkably similar to a photograph of the artist as a young married woman, taken in 1930.

This enigmatic print has been interpreted in different ways (Quance 2001, Lorenzo 2006; 2009). Even its title is a matter of debate. In the little magazine it was presented simply as a 'Linoleum de Norah Borges', which suggests that the artist, who had by then returned to Buenos Aires to live, did not specify a title when she sent it to the editors or to her future husband for delivery. A catalogue of her work made when the artist was quite elderly and infirm records the title as *Sala* (Hall) and gives the date, perhaps retrieved from memory, as 1924 (Martínez Quijano 1996: 31). However, some things can be said for certain about it. The print was not intended as an illusionistic representation, as a copy of an objective reality, for it is immediately obvious that two different kinds of women and two different styles of dress are represented in the same frame, making it difficult to imagine the two figures as being literally in the same room. What we have instead is a subjective impression of two different styles of womanhood, signalled by the radical change in fashion for evening dress.

One woman is dressed in the traditional, conservative manner, with the long evening gown and fan used by the Spanish bourgeoise on formal occasions.[8] The other is dressed like a contemporary fashion plate: in a little black dress with the shorter skirt length that came into fashion after World War I, suggesting a bolder awareness of the body. But one cannot help noticing that the young woman's self-conscious pose contradicts the connotations of her outfit. She sits very awkwardly on the settee in this 'hall', her legs carefully crossed to preserve her modesty. Her slightly tilted head, in itself a sign of timidity, is outlined in such a way as to merge with the curved line of the back of the couch.

A careful symmetry of composition points to allegory: just as the old-fashioned figure is shown sitting beneath a portrait on the wall, so the young woman is seated beneath an ornamental object, as if a binary logic governed the two halves of the print. But the difference from one side to the other is revealing. On the one hand we have a mirroring between the older figure and the style and demeanour of the woman in the portrait of the couple hanging above her head. On the other hand we have an un-mirroring, for the object hanging on the wall above her, although literally a looking glass, does not reflect anything at all. It is an empty mirror, placed so high on the wall that in the dim light its surface is opaque.

---

del Valle. I now base my remarks on a facsimile edition of the little magazine published in 1991 (Sevilla: Renacimiento) as a more reliable source.

[8] Borges included a similar figure in the woodcut *Juerga flamenca* (Flamenco Party), published in the little magazine *Ronsel*, no. 4, in 1924.

Norah Borges's simple print is more complex than appears, for the mirror's blank surface seems to replace the corresponding representation in the other half of the composition. If X is to Y as X' is to Y', then a simple story emerges. While the more conservative of the two seated figures is modelled after the woman in the couple in the portrait, who in my reading represent the older generation, the *abuelos* (grandparents), the younger figure, by contrast, *lacks* a copy or a model from the past for her own life and customs. It would seem possible to read a narrative here of the modern woman and her fears about breaking with tradition, or of not finding her place in the line of generations. Although the conservative woman will shrink like her foremother as she takes her place beside her husband, she *will* have a husband, while the 'advanced' young woman hangs back before an uncertain future, in which she may not find a suitable partner.[9]

For unconscious reasons, perhaps, Norah Borges produced a work in keeping with her brother's famous mistrust of mirrors and their monstrous ability to imitate and reproduce reality. The empty mirror which replaces the human faces of tradition is, thus, in an era that held that all creation was predicated upon destruction of what had gone before, part of a more widespread mistrust of reproducing the past. The point I am making is that the artist is ambivalent about this.

If I read the image as an allegory about the artist (and not just about women like her), it is because several years later, in a photographic portrait, we see Borges assuming a pose remarkably similar to the one depicted in the print. The photograph taken of her at home in Buenos Aires around 1930 (Fig. 2) reveals a woman who, outwardly at least, is the epitome of modern elegance. Then we notice her shyness before the camera, her averted eyes, the care she has taken to sit like a lady, with her knees firmly together, as she leans back stiffly against some sort of recamier. Her husband was photographed in a similar pose reclining against the same couch, but he is confident and poised, looking directly at the camera and exhibiting his stock-in-trade, so to speak (a little magazine) as well as his *gravitas* (Fig. 3), while Norah looks more inhibited and uncomfortable with her part in such publicity.

What happened to Borges when she returned home after the outbreak of the Civil War and resumed married life in Argentina is a chapter of her life that remains to be written. Although her work was more marginalized than it

---

[9] Lorenzo links the print to Jorge Luis Borges's poem *Rosas*, on Argentina's despised nineteenth-century federalist leader, Juan Manuel de Rosas. Referring to it as *Sala federal* (Federal Hall), Lorenzo believes it represents a visit by a young female petitioner to the daughter of the dictator (2006: 16–17; 2009: 76–7). She argues that the figures in the portrait are Rosas and his daughter, yet I am not aware of any real portraits made of father and daughter together.

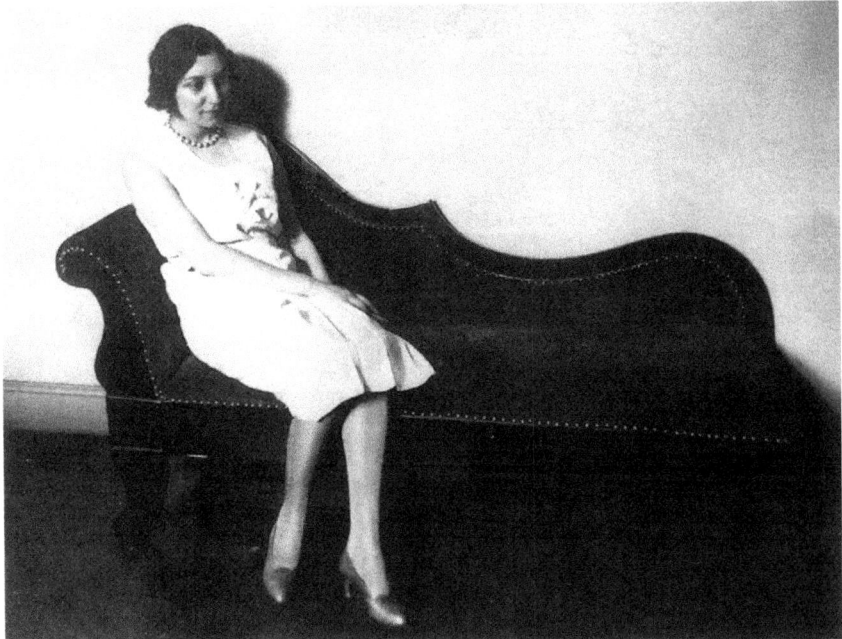

Figure 2. Norah Borges at home, Buenos Aires (1930)

had been before the war, other women of the Spanish avant-garde confronted the aftermath of war with less social protection, facing exile, or ostracism at home. Some, like Ernestina de Champourcín, turned away from the radical Republican ideals of their youth; others, like Concha Méndez, adapted to life in exile and such opportunities as they could find, with husbands or lovers, in Spanish Republican communities.[10]

Remedios Varo, who left Spain during the Civil War, and Maria Zambrano, who fled the country afterward, were able to thrive and produce their best work in exile, Varo no doubt because of the small community of surrealist artists who had settled in Mexico City and the friendship of like-minded women like Leonora Carrington, Zambrano because of a deep sense of mission which led her to bear witness to her Republican political ideals. To judge from their rich body of work, most of which was created after the war, both of these women freed themselves almost completely from the need for a masquerade in Riviere's sense. Perhaps it is no accident that what Varo and Zambrano have in common, despite their very different concerns

[10] This is a complex topic: in Mexico Champourcín experienced a religious crisis and eventually joined Opus Dei (see Comella 2002). Méndez suffered a debilitating isolation (see Ulacia Altolaguirre 1990).

Figure 3. Guillermo de Torre at home, Buenos Aires (1930)

and aesthetics, is the conviction that true freedom lay in being able to leave behind the public persona and its trappings altogether, to place oneself beyond the social demands of a particular time and place. Thus we find the philosopher Zambrano observing that one must be careful not to confuse the idea of personhood with the public persona, lest a public image harden into a mask that will suffocate the self, while Varo presents heroines in a state of constant metamorphosis. As Estrella de Diego points out, Varo clothes her heroines (who may all be versions of the artist) in deliberately anachronistic dress, harking back to the Middle Ages (2007: 40). Both women were devoted to transcending their time and place through a spiritual quest, however different the means with which they sought to gain enlightenment. Through her reading in alchemy, mythology and esoteric spiritual doctrines, Varo ends up placing her heroine beyond fashion altogether. In one of her most striking paintings, *Nacer de nuevo* (To Be Born Again) (1960), her *alter ego* is portrayed at the end of her journeys as someone who has been born anew and who is therefore naked and unadorned, as she bursts through a wall of a pavilion in the woods to lay hands on the Grail (see Ovalle et al. 1994: 185). Zambrano, for her part, has written that it is an enormous relief not to have an image of the self (1989: 29).

The postmodern view of masquerade, as I suggested at the outset, has moved beyond a focus on the psychology of the woman artist and author and real historical experience to concentrate instead on the viewer's contemplation of the represented female as someone whose femininity is always essentially a disguise. This can be assimilated to Butler's argument that feminine identity is not simply constructed but performed and lived as a masquerade. Visual artists' parody of conventions of femininity can therefore be understood as a device which asserts the factitiousness of gender roles and norms. Thus, when Diego notes Varo's interest in masquerade, she concentrates on the painter's fascination with masks and play-acting, situating her penchant for theatrical tableaux within the Parisian surrealist tradition (2007: 47–8) and concluding that Varo's heroines exemplify a sense of the self as intrinsically impossible to capture in any sort of self-representation (2007: 102). Maruja Mallo's extravagant make-up and fashion sense have also been likened to a real-life surrealist masquerade blurring life and art (Zanetta 2006: 92–3). More radical still is the work of a contemporary artist, the photographer Ouka Leele (b.1957), winner of the National Photography Award in 2005, who seems knowingly to fictionalize femininity in her work (Raventós-Pons 2005).[11]

In order to get at the radical difference, we need to consider the question of representation. Let us consider a photograph of 1996 (Plate 8) entitled *El niño la está mirando* (The Child Is Looking at Her), which was published in *Mujeres en el andén / Dones en l'andana* (Women on the Station Platform) (Mit 1999: 37). Like most of Ouka Leele's work this photograph has been staged, with no attempt to pretend otherwise. We are indoors, in the artist's studio, where she offers us the spectacle of a living tableau, a self-portrait of the artist in one of the many guises in which she presumably can see herself. Viewers familiar with religious iconography have no trouble identifying Ouka Leele posing as the Virgin Mary posing with the Infant Jesus in her lap and, more specifically still, imitating the pose in which one finds countless medieval representations of the Virgin and Child scattered throughout Spain. Certain iconic attributes are preserved, such as the pomegranate that the Virgin/artist holds in her left hand (although this is also attributed to

---

[11] Ouka Leele is the professional name of artist Barbara Allende, and this is how she currently spells it. The name has also appeared as 'Ouka Lele'.

Christ as a sign of his future Passion) and the altar-like setting where one sees the Virgin sitting like a queen on her throne.

What is one to make of this photograph? I have not hesitated to call it a parody, because it echoes other art and because I think we need the earlier images it cites to grasp the present subject, but this does not mean that the irony created between copy and original is by any means a destructive one (Hutcheon 1988: 34–35). In Ouka Leele's work viewers are confronted, to begin with, with an ambiguity about the pragmatic meaning of the artist's donning the guise of this mythic figure. The photograph does not venerate the Virgin so much as demythologize her: the figure of Mary could be any mother and the child could be any child. The allusion to one of Lorca's famous gypsy ballads, *Romance de la luna, luna* (Ballad of the Gypsy Moon) suggests that it is the baby boy who creates a goddess as the mother's stature grows in his eyes; in Lorca's poem, we remember, it is the moon, often linked to the Virgin Mary, who appears to the gypsy boy in the forge, dancing and seducing him. Ouka Leele's photograph is a half-playful assertion of how she might as a mother assume the guise of a mythic Virgin in a child's eyes.[12] This is not a denial of the Virgin Mary but a sort of suspended judgment about her reality, which viewers can see according to their own beliefs. Because the photograph is staged, it can be read (however reductively), as a record of a piece of theatre (showing that the artist can use photography, in its origins the genre of documentation, to document a dressing-up, a play-acting); its status as a citation of other works of art blurs reality and representation: the artist in this instance sees herself and gives herself to us to see through prior representations.

Ouka Leele has a rich and varied *oeuvre*. Some of her early photographs from the *movida* period in the early 1980s clearly spoof conventional images of femininity,[13] such as the well-known self-portrait of the artist spilling a glass of water on her bright red dress, the *Autorretrato con agua* (Self-Portrait with Water) of 1980 (see *Ouka Lele* 1987: 21). But in the late 1980s she began to reference religious imagery, even seeing herself through a religious prism. It is hard, given the parody implicit here too, to gauge whether the effect is critical or not – as often happens with postmodern art. In *Semilla* (Seed) of 1993 (Plate 9) (published in *Mujeres* 1994: 97), we see her kneeling on an emerald-green meadow with a young girl behind her (her daughter, who looks impishly at the camera), worshipping an unseen

---

[12] Barbara Allende has informed me that the child is in fact a girl (personal communication of 13 March 2009). This would suggest that the artist is deconstructing the original model of Mother and Infant Jesus to claim the sacred image for women. The photograph challenges us to think about the difference gender can make.

[13] The *movida* ('action', social scene) is the name given to the cultural movement in Spain coinciding roughly with the Transition to democracy from the late 1970s to the mid 1980s.

force in the late-winter woods to the left of the frame, in a scene that recalls popular representations of the apparition of the Virgin at Fatima.

The ambiguity here is of a different order from the other photograph, in that the artist has portrayed herself in the natural world instead of in a studio; in other words, in a place where miraculous apparitions have been said to occur (Quance 2000: 245). But is the light emanating from the woods and tracing an aura about the artist purely natural? The scene's brilliant glow is enhanced by the application of watercolour to a black-and-white photograph, a technique commonly employed by the artist. And, once more, if the viewer is aware of having seen similar images, she is faced with the question of how to interpret a possible parody (of a holy card): is it a deconstruction of the kind of episode that led to the establishment of a cult of the Virgin?[14] Are we to suppose that this simulates what could actually have been, for her or for someone, somewhere, a supernatural episode, or something verging on it? Should we believe that the camera has captured spirit, rather in the way early photographers had imagined was possible? To quote Matei Calinescu on a different topic (1987: 300), 'what does [the] representation represent?'.

Perhaps all of the above possibilities are put into play – all, that is, except the possibility that the artist has captured experience. For the photograph itself, its staging, its references to other works, is the only experience that we are offered. Ouka Leele's art hesitates between masking and unmasking itself, making it impossible to draw any firm conclusions about the artist's identification or lack of identification with her subjects or even her attitude toward them as author. In this sense, we can agree with Raventós-Pons (2005), who has argued that in this body of work the artist has fictionalized (her)self. What remains to be said, however, is that in so doing she has fictionalized experience as well.

In the light of what these religious representations have signified for Spanish women over the centuries, this staged art can radiate irony, playing to the viewer's awareness of the Enlightenment stance on the world and reason's assault on faith. And yet these photographs do not ultimately suggest a clear detachment from the mythical thinking which links women to religion or sees them as the keepers of the faith, as Hegel saw in the archetypal Antigone (Holland 1998). The twentieth-century version of masquerade, which has moved away from Riviere and which we find in some postmodern discussions of gender, thus returns to the problem implicit in the concept of parody: is the imitation a liberation or a permanent bond? Or, more disturbingly still, is this question – posed in regard to this photograph – now beside the point?

---

[14] The artist has noted that this scene set in El Escorial is in fact close to where the Virgin Mary is said to appear to believers (personal communication, 13 March 2009).

As we reflect on the difference between Riviere and Butler and the different kinds of masquerade which these two theorists addressed, we inevitably come back to a key difference between a modern and a postmodern approach to the question of femininity. Women at the beginning of the twentieth century yearned to break out of the conventional gender roles which had been enjoined upon them, and this sometimes led psychologically to the need for an exaggerated display of femininity to compensate for the masculinity they feared in themselves. Riviere's theory explains why some women may have held themselves back in their careers by deferring to men. By the end of the twentieth century, when some theorists are ready to call a display of femininity a performance and a parody, we tend to see the masquerade not as a compulsion but as a flamboyant affirmation of the inessentiality of gender. Perhaps Toril Moi comes closer to an understanding of the violence behind the ascription and assumption of gender when she writes that it is a 'socially imposed definition with real effects. Like all other social categories, the category of woman therefore at once *masquerades as* and *is* an essence' (1999: 290).

Further reading

Heath, Stephen, 1986. 'Joan Riviere and the Masquerade', in *Formations of Fantasy*, ed. Victor Burgin and Cora Kaplan (London: Methuen), pp. 45–61

Mayayo, Patricia, 2003. *Historias de mujeres, historias del arte* (Madrid: Cátedra)

Núñez Jiménez, Marina, 1995. 'Feminidad y mascarada', *Arte, Individuo y Sociedad*, 7: 53–9

Plate 1. Luisa Roldán, *The Virgin and Child with St Diego of Alcalá* (1690–95)

Plate 2. José Ribera, *Assumption of Mary Magdalene* (1636)

Plate 3. Sofonisba Anguissola, *Self-Portrait at the Easel* (c.1556)

Plate 4. Page from a woman's album (author's private collection)

Plate 5. A lady's dance card

Plate 6. Calendar advertising José Ovelar's store

Plate 7. Front cover of the Spanish edition (1924?) of *La Garçonne,* by Victor Margueritte

Plate 8. *El niño la está mirando* (The Child Is Looking at Her), by Ouka Leele (1996)

Plate 9. *Semilla* (Seed), by Ouka Leele (1993)

17

Gender and Change:
Identity and Reform in the Second Republic

FRANCES LANNON

Social historians have traditionally analysed past societies with reference to collective social identities. While the terms race, ethnicity, class, gender, and sexuality all bristle with problems of definition and meaning, we have not found a way of doing without them. They remain useful and necessary categories of analysis. Cultural systems rooted in religion or politics are also particularly powerful markers of identity in any society. The historian cannot write about groups or individuals without reference to such categories, within which personal experience is located and from which each individual derives important assumptions, values, and elements of self-understanding. Human beings are, to a greater or lesser extent, agents of their own experience and narrators of their own stories, but none of us inhabits a neutral space devoid of biologically inherited and socially constructed identities.

Such collective identities have great potency. In the case of gender, which is the subject of this chapter, the social experience of men in any society in any period will be differentiated from that of women not only by biology but also by legal norms, social structures, and cultural conventions based on deeply rooted assumptions about what it means to be male or female. On the other hand, gender also interrelates with, modifies, and is modified by other social identities. Together they form a dynamic matrix within which individuals, families, and groups exist. There can be no straightforward lived identity simply of men as men or women as women that is not subdivided and changed as it intersects with other defining values and interests based on, for example, class, religion, and race. To make matters even more complex, none of these constructed identities is fixed and unchanging. On the contrary, each one of them changes over time, sometimes almost invisibly slowly, and sometimes very rapidly.

The decade of the 1930s in Spain is a particularly interesting period to examine with these observations in mind, because the Second Republic that began in April 1931 was strongly characterized by a determination to challenge and change many existing social relationships, including those based on gender. Many Spaniards, across a broad political spectrum, thought the position of Spanish women in the home, civic life, and the workplace should be improved. But reformers had many other priorities as well. When the monarchy fell and the Second Republic was proclaimed, everyone knew that change and reform were now the order of the day. It was immediately obvious that the new regime would promote a modernizing agenda to change the relations between employers and workers, Church and State, government and society, and women and men. The huge crowds in Madrid and elsewhere who rapturously welcomed the proclamation of the Republic expected it to transform the country and their own experience of being Spanish. Those who feared the Republic did so for the same reason. The great question was how radical change would be, and on how many fronts it would be advanced.

In December 1931 the new Constitution of the Second Republic answered this question. It described Spain as a democratic Republic of workers, and introduced universal suffrage. It separated Church and State, secularized education, and instituted civil marriage and divorce. The Constitution set up a process for the historic regions of Spain to negotiate regional autonomy. It gave the State the right to expropriate property with compensation should a wider social good require such drastic action. Most notably for the topic of this chapter, the Constitution accorded equal civil and political rights to women and men. This legislation constituted a profound and dramatic transformation of the status of women and the opportunities open to them. Implementing the law, however, and translating it into social practice, would depend on the Republic becoming securely established. Unfortunately, the very range and depth of the Constitution's measures alienated many powerful groups and made it likely that the legitimacy of the regime would be contested. In particular, the very ambitious onslaught on Catholic tradition and education, and the perceived threat to property provoked strong opposition. Within only a few years, the prospects for real, sustained reform of the status and social opportunities for women had become dependent on the outcome of a different struggle about class relations and religion.

It is not hard to understand why many social and political commentators in Spain in the 1920s and 1930s were concerned about the situation of women and girls, and wished to improve it. The Spanish economy was still predominantly agricultural, although heavy and manufacturing industry were well established and developing fast in the north and east of the country. The middle class was small. Most workers were unskilled or semi-skilled labourers on the land or in factories, mines, mills, and shipyards. There was almost no social security, and the State education system was woefully inadequate. Yet, even allowing for the hardship and insecurity experienced by large sectors of the population, it is notable that on one measure after another females fared worse than males. The 1930 census recorded a very high level of 32% adult female illiteracy, substantially above the male level of 19%. Those girls who received schooling were almost always educated only to elementary level that gave no access to university or any profession other than elementary-level schoolteaching. Women workers were much less likely than men to be unionized. They were almost always paid at lower rates.

Before the coming of the Republic, married women were legally subordinate to their husbands under Spain's Civil Code of 1889. The supreme importance of the family, and of motherhood, were consistently promulgated by the most powerful cultural force in Spain, the Catholic Church. Catholic teaching provided the ideological basis for gender differences in legal status, educational provision, work, and pay. A woman's vocation was marriage and motherhood. As widely promulgated texts repeatedly proclaimed, she was the 'ángel del hogar' (angel of the hearth), and the heart but not the head of the family. The 1889 Code required wives to obey their husbands. A wife could not acquire or dispose of property without her husband's permission. She had to adopt his nationality. There was no divorce. The manufacture of contraceptive aids and the propagation of artificial methods of birth control was illegal. Although birth rates had gradually decreased, they remained in 1930 at an elevated level of 29 births per 1000 inhabitants. Especially in poor families, however, child mortality was also high. Gregorio Marañón, one of the country's most renowned doctors, pointed out in a famous book published in 1926, *Tres ensayos sobre la vida sexual* (Three Essays on Sexuality) that infant mortality reached almost 50% in poor families known to his own hospital in Madrid. He blamed poverty, disease, ignorance, and the lack of adequate health or welfare provision for this 'heroic but sterile effort of our poor women' (1934: 93–4).

Women who worked in paid employment mainly did so only until they married or had children, unless economic circumstances forced them to continue. According to the 1930 census, only 9.2% of the female population worked. This certainly understates the reality. It did not include significant numbers of women who were seasonal, temporary, or casual workers, or worked without a wage on a family smallholding. But the low percentage, although exaggerated, is nonetheless instructive. The census also recorded that while 24% of single women and 14% of widows formed part of the workforce, only 4% of married women did. By contrast, far and away the largest occupation given for women in the census was being 'members of the family'. Over 9 million women and girls were so described, comprising all women and female children who were not – or were not known to be – wage earners or enrolled as school or college students. 'Members of the family' was an overwhelmingly female category. The 1,765,008 males who were also ascribed to it included no married man or widower, and largely comprised male children below school age or not at school. So the census described a social reality, namely, that a woman's status was established by reference to the household in which she lived, and to the occupation of her husband or father, even though it understated the number of women who worked for a living, whether waged or unwaged.

The single largest paid occupation for women, representing about one-third of the total, was domestic service. This sector fell outside the scope of what few labour laws existed in Spain to regulate working hours or conditions. Pensions and insurance schemes, limited as they were, did not embrace it. And it was not unionized. There was little protection against harsh employers or sexual harassment, and little redress. Many other women worked for pay in their own homes in traditional occupations such as dress-making, embroidery, and lace-making. A law of 31 July 1926 had empowered local committees of employers and employees to set standard prices and wages for home-working, with equal prices for work done by women and men, and had also established a system of inspection. A year later detailed regulation followed to guide implementation. However, the very nature of the work made enforcement difficult. Long hours, low pay, and sometimes miserable conditions often continued to make working from home or in someone else's home a cruel caricature of the domestic haven that was so ubiquitously presented as a woman's privileged sphere.

In work outside the home, women were concentrated in the textile industry, and to a lesser extent in shoemaking, baking, paper manufacture, food-processing, and the tobacco industry. Newer sectors that were opening up by the 1930s included communications, transport, commerce, and the professions. Within the professions education was the only sizeable employer of women. There were very few women lawyers or doctors, but nearly 27,000 teachers. In 1930 teacher training, the *magisterio*, was the solitary gateway to a professional career that was visible to most women. It qualified women to teach at elementary level rather than for pre-university examinations, for which a degree was required. Teaching was gendered in its structures and rewards, just as educational provision was. Although the number of women university students was slowly increasing, in the 1930–31 academic year they still represented a very small and conspicuous minority of the total university student population.

The growing commercial sector employed nearly 40,000 women in shops, hotels, and offices, with a tiny number, under a thousand, finding their way into banks and insurance companies. Change was most noticeable in the rapidly expanding communications sector, in which technological developments brought new opportunities. Over 3,000 mainly young women were employed in the postal, telephone, and telegraph services. In Spain as elsewhere office employment as clerks or typists, or working the switchboards as telephonists, was creating new jobs for lower-middle-class girls and women. But for most Spanish women who worked, employment was simply an economic necessity rather than also being a career. A woman's career was meant to be her family.

Numerous attempts had been made before the 1930s to address the 'woman question' in Spain. The Spanish Socialist Workers' Party (PSOE) had set up a secretariat for women's issues in 1918, although there was always a debate about whether preoccupation about women was a distraction from the primary concern with class. Middle-class feminist organizations emerged at about the same time, to a great extent modelled on earlier movements in Britain, France, and Germany. The largest Spanish organization, the *Asociación Nacional de Mujeres de España* (National Association of Spanish Women) was founded in 1918. ANME, and other smaller organizations, campaigned for female suffrage, the removal of the Civil Code's restrictions on married women, and better female access to education and the professions.

During the dictatorship of General Miguel Primo de Rivera from 1923 to 1930, there were clear signs that change was on the way. In 1926 Primo appointed thirteen women to the National Assembly he convened to discuss a new constitution. He appointed several women to places on municipal councils. In 1926 Primo de Rivera also – no doubt to encourage high levels of natality – introduced family benefits for workers and State employees with a large number of children. And it was under Primo de Rivera that a system of obligatory maternity insurance for women workers was at last established by a law of 22 March 1929 after several years of discussion and preparation. This programme provided medical assistance and a few weeks' paid maternity leave for women workers who had made the qualifying contributions. It did not cover casual workers, or domestic servants. It was modest, but it was also a breakthrough. This was the system that the Republic found ready prepared and itself actually brought into operation on 1 October 1931.

It was to be expected, then, that the reformist Second Republic would be ambitious to change the status and life chances of women. The fundamental statement of principle is found in Article 2 of the 1931 Constitution: 'All Spaniards are equal before the law'. This was further developed in Article 25: 'There can be no foundation for juridical privilege in nature, lineage, sex, social class, wealth, political ideas, or religious beliefs'. Women were given the vote, thirteen years before their sisters in the much older democracy in neighbouring France (Article 36). All public offices and all jobs in public service were opened up to women on the same conditions as men (Article 40). Obligatory, lay, primary education was promised for all, and as far as possible in co-educational schools (Article 48). Whole swathes of the Civil Code of 1889 were swept away. Article 43 applied the concept of equal status and equal rights to marriage, which is where in the old Civil Code it had been most comprehensively denied. The legal subordination of married women to their husbands was ended. And either party could petition for divorce.

On paper, then, the 1931 Constitution represented a revolution in gender relations in Spain. All women were given equal citizenship with men. This was a remarkable change. But in social reality women belonged to a gender category and also to several others that differentiated them powerfully from one another. Of course, whether a woman was rich or poor, socialist or conservative, a devout Catholic or an anticlerical inevitably continued to have a very major effect on the lived reality of her situation. Moreover, it is also true that the gender revolution embedded in the Constitution was at risk precisely because it was inextricably entangled in the other dominant strands of the Constitution's modernizing agenda, which were democratization, devolution, secularizing the Spanish state and society, and the reform of employment law and property relations. Some of the changes in women's status had widespread support. Others were much more controversial. But in the end even those with broad support were undermined because radical and simultaneous change on so many different fronts, many of them not specifically to do with women, proved unacceptable to social groups which felt their religious values, political traditions, or class interests were threatened.

The public and private spaces that women could in reality inhabit would be determined to an extent it is difficult to exaggerate, and over a longer period than anyone in 1931 could have foreseen, by the failure of this extraordinarily ambitious attempt to change every aspect of Spanish life. The Republic was to last only five years before rebel generals rose in arms against the government in July 1936. Their eventual victory in April 1939 marked the definitive end of the constitutional reforms of 1931. The Franco regime revoked the Republic's new deal for women, together with democratization, secularization, devolution, and property reform, for several long decades. If we are to study Spanish women in the Second Republic, the Spanish Civil War, or the Franco regime, it is important to understand how gender issues in the 1930s were affected and eventually determined by conflicts over other kinds of social identity and interest.

It would be false to assume that all those in Spain who favoured the extension of women's rights and opportunities were neatly aligned within clear class, religious, and political categories, and arrayed against equally clearly aligned opponents. It would be similarly erroneous to assume that all women approved the reforms. Female suffrage was the most notorious example of an issue on which women disagreed. It also cut across class, religious, and political divisions. When the main parliamentary debate on this topic took place on 1 October 1931, two parliamentary deputies were women. They had been able to stand for election because the provisional government of the Republic had decreed on 8 May that women were eligible to stand in the forthcoming June elections for the Constituent Assembly even though these were conducted on the existing franchise of adult male suffrage. Clara Campoamor and Victoria Kent were both deputies for Madrid, the former with the Radicals, the latter with the Radical Socialists. They were both distinguished lawyers. In themselves, therefore, they represented a new professional experience that few women in Spain could emulate, and a new political activism at the highest level. This eminence was particularly remarkable in the case of Clara Campoamor because she came from a very modest background and had worked in a variety of quite routine jobs to fund her own education. She was thus the very embodiment of the New Woman in Spain, and worked tirelessly both as a lawyer and as a Republican politician to give other women by legal right the opportunities she had created for herself. She was a member of the parliamentary drafting commission on the Constitution.

To the dismay of feminists but the sardonic amusement of many deputies and journalists, Clara Campoamor and Victoria Kent took opposing sides in the debate on female suffrage. Both in the drafting commission and in the parliamentary debate Campoamor argued on grounds of democratic principle that female suffrage was essential. Kent argued instead on political and pragmatic grounds that female suffrage should be delayed because she feared that middle-class women with little experience beyond the domestic sphere would use their vote to support reactionary politics. This was also the view of a third woman deputy who gained a seat in a by-election in October after this debate had taken place. Margarita Nelken was an intellectual and a Socialist. In her book *La mujer ante las Cortes Constituyentes* (The Woman Question in The Constituent Assembly), published earlier in 1931, she lamented the poor educational level and the clericalism of Spanish women and asserted that 'to give women the vote is today, in Spain, to fulfil one of the greatest desires of the reactionaries' (Nelken 1931: 35).

The Radicals thought of themselves as a progressive party, but all of them voted against female suffrage except Campoamor. They had a long anticlerical tradition, and many of them feared that priests would exert undue political influence on women voters. Campoamor's isolation was painful, and opened up a line of criticism from her colleagues that she was endangering the Republic. The official Socialist line was in favour of female suffrage for reasons of principle like Campoamor's, but some Socialist deputies who shared Nelken's misgivings about the political implications absented themselves from the vote. By contrast, Catholic conservatives had no problem supporting the extension of the franchise to women. Indeed the national Catholic daily *El Debate* (The Debate) had begun campaigning for it back in 1919, seeing no conflict between female suffrage and social conservatism. The woman's vote was carried by 161 deputies in favour against 121 opposed. Only 60% of the deputies voted. The victory was the result of an unusual convergence on this one issue of Republican reformers, Socialists, and Catholic conservatives. It is also an instructive example of how a crucial policy concerning women's rights and citizenly status divided women themselves.

For many feminists the issue was an absolute priority in its own right. This was clearly the case for Clara Campoamor, and also for the many members of ANME who had campaigned for the vote, and crowded into the parliamentary chamber on 1 October to hear the debate. For other women and men it was subordinated to political considerations that seemed to them more urgent and significant.

That is one of the difficulties inherent in studying gender in 1930s Spain. The question of gender relations or the status of women, however important it was seen to be, was not regarded as the supreme issue of the day by very many Spaniards, women or men. In 1931 the end of the monarchy and the arrival of democracy, the future position of Catalonia within Spain, the threat to the social and cultural dominance of the Catholic Church, and disputes over wages and property rights were all fundamental and riveting matters that demanded attention. This was the political reality of this tumultuous decade. Hugely important questions in relation to gender were raised, contested, and settled largely as part of a different agenda with other priorities. For Clara Campoamor herself this was extremely difficult. She found herself hated by many on the Catholic right because of her support for divorce legislation and the secularization of education. But she also had to defend herself against attacks from the left in 1933 when the left lost the first general election conducted on the basis of universal suffrage and it was easy, though erroneous, to argue that the woman's vote had indeed swung the result to the reactionaries. Her book *Mi pecado mortal: el voto femenino y yo* (My Mortal Sin: Female Suffrage and Me) (1936) is her powerful apologia.

The issue on which it was even more obvious that women's interests were interpreted differently by different Spanish women was marriage. ANME and other women's organizations had campaigned during the 1920s for several elements of the old Civil Code to be changed. These included the loss of Spanish nationality by Spanish women who married foreigners, the prohibition on paternity tests, and unequal property rights between husbands and wives. There was little disagreement from any quarter when these were all swept away by the 1931 Constitution. But the introduction of civil marriage and divorce was an entirely different matter. These constituted a direct challenge to the traditional hegemony of the Catholic Church over the regulation of marriage. There had been no great ANME campaign to secularize marriage or permit divorce. But Article 43 of the Constitution did both. It stated that marriage was founded on the equal rights of both sexes and that the family was under the special protection of the State. There was no mention of the Church as having a role at all. The decision about divorce was radical. Divorce had been legal in many European countries for decades before this, but on limited grounds. The Republic, however, made divorce possible simply by mutual consent (a development not agreed in the United Kingdom until 1971), as well as at the petition of one partner with good cause shown. Furthermore, the Divorce Law of March 1932 stipulated that marriage could be dissolved 'whatever the form and the date of its celebration'. The State hereby claimed the right to remove retrospectively the civil effects it had previously given to marriages conducted by the Church under canon law.

It is interesting to compare this with the situation agreed in Italy under the Lateran Accords of 1929. Marriage conducted in a religious ceremony under canon law was given civil effects, and this co-existed with the option of civil marriage. Marriage breakdown could be dealt with by either ecclesiastical or civil courts, depending on the type of marriage in the first place. But the Second Republic had a laicizing and emancipatory agenda that made this kind of compromise unacceptable. Indeed in the 1932 Law it implemented divorce (including for existing marriages that had necessarily been conducted by the Church) before it had even agreed a regulatory framework for civil marriage, which followed in June.

The sense of urgency in this legislation was rooted in compassion for those trapped in unhappy marriages as well as in a determination to end the Church's control of marriage and the family. There was certainly an immediate response. Between the passage of the Law in March 1932 and the end of the following year there were 7,059 divorce petitions, of which nearly 57% were from women (Lezcano 1979: 265–71). The liberating power of the new legislation was evident in these petitions. Some involved women from elite social circles whose decision to divorce became widely known. Constancia de la Mora, granddaughter of Antonio Maura, the famous Conservative leader of the early twentieth century, included in her 1939 autobiography, *In Place of Splendor,* a moving account of her successful petition which was lodged at the very first opportunity, and her happy second marriage. By the time she published the book, however, Franco had triumphed. Already in March 1938 the Franco regime suspended divorce petitions and issued a law that annulled the Civil Marriage Act of June 1932. After the end of the Civil War, a law of September 1939 repealed the 1932 Divorce Law and declared null and void divorces already granted to people – like de la Mora – who had been married under canon law. For them, and for others waiting for a divorce to come through, this reversal was a personal tragedy. The Second Republic wrote civil marriage and divorce into the constitution itself rather than leaving it, as many had urged, to be settled in subsequent legislation that could be more easily revised. It also discounted the possibility of State recognition of Church marriage co-existing with civil marriage. In this haste to modernize and secularize Spanish society it made implacable enemies of large sectors of socially conservative Spaniards, both women and men. Whereas the question of female suffrage had cut across the usual entrenched positions of left and right in Spanish politics, legalizing civil marriage and divorce in the Constitution reinforced them.

There were two further sections of the 1931 constitution aimed directly at changing what it meant to be Spanish and female. One of these concerned education, and the other employment. Article 48 declared that the fostering of culture was 'an essential attribute of the State'. It promised free, obligatory primary education for all. This promised to end the blight of illiteracy for those children denied basic schooling, of whom the majority were girls. But this education was also to be lay, and 'inspired by ideals of human solidarity'. Catholic schools and Catholic culture were to be marginalized. This intention was clear in the statement that in future education would be centred round 'the unified school'. This term held two meanings simultaneously: it referred to schooling that was co-educational instead of single-sex; it also implied that schools not run by State authorities would be endangered. In Catholic tradition there was a strong preference for single-sex education. Moreover, the Catholic Church was far and away the main non-State provider of primary and secondary education in Spain. Giving girls the same education as boys, in the same schools, was therefore entangled in an anticlerical agenda.

Church schools were frequently criticized for their ideological orientation or – especially in the case of girls' schools – their lack of intellectual ambition. But they were also praised by many for the education they provided and the dedication of their staff. They were nearly all run by one or other of the religious congregations that had experienced huge expansion in Spain over the previous fifty or sixty years as powerful suppliers of health and welfare services, and education. The Republic drew back from kicking the religious congregations out of welfare work, with no less a figure than Prime Minister Manuel Azaña pointing out in the debates on the Constitution that Spain really could not at present do without them. Clinics, orphanages, and hospitals would have collapsed. But education was a different matter. Article 26 prohibited the religious congregations from involvement in 'industry, commerce, or education'. Azaña's argument here pitched the stakes very high. He declared that the schools run by the Marist brothers, Jesuits, Escolapios (brothers of the religious schools), or many others for boys, or the Sacred Heart nuns, or Ursulines, or other equivalents for girls, constituted a threat to the Republican State. The very security of the State required their closure. It is certainly true that the religious personnel who ran Catholic secondary schools were fearful of the Republic and all it stood for, and were by tradition and culture usually sympathetic to the fallen monarchical regime. None the less, the outright denial to the religious congregations, but not to other Spanish citizens, of the right to run schools, was extraordinarily harsh and provocative. It inevitably raised the question of what kind of a Republic it was that could not tolerate Catholic schooling.

From the outset, therefore, the Republic's laudable determination to provide more and better education for girls was inextricably linked to its frontal attack on Catholic education. Parents who for profound reasons of belief wanted their daughters – and sons – to be educated in Catholic schools could hardly help but become opponents of the whole Republican enterprise. Azaña and many like him saw the Republic as engaged in a kind of *Kulturkampf* on the model of the culture wars between State and Church in Bismarck's Germany or the French Third Republic. They should not have been surprised that their adversaries took the same view. In this almighty confrontation, the battle over gender roles was important. But it was subsumed into what seemed to almost everyone at the time the bigger war between religion and secularism, Church and State.

Employment reform as applied to women did not raise such wide controversies. All jobs in public service were at least in theory opened up to women on the same conditions as men (Article 40). At the same time, protective labour legislation including the regulation of women's work, and maternity benefits, was promised in Article 46. Because such legislation recognized and emphasized the difference between women and men, and the interests of the family, it provided common ground for conservative reformers and their more radical colleagues. Indeed, the way had been prepared by the maternity benefits legislation of Primo de Rivera. Greater access by women to a wide range of employment would take time, as would the expansion of welfare benefits. They did not have the dramatic immediate impact of the introduction of female suffrage, the closure of Catholic schools, or the introduction of divorce.

Among all the constitutional changes considered in this chapter so far, it is not hard to recognize what might have been a lasting legacy of profound long-term changes in gender relations in Spain. If the Republic had confined itself to the introduction of equal status and equal rights for women and men, female suffrage, broader and better provision of education for girls and employment opportunities for women, and had brought in civil marriage as an option for those who wanted it, with the possibility of its dissolution in civil divorce, the positive impact of such changes over time would have been enormous for women in Spain. As it was, however, the sectarian nature of the 1931 Constitution put all of this at risk by embedding a new deal for women in the attack not just on the Catholic Church as an institution but on Catholic identity and values. There were millions of Spaniards, both women and men, for whom Catholic identity was primary and fundamental. For them there would be no contest when it came to choosing between defence of the Church and defence of the Republic's efforts to promote gender equality.

Some of those efforts fared better than others. Female suffrage was duly introduced, and women voted in the general elections of 1933 and 1936. Political parties rushed to create women's sections to help mobilize the new voters. The 1933 elections were won by the right. In February 1936 the pendulum swung back to the left, and the elections were won by the Popular Front. On both occasions the swing was quite small. The women's vote clearly did not prove the huge influence that had been hoped for or feared. However, many Spanish women were certainly directly involved in political organizations and campaigning in a way that had not been possible before. A few stood successfully for election to parliament and one of these, Dolores Ibarruri, skilfully used parliament as a platform to support her national leadership role in the Communist Party.

The early Republic made valiant attempts to improve female literacy rates. New primary schools were established. But the parallel drive to create unified, co-educational schools, and to ban nuns and other members of religious congregations from teaching petered out when the 1933 elections brought in a government that depended on the support of the mass Catholic party, the *Confederación Española de Derechas Autónomas* (Spanish Confederation of Autonomous Right-Wing Movements). The CEDA had adopted the theme of defending the family, religion, and property, and it adamantly opposed the secularization of marriage and education. The laws giving force to the constitution's decisions were not changed, but in practice they were simply not implemented. The Second Republic is an interesting example of a regime that used a new constitution to bring about some radical social and cultural changes that were unacceptable to large sections of the population. It is not surprising that these could not survive the shift in electoral fortunes from left to right in 1933. Of course, some conservative sectors were simply unsympathetic to any alteration in traditional gender roles. But the Republic's commitment to ending the unequal status of women was also undermined at least in part by associating it with other controversial agendas, and in particular with the campaign to secularize Spanish society.

The Second Republic had considerable success in speeding up the process of change in women's status and opportunities. It expanded educational provision, ended the legal subservience of wives to their husbands, implemented maternity benefits for women workers, and extended the franchise to women. This was an extraordinary achievement. But changing the social reality experienced by so many Spanish women of poor education, low wages, and insecurity could not be the work of just a few years. It required decades. It therefore relied upon the Republic becoming firmly established. The new regime needed to establish its legitimacy right across Spanish society. It needed to be accepted as the framework within which political disagreements and cultural conflicts were expressed. This, however, was never the case. The Constitution posed a direct threat to the interests and values of too many individuals, families, groups, organizations, institutions, and cultures. It was too sectarian and too ambitious. The Popular Front victory in the elections of February 1936 marked the failure by the right to modify or suspend parts of the Constitution by political control of parliament. When faced with a new government that was committed to the same programme as in 1931, many on the right decided that they could not live their values within the Republic. They decided to overthrow it, just as many on the disaffected left had done in the attempted revolution against the right-wing government in October 1934.

Clara Campoamor was in Madrid in July 1936 when the Spanish Civil War began. Two months later she left Spain, and spent the rest of her life in exile. In 1937 she published a book about the conflict in Spain, in Paris (*La Révolution espagnole vue par une républicaine*). She was indeed still a Republican. But she was not an admirer of what the Republic had become. She had become disillusioned with the Radicals. She also feared the anti-parliamentary, revolutionary tendencies of many on the Spanish left which were dramatically demonstrated both in the October 1934 insurrection and the extreme violence on Republican-held territory in the first months of the Civil War. She was appalled that armed revolutionaries killed people just because they were religious, or bourgeois. Of course, she was equally sickened by the repression on the other side, behind Francoist lines. She despaired of what victory by either side would bring. As she anticipated, Franco's victory created a military dictatorship. The new regime reversed the reforms of the Second Republic, and never forgave Clara Campoamor for her role in the Republic's legislation. Her experience illustrates vividly the difficulty of embarking on major reform in Spain in the 1930s without on the one hand being overtaken by more revolutionary currents, and on the other provoking implacable reaction. This was the extremely difficult task facing the Republic in April 1931. With the benefit of hindsight, it seems that the Republic tried to change too much, too quickly, on too many different fronts. Equal rights for women with men were a notable casualty of the Republic's failure and defeat.

Further reading

Campoamor, Clara, [1936] 1981. *Mi pecado mortal: el voto femenino y yo*, ed. Concha Fagoaga and Paloma Saavedra (Barcelona: Lasal)
Capel Martínez, Rosa María, 1982. *El trabajo y la educación de la mujer en España (1900–1930)* (Madrid: Ministerio de la Cultura / Instituto de la Mujer)
——, 1992. *El sufragio femenino en la Segunda República española* (Madrid: Horas y Horas)

18

Invisible Catalan(e)s: Catalan Women Writers and the Contested Space of Home

HELENA BUFFERY AND LAURA LONSDALE

At the end of an insightful essay on Montserrat Roig, Carme Riera draws on a Baudelairian image that for her sums up gendered representation of *fin de siècle* urban experience. She evokes the 'dona fugitiva que apareix i desapareix entre la gentada, engolida per la multitud, entre el clarobscur que propicia la llum de gas' (fugitive/fleeing woman who appears and disappears amidst the throngs, swallowed by the multitude, through the light and shadows of the gas lamps) (1995: 16–17), alluding to its reappearance in later texts, such as Mercè Rodoreda's *Aloma* (1938) and Carmen Laforet's *Nada* (*Nothing*) (1945). For Riera this image is re-imagined and re-presented through the 'mirada bòrnia' (one-eyed gaze) of Roig, with one eye on the world, and one turned inwards on the interior, silent space, on the margins of official culture.

Roig's capacity for observation and for fresh insight into the urban landscape laid out before us in her fictional works is seen as both product and cause of this gendered and politically motivated way of seeing. Indeed, we might surmise that it is her status as a *lectora* (female reader) that produces her *lectora*, as Riera insists in her reading of the lonely and abused Natàlia's flight, in *El temps de les cireres* (*The Cherry Season*) (1977), from the prying eyes of the Rambla and Plaça Urquinaona to the solitude of masturbation in her bathroom:

> No cap altra cosa volia l'escriptora sinó convertir el lector i la lectora en l'ull capaç de sorprendre la fotògrafa en el moment clau per mostrar-nos la seva feblesa. Convertint-nos així en multitud que espia la noia que en tornar a la seva ciutat que [*sic*] encara pensava que podria conquerir-la.
> (Riera 1995: 17)

(The writer wanted nothing more than to transform the reader into an eye capable of surprising the photographer at the very moment that exposes her weakness. Transforming us thus into a multitude that spies on the girl who on returning to her city still believed that she might conquer it.)

The tropological shift from the first to the second image is an important one for this chapter, in which we will attempt to fix one eye on Catalan women's writing, while being aware of the many pragmatic constraints on our ability to see it either in its entirety or in its specificity or singularity. For it is not only our object that appears and disappears amidst the throngs, due to the minority status of Catalan language and culture, as well as to the particular operation of patriarchal structures in twentieth-century Spain and the Catalan-speaking territories, but also the mode of apprehending it that shifts and changes, both inside and out. Convinced that Catalan women writers cannot be fully apprehended without attention to the particular imbrications of gender, language, and class in the context of Catalan culture, we decided to fix our gaze on the impossible image of 'invisible Catalan(e)s', combining theories and approaches from feminist and gender-based critical practice, postcolonial studies, and cultural geography.[1]

Beginning with a brief survey of the place of Catalan women's writing within hispanic studies, we will proceed to assess the potential as well as the limitations of recent critical paradigms to navigate and uncover the layering of discourses within the writings of Esther Tusquets and Carme Riera, re-mapping their relationship to the social and cultural fields in which they are variously located and negotiating the particular spaces of representation they create and explore. We recognize, with Joan Ramon Resina (2008: 128), that the particular history of Catalan culture post-1939, marked by exile, repression, and suppression, has meant that for many writers, including the now undisputedly canonical Mercè Rodoreda, it is the Catalan language itself that came to represent the only recoverable and accessible space of home. Though other writers, educated in Castilian, have felt unable or unwilling to write in Catalan, their writing is nevertheless expressive of the contested space of Catalan culture. Such is the case of Esther Tusquets, whose novelistic trilogy we analyse in this context. We also look at Carme Riera's self-translation of *Cap al cel obert* (Towards the Open Sky) (2000) as *Por el cielo y más allá* (2001), exploring the contested notion of *patria* in her work, alongside evidence of the author's acute consciousness of her readership in the Castilian version of the novel. The decision to focus on Castilian-language texts is undoubtedly controversial in a critical landscape where the fields of Catalan literature and culture are hotly contested (see, for example, Crameri 2000, 2008; King 2005, 2006; Resina 2008). It is important to acknowledge, however, that invisibility is not only determined

---

[1] As in French, the '-*es*' ending indicates the feminine plural, and is used here to present a visible mark of the layering of identity in the case of Catalan women writers.

from the outside, but also generated from the inside, with the excision of Castilian-language writers from their socio-historial context.

Tusquets and Riera negotiate both the spaces and politics of home and language in their work; it is just that this negotiation has tended to be overlooked in favour of gendered readings which do not take into account the other political and cultural forces at work in their writing. In other words, their place within the Catalan landscape is rendered a fleeting and fugitive one, evoking the invisible Catalan(e)s of our title; closer scrutiny of their work soon reveals that questions of national identity are not limited to works in Catalan. However, whilst we will explore the maps of Catalan culture inscribed within these authors' works, and which govern their intelligibility, we would also like to remind our readers of the invisibility of writers who are not voiced, or who can only be heard via major languages like Castilian and English. The politics of translation, as critiqued by postcolonial critics such as Gayatri Spivak (1993), tend to assimilate the foreign into dominant modes of constructing and understanding subjectivity, thus rendering writers of marginalized or minority languages doubly invisible, often simultaneously marking their otherness and/or assimilating their difference into dominant norms. For Spivak, the main way to avoid this is for the reader to have 'the most intimate access to the rules of representation and permissible narratives which make up the substance of a culture, and [...] [to] become responsible and accountable to the writing/translating of the presupposed original' (2000: 13).

In recognition of the many obstacles preventing this level of access to twentieth-century Catalan culture, we will draw on the concept of a 'Catalunya invisible' (invisible Catalonia), developed by Sharon Feldman (2002, 2005), to allude to the critical blind spots that have arisen in relation to the work of Catalan women writers since the Transition. In this concept, Feldman captures a phenomenon observed by other cultural critics: the relative lack of allusion to contemporary Catalan reality in the otherwise realist textual theatre of the late 1980s and early 1990s. On the one hand, this lack is perceived to be a by-product of the need to overcome the perception of minority status, the sense of a need to look beyond the borders of Catalonia – and, more problematically, beyond the borders of Catalan – in order to be seen; on the other, it is presented as a symptom of the particular configuration of Catalan culture, and the contested space of the Catalan territories. Applying this concept to Catalan women writers since the Transition, we explore both the ways in which these writers have become invisible in terms of their cultural specificity, and the ways in which a politics and aesthetics of contested space inhere within their work. Our focus on invisibility through a reading of two authors will ultimately bring us back to focus on the space of contemporary Catalan culture and the woman writer's fluctuating place within it.

It may seem surprising, if not perverse, to allude to the invisibility of Catalan women writers today, after nearly four decades of critical attention, recovery, and celebration. Indeed, since the works of Gabancho (1982) and Arnau (1979) there has been no shortage of studies about contemporary Catalan women writers and the construction of female subjectivity in their texts, that have both made a space for new voices within the academic canon and underlined their difference and otherness, normally, but not exclusively, drawing on the discourses of feminist criticism. In the anglophone world, as has been argued persuasively elsewhere (Miguélez-Carballeira 2005), the reception of Catalan women's writing can be taken as paradigmatic of the development and incorporation of feminist and gender-based critique within hispanism more generally. The work of Rodoreda and Roig in particular was embraced enthusiastically by feminist hispanists seeking to question, critique and/or expand the inexorably masculine canon of hispanic studies in the mid-1980s, seizing above all on Rodoreda's short stories and *La plaça del Diamant* (*The Time of the Doves*) (1962). Indeed, the list of critics who have written on these authors reads like the Who's Who of gender-based criticism in Anglo-American hispanism of the 1980s and 1990s. Stuart Davis (2000) shows how far the predilection for writers like Rodoreda and Roig in the academic canon impacts on the educational canon, finding them to be the Peninsular Spanish women writers with most representation on Anglo-American university curricula. Their very ubiquity might be seen to have contributed to the relative invisibility of other (Catalan) women writers, through the tokenism effect attested by Francesca Bartrina, drawing on Russ (1993):

> És indiscutible el gran nombre i la reconeguda qualitat de les narradores catalanes del segle XX. Però, si ho examinem en detall, podem recordar que, en algun moment, es va negar la genialitat de Mercè Rodoreda i se li va atribuir al seu company Armand Obiols, o es va recordar Helena Valentí només com a musa de Gabriel Ferrater.[...] Cal rellegir com a ficció les novel.les de Dolors Monserdà, Maria Domènech i Maria Aurèlia Capmany, ja que no són només vehicles que transmeten la seva ideologia, sinó que tenen un valor intrínsec [...] Tota la narrativa de Caterina Albert i Mercè Rodoreda és extraordinària, i no tan sols *Solitud, La plaça del Diamant* o *Mirall trencat*. El valor de Roig periodista no ha d'eclipsar la novel·lista; Maria Barbal no escriu només novel·la rural, ni Maria Àngels Anglada només va cultivar el tema hel·lenístic. Les novel·les de Carme Riera, de Maria Antònia Oliver i d'Isabel-Clara Simó no interessen solament les lectores, sinó que també captiven els lectors. (Bartrina 2006: 208)

> (The great number and recognized quality of twentieth-century Catalan women writers are now fully accepted. However, if we look in more detail, we might recall that, at different points, the genius of Mercè Rodoreda was denied and attributed to her partner, Armand Obiols, and that Helena

Valentí was only remembered as Gabriel Ferrater's muse .[...] One must reread as fiction the novels of Dolors Monserdà, Maria Domènech, and Maria Aurèlia Capmany, for they are not just vehicles that transmit the ideology of their authors, but have their own intrinsic value [...] All of the narrative output of Caterina Albert and Mercè Rodoreda is extraordinary, not just *Solitude, The Time of the Doves, A Broken Mirror*. The value of Roig as a journalist should not eclipse that of the novelist; Maria Barbal does not just write rural novels, nor did Maria Àngels Anglada simply cultivate Hellenistic themes. The novels of Carme Riera, Maria Antònia Oliver and Isabel Clara-Simó are of interest not just to female readers, but to male readers as well.)

Yet, at another level, Catalan women writers have been invisible precisely because of the nature of their critical celebration, coming into focus only in so far as they fit in with particular feminist or gender-based critical idioms. At times, as Helena Miguélez-Carballeira (2005) and Laura Lonsdale (2007, 2008) observe in the case of Tusquets, and Resina (1987), Kanyann Short (1995), and Colleen Culleton (2002) redress systematically in the case of Rodoreda's *La plaça del Diamant*, this has led to critical frustration, and to often circular debate about where and how to apply the label of feminist to particular writers. At other times it has resulted in a somewhat limiting view of an author's work, such as the almost exclusive focus on psychology of the female protagonists in Rodoreda. Although the celebration of the 'Any Rodoreda' (Rodoreda Centenary) in 2008 brought more expansive critical attention to relatively neglected works, such as *Quanta, quanta guerra* (What a Lot of War) (1980) *Viatges i flors* (Journeys and Flowers) (1980) and *La mort i la primavera* (*Death in Spring*) (1986), it simultaneously drew attention to the perceived gulf between Anglo-American and home-grown Catalan criticism, at times transmitting the sense that only Catalan critics can fully comprehend Rodoreda's work (see, for example, Mencos 2002: 13; Castells 2008).

The overt appropriation of a series of writers for a particular political agenda has begun to be balanced more recently by attempts to reincorporate these writers – most notably Rodoreda and Roig, but also Caterina Albert (Víctor Català), Maria Aurèlia Capmany, Maria Antònia Oliver, Maria Barbal, and Riera – into their proper socio-historical context, partly in response to increasing frustration at their resistance to Anglo-feminist projects. Yet these new approaches are often marked by a particular critical idiom in which gender and socio-political marginality are intertwined with catch-all ideas of double minority and gender exile, which ultimately take precedence over the real histories (and stories) of the writers concerned. This process, in which gender and nation are brought together, but more often than not conflated, leads to another level of invisibility: one that elides the 'figure in terms of the ground' (Friedman 1998: 137), that is the particular figures cut by these authors and their fictional creations in their particular socio-cultural landscape. To a certain extent this has been countered by the range of excellent studies in Catalan and Spanish, from Bartrina 2001 and Neus Real 1998, 2005, 2006 on pre-Civil War Catalan women writers, to Mónica Jato's recovery of Maria Beneyto (2008) and Montserrat Lunati's superb study of Imma Monsó (2007); as well as by the network of writers and researchers affiliated to the Catalan Pen Club (see especially Marçal 1998, Julià 1999), the journal *Lectora*, and the Unesco-sponsored research centre at the University of Vic.

Projects like that at Vic address specifically the question of the continuing invisibility of women writers within the canon at a number of different levels: through the recovery of hidden figures, communities, and traditions, in both Catalonia and the other Catalan-speaking territories. They also signal increasing attention to the relationship between the Catalan and other traditions, in embracing, as we will here, writers who write in and between Catalan and Castilian or other languages, and in the re-positioning of Catalan women writers whose production is entirely in Castilian. Yet the issue of how far Catalan women writers can become visible within the different systems of cultural value in which they appear and disappear remains critical, and whilst it is a debate that continues to trouble feminist and gender-based criticism more generally, it can be argued that it is exacerbated in the case of Catalan women writers due to their perceived double or triple minority (Marçal 2004: 21–4), due to an experience of exile that may be cultural, political, and gendered.

Particularly influential in implanting this approach to Catalan women's writing has been the work of Geraldine Nichols. In her 1986 study of the representation of exile and marginality in Rodoreda, traces of testimony to the experience of physical exile are subsumed into the wider concept of gender exile as an expression of the feminine experience of submission and dependence in a patriarchal culture. In the more comparative reading of 1989 Rodoreda is placed alongside six other Catalan women authors, including both Catalan- and Castilian-language writers: Roig, Tusquets, Riera, Ana María Matute, Carmen Laforet, and Ana María Moix. Other important texts in this tradition include Randolph Pope's 1991 essay and, of course, McNerney and Enríquez's *Double Minorities of Spain* (1994). Yet whilst at times such a critical focus can contribute to the recovery of specific experiences, as in Dupláa 2000 and Arkinstall 2004, at other times, as in Everly 2003, the different particular socio-historical contexts may disappear from view, according to the critical lens used.

Whilst it is above all the work of Rodoreda that has been continually refracted through this prism (Mencos 2002: 16), Tusquets and Riera also address questions of multiple minority and gender exile. Both authors engage with colonialism – either as a major historical theme (Riera) or as a trope for unequal relationships of power (Tusquets) – and also as a means of deeply problematizing the concepts of home(land) and nation, the politics of belonging. Here we will look at how their texts appear and disappear in the literary landscape, through the modes in which they read or have been read by tradition, and the ways in which they thematize and/or enact a sense of double minority and exile through the evocation of contested space, exploring how this controls the construction and apprehension of feminine subjectivity in their texts.

The emphasis on contested space is drawn from Isobel Armstrong's innovative political and aesthetic association of feminism and postcolonialism through a figure of invaded space (2000): space is a question both of material reality and of the cultural imaginary; the way we imagine space, and imagine ourselves within space, is as important to territorial questions as are more material issues. Drawing on Trinh T. Minh-Ha's (1989) notion of the 'I/i' – the subject who is neither entirely sovereign (I) nor entirely the 'master's subject' (i) – Armstrong describes both colonialism and rape as consequences of '[a] failure to negotiate the space of the highly specific and individuated I/i': this is the 'source of violence' (2000: 220, 225). If colonialism can be understood as an invasion of space and an appropriation of territory, rape, she argues, can be understood in the same terms. Armstrong therefore highlights the located nature of identity, the importance of space to both subjectivity and intersubjectivity. Armstrong's formulation of space in relation to feminist and postcolonialist politics is very suggestive in the context of the narratives of both Tusquets and Riera, because both authors explore the ways in which the contestation of space becomes a highly significant political issue, intimately connected with the individual's formulation of personal identity.

The question of contested space emerges in Riera's *Cap al cel obert* (Towards the Open Sky) (2000) in the historical context of Spanish Cuba in the mid nineteenth century. Although the novel was originally written in Catalan, for the purposes of this essay we will focus on Riera's own Castilian translation, *Por el cielo y más allá* (2001), in which she introduces changes that indicate the unavoidable awareness that she is writing for two different traditions. On the one hand, as in her other self-translations, she employs a radically different intertextual network that draws on her deep but differentiated awareness of both Catalan and Castilian literary traditions; on the other, she sets up a significantly different relationship with her reader, making far more explicit the question of homeland and its relation to the contemporary politics of Catalonia.

Cuba is an island whose political status is in play, and whose future is to be determined largely by the economic self-interest of the ruling classes. But, as an island, Cuba also reflects another island reality, that of Mallorca, underpinning an exploration of individual and collective identity governed by recognition and misrecognition, through the use of mirrors, letters, and intertexts which are (mis)read by the different characters, and which implicate an active and suitably wary (mis)reader. The novel develops the theme of Jewish exile introduced in *Dins el darrer blau* (*En el último azul*) (*In the Last Blue*) (Riera 1994), as a means of foregrounding the problematic politics of homeland and belonging introduced within the novel's historical setting. Furthermore, the novel's concern with slavery highlights the brutal racial exclusivity on which discourses of colonialism and national identity are often founded. Whereas in the Catalan original Riera relies on her reader's recognition of their implication in this history, the Castilian version introduces significant changes to ensure a context of intelligibility. After all, the presence of Catalan, let alone Mallorcan, emigrés in Cuba would be all but invisible to readers whose knowledge of colonial history is framed by the poles of a unitary Spain and the New World.

The fact that the novel's backdrop of territorial politics and violent inequality needs additional explanation for a Castilian-language reader points to a significant extratextual context of unequal and contested space. Against this backdrop, the uprooting and dependency of Mallorca-born María Forteza creates the conditions for her sentimentalized conception of a 'patria del amor' (homeland of love) (Riera 2001: 421), which offers up an alternative vision of homeland conceived in terms of love before territory. María, forced to emigrate to Cuba on her father's death, and transported with her sister (who dies in an on-board epidemic) across a terrifying sea, is tied to Cuba first by necessity, and only later by love. The poem she dedicates to her husband, Joaquín, on their first wedding anniversary associates her newfound love of Cuba with her love for him:

> Esposo:
> Mi patria son tus brazos
> cuando me dan cobijo.
> Pero también la tierra,
> donde crece la palma,
> es mi patria del alma
> donde morir quisiera. (2001: 226)

> (Husband: / My homeland is in your arms/ when they shelter me. / But also the land, / where the palm tree grows, / is the homeland of my soul / in which I hope to die.)

Whilst the Catalan reader encounters only fragments of a rather different poem (Riera 2000: 181 and 324), in which the focus is on the 'sweet land' – and on the recognition of (an)other island home rather than marital duty and love –, in Castilian it is clear that María's patriotism is an offshoot of her love for an individual, her husband, who becomes the very *patria* to which she pledges allegiance. Both poems ultimately point to the roots of this identification in the past, in María's resemblance to the portrait of one of her martyred ancestors, and her receptiveness to Joaquín Fortalesa's tales of his *Xueta* heritage.[2] Her recognition and self-identification with a shared cultural heritage offers a poignant counterpoint to the opening dedication of the novel to the memory of Riera's grandmother, famously the inspiration for her writings in Catalan. Significantly, later in the novel *patria* is identified as the place that provides us with a sense of our own identity or 'identidad propia' (2001: 407), rather than necessarily equating it with the place of our birth. Nevertheless, in the original Catalan this identity is an 'identitat trobada' (found identity) (2000: 321), reminding us of identity's roots in recognition and its interaction with past forms. It is with a deep sense of irony, then, that the narrator describes the prosecutor's attempt to find evidence in this poem of insurrectionist and secessionist national sentiment (2001: 413), given that, for María, any sense of *patria* is deeply sentimental and fundamentally apolitical, born of such historically feminine requisites as duty, necessity, and love.

Of course, the novel itself does not present questions of homeland and patriotism as apolitical. In Riera's novel the borders, boundaries and political allegiances of nations are determined by and for those in power, not least, in Cuba's case, the cynical captain of the island, Rodríguez de la Conca, who is primarily concerned with his own interests. The novel also raises the spectre of that divine right of nations which is at the heart of the imperialist or colonialist project, further exploring the material effects of the exclusivity which shapes imperialist and nationalist discourses. Just as María's story is fundamentally shaped by the legacy of her Jewish ancestry, shared with Joaquín, the very legacy from which he attempted to escape when he first fled to Cuba, so the discovery of this Jewish ancestry contributes in no small part to the miscarriage of justice which condemns María to death at the end of the novel. The inevitable modern resonance of Jewish diaspora, shored up by Riera's own novelistic incursion into the life and death of Joaquín and María's persecuted Jewish ancestors in *Dins el darrer blau*, frames the ways in which the novel problematizes such questions as homeland and belonging. María is paradoxically condemned both as a nationalist insurrectionist and as a wandering Jew, whose claims to national belonging could only ever, in the eyes of Rodríguez de la Conca, be inauthentic and parasitic.

If the contested nature of space emerges in the presentation of both self-interested colonialist politicking and of anti-Semitism, the presence of slavery offers no less a challenge to conceptions of homeland and belonging.

---

[2] *Xuetes* are descendants of Mallorcan *conversos*, or Jews forced to convert to Christianity.

Whilst it could be argued that the novel deals with slavery as a historical reality rather than as a theme in its own right, it is nevertheless notable that Riera should underline, in the epilogue to the Castilian version only, the ways in which contemporary discourses of nationhood ignore the legacy of slavery at everyone's peril:

> trato de reflexionar sobre la historia de nuestro pasado y las contradicciones de nuestro presente, que nos abocan a la más absoluta desmemoria. No hace tanto que fuimos emigrantes y también negreros. La Cataluña *rica i plena* y el industrializado País Vasco, por ejemplo, se levantaron, en gran parte, con capital proveniente de los ingenios esclavistas, y aunque no nos guste, quizá el hecho de reconocerlo nos permitiría ser más generosos y tolerantes con los inmigrantes, con cuantos son diferentes o, simplemente, no piensan lo mismo que nosotros. (Riera 2001: 452)

> (I try to reflect on the history of our past and the contradictions of our present, which lead us to total amnesia. It's not so long since we were emigrants and slave traders. The Catalonia *rica i plena* [rich and complete] and the industrialized Basque country, for example, were built, to a large extent, with capital from mills run on slave labour, and though we might not like it, perhaps if we recognized it we could be more generous and tolerant towards immigrants, and towards those who are different, or who simply think differently, from ourselves.)

The very contemporary concern with immigration in the context of Catalan culture, language, and identity is brought to light with specific reference to a history of colonialism and slavery which an exclusive Catalan nationalism might choose to ignore; and, indeed, this is the political message which Fernando Valls (2000) chooses to foreground in his reading of the Catalan version of the novel. However, whilst there is no doubt that *Por el cielo y más allá* constructs a space for reflection on the violence of the encounter between self and other in the context of colonial violence and its postcolonial response, highlighting its role in the constitution of contemporary national identities, it is less clear that this is intended just as a lesson for Catalan nationalism. Just as María remains elusive throughout the novel, perceived largely through the distorting mirrors of her writing and the perceptions and judgments of others, nor is it entirely clear who the 'our' of 'our past' and 'our present' is intended to include, particularly if we consider Riera's own origins in the Balearic Islands rather than Catalonia, although she now resides in Barcelona and works in Castilian as well as Catalan. Nevertheless, it is interesting that she chooses to make her message about the ambivalent legacy of the nineteenth century so much more explicit for the Castilian-speaking reader; as if they would not make the connection otherwise, due to a lack of knowledge of Catalan cultural history and geography.

Riera's exploration of the themes of homeland, nation, and belonging in the context of Cuba in the mid nineteenth century constitutes a direct attempt to remember – in the face of cultural *desmemoria* (disremembering) (2001: 452) – the discourses and historical experiences on which the modern Catalan-speaking territories are founded. The concept of *patria* is shown to be an ill-defined but powerfully legitimating term for a range of political and economic schemes and practices, as well as a repository for a range of sentiments born of historical, cultural, and personal circumstance. Riera questions this legitimating framework in her presentation of the exclusivity and self-interest invoked in such conceptions. Thus María's fight to determine a definition of *patria* that is both possible and meaningful to her reveals a sense of identity – whether *propia* or *trobada* – that involves both spatial and temporal negotiation, that demands an attentiveness to landscape as well as figure. In this way, *patria* is revealed as a contested space as well as an embattled and highly individualized notion.

Esther Tusquets's writing, though profoundly implicated in the politics of nation, as we will seek to show, is perhaps as evasive as Riera's is overt in dealing with questions of belonging in relation to historical memory. The concern with contested space can, in our view, be located in a number of features of Tusquets's narrative, including the connections it forges between space and subjectivity, the author's employment of a metaphor of colonization for amorous relationships, and the conclusion of her first two novels – *El mismo mar de todos los veranos* (*The Same Sea as Every Summer*) (1978) and *El amor es un juego solitario* (*Love is a Solitary Game*) (1979) – with troubling scenes of unresisted rape. We will argue that this range of evocations of contested space evokes a *terreno fronterizo* (borderland) between different identities which is suggestive in the context of Catalonia's experience of partial colonization and partial decolonization, and productive of new readings of a subjectivity which is both gendered *and* located.

Armstrong highlights the located nature of identity, the importance of space to both subjectivity and intersubjectivity. This is highly pertinent to a reading of Tusquets, given that her writing consistently dwells in intimate, phenomenological spaces, linking spatial awareness to questions of both subjectivity and subjectivity-in-community. The spaces which Tusquets's writing explores and evokes are both vital and political: '[vital space] is always already mediated political space, dominated space' (Armstrong 2000: 223).³ Her writing evokes what Armstrong calls 'the territorial nature

---

³ According to Gaston Bachelard, 'vital space' relates to our first experience of the house: 'our first universe, a real cosmos in every sense of the word'. For him, 'all really inhabited space bears the essence of the notion of home', and thus in the subject's psychological construction of vital space, 'memory and imagination remain associated, each one working for their mutual deepening' ([1958] 1994: 4–5).

of identity when it is imagined, its locatedness in space' (222). Space in Tusquets's narratives is the source of consciousness; the narrator knows herself by the spaces she has occupied (such as her first childhood home), and knows her society by the places it values (such as the *Liceo* theatre, bastion of Barcelona's bourgeoisie). Space in Tusquets's narrative is therefore key to the question of subjectivity, and its consistently metaphorical function lends it a prime aesthetic importance. Furthermore, the author's famously digressive and protracted style conveys, in *El mismo mar*, a sense of tortuous progress through both space and time, challenging the notion of narrative as a journey and suggesting instead a dynamic of constant projection and constant return.

The sense of stasis and the emphasis on space in Tusquets's prose is significant to a consideration of the author's figurative employment of a metaphor of colonization in *El mismo mar*. Tusquets's writing consistently points towards a self-interested, perhaps even treacherous, acquiescence by Barcelona's *haute bourgeoisie* to the linguistic and cultural policies of the Franco regime, and – though Tusquets is herself no Catalanist[4] – this is expressed in an uneasy dynamic of collaboration and resistance most evident in E.'s relationship to her mother, her husband, and her class. Consistently proclaiming and yet resenting her difference and inconformity, E. is painfully and disablingly implicated in a complex network of power relations in which any straightforward relationship between oppressor and oppressed is confounded (see Molinaro 1991: 18). The metaphor of colonization is significant because it frames the dynamic of collaboration and resistance – of belonging and non-belonging – in terms of an uncomfortable and guilty relationship to the sources of dominance and power. The metaphor is most clearly employed in the context of the relationship of the narrator, E., with her young Colombian lover, Clara. E. relentlessly evokes Clara in terms of native exoticism – she is an 'Angélica azteca [...] que recorre cual bacante loca unas selvas inesperadamente tropicales, unas selvas inconfundiblemente amazónicas' (an Aztec Angelica [...] who travels like a mad bacchante through unexpectedly tropical, undoubtedly Amazonian, jungles) (Tusquets [1978] 2002: 78) – and employs the vocabulary of torture and conquest in her description of their lovemaking:

---

[4] Tusquets has contentiously stated that: '[n]o me mueve nada lo catalán, como tampoco lo español. Cataluña es bilingüe, de momento. Si desaparece una de las dos lenguas, y creo que sería muy difícil que lo hiciera el español, no voy a intervenir' (I am not moved in the least by either the Catalan or the Spanish question. Catalonia is bilingual, for the moment. If one of her languages disappears, and I think it would be unlikely to happen to Spanish, I will not intervene) (2001c).

La tumbo de espaldas, la fuerzo a no moverse, la sujeto contra el suelo con mis dos manos, y mi boca empieza un recorrido lentísimo por la garganta fina, palpitante, donde agonizan los gemidos, la garganta de alguien que se está ahogando y que no quiere gritar [...] Y los flancos de Clara arqueados de un modo tan violento y contorsionado, tan pálidos y flacos a la luz de las llamas, evocan imágenes sombrías de terribles torturas ancestrales.
(Tusquets [1978] 2002: 154–5)

(I throw her on to her back, I force her not to move, I pin her against the floor with my two hands, and my mouth begins its slow journey along her fine, palpitating throat, where her moans die out, the throat of somebody who is drowning and who doesn't want to cry out [...] And Clara's flanks, so arched and contorted, so pale and thin in the light of the flames, evoke shadowy images of terrible ancestral torture.)

As Tsuchiya writes, 'by employing the rhetoric of colonization to describe her "conquest" of Clara, who is both her student and a native of Colombia, the narrator transforms Clara into the colonized other' (2003: 222). Nevertheless, if E. is responsible for colonizing Clara, she also collaborates in the colonization – the rape – of her own body by her husband, Julio, when she allows herself to be reclaimed and conquered by him, sexually if not emotionally, on his return at the end of the novel. Unable to identify a third term to the binary of colonizer or colonized, E. fails to recognize that a relationship with Clara might offer something outside this harmful paradigm of oppressor and oppressed.

How do such observations relate to a concern with establishing historical or cultural specificity in relation to women's writing from Catalonia? It is evident that Tusquets's writing, highly lyrical and politically ill-defined, calls for more speculative readings of the politics of space than does, perhaps, Riera's historical novel. Nevertheless, we consider that the spatial qualities and concerns of Tusquets's prose are highly suggestive in the context of Catalonia. Derek Attridge (2004) writes of the South African author J. M. Coetzee that his writing foregrounds, formally and thematically, an impulse of self towards other which can be read in the context of a country facing fundamental questions of inclusion, otherness, and memory. In our view, Tusquets's writing foregrounds an internalization of otherness, an incapacity to negotiate the politics of difference. If Coetzee's writing is the product of a man writing in a country emerging from apartheid, with all that entails in terms of a negotiation of questions of otherness, Tusquets's is the product of a woman writing in a nation already absorbed into another nation, a nation without a state, a contested cultural and linguistic space. The particular historical experience of Catalonia, a nation without a state, is one of partial colonization, and partial decolonization. It evokes a political and cultural borderland between identities which is highly suggestive in the context of Tusquets's writing. As Trinh Minh-Ha's double emphasis on feminism and postcolonialism in the formulation of the 'I/i' model of subjectivity suggests, and as the narratives of both Riera and Tusquets imply, it is not difficult to imagine women as a nation within a nation, a nation without a state, as culturally and linguistically contested, and as variously implicated in complexes of power.

Of course, to include Tusquets in a chapter on Catalan writing inevitably draws attention once more to the relationship between language and the space of home. For the space of Catalan is all but invisible in her earlier works, coming into more explicit focus only in the recent autobiographical *Habíamos ganado la guerra* (We Had Won the War) (2007). Here we have proposed a frame in which to read her work – and that of other Catalan women writers – that is more attentive to the shifting dynamics of gender, space, class, and language, ultimately revealing the colonial conflict that informs the construction of feminine subjectivities in her texts. It is a frame that responds to our conviction that the question of (in)visibility in the context of Catalan women's writing is relevant even to writers who do not fit neatly into the double minority category by virtue of their sex and language, but who nevertheless probe very deeply into the politics of their nation through their exploration of the contested space of home and homeland.

Further reading

Everly, Kathryn A., 2003. *Catalan Women Writers and Artists: Revisionist Views from a Feminist Space* (Lewisburg, PA: Bucknell UP)

Glenn, Kathleen M., Mirella Servodidio, and Mary S. Vázquez (eds), 1999. *Moveable Margins: The Narrative Art of Carme Riera* (London: AUP)

Lonsdale, Laura, 2010. 'The Space of Politics: Nation, Gender, Language and Class in Esther Tusquets' Narrative, in *New Spain, New Literatures (Hispanic Issues)*, ed. Nicholas Spadacini and Luis Martín-Estudillo (Nashville, TN: Vanderbilt UP), pp. 245–61

McNerney, Kathleen, and Cristina Enríquez de Salamanca (eds), 1994. *Double Minorities of Spain: A Bio-Bibliographic Guide to Women Writers of the Catalan, Galician, and Basque Countries (*New York: PMLA)

Nichols, Geraldine Cleary, 1986. 'Exile, Gender, and Mercè Rodoreda', *MLN*, 101: 405–17

19

The Mother and the Nation: Reading Contemporary Women's Autobiographies

XON DE ROS

> 'Nuestro pecado fue partir a buscar una patria – o una *matria*, es igual – y no una hermandad.' Miguel de Unamuno*

'Desde la muerte de Franco habrá notado cómo proliferan los libros de memorias, ya es una peste' (Ever since Franco's death you must have noticed the proliferation of memoirs. It's already a plague) (Martín Gaite 1978: 28). The protestations of the protagonist of *El cuarto de atrás* (*The Back Room*) highlight a phenomenon which was to characterize the literary market of post-Francoism. Critical response followed shortly, with a number of monographs on the genre calling into question the old commonplace that Spaniards are little inclined to reminisce in print (Lara Pozuelo 1991, James Fernández 1992, Caballé 1995, Tortosa 2001). James Fernández records Larra's dismay at what he described as 'Ese torrente sin diques de memorias' (That overflowing stream of memoirs) (1992: 135, n.9), in the aftermath of Ferdinand VII's demise (†1833). A similar outpouring was registered after the 1898 disaster, only to be repeated a few decades later with the numerous testimonials of exiles among the writers of the Generation of 1927.

Nor is the recent trend restricted to Spain. Generally, the concern with selfhood which informs the explosion of autobiographical writing from the late 1970s has been seen as a critical reaction to the perceived anonymity of mass society. The narrowing of attention to the feelings and responses of the experiencing subject may be a consequence of the popularization of Freudianism as well as of the emergence of the therapy industry and self-help culture. In the past, despite its ubiquity, the genre's marginal status in the

---

* 'Our sin was to set out seeking for a fatherland – or a motherland, it's the same thing – and not a brotherhood' ('matria' is Unamuno's neologism for 'madre patria'), quoted in Mainer 1981: 28.

literary field was the reason for its critical invisibility. Traditionally, autobiographies would sit uncomfortably in the history section of booksellers' shelves. Only relatively recently have they been reclaimed by scholars of literature and, from the mid-1970s, with the theoretical work of Philippe Lejeune (1975), the disciplinary parameters of the confessional genre have been established.

In Spain, freedom of expression after Franco's death and the subsequent surge of testimonials previously silenced by the regime contributed to the initial critical appreciation of the genre. Very soon, however, the proliferation of memoirs was causing concern among some critics alarmed by what they perceived as the triviality and insignificance of personal memories (Sanz Villanueva 2000: 262). At the same time, the consumption of autobiographies was attributed to the feminization of the readership and to a concomitant increase in women writers.[1] That in Spain more women than men read books is a documented fact. Moreover, a subjective form of writing has long been associated with women, and women's preference for personal narratives is a widespread assumption and a consequence of their traditional identification with the private sphere. However, whilst it is true that historically the confessional mode in the form of journals or letters has been associated with women, this preference was rather the result of their restricted access to publication. Other factors have contributed to the correlation between women and autobiographical discourse. Among them there is the longstanding association of women with mass culture, which was being visited by a more recent development.

From the 1980s Spain was experiencing a vogue of celebrity memoirs in the pages of women's magazines. The sensational exclusives of popular flamenco singers such as Carmen Sevilla, Sara Montiel, and Lola Flores competing with each other for self-promotion through titillating revelations sold in their millions, first in the *prensa del corazón* and then in the *literatura de quiosco*.[2] Aimed at a wide female audience, these rags-to-riches stories recycled romantic stereotypes and ultimately reinforced normative social standards. Even though these publications were cursorily dismissed as lowbrow by critics, the celebrities' accounts offer interesting narratives of how women negotiate between their professional and their family lives. Despite the sentimentalizing and emotivity, the impact and influence of these popular publications, not only on the practitioners of the genre but also on the views of critics, should not be underestimated. Their structure,

---

[1] Laura Freixas corrects these misconceptions in her chapter 'Aquí y ahora: mitos y datos' (2000: 21–103).

[2] The expression *prensa del corazón* (lit. 'press of the heart') refers to gossip or celebrity magazines marketed for women; *literatura de quiosco* (lit. 'newsstand books') are pulp fiction or airport novels.

narrative conventions, recurrent themes, picaresque elements, and especially the prominence given to women's consciousness and experiences deserve a full investigation in the field of cultural studies.³ At the very least, this phenomenon may help to explain the insistence on maintaining a distinction between autobiography and testimonials on the part of the Spanish literary establishment, when the essential hybridity of the genre has been acknowledged elsewhere.⁴

It may also account for the diversionary tactics of women autobiographers, keen to establish and preserve their still precarious literary reputations. In a country where social control over women's behaviour is still very strong, there is a noticeable fear of exposure on the part of women writers. The presence of two theoretical essays on the subject, with the same title – *La confesión* (The Confession) – by two important autobiographers, María Zambrano (1943) and Rosa Chacel (1971), has been seen as a sign of the problematic nature of the genre for women writers (Freixas 2004: 116–17).⁵ Furthermore, with the virtual exclusion of women from public life during Francoism, few women came into the category of 'historical figure', that, before the rise of social history, defined the main strand of the autobiographical canon.⁶ A consistent tendency among women autobiographers has been to deflect their protagonism, giving themselves the secondary role of witness or partner, or limiting their accounts to fragments of their lives with an emphasis on childhood, in order to avoid too much disclosure. The most noticeable feature of this self-concealment has been to disguise the material, 'bajo la máscara de la novela' (behind the mask of the novel) (Freixas 2004: 120). The close interrelation between autobiography and fiction has been at times self-consciously embraced by the authors themselves (Nichols 1989: 93–4). Two of the most conspicuous examples of this blurring of boundaries between the two modes are the novels of Carmen Martín Gaite and Esther

---

3 Not far from the self-revelatory mood of these publications was a series of books written by women in response to the fame of their significant others: Pilar Valderrama, Antonio Machado's secret lover; Jeanne Rucar, Luis Buñuel's wife; Julia Urquidi, Vargas Llosa's aunt and lover; Josefina Manresa, the widow of Miguel Hernández; Felicidad Blanc, the widow of Leopoldo Panero; and Isabel García Lorca, sister of the poet.

4 A recent example is Sobejano 2003. For the purposes of the present essay, following Leigh Gilmore's assertion that 'autobiographical writing can be expressed in a variety of genres and therefore has few meaningful separable generic traits' (1994: 14), I make no distinction between confession, memoir, and autobiography.

5 See Paul Julian Smith (1992: 14–31) for a discussion of the tensions in the representation of the feminist self in Chacel's autobiography, *Desde el amanecer* (From Sunrise) (1972).

6 Exceptions are the memoirs of women with public roles either in the Republic or in opposition, such as La Pasionaria (Dolores Ibarruri 1984), Federica Montseny (1987), and Clara Campoamor (1936). See the survey by José Romera Castillo, 'Escritura autobiográfica de mujeres en España (1975–1991)': http://cvc.cervantes.es/obref/aih/pdf/11/aih_11_2_017.pdf

Tusquets, but this phenomenon can be found in many of their contemporaries. On the other hand, the fictional autobiography, or 'novela del yo' (the 'I' novel), with a female narrator has been the most prevalent form in the tradition of women novelists from Carmen Laforet's *Nada* (*Nothing*) (1945) onwards (Cipljauskaité 1986, Ballesteros 1994).

Finally, one of the reasons why the confessional mode has been perceived as a feminine genre is the fact that autobiography occupies an important place in feminist debate. The promotion of personal testimonies was already implied in the slogan 'the personal is the political' of the women's movement in the 1960s and 1970s. The use of autobiographical writing became an instrument of political discourse for feminism and has played an important part in the creation of group identity and in the articulation of feminist goals. Rita Felski identifies and discusses two main categories of feminist autobiographical writing, the confession and the novel of self-discovery, and establishes a connection with eighteenth-century epistolary fiction (Felski 1989: 101ff.). This correlation carries a warning for the celebration of feminine values in these texts which, as in the case of their eighteenth-century predecessors, may collude in women's disempowerment. Both traditions favour the subjective voice adopting a first-person narrative with a direct mode of address that presumes an intimacy with the reader, eliciting involvement and identification, and in both there is an emphasis on feelings and personal relationships. As pointed out above, much of the literature currently labelled 'libros de mujeres' (women's reading) conforms to this pattern.[7]

In feminist theory and praxis women's autobiographies became source documents for research into aspects of women's oppression and a springboard for the legitimation of a generalized notion of female experience, whether based on a distinctive psychic identity or on the internalization by women of the dominant ideology of gender difference inculcated through female socialization. Drawing on notions of sexual difference variously theorized by Anglo-American and French feminists (Cixous, Irigaray, and Kristeva), the model predicated on women's life-writing or 'autogynography' (Stanton 1984: 1–20) would reveal woman's anomalous position *vis à vis* dominant forms and discourses, as well as a relational sense of self and an awareness of group identity.[8] Moreover, feminine writing practice (*écriture féminine*) was seen as characterized by linguistic experimentation.

The specificity of feminine autobiographical writing has been contested from different positions. The privileging of gender as the primary constitu-

---

[7] Laura Freixas describes this category as 'works of different genres (essay, biography, novel, short story, and so on), generally but not always written by women, that have women as protagonists and the female predicament as their main concern' (2000: 50).

[8] Among the most influential Anglo-American works are Rowbotham 1973, Chodorov 1978, and Gilligan 1982.

tive category of identity has come under scrutiny and so has the view of the referentiality of the texts as transparent and unmediated. Some critics, such as Lejeune, reject the existence of any but social and cultural differences between male and female autobiographies (1984: 217). From the ranks of feminist scholarship criticism has been directed at the totalizing assumptions of these theories, stressing the diversity and difference of women's experiences. From a post-structuralist perspective, the relationship between author and text became more problematic and, together with a view of subjectivity as a shifting and contingent construction, made the search for distinctive characteristics in women's writing something of a lost cause.

Despite such failings, the foregrounding and celebration of woman's difference fostered a re-evaluation, if not of the feminine self *per se*, then at least of those specific aspects of female experience which had traditionally been devalued as being outside the public domain. Among these, the activities associated with nurturing and motherhood, in particular the relationship between mother and daughter, became an important object of feminist inquiry.[9]

The distinction between mothering and the patriarchal institution of motherhood made by Adrienne Rich in her account of the mutual identification between mother and daughter was a first step in the vindication of motherhood for feminism. According to Rich:

> It is the mother through whom patriarchy early teaches the small female her proper expectations. The anxious pressure of one female on another to conform to a degrading and dispiriting role can hardly be termed 'mothering' even if she does this believing it will help her daughter to survive.
> (1977: 243)

Mothering, by contrast, defined not as self-sacrificial but as a positive role model, supportive and enabling, was deemed to be a source of female empowerment. Rich mentions Hamlet, Lear, and Oedipus among the universal embodiments of human tragedy in order to highlight the absence of cultural recognition of what she calls 'the essential female tragedy' represented in the myth of Demeter and Persephone, that 'of the loss of the daughter to the mother, the mother to the daughter' (1977: 237). Notwithstanding the shortcomings of her assessment, particularly with regard to women's ambivalent feelings about their experience of motherhood, Rich's call for a redress in

---

[9] An interesting case study is that of Hildegart Rodríguez, the subject of a recent monograph by Alison Sinclair (2007).

the critical and theoretical neglect of this area of female experience has had a wide response in the field of women's studies.[10]

In Spain it was not until the mid 1990s that a change could be felt in the perception of the mother-daughter relationship, which up to then had been dominated by a negative portrayal of motherhood. Under the influence of the Catholic Church, the nuclear family was, and to an extent still is, regarded as not only a primary source of stability and security, especially in the case of women, but a model for social and political institutions which incorporate its patriarchal and hierarchical structures. The rigid ideology of motherhood promoted by Franco and the centrality of the mother figure as a personification of the State has been considered responsible for the negative image in dissident films and fiction during Francoism (Gámez Fuentes 2000: 48). According to Christine Arkinstall, 'for almost forty years the body of the mother becomes the dominant element around which sanctioned concepts of femininity, gender, and nationhood are organised' (2002: 48). Moreover, this instrumentalization by the regime resulted in a backlash against motherhood which outlived the dictator by more than twenty years. During that time the birth rate dropped and by the end of the century Spain had achieved the world's lowest fertility rate (Hooper 2006: 133). In women's memoirs of the Franco period, mothers, when not dead or absent, as in the case of Mercedes Salisachs's *Derribos: crónicas íntimas de un tiempo saldado* (Demolitions: Intimate Chronicles of a Paid Time) (1987) and María Campo-Alange's *Mi niñez y su mundo* (My Childhood and Its World) (1956), were portrayed as antagonistic, as in Esther Tusquets's *Correspondencia privada* (*Private Correspondence*) (2001b), Rosa Chacel's *Desde el amanecer* (From Sunrise) (1972), and Clara Janés's *Jardín y laberinto* (Garden and Labyrinth) (1990). Arguably, the weight of the symbolism invested in the mother figure for more than forty years made it hard to imagine her as a force for transformation.

Motherless protagonists featured prominently in the fiction written by women under Franco – Laforet's *Nada* (1945), *Primera memoria* (*School of the Sun*), by Ana María Matute (1960), *La plaça del Diamant* (*The Time of the Doves*), by Mercè Rodoreda (1962).[11] Those fictional orphan girls joined a long tradition in women's literature. Their recurrence has been interpreted as an objective correlative for the social condition of women in general, and

---

[10] Adalgisa Giorgio (2002a) provides a well-informed overview of feminist discourses on the mother-daughter relationship, assessing the impact of these theories on critical approaches to its representation in literature.

[11] Arkinstall offers a survey of the mother-daughter theme in the novels written by women from the 1940s to the 1990s, concluding that 'the principal theme in texts written by women during the early Franco dictatorship is the elegy for the missing mother', whereas from the 1970s she sees a more positive reappraisal of the maternal figure (2002: 52 and *passim*).

as a symbolic reflection on the lack of female literary lineage. On a different note and in a different context, Carolyn Dever has argued that 'for women writers in particular, the absence in narrative of a maternal role model can signify an opportunity for the construction of innovative templates for the young protagonist's identity' in the form of an 'emancipatory ethic of individualism, and self-creation' (1998: 206). It can also be argued that the mother-daughter relation provides a site for the interrogation of established notions not only of individual identity but also, by extension, of national identity (see Arkinstall 2002: 51).

The symbolic association of the nation with the mother goes back well into the past (Boyd 1997: 184ff.). According to historian José Álvarez Junco, in the age of liberal revolutions, Spain was represented by the image of a fierce and haughty Minerva, 'de lineas rectas, belicosas y justicieras' (of severe lines, bellicose, and draconian) (2001: 568). Later, in the course of the nineteenth-century, the figure underwent a transformation and acquired the features of a *mater dolorosa*, as a result of the country's political unrest. Unlike proud Britannia or bold Marianne,

> España era una madre que reclamaba el cariño de sus hijos de una manera muy peculiar: o bien desde el lecho donde yacía, afectada por una mortal dolencia y olvidada por sus ingratos vástagos, seducidos por modas extranjeras; o bien desde la picota donde soportaba mansamente el escarnio de insolentes sayones. (Álvarez Junco 2001: 571)

> (Spain was a mother who laid claim to her children's affection in a peculiar fashion: either from the bed where she was lying mortally ill and abandoned by her thankless offspring, led astray by foreign manners, or else from the pillory where she was meekly enduring the abuse of heartless tormentors.)

From Lorca's Bernarda Alba to the ailing mother of Carlos Saura's *Cría cuervos* (Raise Ravens) (1976) Spanish cultural representations of the mother during most of the twentieth century tend to replicate these two symbolic figurations of the nation: formidable, warlike matron or helpless victim. At the same time, the tragic denouements of these stories exemplify the self-destructive consequences of a concept of self based on the alienation of the feminine.

Interestingly Álvarez Junco situates the nation in the realm of the private sphere, assertying that, 'como la religión o la familia, la nación es un lazo íntimo, personal' (like religion or the family, the nation is an intimate, personal bond (2001: 17), and he suggests, echoing Unamuno, that under the subjection of the father-state, the Spanish nation should be called *matria* instead of *patria*. However, the Spaniards' view of their country's fate was not all tragedy: there was also a resigned irony and ultimately a sense of self-knowledge: '¡Qué lastima y qué irremediable todo lo que le ocurría! Y, a la vez, ¡qué curioso! Pero, también, ¡qué nuestro!' (How sad and hopeless everything that was happening! And at the same time, how odd! But also, how very us!) (2001: 571).

A similar ambivalence between critical distance and self-identification underlies the mother-daughter relationship in literary representations written by women. An example of this symbolic overlapping is found in María Teresa León's *Memoria de la melancolía* (Memory of the Melancholy) (1998, first published in Argentina in 1970), where she reminisces about her life experiences marked by the Civil War and her subsequent exile in Paris, Rome, and Buenos Aires. Hers is the account of a collective experience, that of the Republican diaspora, a memory she wants to rescue from impending oblivion: 'Que recuerden los que olvidaron' (So that those who have forgotten will remember) (1998: 404).

In an illuminating article, Ofelia Ferrán relates León's account of her past to Freud's model of repetitive compulsion associated with traumatic experiences. Just as the child in Freud's example overcomes his anxiety at his mother's dissapearance through a performative act (*fort-da*), León's emphasis on performance is seen as a sign of her working out her own sense of loss (Ferrán 2005: 67). Ferrán points to the way theatrical images in *Memoria de la melancolía* 'function at various levels of the narrative', but she fails to identify one underlying literary discourse, both performative and empowering, which in León's memoir is associated with the maternal and generative: that of the *romancero* (traditional balladry).

In the manner of the women in old Spanish ballads, the narrator takes on the role of the agent of conscience, advocating justice and compassion and raising her voice to denounce the actions of oppressors and to goad the feckless into action (see Odd 1983). The connection with the traditional ballad is not as arbitrary as it might sound since it is suggested by the text itself. Not only does the memoir contain many references to and quotations from both old and modern ballads but it also deploys some of the salient features of the genre such as fragmentarism, lack of closure, emphasis on oral discourse, apostrophizing, strong emotional expression, instability of voice, as it alternates first-, second- and third-person narratives, claims of authenticity over accuracy or aesthetic appeal – 'todo lo que estoy escribiendo no tiene ni deseo de perfección ni de verdad' (nothing I write strives either for perfection or the truth) (León 1998: 69) – , and, above all, its character as a collective testimonial.

León's knowledge of the *romancero* was well-informed. She was the niece of the medievalists Ramón Menéndez Pidal and María Goyri, who introduced her to the ballad tradition as a child. In their home, we are told, she learnt her first Spanish ballads – 'Por primera vez oí la voz del pueblo' (I heard the voice of the people for the first time) – listening to the recordings that the couple had made during their honeymoon, 'siguiendo la ruta del Cid hacia su destierro' (following the Cid's journey into exile) (1998: 151). The word 'destierro' (exile) figures prominently in *Memoria de la melancolía*, where the voice of the people becomes her own and, through her voice, that of the community of exiles whose experience is commemorated in the book.

It was Menéndez Pidal who first drew attention to the fact that women were the main transmitters of the ballads in modern times (Catarella 1990: 331). León adopts not only the traditional ballad's view of women as a stabilizing and humanizing force, but also the role of the female informant, incorporating the critical view of social norms and gender relations that characterizes this tradition (Gómez Acuña 2002).[12] This engagement with a discourse which is both empowering and female is in turn reflected in the mother-daughter relation as portrayed in León's book. In one of the last pages she quotes from Lope de Vega's ballad 'A mis soledades voy / de mis soledades vengo' (In solitude I come and go, / in solitude I wander), expressing an existential fear of disintegration which she swiftly dispels by invoking the mother, who provides her with a reassuring sense of permanence and continuity: 'Aún perdurará por los siglos de los siglos la palabra Madre' (The word Mother will live on for ever and ever) (León 1998: 241).

León's estrangement from her motherland is replicated in the text by a rift between herself and her biological mother as a result of conflicting expectations. In both cases a reconciliation is effected through an act of remembrance whereby the lost objects, Spain and the mother, are internalized by the grieving subject following the pattern described by Freud in his essay on 'Mourning and Melancholia'.[13] At one point in the narrative, León reminds her absent mother of the complexities of their relationship, concluding with a gesture of intimacy and self-knowledge: 'Y sentí como si me llamases para transmitirme tus poderes. La voz tuya, tan admirable, me anunciaba que yo iba a ser como tú, nada más que como tú' (and I felt that you were calling me to transfer your powers to me. Your voice, so admirable, was telling me that I was going to be like you, just like you) (1998: 219). The focus here on the maternal voice brings to mind once again the female character of oral tradition. It is significant that this passage should come immediately after an evocation of the Sephardic community of Salonica and their rich folk song

---

[12] For a feminist reading highlighting León's subversion of patriarchal sexual ideology, see Alda Blanco 1991.

[13] Angel Loureiro, drawing on Kristeva, offers an excellent analysis of León's melancholy, arguing that it reflects a primordial loss related to the separation from the mother, adding to the discussion León's novelized biography of the Cid (2000: 80–87).

tradition, in which the cultural memory of their hispanic heritage is both preserved and kept alive.[14]

What is remarkable in *Memoria de la melancolía* is its assimilation of the spirit of the *romancero* to counteract the anxiety provoked by the threat of oblivion and the sense of personal contingency in the face of history, and the simultaneous identification of this oral tradition with an enabling maternal discourse. Some aspects in this configuration recall the idea of *intrahistoria* theorized by the intellectuals of the Generation of 98 – a notion, as Roberta Johnson demonstrates, also 'imbued with a feminine cast' (2003a: 32).[15] In both cases motherhood is used as a metaphor to describe the sense of belonging and continuity related to the country's intrahistorical tradition. But the treatment of the maternal differs in León's vision. What for Unamuno et al. was defined as domestic, passive, and silent, in *Memoria de la melancolía* is identified with feminine agency and worldliness. However, whereas this perception evokes women's new social roles and public visibility heralded by the Republic, both the title of the book and its disjointed structure suggest a process of bereavement triggered by defeat and exile whose roots are located much more deeply in the psyche of a woman under patriarchal rule. León's memoir records both the hopeful energy of the young Republican militants and their shattered dreams in the aftermath of Franco's victory, but the gendered nature of her loss should not be overlooked (Ferrán 2005: 62). References to the death of León's mother, geographically distanced from her daughter and mentally remote, become an eloquent image of the memoir's prevailing melancholic mood, conveying the protagonist's sense of loss and dislocation *vis à vis* the nation.[16]

As this case illustrates, the textual representation of the mother-daughter bond can be used to link the individual and psychological experiences with collective and social issues. By looking at the articulation of this relation in some of the more recent autobiographies written by women we can identify and examine the forces that have either sustained or fractured this identification in the Spanish collective imagination and, through them, the cultural values of the society that are being reaffirmed or questioned in its construction.

Towards the end of the century there was a perceptible change in the

---

[14] León's involvement in the editorial work and publication of the *Romancero general de la guerra española* (Alberti 1944) must have contributed to her renewed interest in the Spanish ballad tradition.

[15] 'Intrahistoria' is a term introduced by Unamuno to refer to ordinary people's lives and traditions as opposed to the official history. The Generation of 98 was group of writers who reacted to the loss of Spain's last colonies in 1898.

[16] A similar pattern is described by Roberta Johnson (2003a: 261–73) with regard to Zambrano's memoir *Delirio y destino* (Delirium and Destiny) (1989).

way motherhood was experienced and represented in Spain. Emblematic of this reassessment were the films *Solas* (Women on Their Own) (Benito Zambrano, 1999), *Todo sobre mi madre* (*All About My Mother*) and *Volver* (Going Back) (Pedro Almodóvar, 1999 and 2006), in which the mother-daughter connection is explored in a more positive light (see Martin-Márquez 2004). The influence of feminist thinking and theory was certainly behind the publication of the collective volume of essays *Figuras de la madre* (Forms of the Mother) (Tubert 1996) written by a number of women psychoanalysts and cultural critics. Feminism may also have been a contributory factor in the collection of short stories *Madres e hijas* (Mothers and Daughters) published in the same year and edited by Laura Freixas with contributions by fourteen women writers. The volume had an unexpected success with nine reprints in under a year. This reception and the increasing cultural prominence accorded to the theme of motherhood in the following few years suggests a deeper transformation in the psycho-social fabric of the country. Within this process of rehabilitation, the extensive treatment of the mother-daughter relationship in women's autobiographical writing, exemplified in Soledad Puértolas, *Con mi madre* (With My Mother) (2001), Esther Tusquets, *Habíamos ganado la guerra* (We Had Won the War) (2007) and Laura Freixas, *Adolescencia en Barcelona hacia 1970* (Adolescence in Barcelona circa 1970) (2007), offers a vantage point for the examination of the significance and implications of the subject in contemporary Spain.

A number of new inflections come into play in the representations of the mother-daughter relationship in the post-Franco period. According to Akiko Tsuchiya, 'as the nation emerged from totalitarianism, homogeneous and hegemonic ideas of identity, including those of gendered subjects, gave way to the possibility of alternative constructions that allowed for plurality and difference' (2003: 220). Significantly, the social and regional co-ordinates of the family take on a certain importance in women's autobiographies of this period. This is certainly the case in Freixas's book, where disquisitions about the social and ideological differences between her maternal Castilian and her paternal Catalan grandparents occupy a substantial part of the text. Whilst arguably the book's appeal is more sociological than literary, as its reliance on cliché and stereotype suggests, the protagonist's split cultural identity finds a resolution in literature, the practice of which gives her

> la posibilidad de conciliar lo en apariencia irreconciliable: mi vida catalana con la lengua castellana, y mi experiencia de española con la tradición literaria francesa. Una actitud en la vida en la que se unían, sin contradicción, el afán de poseer propio de mi familia catalana (escribimos para guardar, revivir, atesorar), y el refugio en un mundo inmaterial –la música, la lectura, la nostalgia ...– propio de mi familia castellana. Una profesión que me permitía combinar una vida de mujer con la libertad de un hombre.

(Freixas 2007: 198)

(the possibility of reconciling what is apparently irreconcilable: my Catalan life with the Castilian language, and my experience as a Spaniard with the French literary tradition. An attitude to life which would combine, without contradiction, the possessive urge of the Catalan side of my family (we write to preserve, to re-live, to treasure) and refuge in the world of the mind – music, reading, nostalgia – of the Castilian side of my family. A profession which would allow me to combine my life as a woman with the freedom of a man.)

However, the book concludes with the suspicion that writing might, after all, be another form of escapism which is elsewhere associated with her mother's passion for French novels, where she had found refuge from her own contradictions and from the stultifying dullness of Francoist culture. Thus, the fear of repetition, of a life 'de estar y no estar, de buscar la *vraie vie* en el *ailleurs*' (of being there and not being there, of searching for the *vraie vie* in the *ailleurs*), a fate imposed on older generations of Spanish women, still haunts their descendants.

A more nuanced and searching account of the complexities involved in the process of identity formation, also in Barcelona, is Esther Tusquets's memoir of growing up during the first decades of Francoism, *Habíamos ganado la guerra*. Her family belonged to the Catalan upper-middle class who allied themselves with the regime and enjoyed the freedom and privileges that were denied to their own Catalan culture. Reading this book we recognize retrospectively how many characters in Tusquets's fiction were based on her own family. Among them, the narrator's mother looms large, as Tusquets herself acknowledges: 'He escrito mucho sobre mi madre, a veces me parece que sólo he escrito sobre mi madre, sin lograr nunca cancelar el conflicto, pasar página, quedar en paz' (I have written a lot about my mother, sometimes it feels as though I have only written about my mother, without ever being able to cancel out the conflict, turn the page, lay it to rest) (2007: 79). Indeed, at one point in her memoirs she refers to one of her most autobiographical books, *Correspondencia privada* (2001b), and quotes from a letter she addressed to her mother. The passage in question highlights one of the traits of her mother's personality often reiterated in *Habíamos ganado la guerra*: her eccentricity, which mortified Esther as a child but which she has come to appreciate later in life as proof of her mother's free spirit.

Difference from the norm is not only part of her mother's character, but is also attributed to Esther, whose achievement at school is met with the mother's cutting remark: '¡Siempre con tus cosas raras! ¡Siempre teniendo que hacer algo diferente para distinguirte de las demás! (As ever, you and your strange ways! Always wanting to stand out from the crowd!) (2007: 129). Whereas Tusquets recalls feeling, and being made to feel, different while she longed to be as similar as possible to the other children (2007: 98), she now acknowledges her own singularity: 'Yo era una niña rara y supongo que a veces difícil de soportar' (I was a strange girl and I suppose I was sometimes difficult to put up with) (2007: 217).

The fact of being different, one of the few features shared by mother and daughter among the many setting them apart, finds a linguistic correlative in their use of Catalan. This is the language spoken at home by the family – with the significant exception of the writer's younger brother, with whom they all speak in Castilian. Moreover, theirs is a corrupt form of the language: 'el denostado y degradado catalán de los barceloneses' (the scorned and debased Catalan spoken in Barcelona) (2007: 24). Later on, the mother's Castilian-inflected Catalan is underlined – 'el "veraneig" decía en su pésimo catalán' (the *veraneig* [summer holidays] she said, in her appalling Catalan) (2007: 177).[17]

The anomalous position of the Catalan-speaking Francoist bourgeoisie with regard to the regime's linguistic imperialism is paralleled with regard to their defective Catalan *vis-à-vis* a nationalism defined by language. From this perspective, the feelings of strangeness that the protagonist experiences from an early age and the conflictive relationship with her self-centred, emotionally distant mother take on a larger dimension reflecting the problematics involved in the writer's national affiliation.

Finally, in Soledad Puértolas's *Con mi madre* (2001) the relationship with the mother is the exclusive focus of the narrative. The narrator introduces the text as a therapeutic work in the process of coming to terms with the loss of her mother, to whom she felt a strong emotional attachment. The character of the mother is evoked in a series of disconnected recollections filtered through her daughter's feelings of grief and desolation. A pattern of mutual self-identification emerges from the daughter's memories: whilst the mother seems to have lived her life through her daughter's, 'eres como yo, decía satisfecha' (You are like me, she would say with satisfaction) (2001: 65), in the case of the daughter this is presented as a conscious decision, taken at an early age, to uphold her mother's world view: sólo tengo el mérito [...] de haber tomado partido por ella muy pronto, de haber sufrido por las frustraciones y limitaciones que yo imaginaba en su vida' (My only merit [...] is having sided with her very early on, having suffered from the frustrations and limitations I imagined in her life) (2001: 118).

Right from the beginning the mother is defined by her discretion and

---

[17] The word *veraneig* is a hybrid of Spanish *verano* (summer) and the Catalan inflection *-eig*, corresponding to Spanish *-eo*, as in *veraneo*. The Catalan equivalent of *veraneo* is *estiveig*.

self-containedness (2001: 13), two qualities gradually obliterated by illness and old age, which find a correspondence in the book's pervasive imagery of enclosure, from the red room where they were both confined while ill with typhus, to swimming pools, wardrobes, trunks, suitcases, boxes, framed photographs, and letters. These images give the narrator a sense of security and intimacy associated with the maternal presence, which she seeks to recreate within the physical boundaries of the book, against the threat of an emotional and existential spilling-over, provoked by her mother's death. Figured simultaneously as an enabling and constraining force in the life of the daughter, the mother represents the part played by tradition in conceptualizations of subjectivity in relation to the social and to history. In this respect it is worth noting the fact that what the daughter identifies as her mother's symbolic legacy is the city of Madrid, the heart of the Spanish nation.

Moreover, the values and norms of behaviour that, together with her possessions, she hands down to her daughter are couched in ritual and repetition. Like the children's story the young Soledad never tired of listening to, their annual visits to the chapel of San Blas on her birthday or to the Basilica of Nuestra Señora del Pilar on 12 October, the telephone calls at the same time every day, the Christmas dinners, all have a bonding as well as an ideological function. The sense of communality the daughter experiences on these occasions is what makes her comply with social norms: 'Para no herirla, me casé por la Iglesia y, más tarde, bauticé a mis hijos' (I married in the Church and had my children baptized so that she wouldn't be upset) (2001: 12). But with the mother's absence, the gap between practice and belief becomes insurmountable and a feeling of disorientation takes over the daughter's life. Through her memories the narrator tries to recapture the sense of continuity the mother inspired in her. It is significant that the date of the mother's death is the beginning of the 1990s, when the need for new models of social and political behaviour was being voiced by the press and a general interest in the 'memoria histórica' was starting to be felt. This would result in the *Ley de Memoria Histórica* (Law of Historical Memory) of 2007, which signalled the country's desire finally to come to terms with a past that had been silenced hitherto. However, the danger of entering into a solipsistic dialogue with one's past that Unamuno expresses with reference to the writers of his own generation, also applies to contemporary figurations of the *matria* and is dramatized to an extent in the agoraphobia that afflicts the protagonist in Puértolas's memoir.

Woman's autobiographical self has been consistently interpreted in terms of gender politics and, whilst gender has often proved to be a useful category of analysis, yielding many insights into the specific nature of women's experiences, it also runs the risk of excluding those experiences from the historical processes that have configured them (Pulgarín Cuadrado

2004). Moreover, according to historian Anthony D. Smith, of all the social phenomena of collective identity, national allegiances have the strongest hold on individuals, whereas categories of gender, 'geographically separated, divided by class and ethnically fragmented [...] must ally themselves to other more cohesive identities if they are to inspire collective consciousness and actions' (1991: 4).

Whereas the examples discussed here show that the social, historical, and material realities of women's lives are plural and diverse, they all reveal, through the literary treatment of the mother-daughter bond, a desire to reconcile individual and collective identities. As this essay has sought to demonstrate, these intense, often problematic, portraits of the relationship with the mother also describe the writer's search for self-definition in relation to the nation.

Further reading

Arkinstall, Christine, 2002. 'Towards a Female Symbolic: Re-Presenting Mothers and Daughters in Contemporary Spanish Narrative by Women', in *Writing Mothers and Daughters: Renegotiating the Mother in Western European Narratives by Women*, ed. Adalgisa Giorgio (New York and Oxford: Berghahn Books), pp. 47–84

Gámez Fuentes, María José, 2000. 'Never One without the Other: Empowering Readings of the Mother-Daughter Relationship in Modern Spain', in *Mothers and Daughters: Connection, Empowerment and Transformation*, ed. Andrea O'Reilly and Sharon Abbey (Lanham, MD: Rowman & Littlefield), pp. 47–60

Gilmore, Leigh, 1994. *Autobiographics: A Feminist Theory of Women's Self-Representation* (Ithaca, NY: Cornell UP)

Hirsch, Marianne, 1989. *The Mother/Daughter Plot: Narrative, Psychoanalysis, Feminism* (Bloomington: Indiana UP)

Smith, Sidonie, 1987. *A Poetics of Women's Autobiography: Marginality and the Fictions of Self-Representation* (Bloomington: Indiana UP)

20

Tropes of Freedom: Spectacular Eroticism and the Spanish New Woman On-Screen

JESSAMY HARVEY

In the 1970s, the nude female body on the Spanish screen was to become a visual sign of emancipation from sexual repression and ignorance. However, this cannot be linked straightforwardly to the end of the dictatorship as, even prior to Franco's death, the Spanish film industry was to feel anxious about the relaxation of control over erotic and violent content in US and European mainstream cinema, and feared that its inability to show sexual explicitness would inhibit commercial success both within national territory and abroad (Triana-Toribio 2003: 98–9). So although the repressive hypothesis may have appeared attractive in the aftermath of the dictatorship, it has been noted that 'Spanish sexual liberation was based on profit-oriented principles' and that 'there was no fundamental change of mentality' (Legido-Quigley 2002: 211). This period of *destape*, translated as 'lifting the lid off' (Pavlović 2003: 73), 'topless' (Kowalsky 2004: 190), and 'naked moment' (Perriam 2003a: 52), points to the complexities of gender studies and cinematic representation because the erotic display of the female body raises the issue of a retrograde objectification of women. Contradictory responses to nudity are dramatized in the Spanish context, as Mónica Jato has identified, by Alfonso Sastre in *El asesinato de la luna llena* (Murder of the Full Moon) (1996). For although the fictional erotic actress Maritza perceives herself as having been exploited, Teniente Rupérez protests: 'pero no lo llame destape... es el desnudo ... la belleza de su desnudo llegó a nuestro corazón, maltrecho por el franquismo. ¡Era un grito a la libertad!' (but do not call it toplessness ... it is nakedness ... the beauty of your nakedness reached our hearts abused by Francoism. It was a cry to freedom!) (Jato 2006: 146).

This exposure of the naked female body and the depiction of sexual explicitness, heterosexual and otherwise, as a sign of freedom then became a characteristic of democratic cinema, but it also coincided with other radical changes to the image of women on-screen. The dominant destiny outlined had been chaste marriage and sacrificial motherhood, but a cinematic type was to emerge that invited women to recognise themselves as privileged subjects of social change: 'The New Spanish Woman follows the trajectory of her nation; she is educated, liberal, middle-class, often single and/or separated, sexually active and assertive' (Goss 2008: 33). In fact, a generation of actresses, some of whom had bared all during the *destape*, such as Carmen Maura, Ana Belén, and Victoria Abril, were understood to act as 'screen surrogates of the Spanish new woman' (Evans 1999: 271). Thus it can be seen that tropes of freedom attached themselves to both the spectacular erotic female body and the new social type of democratic womanhood, sometimes embodied by the same actress, in ways that need to be seen as problematic rather than straightforward. For although it is tempting to write about the rapid social and cultural changes affecting women during this period in ways which privilege progress, this should not be the only characteristic of the trajectory towards autonomy analysed. In any process of transformation there can be found troubling moments of regression, ambivalence, or disappointment.

This chapter will provide pointers in film feminism, touch upon how the sexual explicitness of democratic cinema has affected the representation of women on-screen, and then move to a specific focus on the character of Desideria in *La pasión turca* (*Turkish Passion*) (1994). I argue that Desideria provides the opportunity to examine how a character can break society's expectations of women whilst confirming them. Additionally, Vicente Aranda's adaptation of Antonio Gala's bestselling novel of the same name (1993) is cited as one of the films of the post-Franco period which re-frames women by granting them agency (Jordan and Morgan-Tamosunas 1998: 271), focusing on their desire for emancipation (Evans 1999: 272), and visualizing the female gaze (Fouz-Hernández and Martínez-Expósito 2007: 167). Although Aranda's work has been described as 'commonly associated with the seedier side of sexuality' (Rob Stone 2002: 171) and is considered part of 'mainstream eroticism' (Kowalsky 2004: 190), it has also been interpreted as cultivating 'a superficial "feminist" sensibility' (Martin-Márquez 1999: 247). A picture that emerges is of a director and a film that manages to appear to articulate discourses of female freedom whilst showing mainstream sexual representations. Contemporary feminist responses to explicit sexual representations of women can be diametrically opposed, as Kath Albury comments (2002: 27):

> Feminist writing on sexuality is as confusing and contradictory as its subject matter. While some writers argue that almost anything which can be recognised as 'sexy' (such as a photograph of a naked woman) is automatically sexist, others commend any expression of female sexuality, even if it has uncomfortable associations.

At this point it would be useful to examine the historical formation of feminism within film criticism to gain a sense of this contested terrain.

Film feminisms

The knowledge that forms the body of this intellectual tradition has been produced by a multiplicity of voices over the last four decades, and has moved from the margins to become institutionalized as an academic discipline. It is important to point out that there are perceived differences between women's studies (which aims to raise consciousness about women's experience through film), feminist film theory (a synthesis of feminism and semiotic or psychoanalytic approaches to film), and gender studies (which widens the focus on femininity to include studies on masculinity on-screen). Some examples of these approaches are: Marjorie Rosen's *Popcorn Venus* (1973), which critiqued the ways in which Hollywood films supported male cultural dominance in their representation of femininity; Laura Mulvey's controversial article 'Visual Pleasure and Narrative Cinema' (1975), which initiated a pervasive and enduring discussion on the male gaze; and Teresa de Lauretis's chapter 'The Technologies of Gender' (1987: 1–30), which discussed the ways in which sexual difference is a product of various technologies, using Foucault's term (1978) as a springboard. These seminal texts, and many others which appear collected in anthologies such as Sue Thornham's *Feminist Film Theory* (1999), are predominantly Anglo-American in origin and application, though the driving force of French theoretical models is also evident. This is linked to the way these film feminisms have a developmental history that scholars link to the emergence of the women's liberation movement in the 1960s through to the 1970s. They are mainly concerned with raising awareness about how patriarchy marginalized, silenced, and oppressed women in America and in some Western European countries – though, crucially, not in Spain during that period.

In using an umbrella term such as film feminisms we may run the risk of obscuring the troubled history of critical approaches to women in film. It is not a corpus exempt of tensions, given that it is both an analytical and a politically prescriptive project. In fact, film feminisms can be seen to be marked by perpetual contestation. They challenge oppression, be it by the Hollywood system, or by male critics developing *auteur* (read 'male director' here) theory, or even the way women's studies or feminist film theory were initially predominantly white, Anglocentric, middle-class, and heterosexual affairs, which neglected to take account of class, colour, alternative sexualities like lesbianism, or non-Western traditions such as Third World cinema. They are responsible not only for initiating processes of recovery by reclaiming forgotten directors like Alice Guy-Blaché (France,

1873–1968), Dorothy Arzner (USA, 1897–1979), and Aziza Amir (Egypt, 1901–52) – a list to which one could now add the names of Spanish women such as Rosario Pi (1899–1967) and Ana Mariscal (1923–95) (see Martin-Márquez 1999) – , but also for exercising all manner of exclusions. As Janet McCabe notes, 'what is chosen from the archive to be retrieved and analysed is dependant on how well the filmmaker fits the feminist world view' (2004: 114), mentioning the rejection of the Nazi propagandist Leni Riefenstahl (1902–2003) as a case in point. Therefore, to understand the development of approaches in film feminisms it is necessary to gain insights into how each generation of critics has built on the work of their predecessors, even if it is in order to distance themselves from them.

The theoretical approaches developed in relation to the study of women on the Spanish screen, or behind the camera, are not disconnected from this contested tradition of film feminisms. However, it is necessary to appreciate the distinct features of the development of a woman-focused critical tradition in relation to Spanish cinema. For example, in the late twentieth century, the disciplines of film studies and gender studies enjoyed rapid growth within the British University system (Perriam 2003b). Although Perriam observed that there was initially an overwhelming focus on Pedro Almodóvar (which often raised debates on Spanish womanhood), and a tendency to privilege films from the post-dictatorship period, there are strong indications that the field has now broadened considerably when reviewing recent publications on national cinema (Triana-Toribio 2003), popular cinema (Lázaro-Reboll and Willis 2004), masculinity (Perriam 2003a, Fouz-Hernández and Martínez-Expósito 2007), and a growing number of introductory guides (Rob Stone 2002, Jordan and Allinson 2005, Bentley 2008). But, where do women, femininity, or feminism fit into this growing bibliography?

Although broader discussions on gender are published (Marsh and Nair 2004), and many aspects of the relationship between women and cinema are examined (see, for example, chapters on sexuality in Rob Stone 2002 and Ballesteros 2001, and on female directors in Jordan and Morgan-Tamosunas 1998); and whereas there is at least one significant journal issue on women and Iberian cinema (Camporesi and Parrondo 2002), as well as a range of journal articles and some edited volumes (Ferrán and Glenn 2002), there is a dearth of monographs that focus solely on women and Spanish cinema. Some exceptions are María Donapetry 1998, María Camí-Vela 2001, and Martin-Márquez, who describes the fragmentation of Hispanist film feminism (1999). She also notes that the growth of feminist practice and theory among those who speak from outside of Spanish academia – she mentions Paul Julian Smith and Marsha Kinder – is distinct from the critical work developed by film scholars or critics based within Spanish academia, criticized for being androcentric (1999: 10). Stephen Marsh and Parvati Nair support this view when they describe the paucity of female film critics within Spanish academia (2004: 5). And Isolina Ballesteros illustrates the paradox of Hispanist film feminism by declaring herself culturally formed by Spanish society, whilst theoretically informed by Anglo-American research, though, importantly, she also values Spanish academia's tendency to focus on film historiography (2001: 25).

The social, political, intellectual, and cultural traditions which impact women's experience across nations, as well as their possibilities of intervening and changing these, are diverse (Martin-Márquez 1999: 11). It is not necessary simply to acquire an understanding of the theoretical tools of film feminism, it is also vital to gain a sense of the particularity of Spanish culture and society in order to understand the national film production and women's role within it; Brooksbank Jones (1997: 144–74), for example, can provide the necessary grounding, as can Jordan and Morgan-Tamosunas (1998: 112–55). All skilfully convey the contradictions of a period of filmmaking when women can be seen to have gained an exceptional degree of emancipation, and yet navigate within a visual culture where their representation as a desiring subject is ambivalent.

Undressing the Spanish New Woman

In homage to the photograph of a naked Marilyn Monroe rolling on red velvet taken in 1949, the poster for *La pasión turca* features a full female nude prostrate on the Turkish flag: Ana Belén as Desideria. However, although audiences would be familiar with the naked body of Ana Belén, she has been cast in roles which project the feminine sexual subject, not merely object. Martin-Márquez has analysed this in the specific case of *La petición* (*The Engagement Party*) (1976) (1999: 264–78). Furthermore, Ana Belén has appeared in films which appear to displace the male to explore female friendships such as in *Jaque a la dama* (*Check to the Queen*) (1979), focusing on a latent lesbian relationship, and the comedy *Rosa Rosae* (1993). Significantly, she has been described by Barry Jordan and Rikki Morgan-Tamosunas as belonging to a group of actresses who 'consistently represent women as complex, multidimensional, thinking subjects in their negotiation of the social, professional, emotional and sexual changes which have characterised post-Franco Spain' (1998: 127). There are a number of key words in this description of the Spanish New Woman on-screen that need highlighting, such as 'negotiation' and, of course women as 'subjects' – not objects – who can be understood as 'complex' and 'multidimensional'. All of these words generate an image of the Spanish New Woman as an individual with agency, one who has the capacity to shape her world through day-to-day choices rather than one who is constrained and determined by social structures. But, importantly, although noting how she embodies progressive agendas, this description also points out that she is not necessarily beyond needing to negotiate conflict or, one could also add, devoid of contradictions herself. Other critics have also agreed with this definition, such as Burkhard Pohl who comments that she is 'expuesta a la tarea de negociar activamente su emancipación, ya no como víctima sino como agente activa de su rol social' (exposed to the task of actively negotiating her emancipation, not now as a victim but as an active agent) (2007: 132).

Of course, the Spanish New Woman is a misnomer, as she is not really new. Indeed, the term has been in use since the late nineteenth century to describe an ideal of a progressive and liberated woman who defies the social conventions of her period. Therefore there is a need to set this particular late-twentieth-century Spanish New Woman within her specific context: on the one hand, to identify what is the weight of tradition that she must challenge at this historical juncture and, on the other, to gauge what options (e.g., education, financial independence, legal rights, ownership of the female body) are available to her so that change can be effected. For although it is possible to identify the similarities and continuities between the late-nineteenth-century ideal and this one, different socio-political circumstances mean that manifestations of the Spanish New Woman do shift across time and space. The end of the twentieth century, with regards to women's participation in Spanish culture as well as their production of it, has been interpreted as a time period characterized by the culmination of a post-dictatorship process of emancipation from the limiting taboos of the Francoist era, namely, in relation to professional and sexual restrictions. However, it is essential to avoid presenting these changes as a straightforward narrative of subversion and liberation from the Franco to the post-Franco period. Anny Brooksbank Jones makes this point as she describes the 'nature of socio-cultural change as it affects women' during the transition period and beyond as 'patchy and often contradictory' (1997: viii).

Angela McRobbie, in discussing the post-feminist masquerade of the 1990s in ways that are also relevant to the Spanish cinematic context in general and to *La pasión turca* in particular, argues that she sees a 'double movement' whereby 'gender retrenchment is secured, paradoxically, through the wide dissemination of discourses for female freedom' (2008: 55). McRobbie is not denying that the feminist agenda has helped to advance the causes of women, but she wants us to be wary of celebrating the new female subject uncritically, in her case the 'can do' girl, which is a style of global femininity. She argues that the global girl as a trope of freedom merely makes patriarchy appear invisible, but does not erase its workings or structures. In Spanish cinema the tropes of freedom attached themselves, first, to the nude woman on-screen during the period of the *destape* and then, secondly, to the Spanish New Woman during the democratic period. But she, nevertheless, continued to get undressed and embody the erotic function. Therefore, rather than continue to maintain the trope that the Spanish New Woman on-screen is always legible as a positive progressive icon, as María Delgado does when she maintains that she is 'increasingly defiant, independent and assertive' (2007: 275), it would be more useful to discern how she may also convey regressive as well as evolving notions of gender, fail to offer solutions, or generate ambivalence. What follows is a comparison between *La pasión turca*, the novel, and *La pasión turca*, the film, to question the tropes of freedom that are sometimes left unquestioned in the discourse of new womanhood and her pursuit of sexual liberation.

La pasión turca on-screen

In her prologue to Antonio Gala's novel Carmen Rigalt explains: 'la novela nació con los ingredientes necesarios para gustar. Turquía, el adulterio, la pasión, el desamor, el engaño y, finalmente, la inmolación' (the novel was created with the necessary ingredients to appeal. Turkey, adultery, passion, indifference, betrayal and, finally, suicide) (Gala 2001: 2). Desideria Oliván, a middle-class, university-educated woman who drifted into an unsatisfactory marriage, becomes obsessed with Yamam – a Turkish tour guide, carpet salesman and drug dealer – after a holiday affair. Eventually, she turns her back on respectability in pursuit of, as it turns out, elusive emotional and sexual fulfilment with the faithless and abusive Yamam. This act of transgression is narrated by Gala as having only one possible outcome: death. And such are the expectations of fidelity haunting the cinematic translation of any literary text that a departure from the original author's intention can be interpreted as violent distortion, as Rigalt does when she lambasts Aranda's version: 'mutilada la obra original (se cambió el único final possible)' (the original was mutilated (the only possible ending was changed)) (Gala 2001: 2). In the context of an exploration of the construction of the Spanish woman as a modern subject striving for emancipation, it is significant that Gala silences his heroine in the novel's conclusion. Desideria tells her own disturbingly degrading story, as the bulk of the novel purports to be the unedited publication of four handwritten notebooks found in a Turkish Delight box, but the epilogue is narrated by a male childhood friend who informs the reader that she has killed herself. As Nicola Gilmour notes, 'Desideria is relegated to a feminized position of silence, losing her narrative voice to the point where even her last words in her suicide note are illegible' (2006: 86–7). However, although the suicide scene was filmed, the cinematic adaptation opted for an alternative ending on its release: to keep Desideria alive, albeit facing an uncharted future after having shot her lover Yamam in the crotch.

The different endings of the novel and the film can be seen as responses to the discourse of New Womanhood and her pursuit of sexual liberation. Whereas the novel presents Desideria as a self-destructive figure whose vanishing act upholds the patriarchal socio-symbolic, the film subverts this passive imperative by re-visioning her as the avenging woman or, as Barbara Creed might say, the *'femme castatrice'* (castrating woman) of 'the woman's revenge film' (1993: 151). Despite this shift, to borrow a line from Kirsten Lentz, 'from being the object of violence (victimization) to being its subject (aggression)' (1993: 377), I would hesitate to state that the film offers a straightforward case for feminist appropriation or, even, that it is a positive representation of female power and control (Jordan and Morgan-Tamosunas 1998: 126). To address the way in which the portrayal of the Spanish New Woman in the adaptation of *La pasión turca* needs to be seen as problematic, as well as bringing into the discussion various approaches developed in film feminism, I will select three key aspects that merit exploration: the female gaze, maternity, and the subject of castration.

The opening scene, as Thomas Deveny notes in his close reading, 'foreshadows exactly where the passion will lead' (1999: 49). The camera switches from a close-up of a woman's eyes through a window to her point of view as the camera pans over a burial ground: '¿quién iba a pensar que mi paisaje cotidiano en esta ciudad tan soñada iba a ser un cementerio?' (who would have thought that my daily view in this desired city would be a graveyard?), she muses out loud.[1] This voice-over technique announces Desideria's ability to tell her own story, and the camera indicates that her subjective viewpoint will be privileged.

A flashback establishes Desideria's back-story, her unsatisfactory marriage to Ramiro, and goes on to explain her presence in Istanbul. A group of married couples travel to Turkey's capital for a holiday which, in Desideria's case, will prove to be a life-changing event. The scene where Desideria encounters Yamam for the first time, on the tour bus travelling from the airport to the hotel, implements a straightforward reversal of the male gaze. As Yamam speaks about the Western imagination's eroticization of his country, the camera switches back and forth between a close-up of Desideria and the front of the coach where he is sitting. Here, the gaze is unidirectional, from female as desiring subject on to male as desired object. The camera shows Desideria's awakening desire, as she gradually lowers her sunglasses, and the way her point of view fragments his body (slicked black hair, three fingers resting on microphone, reflection of moving lips in the mirror). Crucially we do not see his eyes at this stage, so Yamam is filmed in the position of receiving the gaze, as passive object, not returning it.

---

[1] The translations of dialogue are taken from the subtitles to the film.

Now it is important to raise the point that Mulvey rejected the possibility of a female gaze: 'according to the principles of the ruling ideology and the psychical structures that back it up, the male figure cannot bear the burden of sexual objectification' ([1975] 1989: 20). This is because Mulvey was using a psychoanalytical framework (namely, Freud's active/male and passive/female binary) to support her argument that it is the man who actively looks at the woman who passively receives his gaze. This dynamic grants power to the one who is in control of the gaze: he controls the woman through a process of objectification, and then he causes the narrative to progress. The male gaze, therefore, is the focal point of power. However, as Laura Kipnis reminds us, Mulvey's 'theory of the gaze was in relation to a historically specific period of filmmaking', namely, Golden Age Hollywood films. Kipnis raises the point that changes in the industry, narrative form and structure, new plots and images, such as the sexual male body, 'put into question whether Mulvey's theory is still viable' (1993: 8). From the 1980s and through to the 1990s, directors such as Jane Campion in *The Piano* (1993) can be seen to visually address the question of what takes place when the agent of the gaze is female and the object is the male body. Some hispanists (Deveny 1999: 155, Fouz Hernández and Martínez-Expósito 2007:167) do not hesitate to state that *La pasión turca* is a female-gaze film, and this scene in particular appears to shift the balance of power. It certainly inaugurates Desideria's journey of awakening but, meaningfully, she is the tourist and Yamam is the guide.

Later, as they prepare to have covert sex in the bus, Yamam expertly raises her legs to hook them on the chair arms and he flicks Desideria's raised dress over her face. Desideria is so taken with the novelty of sexual fulfilment that she is unaware of his, perhaps casual, veiling gesture. It is one which creates a visual barrier between them and could stand as a metaphor for their inability to understand each other. After the obvious (to all but Ramiro) furtive trysts, Desideria returns home and life appears set to continue as before. Once again the film departs from Gala's novel, bringing to the fore how differently the desiring Spanish New Woman is constructed on the page and on-screen. Gala narrates Desideria's post-holiday relationship as one based initially on business, as she opens a shop in her home town to sell Yamam's Turkish carpets (and, unknowingly, becomes involved in drug smuggling). The film, on the other hand, writes maternity into the plot when Desideria becomes the mother of Yamam's son. In the novel, Desideria uses the business as an excuse to visit Istanbul again and pick up their one-sided relationship, whereas in the film it is the infant's death which propels her to return. Barbara Zecchi has examined the ways in which Spanish films of the 1990s collapse female sexuality and maternity, stating that this erases 'the possibility of freeing female identity from maternal connotations' (2005: 154).

La pasión turca presents sexual and maternal desire as one and the same thing in the character of Desideria, because she wants sex and she wants a child. Once the lovers are reunited, she asks him to pause mid-coitus and says: 'me gusta sentirte así, dentro de mí. ¡Quietecito!' (I like to feel you inside me. Stay still!), barely an instant before telling him that they have had, and lost, a son. She then twice implores '¿tendremos más?' (will we have more?). Fouz-Hernández and Martínez-Expósito, given that their focus is the male body, interpret Desideria's desire as phallic-focused: 'the size of his penis and his sexual prowess are meant to explain the behaviour of the female protagonist!' (2007: 167). Certainly, when Arturo, echoing an earlier exasperated Ramiro, says '¿Pero qué es lo que tiene el turco ese?' (But what does that Turk have?), she indicates with her hands the size of his penis. One can read *La pasión turca* as an expression of a crisis in white Spanish masculinity and Western nationhood (see Santaolalla 1999; Gilmour 2006). However, this should not be at the expense of overlooking the double inscription of Desideria within patriarchal discourses of desire, shown by the bonding of women to their biological destiny and the impossibility of non-phallic female sexuality, which renders complicated any reading of the film as one which explores Spanish New Womanhood and sexual liberation.

Desideria is fascinated with the sensual possibilities of the Arab erotic stereotype: the belly dancer. One evening, alone in the flat she now shares with Yamam, Desideria dances in front of the mirror dressed in exotic garb. Deveny interprets this scene an 'effort at cultural assimilation', because 'as she looks into the mirror' Desideria is 'verbally affirming her own willingness to accept Turkish culture' (1999: 151–2). This reading can be challenged, as her desire for assimilation is selective: not only does Desideria not want to learn the Turkish language but she is trapped by her own banal stereotypification of Orientalism. When Yamam returns, although we cannot see his face, we see him shaking his head, '¿Por qué te has disfrazado así? (Why have you dressed up like this?), and she replies 'porque quiero que mi amo entre en mí' (because I want my master to enter me'), which, as Gilmour notes, can be read as a 'perversion of sexual enslavement' (2006: 82). Desideria places him in the master's position, though Yamam is not comfortable with her subjugation. Later he pushes her away and shouts: 'yo quiero hacer el amor contigo con naturalidad, con alegría, ¡no como si fuera una tragedia!' ('I want to make love with you happily and naturally, not as if it were a tragedy!'). Yamam is objectified by the gaze of Desideria and the camera, as his body is 'constantly fragmented' (Fouz-Hernández and Martínez-Expósito 2007: 184), and here, perhaps, the film elicits a fleeting sympathy for his plight as used object. But although the visual fragmentation serves to underscore Desideria's blindness to Yamam as a person with needs, obligations, and personal desires, it also serves as a strategy to deny the audience insight into his motives, thoughts, or feelings. In contrast, Desideria is laid bare as the camera creates the illusion of complete emotional access by navigating the length of Ana Belén's naked body.

Their relationship is built on a misreading of each other's sexual desire: whereas he seeks to free himself from the pressures of his cultural duties as son, husband, and father through free love, she seeks plenitude through sole ownership of his penis and biological motherhood. It comes as a shock to her that Yamam is already a father: '¿Qué te esperabas?' (What did you expect?), he says, pointing out that he had a life before she arrived. In time, Yamam will break his promise, made under the duress of that paused sexual re-encounter, that they can have children of their own (although her maternal desire is rendered suspect when she emotionally neglects Yamam's children). He makes her have an abortion and, at the same time, a non-consensual hysterectomy; though whether that is due to medical complications or patriarchal collusion remains unclear (the Turkish dialogue between the doctor and Yamam is not subtitled). At this point it becomes evident that Desideria's process of emancipation could have dangerous consequences, as it takes her outside the protection of Spanish society, which is indicated by her conversations with Paulina, an embassy worker. She has no possibilities of getting legal residency, is emotionally and financially dependent on a married – even, as Paulina suggests, violent and criminal – Turkish man, and is losing ownership of her own body. Yamam will demand that Desideria sexually satisfy one of his creditors, to her intense confusion, reducing her to an object of exchange value between men. Distressed, she turns for help to Paulina who – despite Desideria's lack of funds – enables her to return to Spain. As Jordan and Morgan-Tamosunas have commented, this film, like many others about the Spanish New Woman, smooths over financial and logistical difficulties associated with negotiating a change in circumstance (1998: 128–31).

Desideria must face the choice of readmittance into well-heeled bourgeois Spanish society, which her friends warn her comes at a price: she must give up her autonomy and curb her sexual appetite, or accept the role Yamam has outlined for her. In Madrid, Desideria reclaims her place outside conventional society, but on her own terms, when she sleeps with a wealthy man. Back in Istanbul, Desideria becomes Yamam's whore but, erroneously, assumes this means that she owns his penis as he owns her body. In the final scenes, as it becomes clear that Yamam's concept of love involves being with whom he likes – whether male, female, or both at the same time – and when he likes, Desideria enacts revenge. Having acquired a pistol, a gift from a 'client', and angered by Yamam's speech about free love as he kisses and fondles both her and another woman in a restaurant, Desideria castrates him with one bullet. Yamam, although bleeding, allows her to escape without retribution: 'Dejad que Desi huya' (Let Desi get away). As she walks across a bridge that spans the Bosphorous, towards an unknown future, she speaks of her loss: 'Todo ha terminado. No sé a qué mundo pertenezco' (All has ended. I do not know to which world I belong). This is an ambivalent ending, because in expressing his desire to protect her from justice, it can be argued that it is Yamam who is in charge of Desideria's fate, not herself. Wounded, he could be interpreted as the victim of an obsessive woman, and the film would function as a warning to male spectators. And yet, as Desideria crosses the line from victim to avenger, a reading within the logic of female agency is also possible, because the film allows female spectators to take pleasure in witnessing a woman fight back.

What does granting Desideria the power to enact violent revenge mean to the project of film feminism? Castration, either symbolic or displayed on-screen, has been explored by many feminists, often working within the film feminist psychoanalytical framework (Mulvey 1975, Creed 1993). But there has been a move away from universal psychoanalytic concepts towards a socio-historic contextualization of the rise of cinematic female avengers as popular cultural responses to feminism (Clover 1992, Read 2000, Schubart 2007). The decision to distribute *La pasión turca* with an alternative finale was taken by the producer, who 'believed that the suicide ending offered less commercial viability' (Deveny 1999: 154) – an interesting suggestion given that the novel had been successful, but indicative of the way Spanish cinema had become established as a representational space for screening female subject positions in transition from disempowerment towards emancipation.

In bringing back into focus the regressive aspects of this particular film, rather than simply celebrating the subversive elements, this chapter has sought to show how the emergence of the Spanish New Woman on-screen does show, as many critics agree, an individual actively negotiating her own path, but also that she has had to plot a course within a contradictory culture where politics, sexuality, and the market are closely connected.

Further reading

Jordan, Barry, and Mark Allinson, 2005. *Spanish Cinema: A Student's Guide* (London: Hodder Arnold)

Jordan, Barry, and Rikki Morgan-Tamosunas, 1998. *Contemporary Spanish Cinema* (Manchester: Manchester UP)

McCabe, Janet, 2004. *Feminist Film Studies: Writing the Woman into Cinema* (London: Wallflower Press)

Martin-Márquez, Susan, 1999. *Feminist Discourse and Spanish Cinema: Sight Unseen* (Oxford: OUP)

Thornham, Sue (ed.), 1999. *Feminist Film Theory: A Reader* (Edinburgh: Edinburgh UP)

21

Almodóvar's 'Others': Spanish Women Film-Makers, Masquerade, and Maternity

JO EVANS

'It was a small can, a sardine can. It floated there in the sun, a witness to the canning industry, which we, in fact, were supposed to supply. It glittered in the sun. And Petit-Jean said to me – *You see that can? Do you see it? Well, it doesn't see you!* He found this incident highly amusing – I less so.' Jacques Lacan ([1973] 1979: 95)

'Despite the enormous emphasis placed on woman as spectacle in the cinema, woman as woman is largely absent.'
Claire Johnston ([1973] 2000: 25)

'I'd like to draw people's attention to New Zealand being the first place in the world for women to get the vote [...] I think it makes a difference [...] My suspicion is that women aren't used to that [the harsh world of filmmaking], so they must put on their coats of armour and get going.'
Jane Campion speaking at the Cannes Film Festival, 2009[*]

Introduction: Almodóvar's 'others'

The quotations in the epigraph above span the historical period covered in this study of Spanish women's film-making since the end of the Franco regime in 1975. Mindful of the value of recognition (Lacan), the predominance of 'woman as spectacle in the cinema' (Johnston), the importance of their country of origin and the need for women to 'put on their coats of armour and get going' (Campion), this chapter redirects Laura Mulvey's famous question about how classical Hollywood film narrative constructs the female spectator (1975) to ask how the film industry constructs the

---

[*] Campion's comments can be read in full at http://blogs.myspace.com/index.cfm?fuseaction=blog.view&friendId=376458701&blogId=419070011 (accessed 6 June 2009)

woman film-maker. In two sections it examines their representation of feminine masquerade and the *mater dolorosa* and concludes (via Kristeva) that the performance of women film-makers in an industry dominated by oedipal narratives is marked more profoundly by the myth of mobile Io than by Oedipus's compulsive returns.

At the 2009 Cannes Film Festival, Jane Campion was one of the twenty directors in competition, along with two other women, Andrea Arnold from the UK, and Isabel Coixet from Spain. Asked for her views on the predominance of men, Campion's response (above) was widely reported. Coixet's opinion does not appear to have been sought, but the fact that she is one of the women whose presence gave rise to the question is significant.[1] Over the last decade, technological innovation and the success of Almodóvar have brought dramatic changes to the Spanish film industry. Three Oscars for Best Foreign Film have put Spanish film firmly on the international map. Copies of films previously available only in specialist libraries in Spain are now available on DVD. Academic studies are published regularly, and there has been a boom in the number of Spanish women directors (Triana-Toribio 2003: 143–6, Camí-Vela 2005: 17–18, Pérez Millán 2003: 52, Pavlović et al. 2009: 184).

Boom director Azucena Rodríguez describes Pedro Almodóvar's success as 'la demostración palpable de cómo a partir de algo absolutamente localista, nos quitó la vergüenza de España, de nosotros mismos' (visible proof of how something completely local removed our sense of shame about Spain, and ourselves) (Camí-Vela 2005: 175), and her use of the word *vergüenza* (shame) is striking. Almodóvar may have won two Oscars for Best Foreign Film, but his outstanding achievement to date is the Oscar for Best Original Screenplay in 2003 for *Hable con ella* (*Talk to Her*) (2002). This reminds us that the film industry is not just male-dominated, but geographically and linguistically dominated by North America and the English language. Female directors working in other languages need to adopt flexible strategies if they are to negotiate this potential double 'othering', and there is no doubt that Coixet established her international reputation more rapidly by filming in English (Triana-Toribio 2007).

The reference to Almodóvar in the title of this chapter is deliberately provocative. It is a reminder that, although the names of some of Coixet's female peers may be familiar to art-house film-viewers, for the wider film-going public Spanish film *is* Almodóvar, and the words 'Spanish film' and 'women' conjure up female performers like Carmen Maura, Victoria Abril, and Penélope Cruz much more readily than film-makers like Chus Gutiérrez,

---

[1] Coixet discusses her nomination in interview with *El País*: http://www.elpais.com/articulo/cultura/Queria/sexo/fuera/cama/mucha/luz/elpepicul/20090523elpepicul_7/Tes

Gracia Querejeta, Patricia Ferreira, and Icíar Bollaín. This chapter looks, therefore, at Spanish women's film-making since the death of Franco in relation to a wider industry in which 'Almodóvar' functions as a metonym for Spanish film, rather that at single directors who are the subject of excellent studies elsewhere (Martin-Márquez 1999, Camí-Vela 2000, Martínez Carazo 2002, Nair 2002, María Pilar Rodríguez 2002, Collins 2005, Jacqueline Cruz 2005, Santaolalla 2004, Triana-Toribio 2007).[2] It redirects Mulvey's question via Lacan's sardine can to ask how women represent their relationship to the industrial apparatus, then considers their approach to two key aspects of the Almodóvar brand: the representation of gender as masquerade and compulsive returns to the maternal melodrama (Williams 1985, Doane 1984, Ana M. López 1993).

Spanish women film-makers and the sardine can conundrum

The connection Azucena Rodríguez makes between status and shame has correspondences with the psychoanalytical framework of Mulvey's query, subsequently developed by Rodowick (1982), Studlar (1984), Williams (1985), Hansen (1986), and Stacey (1987). However, less attention has been paid to the way the cinematic apparatus (Baudry 1974–75) constructs the female film-maker and to the masquerade she performs in response. Joan Riviere's (1929) Freudian account of the masquerade professional women perform in a male-dominated workplace, is still remembered for the question she raises towards the end about whether *all* femininity is masquerade. The question as to whether gender difference is biological or performative has been revisited many times in the development of women's film theory (Williams 1985, Stacey 1987, De Lauretis 1988), as it has in Almodóvar's films. To rephrase Mulvey's question to apply to the female director, however, it is helpful to return to Lacan's sardine can. The Lacanian Gaze is metaphorical battleground on which we fight for a subjectivity predicated on the extent to which we are recognized ('seen') by the 'other', and our performance is gendered:

> [T]he being gives of himself, or receives from the other, something that is like a mask, a double, an envelope, a thrown-off skin, thrown off in order to cover the frame of a shield [...] It is no doubt through the mediation of masks that the masculine and the feminine meet in the most acute, most intense way. (Lacan [1973] 1979: 107)

This and the sardine can anecdote help to elucidate the ambivalent responses

---

[2] See also Santaolalla's forthcoming full-length study of Icíar Bollaín, in press.

of Spanish women directors to the notion of women film-makers that is discussed below. Lacan wonders why he was so unamused by the sardine can episode and concludes that it was because: 'I, at that moment [...] looked like nothing on earth. In short, I was rather out of place in the picture. And it was because I felt this that I was not terribly amused' ([1973] 1979: 95–6). Although the film industry is clearly not as oblivious to women as the sardine can was to Lacan, it is interesting to see how their humour holds up when asked to consider themselves in the context of an industrial sardine can that so rarely sees them (Martin-Márquez 1999).

This section looks at women film-makers' response to the sardine can conundrum and it is framed with reference to diegetic directors in films by Pilar Miró and Marta Balletbò-Coll. Miró (1940–97) belongs to the generation of women film-makers associated with the Transition to democracy, and she was the first Spanish woman to receive a government position for her work in the film industry. Her melodrama, *Gary Cooper que estás en los cielos* (*Gary Cooper, Who Art in Heaven*) (1980) is about a pregnant film and television director. It is a sharp contrast to Almodóvar's upbeat treatment of a similar theme in *Mujeres al borde de un ataque de nervios* (*Women on the Edge of a Nervous Breakdown*) (1988), as a brief plot summary indicates. The opening establishes Andrea Soriano (Mercedes Sampietro) as a new woman of the Spanish Transition: she has won a prize for her television work; she is directing a television adaptation of Sartre's *Huis clos*; she is about to be offered a long-coveted opportunity to direct an adaptation of Emilia Pardo Bazán's *Los pazos de Ulloa* (The House of Ulloa); and she is pregnant and intends to have her baby, with or without her journalist partner's blessing. Shortly after this opening, however, she discovers she needs to have surgery urgently to remove what may be malignant uterine tumours. The film follows her progress over the next few days as she prepares for an operation she may not survive, and the denouement leaves her on the point of being anaesthetized, accompanied not by her partner, but by an ex, Bernardo, who is married to someone else.

The *mise-en-abîme* of *Huis clos* establishes Andrea's entrapment and existential dilemma, but the wider narrative is a rather more slippery form of *mise-en-abîme*. This is a film about a female film and television director, directed by a woman who has worked in television. Miró was an avowed anti-feminist (Pavlović et al. 2009: 189), and her portrait of women in the film industry is ambivalent. The melodramatic framing of Andrea gazing at a still of Gary Cooper and asking him to watch over her on the operating table may be a satirical comment on the seductive power of the Hollywood star system, but it makes her appear vacuous. This is a cautionary tale for the would-be woman director: the metaphorical threat to Andrea's femininity is gruesomely outlined in the doctor's description of the procedure they will adopt to scrape out her womb; the depiction of the viciousness of women towards other women in an environment in which they are in the minority is harsh; and the decision Andrea is forced to take (whether to go ahead with an operation that may save her life, but will terminate the pregnancy) is a graphic biological metaphor for the catch-22 of domestic and professional demands faced by women.

Miró's film reminds us just how radical a separation of biological and professional personae was required of women in Spain in the 1970s, and the ambivalent framing of the director may be a symptom of her historical context. However, despite the intervening success of Almodóvar and a steady increase in the number of Spanish women film-makers, their response to the notion of women film-makers remains ambivalent (Pavlović et al. 2009: 189). María Camí-Vela's interviews with the women of the boom generation of the 1990s highlight this. Dolores Payás is one of the few who appears comfortable with the woman question, joking that rumours of a boom have been exaggerated ('¿Qué *boom*? Simplemente estamos empezando a equilibrar la situación') (What boom? We're just beginning to redress the balance) (Camí-Vela 2005: 125). Others are reluctant to comment: Helena Taberna acknowledges that the sex of the director makes a difference (ibid.: 202), and Azucena Rodríguez admits that she became aware of a problem when she had children and less time to work (ibid.: 164). Most, however, resist being drawn into discussion in which, as Icíar Bollaín points out, they risk ghettoizing themselves (ibid.: 59–60, and Bollaín 1998).

In his anecdote about how completely his sense of humour failed him Lacan uses humour to illustrate the correlation between visibility and subjectivity. Interestingly, it is the Catalan director Marta Balletbò-Coll whose humour fails her most completely when asked for her views on the woman issue. At first sight this is odd because, like Lacan, Coll uses self-mockery to demonstrate that women are nowhere in relation to the film industry in her first film, *Costa Brava* (1995). Its fast-moving opening shows the would-be director (played by Coll) videoing herself on the roof of her Barcelona apartment. She is in character as a conservative housewife gossiping, in English, about her lesbian neighbour, and Coll performs a hilarious double masquerade as the fictional heterosexual neighbour on (diegetic) video, and as her (diegetic) self on film (masquerading as a lesbian Catalan director trying to get into theatre by producing an English-language video). The jerky editing between film and video adds to the comic balance between self-disclosure and self-parody, and there is a nod to the patriarchal history of women's performance in a cutaway to a white statue of a naked woman. Anyone who has seen her perform this fast-paced, ironic, multilayered masquerade might be surprised that Coll refuses to discuss with Camí-Vela something she addresses so explicitly in her films. Looked at more closely, however, this is a logical paradox. The more explicit diegetic Coll is prepared to be about the difficulties women face getting funding, the more guarded off-screen Coll needs to be about associating herself with women's issues. Coll cuts short her interview with Camí-Vela, summing up her position with succinct black humour:

> A un nivel muy personal yo te diré que lo que yo quiero es facturar. Y cuando estás en colectivos de éstos, facturas muy poco. O sea que a mí es como si me viniera un incendio en mi casa cualquier alusión al tema éste.
> (Camí-Vela 2005: 43).
>
> (On a very personal level I'd say I like to make a living. And when you're in those [women's] collectives, you make very little. So that, for me, any reference to that topic is like watching my own house burn down.)

De Lauretis noted some time ago the 'conceptual paradox corresponding to what is in effect a real contradiction in women's lives: the term, at once, of a sexual *difference* (women are, or want, something different from men) and of a sexual *indifference* (women are, or want, the same as men) (1988: 155). Coll's response highlights the fact that this theoretical paradox is a '*real* contradiction' (my italics) for women. Coll wants the same thing as a male director (funding), so she needs to negotiate very carefully what I am calling the sardine can conundrum. Lacan's lure, the mask that guarantees success or failure in our relationships with others is, in this case, a form of a-transvestism (woman-not-woman), a performance of 'the emperor is not wearing any sex' that requires exactly the kind of fluid, flexible, self-ironic self-construction that Coll performs so well at the beginning of *Costa Brava*.

Masquerade

Given women film-makers' ongoing lack of visibility in the Spanish and international film industry, the link Coll makes between women's groups and watching her house burn down is apt. What is more surprising is that so few of her peers have experimented with the representation of gender as masquerade. Almodóvar's postmodern *mise-en-scène* of identity as performance has allowed him to renegotiate the on-screen representation of sex and sexuality, and one might have thought that his disruption of heterosexual and gender stereotypes with Bakhtinian forms of masquerade would inspire Spanish women directors to produce even more radical on-screen representations of feminine and masculine masquerade. However, Coll is the exception. Spanish women film-makers, unlike the women writers of the post-Franco era (poet Ana Rossetti, for example, or novelist Almudena Grandes) have not produced radical representations of sex and sexuality, and even Coll's postmodern lesbian romances avoid physical contact. This may, of course, be a reaction against the objectification of naked female flesh in 'sexy' Spanish comedies of the 1970s like *No desearás al vecino del quinto* (*Thou Shalt Not Covet Thy Fifth Floor Neighbour*) (1970), as well as in supposedly more highbrow films like Vicent Aranda's *Amantes* (*Lovers*) (1991). Chus Gutiérrez's documentary *Sexo oral* (*Oral Sex*) (1994) does contribute to radical on-screen debates about sex and sexuality, but her cast (mainly consisting of friends and family) do so fully clothed.

To find a film that makes overt the complex link between femininity, performance, and masquerade, we have to go back to *Función de noche* (*Evening Performance*) (1981) directed by Miró's contemporary, Josefina Molina (see Donapetry 2001 and Suárez Lafuente 2003). Like Miró, Molina studied at the Madrid Film School from 1963 and has had a distinguished career in television film-making. Unlike Miró, she was an avowed feminist who is happy to address the 'woman' issue. She comments in an interview prior to filming *Función de noche*, that:

> La mujer está en un momento difícil: busca su nueva identidad. No sabemos todavía quiénes somos. Seguimos mediatizadas por una cultura masculina, no digo machista. La mujer tiene que descubrir sus propios puntos de vista. Y, naturalmente, si los grandes maestros del cine han hablado de sí mismos, lo lógico es que las mujeres hablemos de nosotras, cuando se nos presenta la oportunidad de hacerlo.
>
> (This is a difficult time for women, we are seeking a new identity. We don't yet know who we are, because we are still mediated by masculine, not chauvinist, culture. Women have to find their own point of view. And, naturally, if the great film *maestros* have spoken of themselves, it is logical that we women will speak of ourselves when we have the opportunity to do so.)[3]

She is also frank about her feminist approach to Delibes's novel, *Cinco horas con Mario* (*Five Hours with Mario*), on which *Función de noche* is based, pointing out that 'para mí en la obra no había sólo un cadáver, el de Mario, sino dos. El otro era el de una forma de ser mujer que tenía que desaparecer necesariamente' (the way I see it, there was not just one corpse, Mario's, but two. The other one was a way of life for woman that needed to disappear) (Molina 2000: 89).

The performance of masquerade in this film is, as in Coll's film, multi-layered. *Cinco horas con Mario* is a monologue addressed by a nagging Franco-era widow, Carmen Sotillo, to the dead body of her husband. Molina was directing a stage version of it in Madrid starring the actress Lola Herrera. After a number of performances, Herrera suffered a nervous

---

[3] Josefina Molina, in an interview with H. H. Les, *Tele-radio*, Madrid, 2–8 February 1981, p. 36.

collapse brought on (she explained to Molina) by the gradual realization that Carmen's life mirrored her own, and that a rather unattractive literary character she had initially despised was in the process of teaching her 'los errores de mi vida' (my life's mistakes).[4] Seeing in Herrera's breakdown a metonym for the experience of a generation of Spanish women who had benefited from the Transition, but were unsure who they might be when no longer so repressively, as Molina puts it, 'mediated by masculine culture', Molina decided to document Herrera's experience.

The film shows Herrera masquerading on-stage as Carmen and then offstage, in conversation with her husband, Daniel Dicenta, in her dressing room, and in external sequences with her children, an older female friend, the lawyer who is arranging her divorce, and a doctor she is consulting about whether to have plastic surgery. Molina placed eight hidden cameras in Herrera's dressing room, so the separated couple (both of whom were actors) would not be able to direct their conversation to camera. This makes for an intense and at times uncomfortably voyeuristic viewing experience. The couple have been separated for fourteen years, but are only now legally able to divorce, and their backstage conversations address explicitly Herrera's reassessment of the self-sacrificial role that playing Carmen has forced her so dramatically to reassess. One of the most poignant comments she makes to her husband links her sexual experience directly to new-found awareness of the restrictive roles imposed on her as a single mother and actress during the regime:

> ¿Sabes que he estado con cuatro hombres contándote a ti y nunca he tenido un orgasmo? He perdido la vida, ya no voy a conocer el amor y tengo cuarenta y seis años. He estado toda la vida trabajando y no tengo nada, me he dado cuenta de lo mala que he sido para mí. (You know I've been with four men including you and I've never had an orgasm? I've wasted my life and now I won't find love and I'm forty-six years old. I've worked all my life and I have nothing, and I've realized how bad I've been for me.)[5]

Herrera's blunt self-revelation is a reminder of the reason why Almodóvar's representation of sexual licence in general, and of the housewife's frustration in particular, have become so iconic of the Transition period. However, unlike Almodóvar's fictional *Mujeres al borde...* (*Women on the Verge ...*), this is a lived *ataque de nervios* (nervous breakdown). For Herrera, the

---

[4] Quoted by Javier Ángulo in an article on *Función de noche* in *El País*, 29 September 1981 (source, Filmoteca, Madrid).

[5] Dialogue cited in Ana G. Rivas, 'Lola Herrera: hacer esta película era una forma de tirar fuera toda la basura' (Lola Herrera [says]: making this film was a way of throwing out all the rubbish), *Diario 16*, 28 September 1981, *Espectáculos*, p. 41.

effects of recognizing herself in Carmen were very real, and she describes the experience as cathartic.⁶ However, Molina's interrogation of female masquerade bears no relation to Almodóvar's joyful Bakhtinian parodies, nor is it the effect of a temporary disruption of the symbolic order. Herrera's breakdown is a symptom of the very real contradictions of the conceptual paradox that is patriarchal femininity, made acute by the insights that playing Carmen gave Herrera and by her own need to renegotiate a different form of Transition masquerade. *Función de noche* is an important film for appreciating the grief that accompanies the elation at times of positive social and political change.

Although the next generation tends to avoid such serious on-screen debates about the construction of femininity, one boom generation film that does represent femininity as masquerade is *La Moños* (Mireia Ros, 1997).⁷ Again, it is with reference to a real woman and to Rivierian, not Bakhtinian, masquerade. La Moños was a well-loved Barcelona character of the 1930s, who had taken to roaming the streets of Barcelona flamboyantly dressed up after her lover died and her illegitimate baby was taken away to be brought up by its aristocratic grandmother (as told by Mireia Ros to Camí-Vela 2005: 189). In this filmed homage to a lived, rather than sanctified, *mater dolorosa* of the Franco era, masquerade is psychological defence: 'en vez de suicidarse, decidió continuar adoptando una nueva personalidad porque no podía soportar el dolor' (rather than commit suicide, she decided to carry on, adopting a new personality because she could not bear her pain) (Camí-Vela 2005: 189). The contrast between this lived masquerade and Almodóvar's Bakhtinian, deranged old women is heightened by the appearance of Julieta Serrano in the title role. Serrano, who played the mad ex-wife Lucía in Almodóvar's *Mujeres al borde,* is equally effective here, as a Franco-era *mater dolorosa* fending off maternal grief by performing her life as if she had wandered back in time from an Almodóvar set.

Reconstructing the *mater dolorosa*

Almodóvar's films return compulsively, albeit with postmodern irony, to sacrificial and castrating mothers. He even successfully combines the two in the characters of Gloria in *¿Qué he hecho yo para merecer esto?* (*What*

---

⁶ Diego Galán, 'Josefina Molina ha reintegrado al cine una de sus más ricas posibilidades: la de servir de testimonio mudo de la realidad' (Josefina Molina hsd brought back to our screens one of the richest aspetcs of film-making, which is to serve as a testamente to reality), *El País*, 28 October 1981 (source, Filmoteca, Madrid).

⁷ In Spanish, 'La Moños' is a nickname with connotations of masquerade, as it suggests a woman who is over-dressed, or dressed up in bad taste.

Have I Done to Deserve This?) (1984, and Becky in *Tacones lejanos* (*High Heels*) (1991), and yet it was his most conventional return to the traditional *mater dolorosa* that secured his first Oscar and his first Spanish Goya for Best Director, for *Todo sobre mi madre* (*All About My Mother*) (1999). The strong, self-sacrificing mothers in classic Hollywood maternal melodramas like *Mildred Pierce* (1945), *Stella Dallas* (1937), *Imitation of Life* (1934 and 1959), *All That Heaven Allows* (1955) have been examined repeatedly by women film theorists for the way that they split the representation of the mother into either the sacrificial or the phallic (Kaplan 1992); devalue women by sanctifying maternity (Williams 1985); project masochistic fantasies onto glamorous performers (Doane 1984); return mothers to the domestic sphere (De Lauretis 1985), and/or contribute to the religious iconography of nation-building (Ana M. López 1993). And yet the success of two grieving-mother melodramas in the same year in Spain – *Todo sobre mi madre* and Benito Zambrano's *Solas* – testifies to their enduring appeal. Kristeva's 'Stabat Mater' (1980) eloquently unravelled the compulsive and nostalgic attraction, for men and women, of the oedipal iconography of the *mater dolorosa*. Almodóvar also, consciously or unconsciously, highlights her relationship to oedipal myth in the complex shot of the son's pen writing on the camera lens that leaves open the implication that the rest of the film narrative is his oedipal fantasy of the perfect self-sacrificial mother. But, as Claire Johnston asked back in the mid-1970s, where is 'woman as woman' on-screen?

What is striking about the representation of mothers in Spanish women's film-making is how unlike their melodramatic counterparts they are, and how little the fact that they happen to be mothers limits characterization and narrative trajectory. To consider just a few of the better-known examples: in Coixet's *My Life Without Me* (2003), the children are a concern for the dying mother, but they are one of a number of relationships she takes into account when planning her death. In Bollaín's *Flores de otro mundo* (*Flowers from Another World*) (1999), Patricia is motivated in her search for a partner by the fact that she has children, but she has other autonomous needs. The female protagonist in *Te doy mis ojos* (*Take My Eyes*) (Bollaín, 2003) is also a mother, but the scenes which include the son are a peripheral part of Bollaín's narrative of domestic violence. And in this film Bollaín makes direct reference to the iconography of the Catholic *mater dolorosa* (in the form of a painting in Toledo Cathedral museum) as the sacrificial role model Pilar must reject if she is to free herself from a violent, dysfunctional relationship.

The image of the *mater dolorosa* does recur in Spanish women's film-making in the 1990s, but it functions as a point of departure, rather than as a lure for oedipal returns. In *Todo sobre mi madre*, Almodóvar's classically melodramatic Manuela (played by Cecilia Roth) moves physically between

Madrid and Barcelona and protests at the maternal role Penélope Cruz's dying nun tries to force upon her, but she finds happiness in her return to the maternal role. Unlike Roth's beautiful, doomed *mater dolorosa*, the grieving mothers in films by Spanish women film-makers are mobile: they represent maternity as lived experience rather than as a sanctified icon. Balletbò-Coll's *Sévigné* (2004) features a stage director protagonist who is hoping to get funding to stage a play about Mme de Sévigné (the seventeenth-century French writer famous for the letters she wrote to her daughter). The director is also a mother who is grieving for the loss of her young adult daughter. Coll plays the part of the gauche, adoring, aspiring playwright, who will cajole her into acknowledging the extent to which her emotional petrification is connected to the maternal role she had projected on to her daughter while she was alive. This twist in the representation of maternal grief projects the lost mother on to the dead daughter, so that Coll's *mater dolorosa*, like Kristeva's, is a mobile trope functioning simultaneously as mother, daughter, and wife. In Coll's film, narrative momentum is also produced by her deconstruction, rather than by the compulsive, oedipal returns that may well have contributed to the enormous success of *Todo sobre mi madre*.

The films of the boom generation also use the deconstruction of the *mater dolorosa* as a trope in the interrogation of *desmemoria*, for which the closest English translation may be 'disavowed memory'.[8] Rosa Vergés's *Iris* (2004) uses the character of a grieving mother as a metonym for the process of recovering, and recovering from, Spain's repressed twentieth-century past. This film links maternal grief directly to the effects of Civil War and its aftermath, and here, as in *La Moños*, the grief is for a child who has not died, but has been removed from the mother by an older castrating-mother figure, granted authority by the Nationalist regime. The story unfolds between the Second Republic and the Transition. Iris divorces her first husband during the Second Republic, but the outbreak of Civil War is the catalyst for a sequence of painful events: her mother is shot and killed in a Nationalist attack, Iris is raped by her ex-husband and her second husband, Óscar, is imprisoned. She loses her daughter to her ex-husband's mother and is herself imprisoned for adultery when the divorce laws introduced during the Second Republic are abolished. Later, with the help of the now adult daughter with whom she has regained contact, Iris searches for Óscar, who has been missing throughout the intervening years of the Franco regime. She discovers him living on an island, his memory erased by psychiatric experiments performed on him in prison. This film begins with the death of Iris's mother, but it is the husband who functions as the static icon of

---

[8] The term 'desmemoria' is used to refer to the way the crimes of the Franco regime were suppressed to facilitate a peaceful transition to democracy.

loss (the death of Republican Spain), while Iris, the grieving mother and wife has agency in the role of metaphorical detective who investigates and interrogates the past. Patricia Ferreira's *Para que no me olvides* (*Something to Remember Me By*) (2005) also uses maternal grief as a catalyst for the discovery of a hidden past linked to the Spanish Civil War. Again, and the grieving mother acts as the point of departure, taking on the detective role. Traumatized by the death of her teenage son in a cycling accident, a drama teacher (who works, symbolically, with the blind), is drawn into an alliance with her son's girlfriend. They discover that a house he had been attempting to save from demolition had been lived in by his Republican grandfather during the Civil War, and the discovery of this lost site of family memory plays a positive role in a film that, once again, uses maternal grief as a motif for the reconstruction of a forgotten or silenced past.

Given the radical changes to the social and political situation of women since the end of the regime, it is at first surprising that so many films made by Almodóvar's female contemporaries use maternal grief as a catalyst for their narratives rather than focusing on masquerade as a vehicle of emancipation. The emphasis placed by the regime on the role of the family in the Nationalist mantra of 'Dios, Patria, Familia' (God, Fatherland, Family) may account for the way these films return to deconstruct the nuclear family and mobilize the *mater dolorosa* of Nationalist Catholic myth. Molina's comment that the wife's role in *Cinco horas con Mario* represents a domestic way of life 'que tenía que desaparecer necesariamente' (that needed to disappear) (2000: 89) suggests also that the motif of maternal grief functions as a wider metaphor for the conflicting emotions of emancipation and loss involved in the experience of such a rapidly changing social and domestic role for women, as well as for a lost Spanish twentieth-century history: a liberal past repressed by the Nationalist ideology of the Franco regime, and then suppressed in the interests of the peaceful transition to democracy.

Conclusion: mobility and migration – more Io than Oedipus?

Spain has changed dramatically since the end of the Franco dictatorship, as have theories of representation. Kaja Silverman recently proposed Orpheus, rather than Oedipus, as a potential source of insight into the twenty-first-century unconscious, and there are signs that the Oedipal grip that holds so firm in Hollywood may be slackening.[9] Julia Kristeva wonders whether the

---

[9] Silverman's keynote lecture 'Orpheus Rex' was presented at the Transmission: Cinema / Psychoanalysis Conference, 16–18 September 2008, organised by Jenny Chamarette, Steve Joy, Abigail Loxham and Isabelle McNeill, Centre for Research in the Arts, Social Sciences and Humanities, Cambridge University.

myth of Io might tell us more than Oedipus about the unconscious framework of feminine narratives (1991: 42–6), and this study of the way Spanish women film-makers mobilize the myths of masquerade and maternity suggests she has a point. Io was a young woman who caught Zeus's eye. She was turned into a heifer by the jealous wife Hera, who also had her followed by a gadfly that drove her to run away, to Egypt, maddened by its persistent sting. Io was rediscovered by Zeus on foreign soil and turned back into a woman to give birth to his son, Epaphus, whose name means 'touch-born'. Kristeva suggests that the key to the patriarchal feminine psyche lies with this woman, driven mad and 'condemned to wander as if, as the mother's rival, *no land could be her own*' (1991: 43, my italics).

Spain has now overtaken its Western European neighbours on issues of equal opportunity and for many of the women directors of the boom generation, migration and the *Ley de Extranjería* (Migration Law) are of more concern than maternity and masquerade.[10] This chapter now concludes with a brief look at two recent film-makers whose work suggests there is something, not just of Io, but also of Epaphus (the haptic offspring of touch), in the way women's film-making and theory has developed from the oedipally inclined 1970s to a wider turn of the twenty-first-century concern with the role of affect and the emotional effects of seeing, feeling, and touching on our creative and critical activities (Bruno 2002).

Most of the boom directors were born during the 1950s or 1960s, and as the Film School was closed between 1971 and 1994, they had to leave Spain to study film-making more formally. This situation has now changed dramatically, and two of the most impressive films to emerge from Spain recently were directed by young women as part of an MA degree in documentary film-making at Pompeu Fabra University in Barcelona. Both of these films, Mercedes Álvarez's *El cielo gira* (*The Sky Turns*) (2004) and Ariadna Pujol's *Aguaviva* (2005), address migration and mobile identities. Both return to the rural village to explore the changing structure and geography of the family, and the effects of social, political, and temporal upheaval. Both make the link between identity and the environment that is highlighted in Lacan's sardine can story, and both represent identity as a process of mobile, haptic exchange. It is too early to speculate what this might mean to the next generation of women film-makers, especially at a time when new opportunities to study film in Spain may be overshadowed by the effects of economic recession. The question of funding will, of course, will remain divisive. The

---

[10] Chus Gutierrez's *Poniente* (West) (2002) also uses the grieving mother as its point of departure. It places a multiracial, multilingual, cast against the inhospitable backcloth of the Almería coastal landscape, and uses what appears to be an oedipal narrative of romantic return as a seductive foil to increase the impact of the abrupt explosion of the inter-ethnic violence at the film's denouement.

sardine can conundrum is ongoing, and women will need to get their armour on whether they film in English, like Coixet, or keep an eye on the *absolutamente localista* (absolutely local [issues]), like Almodóvar. Whatever paths the next generation of Spanish women film-makers choose, Pujol and Álvarez's subtle and formally sophisticated documentaries provide new points of departure. They explore changing perceptions of Spanishness without sacrificing attention to cinematography or *mise-en-scène*, or having first to overcome a sense of *vergüenza*, and they remind us (should we still need reminding) that not all Spanish film is Almodóvar and Almodóvar is not all Spanish film.[11]

Further reading

Camí-Vela, María, 2005. *Mujeres detrás de la cámara: entrevistas con cineastas españolas 1990–2004* (Madrid: Ocho y Medio)

Heredero, Carlos (ed.), 1998. *La mitad del cielo: directoras españolas de los años 90* (Málaga: Festival de Cine Español)

Martin-Márquez, Susan, 1999. *Feminist Discourse and Spanish Cinema: Sight Unseen* (Oxford: OUP)

---

[11] A British Academy-funded research trip to Madrid allowed me to view films at the National Library and the *Centro Cultural Conde Duque*, and I should like to thank staff in these libraries, and at the Madrid Filmoteca and the Cervantes Institute in London, who were unfailingly helpful. My thanks are also due to Professor Isabel Santaolalla, for the generous loan of films from her personal collection.

WORKS CITED

Achard, Amédée, 2005. *Un Mois en Espagne (octobre 1846)* (facs. edn: www.elibron.com: Elibron Classics)
Acklesberg, Martha, 1992. '*Mujeres libres*: The Preservation of Memory under the Politics of Repression in Spain', in *Memory and Totalitarianism: International Yearbook of Oral History and Life Studies*, ed. Luisa Passerini (Oxford: OUP), 125–43
——, 2005. *Free Women of Spain: Anarchism and the Struggle for the Emancipation of Women* (Edinburgh: AK Press)
Acuña Villanueva de la Iglesia, Rosario de, 1882. *El lujo en los pueblos rurales*; repr. in microfiche, Simón Palmer 1992
Aguado Higón, Ana M., Rosa María Capel, et al., 1994. *Textos para la historia de las mujeres en España* (Madrid: Cátedra)
Aguilar Piñal, Francisco, 1981–2000. *Bibliografía de autores españoles del siglo XVIII*, 10 vols (Madrid: CSIC)
Ahlgren, Gillian T. W., 1996. *Teresa of Avila and the Politics of Sanctity* (Ithaca, NY: Cornell UP)
Aichinger, Wolfram, 2003. 'Isabel de Villena: la imaginación disciplinada', in *The Querelle des Femmes in the Romania: Studies in Honour of Friederike Hassauer*, ed. Wolfram Aichinger et al. (Vienna: Turia & Kant), pp. 57–69
Alberti, Rafael, 1944. *Romancero general de la guerra española* (Buenos Aires: Patronato Argentino de Cultura)
Alborch, Carmen, 2001. *Solas* (Barcelona: Temas de Hoy)
Albury, Kath, 2002. *Yes Means Yes: Getting Explicit about Heterosex* (London: Allen & Unwin)
Aldaraca, Bridget, 1982. '"El ángel del hogar": The Cult of Domesticity in Nineteenth-Century Spain', in Mora and van Hooft 1982: 62–87
——, 1991. *El ángel del hogar: Galdós and the Ideology of Domesticity in Spain* (Chapel Hill: University of North Carolina Press)
Alejos Morán, Asunción, 1984. 'Un capítulo del grabado valenciano: las xilografías de la *Vita Christi* de sor Isabel de Villena', *Cimal*, 24: 27–32
Alemany, Rafael, 1993. 'Dels límits del feminisme a la *Vita Christi* de sor Isabel de Villena', in Alemany et al. 1993: I, 301–26
——, 1997. 'Lematització provisional del lèxic de la *Vita Christi* de sor Isabel de Villena (A-F)', *Anuari de l'Agrupació Borrianenca de Cultura*, 8: 7–36
——, et al. (eds), 1993. *Actes del Novè Col.loqui Internacional de Llengua i Literatura Catalanes (Alacant –Elx, 1991)*, 3 vols (Barcelona: Publicacions de l'Abadia de Montserrat / Universitat d'Alacant, de València i Jaume I)

—— et al., 1996. *Concordances de la 'Vita Christi' de sor Isabel de Villena CD-Rom* (Alacant: IIFV)
Alexander, Gerard, 1999. 'Women and Men at the Ballot Box: Voting in Spain's Two Democracies', in Enders and Radcliff 1999: 349–74
Alfonso X, el Sabio, 1991. *Partida segunda: manuscrito 12794 de la Biblioteca Nacional*, ed. Aurora Juárez Blanquer and Antonio Rubio Flores, Colección Romania, 3 (Granada: Impredesur)
——, 2001. *Las Siete Partidas*, II: *Medieval Government: The World of Kings and Warriors*, trans. Samuel Parsons Scott and Robert I. Burns (Philadelphia: University of Pennsylvania Press)
Almodóvar, Francisco Jiménez de Góngora y Luján, Duque de, 1781. *Década epistolar sobre el estado de las letras en Francia* (Madrid: Antonio de Sancha)
Altman, Charles F., 1975. 'Two Types of Opposition and the Structure of Latin Saints' Lives', *Medievalia et Humanistica*, n.s., 6: 1–11
Alvar, Manuel (ed.), 1970–72. *'Vida de Santa María Egipciaca': estudios, vocabulario, edición de los textos*, Clásicos Hispánicos, 2.18–19 (Madrid: CSIC)
Álvarez Barrientos, Joaquín, 2006. *Los hombres de letras en la España del siglo XVIII: apóstoles y arribistas* (Madrid: Castalia)
Álvarez Junco, José, 2001. *Mater dolorosa: la idea de España en el siglo XIX* (Madrid: Taurus)
Amar y Borbón, Josefa, 1786. 'Discurso en defensa del talento de las mujeres', *Memorial Literario*, vol. 8, no. 32, pp. 399–430; ed. Carmen Chaves Tesser, *Dieciocho*, 3.2 (1980): 144–59
——, [1790], 1994. *Discurso sobre la educación física y moral de las mujeres*, ed. María Victoria López-Cordón (Madrid: Cátedra)
Amar y Borbón, Josefa: see also Lampillas 1789
Amasuno, Marcelino M., 1996. 'Apuntaciones histórico-médicas al escrito autobiográfico de Leonor López de Córdoba (1362–1430)', *Revista de Literatura Medieval*, 8: 29–71
Amorós, Célia, 2000. *Tiempo de feminismo: sobre feminismo, proyecto ilustrado y postmodernidad*, 2nd edn, Feminismos (Madrid: Cátedra)
Anahory-Librowicz, Oro, 1989. 'Las mujeres no-castas en el romancero: un caso de honra', in *Actas del IX Congreso de la AIH*, ed. Sebastián Neumeister (Frankfurt: Vervuert), I, pp. 321–30
Anderson, Benedict, 2006. *Imagined Communities: Reflections on the Origin and Spread of Nationalism*, rev. edn (London: Verso)
Andrés Martínez, Consuelo de, 1998. 'The Mythological, Historical, and Fictional Portrait of Women in the Works of Don Juan Manuel', unpublished doctoral thesis, University of Sheffield
Andreu, Alicia G., 1995. 'Maternal Discourse in *La cruz del olivar*, by Faustina Sáez de Melgar', *Revista Canadiense de Estudios Hispánicos*, 19.1: 229–40
Andreu, Cristina, 2008. *Isabel Coixet: una mujer bajo influencia* (Barcelona: Sociedad General de Autores y Editores)
Andrews, Margaret, 2006. 'Ethics, Gender and the Internet: An Exploration of

Some Spanish Feminists' Praxis', *Journal of Spanish Cultural Studies*, 7.1: 37–49

Anson, John, 1974. 'The Female Transvestite in Early Monasticism: The Origin and Development of a Motif', *Viator*, 5: 1–32

Archer, Robert, 2005. *The Problem of Woman in Late-Medieval Hispanic Literature*, CT, A214 (Woodbridge: Tamesis)

Arenal, Concepción [1861] 1993. *La mujer del porvenir*, ed. Vicente de Santiago Mulas (Madrid: Castalia)

——, 1883. *La mujer de su casa* (Madrid: Gras & Compañía)

Arenal, Electa and Stacey Schlau (eds), 1989a. *Untold Sisters: Hispanic Nuns in Their Own Words*, trans. Amanda Powell (Albuquerque: University of New Mexico Press)

——, 1989b. '"Leyendo yo e escribiendo ella": The Convent as Intellectual Community', *JHP*, 13: 214–29

Aresti, Nerea, 2001. *Médicos, donjuanes y mujeres modernas: los ideales de feminidad y masculinidad en el primer tercio del siglo XX* (Bilbao: Universidad del País Vasco)

Arkinstall, Christine, 2002. 'Towards a Female Symbolic: Re-Presenting Mothers and Daughters in Contemporary Spanish Narrative by Women', in Giorgio 2002a: 47–84

——, 2004. *Gender, Class, and Nation: Mercè Rodoreda and the Subjects of Modernism* (Lewisburg, PA: Bucknell UP)

Armas, Frederick A. de, 1986. 'Ana Caro Mallén de Soto', in Galerstein 1986: 66–7

——, 1999. 'Mirrors and Matriline: (In)visibilities in Ana Caro's *El conde Partinuplés*', in Hegstrom and Williamsen 1999: 75–92

——, 2003. 'Dreams, Voices, Signatures: Deciphering Woman's Desires in Ángela de Azevedo's *Dicha y desdicha del juego*', in *Woman in the Discourse of Early Modern Spain*, ed. Joan F. Cammarata (Gainesville: UP of Florida), pp. 146–59

Armstrong, Isobel, 2000. *The Radical Aesthetic* (Oxford: Wiley Blackwell)

Arnau, Carme, 1979. *Introducció a la narrativa de Mercè Rodoreda: el mite de la infantesa* (Barcelona: Edicions 62)

Arquiola, Elvira, 1984. 'Biología y política en el *Examen de ingenios* de Huarte de San Juan', *Asclepio*, 36: 85–119

——, 1988. 'Bases biológicas de la feminidad en la España Moderna (siglos XVI y XVII)', *Asclepio*, 40: 297–315

Ashley, Kathleen, 1981. 'Voice and Audience: The Emotional World of the *cantigas de amigo*', in Plummer 1981: 35–45

Attridge, Derek, 2004. *J. M. Coetzee and the Ethics of Reading: Literature in the Event* (Chicago, IL: University of Chicago Press)

Aughterson, Kate, 1995. *Renaissance Woman: Constructions of Femininity in England* (London: Routledge)

Ayerbe-Chaux, Reinaldo (ed.), 1977–78. 'Las *Memorias* de doña Leonor López de Córdoba', *JHP*, 2: 11–33

Bachelard, Gaston, [1958] 1994. *The Poetics of Space*, trans. Maria Jolas, with a foreword by John R. Stilgoe (Boston: Beacon)

Bailey, Matthew, 1993. *The 'Poema del Cid' and the 'Poema de Fernán González': The Transformation of an Epic Tradition*, Spanish Series, 78 (Madison: HSMS)

Ballesteros, Isolina, 1994. *Escritura femenina y discurso autobiográfico en la nueva novela española* (New York: Peter Lang)

——, 2001. *Cine (ins)urgente: textos fílmicos y contextos culturales de la España postfranquista* (Madrid: Fundamentos)

Baños Vallejo, Fernando, 2003. *Las vidas de los santos en la literatura medieval española*, Colección Arcadia de las Letras, 17 (Madrid: Laberinto)

——, and Isabel Uría Maqua (eds), 2000. *La leyenda de los santos: 'Flos sanctorum' del ms. 8 de la Biblioteca de Menéndez Pelayo*, Estudios de Literatura y Pensamiento Hispánicos, 18 (Santander: Año Jubilar Lebaniego / Sociedad Menéndez Pelayo)

Baranda Leturio, Nieves, 2005. *Cortejo a lo prohibido: lectoras y escritoras en la España moderna* (Madrid: Arco)

Barbeito Carneiro, Isabel, 1992. *Mujeres del Madrid barroco: voces testimoniales* (Madrid Dirección General de la Mujer / Comunidad de Madrid)

Barberá y París, María, 1897. *Compendio de higiene para niñas*; repr. in microfiche, Simón Palmer 1992

Barnard, Suzanne, 2002. 'Introduction', in Barnard and Fink 2002: 1–20

——, and Bruce Fink (eds), 2002. *Reading Seminar XX: Lacan's Major Work on Love, Knowledge, and Feminine Sexuality* (Albany: SUNY Press)

Barnett, David, 2006. 'The Voice of the Virgin: Accessible Authority in the Visitation Episode of Isabel de Villena's *Vita Christi*', *La Corónica*, 35: 23–46

Barrett, Michèle, and Anne Phillips, 1992. 'Introduction', *Destabilizing Theory: Contemporary Feminist Debates* (Stanford, CA: Stanford UP), pp. 1–9

Bartrina, Francesca, 2001. *Caterina Albert / Víctor Català: la voluptuositat de l'escriptura* (Vic: Eumo)

——, 2006. 'Narradores', in *Catalanes del XX*, ed. Pilar Godayol (Vic: Eumo), pp. 207–41

Bataille, Georges, [1967] 1988. *The Accursed Share* (New York: Zone Books)

Battesti-Pelegrin, Jeanne, 1985. 'Eaux douces, eaux amères dans la lyrique médiévale traditionelle', in *L'Eau au Moyen Âge*, Sénéfiance, 15 (Aix-en-Provence: Université de Provence), pp. 43–60

Baudry, Jean-Louis, 1974–75. 'Ideological Effects of the Basic Cinematographic Apparatus', trans. Alan Williams, *Film Quarterly*, 28.2 (Winter): 39–47

Beceiro Pita, Isabel, 2003. 'La relación de las mujeres castellanas con la cultura escrita (siglo XIII-inicios del XVI)', in Castillo Gómez 2003: 11–52; repr. 2007 in her *Libros, lectores y biblioteca en la España medieval*, Publicaciones de Medievalia, 2 (Murcia: Nausícaä), pp. 547–86

Bell, Rudolph M., 1985. *Holy Anorexia* (Chicago, IL: University of Chicago Press)

Bellver, Catherine G., 2001. *Spanish Women Poets of the Twenties and Thirties* (Cranbury, NJ: AUP)

Beltrán, Vicente (ed.), 1976. *La canción tradicional* (Tarragona: Tarraco)

Benegas, Noni, and Jesús Munárriz (eds), 1997. *Ellas tienen la palabra: dos décadas de poesía española* (Madrid: Hiperión)

Benito Goerlich, Daniel, 1998. *El real monasterio de la Santísima Trinidad* (València: Consell Valencià de Cultura)

Benito Goerlich, Daniel, and Albert Hauf (eds), 1992. *Speculum animae*, 2 vols (Madrid: Edilán)

Bentley, Bernard P. E., 2008. *A Companion to Spanish Cinema*, CT, A266 (Woodbridge: Tamesis)

Beresford, Andrew M., 2001. '"Una oraçión, señora, que le dixeron que sabías, de Sancta Polonia para el dolor de las muelas": *Celestina* and the Legend of St Apollonia', *BHS*, 78: 39–57

——, 2007a. *The Legend of Saint Agnes in Medieval Castilian Literature*, PMHRS, 59 (London: Dept of Hispanic Studies, QMUL)

——, 2007b. *The Legends of the Holy Harlots: Thaïs and Pelagia in Medieval Spanish Literature*, CT, A238 (Woodbridge: Tamesis)

——, 2010. *The Severed Breast: The Legends of Saints Agatha and Lucy in Medieval Castilian Literature* (Newark, DE: Juan de la Cuesta)

Berg Sobré, Judith, 1979. 'Eiximenis, Isabel de Villena and Some Fifteenth-Century Illustrations of Their Works', in *Estudis de llengua, literatura i cultura catalanes: actes del primer Col.loqui d'Estudis Catalans a Nord-Amèrica, Urbana, 30 de març – 1 de abril de 1978*, ed. Albert Porqueras Mayo, Spurgeon Baldwin, and Jaume Martí-Olivella (Barcelona: Publicacions de l'Abadia de Montserrat), pp. 303–13

Berger, John, 1972. *Ways of Seeing* (London: BBC / Penguin)

Blanco, Alda, 1991. 'Las voces perdidas: silencio y recuerdo en *Memoria de la Melancolía* de María Teresa León', *Anthropos*, 125: 45–49

——, 1995. 'Gender and National Identity: The Novel in Nineteenth-Century Spanish Literary History', in *Culture and Gender in Nineteenth-Century Spain*, ed. Lou Charnon-Deutsch and Jo Labanyi (Oxford: Clarendon Press), pp. 120–36

——, 1998. 'Escritora, feminidad y escritura en la España de medio siglo', in *La literatura escrita por mujer (desde el s. XIX hasta la actualidad)*, Zavala et al. 1993–2000: v, 9–38

——, 2001. *Escritoras virtuosas: narradoras de la domesticidad en la España isabelina* (Granada: Universidad)

Bleiberg, Germán, Maureen Ihrie, and Janet Pérez (eds), 1993. *Dictionary of the Literature of the Iberian Peninsula*, 2 vols (Westport, CT: Greenwood Press)

Bloch, R. Howard, 1991. *Medieval Misogyny and the Invention of Western Romantic Love* (Chicago, IL: Chicago UP)

Blom, Ida, 1991. 'Global Women's History: Organizing Principles and Cross-Cultural Understandings', in *Writing Women's History: International Perspectives*, ed. Karen Offen, Ruth Roach Pierson, and Jane Rendall (Bloomington: Indiana UP), pp. 135–49

Bluestine, Carolyn, 1978. 'The Role of Women in *the Poema de Mio Cid*', *Romance Notes*, 18: 404–9

———, 1986. 'Traitors, Vows and Temptresses in the Medieval Spanish Epic', *Romance Quarterly*, 33: 53–61
Bobes Naves, María del Carmen, 1991. 'Sintaxis narrativa y valor semántico en el exemplo XXVII de *El Conde Lucanor*', in her *Comentario semiológico de textos narratives* (Oviedo: Universidad), pp. 85–100
Bollaín, Icíar, 1998. 'Cine con tetas', in Heredero 1998: 51–2
Bolufer, Mónica, 1998. *Mujeres e Ilustración: la construcción de la feminidad en la España del siglo XVIII* (València: Institució Alfons el Magnànim)
———, 2000. 'Galerías de "mujeres ilustres", o el sinuoso camino de la excepción a la norma cotidiana (ss. XV-XVIII)', *Hispania*, 60/1, no. 204: 181–224
———, 2002. 'Pedagogía y moral en el Siglo de las Luces: las escritoras francesas y su recepción en España', *Revista de Historia Moderna: Anales de la Universidad de Alicante*, 20: 251–91
———, 2003. 'Traducción y creación en la actividad intelectual de las ilustradas españolas', in *Frasquita Larrea y Aherán: europeas y españolas entre la Ilustración y el Romanticismo*, ed. María José de la Pascua and Gloria Espigado (Cádiz: Universidad), pp.137–53
———, 2008. *La vida y la escritura en el siglo XVIII: Inés Joyes, 'Apología de las mujeres'* (València: Universitat)
———, 2009. 'Between Tradition and Modernity: Women of Letters in Eighteenth-Century Spain', in *Eve's Enlightenment: Women's Experience in Spain and Spanish America, 1726–1839*, ed. Catherine Jaffe and Elizabeth F. Lewis (Baton Rouge: Louisiana State UP), pp. 17–32
———, 2010. 'Translation and Intellectual Reflection in the Works of Enlightened Spanish Women: Inés Joyes (1731–1808)', in *Women Writing Back/Writing Women Back: Transnational Perspectives from the Late Middle Ages to the Dawn of the Modern Era*, vol. 16 of *Intersections: Interdisciplinary Studies in Early Modern Culture*, ed. Anke Gilleir, Alicia C. Montoya, and Suzan van Dijk (Brill: Leiden-Boston), pp. 327–45
Bordonada, Ángela Ena (ed.), 1990. *Novelas breves de escritoras españolas 1900–36* (Madrid: Castalia / Instituto de la Mujer)
Bourdieu, Pierre, 1984. *Distinction: A Social Critique of the Judgement of Taste*, trans. Richard Nice (London: Routledge & Kegan Paul)
Bourdieu, Pierre, Alain Darbel, and Dominique Schnapper, 1990. *The Love of Art: European Art Museums and Their Public*, trans. Caroline Beattie and Nick Merriman (Stanford, CA: Stanford UP)
Bowra, C. M., 1952. *Heroic Poetry* (London: Macmillan)
Boyd, Carolyn, 1997. *Historia Patria: Politics, History, and National Identity in Spain, 1875–1975* (Princeton, NJ: Princeton UP)
Braidotti, Rosi, 1994. *Nomadic Subjects : Embodiment and Sexual Difference in Contemporary Feminist Theory* (New York: Columbia UP)
———, 1996. 'Cyberfeminism with a difference', *New Formations*, 29: 9–25
Bratsch-Prince, Dawn, and Montserrat Piera (eds), 2003. 'Critical Cluster: Bringing Iberian Women Writers into the Canon', *La Corónica*, 32: 1–186
Bronfen, Elisabeth, 1992. *Over Her Dead Body: Death, Femininity and the Aesthetic* (Manchester: Manchester UP)

Brooke, Xanthe, 1997. 'Josefa d'Ayala de Óbidos', in *Gaze* 1997: I, 201–03
——, and Peter Cherry, 2001. *Murillo: Scenes of Childhood* (London: Merrell)
Brooksbank Jones, Anny, 1994. 'Feminisms in Contemporary Spain', *Journal of the Association for Contemporary Iberian Studies*. 7.2: 60–5
——, 1997. *Women in Contemporary Spain* (Manchester: Manchester UP)
Brown, Joan L. (ed.), 1991. *Women Writers of Contemporary Spain: Exiles in the Homeland* (Newark: University of Delaware Press)
Brown, Jonathan, 1978. *Images and Ideas in Seventeenth-Century Spanish Painting* (Princeton, NJ: Princeton UP)
——, 2004. 'La monarquía española y el retrato de aparato de 1500 a 1800', in *El Retrato* (Madrid: Fundación Amigos del Prado; Barcelona: Galaxia Gutenberg), pp. 127–44
——, and Robert Engass, 1992. *Italian and Spanish Art 1600–1750: Sources and Documents* (Evaston, IL: Northwestern UP)
Brown, Kenneth, 1987. 'Context i text del *Vexamen* de Francesc Fontanella', *Llengua i Literatura Catalanes*, 2: 172–252
Brown, Robert D. (ed.), 1987. *Lucretius on Love and Sex: A Commentary on 'De rerum natura', IV.1030–1287* (Leiden: Brill)
Brownlee, Marina, 2000. *The Cultural Labyrinth of María de Zayas* (Philadelphia: University of Pennsylvania Press)
Bruno, Giuliana, 2002. *Atlas of Emotion: Journeys in Art, Architecture and Film* (London: Verso)
Bryson, Norman, 1983. *Vision and Painting: The Logic of the Gaze* (London: Macmillan)
—— (ed.), 1988. *Calligram: Essays in New Art History from France* (Cambridge: CUP)
Buenaventura, Ramón, 1985. *Las diosas blancas: antología de la joven poesía española escrita por mujeres* (Madrid: Hiperión)
Bultman, Dana, 2007. *Heretical Mixtures: Feminine and Poetic Opposition to Matter-Spirit Dualism in Spain, 1531–1631*, Albatros-Hispanófila Siglo XXI, 64 (Valencia: Albatros)
Burgos, Carmen de, 1904a. *El divorcio en España* (Madrid: viuda de M. Romero)
——, 1904b. 'Prólogo' to her translation of P. J Moebius, *La inferioridad mental de la mujer* (Valencia: Sempere)
——, 1912. *Influencias recíprocas entre la mujer y la literatura* (Logroño: La Rioja)
——, 1921. *El Artículo 438: Novela* (Madrid: Prensa Gráfica)
——, 1927. *La mujer moderna y sus derechos* (Valencia: Sempere)
Burgos, Elvira, 2008. *Qué cuenta como una vida: la pregunta por la libertad en Judith Butler* (Madrid: Ediciones Antonio Machado)
Butler, Judith, 1990. *Gender Trouble: Feminism and the Subversion of Identity* (London: Routledge)
Buxton, Sarah, 2008. 'A Theory of Narrative Reflection: The Legend of Saint Christopher in Medieval Spanish', in *Reflections: New Directions in Modern Languages and Cultures*, ed. Sarah Buxton et al. (Cambridge: Cambridge Scholars), pp. 17–28

Bynum, Caroline Walker, 1987. *Holy Feast and Holy Fast: The Religious Significance of Food to Medieval Women*, The New Historicism: Studies in Cultural Poetics, 1 (Berkeley: University of California Press)
Caballé, Anna, 1995. *Narcisos de tinta: ensayo sobre la literatura autobiográfica en lengua castellana (siglos XIX y XX)* (Málaga: Megazul)
Cabo Aseguinolaza, Fernando, 1989. 'La perspectiva masculina en la lírica tradicional', *Actas del I Congreso de la AHLM* (Barcelona: PPU), pp. 225–30
Cabrera y Heredia, Dolores, 1850. *Las violetas, poesías* (Madrid: La Reforma)
Cadden, Joan, 1993. *Meanings of Sex Difference in the Middle Ages: Medicine, Science, and Culture* (Cambridge: CUP)
Caldin, Tom, 2007. 'Women and the Limits of Patriarchy', in Poor and Schulman 2007, pp. 91–114
Calinescu, Matei,1987. *Five Faces of Modernity* (Durham, NC: Duke UP)
Calvo Serraller, Francisco (ed.), 1991. *Teoría de la pintura del Siglo de Oro* (Madrid: Cátedra)
Camí-Vela, María Antonia, 2000. 'Flores de otro mundo: una mirada negociadora', in *Cine-Lit 2000: Essays on Hispanic Film and Fiction*, ed. George Caballo-Castellet, Jaume Martí-Olivella, and Guy H. Wood (Portland, OR: Cine-Lit Publications)
——, 2001. *Mujeres detrás de la cámara: entrevistas con cineastas españolas de la década de los 90* (Madrid: Ocho y Medio)
——, 2005. *Mujeres detrás de la cámara: entrevistas con cineastas españolas 1990–2004*, (Madrid: Ocho y Medio)
Campo-Alange, María, [1956] 1964. *Mi niñez y su mundo* (Madrid: Revista de Occidente)
Campoamor, Clara, 1931. 'Discurso en el parlamento español, 1 octubre 1931', <http://www.marxists.org/espanol/tematica/mujer/autores/campoamor/1931/oct01.htm> (accessed 27 November 2008)
——, [1936] 1981. *Mi pecado mortal: el voto femenino y yo*, ed. Concha Fagoaga and Paloma Saavedra (Barcelona: Lasal)
——, 1937. *La Révolution espagnole vue par une républicaine* (Paris: Plon)
Camporesi, Piero, 1991. *Fear of Hell: Images of Damnation and Salvation in Early Modern Europe*, trans. Lucinda Byatt (Cambridge: Polity)
Camporesi Lami, Valeria, and Eva Parrondo Coppel, 2002. 'Cine y mujeres: (re)visiones feministas', *Secuencias: Revista de Historia del Cine*, 15: 4–6
Camps, Victoria, 1998. *El siglo de las mujeres* (Madrid: Cátedra)
Cañadas, Ivan, 2005. *Public Theater in Golden Age Madrid and Tudor-Stuart London: Class, Gender and Festive Community* (Aldershot: Ashgate)
Cañas, Jesús (ed.), 2003. *Libro de Alexandre*, LH, 280 (Madrid: Cátedra)
Cantavella, Rosanna,1986. 'Isabel de Villena, la nostra Christine de Pizan', *Encontre d'Escriptors del Mediterrani*, 2: 80–6
——, 1987. 'El debat pro i antifeminista a la literatura catalana medieval', unpublished doctoral thesis, Universitat de València
——, 1990. 'Medieval Catalan Mary Magdalen Narratives', in Connolly et al. 1990: 27–36

——, 1992. *Els cards i el llir: una lectura de l' 'Espill' de Jaume Roig* (Barcelona: Quaderns Crema)

——, 2000. 'Isabel de Villena', in *Breve historia feminista de la literatura española (en lengua catalana, gallega y vasca)*, Zavala et al. 1993–2000: VI, 40–50

Capdevila-Argüelles, Nuria, 2002. *Challenging Gender and Genre in the Literary Text: The Works of Nuria Amat* (New Orleans, LA: UP of the South)

Capel Martínez, Rosa María, 1982. *El trabajo y la educación de la mujer en España (1900–1930)* (Madrid: Ministerio de Cultura / Instituto de la Mujer)

——, 1986. 'La apertura del horizonte cultural femenino: Fernando de Castro y los Congresos Pedagógicos del siglo XIX', in Durán and Capel 1986: 113–45

——, 1992. *El sufragio femenino en la Segunda República española* (Madrid: Horas y Horas)

——, 2004. *Mujeres para la historia: figuras destacadas del primer feminismo* (Madrid: Abada)

Caro Mallén de Soto, Ana, 1993a. *El conde Partinuplés*, ed. Lola Luna (Kassel: Reichenberger)

——, 1993b. *Valor, agravio y mujer*, ed. Lola Luna, Biblioteca de Escritoras, 39 (Madrid: Castalia / Instituto de la Mujer)

Carrera, Elena, 2005. *Teresa of Avila's Autobiography: Authority, Power and the Self in Mid-Sixteenth-Century* Spain (Oxford: Legenda)

Carrión, María Mercedes, 1999. 'Portrait of a Lady: Marriage, Postponement, and Representation in Ana Caro's *El Conde Partinuplés*', *MLN*, 114: 241–68

Cartagena, Teresa de, 1967. *Arboleda de los enfermos. Admiración operum Dey*, ed. Lewis J. Hutton (Madrid: RAE)

Casamartina i Parassols, Josep (ed.), 2003. *Ángeles Santos: un mundo insólito en Valladolid* (exhibition catalogue) (Herreriano, Valladolid: Museo Patio de Arte Contemporáneo Español, Ayuntamiento de Valladolid / Residencia de Estudiantes, El Norte de Castilla)

Castaños, María Clemencia [pseudonym], 1884. *Bases precisas para la educación de la mujer*; repr. in microfiche, Simón Palmer 1992

Castells, Ada, 2008. 'Made in "Mercè Rodoreda"', *Avui* (3 octubre), p. 40

Castiglione, Baldesar [1528] 1976. *The Book of the Courtier*, ed. and trans. George Bull (Harmondsworth: Penguin)

Castilla Xarava, María Jacoba: see Genlis 1801

Castillo Gómez, Antonio (ed.), 2003. *Libro y lectura en la Península Ibérica y América (siglos XIII-XVIII)* (Salamanca: Junta de Castilla y León)

Castro, Rosalía de, [1866] 1996. 'Las literatas' / 'Bluestockings', trans. Mary Ellen Fieweger in Kaminsky 1996: 471–7

Castro Lingl, Vera, 1998. '*La dama y el pastor* and the Ballads of the *Cancionero general*: The Portrayal of the Experienced Woman', in *'Cancionero' Studies in Honour of Ian Macpherson*, ed. Alan Deyermond, PMHRS, 11 (London: Dept of Hispanic Studies, QMW), pp.133–46

——, 1999. 'El papel de la mujer en las Mocedades de Rodrigo', in *Las Mocedades de Rodrigo: estudios críticos, manuscrito y edición*, ed. Matthew

Bailey and Fátima Alfonso Pinto (London: King's College London CLAMS), pp. 69–88
Catarella, Teresa, 1990. 'Feminine Historicizing in the *Romancero novelesco*', *BHS*, 67: 331–43
Cátedra, Pedro, and Anastasio Rojo. 2004. *Bibliotecas y lecturas de mujeres: siglo XVI*, Serie Maior, 2 (Salamanca: Instituto de Historia del Libro y de la Lectura)
Catena, Elena, 1986. 'El episodio de la reina de las amazonas en el *Libro de Alexandre*', in *Teoría del discurso poético: Actes du Ve Colloque du Séminaire d'Etudes Littéraires*, Travaux de l'Université de Toulouse-Le-Mirail, Série A, 37 (Toulouse: Université de Toulouse-Le-Mirail), pp. 221–6
Cecilla, María Ángeles, 1998. 'Dramaturgas del Siglo de Oro', in *Las mujeres en la sociedad del Siglo de Oro: ficción teatral y realidad histórica. Actas del II Coloquio del Aula-Biblioteca 'Mira de Amescua' celebrado en Granada-Úbeda del 7 al 9 de marzo de 1997, y cuatro estudios clásicos sobre el tema*, ed. Juan Antonio Martínez Berbel and Roberto Castilla Pérez (Granada: Universidad), pp.185–95
Cerezo, Alicia, 2008. 'Ellas se fugan del museo: la narrativa femenina frente a la imagen de la mujer en publicaciones ilustradas españolas del fin de siglo', unpublished doctoral thesis, University of Illinois, Urbana-Champaign
Certeau, Michel de, 1992. *The Mystic Fable, 1: The Sixteenth and Seventeenth Centuries*, trans. Michael B. Smith (Chicago, IL: Chicago UP)
Chacel, Rosa, 1928. 'Chinina-Migone', *Revista de Occidente*, 19, no. 55: 79–89
——, 1971. *La confesión* (Barcelona: Edhasa)
——, 1972. *Desde el amanecer* (Madrid: *Revista de Occidente*)
——, 1980. *Timoteo Pérez Rubio y sus retratos del jardín* (Madrid: Cátedra)
——, 1982. *Alcancía (ida). Alcancía (vuelta)*, 2 vols (Barcelona: Seix Barral)
Charnon-Deutsch, Lou, 1990. *Gender and Representation: Women in Nineteenth-Century Spanish Realist Fiction* (Philadelphia, PA: John Benjamins)
——, 1994. *Narratives of Desire: Nineteenth-Century Spanish Fiction by Women* (University Park, PA: Penn State UP)
——, 2000. *Fictions of the Feminine in the Nineteenth-Century Spanish Press* (University Park, PA: Penn State UP)
——, 2008. *Hold That Pose: Visual Culture in the Nineteenth-Century Spanish Press* (University Park, PA: Penn State UP)
Charnon-Deutsch, Lou, and Jo Labanyi, 1995. *Culture and Gender in Nineteenth-Century Spain* (Oxford: OUP)
Cherner, Matilde [pseudonym Rafael Luna], 1878. *María Magdalena (estudio social)*; repr. in microfiche, Simón Palmer 1992
Chicote, Gloria Beatriz, 1996. 'Jimena, de la épica al romancero: definición del personaje y convenciones genéricas', in *Caballeros, monjas y maestros en la Edad Media (Actas de las V Jornadas Medievales)*, ed. Lillian von del Walde, Concepción Company, and Aurelio González, Publicaciones de *Medievalia*, 13 (México: UNAM / Colegio de México), pp. 75–86
Childs, Sarah, 2008. *Women and British Party Politics: Descriptive, Substantive, and Symbolic Representation* (New York: Routledge)

Chodorov, Nancy, 1978. *The Reproduction of Mothering* (Berkeley: University of California Press)
Chown, Linda E., 1983, 'American Critics and Spanish Women Novelists 1942–1980', *Signs*, 9.1: 91–107
Ciplijauskaité, Biruté, 1986. 'La novela femenina como autobiografía', *Actas del VIII congreso de la AIH*, ed. David Rossoff (Madrid: Istmo), pp. 397–405
——, 1988. *La novela femenina contemporánea (1970–1985): hacia una tipología de la narración en primera persona* (Barcelona: Anthropos)
Cirlor, Victoria, and Blanca Garí, 1999. *La mirada interior: escritoras místicas y visionarias en la Edad Media* (Barcelona: Martínez Roca)
Cixous, Hélène, 1989. 'Castration or Decapitation?', in *Contemporary Literary Criticism: Literary and Cultural Studies*, ed. Robert Con Davis and Ronald Schleifer, 2nd edn (London: Longman), pp. 479–91; trans. 1976, with authorial revisions, by Annette Kuhn from 'Le Sexe ou la tête?', *Les Cahiers du GRIF*, 13: 5–15
Clancy, Patricia A., 1982. 'A French Writer and Educator in England: Mme Le Prince de Beaumont', *Studies on Voltaire and the Eighteenth Century*, 201: 195–208
Claret, Antonio María, ed., [1847] 1859. *Nuevo manojito de flores o sea recopilación de doctrinas para los confesores* (Barcelona: Librería Religiosa)
Clover, Carol J., 1992. *Men, Women and Chainsaws: Gender in the Modern Horror Film* (London: BFI)
Coates, Geraldine, 2008. 'Endings Lost and Found in the *Poema de Fernán González*', *Hispanic Research Journal*, 9: 203–17
——, 2009. *Treacherous Foundations: Betrayal and Collective Identity in Early Spanish Epic, Chronicle, and Drama*, CT, A281(Woodbridge: Tamesis)
Cohen, Judith R., 2002. '*Ca no soe joglaresa*: Women and Music in Medieval Spain's Three Cultures', in *Medieval Women's Song: Cross-Cultural Approaches*, ed. Anne L. Klinck and Ann Marie Rasmussen (Philadelphia: University of Pennsylvania Press), pp. 66–80
Collins, Jackie, 2005. '*Yoyes*: A Space (Place) of One's Own', in *New Studies in European Cinema*, 2, ed. Wendy Everett and Axel Goodbody (Oxford: Peter Lang), pp. 257–71
Comella, Beatriz (ed.), 2002. *Ernestina de Champourcín, del exilio a Dios* (Madrid: Rialp)
Condé, Lisa. P., and S. Hart (eds), 1991. *Feminist Readings on Spanish and Latin-American Literature* (Lampeter: Edwin Mellen)
Connolly, Jane E., Alan Deyermond, and Brian Dutton (eds), 1990. *Saints and Their Authors: Studies in Medieval Hispanic Hagiography in Honor of John K. Walsh* (Madison: HSMS)
Constable, Olivia Remie (ed.), and Kathleen Lacey (trans.), 1997. 'Memoirs of a Castilian Noblewoman: Leonor López de Córdoba, *Memorias*', in *Medieval Iberia: Readings from Christian, Muslim, and Jewish Sources* (Philadelphia: University of Pennsylvania Press), pp. 294–301
Coronado, Carolina, 1846. 'Al señor director', *El Defensor del Bello Sexo*, 8 febrero, p. 97

——, 1993. *Obra poética*, I, ed. Gregorio Torres Nebrera (Mérida: Editorial Regional de Extremadura)

Cortés, Josepa, and Vicent Pons, 1993. 'La biblioteca jurídica de Jaume d'Eixarc (1479)', *Saitabi*, 43: 182–94

Cortés Timoner, María del Mar, 2004. *Teresa de Cartagena, primera escritora mística en lengua castellana* (Málaga: Universidad)

Cotarelo y Mori, Emilio, 1904. *Bibliografía de las controversias sobre la licitud del teatro en España* (Madrid: Revista de Archivos, Bibliotecas y Museos)

Cotoner, Luisa (ed.), 2000. *El espejo y la máscara: veinticinco años de ficción narrativa en la obra de Carme Riera / El mirall i la màscara: vint-i-cinc anys de ficció narrativa en l'obra de Carme Riera* (Barcelona: Destino)

Courcelles, Dominique de, 2000. 'En Mémoire d'elle et en mémoire du sang: la *Vita Christi* de sor Isabel de Villena, abbesse des clarisses de Valence au XVe siècle', *Le Journal de la Renaissance*, 1: 103–20

——, 2001. 'Traduire et citer les Évangiles en Catalogne à la fin du XVe siècle: quelques enjeux de la traduction et de la citation dans la *Vita Christi* de sor Isabel de Villena', in *Essays on Medieval Translation in the Iberian Peninsula*, ed. Tomàs Martínez and Roxana Recio (Castelló: Universitat Jaume I; Omaha, NE: Creighton University), pp. 173–90

Crameri, Kathryn, 2000. *Language, the Novelist and National Identity in Post-Franco Catalonia* (Oxford: Legenda)

——, 2008. *Catalonia: National Identity and Cultural Policy, 1980–2003* (Cardiff: University of Wales Press)

Creed, Barbara, 1993. *The Monstrous-Feminine: Film, Feminism, Psychoanalysis* (New York: Routledge)

Cruz, Anne J., and Mary Elizabeth Perry (eds), 1992. *Culture and Control in Counter-Reformation Spain* (Minneapolis: University of Minnesota Press)

Cruz, Jacqueline, 2005. 'Amores que matan: Dulce Chacón, Icíar Bollaín y la violencia de género', *Letras Hispanas*, 2.1 (Spring): 67–81, http://letrashispanas.unlv.edu/Vol2/JacquelineCruz.pdf (accessed 6 January 2009)

Cuevas, Tomasa, 1985. *Cárcel de mujeres* (Barcelona: Sirocco)

——, 1986. *Mujeres de la Resistencia* (Barcelona: Sirocco)

Culleton, Colleen, 2002. 'Daedalus's Wings: The Effect of Temporal Distance in *La plaça del Diamant*', *Catalan Review*, 16.1–2: 103–19

Cummins, John G. (ed.), 1977. *The Spanish Traditional Lyric* (Oxford: Pergamon)

Curtius, Ernst Robert, [1953] 1990. *European Literature and the Latin Middle Ages*, trans. Willard R. Trask, Bollingen Series, 36 (Princeton, NJ: Princeton UP)

Danckert, Werner, 1976. *Symbol, Metapher, Allegorie im Lied der Völker*, ed. Hannelore Vogel, 4 vols (Bonn: Verlag für Systematische Musikwissenchaft)

Davies, Catherine, 1991. 'Feminist Writers in Spain since 1900: from Political Strategy to Personal Inquiry', *Textual Liberation: European Feminist Writing in the Twentieth Century*, ed. Helena Forsås-Scott (London: Routledge)

——, 1994. *Contemporary Feminist Fiction in Spain: The Work of Montserrat Roig and Rosa Montero* (Oxford: Berg)

——, 1998. *Spanish Women's Writing, 1849–1996* (London: The Athlone Press)

Davis, Stuart, 2000. 'The Hispanic Canon', unpublished M.Phil. thesis, University of Birmingham
De Lauretis, Teresa, 1985. 'Oedipus Interruptus', *Wide-Angle*, 7.1–2: 34–40
——, 1987. *Technologies of Gender: Essays on Theory, Film, and Fiction* (Bloomington: Indiana UP)
——, 1988. 'Sexual Indifference and Lesbian Representation, *Theatre Journal*, 40.2: 155–77
De Lope, Monique, 1985. 'Le Gué et l'aquéduc: l'eau et les discours du passage dans le *Libro de Buen Amor*', in *L'Eau au Moyen Âge*, Sénéfiance, 15 (Aix-en-Provence: Université de Provence), pp. 249–58
Del Valle, Teresa, et al., 1985. *Mujer vasca: imagen y realidad* (Barcelona: Anthropos)
Delgado, María M., 2007. 'Beyond the Muse: The Spanish Actress as Collaborator', in *The Cambridge Companion to the Actress*, ed. Maggie B. Gale and John Stokes (Cambridge: CUP), pp. 272–90
Delgrás, Leopoldo, 1875. *El amigo de las niñas* (Madrid: Librería Hernando)
Deveny, Thomas G., 1999. *Contemporary Spanish Film from Fiction: Literary Tales on Screen* (Lanham, MD: The Scarecrow Press)
Dever, Carolyn, 1998. *Death and the Mother from Dickens to Freud* (Cambridge: CUP)
Devoto, Daniel, 1972. *Introducción al estudio de don Juan Manuel y en particular de 'El Conde Lucanor': una bibliografía* (Madrid: Castalia)
Deyermond, Alan, 1965. '*Mester es sen pecado*', *Romanische Forschungen*, 77: 111–16
——, [1978] 1983. 'Spain's First Women Writers', in Miller 1983: 27–52
——, 1979–80. 'Pero Meogo's Stags and Fountains: Symbol and Anecdote in the Traditional Lyric', *Romance Philology*, 33: 265–83
——, 1988. 'La sexualidad en la épica medieval española', *NRFH*, 36: 767–86
——, 1990. 'Uses of the Bible in the *Poema de Fernán González*', in *Cultures in Contact in Medieval Spain: Historical and Literary Essays Presented to L. P. Harvey*, ed. David Hook and Barry Taylor, King's College London Medieval Studies, 3 (London: King's College London CLAMS), pp. 47–60
——, 1995. 'Las autoras medievales castellanas a la luz de las últimas investigaciones', in *Medioevo y literatura: actas del V Congreso de la AHLM*, ed. Juan Paredes, 4 vols (Granada: Universidad), I, pp. 31–52
——, 1996. 'Building a World: Geography and Cosmology in Castilian Literature of the Early Thirteenth Century', *Canadian Review of Comparative Literature*, 23: 141–59
——, and Peter Bly, 1972. 'The Use of *figura* in the *Libro de Alexandre*', *Journal of Medieval and Renaissance Studies*, 2: 151–81
Diego, Estrella de, 1987. *La mujer y la pintura del XIX español* (Madrid: Cátedra)
——, 2007. *Remedios Varo* (Madrid: Fundación Mapfre)
Dillard, Heath, 1984. *Daughters of the Reconquest: Women in Castilian Town Society, 1100–1300* (Cambridge: CUP)
DiMarco, Vicent, 1991. 'The Amazons and the End of the World', in *Discovering New Worlds: Essays on Medieval Exploration and Imagination*, ed. Scott

D. Westrem, Garland Medieval Casebooks, 2, Garland Reference Library of the Humanities, 1436 (New York: Garland), pp. 69–90

Dinshaw, Carolyn, 1999. *Getting Medieval: Sexualities and Communities, Pre- and Postmodern* (Durham, NC: Duke UP)

——, and David Wallace, 2003. *The Cambridge Companion to Medieval Women's Writing* (Cambridge: CUP)

Doane, Mary Ann, 1984. 'The Woman's Film Possession and Address', in *Re-Vision: Essays in Feminist Film Criticism*, ed. Mary Ann Doane, Patricia Mellencamp, and Linda Williams (Frederick, MD: The American Film Institute / University Publications of America)

——, 1989. 'Veiling over Desire: Close-Ups of the Woman', in *Feminism and Psychoanalysis*, ed. Richard Feldstein and Judith Roof (Ithaca, NY: Cornell UP), pp. 105–41

——, 1991. *Femmes fatales: feminism, film theory, psychoanalysis* (New York: Routledge)

Doménech Rico, Fernando (ed.), 1996. *Teatro breve de mujeres (siglos XVII–XX)* (Madrid: ADE)

——, 1997. 'Autoras en el teatro español: siglos XVI–XVIII', in Hormigón 1997: I, 391–604

Domínguez Prieto, César, 1998. '"De aquel pecado que le acusaban a falsedat": reinas injustamente acusadas en los libros de caballerías (Ysonberta, Florençia, la santa Enperatrís y Sevilla)', in *Literatura de caballerías y orígenes de la novela*, ed. Rafael Beltrán (València: Universitat), pp. 159–80

Donahue, Darcy, 1989. 'Writing Lives: Nuns and Confessors as Auto-Biographers in Early Modern Spain', *JHP*, 13: 230–9

Donaire, María Luisa, and Francisco Lafarga (eds), 1991. *Traducción y adaptación cultural, España-Francia* (Oviedo: Universidad)

Donapetry Camacho, María. 1998. *La otra mirada: la mujer y el cine en la cultura española* (Ann Arbor: University of Michigan Press)

——, 2001. *Toda ojos* (Oviedo: Universidad)

Dopico-Black, Georgina, 2001. *Perfect Wives, Other Women: Adultery and Inquisition in Early Modern Spain* (Durham, NC: Duke UP)

Dougherty, Dru, 1993. 'Dramaturgas españolas: presencia y condición en la escena española contemporánea', *Estreno*, 19: 17–20

Dronke, Peter, 1994. *Women Writers of the Middle Ages: A Critical Study of Texts from Perpetua (d. 203) to Marguerite Porete (d. 1310)* (Cambridge: CUP)

Dubreuil-Blondin, Nicole, 1993. 'A Woman's Touch: Towards a Theoretical Status of Painterliness in the Feminist Approach to Representation in Painting', in *ReImagining Women: Representations of Women in Culture*, ed. Shirley Neuman and Glennis Stephenson (Toronto: University of Toronto Press), pp. 145-59

Ducrot, Osvald, and Tzvetan Todorov, 1989. *Diccionario enciclopédico de las ciencias del lenguaje* (México: Siglo Veintiuno)

Dulumeau, Paul, 1978. *La Peur en occident* (Paris: Fayard)

Dupláa, Cristina, 2000. 'Memoria colectiva y *lieux de mémoire* en la España de la Transición', in *Disremembering the Dictatorship: The Politics of Memory in the Spanish Transition to Democracy*, ed. Joan Ramon Resina (Amsterdam: Rodopi)

Durán, María Ángeles, and Rosa María Capel Martínez (eds),1986. *Mujer y sociedad en España, 1700–1975* (Madrid: Ministerio de Trabajo / Instituto de la Mujer)

Dutton, Brian (ed.), 1981. Gonzalo de Berceo, *'El sacrificio de la Misa', 'La vida de Santa Oria', 'El martirio de San Lorenzo': estudio y edición crítica, Obras Completas de Gonzalo de Berceo*, 5, CT, A80 (London: Tamesis)

——, (ed.), 1990–91. *El cancionero del siglo XV, c. 1360–1520*, Biblioteca Española del Siglo XV, Serie Maior 1–7 (Salamanca: Biblioteca Española del Siglo XV / Universidad)

Dyer, Abigail, 2003. 'Seduction by Promise of Marriage: Law, Sex, and Culture', *Sixteenth Century Journal*, 34: 439–55

Earenfight, Theresa, 2005. *Queenship and Political Power in Medieval and Early Modern Spain* (Aldershot: Ashgate)

Earnshaw, Doris, 1988. *The Female Voice in Medieval Romance Lyric* (New York: Peter Lang)

Eguizábal, Raúl, and Elena Santiago Páez, 2002. *Memoria de la seducción: carteles del siglo XIX en la Biblioteca Nacional* (Madrid: Caja de Madrid / Biblioteca Nacional / Ministerio de Educación, Cultura y Deporte)

Elliott, Alison Goddard, 1987. *Roads to Paradise: Reading the Lives of the Early Saints* (Hanover, NH: UP of New England)

Elliott, J. H., 2002. *Imperial Spain 1469–1716* (London: Penguin)

Enders, Victoria Lorée, 1999. 'Problematic Portraits: The Ambiguous Historical Role of the *Sección Femenina* of the Falange', in Enders and Radcliff 1999: 375–98

——, and Pamela Beth Radcliff (eds), 1999. *Constructing Spanish Womanhood: Female Identity in Modern Spain* (Albany: SUNY Press)

England, John, 1977. '"¿Et non el día del lodo?": The Structure of the Short Story in *El Conde Lucanor*', in *Juan Manuel Studies*, ed. Ian Macpherson, CT, A60 (London: Tamesis), pp. 69–86

—— (ed. and trans.), 1987. Don Juan Manuel, *'El Conde Lucanor': A Collection of Medieval Spanish Tales* (Warminster: Aris & Phillips)

——, 1999. '"Los que son muy cuerdos entienden la cosa por algunas sennales": Learning the Lessons of *El Conde Lucanor*', *BHS*, 76: 345–64

Épinay, Louise Tardieu d'Esclavelle, Marquise d', 1797. *Las conversaciones de Emilia, traducidas sobre la quinta edición del francés al castellano por doña Ana Muñoz* (Madrid: Benito Cano)

[1774], 1996. *Les Conversations d'Émilie*, ed. Rosena Davison (Oxford: The Voltaire Foundation)

Etxebarría, Lucía, 2000. *La Eva futura: la letra futura* (Barcelona: Destino)

Evans, Peter, 1999. 'Culture and Cinema, 1975–1996', in *The Cambridge Companion to Modern Spanish Culture*, ed. David T. Gies (Cambridge: CUP), pp. 267–78

Everly, Kathryn A., 2003. *Catalan Women Writers and Artists: Revisionist Views from a Feminist Space* (Lewisburg, PA: Bucknell UP)
Fagoaga, Concha (ed.), 1999. *1898–1998, un siglo avanzando hacia la igualdad de las mujeres* (Madrid: Dirección General de la Mujer)
Falcón, Lidia, 1992. *Mujer y poder político (fundamentos de la crisis de objetivos de ideología del Movimiento Feminista)* (Madrid: Vindicación Feminista)
Feijóo, Benito Jerónimo, [1726] 2004. *Defensa de las mujeres* (Tuxtla Gutiérrez, Chiapas: Universidad Autónoma de Chiapas)
——, [1726–40] 1986. *Teatro crítico universal, o, Discursos varios en todo género de materias, para desengaño de errores comunes*, ed. Giovanni Stiffoni (Madrid: Castalia)
Feldman, Sharon, 2002. 'Catalunya Invisible: Contemporary Theatre in Barcelona', Special Cluster, 'Barcelona', ed. Brad Epps, *Arizona Journal of Hispanic Cultural Studies*, 6: 269–87
——, 2005. 'Sobre l'aparició i la desaparició: el teatre i Barcelona', *Pausa*, 20: 55–66
Felski, Rita, 1989. *Beyond Feminist Aesthetics: Feminist Aesthetics and Social Change* (Cambridge, MA: Harvard UP)
——, 1995. *The Gender of Modernity* (Cambridge: Polity Press)
Fernández, James, 1990. 'La *Vida* de Teresa de Jesús y la salvación del discurso', *MLN*, 105: 283–302
——, 1992. *Apology to Apostrophe: Autobiography and the Rhetoric of Self-Representation in Spain* (Durham, NC: Duke UP)
Fernández Utrera, María Soledad, 2001. *Visiones de estereoscopio*, NCSRLL, 272 (Chapel Hill: University of North Carolina Press)
Fernández y González, Manuel, n.d. *Las buenas y las malas madres*, vol. 2 (Barcelona: Espasa Hermanos)
Ferrán, Ofelia, 2005. '*Memoría de la melancolía* by María Teresa León: The Performativity and Disidentification of Exilic Memories', *Journal of Spanish Cultural Studies*, 6.1: 59–78
——, and Kathleen M. Glenn, 2002. *Women's Narrative and Film in Twentieth-Century Spain: A World of Difference(s)* (New York: Routledge)
Ferrante, Joan M., 1997. *To the Glory of Her Sex: Women's Roles in the Composition of Medieval Texts* (Bloomington: Indiana UP)
Ferrer Valls, Teresa, 2006. 'Decir entre versos: Ángela de Acevedo y la escritura femenina en el Siglo de Oro', in *Ecos silenciados: la mujer en la literatura española (siglos XII al XVIII)*, ed. Susana Gil-Albarellos and Mercedes Rodríguez Pequeño (Segovia: Fundación Instituto Castellano y Leonés de la Lengua), pp. 213–41
Ferreras, Juan Ignacio, 1972. *La novela por entregas, 1840–1900* (Madrid: Taurus)
Filios, Denise K., 2005. *Performing Women in the Middle Ages: Sex, Gender and the Iberian Lyric* (New York: Palgrave Macmillan)
Fink, Bruce, 1995. *The Lacanian Subject: Between Language and Jouissance* (Princeton, NJ: Princeton UP)

——, 2002. 'Knowledge and Jouissance', in Barnard and Fink 2002: 21–45
Flynn, Elizabeth A., and Patrocinio P. Schweickart (eds), 1986. *Gender and Reading: Essays on Readers, Texts, and Contexts* (Baltimore, MD: The Johns Hopkins UP)
Folguera Crespo, Pilar (ed.), 1988. *El feminismo en España: dos siglos de historia* (Madrid: Pablo Iglesias)
——, 1997a. 'Hubo una revolución liberal burgesa para las mujeres? (1808–1868)', in Garrido González 1997: 451–92
——, 1997b. 'Revolución y restauración. La emergencia de los primeros ideales emancipadores (1868–1931)', in Garrido González 1997: 421–49
Folkart, Jessica, 2002. *Angles on Otherness in Post-Franco Spain: The Fiction of Cristina Fernández Cubas* (Lewisburg, PA: Bucknell UP)
Fonquerne, Yves-René, and Alfonso Esteban (eds), 1986. *La condición de la mujer en la Edad Media: actas del coloquio celebrado en la Casa de Velázquez, del 5 al 7 de noviembre de 1984* (Madrid: Universidad Complutense / Casa de Velázquez)
Foucault, Michel, 1961. *Madness and Civilization: A History of Insanity in the Age of Reason* (London: Tavistock)
——, 1978. *Discipline and Punish: The Birth of the Prison*, trans. Alan Sheridan (New York: Pantheon)
——, 2003. 'On the Genealogy of Ethics', in *The Continental Ethics Reader*, ed. Matthew Calarco and Peter Atterton (New York: Routledge), pp.198–206
Foulché-Delbosc, R., and Jaume Massó y Torrents (eds), 1912. *'Cançoner sagrat de vides de sants': segle xv*, 2 vols (Barcelona: Societat Catalana de Bibliòfils)
Fouz-Hernández, Santiago, and Alfredo Martínez-Expósito, 2007. *Live Flesh: The Male Body in Contemporary Spanish Cinema* (London: I. B. Tauris)
Fracchia, Carmen, 2004. '(Lack of) Visual Representation of Black Slaves in Spanish Golden Age Painting', *Journal of Iberian and Latin American Studies (Tesserae)*, 10: 23–34
——, 2007. 'Constructing the Black Slave in Spanish Golden Age Painting', in *Others and utcasts in Early Modern Europe: Picturing the Social Margins*, ed. Tom Nichols (Aldershot: Ashgate), pp. 179–95
Freedberg, David, 1989. *The Power of Images: Studies in the History and Theory of Response* (Chicago, IL: University of Chicago Press)
Freixas, Laura (ed.), 1996. *Madres e hijas* (Barcelona: Anagrama)
——, 2000. *Literatura y mujeres: escritoras, público y crítica en la España actual* (Barcelona: Destino)
——, 2004. 'Mujeres, literatura, autobiografía: la singularidad española, o consideraciones sobre un eclipse', in her *Autobiografía en España: un balance* (Madrid: Visor), pp. 112–18
——, 2007. *Adolescencia en Barcelona hacia 1970* (Barcelona: Destino)
Frenk, Margit, 1971. *Entre folklore y literatura: lírica hispánica antigua* (México: Colegio de México); 2nd edn 1984
——, 1978. *Estudios sobre lírica antigua* (Madrid: Castalia)

——, 1985. *Las jarchas mozárabes y los comienzos de la lírica románica* (México: Colegio de México)

——, [1992] 2006. 'Poesía de la aristocracia y poesía del pueblo en la Edad Media', first published 1992 in *Heterodoxia y ortodoxia medieval: Actas de las Segundas Jornadas Medievales*, ed. Concepción Abellán et al. (México: UNAM), pp. 1–19; repr. in Frenk 2006: 42–57

——, 1993a. *Symbolism in Old Spanish Folk Songs*, The Kate Elder Lecture, 4 (London: Dept of Hispanic Studies, QMW)

——, [1993b] 2006, 'La canción popular femenina en el siglo de Oro', first published 1993 in *Actas del Primer Congreso Anglo-Hispano*, II: *Literatura*, ed. Alan Deyermond and Ralph Penny (Madrid: Castalia), pp. 139–59; repr. in Frenk 2006: 353–72

——, [1994] 2006. 'Lírica tradicional y cultura popular en la Edad Media hispánica', first published 1994, in *Actas del III Congreso de la AHLM*, ed. María Isabel Toro Pascua, 2 vols (Salamanca: Universidad), I, pp. 41–60; repr. in Frenk 2006: 19–41

——, 2003. *Nuevo corpus de la antigua lírica popular hispánica (siglos XV a XVII)* (México: Facultad de Filosofía y Letras, UNAM / Colegio de México / Fondo de Cultura Económica)

——, 2006. *Poesía popular hispánica: 44 estudios* (México: Fondo de Cultura Económica)

Friedman, Susan Stanford, 1998. *Mappings: Feminism and the Cultural Geographies of Encounter* (Princeton, NJ: Princeton UP)

Frings, Theodor, 1949. *Minnesinger und Troubadours* (Berlin: Deutsche Akademie der Wissenschaften, Vorträge und Schriften)

Fuera de Orden: Mujeres de la Vanguardia Española, 1999. (Exhibition catalogue) (Madrid: Fundación Mapfre Vida)

Fuster, Joan, 1968a. 'El món literari de sor Isabel de Villena', in his *Obres completes*, 7 vols (Barcelona: Edicions 62), I, pp. 153–74.

——, 1968b. 'Jaume Roig i sor Isabel de Villena', in his *Obres completes*, 7 vols (Barcelona: Edicions 62), I, pp. 175–210

Gabancho, Patrícia, 1982. *La rateta encara escombra l'escaleta: cop d'ull a l'actual literatura catalana de dona* (Barcelona: Edicions 62)

Gala, Antonio, [1993] 2001. *La pasión turca*, prologue by Carmen Rigalt (Barcelona: Bibliotex)

Galdona Pérez, Rosa I., 2001. *Discurso femenino en la novela española de postguerra: Carmen Laforet, Ana Marìa Matute y Elena Quiroga* (La Laguna, Santa Cruz de Tenerife: Universidad de la Laguna)

Galerstein, Carolyn (ed.), 1986. *Women Writers in Spain: An Annotated Bio-Bibliographical Guide* (Westport, CT: Greenwood Press)

Galiana Chacón, Juan P., 1991. 'La extracción social de las religiosas en la baja Edad Media valenciana', *Revista d'Història Medieval*, 2: 91–109

Galiana y Albaladejo, Adela, 1861. *El hombre y su corazón: descripción sucinta de las épocas de su vida*; repr. in microfiche, Simón Palmer 1992

Gallego Méndez, María Teresa, 1983. *Mujer, falange y franquismo* (Madrid: Taurus)

Gámez Fuentes, María José, 2000. 'Never One without the Other: Empowering Readings of the Mother-Daughter Relationship in Modern Spain', in *Mothers and Daughters: Connection, Empowerment and Transformation*, ed. Andrea O'Reilly and Sharon Abbey (Lanham, MD: Rowman & Littlefield), pp. 47–60

Gangutia Elícegui, Elvira, 1972. 'Poesía griega "de amigo" y poesía arábigo-española', *Emérita*, 40: 329–96

García Balmaseda, Joaquina, 1882. *La mujer sensata (educación de sí misma): consejos útiles para la mujer y leyendas morales*; repr. in microfiche, Simón Palmer 1992

García de León, María Antonia, 1982. *Las élites femeninas españolas* (Madrid: Queimada)

——, 1996. *Sociología de las mujeres españolas* (Madrid: Universidad Complutense)

García Garrosa, María Jesús, 2007. 'La creación literaria femenina en la España del siglo XVIII: un estado de la cuestión', in *Cambio social y ficción literaria en la España de Moratín*, ed. Teresa Nava Rodríguez (Madrid: Universidad Complutense), pp. 203–18

García Herrero, María del Carmen, 1990. *Las mujeres en Zaragoza en el siglo XV*, Cuadernos de Zaragoza, 62, 2 vols (Zaragoza: Ayuntamiento)

García Lorenzo, Luciano, 2000. *Autoras y actrices en la historia del teatro español* (Murcia: Universidad)

García Miranda, Vicenta, 1855. 'Recuerdos y pensamientos', *Flores del valle* (Madrid: Gerónimo Orduña), pp. 146–53

García Olloqui, María Victoria, 2000. *Luisa Roldán, La Roldana: nueva biografía* (Sevilla: Guadalquivir)

García Sempere, Marinela, 2000. 'La tradició y la originalidad en la *Istòria de la Passió* de Bernat Fenollar y Pere Martines, y en la *Vita Christi* de Isabel de Villena', *Revista de Lenguas y Literaturas Catalana, Gallega y Vasca*, 6: 47–68

—— (ed.), 2002. *'Lo Passi en cobles' (1493): estudi i edició* (Alacant: IIFV; Barcelona: Publicacions de l'Abadia de Montserrat)

Garrido González, Elisa (ed.), 1997. *Historia de las mujeres en España* (Madrid: Síntesis)

Gascón, Christopher D., 2006. *The Woman Saint in Spanish Golden Age Drama* (Lewisburg, PA: Bucknell UP)

Gaylord Randel, Mary, 1982. 'Grammar of Femininity', *Revista Interamericana*, 12: 115–24

Gaze, Delia (ed.), 1997. *Dictionary of Women Artists*, 2 vols (London and Chicago: Fitzroy Dearborn)

Genlis, Stéphanie Félicité Ducrest, Comtesse de, 1785. *Adela y Teodoro, o Cartas sobre la educación*, trans. Bernardo María de Calzada [*Adèle et Théodore*] (Madrid: Ibarra)

——, 1788. *Las veladas de la quinta, o Novelas e historias morales sumamente útiles para que las madres de familia [...] puedan instruir a sus hijos,* trans. Fernando de Guillemán [*Les Veillées du château*] (Madrid: González)

——, 1792. *Los anales de la virtud*, trans. Bernardo María de Calzada [*Les Annales de la vertu*] (Madrid: Imprenta Real)

——, 1801. *Adelaida o el triunfo del amor*, trans. M[aría] J[acoba]C[astilla] X[arava] (Madrid: Pantaleón Aznar)

Geybels, Hans, 2008. *Cognitio Dei experimentalis: A Theological Genealogy of Christian Religious Experience*, Bibliotheca Ephemeridum Theologicarum Lovaniensium Series, 209 (Leuven: Peeters)

Giesen, Bernhard, 1994. *Triumph and Trauma*, The Yale Cultural Sociology Series, 1 (London: Paradigm)

Gilligan, Carol, 1982. *In a Different Voice* (Cambridge, MA: Harvard UP)

Gilmore, Leigh, 1994. *Autobiographics: A Feminist Theory of Women's Self-Representation* (Ithaca, NY: Cornell UP)

Gilmour, Nicola, 2006. 'Turkish Delight: Antonio Gala's *La pasión turca* as a Vision of Spain's Contested Islamic Heritage', *Arizona Journal of Hispanic Cultural Studies*, 10.1: 77–94

Gimeno de Flaquer, Concepción, 1877. *La mujer española: estudios acerca de su educación y sus facultades intelectuales* (Madrid: Imprenta y Librería de Miguel Guijarro); repr. in microfiche in Simón Palmer 1992

——, 1886. 'Las heroínas catalanas', in Sáez de Melgar 1886: 232–44

——, 1900. *Evangelios de la mujer*; repr. in microfiche in Simón Palmer 1992

Giorgio, Adalgisa, ed., 2002a. *Writing Mothers and Daughters: Renegotiating the Mother in Western European Narratives by Women* (New York: Berghahn Books)

Giorgio, Adalgisa, 2002b. 'Writing the Mother-Daughter Relationship: Psychoanalysis, Culture, and Literary Criticism', in Giorgio 2002a, pp. 11–39

Glendinning, Nigel, 1996. *Painting and Poetry in Contemporary Spanish Women Writers*, The Kate Elder Lecture, 5 (London: Dept. of Hispanic Studies, QMW)

Glenn, Kathleen M., and Mercedes Mazquiarán de Rodríguez, 1998. *Spanish Women Writers and the Essay: Gender, Politics and the Self* (Columbia: University of Missouri Press)

Glenn, Kathleen M., Mirella Servodidio, and Mary S. Vázquez (eds), 1999. *Moveable Margins: The Narrative Art of Carme Riera* (London: AUP)

Gold, Hazel, 1988. 'A Tomb with a View: The Museum in Galdós' *Novelas contemporáneas*', *MLN*, 103.2: 312–34

Goldberg, Harriet, ed., 1974. Fray Martín de Córdoba, *'Jardín de nobles donzellas': A Critical Edition and Study*, NCSRLL, 137 (Chapel Hill: University of North Carolina Press)

——, 1983. 'Sexual Humor in Medieval Misogynist *Exempla*', in Miller 1983, pp. 67–83

Gómez Acuña, Beatriz, 2002. 'The Feminine Voice in the *Romancero*'s Modern Oral Tradition: Gender Differences in the Recitation of the Ballad *La bastarda y el Segado*', *Folklore*, 113.2: 183–96

Gómez-Bravo, Ana M., 2003. '"A huma senhora que lhe disse": sobre la práctica social de la autoría y la noción de texto en el *Cancioneiro geral* de Resende y la lírica cancioneril ibérica', *La Corónica*, 32.1: 43–64

Gómez de Castro, Álvar, [1565] 1984. *De las hazañas de Francisco Jiménez de Cisneros* [trans. of *De rebus gestis a Francisco Ximeno Cisnerio, Archiepiscopo Toletano*], ed. and trans. José Oroz Reta (Madrid: Fundación Universitaria Española)

Gómez de la Serna, Ramón, 1930. 'La genial pintora Ángeles Santos encerrada en un sanatorio', *La Gaceta Literaria*, 79 (1 de abril): 1–2

Gómez Redondo, Fernando (ed.), 1996. '*Oración a Santa María Magdalena*', in his *Poesía española*, I: *Edad Media: juglaría, clerecía y romancero*, Páginas de Biblioteca Clásica, 1 (Barcelona: Crítica), pp. 585–90

——, 2002. *Historia de la prosa medieval castellana*, III, *Los orígenes del humanismo: el marco cultural de Enrique III y Juan II* (Madrid: Cátedra)

González Vázquez, Marta, 2000. *Las mujeres de la Edad Media y el camino de Santiago* (Santiago de Compostela: Xunta de Galicia)

Gorfkle, Laura, 1996. 'Re-Staging Femininity in Ana Caro's *Valor, agravio y mujer*', *BCom*, 48: 25–36

——, 1998. 'Female Communities, Female Friendships and Social Control in María de Zayas's *La traición en la amistad*: A Historical Perspective', *Romance Languages Annual*, 10: 615–20

Gornall, John, 1986. '"Por el rio del amor, madre": An Aspect of the *Morenita*', *JHP*, 10: 151-60

——, 1988. 'Transparent Excuses in Spanish Traditional Lyric: A Motif Overlooked', *MLN*, 103: 436-39

Goss, Brian M., 2008. '*Te doy mis ojos* (2003) y *Hable con ella* (2002): Gender in Context in Two Recent Spanish Films', *Studies in European Cinema*, 5.1: 31–44

Goytisolo, Juan, 1977. 'El mundo erótico de María de Zayas', in his *Disidencias* (Barcelona: Seix Barral), pp. 63–115

Grado, Mercedes de, 2004. 'Encrucijada del feminismo español: disyuntiva entre igualdad y diferencia', in *La mujer en la España actual: ¿evolución o involución?*, ed. Jacqueline Cruz and Barbara Zecchi (Barcelona: Icaria), pp. 25–58

Graffigny, Mme de, 1792. *Cartas de una peruana, escritas en francés por Mme de Graffigny* [*Lettres péruviennes*, 1747], trans. María Romero Masegosa y Cancelada (Valladolid: viuda de Santander e hijos)

Graham, Helen, 1995. 'Gender and the State: Women in the 1940s', in *Spanish Cultural Studies: An Introduction*, ed. Helen Graham and Jo Labanyi (Oxford: OUP), pp. 182–95

Grassi y Trechi, Ángela, 1865. *El lujo: novela de costumbres*; repr. in microfiche, Simón Palmer 1992

Greer, Germaine, 1979. *The Obstacle Race: The Fortunes of Women Painters and Their Work* (New York: Farrar, Straus & Giroux)

Greer, Margaret Rich, 2000. *María de Zayas Tells Baroque Tales of Love and the Cruelty of Men* (University Park, PA: Pennsylvania State UP)

——, 2001. 'María de Zayas and the Female Eunuch', *Journal of Spanish Cultural Studies*, 2: 41–53

Grieve, Patricia E., 1987. 'Private Man, Public Woman: Trading Places in *Condesa Traidora*', *Romance Quarterly*, 34: 317–26
——, 1991. 'Embroidering with Saintly Threads: María de Zayas Challenges Cervantes and the Church', *Renaissance Quarterly*, 44.1: 86–106
——, 2009. *The Eve of Spain: Myths of Origins in the History of Christian, Muslim, and Jewish Conflict* (Baltimore, MD: Johns Hopkins UP)
Grössinger, Christa, 1997. *Picturing Women in Late Medieval and Renaissance Art* (Manchester: Manchester UP)
Hale, D. G., 1971. *The Body Politic* (The Hague: Mouton)
Haliczer, Stephen, 2002. *Between Exaltation and Infamy: Female Mystics in the Golden Age of Spain* (Oxford: OUP)
Hall-van den Elsen, Catherine, 1997. 'Luisa (Ignacia) Roldán', in Gaze 1997: II, 1192–93
Hansen, Molly, 1986. 'Pleasure, Ambivalence, Identification: Valentino and Female Spectatorship', *Cinema Journal*, 25.4: 6–32
Harrison, Charles, Paul Wood, and Jason Gaiger (eds), 2007. *Art in Theory 1648–1815: An Anthology of Changing Ideas* (Oxford: Blackwell)
Hart, Thomas R., 2006. *Studies on the 'Cantar de Mio Cid'*, PMHRS, 54 (London: Dept of Hispanic Studies, QMUL)
Haskins, Susan, 1993. *Mary Magdalen: Myth and Metaphor* (New York: Harcourt, Brace & Company)
Hatto, Arthur T. (ed.), 1965. *Eos: An Enquiry into the Theme of Lovers' Meetings and Partings at Dawn in Poetry* (The Hague: Mouton)
Hauf i Valls, Albert, 1987. 'La *Vita Christi* de sor Isabel de Villena y la tradición de las *Vitae Christi* medievales', in *Studia in honorem Prof. M. de Riquer* (Barcelona: Quaderns Crema), II, pp. 105–64
——, 1989. 'Isabel de Villena i la *Istòria de la Passió*', *Segon Congrès Internacional de la Llengua Catalana: Àrea 7, Història de la Llengua*, ed. Antoni Ferrando (València: Institut de Filologia Valenciana; Barcelona: Publicacions de l'Abadia de Montserrat), pp. 541–52
——, 1990. *D'Eiximenis a sor Isabel de Villena: aportació a l'estudi de la nostra cultura medieval*, Biblioteca Sanchis Guarner, 19 (València: IIFV; Barcelona: Publicacions de l'Abadia de Montserrat)
——, 1991. 'Text i context de l'obra de sor Isabel de Villena', in *Literatura valenciana del segle XV: Joanot Martorell i sor Isabel de Villena*, ed. G. Colón et al. (València: Consell Valencià de Cultura, Generalitat Valenciana)
——, 1998. 'Corrientes espirituales valencianas en la baja Edad Media (siglos XIV-XV)', *Anales Valentinos*, 24: 261–302
——, 1999. 'Text, pintura i meditació: el *Speculum animae* atribuït a sor Isabel de Villena i la funció empàtica de l'art religiós', in *Actes del VII Congrés de l'AHLM (Castelló de la Plana 1997)*, 3 vols, ed. Santiago Fortuño Llorens and Tomàs Martínez Romero (Castelló de la Plana: Universitat Jaume I), I, pp. 33–59
——, 2006. *La 'Vita Christi' de sor Isabel de Villena (s. XV) como arte de meditar: introducción a una lectura contextualizada*, vol. 2 of Isabel de Villena, *Vita Christi*, facs. edn (València: Biblioteca Valenciana)

Havelange, Isabelle, and Segolène Le Men, 1988. *Le Magasin des enfants: la littérature pour la jeunesse* (Montreuil: Bibliothèque Robert Desnos / Association du Bicentenaire de Montreuil)

Haywood, Louise M. (ed.), 2000. *Cultural Contexts / Female Voices*, PMHRS, 27 (London: Dept of Hispanic Studies, QMW)

——, 2005. 'El cuerpo como significante en el *exemplum* 44 del *Conde Lucanor* de Don Juan Manuel', in *Textos medievales: recursos, pensamiento e influencia; trabajos de las IX Jornadas Medievales*, ed. Concepción Company, Aurelio González, and Lillian von der Walde, Publicaciones de *Medievalia*, 32 (México: Colegio de México / Universidad Autónoma Metropolitana / UNAM), pp. 205–16

Heath, Stephen, 1986. 'Joan Riviere and the Masquerade', in *Formations of Fantasy*, ed. Victor Burgin and Cora Kaplan (London: Methuen), pp. 45–61

Hegstrom Oakey, Valerie, 2007. '*Comedia* Scholarship and Performance: *El muerto disimulado* from the Archive to the Stage', *Comedia Performance*, 4: 152–78

——, and Anita Stoll, 2002. 'Dramaturgas', in *Diccionario de la comedia del Siglo de Oro*, ed. Frank Casa, Luciano García Lorenzo, and Germán Vega-Luengos (Madrid: Castalia)

——, and Amy Williamsen (eds), 1999. *Engendering the Early Modern Stage: Women Playwrights in the Spanish Empire* (New Orleans, LA: UP of the South)

Henseler, Christine, 2003. *Contemporary Spanish Women's Narrative and the Publishing Industry* (Urbana, IL: University of Illinois Press)

——, and Randolph Pope, 2007. *Generation X Rocks: Contemporary Fiction, Film and Rock Culture* (Nashville, TN: Vanderbilt UP)

Heredero, Carlos (ed.), 1998. *La mitad del cielo: directoras españolas de los años 90* (Málaga: Festival de Cine Español)

Hernández-Girbal, Florentino, 1931. *Una vida pintoresca: Manuel Fernández y González* (Madrid: Imprenta Helénica)

Hernando Pérez, José (ed.), 2001. '*Poema de Fernán González*' *e Hispano Diego García*, Bibliotheca Salmanticensis, Estudios, 227 (Salamanca: Universidad)

Herrmann, Gina, 2010. *Written in Red: The Communist Memoir in Spain* (Champaign: University of Illinois Press)

Hickey, Margarita, 1789. *Poesías varias, sagradas y profanas o amorosas* (Madrid: Imprenta Real)

Hirsch, Marianne, 1989. *The Mother/Daughter Plot: Narrative, Psychoanalysis, Feminism* (Bloomington: Indiana UP)

Holland, Cynthia, 1998. 'After Antigone: Women, the Past and the Future of Feminist Political Thought', *American Journal of Political Science*, 42.4: 1108–32

Hollis, Karen, 1990. 'Teresa de Jesús and the Relations of Writing', in *Conflicts of Discourse: Spanish Literature in the Golden Age*, ed. Peter William Evans (Manchester: Manchester UP), pp. 26–47

Hooper, John, 2006. *The New Spaniards*, 2nd edn (London: Penguin)

Hormigón, Juan Antonio (ed.), 1997. *Autoras en la historia del teatro española (1500–1994)*, 2 vols (Madrid: ADE)

Howe, Elizabeth Theresa, 2002. 'Cisneros and the Translation of Women's Spirituality', in *The Vernacular Spirit: Essays on Medieval Religious Literature*, ed. Renate Blumenfeld-Kosinski, Duncan Robertson, and Nancy Bradley Warren (New York: Palgrave), pp. 283–97

Huarte de San Juan, Juan, [1575] 1989. *Examen de los ingenios para las ciencias*, ed. Guillermo Serés (Madrid: Cátedra)

Huélamo, Ana María, 1993. 'La dominica Sor Constanza, autora religiosa del siglo xv', *Revista de Literatura Medieval*, 5: 127–58

Hurtado, Amparo, 1998. 'Biografía de una generación: las escritoras del Noventa y Ocho', in: *La literatura escrita por mujer (desde el siglo xix hasta la actualidad)*, Zavala et al. 1993–2000: v, 139–54

Hutcheon, Linda, 1988. *A Poetics of Postmodernism: History, Theory, Fiction* (New York: Routledge)

Ibarruri, Dolores, 1984. *Memorias de Pasionaria, 1939–1977* (Barcelona: Planeta)

Ichiishi, Barbara F., 1994. *The Apple of Earthly Love: Female Development in Esther Tusquets' Fiction* (New York: Peter Lang)

Irigaray, Luce, 1985. *The Speculum of the Other Woman*, trans. Gillian C. Gill (Ithaca, NY: Cornell UP)

Irizarry, Estelle, 1983. 'Echoes of the Amazon Myth in Medieval Spanish Literature', in Miller [1978] 1983: 53–66

Irizarry, Estelle, 1993. 'Concepción Arenal', in Levine et al. 1993: 44–53

Jacobs, Fredrika H., 1997. 'Sofonisba Anguissola', in Gaze 1997, I: 188–91

Jagoe, Catherine, 1993. 'Disinheriting the Feminine: Galdós and the Rise of the Realist Novel in Spain', *Revista de Estudios Hispánicos*, 27: 225–48

——, 1994. *Ambiguous Angels: Gender in the Novels of Galdós* (Berkeley: University of California Press)

——, 1998. 'La enseñanza femenina en la España decimonónica', in Jagoe et al. 1998: 105–217

——, Alda Blanco, and Cristina Enríquez de Salamanca, 1998. *La mujer en los discursos de género: textos y contextos en el siglo xix* (Barcelona: Icaria)

Janés, Clara, 1986. *Las primeras poetisas en lengua castellana* (Madrid: Ayuso)

——, 1990. *Jardín y laberinto* (Madrid: Debate)

Jato, Mónica. 2006. 'Los personajes femeninos en los *crímenes extraños* de Alfonso Sastre: una reflexión sobre la cultura española de la democracia', in *Leading Ladies: mujeres en la literatura hispana y en las artes*, ed. Yvonne Fuentes and Margaret Parker (Baton Rouge: Louisiana State UP), pp. 137–50

——, 2008. *El laberinto de la palabra poética* (València: Institució Alfons el Magnànim)

Jay, Martin, 2006. *Songs of Experience: Modern American and European Variations on a Universal Theme* (Berkeley: University of California Press)

Jimeno de Flaquer: see Gimeno de Flaquer

Johnson, Lesley, 1995. 'Imagining Communities: Medieval and Modern', in *Concepts of National Identity in the Middle Ages*, ed. Simon Forde, Lesley

Johnson, and Alan V. Murray, Leeds Texts and Monographs, 14 (Leeds: Leeds UP), pp. 1–21
Johnson, Roberta, 1981. *Carmen Laforet* (Boston: Twayne)
——, 2003a. *Gender and the Nation in the Spanish Modernist Novel* (Nashville, TN: Vanderbilt UP)
——, 2003b. 'Spanish Feminist Theory: Then and Now', *ALEC*, 28.1: 11–19
——, 2005. 'Issues and Arguments in Twentieth-Century Spanish Feminist Theory', *ALEC*, 30.1–2 : 243–72
Johnson, Samuel: see Joyes 1798
Johnston, Claire, [1973] 2000. 'Women's Cinema as Counter-Cinema', in Sue Thornham, *Feminism and Film* (Oxford: OUP), pp. 22–33
Jordan, Barry, and Mark Allinson, 2005. *Spanish Cinema: A Student's Guide* (London: Hodder Arnold)
Jordan, Barry, and Rikki Morgan-Tamosunas, 1998. *Contemporary Spanish Cinema* (Manchester: Manchester UP)
Joyes y Blake, Inés (trans.), 1798. *El Principe de Abisinia* [*Rasselas*, by Samuel Johnson, 1759] (Madrid: Sancha)
Juan Manuel, 1952. *Libro infinido*, in his '*Libro infinido' y 'Tractado de la Asunçión'*, ed. José Manuel Blecua, Colección Filológica, 2 (Granada: Universidad), pp. 3–87
——, 1974. *Libro de los estados*, ed. R. B. Tate and I. R. Macpherson (Oxford: OUP)
——, 1989. *Libro del cavallero et del escudero*, in his *Cinco tratados: 'Libro del cavallero et del escudero'; 'Libro de las tres razone'; 'Libro enfenido'; 'Tractado de la asunçión de la Virgen'; 'Libro de la caça'*, ed. Reinaldo Ayerbe-Chaux (Madison: HSMS), pp. 111–62
——, 1994. *El Conde Lucanor*, ed. Guillermo Serés, intro. by Germán Orduna, Biblioteca Clásica (Barcelona: Crítica)
Julià, Lluisa (ed.), 1999. *Memòria de l'aigua: onze escriptores i el seu món* (Barcelona: Proa)
Kaminsky, Amy Katz, 1993. 'Ana Caro Mallén de Soto', in Levine et al. 1993: 86–97
—— (ed.), 1996. *Water Lilies - Flores del agua: An Anthology of Spanish Writers from the Fifteenth through the Nineteenth Century* (Minneapolis: University of Minnesota Press)
——, 2001. 'María de Zayas and the Invention of a Women's Writing Community', *Revista de Estudios Hispánicos*, 35: 487–509
Kantorowicz, Ernst H., 1957. *The King's Two Bodies: A Study in Mediaeval Political Theory* (Princeton, NJ: Princeton UP)
Kaplan, E. Ann, 1992, *Motherhood and Representation: The Mother in Popular Culture and Melodrama* (New York: Routledge)
—— (ed.), 2000. *Feminism and Film* (Oxford: OUP)
Keene, Judith, 1999. '"Into the Clear Air of the Plaza": Spanish Women Achieve the Vote in 1931', in Enders and Radcliff 1999: 325–48
Keller, John Esten (ed.), 1961. Clemente Sánchez de Vercial, *Libro de los exemplos por a.b.c.*, Clásicos Hispánicos, 25 (Madrid: CSIC)

King, Stewart, 2005. *Escribir la catalanidad: lengua e identidades culturales en la narrativa contemporánea de Cataluña*, CT, A216 (Woodbridge: Tamesis)
——, 2006. 'Catalan Literature(s) in Postcolonial Context', *Romance Studies*, 24.3: 253–64
Kipnis, Laura, 1993. *Ecstasy Unlimited: On Sex, Capital, Gender, and Aesthetics* (Minneapolis: University of Minnesota Press)
Kirk, Else, 1987. 'Images of Amazons: Marriage and Matriarchy', in Macdonald et al. 1987, pp. 27–39.
Kirkpatrick, Susan, 1989. *Las Románticas: Women Writers and Subjectivity in Spain, 1835–1850* (Berkeley: University of California Press)
—— (ed.), 1992. *Antología poética de escritoras del siglo XIX* (Madrid: Castalia / Instituto de la Mujer)
——, 2003. *Mujer, modernismo y vanguardia en España (1898–1931)* (Madrid: Cátedra)
Kitts, Sally Ann, 1995. *The Debate on the Nature, Role and Influence of Women in Eighteenth-Century Spain* (Lampeter: Edwin Mellen)
Klinck, Anne L., 2003. 'Poetic Markers of Gender in Medieval "Woman's Song": Was Anonymous a Woman?', *Neophilologus*, 87: 339–59
Knights, Vanessa, 1999. *The Search for Identity in the Narrative of Rosa Montero* (Lampeter: Edwin Mellen)
Kowalsky, Daniel, 2004. 'Rated S: Softcore Pornography and the Spanish Transition to Democracy, 1977–82', in *Spanish Popular Cinema: Inside Popular Film*, ed. Antonio Lázaro-Reboll and Andrew Willis (Manchester: Manchester UP), pp. 188–208.
Krappe, Alexander H., 1933. 'Le Faucon de l'Infant dans *El conde Lucanor*', *Bulletin Hispanique*, 35: 294–7
Kristeva, Julia, 1980. 'Motherhood according to Giovanni Bellini', in *Desire in Language: A Semiotic Approach to Literature and Art*, ed. Leon S. Roudiez (Oxford: Blackwell)
——, 1984. *Revolution in Poetic Language* (New York: Columbia UP)
——, 1991. *Strangers to Ourselves* (New York: Columbia UP)
Krontiris, Tina, 1992. *Oppositional Voices: Women as Writers and Translators of Literature in the English Renaissance* (New York: Routledge)
Kusche, Maríam, 1989. 'Sofonisba Anguissola en España: retratista en la corte de Felipe II junto a Alonso Sánchez Coello y Jorge de la Rúa', *Archivo Español de Arte*, 52: 391–420
——, 1997. 'La mujer y el retrato cortesano del siglo XVI visto a través de la obra de Sofonisba Anguissola, maestra de pintura y dama de honor de Isabel de Valois', in *La mujer en el arte español* 1997: 69–79
La mujer en el arte español, 1997. VIII Jornadas de Arte, Departamento de Historia del Arte 'Diego Velázquez', Centro de Estudios Históricos, CSIC (Madrid: Alpuerto / CSIC)
Labanyi, Jo, 2000. *Gender and Modernization in the Spanish Realist Novel* (Oxford: OUP)
Laborde, Alice M., 1966. *L'oeuvre de Mme de Genlis* (Paris: A. G. Nizet)

Lacan, Jacques, [1973] 1979. The *Four Fundamental Concepts of Psycho-Analysis*, trans. Alan Sheridan (London: Penguin)

——, 1999. *The Seminars of Jacques Lacan, Book XX: Encore, On Feminine Sexuality: The Limits of Love and Knowledge, 1972–1973*, ed. Jacques-Alain Miller, trans. Bruce Fink (New York: Norton)

Lacarra, María Eugenia, 1988. 'La mujer ejemplar en tres textos épicos castellanos', *Cuadernos de Investigación Filológica*, 14: 5–20

——, 1988–89. 'Notes on the Feminist Analysis of Medieval Spanish Literature', *La Corónica*, 17: 14–22

——, 1990. 'Las paradigmas de hombre y de mujer en la literatura epicolegendaria medieval castellana', in *Estudios históricos y literarios sobre la mujer medieval*, ed. María Eugenia Lacarra et al., Biblioteca de Estudios sobre la Mujer, 4 (Málaga: Diputación Provincial), pp. 7–34

——, 1992. 'La representación de la mujer en algunos textos épicos castellanos', in *Actas del II Congreso Internacional de la AHLM* (1987) (Alcalá: Universidad), I, pp. 395–408

——, 1993. 'Representaciones de la feminidad en el *Cantar de los siete infantes de Salas*', in *Charlemagne in the North: Proceedings of the Twelfth International Conference of the Société Rencesvals* (Edinburgh, 4–11 August 1991), ed. Philip E. Bennett, Anne Elizabeth Cobby, and Graham A. Runnalls (Edinburgh: Société Rencesvals), pp. 335–44

——, 1995. 'Representaciones de mujeres en la literatura española de la Edad Media', in *La mujer en la literatura española*, Zavala et al. 1993–2000: II, pp. 21–68

Lacarra, Eukene, 1999. 'Political Discourse and the Construction and Representation of Gender in *Mocedades de Rodrigo*', *HR*, 67: 467–91

Lacarra, María Jesús (ed.), 1996. *Sendebar*, LH, 304 (Madrid: Cátedra)

——, 1979. *Cuentística medieval en España: los orígenes* (Zaragoza: Universidad)

——, 2007. 'Género y recepción de las *Memorias* de Leonor López de Córdoba (1362/1363–1430)', in *Actas del XI Congreso Internacional de la AHLM (Universidad de León, 20 al 24 de septiembre de 2005)* (León: Universidad), pp. 731–41

Lafarga, Francisco (ed.), 1999. *La traducción en España (1750–1830): libro, literatura y cultura* (Lleida: Universitat)

Laforet, Carmen, 1945. *Nada* (Barcelona: Destino); trans. 1958, *Nothing*, Inez Muñoz (London: Weidenfeld & Nicholson); trans. 2008, *Nada: A Novel*, Edith Grossman (New York: Random House)

Lalaing, María Cayetana de la Cerda y Vera, Condesa de: see Lambert 1781

Lambert, Anne-Thérèse Marguenat de Courcelles, Comtesse de, 1781. *Obras de la marquesa de Lambert*, trans. María Cayetana de la Cerda y Vera, Condesa de Lalaing (Madrid: Manuel Marín)

Lampillas, Xavier, 1789. *Ensayo histórico-apologético de la literatura española*, trans. Josefa Amar y Borbón, 2nd edn [1st edn 1782–83] (Madrid: Pedro Marín)

Laqueur, Thomas, 1990. *Making Sex: Body and Gender from the Greeks to Freud* (Cambridge, MA: Harvard UP)

Lara Pozuelo, Antonio (ed.), 1991. *La autobiografía en lengua española en el siglo xx* (Lausanne: Sociedad Suiza de Estudios Hispánicos)

Larrauri, Elena (ed.), 1994. *Mujer, derecho penal y criminología* (Madrid: Siglo XXI)

Larson, Catherine, 1994. 'Gender, Reading, and Intertextuality: Don Juan's Legacy in María de Zayas's *La traición en la amistad*', *Revista de Literatura Hispánica*, 40–41: 129–38

——, 2000. 'You Can't Always Get What You Want: Gender, Voice, and Identity in Women-Authored *Comedias*', in Stoll and Smith 2000: 127–41

——, 2008. 'Found in Translation: María de Zayas's *Friendship Betrayed* and the English-Speaking Stage', in Paun de García and Larson 2008: 83–94

Lawlor, Teresa, and Ana María Plymen, 2000. 'Images of Women in Spain during Primo de Rivera's Dictatorship: Social Reality v. Advertising – A Case Study from *'Blanco y Negro'*, *International Journal of Iberian Studies*, 13.2: 68–85

Lázaro-Reboll, Antonio, and Andrew Willis, 2004. *Spanish Popular Cinema* (Manchester: Manchester UP)

Le Prince de Beaumont, Jeanne-Marie, 1778. *Almacén y biblioteca completa de los niños, o Diálogos de una sabia directora con sus discípulas de la primera distinción* [*Le Magasin des enfans*, 1756], trans. Mathias Guitet (Madrid: Manuel Martín)

——, 1779–80. *Biblioteca completa de educación para las señoras y jóvenes* [*Instruction pour les jeunes dames*, 1764], trans. José de la Fresa (Madrid: Manuel Martín)

——, 1782. *La devoción ilustrada, o conversaciones familiares entre una sabia directora y algunas personas de distinción,* trans. Juan Manuel Girón (Madrid: viuda de Manuel Martín)

——, 1787. *Almacén de las señoritas adolescentes, o Diálogos de una sabia directora con sus nobles discípulas* [*Le Magasin des adolescentes*, 1760], trans. Plácido Barco López (Madrid: Imprenta de Plácido Barco López)

——, 1795. *Memorias de la Baronesa de Bateville,* trans. José García de Segovia [*Mémoires de Mme la baronne de Batteville, ou la veuve parfaite*, 1766] (Málaga: Luis Carreras)

——, 1796–98. *Cartas de Madama de Montier a su hija* [*Lettres de Mme du Montier à la marquise de *** sa fille,* 1756], trans. María Antonia del Río y Arnedo (Madrid: Josef López)

——, 1797. *La Nueva Clarisa, historia verdadera* [*La nouvelle Clarice, histoire véritable,* 1767] (Madrid: Imprenta de Cruzado)

——, 1807. *Cartas de Emeranza a Lucía, traducidas del francés por N.D.N.* (Madrid: viuda de Barco López)

Legido-Quigley, Eva 2002. 'Eroticism in Contemporary Spanish Women Writers' Narrative', in *The Feminist Encyclopedia of Spanish Literature*, ed. Janet Pérez and Maureen Ihrie, 2 vols (Westport, CT: Greenwood Press), I, pp. 210–16

Lejeune, Philippe, 1975. *Le Pacte autobiographique* (Paris: Seuil, 1975)
——, 1984. 'Women and Autobiography at Author's Expense', in Stanton 1984: 205–18
Lemaire, Ria, 1983. 'Relectura de una cantiga de amigo', *NRFH*, 32: 289–98
——, 1986. 'Explaining Away the Female Subject: The Case of Medieval Lyric', *Poetics Today*, 4: 729–43
——, 1987. *Passions et positions: contribution à une sémiotique du sujet dans la poésie lyrique médiévale en langues romanes* (Amsterdam: Rodopi)
Lentz, Kirsten M., 1993. 'The Popular Pleasures of Female Revenge (or Rage Bursting in a Blaze of Gunfire)', *Cultural Studies*, 7.3: 374–405
León, María Teresa, [1970] 1998. *Memoria de la melancolía*, ed. Gregorio Torres Nebrera (Madrid: Castalia)
Letourneux, Nicolas, 1774. *Instrucciones cristianas sobre el sacramento del matrimonio*, trans. María Francisca de Sales Portocarrero, Condesa de Montijo (Barcelona: Bernardo Pla)
Levine, Laura, 1994. *Men in Women's Clothing: Anti-Theatricality and Effemination, 1579–1642* (Cambridge: CUP)
Levine, Linda Gould, and Gloria Feiman Waldmen, 1980. *Feminismo ante franquismo: entrevistas con feministas de España* (Madrid: Editora Universal)
——, Ellen Engelson Marson, and Gloria Feiman Waldman (eds), 1993. *Spanish Women Writers: A Bio-Bibliographical Source Book* (Westport, CT: Greenwood Press)
Lezcano, Ricardo, 1979. *El divorcio en la Segunda República* (Madrid: Akal)
Lida de Malkiel, María Rosa, 1952. *La idea de la fama en la Edad Media castellana* (México: Fondo de Cultura Económica)
Linehan, Peter, 1997. *The Ladies of Zamora* (Manchester: Manchester UP)
Lombroso, Cesare, 1896. *La femme criminelle et la prostituée* (Paris: Alcan. Saint-Aubin)
Lonsdale, Laura, 2007. 'Feminism and Form: Reading for Ambiguity in Esther Tusquets' *El mismo mar de todos los veranos*', in *Reading Iberia: Theory/History/Identity*, ed. Helena Buffery, Stuart Davis, and Kirsty Hooper (Bern: Peter Lang), pp. 159–75
——, 2008. 'Feminism and Form in the Fiction of Rosa Montero and Esther Tusquets', unpublished doctoral thesis, University of Birmingham
——, 2010. 'The Space of Politics: Nation, Gender and Class in Esther Tusquets' Narrative', in *New Spain, New Literatures (Hispanic Issues)*, ed. Nicholas Spadacini and Luis Martín-Estudillo (Nashville, TN: Vanderbilt UP), pp. 245–61
López, Ana M., 1993. 'Tears and Desire: Women and Melodrama in the 'Old' Mexican Cinema', in *Mediating Two Worlds: Cinematic Encounters in the Americas*, ed. John King, Ana M. López, and Manuel Alvarado (London: BFI), pp. 147–63
López-Baralt, Luce, 1985. *Huellas del Islam en la literatura española: de Juan Ruiz a Juan Goytisolo* (Madrid: Hiperión)
——, 1992. *Islam in Spanish Literature, from the Middle Ages to the Present*, trans. Andrew Hurley (Leiden: Brill)

López-Cordón, María Victoria, 1996. 'Traducciones y traductoras en la España de finales del siglo XVIII', in *Entre la marginación y el desarrollo: mujeres y hombres en la historia: homenaje a Mª Carmen García-Nieto,* ed. Cristina Segura and Gloria Nielfa (Madrid: Ediciones del Orto), pp. 89–112

——, 2005. 'La fortuna de escribir: escritoras de los siglos XVII y XVIII', in Morant 2005–06: II, 193–234

López de Córdoba, Leonor, 1996. 'Autobiography' [*Memorias*], trans. Amy Kaminsky and Elaine Dorough Johnson, in Kaminsky 1996: 19–32

López Estrada, Francisco, 1978. '*Mester de clerecía*: las palabras y el concepto', *JHP*, 2: 165–74

——, 1986. 'Las mujeres escritoras en la Edad Media castellana', in Fonquerne and Esteban 1986: 9–38

López-Mayhew, Bárbara, 2004. 'From Manuscript to 21st Century Performances: *La traición en la amistad*', *Comedia Performance*, 1: 174–91

Lorenzo Alcalá, May, 2006. 'Contrapunto borgiano', http:/www.maylorenzoalcala.com. (accessed 21 November 2008)

——, 2007. *Norah Borges: mito y vanguardia* (exhibition catalogue) (Neuquén: Museo Nacional de Bellas Artes)

——, 2009. *Norah Borges: la vanguardia enmascarada* (Buenos Aires: Eudeba)

Lorenzo Gradín, Pilar, 1990. *La canción de mujer en la lírica medieval* (Santiago de Compostela: Universidade)

Louis, Anja, 2005. *Women and the Law: Carmen de Burgos, an Early Feminist* (Woodbridge: Tamesis)

Loureiro, Ángel G., 2000. 'María Teresa León: The Ruin of Memory', in his *The Ethics of Autobiography: Replacing the Subject in Modern Spain* (Nashville, TN: Vanderbilt UP), 64–99

Ludmer, Josefina, 1984. 'Tretas del débil', in *La sartén por el mango: encuentro de escritoras latinoamericanas,* ed. Patricia Elena González and Eliana Ortega (Río Piedras: Huracán), pp. 47–55

Luna, Lola, 1995. 'Ana Caro, una escritora "de oficio" del Siglo de Oro', *BHS*, 72: 11–26

——, 1996. *Leyendo como una mujer la imagen de la mujer* (Barcelona: Anthropos)

Lunati Maruny, Montserrat, 2007. *Imma Monsó: la narrativa de la ironia i la diferència* (Vic: Eumo)

McCabe, Janet, 2004. *Feminist Film Studies: Writing the Woman into Cinema* (London: Wallflower Press)

Macdonald, Sharon, 1987. 'Drawing the Lines – Gender, Peace and War: An Introduction', in Macdonald et al., 1987, pp. 1–26

——, Pat Holden, and Shirley Ardener (eds), 1987. *Images of Women in Peace and War: Cross-Cultural and Historical Perspectives* (London: Macmillan / Oxford University Women's Studies Committee)

McKendrick, Melveena, 2006. 'Representing Their Sex: Actresses in Seventeenth-Century Spain', in *Rhetoric and Reality in Early Modern Spain,* ed. Richard Pym (Woodbridge: Tamesis), pp. 72–91

McNerney, Kathleen (ed.), 1999. *Voices and Visions: The Words and Works of Mercè Rodoreda* (Selinsgrove, PA: Susquehana UP)
——, 2001. 'Isabel de Villena', *Catalan Review*, 15: 151–3
——, and Cristina Enríquez de Salamanca (eds), 1994. *Double Minorities of Spain: A Bio-Bibliographic Guide to Women Writers of the Catalan, Galician and Basque Countries* (New York: PMLA)
McRobbie, Angela, 2008. *The Aftermath of Feminism: Gender, Culture and Social Change* (London: Sage)
Mainer, José Carlos, 1981. *La edad de plata (1902–1939): ensayo de interpretación de un proceso cultural* (Madrid: Cátedra)
Mainz, Valerie, 1997. 'Court Artists', in Gaze 1997: I, 37–43
Mâle, Émile, 1932. *L'art réligieux après le Concile de Trente: étude sur l'iconographie de la fin du XVIe siècle, du XVIIe et du XVIIIe siècle, Italie, France, Espagne, Flanders* (Paris: A. Colin)
Maneikis Kniazzeh, Charlotte S., and Edward J. Neugaard (eds), 1977. *'Vides de sants rosselloneses': text català del segle XIII*, 3 vols, Publicacions de la Fundació Salvador Vives Casajuana, 48, 51, 53 (Barcelona: Fundació Salvador Vives Casajuana)
Mangini, Shirley, 1995. *Memories of Resistance: Women's Voices from the Spanish Civil War* (New Haven, CT: Yale UP)
——, 2001. *Las modernas de Madrid: las grandes intelectuales españolas de la vanguardia* (Barcelona: Península)
——, 2010. *Maruja Mallo and the Spanish Avant-Garde* (New York: Ashgate)
Manteiga, Roberto, Carolyn Galerstein, and Kathleen McNerney (eds), 1988. *Feminine Concerns in Contemporary Spanish Fiction by Women* (Potomac, MD: Scripta Humanistica)
Marañón, Gregorio, [1926] 1934. *Tres ensayos sobre la vida sexual: sexo, trabajo y deporte, maternidad y feminismo, educación sexual y diferenciación sexual*, 7th edn (Madrid: Biblioteca Nueva)
——, 1960. *Ensayos sobre la vida sexual* (Madrid: Espasa-Calpe)
Marçal, Maria-Mercè, 1990. 'Isabel de Villena i el seu feminisme literari', *Revista de Catalunya*, 44: 120–30
—— (ed.), 1998. *Cartografies del desig: quinze escriptores i el seu món* (Barcelona: Proa)
——, 2004. *Sota el signe del drac: proses 1985–1997* (Barcelona: Proa)
Marchal, Roger, 1991. *Mme de Lambert et son milieu* (Oxford: The Voltaire Foundation)
Marcos Marín, Francisco (ed.), 1987. *Libro de Alexandre* (Madrid: Alianza)
Margueritte, Victor, 1924 (?). *La garzona [La Garçonne, 1922]*, trans. Antonio de Vergara, n.d. (Madrid: [A-Marzo])
Marimón Llorca, Carmen, 1990. *Prosistas castellanas medievales* (Alicante: Caja de Ahorros Provincial)
Maroto Camino, Mercedes, 1996. '"Ficción, afición y seducción": Ana Caro's *Valor, agravio y mujer*', *BCom*, 48: 37–50
——, 1999. 'María de Zayas and Ana Caro: The Space of Woman's Solidarity in the Spanish Golden Age', *HR*, 67: 1–16

——, 2001. 'Transvestism, Translation and Transgression: Ángela de Azevedo's *El muerto disimulado*', *Forum for Modern Language Studies*, 37: 314–25
Marsh, Steven, and Parvati Nair, 2004. *Gender and Spanish Cinema* (Oxford: Berg)
Martín Gaite, Carmen, 1978. *El cuarto de atrás* (Barcelona: Destino); trans. 1983, *The Back Room*, Frances López Morillas (New York: Columbia UP)
——, 1987. *Usos amorosos de la postguerra española* (Barcelona: Anagrama)
Martín-Gamero, Amalia (ed.), 1975. *Antología del feminismo* (Madrid: Alianza)
Martín González, Juan José, 1993. *El artista en la sociedad española del siglo XVII* (Madrid: Cátedra)
Martin-Márquez, Susan, 1999. *Feminist Discourse and Spanish Cinema: Sight Unseen* (Oxford: OUP)
——, 2004. 'Pedro Almodóvar's Maternal Transplants: From *Matador* to *All About My Mother*', *BHS*, 81: 497–509
Martínez Carazo, Cristina, 2002. '*Flores de otro mundo*: la pluralidad cultural como propuesta', *Letras Peninsulares*, 15.2: 377–90
Martínez Cuadrado, Miguel, 1973. *La burguesía conservadora (1874–1931)* (Madrid: Alianza)
Martínez de Toledo, Alfonso, 1981. *Arcipreste de Talavera o Corbacho*, ed. J. González Muela, Clásicos Castalia, 24 (Madrid: Castalia)
Martínez Quijano, Ana (ed.), 1996. *Norah Borges, cien años de pintura* (Buenos Aires: Centro Cultural Borges)
Martínez Sierra, Gregorio, 1917. *Feminismo, feminidad, españolismo* (Madrid: Renacimiento)
Martínez y Martínez, Francisco, 1945. 'Una visita al cenobio de la Santísima Trinidad de Valencia, sepultura de la reina doña María', *Anales del Centro de Cultura Valenciana*, segunda época, 4: 167–85
Masera, Mariana, 1999. '"Que non sé filar, ni aspar, ni devanar": erotismo y trabajo femenino en el cancionero hispánico medieval', in *Discursos y representaciones en la Edad Media*, ed. Concepción Company, Aurelio González, and Lilian von der Walde Moheno (México: UNAM), pp. 215–31
——, 2000. '"Fue a la ciudad mi morena: / si me querrá cuando vuelva?": la voz masculina en la antigua lírica tradicional', *Medievalia*, 31: 47–57
——, 2001. *'Que non dormiré sola, non': la voz femenina en la antigua lírica hispánica* (Barcelona: Azul)
Massanés, Josefa. 1886. 'La florista', in Sáez de Melgar 1886: 803–21
Mata López, Manuel, 1967. 'Obras en el real monasterio de la Santísima Trinidad (siglo XV)', *Saitabi*, 17: 43–50
Mateu y Llopis, Felipe, 1956. 'Notas sobre archivos eclesiásticos y de protocolos del reino de Valencia', *Revista de Archivos, Bibliotecas y Museos*, 62: 699–737
Matute, Ana María, 1960. *Primera memoria* (Barcelona: Destino); trans. 1989, *School of the Sun*, Elaine Kerrigan (New York: Columbia UP, 1989
Mayayo, Patricia, 2003. *Historias de mujeres, historias del arte* (Madrid: Cátedra)

Mayoral, Marina (ed.), 1990a. *Escritoras románticas españolas* (Madrid: Fundación Banco Exterior de España)

——, 1990b. 'Las amistades románticas: confusión de fórmulas y sentimientos', in Mayoral 1990a: 43–71

Mederos, Alicia (ed.), 2001. *Los álbumes de Josefina de la Torre: la última voz del 27* (Madrid: Residencia de las Estudiantes)

Mencos, Maria Isidra, 2002. *Mercè Rodoreda: una bibliografia crítica (1963–2001)* (Barcelona: Fundació Mercè Rodoreda / Institut d'Estudis Catalans)

Menocal, María Rosa, 1990. *The Arabic Role in Medieval Literary History: A Forgotten Heritage* (Philadelphia: University of Pennsylvania Press)

Merced, Leslie Anne, 2004. 'Writing in the Raw: Rhetorical Moves of Female Essayists during the Spanish *Fin de Siglo*', unpublished doctoral thesis, University of Illinois, Urbana-Champaign

Mérida Jiménez, Rafael M., 2002. *Women in Medieval Iberia: A Selected Bibliography* (Eugene: University of Oregon, Society for Medieval Feminist Scholarship)

——, 2008. *Damas, santas y pecadoras: hijas medievales de Eva*, Icaria, Mujeres y Cultura, 98 (Barcelona: Centre Dona i Literatura)

Michael, Ian, 1960. 'Interpretation of the *Libro de Alexandre*: The Author's Attitude Towards His Hero's Death', *BHS*, 37: 205–14

——, 1965. 'The Description of Hell in the Spanish *Libro de Alexandre*', in *Medieval Miscellany Presented to Eugène Vinaver* (Manchester: Manchester UP), pp. 220–9

——, 1970. *The Treatment of Classical Material in the 'Libro de Alexandre'* (Manchester: Manchester UP)

Miguélez-Carballeira, Helena, 2005. 'Renewing Old Acquaintances: The Conflation of Critical and Translational Paths in the Anglo-American Reception of Mercè Rodoreda, Esther Tusquets and Rosa Montero', unpublished doctoral thesis, University of Edinburgh

Mill, John Stuart, 1869. *The Subjection of Women* (London: Longmans, Green, Reader & Dyer)

Miller, Beth, [1978] 1983. *Women in Hispanic Literatura: Icons and Fallen Idols* (Berkeley: University of California Press)

Minh-Ha, Trin T., 1989. *Woman, Native, Other: Writing Postcoloniality and Feminism* (Bloomington: Indiana UP)

Mirrer, Louise, 1992. *Upon My Husband's Death: Widows in the Literature and Histories of Medieval Europe* (Ann Arbor: University of Michigan Press)

——, 1994. 'Representing "Other" Men: Muslims, Jews, and Masculine Ideals in Medieval Castilian Epic and Ballad', in *Medieval Masculinities: Regarding Men in the Middle Ages*, ed. Clare A. Lees (Minneapolis: Minnesota UP), pp. 169–86

——, 1995. 'Men's Language, Women's Power: Female Voices in the *Romancero Viejo*', in *Oral Tradition and Hispanic Literature: Essays in Honor of Samuel G. Armistead*, ed. Mishael M. Caspi et al. (New York: Garland), pp. 522–47

——, 1996. *Women, Jews, and Muslims in the Texts of Reconquest Castile* (Ann Arbor: University of Michigan Press)

Mit, Geles (ed.), 1999. *Mujeres en el andén / Dones en l'andana* (València: Generalitat Valenciana)
Mohedano Hernández, José María (ed.), 1951. *'El espéculo de los legos': texto inédito del siglo xv* (Madrid: CSIC)
Moi, Toril, 1999. *What Is a Woman? And Other Essays* (Oxford: OUP)
Molina, Josefina, 2000. *Sentada en un rincón* (Valladolid: 45 Semana Internacional de Cine)
Molinaro, Nina L., 1991. *Foucault, Feminism and Power* (Lewisburg, PA: Bucknell UP)
Moliner, María, 1966. *Diccionario del uso del español* (Madrid: Gredos)
Moll, Jaime, 1982. 'La primera edición de las *Novelas amorosas y exemplares* de María de Zayas y Sotomayor,' *Dicenda: Cuadernos de Filología Hispánica*, 1: 177–9
Monlau, Pedro Felipe, 1857. *Elementos de higiene privada, o arte de conservar la salud del individuo* (Madrid: Rivadeneyra)
Monreal de Lozano, Luciana Casilda, 1884. *Cartilla de higiene y economía doméstica para uso de las escuelas de niñas*; repr. in microfiche, Simón Palmer 1992
Monroe, James T., 1981–82. '¿Pedir peras al olmo? On Medieval Arabs and Modern Arabists', *La Corónica*, 10: 121–47
Montaner, Alberto (ed.), 2007. *Cantar de mio Cid*, Biblioteca Clásica (Barcelona: Galaxia Gutenberg)
Montesa Peydro, Salvador, 1981. *Texto y contexto en la narrativa de María de Zayas* (Madrid: Dirección General de la Juventud y Promoción Sociocultural)
Montijo, María Francisca de Sales Portocarrero, Condesa de: see Letourneux 1774
Montseny, Federica, 1987. *Mis primeros 40 años* (Barcelona: Plaza y Janés)
Moore, John K., 2003. 'Conventional Botany or Unorthodox Organics? On the *Meollo/ Corteza* Metaphor in *Admiraçión operum Dey* of Teresa de Cartagena', *Romance Notes*, 44: 3–12
—— (ed.), 2008. *'Libro de los huéspedes': Escorial MS h.I.13*, Medieval and Renaissance Texts and Studies, 349 (Tempe, AZ: Arizona Center for Medieval and Renaissance Studies)
Mora, Constancia de la, 1939. *In Place of Splendor: The Autobiography of a Spanish Woman* (New York: Harcourt Brace)
Mora, Gabriela, and Karen S. van Hooft (eds), 1982. *Theory and Practice of Feminist Literary Criticism* (Ypsilanti, MI: Bilingual Press)
Morales Blouin. Egla, 1981. *El ciervo y la fuente: mito y folklore del agua en la lírica tradicional* (Potomac, MD: Studia Humanitatis)
Morán Turina, Miguel, and Javier Portús, 1997. *El arte de mirar: la pintura y su público en la España de Velázquez* (Madrid: Istmo)
Morant, Isabel, et al. (ed.), 2005–06. *Historia de las mujeres en España y America Latina*, 4 vols (Madrid: Cátedra)
Morcillo, Aurora, 2000. *True Catholic Womanhood: Gender Ideology in Franco's Spain* (Dekalb: Northern Illinois Press)

Mujeres: 10 fotógrafas / 50 retratos, 1994. (Madrid: Fundación Arte y Tecnología)
Mujica, Barbara, 1999. 'Women Directing Women: Ana Caro's *Valor, agravio y mujer* as Performance Text', in Hegstrom and Williamsen 1999: 19–50
——, 2004. *Women Writers of Early Modern Spain: Sophia's Daughters* (New Haven, CT: Yale UP)
——, 2008. 'María de Zayas's Friendship Betrayed à la Hollywood: Translation, Transculturation and Production', in Paun de García and Larson 2008: 240–53
Mulvey, Laura, 1975. 'Visual Pleasure and Narrative Cinema', *Screen*, 16.3 (Autumn): 6–18; repr. 1989 in her *Visual and Other Pleasures* (Basingstoke: Macmillan), pp. 14–26
Muñoz, Ana: see Épinay 1797
Muñoz Fernández, Ángela, 1995. *Acciones e intenciones de mujeres: vida religiosa de las madrileñas (ss. XV-XVI)* (Madrid: Horas y Horas)
Muñoz López, Pilar, 2003. *Mujeres españolas en las artes plásticas: pintura y escultura* (Madrid: Síntesis)
Múzquiz-Guerreiro, Darlene, 2005. 'Symbolic Inversions in Ángela de Azevedo's *El muerto disimulado*', *BCom*, 57: 147–63
Nacimiento, Cecilia del, 1970. *Obras completas*, ed. José M. Díaz Cerón (Madrid: Editorial de Espiritualidad)
Nair, Parvati, 2002. 'In Modernity's Wake: Transculturality, Deterritorialization and the Question of Community in Icíar Bollaín's *Flores de otro mundo*', *Postscript*, 21.2: 38–49
Nash, Mary (ed.), 1983. *Mujer, familia y trabajo en España (1875–1936)* (Barcelona: Anthropos)
——, 1994. 'Experiencia y aprendizaje: la formación histórica de los feminismos en España', *Historia Social*, 20: 151–72
——, 1995. *Defying Male Civilization: Women in the Spanish Civil War* (Denver, CO: Arden Press)
Navarro, Ana (ed.), 1989. *Antología crítica de escritoras de los siglos XVI y XVII*, Biblioteca de Escritoras, 1 (Madrid: Castalia / Instituto de la Mujer)
Nelken, Margarita, 1931. *La mujer ante las Cortes Constituyentes* (Madrid: Castro)
Nichols, Geraldine Cleary, 1986. 'Exile, Gender, and Mercè Rodoreda', *MLN*, 101: 405–17
——, 1989. *Escribir, espacio propio: Laforet, Matute, Moix, Tusquets, Riera y Roig por sí mismas* (Minneapolis: Institute for the Study of Ideologies and Literature)
——, 1992. *Des/cifrar la diferencia: narrativa femenina de la España contemporánea* (México: Siglo XXI)
Nieto Soria, José Manuel, 1987. 'La monarquía bajomedieval castallana ¿una realeza sagrada?', in *Homenaje al profesor Juan Torres Fontes* (Murcia: Universidad / Academia Alfonso X el Sabio), II, pp. 1225–3
——, 1988. *Fundamentos ideológicos del poder real en Castilla (siglos XIII y XVI)* (Madrid: Eudema)

Nieva de la Paz, Pilar, 1993. *Autoras dramáticas españolas entre 1918 y 1936* (Madrid: CSIC)
Núñez Jiménez, Marina, 1995. 'Feminidad y mascarada', *Arte, Individuo y Sociedad*, 7: 53–9
O'Connor, Thomas Austin, 2000. *Love in the 'Corral': Conjugal Spirituality and Anti-Theatrical Polemic in Early Modern Spain* (New York: Peter Lang)
O'Leary, Catherine, and Alison Ribeiro de Menezes, 2007. *A Companion to Carmen Martín Gaite* (Woodbridge: Tamesis)
Obregón, Ignacio, 1784. *Elogio histórico de Madama Le Prince de Beaumont* (Madrid: Pedro Marín)
Odd, Frank, 1983. 'Women of the *Romancero*: A Voice of Reconciliation', *Hispania*, 66: 360–8
Oehrlein, Josef, 1993. *El actor en el teatro español del Siglo de Oro*, trans. Miguel Ángel Vega (Madrid: Castalia)
Offen, Karen, 1988. 'Defining Feminism: A Comparative Historical Approach', *Signs* 14.1 (Autumn): 119–57
——, 2000. *European Feminisms, 1700–1950: A Political History* (Stanford, CA: Stanford UP)
Olinger, Paula, 1985. *Images of Transformation in Traditional Hispanic Poetry* (Newark, DE: Juan de la Cuesta)
Olivares, Julián (ed.), 2009. *Studies on Women's Poetry of the Golden Age: Tras el espejo la musa escribe*, CT, A273 (Woodbridge: Tamesis)
——, and Elizabeth S. Boyce (eds), 1993. *Tras el espejo la musa escribe: lírica femenina de los Siglos de Oro* (México: Siglo Veintiuno)
Ordóñez, Elizabeth J., 1982. 'Reading Contemporary Spanish Narrative by Women', *ALEC*, 7: 237–51
——, 1991. *Voices of Their Own: Contemporary Spanish Narrative by Women* (Lewisburg, PA: Bucknell UP)
Orr, Clarissa Campbell, 2005. 'Aristocratic Feminism, the Learned Governess, and the Republic of Letters', in *Women, Gender and Enlightenment*, ed. Sarah Knott and Barbara Taylor (London: Palgrave), pp. 306–25
Ortega Costa, Milagros, 1989. 'Spanish Women in the Reformation', in *Women in Reformation and Counter-Reformation Europe*, ed. Sherrin Marshall (Bloomington: Indiana UP), pp. 89–119
Ortega y Gasset, José, [1925] 1998. *La deshumanización del arte y otros ensayos* (Madrid: Alianza)
Orts Molines, Josep Lluís, 1993. 'A propòsit de l'*estil femení* de sor Isabel de Villena', in Alemany et al. 1993: I, 315–26
Osuna, Francisco de, [1527] 1972. *Tercer abecedario espiritual*, ed. Andrés Melquíades (Madrid: Editorial Católica)
Ouka Lele: Fotografía 1976–1987, 1987. Intro. by Francisco Calvo Serraller (Madrid: Galería Moriarti)
Ovalle, Ricardo, Walter Gruen, et al., 1994. *Remedios Varo: Catálogo razonado / Catalogue raisonnée* (Mexico: Era)
Pacheco, Francisco, [1649] 1990. *Arte de la pintura: antigüedad y grandeza*, ed. Bonaventura Bassegoda i Hugas (Madrid: Cátedra)

——, 2007. *The Art of Painting, Its Antiquity and Greatness* (1649), selected extracts from Pacheco 1649, trans. Nicholas Walker, in Harrison et al. 2007: 30–8

Palacios, Emilio, 2002. *La mujer y las letras en la España del siglo XVIII* (Madrid: Laberinto)

Palafox, Eloísa, 1998. *Las éticas del 'exemplum': los 'Castigos del rey don Sancho IV', 'El Conde Lucanor' y el 'Libro de buen amor'*, Publicaciones de *Medievalia*, 18 (México: Colegio de México / Universidad Autónoma Metropolitana / UNAM)

Palomino, Antonio, [1724] 1986. *Vidas*, ed. Nina Ayala Mallory (Madrid: Alianza)

——, 1987. *Lives of the Eminent Spanish Painters and Sculptors*, ed. and trans. Nina Ayala Mallory (Cambridge: CUP)

Papa, Cristina, 1994a. '*Car vós senyora sou la gran papesa*: mariologia e genealogie femminili nella *Vita Christi* di Isabel de Villena', in *Las sabias mujeres: educación, saber y autoría* (siglos XIII-XVII), ed. María del Carmen Graña Cid (Madrid: Asociación Cultural Almudaina), pp. 213–25

——, 1994b. '*... l'avrebbe adorata come Dio, se la fede cristiana non l'avesse trattenuto*: la *Vita Christi* di Isabel de Villena', *Hagiographica*, 1: 287–314

Pardo Bazán, Emilia, 1890. 'Dos palabras', *Poesías por Carolina Valencia* (Valencia: Alonso y Menéndez), pp. x–xi

——, [1892] 1981. 'La mujer española', in her *La mujer española*, ed. Leda Schiavo (Madrid: Editora Nacional)

——, [1892] 1999a. *'La mujer española' y otros escritos*, ed. Guadalupe Gómez-Ferrer (Madrid: Castalia)

——, [1892] 1999b. 'La educación del hombre y la de la mujer: sus relaciones y diferencias', in *'La mujer española' y otros escritos*, ed. Guadalupe Gómez-Ferrer (Madrid: Castalia), pp. 149–77

——, [1896] 2004. *Memorias de un solterón* (Madrid: Cátedra)

——, [1909] 1996. *'Náufragas', 'El encaje roto' y otros cuentos*, ed. Joyce Tolliver (New York: MLA), pp. 101–9

——, [1910] 1990. 'La manga', in *Cuentos completos*, ed. Juan Paredes Núñez (A Coruña: Fundación Pedro Barrie de la Maza, Conde de Fenosa), III, pp. 382–4

——, [1913] 1996. *Cocina española antigua y moderna* (San Sebastián: R & B)

Parker, Rozsika, and Griselda Pollock, 1981. *Old Mistresses: Women, Art and Ideology* (London: Pandora)

Parsons, Deborah L., 2003. *A Cultural History of Madrid: Modernism and the Urban Spectacle* (New York: Berg)

Pattison, David, 2007. 'The Role of Women in Some Medieval Spanish Epic and Chronicle Texts', in *The Place of Argument: Essays in Honour of Nicholas G. Round*, ed. Rhian Davies and Anny Brooksbank Jones (Woodbridge: Tamesis), pp. 17–30

Paun de García, Susan., and Donald Larson (eds), 2008. *The Comedia in English Translation and Performance* (Woodbridge: Tamesis)

Pavlović, Tatjana, 2003. *Despotic Bodies and Transgressive Bodies: Spanish Culture from Francisco Franco to Jesús Franco* (Albany: SUNY Press)
——, et al., 2009. *100 Years of Spanish Cinema* (Malden, MA: Wiley-Blackwell)
Pérez, Janet, 1988. *Women Writers in Contemporary Spain* (Boston: Twayne)
——, 1995. *Modern and Contemporary Spanish Women Poets* (New York: Twayne)
Pérez, Jaume, 1485. *Expositio super cantica evangelica* (Valentia: Alphonsus Fernandez de Corduba)
Pérez, Louis Celestino (ed.), 1988. *The Dramatic Works of Feliciana Enríquez de Guzmán* (Valencia: Albatros Hispanófila)
Pérez, Miquel (trans.), 1491. *Gerson: De menyspreu del mon / Imitatio Christi et de contemptu mundi* [by Thomas à Kempis], splanat del lati per Miquel Pereç (Valencia: Pere Hagenbach & Leonard Hutz)
Pérez Galdós, Benito, [1881] 2000. *La desheredada*, ed. Germán Gullón (Madrid: Cátedra); trans. 1976, Lester Clark, *The Disinherited* (London: Folio Society)
——, [1881] 2005. *La desheredada* (Madrid: Alianza).
——, [1884] 1983. *La de Bringas*, ed. Alda Blanco and Carlos Blanco Aguinagua (Madrid: Cátedra); trans. 1996, Catherine Jagoe, *That Bringas Woman* (London: Dent)
——, [1884–86] 1997. *Fortunata y Jacinta,* ed. Francisco Caudet, 2 vols (Madrid: Cátedra); trans. with intro., 1987, Agnés Moncy Gullón, *Fortunata and Jacinta* (London: Viking)
——, 1923. 'El coleccionista', in *Fisionomías sociales*, vol. 1 of *Obras inéditas*, ed. Alberto Ghiraldo (Madrid: Renacimiento), pp. 197–208
Pérez Millán, Juan Antonio, 2003. 'Women Are Also the Future: Women Directors in Recent Spanish Cinema', *Cineaste*, 29.1: 50–55
Pérez Priego, Miguel Ángel, 1990. *Poesía femenina en los cancioneros*, Biblioteca de Escritoras, 13 (Madrid: Castalia / Instituto de la Mujer)
Pérez-Romero, Antonio, 1996. *Subversion and Liberation in the Writings of St Teresa of Avila* (Amsterdam: Rodopi)
Perlingieri, Ilya Sandra, 1992. *Sofonisba Anguissola: The First Great Woman Artist of the Renaissance* (New York: Rizzoli)
Pernarnau Espelt, Josep, 1982. 'La butlla de Gregori XI relativa a l'escriptora catalana sor Ramoneta Oller', *Arxiu de Textos Catalans Antics*, 1: 269–70
Perriam, Chris, 2003a. *Stars and Masculinities in Spanish Cinema: From Banderas to Bardem* (Oxford: OUP)
——, 2003b. 'Iberian Studies in the UK', Subject Centre for Languages, Linguistics and Area Studies Good Practice Guide, http://www.llas.ac.uk/resources/gpg/1447 (accessed October 2008)
Perry, Mary Elizabeth, 1990. *Gender and Disorder in Early Modern Seville* (Princeton, NJ: Princeton UP)
Pick, Lucy K., 2004. *Conflict and Coexistence: Archbishop Rodrigo and the Muslims and Jews of Medieval Spain* (Ann Arbor: University of Michigan Press)

Piera, Montserrat, 2003. 'Writing, *Auctoritas* and Canon Formation in Sor Isabel de Villena's *Vita Christi*', *La Corónica*, 32: 105–18

——, 2006. 'Mary Magdalene's Iconographical Redemption in Isabel de Villena's *Vita Christi* and the *Speculum Animae*', *Catalan Review*, 20: 313–28

Plagnol-Diéval, Marie-Emmanuelle, 2000. 'Aimer ou haïr Mme de Genlis', in *Portraits de femmes,* Études sur le XVIIIe Siècle, vol. 28, ed. Roland Mortier and Hervé Hasquin (Bruxelles: Université), pp. 89–98

Plummer, John F. (ed.), 1981. *Vox Feminae: Studies in Medieval Woman's Song*, Studies in Medieval Culture, 15 (Kalamazoo: Medieval Institute Publications, Western Michigan University)

Pohl, Burkhard, 2007. 'El lado oscuro de la nación: *La comunidad* (Álex de la Iglesia, 2000)', in *Miradas glocales: cine español en el cambio de milenio*, ed. Burkhard Pohl and Jörg Türschmann (Frankfurt: Iberoamericana Vervuert), pp. 119–38

Pollock, Griselda, 1988. *Vision and Difference: Femininity, Feminism and the Histories of Art* (New York: Routledge)

Poor, Sara S., and Jana Schulman (eds), 2007. *Women and Medieval Epic: Gender, Genre, and the Limits of Epic Masculinity* (New York: Palgrave Macmillan)

Pope, Randolph F., 1991. 'Mercè Rodoreda's Subtle Greatness', in Joan L. Brown 1991: 116–35

Porqueras Mayo, Alberto, 1972. *Preceptiva dramática española* (Madrid: Gredos)

Portús, Javier, 2002. *The 'Sala Reservada' and the Nude in the Prado Museum* (Madrid: Museo Nacional del Prado)

——, 2004. *El retrato español: del Greco a Picasso* (Madrid: Museo Nacional del Prado)

Puértolas, Soledad, 2001. *Con mi madre* (Barcelona: Anagrama)

Pulgarín Cuadrado, Amalia, 2004. 'Discurso autobiográfico y escritura femenina en la década de los noventa', *Autobiografía en España: un balance*, ed. Celia Fernández and María Ángeles Hermosilla (Madrid: Visor), pp. 563–76

Quance, Roberta, 2000. *Mujer o árbol: mitología y modernidad en el arte y la literatura de nuestro tiempo* (Madrid: Ediciones Antonio Machado)

——, 2001. 'Un espejo vacío: sobre una ilustración de Norah Borges para el ultraísmo', *Revista de Occidente*, 239 (marzo): 134–47

Quispe Agnoli, Rocío, 1995. 'El espacio medieval femenino entre la escritura y el silencio: *Admiraçión operum Dey* de Teresa de Cartagena', *Lexis: Revista de Lingüística y Literatura*, 19.1: 85–102

Ramírez, Antonio, 1999. *Medios de masas e historia del arte* (Madrid: Cátedra)

Ramos Pérez, Rosario (ed.), 2003. *Ephemera, la vida sobre papel: colección de la Biblioteca Nacional* (Madrid: Biblioteca Nacional / Ministerio de Cultura y Deporte)

Ratcliffe, Marjorie, 1987. 'Women and Marriage in the Medieval Spanish Epic', *Journal of the Rocky Mountain Medieval and Renaissance Association*, 8: 1–13

——, 1988. '"*Matris et munium ...*"': Marriage and Marriage Law in Medieval Spanish Legislation', *Revista Canadiense de Estudios Hispánicos*, 13: 93–109
Raventós-Pons, Esther, 2005. 'Ouka Lele y sus retratos: la ficcionalización del ego', *Confluencia: Revista Hispánica de Literatura y Cultura,* 21.1: 195–209
Read, Jacinda, 2000. *The New Avengers: Feminism, Femininity and the Rape-Revenge Cycle* (Manchester: Manchester UP)
Real, Neus, 1998. *El Club Femení i d'Esports de Barcelona, plataforma d'acció cultural* (Barcelona: Publicacions de l'Abadia de Montserrat)
——, 2005. *Mercè Rodoreda: l'obra de preguerra* (Barcelona: Publicacions de l'Abadia de Montserrat)
——, 2006. *Dona i literatura a la Catalunya de preguerra* (Barcelona: Publicacions de l'Abadia de Montserrat)
Reames, Sherry L., 1985. *The 'Legenda aurea': A Reexamination of Its Paradoxical History* (Madison: University of Wisconsin Press)
Recio, Roxana, 1993. 'Las interpolaciones latinas en la *Vita Christi* de sor Isabel de Villena: ¿traducciones, glosas o amplificaciones?', *Anuario Medieval*, 5: 126–40
Reckert, Stephen, 1970. *Lyra minima: Structure and Symbol in Iberian Traditional Verse* (London: King's College)
——, 1993. *Beyond Chrysanthemums: Perspectives on Poetry East and West* (Oxford: Clarendon Press)
Redondo Goicoechea, Alicia (ed.), 1993. *Relatos de novelistas españolas (1939–69)* (Madrid: Castalia / Instituto de la Mujer)
——, 2003. *Mujeres novelistas: jóvenes narradoras de los noventa* (Madrid: Narcea)
Reilly, Bernard, 1982. *The Kingdom of León-Castilla under Queen Urraca, 1109–1126* (Princeton, NJ: Princeton UP)
Reina Ruiz, María, 2005. *Monstruos, mujer y teatro en el barroco: Feliciana Enríquez de Guzmán, primera dramaturga española* (New York: Peter Lang)
Resina, Joan Ramon, 1987. 'The Link in Consciousness: Time and Community in Rodoreda's *La plaça del Diamant*', *Catalan Review*, 2.2: 225–46
——, 2008. *Barcelona's Vocation of Modernity: Rise and Decline of an Urban Image* (Stanford, CA: Stanford UP)
Rhodes, Elizabeth, 2005. 'Redressing Ana Caro's *Valor, agravio y mujer*', *HR*, 73: 309–28
Rich, Adrienne, 1977. *Of Woman Born: Motherhood as Experience and Institution* (London: Virago)
Rico, Francisco, 1985. 'La clerecía del mester', *HR,* 53: 127–50
Riddel, María del Carmen, 1995. *La escritura femenina en la postguerra española* (New York: Peter Lang)
Riego, Bernardo, 2001. *La construcción social de la realidad a través de la fotografía y el grabado informativo en la España del siglo XIX* (Santander: Universidad de Cantabria)
——, 2003. *Impresiones: la fotografía en la cultura del siglo XIX (antología de textos)* (Girona: Centre de Recerca i Difusió de la Imatge / Ajuntament de Girona)

Riera, Carme, 1994. *Dins el darrer blau* (Barcelona: Destino); trans. 1996, *En el último azul*, Carme Riera (Madrid: Alfaguara); trans. 2007, *In the Last Blue*, Jonathan Dunne (New York: Overlook Press)

——, 1995. 'Montserrat Roig: una altra mirada de Barcelona', *Lectora: Revista de Dones i Textualitat*, 1 (octubre): 7–17

——, 2000. *Cap al cel obert* (Barcelona: Cercle de Lectors)

——, 2001. *Por el cielo y más allá*, trans. of *Cap al cel obert* (Madrid: Alfaguara)

Riera i Sans, Jaume, 1993. 'Falsos dels segles xii, xiv i xv', in Alemany et al. 1993: I, 425–91

Ringrose, David R., 1996. *Spain, Europe, and the 'Spanish Miracle', 1700–1900* (Cambridge: CUP)

Río y Arnedo, María Antonia del (trans.), 1795. *Sarah Th.* [French original by Jean François de Saint-Lambert] (Madrid: Imprenta de José López)

Río y Arnedo, María Antonia del: see also Le Prince 1796–98

Ríos, Blanca de los, 1886. 'La gitana', in Sáez de Melgar 1886: 589–607

Rípodas Ardanaz, Daysi, 1993. 'Una ignorada escritora en la Charcas finicolonial: María Antonia de Río y Arnedo', *Investigaciones y Ensayos*, 43 (Buenos Aires: Academia Nacional de la Historia), pp. 165–207

Riquer, Martí de, 1964. *Història de la literatura catalana: part antiga* (Barcelona: Ariel), III, pp. 480–2

Rivera Garretas, María Milagros, 1992. 'La admiración de las obras de Dios de Teresa de Cartagena y la querella de las mujeres', in Segura Graíño 1992: 277–300

——, 1997. 'Las prosistas del humanismo y del Renacimiento (1400–1550)', in *La literatura escrita por mujer: desde la Edad Media hasta el siglo XVIII*, Zavala et al. 1993–2000: IV, 83–130

Riviere, Joan [1929], 1986. 'Womanliness as a Masquerade', in *Formations of Fantasy*, ed. Victor Burgin, James Donald, and Cora Kaplan (London: Methuen), pp. 35–44; trans. 1979 as 'La femineidad como máscara', in *La femineidad como máscara*, ed. Alicia Roig (Barcelona: Tusquets)

Robertson, Elizabeth, 1991. 'The Corporeality of Female Sanctity in *The Life of Saint Margaret*', in *Images of Sainthood in Medieval Europe*, ed. Renate Blumenfeld-Kosinski and Timea Szell (Ithaca, NY: Cornell UP), pp. 268–87

Rodado Ruiz, Ana María, 1990. '*Vida de Santa Pelagia*', in Connolly et al. 1990: 169–80

Rodoreda, Mercè, 1938. *Aloma*, revised edn, 1969 (Barcelona: Edicions 62)

——, 1962. *La plaça del Diamant* (Barcelona: Club Editor); trans. 1980, *The Time of the Doves*, David H. Rosenthal (New York: Tapplinger)

——, 1980. *Quanta, quanta guerra ...* (Barcelona: Club Editor)

——, 1980. *Viatges i flors* (Barcelona: Edicions 62)

——, 1986. *La mort i la primavera*, ed. Núria Folch (Barcelona: Club Editor); trans. 2009, *Death in Spring*, Martha Tennent (Rochester, NY: Open Letter)

Rodowick, David, 1982. 'The Difficulty of Difference', *Wide Angle*, 5.1: 4–15

Rodrigo, Antonina, 1988. *Mujeres de España: las silenciadas* (Barcelona: Círculo de Lectores)

———, 1999. *Mujer y exilio 1939* (Madrid: Compañía Literaria)
Rodríguez, María Pilar, 2000. *Vidas im/propias: tranformaciones el sujeto femenino en la narrativa española contemporánea* (West Lafayette, IN: Purdue UP)
———, 2002. 'Filmar el terror, filmar la política, filmar la experiencia: *Dias contados* de Imanol Uribe y *Yoyes* de Helena Taberna', in *Mundos en conflicto: aproximaciones al cine vasco de los noventa* (San Sebastián: Universidad de Deusto), pp. 135–71
Rodríguez Magda, Rosa María, 1994. *Femenino fin de siglo: la seducción de la diferencia* (Barcelona: Anthropos)
Rodríguez Rivas, Gregorio, 1992. 'La *Arboleda de los enfermos* de Teresa de Cartagena, literatura ascética en el siglo XV', *Entemu*, 3: 117–30
Roig, Jaume, 2006. *Espill*, ed. Antònia Carré (Barcelona: Quaderns Crema)
Roig, Montserrat, [1977] 1995. *El temps de les cireres* (Barcelona: Edicions 62)
Rojas, Fernando de, [1499] 1969. *La Celestina tragicomedia de Calisto y Melibea*. Prologue by Stephen Gilman. Edn. and notes by Dorothy S. Severin (Madrid: Alianza)
Romero Masegosa y Cancelada, María (trans.), 1792. *Cartas de una peruana, escritas en francés por Mme de Graffigny* [*Lettres péruviennes*, 1747] (Valladolid: viuda de Santander e hijos)
Romeu, Josep (ed.), 1957. '*Consueta de Santa Àgata*', in his *Teatre hagiogràfic*, Els Nostres Clàssics, A79–82 (Barcelona: Barcino), pp. 35–66
Romeu Alfaro, Fernanda, 1994. *El silencio roto: mujeres contra el franquismo* (Madrid: Fernanda Romeu Alfaro)
Ros, Xon de, 2007. *Primitivismo y modernismo: el legado de María Blanchard* (Bern: Peter Lang)
Rowbotham, Sheila, 1973. *Woman's Consciousness, Man's World* (Harmondsworth: Penguin)
Ruiz García, Elisa, 2003. 'Los libros de Isabel la Católica: una encrucijada de intereses', in Castillo Gómez 2003: 53–78
Ruiz Gómez, Leticia, 1998. *La colección de estampas devocionales de las Descalzas Reales de Madrid* (Madrid: Fundación Universitaria Española)
Rummel, Erika, 1999. *Jiménez de Cisneros: On the Threshold of Spain's Golden Age* (Tempe, AZ: Arizona Center for Medieval and Renaissance Studies)
Russ, Joanna, 1993. *How to Suppress Women's Writing* (London: Women's Press)
Sáez de Melgar, Faustina, 1886. *Las mujeres españolas, americanas y lusitanas pintadas por sí mismas* (Barcelona: Juan Pons)
Sales y Alcalá, Agustín de, 1761. *Historia del real monasterio de la Santísima Trínidad* (València: Joseph Esteban Dolz, Impressor del S[anto] Oficio)
Salisachs, Mercedes, 1987. *Derribos: crónicas íntimas de un tiempo saldado* (Barcelona: Plaza y Janés)
Salisbury, Joyce E., 1991. *Church Fathers, Independent Virgins* (New York: Verso)
San Alberto, María de, 1998. *Viva al Siglo / Muerta al Mundo: Selected Works*

/ *Obras escogidas by / de María de San Alberto (1568–1640)*, ed. Stacey Schlau (New Orleans, LA: UP of the South)

San Félix, Sor Marcela de, 1988. *Obra completa: coloquios espirituales, loas y otros poemas*, ed. Electra Arenal and Georgina Sabàt de Rivers (Barcelona: PPU)

Sánchez, Magdalena S., 1998. *The Empress, the Queen, and the Nun: Women and Power at the Court of Philip III of Spain* (Baltimore, MD: Johns Hopkins UP)

——, and Alain Saint-Saëns (eds), 1996. *Spanish Women in the Golden Age: Images and Realities*, Contributions in Women's Studies, 155 (Westport, CT: Greenwood Press)

Sánchez Llama, Íñigo, 2000. *Galería de escritoras isabelinas: la prensa periódica entre 1833 y 1895* (Madrid: Cátedra)

Santaolalla, Isabel, 1999. 'Close Encounters: Racial Otherness in Imanol Uribe's *Bwana*', *BHS*, 76: 111–22

——, 2004. 'The "Road that Turning Always ...": Re-Placing the Familiar and the Unfamiliar in Icíar Bollaín's *Flowers from Another World* (1999)', in *Studies in European Cinema*, 1.2: 129–38

——, forthcoming. *Icíar Bollaín* (Manchester: Manchester UP)

Sanz Villanueva, Santos, 2000. 'Poética postmoderna y novela', in *Los nuevos nombres: 1975–2000. Primer suplemento, Historia y crítica de la literatura española*, 9/1, ed. Jorge García (Barcelona: Crítica), pp. 257–63

Sargent, Michael G. (ed.), 2005. Nicholas Love, *The Mirror of the Blessed Life of Jesus Christ* (Exeter: Exeter UP)

Satué, Enric, 1985. *El libro de los anuncios, I: la época de los artesanos (1830–1930)* (Barcelona: Alta Fulla)

Saugnieux, Joel, 1982. 'Berceo y el apocalipsis', in his *Berceo y las culturas del siglo XIII*, Colección Centro de Estudios 'Gonzalo de Berceo', 7 (Logroño: Instituto de Estudios Riojanos), pp. 149–69

Scanlon, Geraldine, [1976] 1986. *La polemica feminista en la España contemporánea (1868- 1974)* (Madrid: Siglo XXI); 2nd edn 1986 (Madrid: Akal)

Scholberg, Kenneth R., 1977. 'Figurative Language in Juan Manuel', in *Juan Manuel Studies*, ed. Ian Macpherson, CT, A60 (London: Tamesis), pp. 143–55

Schubart, Rikke, 2007. *Super Bitches and Action Babes: The Female Hero in Popular Cinema, 1970–2006* (Jefferson, NC: McFarland)

Schulenburg, Jane Tibbetts, 1978. 'Sexism and the Celestial *gynaeceum* from 500 to 1200', *Journal of Medieval History*, 4: 117–33

Schumm, Sandra J., 1999. *Reflections in Sequence: Novels by Spanish Women, 1944–88* (Lewisburg, PA: Bucknell UP)

Schwartz, Vanessa R., 1995. 'Museums and Mass Spectacle: The Musée Grévin as a Monument to Modern Life', *French Historical Studies*, 19.1 (Spring): 7–26

Sedgwick, Eve Kosofsky, 1985. *Between Men: English Literature and Male Homosocial Desire* (New York: Columbia UP)

Segura, Isabel, and Marta Selva, 1984. *Revistes de dones (1846–1935)* (Barcelona: Edhasa)

Segura Graíño, Cristina (ed.), 1992. *La voz del silencio, I: Fuentes directas para la historia de las mujeres (siglos VIII–XVIII)* (Madrid: Asociación Cultural Al-Mudayna)

Seidenspinner-Núñez, Dayle,1993. '"Él solo me leyó": Gendered Hermeneutics and Subversive Poetics in *Admiraçión operum Dey* of Teresa de Cartagena', *Medievalia*, 15: 14–23

——, 1997, 'But I Suffer not a Woman to Teach: Two Women Writers in Late Medieval Spain', in *Hers Ancient and Modern: Women's Writing in Spain and Brazil*, ed. Catherine Davies and Jane Whetnall, Manchester Spanish and Portuguese Studies, 6 (Manchester: University), pp. 1–14

——, 1998. *The Writings of Teresa de Cartagena* (Cambridge: D. S. Brewer)

——, and Yonsoo Kim, 2004. 'Historicizing Teresa: Reflections on New Documents regarding Sor Teresa de Cartagena', *La Corónica*, 32.2: 125–50

Sendebar: see María Jesús Lacarra 1996

Serrano de Tornel, Emilia [Baronesa de Wilson], 1861. *Las perlas del corazón: deberes y aspiraciones de la mujer en su vida íntima y social)*; repr. in microfiche, Simón Palmer 1992

Serrano y Sanz, Manuel [1901], 1975. *Apuntes para una biblioteca de escritoras españolas desde el año 1401 hasta 1833*, 2 vols, BAE, 268–71, 2nd edn (Madrid: Atlas)

Servodidio, Mirella, 1987. *Reading for Difference: Feminist Perspectives on Women Novelists of Contemporary Spain, ALEC,* 12.1–2 (Special Issue)

Seybolt, Robert Francis, 1946a. 'Fifteenth-Century Editions of the *Legenda aurea*', *Speculum*, 21: 327–38

——, 1946b. 'The *Legenda aurea*, the Bible, and *Historia scholastica*', *Speculum*, 21: 339–42

Shergold, N. D., 1967. *A History of the Spanish Stage: From Medieval Times until the End of the Seventeenth Century* (Oxford: Clarendon Press)

Short, Kanyann, 1995. 'Too Disconnected / Too Bound Up: The Paradox of Identity in Mercè Rodoreda's *The Time of the Doves*', in *International Women's Writing: New Landscapes of Identity*, ed. Anne E. Brown and Marjanne E. Goozé (Westport, CT: Greenwood Press), pp. 187–95

Simmel, Georg, 1923. 'Filosofía de la moda', *Revista de Occidente*, 1.1, 2: 43–66; 211–30

Simón Palmer, María del Carmen, 1991. *Escritoras españolas del siglo XIX: manual bio-bibliográfico* (Madrid: Castalia)

—— (ed.), 1992. *Escritoras españolas, 1500–1900* [2,000 microfiches] (Madrid: Biblioteca Nacional; London: Chadwyck Healey)

Simpson, Lesley Byrd (trans.), 1959. *Little Sermons on Sin: 'The Archpriest of Talavera', by Alfonso Martínez de Toledo* (Berkeley: University of California Press)

Sinclair, Alison, 1998. *Dislocations of Desire: Gender, Identity and Strategy in 'La Regenta'*, NCSRLL, 255 (Chapel Hill: University of North Carolina Press)

——, 2005. '"Though I speak with the tongues of men and of angels ...":

Rhetorical Practices in Medical and Religious Discourse in 19th-Century Spain', *Nineteenth-Century Prose*, 32.1: 97–127
——, 2007. *Sex and Society in Early Twentieth-Century Spain: Hildegart Rodríguez and the World League for Sexual Reform* (Cardiff: University of Wales Press)
Sinués de Marco, María del Pilar, 1859. *El ángel del hogar: obra moral y recreativa dedicada a la mujer* (Madrid: Imp. Nieto y Cia.)
——, [1859] 1904. *El ángel del hogar: estudios morales acerca de la mujer*, 8th edn (Madrid: Liberería General Victoriano Suárez)
Slade, Carole, 1995. *St Teresa of Avila, Author of a Heroic Life* (Berkeley: University of California Press)
Sluhovsky, Moshé, 2007. *Believe Not Every Spirit: Possession, Mysticism and Discernment in Early Modern Catholicism* (Chicago, IL: Chicago UP)
Smith, Anthony D., 1991. *National Identity* (London: Penguin)
Smith, Paul Julian, 1989. *The Body Hispanic: Gender and Sexuality in Spanish and Spanish American Literature* (Oxford: Clarendon Press)
——, 1992. *Laws of Desire: Questions of Homosexuality in Spanish Writing and Film, 1960–1990* (Oxford: Clarendon Press)
Smith, Sidonie, 1987. *A Poetics of Women's Autobiography: Marginality and the Fictions of Self-Representation* (Bloomington: Indiana UP)
Smith, Theresa Ann, 2003. 'Writing out of the Margins: Women, Translation, and the Spanish Enlightenment', *Journal of Women's History*, 15.1: 116–43
——, 2006. *The Emerging Female Citizen: Gender and Enlightenment in Spain* (Berkeley and Los Angeles: University of California Press)
Sobejano, Gonzalo, 2003. 'The Testimonial Novel and the Novel of Memory', in Turner and López 2003: 172–92
Soler, Colette, 2002. 'What Does the Unconscious Know about Women?', in Barnard and Fink 2002: 99–108
Solomon, Michael R., 1997. *The Literature of Misogyny in Medieval Spain: The 'Arcipreste de Talavera' and the 'Spill'* (Cambridge: CUP)
Soufas, Teresa Scott, 1991. 'Ana Caro's Re-Evaluation of the *Mujer varonil* and Her Theatrics in *Valor, agravio y mujer*', in Stoll and Smith 1991: 85–106
——, 1997a. *Dramas of Distinction: A Study of Plays by Golden Age Women* (Lexington: UP of Kentucky)
——, 1997b. *Women's Acts: Plays by Women Dramatists of Spain's Golden Age* (Lexington: UP of Kentucky)
——, 2000. 'The Absence of Desire Leonor de la Cueva's *La firmeza en la ausencia*', in Stoll and Smith 2000: 142–55
Spitzer, Leo, 1952. 'The Mozarabic Lyric and Theodor Fring's Theories', *Comparative Literature*, 4: 1–22
Spivak, Gayatri Chakravorty, 1993. 'The Politics of Translation', in her *Outside in the Teaching Machine* (New York: Routledge), pp. 179–200
——, 2000. 'Translation as Culture', *Parallax*, 6.1: 13–24
Sponsler, Lucy A., 1975. *Women in the Medieval Spanish Epic and Lyric Traditions*, Studies in Romance Languages, 13 (Lexington: UP of Kentucky)

Stacey, Jackie, 1987. 'Desperately Seeking Difference', *Screen*, 28:1; repr. in Kaplan 2000: 450–65

Stanton, Donna C. (ed.), 1984. *The Female Autograph: Theory and Practice of Autobiography from the 10th to the 20th Century* (Chicago, IL: University of Chicago Press)

Staunton, George, 1798. *Viage al interior de China y Tartaria hecho en los años 1792, 1793, 1794 por el lord Macartney [...] recopiladas de los escritos del Lord Macartney, de los de sir Erasmo Gower [...] por sir Jorge Staunton [...]*, vol. 1, trans. [from the French] by D[oña] M[aría] J[osefa] L[uzuriaga] (Madrid: Sancha)

Stewart, Joan H., 1993. *Gynographs: French Novels by Women of the Late Eighteenth Century* (Lincoln: University of Nebraska Press)

Stoll, Anita, 1999. '"Tierra de en medio": Liminalities in Angela de Azevedo's *El muerto disimulado*', in Hegstrom and Williamsen 1999: 151–64

——, and Dawn L. Smith (eds), 1991. *The Perception of Women in Spanish Theater of the Golden Age* (Lewisburg, PA: Bucknell UP)

——, and —— (eds), 2000. *Gender, Identity, and Representation in Spain's Golden Age* (Lewisburg, PA: Bucknell UP)

Stone, Marilyn, and Carmen Benito-Vessels (eds), 1998. *Women at Work in Spain: From the Middle Ages to Early Modern Times* (New York: Peter Lang)

Stone, Rob, 2002. *Spanish Cinema* (Harlow: Longman)

Stratton, Jon, 1996. *The Desirable Body: Cultural Fetishism and the Erotics of Consumption* (Urbana: University of Illinois Press)

Stratton, Suzanne L., 1994. *The Immaculate Conception in Spanish Art* (Cambridge: CUP)

Stroud, Matthew D., 1986. 'La literatura y la mujer en el Barroco: *Valor, agravio y mujer* de Ana Caro', in *Actas del VIII Congreso de la AIH*, ed. David A. Kossoff et al., 2 vols (Madrid: Istmo), II, pp. 605–12

Studlar, Gaylyn, 1984. 'Masochism and the Perverse Pleasures of the Cinema, *Quarterly Review of Film and Video Studies*, 9.4: 267–82

Suárez Lafuente, María, 2003. 'Women in Pieces: The Filmic Re/Constructions of Josefina Molina', *European Journal of Women's Studies*, 10: 395–407

Subirats, Eduardo, 1983. *El alma y la muerte* (Barcelona: Anthropos)

Sullivan, Constance A., 1992. '"Dínos, dínos quien eres": The Poetic Identity of María Gertrudis Hore (1742–1801)', in *Pen and Peruke: Spanish Literature of the Eighteenth Century*, ed. Monroe Z. Hafter, Michigan Romance Studies, 12 (Ann Arbor: University of Michigan), pp. 153–83

Sullivan, Henry W., 1999. 'Don Quixote & the "Third Term" as Solvent of Binary Dualisms: A Response to Howard Mancing', *Cervantes*, 19.1: 177–97

Surtz, Ronald, 1995. *Writing Women in Late Medieval and Early Modern Spain: The Mothers of Saint Teresa of Avila* (Philadelphia: University of Pennsylvania Press)

Sutherland, Ann Harris, and Linda Nochlin, 1976. *Women Artists: 1550–1950* (Los Angeles: Los Angeles County Museum of Art; New York: Random House)

Talavera: see *Martínez de Toledo 1981*

Tavani, Giuseppe, 1969. *Poesia del Duecento nella Penisola Iberica: problemi della lirica galego-portoghese* (Roma: Ateneo)

Tejero, Delhy, 2004. *Los cuadernines (diarios 1936–1968)* (Zamora: Diputación)

Teresa de Jesús, 1957. *The Life of Saint Teresa of Ávila by Herself*, trans. J. M. Cohen (Harmondsworth: Penguin)

——, 1986. *Cuentas de conciencia*, in *Obras completas*, ed. Efrén de la Madre de Dios and Otger Steggink (Madrid: Biblioteca de Autores Cristianos), pp. 585–634

——, 1990. *Libro de la Vida*, ed. Dámaso Chicharro, LH, 98 (Madrid: Cátedra)

Thacker, Jonathan, 2007. *A Companion to Golden Age Theatre* (Woodbridge: Tamesis)

Thomas, Antoine-Léonard, 1773. *Historia o pintura del carácter, costumbres y talentos de las mujeres en los diferentes siglos* (Madrid: Miguel Escribano)

Thompson, Billy Bussell, 1990. '"Plumbei cordis, oris ferrei": la recepción de la teología de Jacobus a Voragine y su *Legenda aurea* en la Península', in Connolly et al. 1990: 97–106

——, and John K. Walsh (eds), 1977. *'La vida de Santa María Egipçiaca': A Fourteenth-Century Translation of a Work by Paul the Deacon*, EHT, 17 (Exeter: Exeter UP)

——, and ——, 1986–87. 'Old Spanish Manuscripts of Prose Lives of the Saints and Their Affiliations', *La Corónica*, 15: 17–28

Thompson, Stith, 1955–58. *Motif-Index of Folk-Literature: A Classification of Narrative Elements in Folktales, Ballads, Myths, Fables, Mediaeval Romances, Exempla, Fabliaux, Jest-Books, and Local Legends*, 7 vols, 2nd edn (Bloomington: Indiana UP)

Thornham, Sue (ed.), 1999. *Feminist Film Theory: A Reader* (Edinburgh: Edinburgh UP)

Tinagli, Paola, 1997. *Women in Italian Renaissance Art: Gender, Representation, Identity* (Manchester: Manchester UP)

Tolliver, Joyce, 1998. *Cigar Smoke and Violet Water: Gendered Discourse in the Stories of Emilia Pardo Bazán* (Lewisburg, PA: Bucknell UP)

Torre, Guillermo de, [1925] 2001. *Literaturas europeas de vanguardia*, ed. José María Barrera López (Sevilla: Renacimiento / Biblioteca del Rescate)

Tortosa, Virgilio, 2001. *Escrituras ensimismadas: la autobiografía literaria en la democracia española* (Alicante: Universidad)

Triana-Toribio, Núria, 2003. *Spanish National Cinema* (London: Routledge)

——, 2007. 'Anyplace North America: On the Transnational Road with Isabel Coixet', *Studies in Hispanic Cinema*, 3.1: 47–64

Trusted, Marjorie, 1996. *Spanish Sculpture: A Catalogue of the Collection in the Victoria and Albert Museum* (London: V&A)

——, 2007. *The Arts of Spain: Iberia and Latin America 1450–1700* (London: V&A)

Tsuchiya, Akiko, 2002. 'The "New" Female Subject and the Commodification of Gender in the Works of Lucía Etxebarria', *Romance Studies*, 20: 77–87

——, 2003. 'Women and Fiction in Post-Franco Spain', in Turner and López 2003, pp. 212–30

Tubert, Silvia (ed.), 1996. *Figuras de la madre* (Madrid: Cátedra)
Turner, Bryan S., 1996. *The Body and Society: Explorations in Social Theory* (London: Sage)
Turner, Harriet, and Adelaida López de Martínez (eds), 2003. *The Cambridge Companion to the Spanish Novel: From 1600 to the Present* (Cambridge: CUP)
Tusquets, Esther, [1978] 2002. *El mismo mar de todos los veranos* (Barcelona: Anagrama); trans. 1990, *The Same Sea as Every Summer*, Margaret E. W. Jones (Lincoln: University of Nebraska Press)
——, [1979] 2001a. *El amor es un juego solitario* (Barcelona: Anagrama); trans.1986, *Love Is a Solitary Game*, Bruce Penman (London: Calder)
——, [1980] 1998. *Varadas tras el último naufragio* (Barcelona: Anagrama); trans. 1992, *Stranded*, Susan E. Clark (Elmwood Park, IL: Dalkey Archive Press)
——, 2001b. *Correspondencia privada* (Barcelona: Anagrama); trans. 2008, *Private Correspondence*, Barbara F. Ichiishi (Cranbury, NJ: AUP)
——, 2001c. Interview with Ángel Molina. *ABC*, 15 May 2001 <www.joanducros.net/corpus/Esther%20Tusquets.html>
——, 2007. *Habíamos ganado la guerra* (Barcelona: Bruguera)
Twomey, Lesley K., 2003a. 'Sor Isabel de Villena: A Gendered Perspective on the Immaculate Conception', *Journal of Catalan Studies*, 6
——, 2003b. 'Sor Isabel de Villena, Her *Vita Christi* and an Example of Gendered Immaculist Writing in the Fifteenth Century', *La Corónica*, 32.1: 89–103
——, 2005. 'Una relectura del color rojo: la alegoría en la *Vita Christi* de Isabel de Villena', in *Las metamorfosis de la alegoría: discurso y sociedad en la Península Ibérica desde la Edad Media hasta la edad contemporánea*, ed. Rebeca Sanmartín and Rosa Vidal Doval (Madrid: Iberoamericana-Vervuert), pp. 189–202
——, 2007. 'Poverty and Richly Decorated Garments: A Re-Evaluation of Their Significance in the *Vita Christi* of Isabel de Villena', in *Medieval Clothing and Textiles*, ed. Robin Netherton and Gale R. Owen-Crocker (Woodbridge: Boydell & Brewer), III, pp. 119–34
——, forthcoming. *The Fabric of Marian Devotion in Isabel de Villena's 'Vita Christi'* (Woodbridge: Tamesis)
Ugarte, Sharon K. (ed.), 1991. *Conversaciones y poemas: la nueva poesía femenina española en castellano* (Madrid: Siglo XXI)
Ulacia Altolaguirre, Paloma, 1990. *Concha Méndez: memorias habladas, memorias armadas* (Madrid: Mondadori)
Uría Maqua, Isabel, 1996. 'La soberbia de Alejandro en el poema castellano y sus implicaciones ideológicas', *Anuario de Estudios Filológicos*, 19: 513–28
——, 2000. *Panorama crítico del mester de clerecía* (Madrid: Castalia)
Urruela, María Cristina, 2001. 'Becoming "Angelic": María Pilar Sinués and the Woman Question', in Vollendorf 2001b: 160–75
Urzainqui, Inmaculada, 1991. 'Hacia una tipología de la traducción en el siglo XVIII: los horizontes del traductor', in Donaire and Lafarga 1991: 623–38

Valero-Costa, Pilar, 2002. 'El poder de la palabra: la política de género en la autobiografía de doña Leonor López de Córdoba', *Medievalia*, 34: 33–42

Valis, Noël, 2002. *The Culture of 'Cursilería': Bad Taste, Kitsch, and Class in Modern Spain* (Durham, NC: Duke UP)

Valls, Fernando, 2000. 'Primera lectura de *Cap al cel obert*', in Cotoner 2000, pp. 305–17

Van Ginhoven, Christopher, 2010. 'The Theurgic Image: Ignatius of Loyola, Teresa of Avila, and the Institutional Praxis of the Counter-Reformation', unpublished doctoral thesis, New York University

Vaquero, Mercedes, 2005. *La mujer en la épica castellano-leonesa en su contexto histórico*, Textos de Difusión Cultural, Serie El Estudio (México: UNAM)

Vargas Ponce, José, 1827. *Proclama de un solterón a las que aspiren a su mano* (Marsella: Librería de Camoin)

Vasari, Giorgio, [1568] 1878–85. *Le vite de' più eccellenti pittori, scultori ed architettori*, ed. Gaetano Milanesi, 9 vols (Florence: Sansoni)

Vasvári, Louise O., 1999. *The Heterotextual Body of the 'Mora Morilla'*, PMHRS, 12 (London: Dept of Hispanic Studies, QMW)

Vázquez, Oscar E., 2001. *Inventing the Art Collection: Patrons, Markets, and the State in Nineteenth-Century Spain* (University Park: Pennsylvania UP)

Veeser, H. Aram (ed.), 1989. *The New Historicism* (London: Routledge)

Vega, Lope de, [1609] 2006. *Arte nuevo de hacer comedias*, ed. Enrique García Santo-Tomás (Madrid: Cátedra)

Veinte ilustradores españoles (1898–1936), 2004. (Madrid: Ministerio de Educación, Cultura y Deporte)

Velázquez, 2006. (London: National Gallery)

Vélez, Pilar, 1998. *El cromo a Catalunya, 1890–1936* (Molins de Rei: Ajuntament)

Vélez-Sainz, Julio (ed.), 2009. Álvaro de Luna, *Libro de las virtuosas e claras mugeres*, LH, 647 (Madrid: Cátedra)

Verhaeghe, Paul, 2002. 'Lacan's Answer to the Classical Mind/Body Deadlock: Retracing Freud's *Beyond*', in Barnard and Fink 2002: 109–39

Victorio, Juan, 1986. 'La mujer en la épica castellana', in Fonquerne and Esteban 1986, pp. 75–84

—— (ed.), 1988. *Poema de Fernán González*, LH, 151 (Madrid: Cátedra)

Vidal, Hernán (ed.), 1989. *Cultural and Historical Grounding for Hispanic and Luso-Brazilian Feminist Literary Criticism* (Minneapolis: Institute for the Study of Ideologies and Literature)

Vilarós, Teresa, 1995. *Galdós: invención de la mujer y poética de la sexualidad (lectura parcial de 'Fortunata y Jacinta')* (Madrid: Siglo XXI)

Villaseñor Black, Charlene, 2006. *Creating the Cult of St Joseph: Art and Gender in the Spanish Empire* (Princeton, NJ: Princeton UP)

Villena, Isabel de, 1916. *Llibre anomenat 'Vita Christi'*, ed. Ramon Miquel y Planas, 3 vols (Barcelona: Biblioteca Catalana)

——, 1986. *Vita Christi: Antología*, ed. Lluïsa Parra (València: Institució Alfons el Magnànim)

——, 1987. *Protagonistes femenines a la 'Vita Christi'*, ed. Rosanna Cantavella and Lluïsa Parra (Barcelona: laSal)
——, 1992. *Vita Christi*, ed. Josep Almiñana Vallés and Juan Costa Català, 2 vols (València: Ajuntament)
——, 1995. *Vita Christi: selecció*, ed. Albert Hauf, Millors Obres de la Literatura Catalana, 115 (Barcelona: Edicions 62 / 'la Caixa')
——, 2008. *Femmes dans la Vie du Christ* [= Villena 1987], trans. Patrick Gifreu (Perpignan: Éditions de la Merci)
Vollendorf, Lisa, 2001a. *Reclaiming the Body: María de Zayas's Early Modern Feminism*, NCSRLL, 270 (Chapel Hill: University of North Carolina Press)
—— (ed.), 2001b. *Recovering Spain's Feminist Tradition* (New York: PMLA)
——, 2005. 'The Value of Female Friendship in Seventeenth-Century Spain', *Texas Studies in Literature and Language*, 47: 425–45
Voros, Sharon, 1997. 'Armesinda's Dream: Leonor de la Cueva's Challenge to Patriarchy in *La firmeza en la ausencia*', *Revista Monográfica*, 13: 74–86
——, 2000. 'Fashioning Feminine Wit in María de Zayas, Ana Caro, and Leonor de la Cueva', in Stoll and Smith 2000: 156–77
——, 2008. 'Zayas's Comic Sense', in Paun de García and Larson 2008: 229–39
——, 2009. 'Leonor's Library: The Last Will and Testament of Leonor de la Cueva y Silva', in *Studies in Honor of Robert L. Fiore*, ed. Chad M. Gasta and Julia Domínguez (Newark, DE: Juan de la Cuesta), pp. 521–34
Vozzo Mendia, Lia (ed.), 1992. *Leonor López de Córdoba, Memorie* (Parma: Pratiche)
Vries, Jan de, 1963. *Heroic Song and Heroic Legend*, trans. B. J. Timmer (London: OUP)
Walker, Roger M. (ed.), 1977. *Estoria de Santa María Egiçiaca*, 2nd edn, EHT, 15 (Exeter: Exeter UP); 1st edn 1972, EHT, 1
Ward, Benedicta, 1987. *Harlots of the Desert: A Study of Repentance in Early Monastic Sources* (London: Mowbray)
Wardropper, Bruce W., 1960. 'The Color Problem in Spanish Traditional Poetry', *MLN*, 75: 415–21
——, 1986. 'The Impact of Folk Song on Sacred and Profane Love Poetry in Post-Tridentine Spain', *The Sixteenth Century Journal*, 4: 483–98
Warner, Marina, 1976. *Alone of All Her Sex: The Myth and the Cult of the Virgin Mary* (London: Weidenfeld & Nicholson)
Weber, Alison, 1992. 'Saint Teresa, Demonologist', in Cruz and Perry 1992: 171–95
——, 1996. *Teresa of Avila and the Rhetoric of Femininity* (Princeton, NJ: Princeton UP)
Weisl-Shaw, Andreea Marina, 2010. 'The Comedy of Didacticism and the Didacticism of Comedy in Medieval Spanish and French Comic Tales', unpublished doctoral thesis, University of Cambridge
Weiss, Julian, 2006. *The 'Mester de Clerecía': Intellectuals and Ideologies in Thirteenth-Century Castile*, CT, A231 (Woodbridge: Tamesis)
Weissberger, Barbara, 2004. *Isabel Rules: Constructing Queenship, Wielding Power* (Minneapolis: University of Minnesota Press)

Westerhof, Danielle, 2008. *Death and the Noble Body in Medieval England* (Woodbridge: Boydell & Brewer)
Whetnall, Jane, 1984. '*Lírica femenina* in the Early Manuscript Cancioneros', in *What's Past is Prologue: A Collection of Essays in Honour of L. J. Woodward*, ed. Salvador Bacarisse et al. (Edinburgh: Scottish Academic Press), pp. 138–50
——, 1992. 'Isabel González of the *Cancionero de Baena* and Other Lost Voices', *La Corónica*, 21.1: 59–82
Whilelm, James J., 1990. *Lyrics of the Middle Ages: An Anthology*, Garland Reference Library of Humanities, 1268 (New York: Garland)
Whitenack, Judith, 1999. 'Ana Caro's *Partinuplés* and the Chivalric Tradition', in Hegstrom and Williamsen 1999: 51–74
Wilcox, John, 1997. *Women Poets of Spain, 1960–1990: Towards a Gynocentric Vision* (Urbana: University of Illinois Press)
Wilkins, Constance L. (ed.), 1998. Constanza de Castilla, *Book of Devotions. Libro de devociones y oficios*, EHT, 52 (Exeter: Exeter UP)
——, 2003. '"En memoria de tu encarnaçión e pasión": The Representation of Mary and Christ in the Prayerbook by Sor Constanza de Castilla', *La Corónica*, 31.2: 217–35
Williams, Linda, 1985. 'Something Else Besides a Mother: *Stella Dallas* and the Maternal Melodrama', *Cinema Journal*, 24.1: 2–27; repr. in Kaplan 2000: 479–504
Williamsen, Amy, 1992. 'Re-writing in the Margins: Caro's *Valor, agravio y mujer* as Challenge to Dominant Discourse', *BCom*, 44: 21–30
Willis, Raymond S., 1935. *The Debt of the Spanish 'Libro de Alexandre' to the French 'Roman d'Alexandre'* (Princeton, NJ: Princeton UP)
——, 1956–57. '*Mester de Clerecía*: A Definition of the *Libro de Alexandre*', *Romance Philology*, 10: 212–24
——, 1965. *The Relationship of the Spanish 'Libro de Alexandre' to the 'Alexandreis' of Gautier de Châtillon* (New York: Kraus)
Winstead, Karen A., 1997. *Virgin Martyrs: Legends of Sainthood in Late Medieval England* (Ithaca, NY: Cornell UP)
Wolf, Kirsten, 1997. 'The Severed Breast: A Topos in the Legends of Female Virgin Martyr Saints', *Arkiv för Nordisk Filologi*, 112: 97–112
Woods-Marsden, Joanna, 1998. *Renaissance Self-Portraiture: The Visual Construction of Identity and the Social Status of the Artist* (New Haven, CT: Yale UP)
Wynn, Sir Richard, [1623] 1996. *A Brief Relation of What Was Observed by the Prince's Servants in Their Journey into Spain, in the Year 1623*, ed. Dámaso López García (Santander: Proases)
Wyszynski, Matthew A., 1998. 'Friendship in María de Zayas's *La traición en la amistad*', *BCom*, 50: 21–33
Zambrano, María, 1943. *La confesión: género literario* (Méjico: Luminar)
——, 1989. *Delirio y destino: los veinte años de una española* (Madrid: Mondadori)
Zanetta, María Alejandra, 2006. *La otra cara de la vanguardia: estudio compa-*

rativo de la obra artística de Maruja Mallo, Ángeles Santos y Remedios Varo (Lampeter: Edwin Mellen)

Zavala, Iris M., et al., 1993–2000. *Breve historia feminista de la literatura española (en lengua castellana)*, 6 vols (Barcelona: Anthropos)

Zayas y Sotomayor, María de, 1637. *Novelas amorosas y ejemplares* (Zaragoça: Hospital Real y General de Nuestra Señora de Gracia, a costa de Pedro Esquer)

——, 1948. *Novelas amorosas y ejemplares*, ed. Agustín G. de Amezúa y Mayo (Madrid: RAE)

——, 1983. *Parte segunda del Sarao y entretenimiento honesto (Desengaños amorosos)*, ed. Alicia Yllera, LH, 179 (Madrid: Cátedra)

——, 1999. *La traición en la amistad. Friendship Betrayed*, ed. Valerie Hegstrom, trans. Catherine Larson (Lewisburg, PA: Bucknell UP)

——, 2000. *Novelas amorosas y ejemplares*, ed. Julián Olivares, LH, 482 (Madrid: Cátedra)

——, 2003. *La traición en la amistad*, ed. Barbara López-Mayhew (Newark, DE: Juan de la Cuesta)

——, 2006. *La traición en la amistad*, ed. Michael J. McGrath (Newark, DE: Cervantes & Co. Spanish Classics)

——, 2009. *Exemplary Tales of Love and Tales of Disillusion*, ed. and trans. Margaret R. Greer and Elizabeth Rhodes (Chicago, IL: University of Chicago Press)

Zecchi, Barbara, 2005 'All About Mothers: Pronatalist Discourses in Contemporary Spanish Cinema', *College Literature*, 32.1: 146–64

Zizek, Slavoj, 1991. *Looking Awry: An Introduction to Jacques Lacan through Popular Culture* (Cambridge, MA: MIT Press)

Zulueta, Carmen de, 1992. *Cien años de educación de la mujer española. Historia del instituto internacional* (Madrid: Cátedra)

INDEX

Abril, Victoria: *see* female actors in the twentieth century
Academia de Bellas Artes de San Fernando: 135, 259
Achard, Amédée: 190
Advertisement industry: 191, 200, 202, 203–4, 207–8
   and female images: 193, 194, 195, 196, 197, 199, 200, 201, 202, 203, 205, 206, 207
   and ideals of femininity: 190, 205, 207–8; *see* ángel del hogar; conduct manuals
   in nineteenth century:
     commercial posters, 191, 204, 204n
     calendars: 190–1, 200
Aguirre, Cayetana: *see* women translators in the eighteenth century
Albert, Caterina (Víctor Català): 290–1
Alberti, Leon Battista: 132
Aldaraca, Bridget: 13, 212–14
Alemany, Rafael: 106
Alexander, Gerald: 248
Alfonso V: 98
Alfonso X: 31, 69–72, 71n, 77, 79
   see Siete Partidas
Almodóvar, Pedro: 21, 310, 311, 320, 329–34, 336–9, 340, 342
   and maternal melodramas: 21, 311, 337–40
alumbradas (Illuminists): 115
Álvarez Junco, José: 307
Álvarez, Mercedes: *see* women filmmakers documentarists
Amar y Borbón, Josefa: 15, 177, 178, 179, 180, 185, 228–9, 244
Amat, Nuria: 14
Amorós, Celia: 255
Anderson, Benedict: 27

Andreu, Alicia: 252
ángel del hogar, ideology of: 13, 198, 212, 232–3, 237, 252, 252n, 275
   see also María Pilar Sinués de Marco
Anglada, Maria Àngels: 290–1
Anguissola, Almicare: 131
Anguissola, Sofonisba: 11, 129–32, 132n, 139, 140, 141–2
Anson, John: 62
Aranda, Vicente: 21, 318, 321–6, 328, 335
Arenal, Concepción: 15, 17, 237–8, 251
Armstrong, Isobel: 293, 297
Arnold, Andrea: 330
Asociación Femenina de Educación Cívica: 253
Asociación Nacional de Mujeres Españolas (ANME): 247, 277, 280
Astell, Mary: 244
Autobiographies: 10, 20, 84, 111–26, 281, 301–2, 303n, 304–5, 308–15
   and memoirs: 82–6, 222–5, 301–2, 303n, 306, 312
   and feminism: 20, 303n, 304
Avant-garde: 14, 17, 18n, 257, 260, 263–9, 263n
Ayala de Óbidos, Josefa: *see* women painters of the Golden Age
Aylmer, John: 161
Azevedo, Ángela de: *see* women dramatists of the Golden Age

Bachelard, Gaston: 297n
Balletbò-Coll, Marta: *see* women filmmakers of the boom
Barbal, Maria: 290–1
Barberá y París, Dolores: 217–18
Barnett, David: 106
Bataille, Georges: 211, 212

Belén, Ana: 318, 321, 327
Benedict XIII (Pedro Luna): 92
Beneyto, Maria: 292
Benito Goerlich, Daniel: 98n, 99n, 102–3, 105, 106n
Berg, Judith: 106
Bergnes, Juana: *see* women translators in the eighteenth century
Bernard of Clairvaux: 110
BIESES (Bibliografía de Escritoras Españolas): 4n, 81n
Blanchard, María: *see* women painters of the avant-garde
Blanco, Alda: 3, 232, 236, 309n,
Blázquez de Frías, Baltasar: 169
Blom, Ida: 249, 253, 255
Boccaccio, Giovanni: 145
Boethius: 91
Boehl von Faber, Cecilia (Fernán Caballero): 233, 236
Bollaín, Icíar: 21, 331, 333, 338
Borges, Norah: 18, 18n, 257–8, 262–3, 264, 265–6, 267
Bourdieu, Pierre: 192, 214
Braidotti, Rosi: 4
Bronfen, Elizabeth: 16, 211–12, 220, 223, 225
Bryson, Norman: 11, 129
Burgos, Carmen de (Colombine): 15, 239–40, 247
Burgos, Elvira: 261
Butler, Judith: 257, 263n, 269, 272

Cabrera y Heredia, Dolores: 235
Calinescu, Matei: 271
Campion, Jane: 325, 329–30
Campoamor, Clara: 15, 248, 279–80, 285, 303n
Capmany, Maria Aurèlia: 290–1
Carducho, Vicente: 132
Caro, Rodrigo: 160
Caro Mallén de Soto, Ana: *see* women dramatists of the Golden Age
Carrington, Leonora: 267
Cartagena, Alfonso de: 92
Cartagena, Teresa de: 9, 81, 90–4
Casanova, Sofía: 238–40
Castiglione, Baldassare: 132
Castilla, Constanza de: 9, 81, 86–7, 90
Castilla Xarava, María Jacoba: *see* women translators in the eighteenth century
Castillo Solórzano, Alonso de: 160
Castro, Rosalía de: 245, 246
Catalan nationalism: 288, 289, 313
and language: 296, 313
Catalan Pen Club: 292
Catalan women writers: 19–20, 57, 287–300, 311–13
Medieval: 81, 81n, 99–100, 107n,
and cultural specificity: 288–9, 299
as 'double minority': 19, 291–3, 300
and 'gender exile': 19, 291–2
and sense of homeland: 293–5, 297, 300
critical reception of: 19–20, 288, 290–2
see entries for individual writers
Catholic Church: 116, 205, 275, 280, 282
and education: 104, 137, 274, 275, 282–3
and religious discourse: 87–90, 99, 104, 116, 215, 305
and religious orders: 5, 55, 86, 89, 98, 98n, 101, 102–4, 111, 137, 151, 159, 176, 228, 282, 284
Censorship: 178, 182
Cerezo, Alicia: 252
Cervantes de Saavedra, Miguel: 145, 147, 154, 169
Charles I: 157
Charles II: 131
Chacel, Rosa: 15, 240, 257–9, 303, 303n, 306
Champourcín, Ernestina de: 259, 267, 267n
Charnon-Deutsh, Lou: 13, 16, 198, 211–12, 223
Cherner, Matilde (Rafael Luna): 220–5
Childs, Sarah: 244
Cinema: 2, 3, 14, 17, 21–2, 240, 306, 310, 317–28, 329–42, 340n
sexy Spanish comedies: 335
Cisneros, Francisco Ximénez de: 124
Civil War: 13, 258–9, 263, 266–7, 278, 281, 285, 308, 339–40
Cixous, Hélène: 1, 76, 254, 304
Coixet, Isabel: 14, 330, 338, 342
Comedia: 145, 157–71
and cross-dressing: 158, 164, 170

Condesa de Lalaing (Cayetana de la Cerda y Vera): *see* women translators in the eighteenth century
Condesa de Montijo (María Francisca de Sales y Portocarrero); *see* women translators in the eighteenth century
Condesa Catalina Caso: *see* women translators in the eighteenth century
Conduct manuals: 16, 134, 197, 208, 211, 214, 216, 220, 225, 232, 239
    primers and chapbooks: 198, 199
    see also Joaquina García Balmaseda; Luciana Monreal de Lozano; Emilia Serrano de Tornel
Confederación Española de Derechas Autónomas (CEDA): 284
Constantine I: 61
Consumerism: 189, 190, 214, 218, 225, 239
    and excess: 16, 211–18, 220–1, 262
    see also fashion
Conversos: 90, 114n, 295n
Córdoba, Fray Martín de: 59
Coronado, Carolina: 230–1, 233
Cortes Constituyentes: 247, 279
Count Julian: 29, 29n
Count of Lemos (Pedro Fernández de Castro): 144
Counter Reformation: 5, 11, 110n, 133, 137, 144, 151, 155
Courtly love: 64, 66, 169
Cruz, Penélope: *see* female actors in the twentieth century
Cultural Studies: 2–3, 130, 303
Cursilería: 13, 214, 219

Davies, Catherine: 12n, 13, 14n, 15n, 251–2
Death: 5, 19, 35–9, 61–3, 74–5, 83, 85, 99, 143–4, 146, 150–6, 159, 162–8, 213, 220, 223–5, 339–40
    and the undead: 143–56
de la Cruz, Sor Juana Inés: *see* women dramatists of the Golden Age
de la Cueva y Silva, Francisco: 169
de la Cueva y Silva, Leonor: *see* women dramatists of the Golden Age
de la Mora, Constancia: 281
de la Torre, Josefina: 257n, 259
De Lauretis, Teresa: 319, 331, 334, 338
de los Arcos, Luis Antonio, 131

de los Ríos, Blanca: 238, 240, 252
De Medici, Catherine: 161
del Nacimiento, Cecilia: *see* women dramatists of the Golden Age
del Río y Arnedo, María Antonia: *see* women translators in the eighteenth century
Delibes, Miguel: 335–7
Deyermond, Alan: 2, 25n, 26n, 28n, 35n, 38, 38n, 41, 42n, 49n, 50, 51n, 52n
Dicenta, Daniel: 336
Diego, Estrella de: 14, 268
Dillard, Heath: 5, 26, 69, 80
do Ceo, Sor Maria: *see* women dramatists of the Golden Age
Domènech, Maria: 290–1
Domestic (private) sphere: 11, 13, 16, 27, 102, 137, 165, 190, 220, 232, 234–6, 276, 279, 302, 307, 338
    see also ángel del hogar; and public sphere
Duke of Almodóvar (Pedro Francisco Jiménez de Góngors y Luján): 179

Earnshaw, Doris: 42–4, 42n, 49, 52–3
écriture féminine: 2, 304
Egual, María: *see* women dramatists of the Golden Age
Eiximenis, Francesc: 100, 103, 103n, 106n
El Greco (Domeniko Theotokopoulos): 132
Elizabeth I: 161
Enders, Victoria Lorée: 3, 249
Enlightenment: 15, 175–87, 228–9, 244, 255, 258, 271
Enríquez de Guzmán, Feliciana: *see* women dramatists of the Golden Age
Epic poetry: 7, 25–39
Eroticism: 47–53, 57, 64, 135–7, 167, 235, 317–18
Espéculo de los legos: 59
Espina, Concha: 240
Everyday life: 2, 4, 55, 189–90, 200, 203
    and ephemera in print media: 16, 189–91, 189n, 199–200, 200n, 207
    collections: 189n, 200n,
    photographs: 190, 192, 195, 199
    holy images: 190–1, 199, 205, 205n, 271

and objects: 16, 190–1, 197, 205, 207–8
  albums: 190–1, 192n, 205
  fans: 190, 198n, 200
  and penny novels: 197
  see consumerism and fashion
Exemplary literature: 11, 59, 62, 69–80, 84–6, 92–4, 143–5, 221
Exile: 19, 83, 267, 285, 291–4, 301, 308–10

Don Fadrique de Castilla: 70
Falcón, Lidia: 13n, 254
Fashion: 3, 16, 193, 194, 195, 205, 211, 213–14, 216–23, 228, 262, 265, 268–9
  and cosmetics: 202, 203, 208
  as luxury: 16, 192, 198, 211–13, 216–17, 219–20
  and lust: 16, 211–13, 215
  and social distinction: 213, 221
  and vanity: 198, 213–14, 217, 219–20, 223
  see also consumerism
Feijóo, Benito Jerónimo: 179, 244
Felipe II: 11, 132n, 139
Felipe III: 6, 132
Felipe IV: 145, 169
Felipe V: 131
Felski, Rita: 261, 304
Female actors:
  in the comedia: 11–12, 158
  in twentieth-century: 21, 318,321, 330, 335–7, 336n
  see Ana Belén
Female body: 10, 11, 21, 77, 109–27, 135, 138–9, 143–4, 152–5, 208, 222–4, 299.
  humoral balance of: 139, 147
  and sickness: 92–4, 222, 224
  on-screen: 20, 21, 222–3, 251, 317–19, 320, 322, 327
  and 'destape': 317–18, 322
  as spectacle: 61, 208 158, 269, 317, 327, 329
Female desire: 8, 9, 41–54, 64, 67, 114, 143, 159, 220, 231–35, 324, 326
  as illness: 224
Female friendship: 160, 165, 165n, 166–8, 171, 231, 235, 267, 321
Female gaze: 129, 135, 137, 139, 155, 318, 324–6, 331

and spectatorship: 2, 89, 141, 155, 318, 324–6, 331
Female literacy: 5, 56, 228, 232, 239, 248 275, 282, 284, 302
Femininity: 3, 21, 60, 181, 190, 205, 207–8, 218, 225
  see also masquerade
Feminism:
  definition: 245
  French theorists: 1, 147, 204, 254, 304, 309n, 319, 338–9, 340–1
  Anglo-American theorists: 3, 19, 21, 259–50, 253, 290, 292, 304, 319, 321
  and relational versus individualist: 249–51, 254–5
  and cultural geography: 288
  and intersectionality: 17–19, 94, 155, 244–5, 253, 273–85
  and Post-Structuralism: 2, 293, 300, 305
  and Postcolonial studies: 289, 293,296, 300
  and gender studies: 319
  and feminist film theory: 319
  in Spain: 12–18, 216, 218, 227, 237–8, 239, 243, 245–56, 261–2, 279–80, 311
    proto-feminism: 100, 105, 143, 152, 164, 185, 228–9, 244
  in film-criticism: 320–1
Feminist magazines: 13n, 254, 292
Istòria de la Passió: 104n
Fernández, James: 110, 115n, 117
Fernández y González, Manuel: 198, 198n
Ferrán, Ofelia: 308, 310, 320
Ferrater, Gabriel: 290–1
Ferreira, Patricia: see women film-makers of the boom
Ferreira de la Cerda, Bernarda: see women dramatists of the Golden Age
Film studies: 2–3, 319–21
  and Psychoanalysis: 319, 340n
  and Feminism: 21, 318–20, 324, 328, 319, 331
folklóricas: 302
Fontanella, Francesc: 145
Forteza, María: 294
Foucault, Michel: 116, 215, 319
Franco regime: 15, 19, 248–49, 258–9,

278, 281, 298, 303, 306, 312–13, 317, 329, 339–40, 339n
Freixas, Laura: 20, 302n, 303, 304n, 311
Frenk, Margit: 8, 8n, 41–3, 41n, 44n, 45, 49–51, 51n
Freud, Sigmund: 148, 223, 301, 308–9, 325, 331
    see also Psychoanalysis
Frings, Theodore: 43

Galen: 147
Gallego Méndez, María Teresa: 248
Gangutia, Elvira: 42
García Balmaseda, Joaquina: 217
García Lorca, Federico: 270, 303n, 307
    and Bernarda Alba: 307
García Sempere, Marinela: 106
Gender studies: 19, 61, 63, 82, 130, 149, 154, 158, 198, 229, 244–5, 249–51, 255, 262, 269, 273, 280, 288, 290–2, 204–5, 317–20, 331
    see feminism
Gender difference: 11, 148–50, 232, 304, 331
    essentialist theories of: 2, 18, 148, 254, 304, 331 257, 325
    and national identity: 26, 236, 280, 289–91, 297, 306, 310–5
Gender equality: 11, 12n, 19, 143–4, 148, 152–3, 179, 238, 240, 243, 244n, 246, 249, 251, 254, 258, 283
    see legislation
Generation of 1898: 310, 310n *see* Miguel de Unamuno
Generation of 1927: 261, 301
Gerson, Jean: 109
Giesen, Bernhard: 28
Gimeno de Flaquer, Concepción: 218, 251–3
Gómez de Avellaneda, Gertrudis: 230, 251
Góngora, Luis de: 169
Goyri, María: 308
Goytisolo, Juan: 146–7
Grado, Mercedes de: 254
Grassi y Trechi, Ángela: 220
Grau, Julián: 260
Greer, Germaine: 130, 131
Gutiérrez, Chus, 21, 330, 335, 341n
Hagiography: 55–67, 81, 109–27, 131, 133, 135, 169

    see also saints
Hapsburg, House of: 129, 131, 141–2
Hart, Stephen: 2
Hauf, Albert: 81n, 89n, 100, 102n, 103–6, 103n
Henry II: 82, 88n
Herrera, Lola: *see* female actors in the twentieth century
Hickey, Margarita: *see* women translators in the eighteenth century
Historical memory: 15, 36, 297, 308, 309, 314, 339, 340
    and desmemoria, 296–7, 339, 339n
History of Art: 3, 14, 105,129, 130, 132, 133, 134, 261
    and feminism: 14, 130, 132–3, 141
Hore, Gertrudis María: 228–9
Horizonte: 264, 264n
Huarte de San Juan, Juan: 11, 139, 147
Hurtado, Amparo: 240

Ibarruri, Dolores (La Pasionaria): 284, 303n
Inquisition: 133, 135
Instituto de la Mujer: 12, 12n, 285n
Intrahistoria: 310, 310n *see* Miguel de Unamuno
Irigaray, Luce: 1, 304, 319
Isabel de Borbón: 169
Isabel de Valois: 132, 140
Isabel I of Castile (la Católica): 6, 7, 99, 161
Isabel II: 236
    and the Revolution of 1868: 236
Istòria de la Passió: 104n

Jimeno de Flaquer, Concepción *see* Gimeno de Flaquer
Juan II de Castilla: 70, 88n
Johnson, Roberta: 3, 12–13, 22
Joyes, Inés: *see* women translators in the eighteenth century
Don Juan Manuel: 9, 70, 70n, 72–80, 73n
Juan Ruiz: 69
Junta de Damas (of the Madrid Royal Economic Society): 229

Katherine of Lancaster: 83, 88n
Kahlo, Frida: 257
Keene, Judith: 248

Kent, Victoria: 15, 18, 247–8, 279
Kirkpatrick, Susan: 2, 13–14, 16–17, 231, 234–5, 239, 246, 247n, 252n
Kristeva, Julia: 1, 22, 147, 304, 309n, 330, 338, 340–1

La Cava: 29, 29n
Labanyi, Jo: 13n, 212, 218
Lacan, Jacques: 11, 143n, 144, 148, 149, 152, 154–5, 263n, 329, 331–4, 34–2
Laforet, Carmen: 12, 12n, 13n, 287, 292, 304, 306
Larrea, Francisca: *see* women translators in the eighteenth century
Legislation
  Siete Partidas: 70–1, 77, 79
  and 1889 Civil Code: 214,247, 275, 277, 278
  Constitution of 1931: 241, 247, 274
  on civil marriage: 278, 280–3
  on divorce: 248, 274, 275, 278, 280–2, 283, 336, 339
  on equal gender rights: 27, 198, 243, 283
  on woman suffrage: 17–18, 239, 247–8, 253, 262, 278, 283–4
Ley de Memoria Histórica (2007): 314
Ley de Extranjería: 341
Lejárraga, María (María Martínez Sierra): 251, 253
León, María Teresa: 15, 20, 259, 308–10
  and exile: 308–10
  and the Romancero: 308, 309n, 310, 310n
León Garavito, Francisco de: 159
Lesbianism: 319, 321, 333, 334
Libro de Alexandre: 7, 25–6, 26n, 27n, 28–29, 32, 33n, 36–8, 36n, 38n
Libro de las tribulaciones: 92
Libro de los cien capítulos: 78
Liga de Amas de Casa: 253
Linehan, Peter: 80
Literary market: 175, 177, 229, 232, 239, 301–2
Lombroso, Cesare: 221
López de Córdoba, Leonor: 7, 9, 81–6
Lorenzo, May: 263, 265, 266n
Louis, Anja: 240
Luna, Álvaro de: 59
Luzuriaga, María Josefa: *see* women translators in the eighteenth century

Lyceum Club: 261
Lyrical sisterhood: 231, 233, 238
Llull, Ramón: 92

Mallo, Maruja: *see* women painters of the avant-garde
Mangini, Shirley: 14–15, 14n, 240, 261
Manrique de Lara, Doña Inés Jacinta: 160
Mañé, Teresa (Soledad Gustavo): 240
Marañón, Gregorio: 262, 275
Marçal, Maria Mercè: 105n, 292
Margaret of Hungary: 161
Margueritte, Victor: 262
María of Castile, Queen Consort of Aragon and Naples: 98
Mariana, Juan de: 157
Mariscal, Ana: *see* women film-makers of the Frenco period.
Marquesa de Espeja (Josefa de Alvarado): *see* women translators in the eighteenth century
Martínez de Toledo, Alfonso: 9, 70, 73–5
Mary of Guise: 161
Mary Tudor: 161
Marriage: 5, 9, 19, 45, 65, 70–80, 151, 154, 159, 164–5, 167, 169, 182–3, 187, 233, 240, 260, 263, 274–5, 278, 280–4, 318, 323–4
  polygamy: 70
  sponsa Christi (bride of Christ): 8, 64–5
  and widowhood: 5, 61–3, 158, 238, 275, 335
Mass-market fiction (literatura de quiosco): 302, 302n
Massanés, Josefa: 230, 252
Martín Gaite, Carmen: 12, 13n, 15n, 301, 303
Masculinity: 16, 38, 218, 223–4, 262, 272, 319–20, 326
  crisis of: 326
  and castration: 76, 148, 154, 251–3, 324, 328
Masquerade: 4, 18–19, 21–2, 149, 257–72, 322, 329–41
  Bakhtinian: 334, 337
  post-feminist: 322
  see Joan Riviere; and Judith Butler
Matos Fragoso, Juan de: 161
Matute, Ana María: 12, 12n, 13n, 292, 306

Maura, Carmen: *see* female actors in the twentieth century
McNerney, Kathleen: 2, 12n, 105, 292
Medical discourse: 3, 9, 16, 70, 147–8, 215, 275
Melodrama: 147, 240, 332
  and maternal grief: 313, 337, 331, 338, 339–40
  and Almodóvar: 21, 338–9
Memorial literario, instructivo y curioso de la Corte de Madrid: 179
Méndez Cuesta, Concha: 259
Menéndez Pidal, Ramón: 308–9
Mérode, Cléo de: 262
Mester de Clerecía: 7, 26, 26n, 27, 34, 39
Miller, Beth: 1, 7
Minh-Ha, Trinh T.: 293, 300
miracles: 60, 84–6, 101, 114, 154, 271
Miró, Pilar: 21, 332–3, 335
Misogyny: 10, 29, 63, 70, 75, 82, 102n, 167
  and violence: 60, 61, 62, 65, 73–6, 143, 151, 154, 247, 293, 338
  and rape: 29, 29n, 71, 151, 162–3, 293, 297, 299, 339.
  and female slavery: 138, 142, 151, 162
Models of womanhood: 232, 261, 265, 320
  the Modern Woman: 197, 266
  the New Spanish Woman: 250, 279
  post-Frenco: 21, 317–28, 332
  on screen: 323–4, 326
  see ángel del hogar
Modernity: 17–18, 142, 227–41, 258, 261
  and modernization: 227
  and modernism: 13, 14, 17, 18, 258, 259–69
Moi, Toril: 272
Moix, Ana Maria: 292
Molina, Josefina: 21, 335–7, 336n, 337n, 340
Monlau, Pedro Felipe: 215
Monreal de Lozano, Luciana Casilda: 217
Monroe, James: 42
Monserdà, Dolors: 290–1
Monsó, Imma: 292
Montseny, Federica: 15, 247, 250, 303n
Montsoriu, Abbess Aldolça de: 99, 103, 103n

Mor, Anthonis: 139
Mother: 61, 275, 305–6, 310–11, 318, 327
  and daughter relationship: 4, 20, 46, 46n, 180, 211, 232, 305–11, 306n, 313–15
  literary representation of: 20, 46, 46n, 306n, 298, 306–14
  in cinema: 310, 338, 339
  as mater dolorosa: 21, 330, 337–40
  and the nation: 307–15
  and orphans: 150, 220, 234, 305, 306
  under Franco: 306
  in post-Franco Spain: 310
Mujeres Libres: 250
Mulvey, Laura: 21, 319, 325, 328
Murillo, Bartolomé Esteban: 11, 129–30, 136, 137
Muñoz, Ana: *see* women translators in the eighteenth century
Myth: 49, 159–60
  Io: 22, 330, 340–1
  Oedipus: 22, 305, 330, 338, 340–1
  Demeter and Persephone: 305
  Antigone: 271
  Psyche: 162
  Venus: 141, 160
Mysticism: 65, 109–27, 260

Nash, Mary: 2–3, 15, 250
Nelken, Margarita: 15, 247–8, 251, 279
New Historicism: 7
Nieto Soria, José Manuel: 78

Obiols, Armand, 290
Offen, Karen: 244n, 245, 249–50, 253, 255–6
Olivares, Count-Duke of: 145
Oliver, Maria Antònia: 290–1
Oller, Sor Ramoneta: *see* Women writers, in fourteenth century
Oral tradition: 33, 43, 53, 309–10
  and Romancero: 308, 310, 309n, 310n
Orientalism: 326
Ortega y Gasset, José: 261
Osuna, Francisco de: 6, 110, 118–9, 122–3
Ouka Leele (Bárbara Allende Gil de Biedma): 19, 269–71, 269, 270, 269n
Pacheco, Francisco: 133–5, 139
Painting: 129–42, 197, 257–69

portraiture: 129, 137, 139, 139n, 142, 267, 265–66, 266n
self-portraiture: 141–2, 265
Palomino, Antonio: 133–4
Pardo Bazán, Emilia: 15–8, 227–8, 332, 237–9, 246, 247n, 250–2, 232
Paris 1889 Exhibition: 192
Parker, Rozsika: *see* History of Art and feminism
Partido Feminista: 254
Patriarchy:
  ideology of: 1, 26, 38, 130, 142, 148, 150, 154–5, 164, 225, 256, 292, 305, 322, 324, 327
  social structure: 9, 11, 79, 80, 137, 142–3, 153, 245, 288, 305–6, 310, 319, 326, 337, 341
Payás, Dolores: *see* women film-makers of the boom
Pedagogical Congress (1892): 238
Pedro I: 83, 86, 88n
Pereç, Jaume: 98n, 104n
Peres, Miquel: 98, 103, 104n
Pérez de Montalbán, Juan: 145, 160
Pérez Galdós, Benito: 191–2, 207, 214, 217, 220
Periodical press: 177, 183, 219, 228–30, 237, 240, 279
  and women writers: 177, 179, 183, 185, 228–30, 237, 240
Picón, Jacinto Octavio: 191
Photography: 16, 190. 191, 192, 192n, 195, 199, 239, 269–72
  see Ouka Leele
Pi, Rosario: *see* women film-makers of the Frenco period
Piera, Montserrat: 3, 105n, 107
Pinar, Florencia: 81
Pizan, Christine de: 102
Plato: 149
Poema de Fernán González: 7, 25–6, 28–30, 34, 36, 38
Pollock, Griselda: *see* History of Art and feminism
Ponce Solís y Farfán, Cristóbal: 159
Pons, Vicent: 104n, 105, 105n
prensa del corazón: 302, 302n
Primo de Rivera, Miguel: 244, 277, 283
Psychoanalysis: 2, 13, 75, 325, 328, 331, 340n

  see Sigmund Freud; and Jacques Lacan
Public sphere: 13, 16, 27, 190, 220
  women's role in: 228–41, 243–4, 279–80
  and employment, 275–77
  see domestic sphere
Puértolas, Soledad: 20, 311, 313–14
Pujol, Ariadna: *see* women film-makers documentarists

Quance, Roberta: 14, 18, 260, 262, 265, 271
Querejeta, Gracia: *see* women film-makers of the boom
Querelle des femmes: 91, 102n

Ramos Pérez, Rosario: 189n, 190, 199–200, 200n
Readership: 183–4, 186, 195, 239, 288, feminization of, 183, 239, 302
Recio, Roxana: 106, 106n
Reconquest: 26, 34, 56
Rembrandt (Rembrandt van Rijn): 142
Residencia de Señoritas: 259
Restauración: 236
Revolution of 1868: 236
Ribera, José: 11, 129–30, 135
Rich, Adrienne: 305
  and mother-daughter bond: 305
Richardson, Samuel: 181
Riego, Bernardo: 190–2
Riera, Carme: 14, 20, 287–97, 299–300
Riquer, Martí de: 103
Riviere, Joan: 18, 257–8, 262, 264, 267, 271–2
Rodoreda, Mercè: 3, 12, 287–8, 290–2, 306
Rodríguez Magda, Rosa: 254–5
Rodríguez, Azucena: *see* women film-makers of the boom
Roig, Jaume: 10, 102, 102n
Roig, Montserrat: 287, 290–2
Roldán, Luisa Ignacia: 129, 130–1, 133, 133–4, 142
Roldán, Pedro de: 131
Romancero general de la guerra española: 309n–310n
Romancero: 42, 53, 160, 308, 310
Romanticism: 17, 230–6

Romero Masegosa, María del Rosario: *see* women translators in the eighteenth century
Romero, Marina: 259
Ros, Mireia: *see* women film-makers of the boom
Rousseau, Jean-Jacques: 181, 185, 229

Sáenz de Tejada, Victorina: 234
Sáez de Melgar, Faustina: 193, 232, 235n, 236, 251, 252, 252n
Saints:
  female: 8, 55–67, 81, 126, 135, 139, 169
    see also Teresa de Jesús
  male: 57, 109, 131, 133, 137
    St Paul: 62, 148, 183
  virgin martyrs: 8, 55, 60, 63–5
Sala Parés (Barcelona):195
Salinas, Juan de: 169
Salisbury, Joyce E.: 63
Salon culture (tertulias): 176, 228
  in eighteenth century: 176, 228
San Alberto, María de: *see* women dramatists of the Golden Age
San Félix, Sor Marcela de: *see* women dramatists of the Golden Age
Sánchez Coello, Alonso: 139
Sánchez de Vercial, Clemente: 59
Sánchez Llama, Iñigo: 236
Sánchez, Josefa: *see* women painters of the Golden Age
Santa María, Pablo de, Bishop of Cartagena (Salomón Ha Levi): 90
Santos, Ángeles: 14n, 260, 260n
Sartre, Jean Paul: 332
Sastre, Alfonso: 317
Saura, Carlos: 307
Scanlon, Geraldine: 12, 238–9, 247, 260
Sección Femenina de la Falange: 249–50
Second Republic: 17–19, 247–8, 273–4, 277–8, 281, 284–5, 339
*Sendeba*r: 9, 69n, 70–1, 79
Serrano de Tornel, Emilia: 216, 220
Serrano, Julieta: *see* female actors in the twentieth century
Sexuality: 57, 61, 142, 145, 151, 155–6, 213, 215, 225, 257, 262, 317–19, 321–3, 334
  and intersexuality: 262
  see female desire

Showalter, Elaine: 1
Siete Partidas: *see* legislation
Simmel, Georg: 214
Simó, Isabel-Clara: 290–1
Sinués de Marco, María Pilar: 193, 232–4, 235n, 236, 238, 251–2, 252n
Social History: 303
Soufas, Teresa Scott: 11, 158–61, 159n, 161n, 162n, 163, 166, 168–70, 169n, 170n
Sousa, Juana Teodora de: *see* women dramatists of the Golden Age
Spain, representations of:
  as *mater dolorosa*: 307
  as Minerva: 307
Spitzer, Leo: 43
Spivak, Gayatri Chakravorty: 289
suffrage: 17–18, 19, 239, 243, 244n, 247–8, 253, 260, 274–84, 239
  see legislation

Tavani, Giuseppe: 43
Taverna, Helena: *see* women film-makers of the boom
Tejero, Delhy (Adela): 259–60
Teresa de Jesús / of Avila: 10, 109–26
The Spanish Socialist Workers' Party (PSOE): 277
Toledo, García de: 111
Torre, Guillermo de: 263, 268
Traditional lyric: 2, 8, 41–5, 48–9, 50, 51n, 53
  female: 2, 42–53
Transvestites: 62–3, 163, 324
Tusquets, Esther: 12, 12n, 20, 288–9, 291–3, 297–300, 298n, 304, 306, 311–12
Twomey, Lesley K.: 81n, 106, 106n

Unamuno, Miguel de: 301, 301n, 307, 310, 310n, 314 *see* generation of 1898

Valdés Leal, Juan de: 152
Valentí, Helena: 290–1
Valera, Juan: 233
Valis, Noël: 13, 214
van Hemessen, Catherina: *see* women painters of the Golden Age
Vargas Ponce, José: 177
Varo, Remedios: *see* women painters of the avant-garde

Vega, Lope de: 158–60, 158n, 159n, 169, 171, 303, 309
Velázquez, Diego: 11, 129–30, 132–3, 137–8, 138, 141–2
Vélez de Guevara, Luis: 160
Vergés, Rosa: 339
Villena, Enrique de: 97, 105
Villena, Isabel de (Elionor): 9–10, 81, 81n, 89n, 97–107
virago (mujer varonil): 163
Vives, Juan Luis: 107, 135
Voragine, Jacobus de: 56–7, 59, 62–3

Weber, Alison: 110, 114, 118–19
Weiss, Julian: 26, 27n, 38
Witiza, King of Visigoths: 28
Woman question: 17, 245, 251, 253, 277, 279
Women, mythologies of:
    Amazons: 37, 37n, 38
    Antigone: 271
    Celestina: 221
    Eve: 63, 223
    Immaculate Conception: 106, 134, 135, 139, 144
    Mary Magdalen: 10, 56, 60, 100–2, 135
    Virgin Mary: 10, 55, 89, 94, 106, 151, 154, 223, 269–70, 271n
    see ángel del hogar
Women artists:
    and painting:
        in the Golden Age: 130–1, 141
            see Sofonisba Anguissola
        in the avant-garde: 14n, 257, 259, 263, 267, 269
            see Norah Borges
    and photography:
        see Ouka Leele
    and sculpture:
        see Luisa Ignacia Roldán
Women dramatists:
    in Golden Age: 12, 157–70
        see María de Zayas y Sotomayor
Women film-makers:
    of the Franco period: 320
    after Franco: 21, 331–3, 335–8, 336n, 337n, 340
    of the boom: 14, 21, 330–9, 340, 342.
        see Isabel Coixet, and Icíar Bollaín
    documentarists: 22, 341–2

Women translators:
    in eighteenth-century Spain: 175–88
        see Josefa Amar y Borbón
Women writers:
    essay: 16–18, 176–86, 232–3, 237, 238, 243, 256, 303, 311
    devotional: 86–94, 99–107, 111–27
        see also conduct manuals
    fiction:
        seventeenth century: 143–56
        nineteenth century: 177, 220–4, 233, 236
        twentieth century: 16, 240, 247, 288–300, 303–4, 306, 318, 323–25, 328, 334–5
            see also exemplary literature
    poetry: 2, 7, 13, 56, 145–6, 176, 259, 334
        medieval: 81
        Epic: 7, 25, 27–39
        Lyric: 41–53
        Religious: 56
        in the Golden Age: 160, 164, 168, 169
        in nineteenth century: 227, 228–31, 223–5, 238, 241
Women's crafts: 197, 276
Women's liberation movement: 304, 319
Women's magazines:
    in the nineteenth century: 192, 193, 193n, 195, 195n, 196, 199, 260
    see women's visual culture; and prensa del corazón
Women's organizations
    see Asociación Nacional de Mujeres Españolas (ANME); Asociación Femenina de Educación Cívica; Mujeres Libres; Liga de Amas de Casa; Partido Feminista
Women's studies
    as an academic discipline: 1–2ff
    and gender studies: 319
    and queer theory; 26n, 69
    and social history: 273
    in Hispanism: 1–7, 12–15, 69, 97, 99, 306
Women's visual culture
    and decorative arts: 197
        see women's magazines
    and feminine imagery: 189, 193, 200
    in stationery: 191, 200

and nineteenth century weeklies: 192, 195, 196, 199, 202, 260
Wynn of Gwydir, Sir Richard: 157–8, 157n, 171

Zambrano, Benito: 310, 338
Zambrano, María: 3, 15, 259, 267–9, 303

Zayas y Sotomayor, Fernando de: 144
Zayas y Sotomayor, María de: 7, 11–12, 143–56, 160, 165–8, 170, 186
Zizek, Slavoj: 155

www.ingramcontent.com/pod-product-compliance
Ingram Content Group UK Ltd.
Pitfield, Milton Keynes, MK11 3LW, UK
UKHW022122230426
12048UKWH00011BA/668